ART AND JUDAISM IN THE GRECO-ROMAN WORLD

Art and Judaism in the Greco-Roman World: Toward a New Jewish Archaeology explores the Jewish experience with art from the Hellenistic era through the rise of Islam. It starts from the premise that Jewish art in antiquity was a "minority" or "ethnic" art and surveys ways that Jews fully participated in, transformed, and at times rejected the art of their general environment. *Art and Judaism* focuses on the politics of identity in the Greco-Roman world, even as it discusses ways that modern identity issues have sometimes distorted and at other times refined scholarly discussion of ancient Jewish material culture. *Art and Judaism*, the first historical monograph on ancient Jewish art in the English language in fifty years, evaluates earlier scholarship as it sets out in new directions. Placing literary sources in careful dialogue with archaeological discoveries, this "New Jewish Archaeology" is an important contribution to Judaic studies, religious studies, art history, and classics.

Steven Fine is Jewish Foundation Professor of Judaic Studies at the University of Cincinnati, where he specializes in the history of Judaism during the Greco-Roman period. His particular interest is the relationship between ancient Jewish literature (particularly rabbinic literature) and archaeology and art.

ART AND JUDAISM IN THE GRECO–ROMAN WORLD

TOWARD A NEW JEWISH ARCHAEOLOGY

STEVEN FINE
UNIVERSITY OF CINCINNATI

CAMBRIDGE
UNIVERSITY PRESS

CAMBRIDGE UNIVERSITY PRESS
Cambridge, New York, Melbourne, Madrid, Cape Town, Singapore, São Paulo

Cambridge University Press
32 Avenue of the Americas, New York, NY 10013-2473, USA

www.cambridge.org
Information on this title: www.cambridge.org/9780521844918

First published 2005
Reprinted 2006 (twice)

Printed in the United States of America

A catalog record for this publication is available from the British Library

Library of Congress Cataloging-in-Publication Data
Fine, Steven.
Art and Judaism in the Greco–Roman world: toward a new Jewish archaeology / Steven Fine.
p. cm.
Includes bibliographical references and indexes.
ISBN 0-521-84491-6 (hardback)
1. Jewish art and symbolism. 2. Judaism – History – Post-exilic period, 586 B.C.–210 A.D.
3. Judaism – History – Talmudic period, 10–425. 4. Synagogue art. 5. Synagogue
architecture. 6. Judaism and art – History – To 1500. 7. Archaeology and religion. I. Title.
NK1672.F56 2005
704.03'924038 – dc22   2004019667

ISBN   978-0-521-84491-8 hardback

For Leah

נר מאיר על מנורת קדש

ויפי פנים על קומה זקופה

A lamp shines on the holy menorah,

and a beautiful face on an upright figure.

Ben Sirah 26

CONTENTS

CONTENTS

ILLUSTRATIONS

ABBREVIATIONS

In deference to readers from numerous disciplines who might use this volume, abbreviations have been kept to a bare minimum.

AJR	*Ancient Jerusalem Revealed*, ed. H. Geva. Jerusalem: Israel Exploration Society, 1994.
AJAAD	R. Hachlili, *Ancient Jewish Art and Archaeology in the Diaspora*. Leiden: E. J. Brill, 1998.
AJAALI	R. Hachlili, *Ancient Jewish Art and Archaeology in the Land of Israel*. Leiden: E. J. Brill, 1988.
ASHAAD	*Ancient Synagogues: Historical Analysis and Archaeological Discovery*, eds. D. Urman and P. V. M. Flesher. Leiden: E. J. Brill, 1995.
ASR	*Ancient Synagogues Revealed*, ed. L. I. Levine. Jerusalem: Israel Exploration Society, 1981.
b.	*Babylonian Talmud.*
EJ	*Encyclopedia Judaica.* Jerusalem: Keter, 1972.
FDS	*From Dura to Sepphoris: Studies in Jewish Art and Society in Late Antiquity*, eds. L. I. Levine and Z. Weiss. *Journal of Roman Archaeology Supplementary Series*. Portsmouth, RI, 2000.
GLAJJ	*Greek and Latin Authors on Jews and Judaism*, ed. M. Stern. Jerusalem: Israel Academy of Sciences and Humanities, 1976–84.
JCP	*Jews, Christians and Polytheists in the Ancient Synagogue: Cultural Interaction During the Greco–Roman Period*, ed. S. Fine. London: Routledge, 1999.
JE	*The Jewish Encyclopedia: A Descriptive Record of the History, Religion, Literature, and Customs of the Jewish People from the Earliest Times to the Present Day*. New York: Funk and Wagnalls, 1901–6.
JLA	*Judaism in Late Antiquity, Part 3: Where We Stand: Issues and Debates in Ancient Judaism, Volume Four: The Special Problem of the Synagogue*, ed. J. Neusner. Leiden: E. J. Brill, 2001.
m.	*Mishnah.*
NEAEHL	*New Encyclopedia of Archaeological Excavations in the Holy Land*, ed. E. Stern. Jerusalem: Israel Exploration Society and Carta, 1993.
NJPS	*Tanakh, A New Translation of the Hebrew Scriptures According to the Traditional Hebrew Text*, Philadelphia: Jewish Publication Society of America, 1985.

OCD	*Oxford Classical Dictionary*, eds. S. Hornblower and A. Spawforth, 3rd ed. New York: Oxford University Press, 1996.
OENEA	*Oxford Encyclopedia of Near Eastern Archaeology*, ed. E. M. Meyers. New York: Oxford University Press, 1996.
t.	*Tosefta*. Unless otherwise noted, ed. S. Lieberman (New York and Jerusalem: Jewish Theological Seminary, 1992) is cited through tractate *Baba Batra*, ed. M. S. Zuckermandel (Jerusalem: Wahrman, 1970) is cited from *Sanhedrin* through *Uqtsin*.
y.	*Jerusalem* (or *Palestinian*) *Talmud*.

PREFACE

On a sunny January afternoon in the year 2000, I boarded a white tram for the descent from the elegantly situated J. Paul Getty Center above Los Angeles to Sepulveda Canyon below. My mind was racing. I had just met with Catherine Soussloff, editor of *Jewish Identity in Modern Art History* (1999),[1] and Margaret Olin, whose *The Nation Without Art: Examining Modern Discourses on Jewish Art*[2] was nearing completion. Both were then Fellows at the Getty. It was an eventful lunch. Soussloff and Olin were studying the difficult attitude of modern scholarship toward Jewish visuality. I, by contrast, had lived it. They researched the giants of Jewish art scholarship, whereas I had studied with some of them, met others late in their lives, or known their students. They articulated the disdain toward this material in much of the scholarly discourse, whereas as a young student I had been stung by the arrogance of scholars who "knew" that Jewish art was inferior – or even nonexistent. This situation had so perplexed me that after completing my M.A. in art history in 1984, I left this discipline behind to try my luck in the study of ancient Judaism – where years later I realized that this attitude had also left its mark. Taking my leave of Olin and Soussloff and energized by their postmodern perspective, I decided that the time was finally right to write the volume that you hold in your hands – a project for which I had been preparing myself since my first visit to Israel as a high school student. Since those days during the mid-1970s, I have worked to gain some of the skills necessary to interpret Jewish history, rabbinic literature, the history of art, and the history of religions. More recently, I have focused on developing some of the professional maturity and sophistication necessary to integrate these disciplines.[3]

Before presenting the results of this study, I am pleased to thank all those who have supported this project. I thank the Society of Biblical Literature for support of my visit to study Jewish remains in Rome and vicinity and Robert O. Freedman of Baltimore Hebrew University for my sabbatical in 2001–2, which I spent in Israel. The Charles Phelps Taft Memorial Fund at the University of Cincinnati awarded me a Faculty Research Fellowship for study in Israel during the Summer of 2004 that allowed for some last-minute tuning of this manuscript. Libraries, museums, and archives have been extremely generous with their time and resources. In Baltimore I thank the Joseph Meyerhoff Library of Baltimore Hebrew University, the Milton S. Eisenhower Library at Johns Hopkins University, and the library of the Walters Art Museum. Israeli institutions include the A-B Institute of Samaritan Studies, the Central Zionist Archive, the Hebrew University Archives, Genazim: The Archives of the Hebrew Writers' Association in Israel, the Hebrew University Institute of Archaeology Library and Slide Library, the Israel Antiquities Authority Archives, the Israel Exploration Society, the Israel Film

Archive–Jerusalem Cinematheque, the Israel Museum, the Israel State Archives, the Jewish National and University Library, the Shalom Hartman Institute, the Steven Spielberg Jewish Film Archive, and the Yad Izhak Ben-Zvi Institute Library. In Cincinnati, I am most grateful to the University of Cincinnati Library System, the Hebrew Union College–Jewish Institute of Religion's Klau Library, the Comprehensive Aramaic Lexicon, and the Jacob Rader Marcus Center of the American Jewish Archives. I also thank the Semitic Museum at Harvard University, the Beinecke Rare Book and Manuscript Library at Yale University, and the Palestine Exploration Fund in London for their assistance. This volume was published with the help of the Charles Phelps Taft Memorial Fund of the University of Cincinnati.

My students in Baltimore, Jerusalem, and Cincinnati have greatly contributed to this volume. I especially thank Bonnie Gracer, Sara Lewis, Heather Murphy, J. Renee Dunnagan, Gerdy Trachtman, Derika Wellington, and Libby White for their challenges and insights. More than I can recount, colleagues, friends, and teachers near and far have helped to make this a better book. I particularly thank Dan Barag, Albert Baumgarten, Joseph Baumgarten, George Berlin, John Brolley, Isaiah Gafni, Stephen A. Kaufman, Lee I. Levine, Eric M. Meyers, Gila Naveh, Jacob Neusner, Benyamim Tsedaka, Steven M. Wasserstrom, and Anthony D. York for their assistance at various stages. Steven Bowman, David Ellenson, Louis Feldman, Elka Klein, Frederic Krome, Ruth Langer, Stuart S. Miller, Rachel Neis, Margaret Olin, Tessa Rajak, Richard S. Sarason, Jonathan D. Sarna, and the late Joseph Gutmann read and commented on specific chapters, adding much to my process. Mark Chancey, Jaś Elsner, Yaacov M. Moses, Lawrence H. Schiffman, and Ziony Zevit read the entire manuscript, for which I am especially grateful. Andrew Beck and his staff at Cambridge and Eleanor Umali and the people of Techbooks have made the final stages of this project most pleasant, for which I owe them much. J. Renee Dunnagan prepared the Index of Primary Sources. I would be remiss if I were not to thank my teachers, many of whose footprints may be felt throughout this volume. I particularly thank Yearl E. Schwartz, Richard D. Hecht, Bezalel Narkiss, Dov Noy, Dov Berkowitz, Selma Holo, Pratapaditya Pal, Bruce Zuckerman, Daniel Landes, Elieser Slomovic, Arie Strikowsky, Lee I. Levine, Avigdor Shinan, and Lawrence H. Schiffman, and remember the late Stephen S. Kayser, Amos Funkenstein, and Menahem Stern.

Most of all, I thank my wife, Leah Bierman Fine, for her loving and constant support, for her unwavering concern for all that I find exciting – and for pushing me to keep my writing "interesting." The reader will decide if I have succeeded in this task. Our elder son, Elisha Nir Fine, now thirteen, is my tireless travel companion, discussion partner, and sometimes research assistant. The contribution of our preschooler, Yaakov Meir Fine, to this project resides in his ability to effortlessly interrupt my deepest concentration with a giggle and with a glimmer of his shining eyes to teach me what is really important. Leah, Elisha, and Koby are my constant reminders that human beings, created in the image of the Divine, are the only true "Jewish symbols."[4]

Jerusalem, Israel
Tammuz, 5764
July 2004

A NOTE ON TRANSLITERATION
AND TRANSLATION

Transliteration of Hebrew and Aramaic characters follows the "general" system used by the *Encyclopedia Judaica* (Jerusalem: Keter, 1972, 1:90) with the exception that the letter *qof* is transliterated with a "q." Hebrew and Greek nouns that appear in the *American Heritage Dictionary: Second College Edition* (Boston: Houghton Mifflin, 1991) are treated as English words. Names that appear in Biblical literature are spelled in standard English forms, except when other transliterations have become standard in scholarly literature. *The Holy Bible: Revised Standard Version* (London: Nelson, 1965) generally served as the starting point for translations of the Hebrew Scriptures, New Testament, and the Apocrypha.

INTRODUCTION

J EWISH ARCHAEOLOGY IS A TERM THAT HAS BEEN USED VERY sparingly during the past half century. It was popular, however, during the period between the end of World War I and the early 1950s. Jewish archaeology was used by Jewish scholars to describe ancient Jewish remains of the Greco–Roman period – from the ruins of Herod's Temple to ancient coins, synagogue remains, tombs, and villages. It was the Jewish equivalent of "Christian archaeology," a term commonly used in Catholic scholarship around the turn of the twentieth century. The hallmark of this Jewish archaeology was the placement of Jewish artifacts in dialogue with ancient Jewish literature, in the hopes of understanding more about Jewish culture than either the extant literary texts or excavated artifacts could yield on their own.

"Palestinian" Jewish archaeologists Nahum Slouschz, Eleazar Lipa Sukenik, Hungarian Talmudist Ludwig Blau, and other Jewish scholars who engaged Jewish archaeological remains were an excited lot, dedicated to interpreting ever more dramatic discoveries within the full context of Jewish literature and history. Their scholarly output was prodigious, their discoveries significant. Between the two world wars, major discoveries, including most spectacularly the Na'aran and Beth Alpha synagogues and the Beth She'arim catacombs in Palestine and the Dura Europos synagogue in Syria, sparked heated scholarly discussion and publication programs. These scholars were determined to prove, once and for all, that Judaism and the Jews possessed a significant and meaningful visual culture in antiquity. They were successful.

"Jewish archaeology" was the product of deep Jewish insecurity and – for some – profound national hope. Jewish scholars, Zionists and Jewish culturalists alike, were out to show that Jews, like all other nations, created beautiful and exciting art throughout their long history. The odds were high and from the beginning were stacked against them – at least in the Protestant world. Among Protestants, particularly in Germany, it was a "given" that Judaism was an "aniconic" and "iconoclastic" religion, devoid of art. Because the existence of a national art was an essential feature of nineteenth-century romantic nationalism, Jews who were committed to the maintenance of Jewish peoplehood needed the existence of a strong and vital "Jewish art."

During the second half of the twentieth century, a very different ideological stance dominated American scholarly discussions of Jewish archaeological discoveries. Yale's Erwin R. Goodenough, Columbia University's Morton Smith, and some of Smith's students knew that ancient Jews did in fact "do art." Unfortunately, they did not grasp the full depth of what I call the "Jews don't do art" trope. They simply tempered its implications. They hence asserted that only the ancient rabbis were "aniconic" – or, at least, very troubled by art. The trope changed from "Jews don't do art" to "rabbis don't do art." This model informed much of contemporary American scholarship on ancient Judaism and revealed important distinctions within the late antique Jewish community, although these were sometimes overstated. This trope, which allowed Jewish archaeological remains to be used for the construction of "nonrabbinic Jews" as a distinct culture group in late antique Palestine, supports specific ideological perspectives within liberalizing elements of the contemporary American Jewish community. The construction of modern nonrabbinic Jews was thus provided with ancient roots. It is an excellent example of the ways that scholarship and ideology intersect in the study of ancient Judaism. In *Art and Judaism in the*

Greco–Roman World: Toward a New Jewish Archaeology, I hope to finally lay to rest the last vestiges of the insidious (and often anti-Semitic or anti-rabbinic) trope of Jewish "aniconism" in antiquity by exposing its roots as it pertains to the Greco–Roman period. In this task, I build upon recent studies that that have analyzed this approach in scholarship in relation to later periods. To this purpose, I resurrect the term "Jewish archaeology" and the legacy of the early interpreters of ancient Jewish material culture while integrating more recent innovations in the study of antiquity – and particularly of ancient Judaism.

Art and Judaism in the Greco–Roman World: Toward a New Jewish Archaeology builds upon the project of reading ancient Jewish texts, particularly rabbinic literature, in close conversation with archaeology. Great discoveries in both of these (usually) self-contained disciplines during the last century offer rich opportunities for dialogue and for better understanding the place of art in Judaism than has ever before been possible. This volume is divided into four parts. The first section, "The '*Most Unmonumental People*' of the World": Modern Constructions of Ancient Jewish Art," sets out the history of this discipline through a series of case studies. I begin by discussing nineteenth- and early-twentieth-century attitudes in Western Europe and America, both Protestant and Catholic, and how these influenced Jewish conceptions. This will be accomplished through the focal lens of one building and its architect, Arnold W. Brunner and his Henry S. Frank Memorial Synagogue in Philadelphia. The Frank synagogue, loosely modeled on the ancient Galilean synagogue of Kefar Baram by America's premiere Jewish architect of the period, is an excellent point from which to examine the situation before World War I.

I then turn to the Zionist context, exploring Zionist interpretation of ancient Jewish art and the implications of Zionist perspectives. Here I focus on the "first Hebrew excavation," carried out by Nahum Slouschz in 1921, and the career of the legendary E. L. Sukenik, its interface with Ludwig Blau's conception of "Jewish archaeology," and the implications of their research for the interpretation of Jewish material culture.

This section continues with a discussion of the ways that ancient Jewish art were interpreted by E. R. Goodenough, Morton Smith, and some of their students. Finally, we turn to the art historical context. Here we explore the ways that Jewish art is construed – and sometimes misconstrued – in current introductory textbooks. "Toward a New Jewish Archaeology: Methodological Reflections" concludes this survey of twentieth-century approaches. I suggest what may be learned from previous research as well as what is no longer useful.

The bulk of the volume deals with the interpretation of the archaeological and textual artifacts and hence the cultures that they bespeak. Here I discuss the relationship between "art" and "Judaism" as I see it. A note on terminology: The word "art" is an imperfect cipher to describe the material culture of the Greco–Roman period.[1] Art in the modern romantic sense did not exist in antiquity. In fact, no word for fine arts existed in Hebrew until the twentieth century! The Greek word *téchne* and the Aramaic *umanut* come closest – both refer to craftsmanship. By "art," I refer to material culture that ancients might have considered to be well-designed or crafted. Defining "Judaism" is far more complex. In this context, I mean the web of practices, beliefs, sacred stories ("myths"), and cultural inclinations (in no particular order) out of which Jews built their identities – both those elements that were shared across intragroup boundaries and those that were disdained in other Jews. Each of these components was (and still is) given different weights by various elements within the community. These were the elements, nonetheless, by which one Jew would recognize another – even when they spoke different languages or fundamentally disagreed – and often also by which non-Jews might recognize members of the Jewish community. This definition is sloppy – as all definitions of a phenomemon as complex as Judaism must be. It encompasses the "broad agreement" regarding theology and praxis that E. P. Sanders believes connected the varied forms of Judaism during the Second Temple period and which he calls "common Judaism." It also includes the diversity of opinions. In an earlier study, I demonstrated the validity of this approach for late antiquity.[2] I sometimes refer to this shared religion as a Jewish *koiné*, paraphrasing the "Mediterranean *koiné*" and "Christian *koiné*" that historian Peter Brown suggests united the many faces of late antique Christianity.[3]

This volume focuses on significant issues in the history of the Jewish experience with art during the Greco–Roman period – from the Hellenistic period through the rise of Islam. Throughout this very long period, one of the constant connecting threads was Jewish reflection on the place of "art" within Jewish culture. I write from the premise that Jewish art in antiquity was a "minority" or "ethnic" art, and explore the ways that Jews fully participated in, transformed, and at times rejected the art of their general environment. I focus on the politics of identity during the Greco–Roman period and the ways in which Jewish identity was formed and transformed through contact with the art of the Hellenistic and later Roman, Byzantine, and Islamic worlds.

The second major section is called "Art and Identity in the Greco–Roman World." This section discusses the ways art and identity were interwoven in each of the formative contexts in which Jews lived: the Second Temple period Judaea, late antique Palestine, and diaspora communities from Spain in the west to Sassanian Persia in the east. Two monuments serve as focal points for this discussion – the no-longer-existing tomb of the Hasmonian royal house at Modi'in in Israel and the synagogue of Na'aran near Jericho.

Next, in the third section I explore "Jewish 'Symbols' in the Greco–Roman World," focusing on how specific visual images were used. I highlight two: the date palm and the menorah. In this section, I interpret these images within specific contexts and the ways that they functioned within those contexts. I argue for a rather broad and open-ended interpretation, one that takes into account all available literary and visual sources without giving undue emphasis to any one type.

The last section of this volume – "Reading Holistically: Art and the Liturgy of Late Antique Synagogues" – interprets the remains of ancient synagogues in terms of the liturgies that took place within them. I suggest that ancient synagogues were, first and foremost, contexts that were carefully constructed as liturgical spaces. In the first chapter of this section, I provide a liturgical interpretation of the Dura Europos Synagogue, interpreting the art of this outstanding monument first in terms of other literary and artistic remains discovered in this city of the Syrian Desert. I then turn to the Palestinian context, where I interpret synagogues decorated with carpet mosaics, principally the Sepphoris and Beth Alpha mosaics, in terms of the literature and liturgical lives of the Jews who built them. Here I focus on two themes in the art of Palestinian synagogues – the role of Scripture and liturgy in determining the structure and decoration of these buildings and the significance of the zodiac in synagogue art and in Jewish liturgical practice. Finally, I turn to the question of sanctity as a significant leitmotif in the development of synagogue art in late antique Palestine.

In this volume, I build upon the Jewish archaeology of old, and recent studies of late antique religion and art – particularly the most important insights of the Good-enough/Smith approach – to suggest a viable and multifaceted interpretation of the Jewish content of ancient Jewish art. In the end, my gaze is set not upon the artifacts nor upon the texts that have been preserved, although these are the sources that I study. Rather, my focus is the flesh-and-blood Jews who made, used, and sometimes avoided and destroyed "art" in the Greco-Roman world.

PART ONE

"THE '*MOST UNMONUMENTAL PEOPLE*' OF THE WORLD"

———————

MODERN CONSTRUCTIONS OF ANCIENT JEWISH ART

The Jews have been called the "*most unmonumental people*" of the world. This assertion is based on the sad fact that few Jewish monuments are known. . . .

Ludwig Blau, 1926[1]

The conception of Jewish art may appear to some to be a contradiction in terms. . . .

Cecil Roth, 1956[2]

For some time now I have felt the need for a comprehensive study, which would support my thesis for the existence of an ancient Jewish art. . . .

Rachel Hachlili, 1988[3]

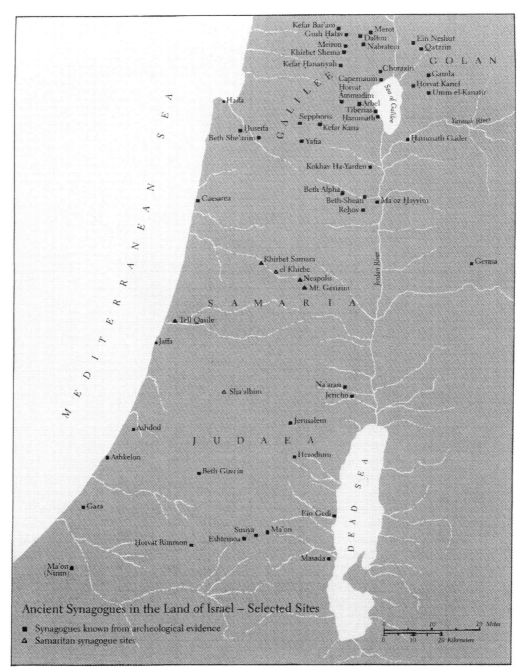

1. Ancient synagogues in the Land of Israel (courtesy of Yeshiva University Museum).

MY STUDY OF THE RELATIONSHIP BETWEEN ART AND Judaism in antiquity begins with a discussion of the ways that this relationship has been constructed by modern scholars. A subject of academic research for over a century, the relationship between Judaism and art is a test case for understanding more than either category alone. Art has been a litmus test for interpreting the place of the Jew in modern society. Without understanding this phenomenon and the people who gave it voice, it is impossible to take what is best from earlier scholarship and to suggest interpretations that better reflect the relationship between art and Judaism in antiquity.

Beginning during the last years of the nineteenth century and continuing throughout the twentieth century,

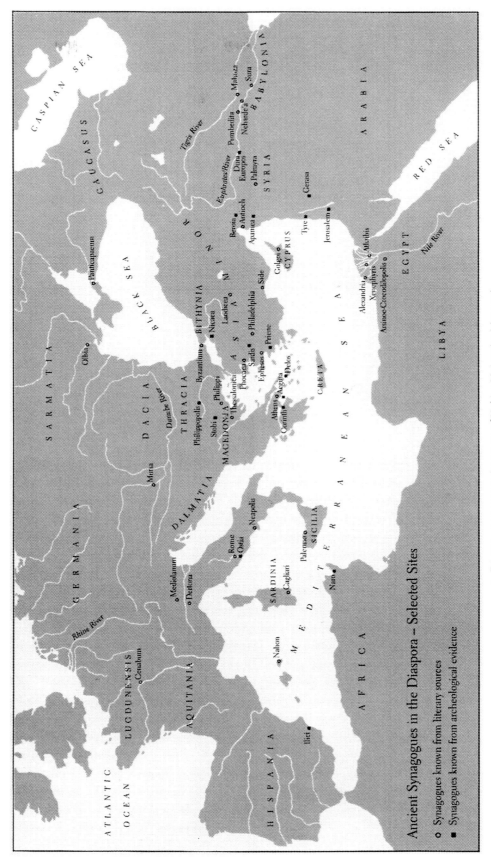

Ancient Synagogues in the Diaspora – Selected Sites

○ Synagogues known from literary sources
■ Synagogues known from archeological evidence

2. Diaspora synagogues (courtesy of Yeshiva University Museum).

elements within the Jewish community set out to prove the existence and respectability of "Jewish art." This concern was much more than academic. During the nineteenth and early twentieth centuries, Jews – both as individuals and communities – undertook to remake themselves into "ideal" Westerners: Frenchmen, Englishmen, Germans, Hungarians, Poles, Italians, Americans, and "Hebrews." With amazing speed, they adopted the national identities, languages, and attitudes of the lands where they lived, conforming to the demands and prejudices of the nations that most hoped so resolutely to join.

When common prejudice asserted, for example, that Jewish men were effeminate and weak, Jews built communal gymnasia (e.g., the Jewish community centers movement in North America) where they could strengthen their supposedly weak physiques.[4] Zionists internalized this prejudice, asserting the importance of "muscular Judaism" for the "New Jew," now called a "Hebrew" (later, Israeli). To prove their physicality and their loyalty to their nation-states, Jews celebrated their participation in the military. Books like *Jews Fight Too* – published soon after America's victory in World War II with an introduction by Boston's colorful mayor, James M. Curley[5] – vividly reflect Jewish adaptation to the mores of their new homeland and the obstacles that were set before them in the process.[6] The celebration of military prowess among Zionists was a similar phenomenon, albeit constructed in response to very different considerations.[7] "Nose jobs" – plastic surgery to diminish large "Jewish" noses, popular with American Jewish women in the post–World War II years – were another manifestation of this desire to fit the standards of the general society, even to the point of undergoing surgery to accomplish conformity.[8] Within the liturgical sphere, synagogue services, architecture, liturgical music, and especially Jewish theology and practice were transformed by Jews of all degrees of "traditionalism" in ways that might have been unrecognizable to previous generations – but would be familiar and often considered laudatory by the majority culture.[9]

This attempt to "fit" the mores and expectations of the majority is particularly evident in regard to art. Art was generally considered antithetical to Judaism, or at best as a context where Jews were less than proficient. Some even thought that Jews were genetically deficient when it came to all things visual. Great efforts were made by some Jews to remedy this situation. Because the possession of a national art was considered an essential characteristic of a national spirit, Jews interested in maintaining Jewish peoplehood (including Zionists) often strove to construct a Jewish art. Others, mainly the more assimilationist streams, asserted the superiority of Judaism specifically because it was construed as a noniconic religion (like the so-called aniconic Protestant churches, and unlike deeply visual Roman Catholicism). These constructions were not generally based in any firsthand knowledge of Jewish visual culture. Rather, they were rooted in Christian theological assumptions, often historicized, of what ancient Judaism (and thus the earliest church)[10] "ought" to have been. Protestants, who imagined the earliest Christians to have been aniconic, imagined that ancient Jews were precursors of their own approaches. Defending their own visual traditions, Catholic scholars projected a rich artistic tradition upon ancient Jews.[11]

Beginning near the turn of the twentieth century, a pro-Jewish art camp developed that set out to change the cultural narrative regarding Judaism and art by highlighting actual artifacts. This battle was fought using both the tools of then-regnant academic scholarship and through popular dissemination of Jewish visual culture. At first this included the preparation of scholarly studies (particularly of medieval Hebrew manuscripts) and the organization of archaeological excavations and expeditions to collect folk art – all of which provided the legitimization and patina of objective Western scholarship, especially when carried out by non-Jews.[12] Many Jewish scholars lauded and accepted any evaluation of their ancient art, even when it was treated only for its value as a precursor of Christian art, and even when the "complement" served the most blatantly anti-Semitic scholarly agendas. Just as importantly, they set out to change popular conceptions through profusely illustrated popular and semipopular publications, the establishment of Jewish museums, and especially through contemporary synagogue architecture. Popularizing volumes were often quite apologetic in tone, and might together be called, albeit uncharitably, a *Jews Do Art Too!* literature.[13] The finest example of this phenomenon is Cecil Roth's co-edited volume, *Jewish Art: An Illustrated History*, which appeared in Hebrew in 1956/7 and later in English and German. It is simply astonishing that more than fifty years after the start of the pro-Jewish art campaign began, Roth felt compelled to introduce *Jewish Art* on the apologetic note cited at the start of this chapter.[14] The context occasioning Roth's volume was the recent birth of the Jewish state in 1948, and hence the renewed sense of urgency to create a national art. The *raison d'être* of this extremely popular volume (still in print in Hebrew) was to tell the story of the art of a nation, from its Biblical origins through the most contemporary of art. As we are told on the dust jacket of the first Hebrew edition (and less explicitly in the text itself): "the [artistic] advances of the present, for each and every people, are the fruit of an ancient and well-rooted tradition" (my translation). Significantly, apologetic was restricted to the front matter and dust jacket only. An important factor in the rhetoric of this text was the breadth of objective research by eighteen renowned scholars. The circular town plan of the modern Galilean village of Nahalal is set at the end of a unified architectural tradition that flows through Canaanite temples; the Tomb of the Patriarchs in Hebron; and ancient, medieval, and modern synagogues. Similarly, the Dura Europos synagogue paintings of the mid-third century are part of a figurative tradition that is traced, if only implicitly, back to Biblical Israel and forward through medieval manuscripts, Hebrew books, and the paintings of such moderns as Amedeo Modigliani and Marc Chagall. I could suggest many more such correspondences, but this is enough to make the point. Just as Italians, Germans, Britons, and even Americans possess a venerable, distinctive and vibrant national art, so too – this volume argues – do the Jews.

As late as 1988, Israeli archaeologist Rachel Hachlili fell into the *Jews Do Art Too!* paradigm. Introducing her important survey of *Ancient Jewish Art and Archaeology in the Land of Israel*, Hachlili legitimized her work by claiming that the volume was intended to "support my thesis for the existence of an ancient Jewish art"[15] – this more than a century after the first discoveries of synagogue remains in the Galilee, followed by the exploration of the Jewish catacombs in Rome, synagogue discoveries from Dura Europos to Beth Alpha and Sardis, and major excavations of Second Temple Jerusalem! As a student of Jewish art during the late 1970s and 1980s, I often found myself mouthing apologetics for my discipline and on occasion experienced prejudice against it within academic and museum circles. Apologetics were part and parcel of Jewish art scholarship.

The historical background for this astonishing situation has recently come under intense scholarly scrutiny. The first to address these issues was Annabelle Wharton of Duke University, in regard to interpretations of the Dura Europos synagogue.[16] Kalman Bland, also of Duke, discussed the nineteenth-century philosophical roots of this phenomenon in his *The Artless Jew: Medieval and Modern Affirmations and Denials of the Visual*,[17] which he traces to the thought of Immanuel Kant, who praised Jews for being aniconic like German Protestants, and G. W. F. Hegel, who damned them for the same supposed aniconicism. Catherine Soussloff's edited volume, *Jewish Identity in Modern Art History*, published in 1999, suggests the absolute ambivalence (if not contempt) that art historical scholarship, often carried out by Jews, has shown toward Judaism and Jewish art. Margaret Olin's *The Nation Without Art: Examining Modern Discourses on Jewish Art* presents case studies in the historiography of art history regarding Jews. Olin's discussions of nineteenth- and twentieth-century conceptions in the German academy and Jewish responses to this artlessness are particularly relevant. The dust jacket of Olin's volume bespeaks the tone of righteous indignation that she, as well as Wharton and Bland, bring to their studies. An illuminated detail of "Abraham smashing the idols, from *The Copenhagen Haggadah*, Altona, 1739" appears beneath the title of the volume. In this northern German manuscript, Abraham is shown within a columned temple destroying his father's idols, while idolaters sacrifice outside. Paradoxically for the reigning paradigm, this midrashic tradition of patriarchal aniconicism is presented visually. Central to Olin's rhetoric is the sense that she too has come to break the idols of academic art history's fathers. This body of work parallels a rethinking of the place of art and literature in the history of the early church. Paul Corby Finney's *The Invisible God: The Earliest Christians on Art* (1994), for example, questions the commonplace among art historians that the pre-Constantinian church was aniconic, following upon supposed Jewish models.[18] Finney marshals literary, iconographic, and historiographic tools to show that this conception of the early church as aniconic was incorrect. Finney assumes, however, that earliest Judaism nevertheless was antagonistic toward art. The writings of Blank, Olin, and others began the process of overturning this vestegal truism.

Israelis have studied the place of art within the Zionist milieu in some detail. Intellectual historian Yaakov Shavit's *Athens in Jerusalem: Classical Antiquity and Hellenism in the Making of the Modern Secular Jew* was the first monograph to approach the place of art in Zionist culture.[19] Nuancing some of Shavit's generalizations, in 1999 literary scholar Avner Holtzman turned to the question of *Aesthetics and National Revival – Hebrew Literature Against the Visual Arts*.[20] In *Lo and Behold: Zionist Icons and Visual*

Symbols in Israeli Culture (2000), Alec Mishory focuses on specific themes in Zionist iconography, setting them in the context of Zionist and Israeli literature and history.[21] Astonishingly, an entire discourse and reevaluation of the development of Western attitudes toward Jewish art has thus appeared in print in very short order. This revision of the scholarly narrative is in fact playing catch-up with the general narrative transformation within the Jewish community. The proliferation of coffee table books, Jewish museums, galleries, and archaeological parks – not to mention the associated jewelry, reproductions, posters, placemats, coasters, scarves, postage stamps, and coins – has worked to virtually wipe out all vestiges of inferiority regarding art among Jews born during the latter twentieth century – and may even have overcompensated just a bit.[22]

My purpose in this section is not to relate the full details of this academic paradigm shift, a transformation that is still in motion.[23] Rather, I explore what I consider some of the most important contexts in which the previous paradigm has been influencial. The choice of contexts is at some level very personal in that each has been central to my own intellectual development. However, I believe (perhaps with some egocentrism) that each has been central as well to the general development of our theme – American and Israeli Judaic studies (with their intertwined tendrils and roots in the German *Wissenschaft des Judentums*), the history of religions, and the history of art.

This section is constructed of four very specific contexts, each of which sheds light on broader issues in the modern construction of ancient Jewish art. Through these thick descriptions, I hope to tease out some of the nuances of this scholarship. I begin with "Building an Ancient Synagogue on the Delaware: Philadelphia's Henry S. Frank Memorial Synagogue and Constructions of Jewish Art at the Turn of the Twentieth Century." Here I explore attitudes toward the visual in Judaism as they existed during the latter nineteenth century through the focusing lens of an American synagogue built in 1901. Designed by noted American architect Arnold W. Brunner on the grounds of Philadelphia's Jewish Hospital, the Frank Memorial Synagogue exemplifies American trends in the construction of Jewish art at the turn of the twentieth century. The Frank Memorial Synagogue was modeled upon a late antique Galilean synagogue that was explored and published by British scholars a few decades earlier. Through Brunner's writings, we see an example of how Protestant and Catholic perspectives affected Jewish perceptions of their ancient art. We also show ways that the German–Jewish elite of turn-of-the-century America sought to write a new narrative of Jewish artistic continuity through the medium of ancient synagogue discoveries in the Land of Israel. The Frank Synagogue is an excellent vantage point from which to view the Jewish art (and particularly the Jewish archaeology) paradigm as it existed during the latter nineteenth century, and the transitions in attitude that led to massive revisions of this paradigm in the new century.

In the second section, I focus on Zionist perceptions of Jewish archaeology and ways that early Zionists utilized archaeology in the writing of the Zionist narrative. "The Old–New Land: Jewish Archaeology and the Zionist Narrative" explores aspects of the way that ancient Jewish remains served in writing a new narrative of the Jewish past (and future). The Palestinian/Israeli context – completely interwoven with American trends, personalities, and perceptions – has determined much of our interpretation of ancient Jewish art, and to my mind offers a model that is in many ways still useful. I begin with the first synagogue excavation carried out under Jewish auspices, at Hammath Tiberias on the Sea of Galilee in 1921. We then turn to the father of Jewish archaeology in Palestine, Eleazar Lipa Sukenik. Sukenik's development and scholarship are assessed through his correspondence with his patron and mentor, Hebrew University President Judah L. Magnes. Taken together with our discussion of the American context, this discussion of Zionism presents ways that Jewish culturalists during the first half of the twentieth century constructed Jewish archaeology and integrated it into the warp and woof of both the national enterprise and academic Judaic studies.

The third section looks at ways that the search for nonrabbinic Jews set the agenda for American Jewish scholarship during the second half of the twentieth century, and how these perceptions have affected Jewish scholarship and even the Jewish communal discourse. Ludwig Blau, a leading Hungarian Talmudist, was apparently the first to suggest that archaeology might reveal Jews who did not follow the ancient rabbis. This aspect of his approach was taken over by E. R. Goodenough. Goodenough's mammoth project, *Jewish Symbols in the Greco–Roman Period*, has set the tone of much of modern scholarship on ancient Judaism and its art for nearly a half century, and profoundly influenced Jewish self-perceptions.[24] In "Archaeology and the Search for Nonrabbinic Judaism," I explore the context in which

Goodenough's work developed, its continuing influence, and its contemporary significance.

Approaches and prejudices in the history of art hover over our discussions of early-twentieth-century interpretations of ancient Jewish art. Olin and Wharton have discussed this phenomenon in detail. In the final section, "Art History: Textbooks and the Rhetoric of Jewish Artlessness," I build upon their research and explore the ways that the Dura Europos synagogue and Judaism in general are presented in contemporary introductory art history textbooks. Reflecting a century of deep ambivalence within art historical scholarship toward Jewish art, most of these texts continue to spread the gospel of Jewish art as "a contradiction in terms" to undergraduates throughout the English-speaking world. Even so, there is evidence that a new paradigm of Jewish art is beginning to take hold in art history. Concluding this section, I draw out what I see as the most useful elements of this century of scholarship. I then turn my "real" task: the reinterpretation of the sources for *Art and Judaism in the Greco-Roman World.*

CHAPTER ONE

BUILDING AN ANCIENT SYNAGOGUE ON THE DELAWARE

———————

PHILADELPHIA'S HENRY S. FRANK MEMORIAL SYNAGOGUE AND CONSTRUCTIONS OF JEWISH ART AT THE TURN OF THE TWENTIETH CENTURY

THE HENRY S. FRANK MEMORIAL SYNAGOGUE WAS DEDICATED on September 12, 1901, in a grand celebration on the grounds of the Jewish Hospital of Philadelphia.[1] In attendance was the leadership of Philadelphia Jewry – lay leaders and rabbis, traditionalists and reformers alike. As the assembly entered the new synagogue, the hospital reader chanted in Hebrew, "Open to me the gates of the righteous that I may enter them and praise the Lord." From within the synagogue, Cantor Leon Elmaleh and the boys' choir of Congregation Mikve Israel responded, "This is the gate of the Lord; the righteous may enter" (Psalm 118: 19–20).[2]

Measuring 33 by 37 feet, the Frank Memorial Synagogue drew inspiration from ancient synagogues preserved in the Galilee (Figures 3, 4). At the thirty-sixth annual meeting of the Jewish Hospital Board, President William Bowers Hackenburg, who himself was "largely responsible for its development into a major public institution,"[3] assured the board and membership that the "little

3. The Henry S. Frank Memorial Synagogue (photograph courtesy of the Albert Einstein Healthcare Network).

4. The Henry S. Frank Memorial Synagogue, main entrance (photograph by Steven Fine).

synagogue will be one of the most beautiful and completely furnished houses of worship in the country." The design was to be "after the style of architecture . . . in the synagogues of Palestine in the first and second centuries. . . . The inscription over the outer entrance is literally copied from one of these."[4] The models for the Frank Memorial Synagogue were drawn from the well-preserved large synagogue in the Upper Galilean village of Kefar Baram, near the present border with Lebanon (Figure 5); a smaller synagogue at Kefar Baram; as well as the nearby synagogue of Nabratein. The gray Indiana limestone and granite used, very popular in turn-of-the-century America, vaguely resemble weathered Palestinian limestone, particularly as it appears in contemporary photographs. These synagogues had been explored and publicized by the British Palestine Exploration Fund during the late nineteenth century,[5] and a full-page plate of the large Baram synagogue appeared in that pride of American Jewry, *The Jewish Encyclopedia.*[6]

In fact, the main portal of the large Baram synagogue was the inspiration for the main portal of the Frank Memorial Synagogue and for the repeating window frames of the building. Within the round Syrian arch of the Baram synagogue, the architect placed a menorah encircled by a wreath, based on an image from Nabratein. On the architrave, the architect placed a Hebrew inscription (written in turn-of-the-twentieth-century Hebrew script) that had been discovered on the lintel of the small Baram synagogue. Now in the Louvre, the inscription translates: "Peace be upon the place, and on all the places of Israel."[7] The pavement of the synagogue's porch was set in mosaic, reminiscent of Roman flooring – Palestinian synagogues with mosaic pavements had not yet been discovered. On each side of the ark were placed seven-branched menorahs. The candlesticks were loosely modeled on the menorah on the Arch of Titus in Rome.[8] The ark, flanked by menorahs, parallels designs on gold glasses from Rome that were illustrated in *The Jewish Encyclopedia.*[9]

Arnold W. Brunner, the architect, in effect built an ancient synagogue in what was then suburban Philadelphia. This was an amazing feat, one that was not repeated anywhere else in the world. What prompted Brunner to design such a building and the Jews of Philadelphia to construct it? An answer to this question may provide us with a sense of the complexities involved in the ways in which Jews and non-Jews alike viewed the visual in Jewish life as the twentieth century dawned.

5. The large synagogue at Kefar Baram (after *The Jewish Encyclopedia*, 11: 621).

Arnold W. Brunner (1857–1925) was among the most accomplished architects of his day and may have been the first American-born Jewish architect.[10] A member of the German–Jewish elite at a time when Philadelphia was the "capital of Jewish America,"[11] Brunner's projects included, as Felix M. Warburg eulogized in the *Proceedings of the American Historical Society*, "the most beautiful private homes, school buildings, playgrounds, stadiums, university buildings, state capitols, synagogues, temples, halls for music, etc."[12] Brunner's early synagogue projects were neo-Romanesque buildings with Islamic and Byzantine elements. Throughout the 1890s, Brunner accomplished major synagogue projects using this style, as evidenced by his buildings for the Beth El (1891) and Shaaray Tefila (1894) congregations in New York and for Mishkan Israel in New Haven, Connecticut (1897). By the end of the century, however, he had become increasingly uncomfortable with contemporary reliance on Christian and Muslim models for synagogue architecture. Implicit in Brunner's problem was the modern dilemma of creating monumental synagogues where few had existed before.[13] No longer satisfied with adapting Christian and Moorish architecture and decoration, Brunner sought out a medium that was drawn from neither church nor mosque but would somehow uniquely express Jewish conceptions. He found this

medium in the then popular neoclassical architecture, which he considered preeminently appropriate for synagogue buildings. Brunner's first neoclassical synagogue was built for Shearith Israel in New York in 1897, followed by the Frank Memorial Synagogue in 1901.[14]

Brunner wrote two major essays and one shorter piece on synagogue architecture, all from the standpoint of a practicing architect. These articles document the development of Brunner's conception of synagogue architecture from Romanesque and Moorish revival forms to neoclassicism. This transition reflects more than architectural development: It represents a complete reassessment of Jewish aesthetics.

Brunner's first article, "Synagogue Architecture," appeared with numerous illustrations in *The Jewish Encyclopedia* in 1902.[15] There he surveyed synagogue architecture, described building types, and assessed their continued validity. Brunner was particularly critical of what he called "pseudo-Moorish" buildings as "presenting in many cases a grotesque appearance rather than the dignity and simplicity that should have been attained."[16] By contrast, he wrote admiringly that "the use of Classic orders seems especially adapted to the synagogue, and many variations in design are possible."[17] Brunner began his survey with an evaluation of synagogue architecture that, as we shall see later, fits well within the spirit of other *Jewish Encyclopedia* articles:

Ancient Jewish art is mainly represented by the Temple and its fittings, of which all that is left to contemplate is the lower portion of the fortified wall. Even if this overstates the fact, it is most probable that very little distinctively Jewish art ever flourished for an extended period. The position of Judea and its history naturally discouraged the development of art, however vigorous its beginnings may have been. The remains of the ancient synagogues that are now extant present very meager data, and the best preserved of the ancient ones, such as the great synagogue in Kafr Bir'im, while containing much of interest and many characteristic forms, gives but little inspiration to the synagogue builder.

Brunner seems to be generally disappointed that the Baram synagogue provides "so little inspiration." Between his penning of this article and its publication in the *Jewish Encyclopedia* in 1902, however, he seems to have had a change of heart — as evidenced by his plans for the Frank Memorial Synagogue. In this building, the architect drew more than a "little inspiration" from the Baram synagogue.

Brunner's evaluation of Baram was much more enthusiastic in a subsequent two-part article, "Synagogue Architecture," which appeared in 1907 in a general architectural journal known as *The Brickbuilder: Devoted to the Interests of Architecture in Materials of Clay*.[18] There he provided a broad program for synagogue architecture, again praising neoclassicism over other contemporary styles. In designing the Frank Memorial Synagogue, Brunner followed his own sense, presented in *The Brickbuilder*, of "the many laws governing synagogue architecture":

The door of the synagogue faced the west; the ark was at the eastern end; the desk, from which the law was read, was approximately in the center of the building; the space on either side contained benches for the men, and a gallery was constructed for the exclusive use of women. This plan taken as a basis was developed and improved, but there was no deviation from the main ideal. The building was always rectangular,[19] with or without columns. There was no transept, the plan of the basilica being invariably adopted. The ark at the eastern end was erected on a platform reached by steps and the perpetual lamp was suspended in front of it. . . .[20]

Brunner maintained his prescribed rectangular form in the Frank Memorial Synagogue.[21]

Brunner's essay began by broadly attacking the proposition that "it is generally stated that there is no Jewish

architecture."[22] Only then did he turn to the details of synagogue design. His initial polemic was directed against the French architectural historian Julien Gaudet and his 1905 *Éléments et théorie de l'architecture*. As Brunner paraphrased Gaudet's analysis:[23]

It was to have been expected that the Israelites, with a religion older than Christianity, would have produced an architecture with a history, but they did not. Accordingly, the synagogue to-day, the direct descendant of the Temple, is to us a modern problem not materially different from that of the contemporary churches.[24]

Brunner's view of the apparent lack of a Jewish architectural tradition was completely different:[25]

The reason for this lies in the history of the Jewish people. That there were expressions of art in ancient Judea and aspirations for beauty and a fine sense of form are not to be doubted. The use of colors and their combinations was understood, and embroidery, engraving on metals and other ornamental work were extensively practiced. We know, not alone from the scriptures and from the detailed descriptions of the Temple in Josephus, but from the results of actual explorations in Palestine, that the beginnings of Jewish art were vigorous and promising. The state of Judea, however, was not allowed to pursue the arts of peace for any considerable period of time, and the dispersion of the Jews was necessarily fatal to any continuance or development of native art.

Brunner went on to describe with great enthusiasm the remains of the Temple Mount in Jerusalem, where

the stones are laid perfectly true, without mortar. The remains of the great arch that connected the Temple are to be seen, and we find that ancient Judaic architecture employed not only the arch, but vaults, moldings, and sculptured decorations, and there are many other evidences of advanced architectural skill.[26]

This statement is amazingly positive toward Jewish archaeological remains, especially in light of Brunner's earlier comments in the *Jewish Encyclopedia* article. Brunner then moved on to the subject of ancient synagogue architecture, for which he expressesd considerable sympathy. Even as he granted that "the exterior of the majority of the ancient synagogues possessed very little architectural interest and what we call interior decoration hardly existed,"[27] Brunner wrote that

Among the remains of the early synagogues that we know, those in Galilee, described by the Palestine Exploration Society, are among the best preserved, but they give us only scant information. However, there are many details of ornamentation and construction that are most suggestive. The so-called Great Synagogue at Kifr Birim presents, perhaps, the best indication of the early style of architecture employed for these structures.[28]

Brunner then described the architectural features of the Kefar Baram synagogue, concluding with a perceptive dating of this building that has only recently been accepted by most scholars:

We must be impressed by the characteristic and distinctive treatment of sculptured palms, garlands, discs, grapes suspended from knotted cords, olive and vine leaves all cut with a crispness suggesting Byzantine work of the fifth or sixth century.[29]

Brunner drew support for his revised position on Jewish architecture from Eugène-Emmanuel Viollet-Le-Duc, the most significant historian of architecture in nineteenth-century France. Viollet-Le-Duc was responsible for the restoration (some today would say violation) of numerous medieval churches, including the abbey church at Saint-Denis and the cathedrals of Amiens and Notre Dame de Paris. In his extremely influential work *Entretiens sur l'architecture* (1858–72), cited by Brunner from the English translation,[30] Viollet-Le-Duc, Brunner said, "contends that early Jewish art provided inspiration from the Greeks, whom he believes borrowed many details from these primitive buildings. . . ."[31] There is ample reason why Brunner only paraphrases Viollet-Le-Duc's comments. Viollet-Le-Duc did not single out Judeans alone for this early influence on the Greeks, but his rather odd comments included Phoenicians as an influence as well:[32]

During this period [of the Peloponnesian War] – so short and brilliant – the arts of the Greeks radiated far and wide, and their influence extended to the Bosporus, and probably over a part of the coast of Syria. There, however long previous to that glorious epoch, there existed a powerful civilisation, possessing arts marked by a vigour altogether primitive. Phoenicia and Judaea built, traded and colonized, long anterior to the historic times of the Hellenic Peninsula.

Viollet-Le-Duc is clearly pro-Jewish in orientation, attributing Roman architecture to Phoenician and Judaean influence,[33] and Byzantine art to the influence of Second Temple period Jewish architecture.[34] Brunner's reference to Viollet-Le-Duc is used to rhetorical advantage, even as he himself remains unconvinced by Viollet-Le-Duc's thesis:

Upon examining the ruined remains that exist today [of ancient synagogues and tombs] it is evident that whether this art inspired the Greek, or was inspired by the Greeks, it was serious and important, and if circumstances had allowed it to develop, it would have probably continued on much the same lines as the art of Greece.

For Arnold Brunner, neoclassicism had become a distinctly Jewish architectural form, reflecting ancient Jewish architectural principles. Brunner went still further. Based on the remains of the temple and later synagogue ruins, Brunner developed his own rather odd notion of interrupted continuity between ancient classical architecture and modern neoclassicism. He believed that had the Jews not been exiled from Palestine,

As far as one may see, the style of the early Judean buildings, if it had been allowed to progress and develop, might not unreasonably have become to-day what we may call modern classic architecture, the type which is being used very generally for churches in America and elsewhere.

For Brunner, the arrested Jewish architecture of late antiquity would surely have developed into the neoclassicism of his own day. This claim is as naïve as it is ingenious. It provides a seal of authenticity for the only historicized architectural form that Brunner believed could reasonably be used for contemporary synagogue buildings. Brunner's *Brickbuilder* article is prescriptive:

In selecting a style [of synagogue architecture] to-day, I believe firmly that we should either go back to the early Judean architecture, or follow the general custom that prevailed in building synagogues since the dispersion of the Jews, and conform to the style that is in vogue in the land in which the synagogue is erected.

Brunner here articulates a new vision for his work, which he first expressed, as we have seen, in New York's Shearith Israel congregation.[35] He was never again to build a Romanesque synagogue. Brunner designed a "classically styled" home for the Jewish Theological Seminary in New York in 1903, although there he used no specifically Jewish iconography,[36] and again in the neoclassical Union Temple in Brooklyn (1926).[37] In Philadelphia, Arnold Brunner experimented with specifically Jewish iconography, building the Frank Memorial Synagogue based upon principles that he later laid out in *The Brickbuilder*. In the chapel of the Jewish Hospital of Philadelphia, Brunner created a Judaized neoclassical iconography.

Brunner's Judaized neoclassicism was a fitting addition to the religious landscape of late-nineteenth and early-twentieth-century America, where neo-Gothic buildings, each designed in accord with the specific theology of its denomination, were ubiquitous. The Jews built a neoclassical building in their "own" vernacular form on the campus of the Jewish Hospital.

The sophistication of the Frank Memorial Synagogue project fits well with the high level of both Jewish and secular sophistication that was to be found among the German–Jewish elite in turn-of-the-century Philadelphia. Mayer Sulzberger, jurist, communal leader and "patriarch" of Philadelphia Jewry,[38] for example, intended to receive the synagogue on behalf of the hospital at the dedication ceremony.[39] Rabbi Marcus Jastrow, the renowned academic Talmudist and rabbi of Philadelphia's Rodeph Shalom Congregation, spoke. His son, Morris Jastrow, a librarian and research professor of Assyriology at the University of Pennsylvania, led High Holy Day services in the synagogue in 1901. Brunner was in close contact with Philadelphian Cyrus Adler, who himself authored the entry on Brunner in the *Jewish Encyclopedia*. In 1913, Adler described Brunner as "the advisor on all matters of art and antiquity" to another prominent member of the German–Jewish aristocracy.[40] As previously mentioned, Brunner was eulogized by Felix M. Warburg, who himself financed the Harvard excavations of Samaria.[41] Warburg concludes his obituary for Brunner with the rhetorical question: "Is it any wonder that he was beloved, and his untimely death mourned by so many?" The Jewishly and secularly learned, often traditionally observant, German–Jewish elite of late-nineteenth-century and early-twentieth-century Philadelphia provided rich soil for the construction of the Frank Memorial Synagogue. Jonathan D. Sarna describes the sense of purposefulness that this Jewish elite felt as "they attempted, through works of culture, to promote a sense of Jewish identity":[42]

However much they argued among themselves over religious and other issues, they nevertheless championed the idea of a unified Jewish cultural tradition, rooted in history, ideas, values, and sacred texts, that linked American Jews one to another, as well as backward through time.

Built on Jewishly neutral ground, at a site belonging to the entire Jewish community but to neither traditionalists nor reformers exclusively, the new synagogue was an ideal context through which to express this unity. The Frank Memorial Synagogue bespoke a shared religious tradition, but in an idiom that was detached from traditional and well-known Jewish iconography or the traditional textual canon of Jewish knowledge. Its architecture was in some measure an expression of traditional religion that stemmed ultimately from nontraditional sources. In terms of ancient Judaism, this shared tradition, cleansed of many of its more "folkish" (and thus embarrassing) Eastern European elements, was called the religion of "Catholic Israel" by Solomon Schechter[43] and later "normative Judaism," by American Protestant scholar George Foot Moore.[44] The Frank Memorial Synagogue represented the religion of "Catholic Israel" in brick and mortar. In scholarly terms, this shared tradition was not the religion of traditional Orthodoxy, even for the Orthodox. Rather, it was Jewish tradition as read through the shared agency of modern academic scholarship, the *Wissenschaft des Judentums*.

Scholarship at the time the Frank Synagogue was built was beginning to integrate archaeological remains into its understanding of ancient Judaism. The focal point of this interest was Budapest, among students of the legendary *Wissenschaft* scholar David Kaufmann – who, among other things, was the first Jewish art historian.[45] The multinational Hapsburg Empire, and Budapest in particular, were fertile soil for such scholarship. Ludwig Blau and Samuel Krauss, both of whom were scholars of rabbinic literature, shared a profound interest in setting Jewish sources within the broadest possible context. Each a contributor to the *Jewish Encyclopedia*, they were among the first to actively interpret archaeological evidence in full light of their immense knowledge of rabbinic literature. Krauss, the more conservative of the two, seems to have been closest in spirit to rabbinics' scholarship in turn-of-the-century America. A traditionalist as well as a Zionist, he asserted absolute continuity between Jewish archaeological discoveries, rabbinic literature, and classical sources. Krauss's *Talmudische Archäologe*, published in 1910/11,[46] is a classic of this approach. This work is still the foundational work for a small but influential group of academic Talmudists who continue to incorporate archaeological discoveries in their interpretations of rabbinic literature. As Saul Lieberman of the Jewish Theological Seminary later wrote, "it is impossible to explain correctly neither the *Halakhah* nor the *Aggadah* without understanding the form of the millstone [the subject of Lieberman's article], its history, development and use."[47]

A renewed, modernized study of ancient Jewish sources motivated Jewish scholars in America and in Western Europe at the turn of the twentieth century. This dedication to a shared, ancient tradition studied in new ways was expressed through support of Palestinian archaeology in the years following World War I. This is well expressed in a 1929 letter encouraging funding of the Jewish Palestine Exploration Society. Instructively, the letter was signed by the presidents of all American rabbinical seminaries, accomplished *Wissenschaft* scholars in their own right: Cyrus Adler, of the Jewish Theological Seminary; Stephen S. Wise of the Jewish Institute of Religion (which later merged with Hebrew Union College); Julian Morgenstern of the Hebrew Union College; and Bernard Revel representing Yeshiva University. Adler, Wise, and Morgenstern all were involved in financing Hebrew University of Jerusalem excavations, Morgenstern and Wise in a Hebrew University plan to purchase and excavate ancient synagogues.[48] It is worthy of note that whereas the Rabbi Isaac Elchanan Seminary of Yeshiva University (1928) was built in a modernized Moorish repertory, the floor of the southern Amsterdam Avenue entrance was paved with a zodiac. One wonders whether this was done as a reference to the Na'aran synagogue mosaic and its zodiac (discovered in 1918).[49] Just as the American Jewish elite strove to meld a modernized pan-Jewish tradition with Americanism, Brunner's Frank Memorial Synagogue consciously melds Jewish and classical architectural traditions with a new concern for what later came to be called "Jewish archaeology."[50]

Some Jews looked to archaeology for a model of Jewish normality that they believed existed before the much-maligned medieval period. In 1924, Blau made this explicit in the course of a discussion of Jewish languages in the inaugural volume of the *Wissenschaft* journal of American Reform, the *Hebrew Union College Annual:*[51]

In every age the Jews adopted the language and customs of the peoples with whom they dwelt, without, however, losing their identity among them. This fact, the most important which history can confirm regarding the Jewish people, shall not be elaborated on in detail in this article, but we shall content ourselves merely with observing that the same statement may be made and confirmed with reference to Jewish script, if we leave out of consideration the period from the sixteenth to the eighteenth centuries in Eastern Europe, i.e. Poland and the contiguous countries. The Jews originally were not a Ghetto people, and did not become one until they were driven to it.

Accordingly the script and language they employ are infallible witnesses as to their environment and condition. . . .

Blau's agenda in this article, shared to some extent by all of the American Jews we have discussed, was the search for a premedieval balance between participation in the general culture and Jewish particularity that could serve as a model for the present. The dichotomy between "Hellenism" and "Hebraism," so common in contemporaneous thought, finds no quarter here, as it did not in the Frank Memorial Synagogue.[52] The classical styling of the Frank Memorial Synagogue exterior (which only initiates would know is related to ancient synagogues) is in harmony with the extended Hebrew inscription from the Baram synagogue on the cornice. By virtue of this inscription, Jews and non-Jews who could not read Hebrew would certainly recognize this to be a Jewish building, and those with Jewish knowledge would recognize the prayer book-like phraseology. Once again, the initiates – people like the Jastrows and Adler, would know that this inscription derives from an ancient synagogue ruin in Palestine. The Frank Memorial Synagogue is an architectural projection of the old yet new hybrid Jewish–Americanism that Jews within Brunner's social sphere so thoroughly cherished and sought to build.[53] It is both "Hellenic" and "Hebraic" at the same time.

Brunner's apology for Jewish architecture goes much deeper than these local or even national considerations. Brunner's attitude is in marked contrast to that expressed in the reports of the Palestine Exploration Society, which he clearly studied in detail. Their *Surveys of Western Palestine* presented accurate description of the state of Jewish material culture in Palestine, describing not only the great monumental remains of throughout Palestine, including the Upper Galilee, but also smaller remains as well. The principle investigator of the synagogue, H. H. Kitchener, concluded as early as 1878 that the Galilean-type synagogues whose remains he meticulously described at Capernaum, Chorazin, Kefar Baram, Meiron, and elsewhere were constructed by Romans on behalf of the Jewish community:[54]

The Jews themselves, having taken to commercial pursuits, were unable to perform works of this sort, and by using Roman workmen obtained much finer results than we are led to think they would themselves be capable of. . . . We may therefore suppose that they were forced upon the people by the local Roman rulers at a time when they were completely submissive to that power, and that [as] directly [as] they were able, they deserted such Pagan buildings, a disloyalty to their religion.

This evaluation was repeated in *The Survey of Western Palestine, Special Papers* in 1881.[55] Brunner clearly did not accept Kitchener's historical conclusion, which he passed over in damning silence in both of his articles. Kitchener assumes a religious and economic rationale for the perceived lack of "works of this sort" made by Jews, projecting into antiquity anti-Semitic stereotypes regarding Jewish business acumen and nonparticipation in arts and crafts. Kitchener's model for interpreting ancient synagogues was carried on by two of the most esteemed archaeologists of turn-of-the-century Germany, Heinrich Kohl and Karl Watzinger. Between 1905 and 1907, Kohl and Watzinger explored and partially excavated many of the Galilean synagogues that the Palestine Exploration Society had previously explored. They essentially adopted Kitchener's position as a given. Perhaps, this interpretation is not so odd when we consider that between 1790 and 1840, a series of round synagogues was built in Germany that reflect a relationship to local authority that parallels Kitchener's approach. These were built on the property of local rulers in conformity with "the worldly taste of the Christian rulers and the Jewish elite who commissioned them from Christian architects."[56] Perhaps the best example is the synagogue of Wörlitz in Germany. Carole Krinsky's description of the relation of the Jews to the local rulers is reminiscent of Kitchener's evaluation of ancient Galilean Jews. According to Krinsky, this synagogue[57]

built in 1789–90 by court architect Friedrich Wilhelm von Erdmannsdorf was a round pavilion in the gardens of the Jews' patron; the synagogue was also known as the Temple of Vesta — which shows the congregation's position before emancipation as the private domain of the Grand Duke of Anhalt-Dessau.

The strands that come together in Brunner's treatise and ultimately in the Frank Memorial Synagogue reflect a century of Western reflection on the place of art in Judaism. This reflection was recently surveyed, as I have mentioned, by Margaret Olin and Kalman P. Bland.[58] Bland distinguishes between attitudes toward art and Judaism in Protestant and Catholic contexts. Bland shows that in Protestant Germany, pivotal thinkers such as Immanuel Kant and Georg Wilhelm Friedrich Hegel constructed the notion that Jews are "artless," as part of their continuing

"protest" against Catholicism.[59] Seeing themselves as the true Israel, Protestants bashed Catholic iconicism by positing an aniconic Judaism that was the model of Biblical truth. This originally German Protestant attitude was thoroughly absorbed by leading elements within Western Jewry. In an article published in the *Jewish Quarterly Review* in London in July 1901, for example, British painter Solomon J. Solomon aligned Judaism firmly with Protestantism, stating that "a great part of Israel's mission is fulfilled in the teaching of the Protestant Church."[60] He continues that "it is clear that in religious thought Israel is more closely allied to the Protestant than to any other sect." By "sect," Solomon refers to Roman Catholicism and Anglicanism, which he believed were on the wane.[61] For this author, the similarity between Judaism and Puritanical Protestantism is expressed in attitudes toward the visual, our author asserting that "art plays no part" in the ideal forms of either tradition.

For German Protestants, the aniconic evaluation of Judaism contained within it what would soon be a troubling nationalistic aspect. The artlessness of the Jews mirrored German doubts as to the viability of their own national art, especially when compared with French art. Self-doubts as to the quality and depth of German national culture, especially art, set an important context for understanding how German Protestants assessed Jewish art. The useful Jews of necessity fared badly when set up as the alter ego of the self-critical Germans. As Hans Belting notes in his *The Germans and Their Art: A Troublesome Relationship*, "Nationalistic overtones had always functioned to exaggerate the importance of [German] art in order to compensate for the public's lack of conviction in it. When German art did not seem to measure up, it was raised to symbolizing a national ideal in constant struggle against an antagonistic modern movement."[62]

The Protestant assessment pervades the central articles on the visual within *The Jewish Encyclopedia*. It is expressed, as we have seen, by Brunner in his "Synagogue Architecture." This notion was so thoroughly engrained that the *Jewish Encyclopedia* affords veracity to a pseudo-scientific evaluation of this supposed lack of artistic capacity. The German Protestant theologian and orientalist Immanuel Benzinger wrote in "Art Among the Ancient Hebrews" that[63]

Such a command as that of the Decalogue (Ex. xx. 4; Deut. v.) would have been impossible to a nation possessed of such artistic gifts as the Greeks, and was carried to its ultimate consequences – as to-day in Islam – only because the people lacked artistic inclination, with its creative power and imagination. . . . The same reason, to which is to be added a defective sense of color, prevented any development of painting.

On the next page of the same volume, the noted Reform scholar Kaufmann Kohler, steeped in the intellectual culture of German Protestantism, takes virtually the same approach. Kohler suggests that because of the Second Commandment, "it is . . . somewhat incorrect to speak of Jewish art."[64]

Yet within the *Jewish Encyclopedia*, another voice can be heard, although not textually. Within the pages of the encyclopedia, the editors placed and showcased literally thousands of "illustrations." This vast resource (developed cumulatively with the serial publication of the twelve volumes), constitutes one of the finest repositories of Jewish material culture to this day. The editors clearly considered "one of the special aims of the Encyclopedia to bring together as full a body of illustrative material as possible."[65] Still only "illustrations," and not called art, the editors, led by Cyrus Adler, believed that this assemblage would "prove of great educational value in every Jewish household." The illustrations are the last feature of the encyclopedia to be discussed in the preface to volume one. They are the only area of the *Jewish Encyclopedia* that appeals to "the Jewish household" for legitimization and not to scholarship. Nevertheless, the illustrations clearly belie the anti-Jewish art arguments bespoken in various academic articles. The illustrations of the *Jewish Encyclopedia*, many of them in color, present what might be construed as a countervoice to the academic arguments. Whereas the articles argued that Jewish art is a contradiction in terms, the illustrations shout out its vitality.[66] This second voice – the nonliterary one – parallels the celebration of ancient Jewish architecture expressed in Brunner's Frank Memorial Synagogue in 1901. It is a harbinger of a change in Jewish self-awareness that would only reach written form later in the first decade of the twentieth century.

Brunner does not resort to the German Protestant model in his *Brickbuilder* article. Rather, he rejects it through omission. It is not the German intellectual tradition, exemplified in the *Jewish Encyclopedia* articles, that resulted in Brunner's ancient synagogue on the Delaware. Brunner found support in the intellectual oeuvre of French Catholic scholarship. Bland has shown that Catholics took a position diametrically opposed to that of Protestant scholarship.

Seeing themselves and not the Protestants as the "true Israel," Catholics retorted that Jews in Biblical times had a rich visual culture, drawing their proof from descriptions of the Biblical Tabernacle and Temple.

Viollet-Le-Duc's assertions that Greek and Roman architecture are indebted to Phoenicians and Judaeans, and his claim that Byzantine architecture is influenced not by Roman but by ancient Jewish architecture, as preserved in Jerusalem, reflects this Catholic response to attacks on church art:[67]

Psychological considerations therefore combine with the investigations of monumental remains, to render it probable that Byzantine Art derived some of its decorative constituents from Palestine. I am aware of the prejudices that oppose this hypothesis: we have none of us forgotten the opinions of Voltaire respecting the Jewish people; But Voltaire had no conception of the nature and value of the primitive arts of Syria; and I suggest that his very persistence in endeavouring to depreciate that people and the wit he employs in making it ridiculous, should put us on our guard against his views on the question. One does not take so much pains to destroy that which has no veritable basis; and the warmth of Voltaire's attack on this inconsiderable Jewish people is an indication if its real importance.

Voltaire's anti-Judaism is well known. It was deeply intertwined with his disdain of Christianity and particularly of Roman Catholicism.[68] Viollet-Le-Duc is responding to Voltaire's oft-repeated and reformulated position that the Jews "were a wretched Arabic tribe without art or science, hidden in a small, hilly and ignorant land."[69] By defending the Jews and particularly ancient Jewish artistic creativity, Viollet-Le-Duc was defending the visual traditions of the Catholic Church. Asserting the Jewish rather than classical origins of Byzantine art, Viollet-Le-Duc further removed Christian art from the claim that it was idolatrous. In adopting Viollet-Le-Duc's platform, Brunner adopted the positive Catholic evaluation of Jewish art over the negative Protestant assessment that he himself had accepted in his *Jewish Encyclopedia* article. This transformation within Brunner is striking, and is related to a more general trend toward greater Jewish awareness and a less assimilationist attitude within American Jewry as the new century dawned. Brunner has done nothing less than rewrite in stone the narrative of Jewish artlessness.

To conclude: Through the focusing lens of the Frank Memorial Synagogue, I have provided a thick description of the process by which Arnold Brunner rewrote the story of Jewish architecture, bringing to the fore ancient, yet new, Jewish sources to mold a neoclassical Jewish architecture, one that was revolutionary in its "traditionalism."[70] Brunner's personal development, evidenced in his writings as in his architecture, reflects a reevaluation among Jews of his social circle of their artistic heritage. Although in the text of the *Jewish Encyclopedia* (though not in the illustrations) Jews were willing to posit their own artlessness, by the end of the first decade of the twentieth century, American Jews were questioning this approach and their own assimilationist tendencies. In Brunner's case, this transformation resulted from rejection of German Protestant conceptions of Jewish artlessness and his embrace of French Catholic positive attitudes toward Jewish art. A new Jewish art was developing — or, to be more precise, a new Jewish evaluation of traditional Jewish artistic production and the possibilities resonating within it. This interest in art was not merely aesthetic or academic — the existence of Jewish art was essential for the acceptance of Judaism and the Jews in the company of twentieth-century religions and nations.

CHAPTER TWO

THE OLD–NEW LAND

JEWISH ARCHAEOLOGY AND THE ZIONIST NARRATIVE

. . . the study would be facilitated to a certain extent by the listing and systematic examination of the material which is still at hand and yet widely scattered (in Rome, Paris, London and other places). Whereas at universities and Christian seminaries such museums have been established as an auxiliary of theological instruction, the rabbinical seminaries do not possess any monuments at all, or at least, they contain nothing worth mentioning. In fact, it does not occur to anyone to read about the Jewish monuments, and, as far as I know, such a subject of study figures in no curriculum and there exists no Jewish archaeologist in the sense of the term employed here. . . . *To America, which has at its disposal the means and the teaching staff, there is here offered a grateful field of activity – the founding of Jewish archaeology. It is well worth the exertion and the money of the noble.* The carrying out of this plan would not be difficult, because in such a museum first of all *copies* could be procured, which in the course of time would be able to be increased by the systematic acquisition of *originals*. Copies would be of great service in instruction. In Palestine there has been founded a Jewish Archaeological Society which, let us hope, will carry on its labors successfully. This society, as is quite natural, confines itself exclusively to the Holy Land, but that which I am proposing has reference to all lands, a plan which only America would be able to carry in view of the present conditions. It would be a religious and national achievement at the same time, even as it would be a furtherance of general science, not *only* Jewish science. A general exhibition of the Jewish monuments would level the way for the establishment of institutions to carry out this suggested task, a work which enthusiastic men would be in a position to accomplish.

S O WROTE LUDWIG BLAU IN THE *Hebrew Union College Annual* of 1926. Writing from impoverished post-war Budapest, Blau looked to American Jewish institutions, which at the time were modestly subsidizing his own seminary,[1] to found Jewish archaeology. It was Palestine, however, where this approach developed its vital energy and where "enthusiastic men" set out to create Jewish archaeology. A fascinating group of cultural Zionists came to see in archaeology a potent tool for rewriting the Jewish past in the image of their own aspirations for a very different Jewish future. Archaeology was construed to be a tangible link to the Land of Israel and increasingly seen as a kind of "deed" hidden in the soil of Palestine – waiting to be dug up by modern archaeologists.[2] It was enlisted in the national project of taking physical possession of the "ancestral homeland," and provided historical Jewish content and legitimacy in the construction of what the founder of political Zionism, Theodor Herzl, called the *Altneuland*, the "Old–New Land."[3] At the same time, archaeology provided ancient Jewish art for cultural Zionists concerned – often in tandem with American and European culturalists who were not Zionists – with creating a contemporary Jewish artistic tradition.

Early Zionist interest in archaeology was concerned first and foremost with synagogue archaeology. The two most important early excavators of synagogues at the formative stage of this discipline were Nahum Slouschz and E. L. Sukenik. Slouschz conducted the first "Hebrew excavation," carried out by the Jewish Palestine Exploration Society (the same organization to which Blau refers). E. L. Sukenik was the true father of Jewish archaeology. I show that Sukenik's career closely parallels the plan set out by Blau for the formulation of Jewish archaeology. I continue with a discussion of ways that Zionist interests have fashioned scholarly interpretation of ancient Jewish art and archaeology.

THE JEWISH PALESTINE EXPLORATION SOCIETY AND THE BIRTH OF HEBREW ARCHAEOLOGY

Jewish participation in the archaeological exploration of Palestine began with the acquisition of the synagogue ruins at Meiron in the Upper Galilee by a society led by Jerusalem educator and scholar David Yellin, sometime near the close of World War I.[4] This was called the "Fund for the Redemption of Historical Sites," *Qeren le-Geulat Meqomot Histori'im.*[5] The title parallels the *Qeren Kayemet Le-Geulat Eretz Yisrael* (the "Fund for the Redemption of the Land of Israel," the Jewish National Fund), both titles making secularized use of traditional Jewish redemptive language. The founding of the Jewish Palestine Exploration Society (JPES) in 1913 – and its revitalization in 1920 – gave institutional expression to growing Zionist interest in the archaeology of Palestine. The JPES, later the Israel Exploration Society, marked the entry of the Jews into the European competition to possess Palestine through archaeological exploration. The board of overseers of the postwar society included the greatest luminaries of early cultural Zionism: Yellin; Eliezer Ben-Yehuda, celebrated as the "father of modern Hebrew"; Joseph Klausner, a literary critic and historian; Boris Schatz, founder of the Bezalel Art Institute; and Professor Nahum Slouschz (pronounced Slousch). Tel Aviv resident Chaim Nahman Bialik, dubbed the "poet laureate of Israel," helped to procure resources for the society.

"Professor Slouschz" (as he was always called) was one of the first important Zionist academics, having held the newly founded chair of modern Hebrew language and literature at the Sorbonne (1904). A member of the pre-Herzl *Ḥovevei Zion* movement, Slouschz also wrote the first ethnography of North African Jewry, prepared corpora of Semitic inscriptions, and wrote a cultural history of the Mediterranean.[6] In 1921 the editor of the *Menorah Journal* wrote: "Savant, traveler, discoverer, master of tongues Western and Oriental, Dr. Nahum Slouschz is surely one of the most versatile and 'legendary' of modern Wandering Jews."[7] After the war, Slouschz settled in Palestine and, by revitalizing the Jewish Palestine Exploration Society, fulfilled a longtime goal of engaging in archaeological excavation of the Holy Land. His participation in the JPES provided academic prestige and credentials for the project, and in Zionist circles presumed archaeological competence. Slouschz seems to have had a well-developed sense of the dramatic, sparking the usually staid W. F. Albright's comment that "unfortunately he (Slouschz) had not received any real training in either epigraphy or archaeology, and his part was important chiefly because of his flair for publicity and his success in interesting the public in the Jewish archaeology of Palestine."[8]

The first excavation carried out by the Jewish Palestine Exploration Society took place in 1920/21 at Hammath Tiberias (the hot springs of Tiberias), on the shores of the Sea of Galilee just south of Tiberias. Often overlooked, this project is of singular importance for interpreting Zionist archaeology. Slouschz not only recovered artifacts that were deemed meaningful, but also set in place many of the essential ideological contours of the Zionist "Old–New Land." Evidence for this excavation is broad, spanning the artifacts themselves (now in the collection of the Institute of Archaeology of the Hebrew University of Jerusalem), Slouschz's scholarly and popular reports, and early motion picture footage by pioneering cinematographer Yakov Ben Dov.[9]

Happily for all concerned, the discoveries were quite spectacular. Slouschz found remains of an ancient "chancel" screen, a mosaic, a capital decorated with menorahs, and, most important, an intact limestone menorah. Slouschz described his discoveries in the first issue of the Hebrew-language *Journal of the Jewish Palestine Exploration Society*, where it was the lead article:[10]

Under the paving stones, a stone with carving was discovered. It was located a bit below the level of the floor, and a bit protruded from under the stones that were missing in the center of that place. When we cleaned some of the dust that was above it, revealed before us was a large menorah, in the form of the menorah of the Temple in every detail, as it is written in the book of Exodus, chapter 25 and chapter 37. It is made of limestone similar to marble (and not local stone, in any event). . . .

Slouschz then describes the menorah, using terminology from the Biblical description in Exodus. He continued:

I realized that, before me was a menorah made exactly (*mamash*) in the form of the holy menorah, which served in the ancient synagogue, and which they [the ancients] hid away for their own reasons for which I will soon return. The significance of this discovery gave me hope in my heart for future finds. Also the workers were very impressed by the

6. Nahum Slouschz (center) and his team with the Hammath Tiberias menorah (courtesy of the Israel Exploration Society).

discovery of a beautiful physical relic of our past, that is of visual interest and not of faint letters and images.

. . . We carried it to the sea and we washed it in water so as to remove from it the layer of dust, and the photographer returned and photographed the menorah and the workers around it (Figure 6). News of the discovery spread in the local area, and Jewish and non-Jewish visitors came in great numbers, so much so that I decided to open the antiquities room, which the government authorities had placed at my disposal in the bath house, to the public who come in great numbers. This was on Tuesday, the ninth of Iyar (May 11, 1921).

Slouschz appended to his discussion a footnote that represents both his patronizing attitude toward his Sephardi workmen and reflects through the prism of rabbinic Hebrew the excitement of the moment:

Whoever had not seen the festive joy (*ha-simha ha-hogeget*) of the Sephardi workers when they carried the menorah has never seen the happiness of the pure (*temimim*)!

In this final report on the synagogue, Slouschz does not spell out the background for his "great happiness" in any concentrated manner. This, it seems, would have been considered unscientific – and thus not appropriate for a scholarly presentation. Fortunately for us, in an article written for a more general learned audience in *Hashiloach*, Slouschz explained the significance of his work in some detail.[11] I translate here a large block of this text, which expresses well the ideological underpinnings of early Zionist archaeology:

It has been many decades since the scholars of the nations began to excavate in the depths of the soil of our ancestors. They have already succeeded in spreading light over the darkness covering its great past. This is not the place to detail the results of these excavations, which have been carried out in various places: in Gezer, in Lachish, in Taanak, in Meggido, in Beth Shemesh, and recently in Jericho and Samaria. The point is that owing to these projects it has become clear to us that also the soil of the Land of Israel covers significant remnants of the material culture of its past inhabitants, and that uncovering these remnants will shed considerable light upon the riddle of the political, economic and cultural life that was distinctive to Israel in its land. If this is so, how can we, the offspring of Hebrew culture and its builders for the future, stand at a distance and watch as our work is done by others?

For that which has been done in this discipline thus far is minute, and our ideology and purpose is different from that of most Gentile scholars. It is not accidental that the important excavations that have been carried out until now have focused upon sites known as Canaanite and Greek centers, and that the only Hebrew site where anything at all has been done is on account of the desire and subvention of a single wealthy Jew?[12] Even there it was only a start, though the beginnings were promising.

It is clear, therefore, that there is room for us to distinguish ourselves. We truly strive to learn and to know what the people of Israel accomplished and created during the period when their political lives were normal. We greatly desire to trace the development of our language, crafts and industry throughout the generations when material and political existence had still not been pushed aside by the life of religion and the spirit. We are hungry to know the secret of the existence of our people in its land even after the destruction of its political life, and the secret of its great spiritual creativity.

In addition, there are entire periods that are important to us, the Jews, for which the nations have no need. For example, the period when Israel lived on its soil in the Galilee and worked in crafts, farming, and other skilled activities. Further, we know much about the lives of our ancestors in the days of the Tannaim and the Amoraim, but we know virtually nothing of the [later] period when the *masorah* [standardizing the Biblical text], *niqud* [Hebrew system of vocalization] and *piyyut* [liturgical poetry] developed and our language was revitalized. Who will wipe away the dust from the eyes of Yose son of Yose, Yannai and Eleazar ha-Qallir so as to tell us of their history and reveal their birthplaces and tombs?

Questions such as these, which are of little importance to the Christians, are an entire Torah for us and we must learn it. Because the members of the "Hebrew Society for the Exploration of Eretz Israel and its Antiquities" in Jerusalem

understand the importance of answering these questions, they saw fit to conduct the first excavations in the Land of Israel by Jews, to begin work on the site where the ancient city of Tiberias stood – the city that is second to Jerusalem in its national value. There dwelled the patriarchs, the sages of the Talmud, the *masorah* and *piyyut*. [Tiberias] served as the spiritual center of Israel more than 800 years. . . .

Slouschz saw in archaeology access to a period when Jews were a nation imbedded in their land, speaking their language, and in keeping with the romantic nationalism of his day, possessing their own "crafts and industry." Archaeology was a key to rediscovering independent Jewish political life that was not yet encumbered with the presumed ills of diaspora life. This was a standard classical Zionist rationale for studying the Jewish past in the Land of Israel, one that readers of *Hashiloach* would recognize.

Slouschz believed that the Hammath Tiberias excavation was especially important because it involved a post-Biblical site, and not the earlier periods that Christian archaeologists often found of interest. This was a Jewish site, revealing Jewish content that fit well with the interests of both traditional scholarship and the *Wissenschaft des Judentums*. In both contexts, rabbinic literature stands at the center of the canon; the study of Scripture unmediated by the rabbis was of considerably less interest.[13] His interest in discovering the tombs of liturgical authors, many of whose works were virtually unknown at that time but were of interest to *Wissenschaft* scholars, bespeaks traditionalist moorings, a bit of sappy popularizing, and Slouschz's earnest hope that archaeology would form an integral part of Zionist scholarship. Slouschz's rabbinic orientation is imbedded in the language of his articles, which like all literary Hebrew of his day, are written in an idiom strongly influenced by rabbinic Hebrew.

Slouschz reports in *Hashiloach* that the discoveries at Hammath Tiberias made quite a sensation. At one point, he writes of the Jewish workers in the recently formed Zionist Labor Brigade (*Gedud ha-Avodah*) who not only discovered the first remains of the synagogue in the course of road building on the shore of the Sea of Galilee, but also remained interested throughout the excavations. Slouschz describes these Eastern European "refugees from destruction" excitedly coming "out of their tents" (a Biblical idiom with distinctly contemporary resonance) to see each new discovery.[14] At another point he tells how:[15]

Almost all of the residents of Tiberias, with them the Governor [Herbert Samuel] and later Edwin Samuel and his wife, came to celebrate the sight that was revealed from beneath the soil. Teachers and their students also came. The Arab teacher explained to his students with all seriousness that the seven-branched menorah proves that this shrine was built by "Sultan Solomon" (King Solomon).

The holiness of Rabbi Meir,[16] which envelopes this place, influenced the Sephardi sages and the Sephardi population especially. When I explained my position that on the site of the building was once the famous synagogue known in the Talmud at the "Synagogue of Ḥammatan" where the *tanna* Rabbi Meir publicly taught Torah, the notion was well received by the sages of Tiberias. On Friday a congregation of rabbis and dignitaries came and prayed [the afternoon] *minḥah* prayers publicly and thus sanctified the place that was abandoned and hidden for many, many generations.

In describing the visitors to the Hammath Tiberias site, Slouschz included representatives of virtually the entire body politic of Jewish Palestine. Within this hierarchy, representatives of the British colonial government and Eastern European secular Zionist road builders fare best. Sephardi rabbis and their followers are also treated with a modicum of respect, not the least because they accepted Slouschz's interpretation of the site in light of rabbinic sources. Missing is the then-declining Ashkenazi religious elite of the "Old *Yishuv.*" For these traditionalists, "secular" Zionism, however clothed in a rhetoric of tradition, was heretical. They would have none of the Zionist usurpation of their historic right to interpret the Jewish past. In the decades to follow, this constituency was to voice antagonism toward Zionist archaeology.[17] In his *Hashiloach* article, Slouschz even includes Arabs, although his treatment is distinctly condescending ("orientalizing") toward the well-meaning Arab teacher. Slouschz is vitally interested in proving the significance of archaeology for Jewish self-definition during the twentieth century. The secularized nationalist identity that he advocates is bolstered "scientifically" by archaeology and supported by secular Ashkenazim, by Sephardi rabbis, by the ruling British Empire, and even by the primitive and otherwise acquiescent Arabs. Hammath Tiberias was first and foremost an internal Jewish affair – or, more particularly, an accomplishment of the old–new "Hebrew" society in the making.

Another indication of the significance of the Hammath Tiberias excavation for the Zionist enterprise resides in the then-nascent Palestinian film industry. Ben Dov, the Bezalel-trained photographer turned cinematographer, included a sequence lasting just over six minutes in his 1921 silent Zionist propaganda film, *Shivat Zion* (*Return to Zion*). This film preserves the most important photographic record of the Hammath Tiberias excavation. Although Ben Dov arrived at Hammath Tiberias after the initial clearance of the synagogue, an attempt at dramatic contemporaneity is made when a brush is shown whisking dust off the synagogue mosaic. The prayer hall was photographed after excavation (these are virtually the only extant photographic images of this project), and the artifacts are shown in detail – apparently as displayed by Slouschz to the local public. In presenting Hammath Tiberias, Ben Dov was particularly interested in artifacts with images of the menorah, although unlike Slouschz's article in *Hashiloach*, he does not stress the stone menorah. The presence of the Labor Brigade is a major focus in this sequence, as it is throughout *Shivat Zion.* The Sephardi workers are not highlighted. Ben Dov consciously valorized the excavation and the excavators, turning Slouschz into a culture hero and the (Ashkenazi) Labor Brigade members into officiates of the cult. The presence of the British inspector of archaeology provides an aura of professional and legal legitimization to the excavation and the excavators.

In one extended sequence, Ben Dov presents Slouschz directing members of the Labor Brigade as the Zionist workers open a Roman-period sarcophagus and the government inspector looks on. Inside, a well-preserved skeleton is revealed. Slouschz excitedly removes a glass drinking cup and shows it to the assembly. There is no positive archaeological evidence whereby to assert the Jewishness of the interned. This is exactly what Slouschz did, however, in his *Hashiloach* article. As in the film, his status as discoverer and interpreter of the discoveries is emphasized (Figure 7):[18]

Thus four large sarcophagi were uncovered within fifteen meters from the shrine, one beside the other – a remnant of an ancient cemetery. On the surfaces of the sarcophagi images of circles were found, half-circles, and lines similar to those that we find on the marble tablets and other utensils (from the synagogue) that were made by Jews of those generations. We removed the cover from the second sarcophagus – and I found the skeleton of a man, fragments of a glass bottle and a glass cup. It is possible that this is a cup for hand washing (*netilat yadaim*) for the [eschatological] future.

In the excitement of the cinematographic moment, the skeleton undergoes a sort of redemption – almost a reviviation of Ezekiel's dry bones, thanks to Slouschz, the Zionist road workers, the benevolent British mandatory

7. Nahum Slouschz with a British inspector and workmen, Hammath Tiberias Synagogue excavations. From Yakov Ben Dov's 1921 film *Shivat Zion* (courtesy of the Steven Spielberg Jewish Film Archive).

government, science, and the Zionist dream of a secularized "redemption" of the Jews in "their own land." This parallels the reviviation of the newly muscular Labor Brigade members who excavate his remains, as these new immigrants sink their roots into the Land of Israel. This moment of redemption exemplifies the sense of secularized messianic time that Palestinian Jews felt was upon them as a result of the Balfour Declaration of 1917 expressing British support for "the establishment in Palestine of a national home for the Jewish people," and the subsequent establishment of the British mandate under high commissioner Herbert Samuel – a British Jew who likened himself to a "new Nehemiah." The film ignores the fact that disturbing the dead is widely frowned upon by Jewish tradition. Slouschz seems to be aware of this in his article, tentatively (and outlandishly) identifying the glass cup found with the body as a washing cup used to remove ritual defilement. Slouschz was raised traditionally and had spent World War I teaching Jewish history at the precursor institution to Yeshiva University[19] (having been exiled from Ottoman Palestine along with his relative, Izhak Ben Zvi).[20] *Shivat Zion*, like Slouschz's rhetoric in his *Hashiloach* article and "secular" Zionism itself, makes use of traditional Jewish categories throughout, categories clearly reinvested with contemporary Zionist meaning. Ben Dov came to Hammath Tiberias to record and valorize the happy coincidence of Zionist road building, the scientific discovery of Jewish archaeological remains from the Talmudic period,[21] and, most of all, the "redemptive" return of the Jews to their land. Ben Zvi, later the second president of Israel, described

both Slouschz's approach and the ideology of early Zionist scholarship: "More than being drawn toward the frozen past, he (Slouschz) is passionately drawn to the present that is being renewed and to the vision for future. . . . This vision for the future is reflected in each and every line of his studies and articles."[22]

The excavation of Hammath Tiberias – celebrated in public exhibition, print, and film – was a significant moment in the ideological development of Zionism. As such, it set the tone for all later Zionist archaeology – both in its attempt at scholarly rigor and as a popular ritual of the cult of the "Old–New Land." It is the first example of many to follow in which archaeological excavation became a central form of secular Zionist ritual drama – a new way of possessing the Land. This element was promoted by Slouschz in writing and by Ben Dov in the new medium of film. Beginning with Hammath Tiberias, "digging" became a nationalistic ritual, for the participants as well as vicariously for distant observers and museum visitors who witnessed the "relics" uncovered. As a result, the archaeologist emerged as both a cult hero and a cult officiate.[23]

The important work that lies before me is the creation of Jewish Archaeology.

E. L. Sukenik, personal journal, July 1928[24]

It is astonishing how closely Sukenik's career parallels the plan suggested by Blau in 1926. Born in Bialystok, Poland in 1889 of a traditional upbringing, Sukenik spent four years as a student of the Slobodka Yeshiva, one of the leading *yeshivot* of his day. He came to Palestine in 1912. Early on, Sukenik set out to be the "Jewish archaeologist" par excellence, spending a year studying archaeology at the University of Berlin in the early 1920s. A profound influence on Sukenik's scholarship was the American scholar and father of Biblical archaeology, William Foxwell Albright. But whereas Albright was dedicated to creating Biblical archaeology, Sukenik's focus was the national archaeological movement of the Jewish people (following upon themes in contemporary German scholarship),[25] with a sweep from Biblical times to the Talmudic period, in Palestine and in the diaspora. This approach he called "Jewish archaeology," borrowing from the Catholic approach known as "Christian archaeology."

Sukenik's career was heavily promoted by another American, Hebrew University president Judah L. Magnes. Magnes conceived the need for the new university to develop a program in Jewish archaeology as part of his broader vision for modern Jewish culture and particularly for cultural Zionism. In supporting Sukenik, Magnes was out of step with the developing faculty of his own university, which kept Sukenik at bay and outside of the Institute for Jewish Studies. Magnes's approach was well in tune, however, with the approach to Jewish culture that had developed among the German–Jewish elite of America since the turn of the century, particularly its interest in the ancient synagogue. American Jewry did not found Jewish archaeology as a field in America, as Blau had hoped it would. Rather, America's vision of an ancient yet renewed Jewish culture facilitated Jewish archaeology in Palestine. Magnes's personal relationships were essential to this support. It should be remembered that Magnes was previously assistant rabbi of New York's prestigious Congregation Emanuel, and that his wife was the sister of the prominent American Louis Marshall, for a time president of Congregation Emanuel.[26]

Utilizing his personal connections in America to the fullest, Magnes sent Sukenik to Philadelphia's Dropsie College for Hebrew and Cognate Learning to complete his doctoral studies. The minutes of a 1926 faculty meeting contain a detailed "Report on the Thesis of Mr. E. L. Sukenik." According to this report,[27]

The thesis presented by Mr. E. L. Sukenik on the ancient synagogues of Palestine consists of eighty pages in Hebrew, with the chapter on Naaran being translated into English on thirty-three pages. The whole is accompanied by an album of photographs and reproductions. The first four chapters (pages 1–11), given here only in summary, are to be enlarged in the future. Chapter 1 deals with the history of discovery and research, chapter 2 with the architectural plan of the structures, 3 with the orientation and 4 with the ornamental decorations. Mr. Sukenik then treats in all the ruins of the synagogue at Capernaum, of the court and terrace about the synagogue and of the inscriptional material. The other synagogues described, are those of Chorazin, Meron, Kefr Birim and Naaran. In dealing with Naaran, the author treats most minutely the inscriptional material.

This dissertation was directly the result of Sukenik's work at the Hebrew University under Magnes's patronage.

8. E. L. Sukenik in the Arbel Synagogue (courtesy of the E. L. Sukenik Archive, Institute of Archaeology, Hebrew University of Jerusalem).

Reading the correspondence between Sukenik and Magnes and others at the university from the mid-1920s through the early 1930s, preserved in the archives of the Hebrew University, one is struck by the excitement with which Sukenik set about creating Jewish archaeology. Sukenik's reports contain electrifying descriptions of his most recent discoveries and organizational triumphs. I translate from the Hebrew one particularly colorful example, written to the management of the Institute for Jewish Studies on "13 Adar II 5687," March 17, 1927 (Figure 8):[28]

On Sunday this week I visited the ruins of Arbel (*Ḥorvat Arbel*). We came there by way of Wadi Hamam, next to Migdal. This path is not easy, but it is superlative in its natural beauty. As I later understood, it is easier to arrive to this site by way of Kefar Hittin. The view from the site of the synagogue is fantastic. To the east the Hermon may be seen in all its glory and the plain of Ginnosar in all its breadth. To the north stand the mountains of the Upper Galilee and to the west spreads forth the Valley of Hittin – or as it was once called, the Valley of Arbel. Potsherds are scattered all around and show the community that was here. In the synagogue and its surroundings we prepared approximately ten photographs. There are few remains. Only one of the lintels and a corner column are still in situ. There are other fragments of pavement, though, I am sorry to say that we could not photograph them due to the numerous wild plants that today cover the site. Excavation of the site will certainly reveal more elements of the synagogue. . . .[29]

Magnes and Sukenik's shared vision called for the creation of a center for the study of Jewish archaeology at the Hebrew University. Sukenik set about to collect objects of Jewish antiquity (including facsimiles),[30] either through purchase or excavation, to publish them in a scholarly manner, and to build a national museum to house them on the Hebrew University's Mt. Scopus campus. This project was intended to reach beyond Palestine to include the Jewish diaspora as well. Magnes and Sukenik began work to acquire ancient synagogue sites in the Galilee, at Chorazin, Baram, Gush Ḥalav, Nabratein, Khirbet Shema, and Arbel. Congregation Emanuel, Cincinnati's Hebrew Union College (Magnes's alma mater) under president Julian Morgenstern, and Stephen S. Wise's Free Synagogue in New York were enlisted to adopt ancient synagogues and thus support the Hebrew University's project to "redeem" synagogue ruins. The goal was to excavate and reconstruct these synagogues, creating what can only be called Zionist archaeological parks, parallel to the Franciscan site at Capernaum.[31] These Zionist sites would assert the significance of ancient Jewish culture in the old–new land, just as the new Zionist settlements epitomized modern Jewish colonization.[32]

Magnes went so far as to offer Louis Marshall the stone of a Galilean synagogue to serve as the cornerstone of Congregation Emanuel's new building at Fifth and 65th Streets in Manhattan.[33] This flare for the dramatic was a hallmark of his leadership of the Hebrew University. A historically significant stone was in fact set as the cornerstone of the Hebrew University's Museum of Jewish Antiquities. Opened in 1941, this Bauhaus-style building was literally "built on a corner stone taken from the Third Wall of Jerusalem (begun by Agrippa I about A.D. 40)."[34] The discovery of the Third Wall of Second Temple period Jerusalem was among Sukenik's crowning achievements. Through a combination of careful scholarship and good luck, he and L. A. Mayer identified the wall in 1925–7 – in a location that other scholars had rejected.[35] A carved ashar from the Third Wall was set as the cornerstone of the Museum of Jewish Antiquities. Visible in early photographs, this well-carved stone was buried beneath planting soil and forgotten in recent renovation of the Mt. Scopus campus. It was rediscovered by Dan Barag and the author on May 29, 2001. This use of ancient Jewish masonry to draw a direct connection between the ancient Jewish presence in Palestine and the Zionist endeavor goes a long way toward explaining the ideological background of Sukenik's project. Beyond his academic achievements, Sukenik provided the nascent state with an archaeological

Abb. 582. Siebenarmiger Leuchter aus der grossen Kirche.

9. Menorah from a synagogue in Priene. The German caption below translates: "Seven-armed Candelabrum from the large Church" (T. Wiegand and H. Schrader, *Priene: Ergebnisse der Ausgrabungen und Untersuchungen in den Jahren 1895–1898* [Berlin: G. Reimer, 1904], 481).

heritage that well-suited Zionism's self-perception as an old–new national movement. His academic pursuits served a far broader program of nation building.

Sukenik consciously fashioned himself as more than "just" a "Hebrew archaeologist." He intended to be *the* world-renowned scholar of all Jewish antiquities and to make the Hebrew University the global center for the study of Jewish archaeology – an ambition that meshed well with the university's own goal of becoming a world-class institution. In 1928 Sukenik set out for Greece, his trip financed by the Hebrew University.[36] There he participated in the excavation of a synagogue mosaic on the island of Aegina. In Athens, Sukenik frequented the library of the German Archaeological Institute. With great excitement, he wrote to Magnes that he had "discovered" the synagogue at Priene in Asia Minor while in this library.[37] His discovery came when Sukenik opened the final report of the German excavations published in 1904 (unavailable to him in Palestine) and found an early synagogue described as a *hauskirche*, a "house church."[38] The fact that the large menorah plaque from Priene was found in a Byzantine church blinded the scholars to the synagogue remains, which they thought were Christian (Figure 9). Sukenik was indeed the first to identify the Priene synagogue as a synagogue, as he was the first in so many other areas of Jewish archaeology.

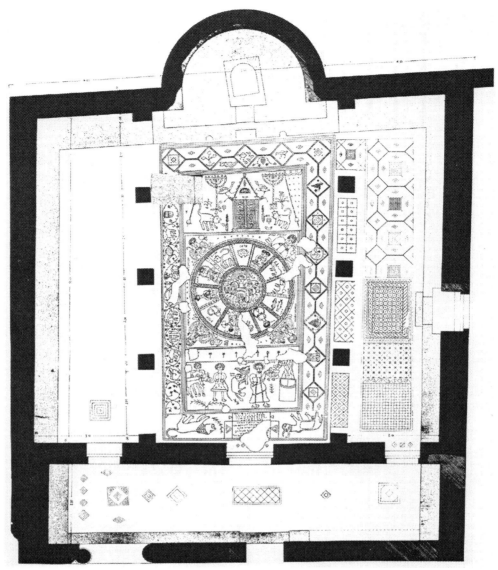

10. Drawing of the Beth Alpha Synagogue mosaic (After E. L. Sukenik, *The Ancient Synagogue of Beth Alpha* [Jerusalem: Hebrew University, 1932], pl. 10).

Sukenik's towering achievement during this period was the result of another chance discovery. In late 1928, the digging of an irrigation canal at Beth Alpha in the Jezreel Valley had revealed a beautiful floor mosaic. Sukenik excavated the synagogue in early 1929, which became a sensation throughout Jewish Palestine and around the world.[39] Sukenik's report, published in Hebrew as well as English, was financed by Congregation Emanuel using the funds allocated by Marshall (Figure 10).[40] The discoveries at Beth Alpha did much to elevate the status of archaeology within Zionist academic contexts, although it still was not accepted among the disciplines of the Institute for Jewish Studies of the Hebrew University and Sukenik's academic

status as a result was left unresolved through much of his career. A summary presentation of Sukenik's scholarly odyssey, *Ancient Synagogues in Palestine and Greece* (1934), was presented orally as the highly prestigious Schweich lectures of the British Academy in 1930. This volume capped the first part of his career and established Sukenik as the preeminent Jewish archaeologist he had hoped to be.

In *Beth Alpha* and in *Synagogues in Palestine and Greece*, Sukenik is comfortable with a vast quantity of sources – from Hebrew, Aramaic, and Greek to art history and rabbinic literature. Sukenik's interpretative approach – following Slouschz and, more importantly, Albright – assumed continuity between sacred texts and archaeological discovery.

This textual interest built upon his own traditionalist upbringing, although it should be emphasized that Sukenik saw himself first and foremost as an archaeologist. Until the discovery of the Dead Sea Scrolls, he engaged in little textual scholarship (other than inscriptions). Sukenik worked actively to bridge the gap between his work and the text scholars of the Institute of Jewish Studies – with varying degrees of success. His first survey article on synagogue archaeology reflects his interest in engaging text scholars. It appeared early in Sukenik's career, in *Rimon: A Hebrew Magazine of Art and Letters*, edited in Berlin by Rachel Wischnitzer in 1923. He concluded his description of the synagogue at Hammath Tiberias with a discussion of its menorah. Sukenik wrote with obvious pleading that "every interpreter of Holy Scripture will need to take into account the image of this menorah that was buried in the past, certainly during a period of danger, and revealed to us in the first Hebrew excavations in the Land of Israel."[41]

Sukenik's sense of accomplishment is evident in the conclusion to the Schweich lectures in 1930:[42]

New discoveries are constantly being made, in Palestine as well as in the centres of the Diaspora, which will undoubtedly add new details to our conception of the early synagogues. But even now we may safely predict that these details will not change the conception as a whole.

No sooner had he spoken these words than our author's smugness was overtaken by new discoveries – which he immediately embraced. An appendix to the published version, *Ancient Synagogues in Palestine and Greece*, belies his own conclusion; Sukenik discussed finds made between the close of the lectures and their publication in 1934. These include the synagogue at Stobi, discovered in 1931, the first report of which was published in Serbia in 1932; the Hammath Gader synagogue, which Sukenik excavated in 1932; the Dura Europos synagogue, discovered in 1932 and visited by Sukenik in 1933; and the Huseifa synagogue, first uncovered in 1933. Reflecting back upon his comment in 1949 with the wisdom of age, Sukenik wrote that "in some ways my assumption was justified, but, as is usual with predictions (and to my great satisfaction in this case), fate dealt otherwise."[43]

Dura Europos was by far the most spectacular of these "new" finds. Sukenik took up the challenge of this monument with characteristic vigor, producing a monograph, *The Dura Europos Synagogue and Its Pictures* (in Hebrew), whose publication was delayed until 1947 by World War II.[44] It was the work of a mature scholar: a careful analysis of each painting in terms of ancient Jewish literature, particularly rabbinic literature. Today, he is still the only Dura interpreter to have made full use of inscriptions and the Dura Jewish liturgical parchment. Throughout his oeuvre, Sukenik's interpretations are marked by their lack of tendentious meta-theories. He provides a cautious and measured statement of the synagogue in light of extant parallel literature. Sukenik's Dura volume is generally unknown outside of Israel, mainly because it was written in Hebrew and never translated into a European language. His analysis was not superceded, however, by Carl Kraeling's final report of the Dura synagogue. In 1949, with the war over and Israel's independence secured, Sukenik inaugurated the Louis M. Rabinowitz Fund for the Exploration of Ancient Synagogues, dedicated to synagogue studies and financed by the noted American Jewish philanthropist Louis M. Rabinowitz (who also supported the publication of Kraeling's final Dura synagogue report).

This brief survey of Sukenik's life as a scholar of synagogues is nothing less than the history of a scholarly discipline. Sukenik's overwhelming significance for synagogue studies is evidenced by A. T. Kraabel's title of his own comprehensive survey of diaspora synagogues some thirty years later – "The Diaspora Synagogue: Archaeological and Epigraphic Evidence Since Sukenik."[45]

ZIONIST DISCOVERY AND SCHOLARLY INTERPRETATION

From Blau to Slouschz to Sukenik, the field of Jewish archaeology truly came into its own during the interwar years. It must have been a heady experience for Sukenik and his fellow travelers: They were able to literally create a new scholarly discipline and at the same time to discover Jewish "roots" in the soil of Palestine. Like traditional Jewish imagery of all sorts, archaeological discoveries of the Talmudic period were woven into the secularized fabric of Zionist visual iconography. These images provided the visual trappings of authentic continuity that were essential for the Zionist revolution – much, for example, as the use of classical Greek architecture and coin types had for pre-Euro modern Greece and the way that nineteenth-century neo-Gothic architecture connects the House of Parliament to the Westminster Abbey, to the Magna Charta, and back to William the Conqueror. Discovery was a prerequisite of this

Zionist project, and archaeology the vehicle for recovering a Jewish/"Hebrew" artistic heritage. Zionist scholars interpreted the artistic production of previous generations in terms of the national project, creating this old–new national artistic tradition.[46] Even images of stylized mosaic floors with no specific Judaic content became subtle shorthand statements of Jewish rootedness in Palestine. Note, for example, 50 and 100 mils banknotes issued by the new State of Israel in 1948. These were decorated with mosaics from the Beth Alpha synagogue, although geometric pavements without any specific Jewish content.[47]

Mosaic art itself came to be seen as a Jewish Palestinian (later Israeli) art form.[48] These motifs were interpreted in terms of the Jewish connection to the Land, and often described in terms of Jewish messianic longings (albeit in a secularized guise). Imagery on ancient Jewish coins was given specifically Jewish interpretations by numismatists and artists eager to create a Jewish iconographic vocabulary. Thus, images on ancient coins such as grapes, pomegranates, wheat, *lulav* bunches (a palm frond bound to willow and myrtle twigs and set beside a citron [*etrog*]), palm trees and palm fronds, all symbols with special currency in Zionist art,[49] were described by Jewish authors first and foremost in terms of Jewish literary sources – even when these sources postdated the coins by centuries.[50] These images, together with the menorah, the Torah shrine, and even the zodiac wheel were, identified as "messianic symbols" in the hands of some interpreters – although to his credit, not Sukenik.[51] The messianic/salvic/escatological interpretation of ancient Jewish iconography aligned well with approaches utilized by Western archaeologist and art historians. Jewish and pagan artifacts were interpreted in terms of salvation themes, in keeping with the Christian popular and academic preoccupation with salvation and fitting nicely with the Zionist rhetoric of redemption.[52]

Scholars formed an essential and unique element within the formative Zionist enterprise. Slouschz's status as a former professor of modern Hebrew literature at the Sorbonne brought him a considerable cachet. Eleazar Lipa Sukenik was another. Zionist scholars, particularly those associated with the Hebrew University, were intimately involved in the national project.[53] Sukenik served on the Committee on the Symbol and the Flag of the Provisional Government of Israel,[54] and Gershom Scholem, perhaps Jerusalem's most famous scholar, interpreted the Shield of David for a broadly learned Hebrew-speaking audience in 1949.[55]

Numismatists have been intimately involved in designing Israel's coinage.

It is astonishing that despite the strongly ideological tenor of Zionist interest in archaeology, scholarly writings on ancient Jewish material culture by the Jerusalem School betray relatively little blatant ideology. The heritage of Western European academic scholarship and particularly of its Jewish manifestation, the *Wissenschaft des Judentums*, led to the construction of a well-developed rhetoric of scholarly detachment to separate between openly ideological reflection and scholarship.[56] We have seen this in Slouschz's academic report on the Hammath Tiberias excavation. In his scholarly publication of the Beth Alpha synagogue, Sukenik is extremely restrained in describing "just the facts" of the excavation, with a minimum of ideology.[57] The Beth Alpha report was to be just another well-published site and not a locus for ideological pontification. This was thought to provide a scientific legitimacy to the undertaking. Consider, for example, Sukenik's study of the Dura Europos synagogue, the work of his students Maximillian Kon and Nahman Avigad on funerary monuments, and Mordecai Narkiss's *Ancient Jewish Coinage* and his numerous studies on later periods – none are overtly ideological in Zionist terms.[58] What unifies them is an assertively positive attitude toward Jewish visual culture. The rhetoric of these studies is often couched in a distinct pleasure at recent discoveries of Jewish national art and identification with that art.[59] This focus was given visual expression in the beautifully produced final report of the Beth Alpha excavation, which appeared in English as well as Hebrew.[60] It was generally not overt. These scholars sought acceptance of their material and interpretations within the international scholarly community – just as Zionism itself was seeking out international legitimization.

Beginning with Slouschz, early Zionist archaeologists interpreted discoveries to show Jewish national art in its best light. Blau, Sukenik, and others happily enlisted the work of the anti-Semitic Austrian art historian Josef Strzygowski, who placed the origins of Christian art firmly in the East, in a Jewish context.[61] Strzygowski "blamed the demise of all things Graeco–Roman on the Oriental, and specifically Semitic, take-over of early medieval European and Christian forms by the arts of the East."[62] This focus on a supposed Jewish predecessor to Christian art was not meant as a compliment. In fact, it was, as Jaś Elsner calls it, a "proto-Nazi art history":

This proposition . . . appeared proved by the archaeological finds of the 1920's and 1930's, which themselves coincided with the onward march of the movement that was to establish the 1000-year Reich in the year after the discovery of the Dura synagogue.[63]

As Margaret Olin nicely puts it: "The ardor of art historians who looked for origins as signs of irreducible Jewish essences, however, posthumously [sic] transformed the anti-Semite Strzygowski into a champion of Jewish art."[64] For Sukenik, like Blau before him, this was not the determining factor of his research, although he was deeply impressed by Strzygowski's approach.[65]

Beginning during the 1960s, art historian Bezalel Narkiss and his developing circle accepted the claim now associated most closely with philo-Semitic scholar Kurt Weitzmann – that the origins of early Christian art are to be found in preexisting Jewish Biblical illustration.[66] This provided legitimacy for ancient Jewish art within the broader art history community, as well as rhetoric that might serve to legitimize and integrate Jewish art into the Judaic studies canon. The price paid, however, was that Jewish creativity was often harnessed to the ideologically driven narrative of Christian art history and was not always approached for its own intrinsic worth.

Ideology was not far below the surface of early Jewish archaeology, however. As a respected chemist, explorer, and collector of antiquities, Adolf Reifenberg was more free to assert ideology than Sukenik and his colleagues were. An amateur closely integrated into the archaeological community (he was the founder of the *Israel Exploration Journal* and was ultimately buried meters away from Sukenik in Jerusalem's Sanhedria Cemetery), Reifenberg provided an ideological rationale for Jewish archaeology. His works included *Palästinensische Kleinkunst*,[67] *Denkmäler der jüdischen Antike*,[68] and *Ancient Jewish Coins*,[69] with many of the illustrations drawn from his personal collection. *Denkmäler der jüdischen Antike* (*Monuments of Jewish Antiquity*) is perhaps the most interesting of these studies. This well illustrated volume appeared in 1937 in the Schocken Bücherei – a series which was itself an act of resistance against the Nazi narrative about Jews and Judaism, published in Berlin by cultural Zionist Salman Schocken. Reifenberg sets Jewish art at the center of the Western artistic canon in a manner reminiscent of Catholic scholars such as Violet le-Duc and of the anti-Semitic Strzygowski. I cite from the English version of this work published by Schocken Books in New York in 1950 – now called *Ancient Hebrew Arts*:[70]

To be sure, the material remains of Jewish antiquity from the period of the Maccabees are modest, but they have significance as the foundation of synagogue art. The products of the first centuries CE were closely connected with Jewish ideology and ritual. They represented a marked contribution to the development of Jewish art, made their impression on the Jewish Middle Ages and are part of Jewish art consciousness to this day. Influences exerted by Jewish antiquities beyond the national confines or upon later developments had their beginnings before the period of synagogue art. Hebrew motives pervaded not only the Greek world but later Jewish antiquity and early Christian art. . . .

The influence of Jewish synagogue art reaches deeper. It forms the connecting link between antiquity and Christian – Byzantine architecture. In the synagogue secular pagan architecture was first adapted to the religious needs of a non-pagan community. The architectural details and particular architectonic features of the Christian basilicas occurred previously in the synagogue. Jewish pictorial synagogue art influenced the art of the Christian church.

It is probable that future finds and research will result in many corrections of currently held opinions. However, it appears certain that they will maintain or strengthen the thesis that an authentic expression, genuinely Hebraic ideas and motives, is found in the remains of Jewish antiquity and that here as elsewhere early Judaism exerted its influence upon other cultures and peoples.

Significantly, in 1937 Reifenberg's Schocken Bücherei volume was introduced by L. A. Mayer, who begins with a refutation of the notion that Judaism is a religion without art. Reifenberg himself does not engage in this now ritualized apology, and it does not appear in his 1950 English volume. Reifenberg's own apology is far more revolutionary. For him, the roots of Western art are to be found in Jewish art. Academic Zionist scholars responded to charges of Jewish artlessness by positively asserting the significance of Jewish visual culture – both for Jews and for everyone else. By pushing Jewish art to the center of the art historical canon, these scholars set out to subvert through erasure (rather than through argumentation) the generally accepted view of Jews and art. For early Zionist authors, this subterfuge was a requirement of the national project. The existence of an antique and venerable Jewish art was seen as a necessary manifestation of the national spirit, just as English art manifested the British spirit and French art the French spirit.[71] Zionist authors set about constructing their national art from antiquity up.

Another problem for the legitimacy of Jewish art came from within the Jewish academic community itself, with its then strict focus on literary texts and general disinterest in the visual side of Jewish culture. Other than the Budapest-based David Kaufmann and his students, Krauss and Blau, few *Wissenschaft* scholars exhibited any interest in the visual.[72] Most scholars comfortably accepted the standard association of Judaism with aniconism. Filled with the hope that their discipline would be accepted within Judaic studies, artifact-based scholars interpreted ancient Jewish remains against the background of Jewish literary sources. They thus succeeded in weaving the visual firmly into the fabric of Jewish sacred texts. In this way, the visual gained legitimacy in Jewish eyes through association with the Bible, Talmud, and related documents – an association that was ideologically vital within the "textocentric" world of Judaic studies at the time. This association served de facto to breach the barrier between art and Jewish texts. We have seen the way that Slouschz followed by Sukenik attempted to bridge this gap.

Beginning with Slouschz, the close linking of archaeology and rabbinic literature became a hallmark of Zionist scholarship, where general continuities between the two have largely remained a commonplace of the academic culture to the present day. This approach served to reinforce the perception that the religion of the rabbis was the driving force in Jewish culture of the time. At the same time that American Jews strove to assert a mildly Hellenized yet shared "normative Judaism," Zionists, holding similar assumptions, saw in the close proximity between archaeology and rabbinic literature a strong statement of the old–new "Hebrew" culture in Palestine. This twinning presented a model of Jewish leadership within a strongly Jewish yet nonghettoized and unproblematically aesthetic culture in the Land of Israel. The focus upon culture is significant. Just as usefully, Jewish archaeology revealed a Jewish culture that was both religious and Hellenized, providing "religious" and "secular" Zionists alike with raw materials for ideological constructions and scholarly investigation.[73]

To sum up: Writing for an audience that was itself in the process of subverting the "diaspora" image of the Jew, early Zionist archaeology set out to erase contrarian opinions regarding art and ancient Judaism. During this period, Jewish and particularly Zionist scholarship was in the process of rewriting the script of Jewish artlessness. Early Zionist archaeologists did their part, often supported by American donors. Some Zionists explicitly placed Jewish archaeology at the very center of both the Jewish and the Western artistic tradition. More than that, the unassailable antiquity of archaeological evidence, discovered and interpreted by "unbiased" modern scholars, made archaeology a particularly attractive tool and metaphor for the Zionist endeavor. Read in tandem with rabbinic literature, archaeology provided a vivid antecedent to the modern "return of the Jews to their land" – even as it provided a script for the Jewish past that contrasted with the "Dark Ages" of European Jewish traditionalism (within which all of the major early practitioners were raised and against which they had rebelled in their youths).

This construction of Jewish art is well illustrated through reference to the volume with which we opened this chapter, Ephron and Roth's *Jewish Art*. The beautifully designed dust jacket of the first Hebrew edition is decorated with a drawing based upon the personified seasons of the zodiac in the Beth Alpha synagogue mosaic. This ancient mosaic, discovered in the Zionist present, is redesigned here as a kind of portrait. It is no longer the personification of a season that it once was. This reworking of the mosaic binds the paintings of Modigliani, Chagall, and Reuben Rubin to an ancient, yet pointedly refreshed visual tradition. The use of the Beth Alpha "portrait" is distinctive in its nonuse of a distinctly Jewish symbol, just as the letter script used on the dust jacket also reflects an old–new orientation. It is a modernized version of an ancient Jewish scribal font. A similar font, this one drawn from the Dead Sea Scrolls, was used on Sukenik's unique burial monument – itself decorated with motifs drawn from ancient ossuaries, resting on a base of miniature Herodian ashlars. The Hebrew inscription on the tomb translates: "Eleazar Lipa Sukenik, discoverer and interpreter of Jewish antiquities" (*megaleh ve-ḥoker qadmoniot Yisrael*). It is likely that Sukenik was the first Jew whose tomb was decorated with Second Temple motifs in almost 2,000 years. Both the dust jacket of *Jewish Art* and Sukenik's tomb serve as visual metaphors for the place that was being created for art and archaeology in Zionist iconography and thought. Through the archaeological enterprise, early Zionist scholars laid the intellectual foundations for an old–new Jewish national art that made the Jews a "real" nation rooted in the art of "Eretz Israel."

CHAPTER THREE

ARCHAEOLOGY AND THE SEARCH FOR NONRABBINIC JUDAISM[1]

We know from the Talmud everything about the lives of the literates. What we wouldn't give if we knew about the *am ha'aretz,* the peasant, the simple man; his clothes, the food he ate, his faith and beliefs.

Ludwig Blau[2]

To maintain with some scholars that the people who erected the synagogues were ignorant of the law against images, or cared little for the interpretation thereof by the Rabbis, amounts to explaining the past by the present. . . .

Letter from Louis Ginzberg to Louis Marshall, 1927[3]

. . . For some years I have been approaching the problem primarily from the Greek angle, an angle which quickly brought me to Philo and Hellenistic Judaism. To begin to dip into the great literature of the rabbis and Kabalists is a perilous undertaking. I shall have to do so, as I am dipping all about, but I distrust in advance any conclusions I may come to. Still, very few of the rabbis have any real comprehension of the Greek spirit, and the problem can only be discussed by one who is not afraid to work in fields where a specialist will think he has no business.

Letter from E. R. Goodenough to Gershom Scholem, April 27, 1937[4]

LUDWIG BLAU SPENT HIS ENTIRE PROFESSIONAL career seeking to set rabbinic literature within the broad context of Greco–Roman culture. He did this as a faculty member and then director of the Jewish Theological Seminary of Budapest (until the defeat of the Hapsburgs in World War I, called the Franz-Josef Landesrabbinerschule). The intellectual environment in which Blau functioned was harnessed to training rabbis to seek a balance between Judaism and full participation in general Hungarian culture, "to produce a type of Rabbi who would regard the Magyarization of the Israelite religion his calling."[5] Through modern scholarship, Blau sought to integrate the Jews into the general culture, both in late antiquity and in early-twentieth-century Hungary. Whether writing about Jewish marriage documents and their relationship to Egyptian papyri or about Jewish magic in the context of Greco–Roman magic, Blau was more concerned than most scholars with presenting Jewish sources in their Greco–Roman setting.[6] Unlike his contemporaries, however, Blau's focus was the people behind texts and artifacts, not exclusively the explication of texts. With the imagination of a historian, Blau clearly understood the limits of rabbinic sources for understanding ancient Jewry, and actively sought out alternative sources and alternative voices within traditional sources. Blau read rabbinic sources against the grain in order to discover ancient Jewish culture beyond rabbinic circles.

Ludwig Blau published "Early Christian Epigraphy from the Jewish Point of View" in 1923 and "Early Christian Archaeology from the Jewish Point of View" in 1926, both in the *Hebrew Union College Annual*. The latter article is of greater interest to us here, for in it Blau discusses correspondences between archaeological and literary sources in concrete ways and, as we have seen, urges the creation of "Jewish archaeology." With Sukenik, Blau appreciated the fact that Strzygowski had placed Jewish "oriental" art at the center of the scholarly discussion. It was the positively disposed scholarship of Carl Maria Kaufmann and the Counter-Reformation field known as "Christian archaeology," however, that most engaged Blau. As early as 1886, Blau's teacher, David Kaufmann, referred to "archéologie

juive" as a companion to "archéologie chretiénne."[7] Following in the tradition of his teacher, Blau's twin articles on "Christian Epigraphy" and "Christian Archaeology" are prolonged reflections on C. M. Kaufmann's important *Handbuch der Christlichen Archaeologie*.[8] Like Viollet-Le-Duc, this preeminent Catholic scholar viewed Jewish art quite positively, treating the art of the Church as a natural development out of Jewish material culture. His positive assessment clearly nurtured Blau's call for the establishment of "Jewish archaeology." Unlike C. M. Kaufmann on Christianity and Krauss and his "Talmudic archaeology," however, Blau was interested in finding discontinuity between the archaeological sources for ancient Judaism and rabbinic literature (thus for him, "Jewish archaeology"). Ludwig Blau was the first rabbi/scholar of whom I am aware to highlight discontinuity between the rabbis and other Jewish communities during late antiquity using archaeological sources. Although clearly in the service of a liberalizing political agenda, his comments are usually cautious and convincing.

Blau was not the last twentieth-century scholar to search these corpora for "nonrabbinic Jews," nor the last Jewish scholar to harness Jewish material culture to a Jewish liberalizing agenda. The search for nonrabbinic Judaism was the theme of much of the American scholarly discussion on ancient Judaism throughout the second half of the twentieth century, an approach most profoundly heralded by E. R. Goodenough. No single work influenced the historiography of ancient Judaism in America during the Cold War years more than Goodenough's thirteen-volume *Jewish Symbols in the Greco-Roman Period* (1954–68). To understand Goodenough's contribution to the study of Jewish archaeology, I contextualize it in terms of the scholarship that preceded *Jewish Symbols* and that which flowed from and reacted to it.

Scholarship on ancient Judaism, whether or not it took account of archaeology, generally assumed the rabbi-centered approach that G. F. Moore called "normative Judaism." The religion of the *Jewish Encyclopedia* was pervasive, whether written by "Orthodox" scholars or by Talmudists associated with Conservative or Reform institutions. Those who wrote about archaeology assumed absolute continuity between classical sources and the new discoveries, as is evident not only in the works of Samuel Krauss, but also of Louis Ginzberg, J. N. Epstein, Saul Lieberman, and E. E. Urbach.[9] E. R. Goodenough's *Jewish Symbols* approached the problem from the perspective of

New Testament studies, not Jewish studies. Although dealing with the same period and often with the same texts, Jewish study of the latter Second Temple period and Christian "New Testament history" have, for most of their respective histories, run on parallel tracks. The questions and motivations of each discipline have seldom merged. Goodenough's work is a good example of this phenomenon at mid-century, his approach merging into Jewish scholarship (as it veered from the Christian mainstream), gaining success through the agency of another American, Columbia's Morton Smith, and his cadre of students.

Goodenough's concern was to find Jews who were so thoroughly Hellenized that they could have quickly been absorbed into the early Christian movement. Goodenough ultimately located these Jews in the archaeological record and in the writings of Hellenistic authors such as Philo of Alexandria. This turn to archaeology has a long history in German Protestant circles. German Protestant scholars looked to the pre-Constantinian church for the archaeological roots of their own theologically based aniconism. They suggested that the first Christians, "like the Jews" were theologically "aniconic." It was only when a degenerate Catholic impulse took over in the fourth or fifth century that figurative art – which they considered to be pagan to the core – could enter and profane the Church. Goodenough assumed a similar model for Jews, although he was interested precisely in discovering and highlighting the history of nonnormative, "Hellenistic Judaism." His study was written with a definite Christian theological agenda (even as it was anticlerical), clothed in then-popular secularist terms as the "History of Religion." Trained as a Methodist minister and later as a historian of Christianity, Goodenough offered a counterhistory to the Judaism that Moore and the normative Judaism community held to be axiomatic.[10]

According to Goodenough, the Pharisees dominated Judaism before the destruction of the Temple. With this assumption, he fit within the normative Judaism consensus. To Goodenough, the continuers of the Pharisees – the rabbis – were much reduced after 70 C.E.; they did not influence anyone but themselves. During this period, a mystical "Hellenistic Judaism" developed. The influence of the rabbis resumed during the Byzantine and early Islamic period, squelching Hellenistic Judaism. Goodenough's interest was not the rabbis, as it was for most Jewish scholars, but in the "mystical Judaism" beyond the rabbis. Goodenough found evidence for his position in a source

that had not often been considered by his predecessors – archaeology. In his binary construction of Hellenized Judaism in conflict with non-Hellenized Pharisaic/rabbinic Judaism, Goodenough saw the rabbis as being "like New England 'society,' a puritanical sect walled up in its self-made ghetto, while outside was the wonderful world of Hellenized Judaism, mystic, artistic and free."[11] More to the point, Goodenough saw the rabbis through the templates of both historical Christian antagonism toward the Pharisees and rabbinic literature and the self-perceived strict, legalistic Methodism of his youth – a religion that he himself had abandoned.

Goodenough described his approach succinctly in a letter dated November 18, 1947:[12]

The Jews of [the Greco–Roman] period, living for the most part before the Talmud was written, and so with only their Bible (in Greek translation) to go by, kept their devotion to the Torah, to the festivals and Sabbaths and dietary laws as well as they could simply from their Bible and from local and unstandardized traditions. They were certainly loyal to Judaism as they understood it, or they would not have continued building their synagogues in the teeth of pagan, and later Christian, opposition. But the symbols seem to tell us that these Jews were led by the growing Gnosticism, Neo-Platonism, and other forms of mysticism. That is, I believe that in these centuries was laid the foundation for the type of Judaism which later flowered and persisted as Cabala. When a rabbinate based upon the legalism of the Talmud became supreme it suppressed the mystical type of Judaism (or the mystical types, for there must have been varieties), drove it out of general favor, but could not prevent its continuing and reviving in such medieval Cabalism as the *Zohar*. This the borrowed pagan symbols and the biblical illustrations at Dura seem to me to agree in telling us.

Since written texts from the Jews who used this art do not exist, the method of research by which the symbols are evaluated has to be to take the symbols and paintings themselves, but primarily the symbols, and to trace them back as they go from one religion to another. These symbols quickly reveal themselves as the essential vocabulary of the lingua franca of most religions of antiquity, one which still survives in Christianity . . . . But even tracing the symbols from one religion to another in antiquity forces one to open up the general subject of the subject of religious symbols. I have reached the conclusion that while each religion gives symbols of its own explanation, in terms of its own gods and myths, there is a constant religious "value" as I am calling it which a symbol never loses in such transition. The presumption would then be that Jews felt free to borrow the symbol because they wanted the "value" the symbols represented for their own religion, and had found a way to explain that value in terms of their own traditions or biblical proof-texts.

Goodenough's thought developed considerably between the publication of volumes one–four in 1954 and the completion of the posthumously published conclusion in volume twelve in 1968. In the face of a mountain of scathing reviews, in his final volume Goodenough softened his position regarding the extent of mystical Judaism, limiting such beliefs to an elite and not to the general population. Feeling considerable pressure (evidenced by the slackening of his usual gentility), Goodenough restated the genesis of his question:[13]

If the reader of this series is to recognize at all what its author is trying to do he must understand that the study of Jewish symbols is itself part of a larger investigation. For many years the author has been trying to answer the question how Christianity, starting with the teachings of a Galilean carpenter, could so quickly have become a religion of salvation from the world and the flesh, of a Savior who in his person brought divinity to a lost humanity, a religion of sacraments, organized priesthood, and theological formations – that is, a Greco-Roman religion even though it called itself the Verus Israel.

Goodenough's *Jewish Symbols* was an attempt to fill the gap between Judaism and Christianity, between what he perceived as the "sternness" of the Pharisees/rabbis and the Hellenism of the early Church. He began his studies with a dissertation on Justin Martyr's *Conversation with Trypho*,[14] then moved to the writings of Philo of Alexandria. His project ultimately settled on the archaeological evidence for ancient Judaism as read through the lens of Jungian psychology. In his personal life, Goodenough spent considerable energies rebelling against Methodism into a kind of mystically oriented if sardonic anti-Protestantism.[15] Ancient Judaism was the battleground where he worked his personal transformation. Goodenough's personal and his academic passions were thus in full consort.

Goodenough relates that his interest in ancient Jewish art began while he was still a young graduate student at Oxford University. There, looking for Jewish precursors of early Christian art, Goodenough was "gently" told by his "dons" that "it had no possible foundation. Jewish Scripture and tradition alike forbade the making of images, and so long as a group was loyal to Judaism at all it would have had nothing to do with art."[16] Seven or eight years later, this time at Yale, Goodenough's senior colleague, Paul Baur, wrote an article in which he asserted a Christian interpretation of an oil lamp bearing the image of David and Goliath. Goodenough questioned this Christian attribution, suggesting to Baur that the lamp might have been Jewish. Baur's response to Goodenough is indicative of the then-regnant paradigm: "there is no such thing as Jewish art, and that such a suggestion about the lamp would be nonsense."[17] From this truism, so deeply grounded in the nationalist ideologies of the nineteenth century, Goodenough's study of Jewish archaeology began. Goodenough found in Jewish material culture an "unknown" resource to tap; and in the exoticness of this material, his tool for discovering nonrabbinic ancient Judaism. He first collected the evidence, bit by bit – ultimately producing a convenient repository of almost all known ancient Jewish art.

Based on his "discoveries," Goodenough then set about constructing a salvation-based mystery religion. That this was the Judaism that Goodenough "discovered" in the visual imagery of ancient Judaism is not in itself surprising. The salvation trope had long been applied to Jewish archaeological remains. Goodenough's focus on "symbols" as a supposedly unmediated tool for understanding what was "true" about Judaism during antiquity – and of archetypes in general – is also to be understood in terms of the intellectual history of his own period.

Goodenough found in Jungian psychology access to the universal "human psyche," and in "Jewish symbols," the concretization of an otherwise unknown nonrabbinic Judaism. He was in good company in his ahistorical endeavor. Working contemporaneously with such giants of the mid-twentieth century as Mircea Eliade and Henry Corbin, Goodenough created an equally ahistorical conception of religion. Unlike Eliade and Corbin, however, Goodenough saw himself fully as a philologically based historian. In this sense, he was more like Gershom Scholem, if only superficially. Scholem's philological acumen was (and still is) legendary. Like Scholem, Goodenough was committed to a counterhistory of Judaism, to rewriting the Jewish past "based upon the belief that true history lies in a subterranean tradition that must be brought to light."[18] But where Scholem found evidence for his reconstruction in the literature of Jewish mysticism (loosely called *Kabbalah*), for Goodenough archaeology provided the raw material for his counterhistory. Goodenough saw his work as the corollary of Scholem's – although Scholem himself dismissed Goodenough's dichotomy between the rabbis and mysticism. Still, Scholem was publicly respectful toward

Goodenough. In a 1965 letter to Jacob Neusner, he wrote: "I am sure that Goodenough has put his hand on a very important problem, which other people have tried to evade. As to the solution, it seems to be still very far off."[19]

For Goodenough, the "discovery" of Jewish art was the "discovery" of a nonrabbinic Judaism that he consciously grafted to Scholem's work on Jewish mysticism. Goodenough cited Scholem's work in support of his division between Jewish mysticism and rabbinic legalism – a distinction that Scholem never accepted. In fact, against the normative Judaism consensus that might have supported Goodenough's binary model, Scholem considered mysticism to have been an essential element of Talmudic religion.[20] Like Scholem, Goodenough was convinced of the truth of carefully constructed meta-theories that tie together all of the available evidence. For Scholem, it was the grand progression from the Spanish Expulsion through Sabbatianism, Frankism, Hassidism, and ultimately Jewish Reform and Zionism. For Goodenough, it was the all-encompassing interpretation of Jewish symbols through the ages based on Jungian archetypes.[21]

Goodenough's strong interest in Jung brought him into the greatly esteemed company of the Eranos group of scholars whom Jung convened yearly in Ascona, Switzerland, to discuss and develop the "History of Religions." Steven M. Wasserstrom has characterized this intellectual community in his recent monograph, *Religion After Religion: Gershom Scholem, Mircea Eliade and Henry Corbin at Eranos.*[22] A lesser member of this group, Goodenough – like his colleagues – saw himself as the incarnation of the tradition that he researched. As he quipped at the first session of a course taught at Brandeis University in 1962: "This will be a course in Goodenough."[23] Wasserstrom suggests that this sense of virtuosity is a hallmark of the Eranos members. Goodenough's "own intellectual and spiritual sojourn" was the text – both in his Brandeis course and in his scholarship. The virtuosos of Eranos privileged virtuoso religion over more general forms of praxis or cultural history that were more common to the members of each religious group. Although Scholem distanced himself from the more extreme psychological elements of Eranos, Wasserstrom has shown just how integral Scholem was to the community that assembled at Ascona. With his Eranos contemporaries, Goodenough privileged mysticism, myth, and "gnosis" – characterized by Wasserstrom as a "*mystocentric* conception of religion" and as a "gnostic

History of Religions."[24] Each in his own way, the scholars of Eranos considered "symbols" to be essential to religion in general, and to the religious traditions in which they were revered experts in particular. These symbols were thought to transcend all religions, being common to all.

Goodenough's work sparked an eruption of scholarly response, some of it of the most visceral kind. He rocked both the American and the Israeli variants of the normative Judaism consensus. For American Jews, the sense of a shared rabbinic religion was at stake, as was a shared national heritage for Israelis. Under the influence of Scholem, Zionists and (to a lesser extent) American scholars were aware that ancient Judaism included important mystical trends that had been disparaged or unacknowledged by the *Wissenschaft des Judentums*. Blau – and apparently following upon him, Judah L. Magnes – had earlier seen in archaeology the voice of the nonrabbinic, providing a Jewish precursor for Goodenough's approach that parallels similar attempts to discover heresies in the art of early Christianity. Goodenough's binary counter-Judaism, however, was considered to be lacking in nuance by most and otherwise beyond the bounds of even these adaptations of the regnant paradigm. Goodenough's ahistorical assumptions were evident to scholars who were not Eranos initiates (as they were to Scholem), as was his essential ignorance of rabbinic literature. The wedge that he emphasized between the rabbis and archaeology was acknowledged by many, however, to be a useful contribution.

It should not be surprising that scholars of rabbinic literature were particularly dismissive of Goodenough's approach – as he had anticipated they would be. A plethora of studies on the relationship between the rabbis and art followed, particularly in Jewish contexts. The most important responses were carried out by the doyen of Israeli Talmudic scholarship – the Breslau-trained E. E. Urbach – and by two American Talmudists: Joseph Baumgarten, a student of Albright, and the Yeshiva University-trained Talmudist Gerald J. Blidstein (a student of the famed rabbinics scholar Abraham Weiss).[25] With vigorous disdain, Urbach brought vast amounts of rabbinic material to bear in order to dispel Goodenough and assert a seamlessness between the archaeological evidence and rabbinic sources. Urbach's study became the essential statement for Israeli scholarship on the place of art in ancient Judaism. Both Baumgarten's and Blidstein's studies are at some level influenced by Goodenough's distinction between the rabbis and synagogue communities, even as they are largely focused on rabbinic texts. Like Albright before him, Baumgarten strove to maintain a balance between archaeology, text, and community. Both he and Blidstein steer a course between the excesses of Urbach and Goodenough. Their work is nuanced by their presentations of relationships between the rabbis and other communities mainly in late antique Palestine using both literary and archaeological evidence. Both distinguish attitudes toward the visual in different segments of Palestinian Jewish society, in Palestine and Babylonia, closely "reading" rabbinic and some archaeological sources.

Jewish Symbols marked something of a turning point. Non-Jewish scholars (and some Jews as well) were astounded by the breadth of Goodenough's collection of artifacts and sites. This astonishment had more to do with the sociology of knowledge, however, than the evidence itself. Goodenough collected the vast majority of images for his impressive collection from previous publications. This is made clear from his extensive and bibliographically annotated files of negatives and photographs (now at the Harvard Semitic Museum), only a few of which were procured from museum collections and nearly all of which were copied from scholarly publications. Goodenough lavishly acknowledged his predecessors in the preface to volume one.[26] Even so, the efforts put forth by Goodenough in the age before scanners, photocopiers, or even speedy mail communication is quite impressive. In a 1937 letter to Scholem, he wrote that "this is a tremendously time-consuming task, and I grow very discouraged with my slowness, but I am really getting together some striking material."[27] The large and impressive volumes prepared by Goodenough, financed by the Eranos-related Bollingen Foundation (named for the Swiss village near which Jung built his retreat), were intended to assert position through the force of the argument, the extensiveness of the photographic collection (which included specially commissioned color images of the Dura Europos synagogue), and by the considerable shelf space the thirteen oversized folio volumes require in library stacks. In this way, Goodenough, supported by Bollingen, made sure that his work could not be overlooked. Morton Smith's comment that before Goodenough Jewish archaeological discoveries were mostly "neglected, and almost all of it misinterpreted" is simply not true.[28] Goodenough himself would certainly have quickly denied it. The synthetic work of Samuel Krauss, Blau, Sukenik, and others belie this statement.

Goodenough claimed Jewish archaeology for his own through the careful collection and interpretation of Jewish archaeological finds. He claimed Jewish art of late antiquity as the missing link between Paul and Nicaea in the history of Christianity. The very act of publication reflects a receptivity to this project in post-war America that in all likelihood would not have been found in previous decades. The gradual elevation of Judaism to the triumvirate of American religions (Protestantism, Catholicism, Judaism),[29] the founding of the State of Israel, the organization of American Jewish museums, renewed movement in Christian circles in viewing early Christianity within a Jewish context, and movement in Jewish circles to interpret ancient Judaism broadly within the Greco-Roman context (as they read the Jewish experience in North America broadly within the American context) provided the backdrop for this paradigm shift.

Jewish Symbols continues to deeply influence Jewish scholarship, although Goodenough's influence in Christian circles is comparatively small.[30] His influence within Jewish circles may in part be attributed to the similarity between his thought and that of Goodenough's junior colleague, the former Episcopalian priest turned historian of religion, Morton Smith, and Smith's cadre of Jewish Theological Seminary-trained, Conservative rabbi–doctoral students. Smith was the first Christian graduate of the Hebrew University of Jerusalem, having written his first dissertation in that university's flagship Talmud department.[31] The dissertation was completed after his return to America "under the supervision of Prof. Lieberman and to his satisfaction" and in close contact with Hebrew University registrar Gershom Scholem.[32] Smith's connections to both Jewish and Christian scholarship were thus irreproachable, even as his personal connection to Christian piety slackened and grew adversarial. Smith was particularly close to Scholem and was eventually the translator of his *Jewish Mysticism, Jewish Gnosticism, Merkabah Mysticism and Talmudic Literature* (1960).[33] Smith's ability to influence Judaic studies was thus substantially greater than that of Goodenough. This distinguished Smith from Goodenough, who was ever the outsider.

Smith and Goodenough shared numerous biographical, religious, and scholarly affinities. Like Goodenough, Smith rebelled against normative Judaism (as both had done against orthodox Christianity – in its past and present manifestations). Each of these scholars wrote counterhistories of ancient Judaism and Christianity. Smith, like his colleagues Goodenough and Scholem, focused on historical resources that had previously been considered marginal to understanding Jewish religious history, and moved them from the periphery to the very center of scholarly discourse. Well-trained in rabbinic literature, Smith did not accept Goodenough's mystical Judaism, although "like Goodenough, Smith argued that Jewish magic and art provided clear evidence that non-rabbinic Judaism persisted well into 'the rabbinic period.'"[34] It should come as no surprise that the most penetrating critique of Goodenough's work and the scholarship that preceded it was penned by Morton Smith – which he published only after the elder scholar's death.

Smith's critique of the normative Judaism model was no less disparaging than was Goodenough's. The difference is that Smith denied, as Scholem did, Goodenough's binary relationship between rabbinic Judaism and Hellenistic Judaism. This emerges in Smith's estimation of Moore's *Judaism:* "Although it too much neglects the mystical, magical and apocalyptic sides of Judaism, its apology for tannaitic teaching as a reasonable, humane, and pious working out of biblical tradition is conclusive and has been of great importance not only for Christians, but also for Jewish understanding of 'Judaism.'"[35] Still, Smith, like Goodenough, gave prominence to the notion that the rabbis were a minority voice, not the arbiters of "normative Judaism."[36] Smith's focus on the religion of Jews beyond "normative Judaism" is influenced by developments in the German Protestant study of early Christianity, particularly Walter Bauer's *Heresy and Orthodoxy in Earliest Christianity.*[37] This approach was clearly central to both Goodenough's interests and to Smith's focus on the "mystical, magical and apocalyptic" sides of both Christianity and early Judaism. As Shaye J. D. Cohen notes, "Smith saw his own work as complementing that of Walther Bauer on early Christianity and Erwin Goodenough on early Judaism."[38] Both Goodenough and Smith filled the void created between sources that had once been filled by "normative Judaism" by ascribing central value to texts and artifacts that were formerly considered marginal. Smith filled the void with a mixture of the "mystical, magical and apocalyptic" together with a large dose of anticlerical cynicism regarding the efficacy of ancient (and modern) Jewish and Christian "orthodoxies." This approach was recently lionized in terms of rigorously applied "hermeneutics of suspicion" by one of the last Smith students, Seth Schwartz, now of the Jewish Theological Seminary of America.[39] Truth be told, Goodenough

and Smith and their most ardent followers set out to regrout the mosaic of ancient sources in ways that were often no less "normative" in effect than that which they intended to replace.

It should not be taken lightly that among Smith's most prominent students were American-born Conservative rabbis. Among the most prominent of these students are Jacob Neusner, Lee I. Levine, and Shaye J. D. Cohen. Smith, followed particularly by Levine and Neusner, found in Goodenough's emphasis on the non-"Orthodox" a point of departure for their own studies of rabbinic influence in late antique Jewish culture.[40] During the late 1950s and 1960s, in studies both at Columbia University and the adjacent Jewish Theological Seminary, the scholarship of each reflects a strong interest in the balance between tradition and modernity together with questions related to rabbinic authority. Such questioning became a leitmotif of this religious community. Historiography was seen by historian – and later chancellor – Gerson D. Cohen as a bridging tool between tradition and modernity – and between the seminary and its Americanizing constituency. For Cohen, "the study of Jewish history . . . could help span the abyss between textual scholarship and issues of concern to the contemporary Jew."[41] In this, Cohen followed closely on his immediate predecessor, Louis Finkelstein's lead. Unlike his predecessors as chancellor, all but one of whom were renowned Talmudists[42] and all of whom actively styled the seminary as a nondenominational and traditionally observant *Wissenschaft*-focused institution, Cohen's leadership was keenly denominational.[43] He sought to bridge the growing gulf between the seminary and increasingly denominational (read, less "Orthodox") Conservative congregational life through the denominationalization of the Jewish Theological Seminary. A perusal of Cohen's scholarly and rabbinic writings suggests a keen interest in questions of authority in Jewish history, particularly on the place of the non-"Orthodox," in ways that are antithetical to Finkelstein's generally traditionalist approach to history. Finkelstein strove to assert a direct lineage from the Prophets through the ancient rabbis, the medieval period until the rabbinic greats of the modern period, and finally to contemporary Talmudic scholars of the Jewish Theological Seminary.[44] By contrast, Cohen, a model *Wissenschaft* scholar who edited and was the translator and major commentator of a major medieval lineage of rabbinic authority – Ibn Daud's *Sefer ha-Qabbalah*[45] – eventually chose to reexamine in practical ways the notion of rabbinic authority within Conservative Judaism. As chancellor of the Jewish Theological Seminary, Cohen modified the normative Judaism consensus regarding shared origins. Just as significantly, he sought to replace traditional "Orthodoxy" as the legitimate heir of ancient and medieval Judaism (even within the Jewish Theological Seminary), and to create in its place a liberalizing and strongly denominational Conservative Judaism.

With his ties to Israeli and American Jewish scholarship, particularly with Lieberman and Scholem, Smith supported his rabbi-students in their search for a counterweight to the normative Judaism consensus and provided an entrée to his counterhistorical approach. Each in his own way, these rabbi-students dedicated their careers to sorting out the place of the rabbinic community in Jewish culture. For Levine, and to a far lesser extent for Neusner, archaeology provided an external vantage point from which to view the ancient rabbis.

Levine considers Moore and Goodenough to be "two of the most important scholars of Judaism during the period of the Second Temple and the Talmud."[46] Following Smith, Levine believes that "Goodenough's contribution was first and foremost in the collection of archaeological materials that provide witness to the broad utilization of art, multifaceted as it was, among Jews of those generations. . . ."[47] For Levine, discovery of this "multifaceted" world is Goodenough's unique contribution. Introducing his 1998 volume *Judaism and Hellenism in Antiquity: Conflict or Confluence?*, Levine wrote:[48]

These two ostensibly different cultures clashed on occasion, yet in most instances contacts of Jews and Judaism with the Hellenistic-Roman world proved immensely fructifying and creative. Some Jews may have been intimidated by this culture, but many found it attractive, stimulating and even indispensable.

One need only replace the phrase "Hellenistic–Roman" in this formulation with "modern" in order to find a worldview that comports with Conservative ideology on the place of Jews and Judaism in modern America. This approach posits positive interaction and integration of Jews into the majority culture, even as Jews become part and parcel of that culture. Historiographically, this approach is related to Columbia University historian Salo W. Baron's rejection of what he calls "the lachrymose conception of Jewish history."[49] For Jewish historiography before Baron, Jewish history was often conceived as a long series of persecutions. Baron precipitated a paradigm shift, whereby Jews were no longer seen as powerless but as holding significant power owing to their "social and economic" positions in various societies. No less than the historical context, this model reflects the growing comfort of Jews in Western, and particularly American, culture. Levine, as a student of Cohen and of Cohen's teacher, Baron, is not alone among contemporary archaeologically focused scholars in adopting this counterhistory – what Robert Bonfil has called in another historical context an "anti-lachrymose conception of Jewish history."[50] Art historian Kurt Weitzmann's conception of an "Age of Spirituality" when Jews, Christians, and polytheists lived together in harmony, for example, was formed as a protest against Nazi racial law, and developed further in tolerant yet religious post-war America.[51] Archaeology serves an important role in Levine's construction of a late antiquity that was "immensely fructifying and creative." Significantly, his recent 748-page monograph, *The Synagogue: The First Thousand Years* (2000), contains very limited discussion of the negative influence of Christian Rome on the synagogue, which included confiscations, burnings, rededications as churches, and other restrictions – both in diaspora communities and in Palestine.[52] Rather, Levine emphasizes positive elements of Christian influence on the synagogue, implicitly suggesting a more-or-less happy coexistence.

This scholar imagines a rabbinically friendly – although not rabbinically dominant – Jewish antiquity, where nonrabbinic Judaism flourished. To Levine, the rabbis were set off from (negatively defined) nonrabbinic Judaism as a distinct "class." The term "class" imbeds in his analysis sociological models of class conflict, although the implications of this model are not spelled out.[53] Peaceful urbanism without clear rabbinic dominance is expressed, Levine suggests, in the archaeological record. Israeli reviewer Yoram Bronowski captured the strongly American tone of Levine's *Judaism and Hellenism* when he described it as "a quiet song of praise (*shir hallel*) . . . to this blending (*mizug*) [of Judaism and Hellenism]."[54] The anti-lachrymose blending posited by Levine seems particularly attractive when read against the background of 9/11, now that the complexities of Jewish existence have become ever more apparent – even in America.

Jacob Neusner was a personal friend of Goodenough's in his later years and today is executor of his literary estate. Neusner not only edited Goodenough's memorial volume, but also claimed in a 1964 letter to Scholem to have had a hand in the revision of Goodenough's thesis. In this letter, Neusner took considerable credit for having helped Goodenough "revise his historical explanation of the 'symbols'" in his summary statement, volume twelve.[55] This is clearly the case, for there is considerable similarity between Neusner's formulation in a 1963 article, "Jewish Use of Pagan Symbols after 70 C.E." and Goodenough's revised thesis. Neusner suggests that[56]

Obviously, Jews throughout the Greco-Roman and Iranian worlds shared much in common; there is no reasonable ground to doubt that the main elements of law and doctrine were widespread. There is considerable reason to suppose, however, that local variations and modulations of ideas, emphasis, and interpretation of law and doctrine were far more substantial than we have hitherto supposed.

Compare this to Goodenough's formulation in volume twelve, published in 1965:[57]

Wherever we find Jewish remains, such as synagogues or collective burial grounds, we may, I believe, suppose that this minimal Judaism existed, else I cannot imagine why synagogues would have been built at all. But we cannot take anything beyond this for granted. Usually we do not have to look far to find the Jews of a given group were observing the sabbaths and festivals, though the forms of their observance would vary greatly when local customs, usually under the influence of gentile religions about them, as with modern Reform Jews, came to be included in Jewish ritual. The peculiar observances of the Essenes, Therapeutae, and Qumran sects probably reflect only a small part of such divergent observances in the ancient world.

Neusner's approach here certainly does parallel that of the revised Goodenough thesis, with its "minimal Judaism," or as he calls it a page earlier, a Jewish "common denominator"[58] – a formulation that E. P. Sanders stated positively in his study of the "common Judaism" of the period. Goodenough acknowledges Neusner's contributions broadly in the preface to volume twelve, describing "the critical aid that a recent acquaintance, a brilliant young scholar, has given during the last two years, Jacob Neusner."[59] Neusner's revelation of his part in reformulating Goodenough's thesis is illuminating, particularly because it affirms at some level Scholem's intuition in an earlier letter to Neusner (March 3, 1964) in which Scholem wrote:[60]

I am not sure whether your polemical remarks about Prof. Urbach are justified. You say that he grossly exaggerated the contrast [of great rabbinic power pre-70, and slackened influence after the destruction of the Temple] which Goodenough proposed.[61] On the face of Goodenough's formulation I would not say that he did. I think it is rather you who tries to smooth out the somewhat extravagant formulations of Goodenough. . . .[62]

Scholem's comment, harsh as it was, hits the mark. Goodenough's challenge to "normative Judaism" clearly had a powerful influence on Neusner's thinking. Although Neusner was aware of Goodenough's excesses, the Goodenough of volume twelve shares many basic assumptions with Neusner's contemporaneous writings. The volume reflects a narrowing of the gulf between Neusner's methodological assumptions and those of E. R. Goodenough.

Since those early days, Neusner has repeatedly taken up Goodenough's thesis, postulating a great gulf between rabbinic literature and synagogue remains.[63] It is not surprising that Jacob Neusner has served as principal propagator of Goodenough's legacy, in a sense as Goodenough's Boswell. Neusner published an abridged version of *Jewish Symbols*, to which he added his own notes, thus replicating the blending of his ideas with Goodenough's that is implicit in volume twelve of *Jewish Symbols*.[64] In all of Neusner's writings about Goodenough, one senses both genuine affection and identification with Goodenough, as well as a desire to safeguard his reputation and contribution.

Following upon Goodenough and Smith, Neusner, Levine, and Shaye Cohen have focused on the extent of rabbinic power, influence, and authority. Unlike Goodenough and, to a lesser extent, Smith, these scholars never overcompensated in their own studies of rabbinic literature by stressing elements in ancient Judaism that are most characteristic of magical or mystic virtuosos over the literature of the ancient rabbis. These scholar–rabbis have their eyes fixed squarely on the world of the Talmudic rabbis. Each in his own way, Shaye Cohen, Levine, and Neusner found that the social position of ancient rabbis was "ambiguous" in ways that the reader might easily compare to the status of modern (particularly Conservative) rabbis.[65] While not abandoning the Talmud focus that they inherited from their seminary education, each of these scholars set out to present the image of an ancient Judaism that was not wholly rabbinic. A root of their question, I would argue, is to be found in the transformations occurring almost simultaneously at the Jewish Theological Seminary and within the Conservative movement. These scholar–rabbis reflect the spirit of their day, their work paralleling a distancing of the Conservative Jewish community from traditional models of authority and a concomitant embrace of the social sciences (especially history) for formulating a less "normative" identity and more "pluralistic" communal norms. Some were cognizant of the communal uses of their scholarship; others were not.[66]

It should be remembered that history has never been just a secular social science for Conservative Judaism, but a hermeneutic for uncovering religious truths. The wedding of historiography with Jewish jurisprudence (*halakha*) is seen by Conservative Jews as a feature that distinguishes their religious system from both Orthodox and Reform practice.[67] Historiography served both de facto and de jure as a tool for approaching traditional sources in a modern "scientific" way and at the same time fashioned a chasm between the past and contemporary practice and belief. Within this community, the historian serves as both mediator/formulator of that tradition and often as a culture hero – particularly when cloaked in the mantle of the professor–rabbi that often set him (and now, her) at the apex of the religious system. This status was expanded under Chancellor Cohen and current Chancellor Ismar Schorsch, both historians. Historians became the arbiters of Conservative doctrine, replacing in this role the once-dominant law-focused Talmud department of the Jewish Theological Seminary. The fact that Saul Lieberman died in 1983 and that the decision to ordain women to the Conservative rabbinate came in the same year after a gruesome fight is not coincidental.[68] These were pivotal events for the Conservative movement. Conservative scholarship on ancient Judaism provided a usable past for a liberalizing Conservative movement.

Thus, Goodenough's and Smith's theological–historical goals and those of American Jews in search of a new balance between Judaism and "Hellenism" (read in the current context of 1960s and 1970s American culture) were mutually supportive.[69] In fact, Goodenough saw his mystical Judaism as a kind of ancient Reform movement. Historical scholarship at Reform seminaries showed comparatively less interest in *Jewish Symbols*.[70] Reform had distanced itself from Talmudic authority long before, and so this issue was not of vital significance for the present as it was for Conservative Judaism. A new historiography of ancient Judaism, first actualized as ideology under the chancellorship of historian Gerson D. Cohen, served to bridge the gulf between the Jewish Theological Seminary and the

increasingly liberalized Conservative synagogue movement, breaking down the old consensus in favor of a somewhat more "democratized" (or, in contemporary Conservative parlance, "egalitarian")[71] religious ideology that aligns with parallel trends and transformations in American mainline Protestantism.[72]

With the vantage point of fifty years since the first volumes of *Jewish Symbols* appeared, some of the errors of Goodenough's analysis are more evident than they were to earlier interpreters. Goodenough misunderstood the rabbis, as many of his reviewers stressed. He also erred in his creation of the binary opposite "mystical Judaism." Goodenough's overstatement was all the more monumental (and even colonialist) owing to his almost complete unfamiliarity with rabbinic sources in the original languages, a gap of which he was painfully aware. By his own admission, Goodenough did "not read Hebrew"[73] and knew rabbinic literature only in translation. He made no use of the vast literature of Byzantine-period Jewry, particularly *piyyutim* that had been preserved in traditional collections or discovered in the Cairo Genizah – not because many of these documents were unpublished in his day, but apparently because they appeared (and despite massive publication programs, still appear) almost exclusively in Hebrew. To be fair, the then-accepted dating of the "Galilean-type" synagogues – Baram, Gush Ḥalav, Meiron, Nabratein, Capernaum, Chorazin, and Arbel – to the second century allowed for the use of Classical rabbinic sources to interpret these buildings. This is no longer the case, however, as we now know (as Brunner intuited) that these synagogues date to the Byzantine period.[74]

Still, it is indicative of his difficulty with the Hebrew and Aramaic literature of ancient Judaism that Goodenough makes no reference to Byzantine-period liturgical texts in the course of his interpretation of late-fifth- and sixth-century buildings such as Na'aran and Beth Alpha. This is particularly the case in light of the thematic parallels between the synagogue remains and the poetry that Slouschz, Sukenik, and others had noted. Indicative of Goodenough's difficulty with Hebrew and Aramaic texts is the fact that a fragment of a Jewish liturgical parchment discovered near the Dura Europos synagogue was below Goodenough's "radar screen." He missed it altogether. This is startling for a scholar as careful as Goodenough, especially because this most important document was first published by C. Torrey in English 1936[75] and discussed by R. de

Mesnil du Buisson in French in 1939[76] and in Hebrew by S. Lieberman in 1940,[77] L. Ginzberg in 1941,[78] and E. L. Sukenik in 1947.[79]

As Smith, A. D. Noch, and other Christian scholars expressed[80] – and Jewish scholars did not discuss in print – Goodenough reinterpreted the material remains of Judaism in keeping with his own Christian theological–historical suppositions and background. For him, the rabbis paralleled directly the aniconic and strict Christianity of his youth.[81] Goodenough's approach was facilitated by the removal of each "symbol" from its original setting (be it a catacomb, synagogue, or whatever) and reorganization of that material according to themes. This is as much a function of the technology that he used as of his own proclivities. The cataloging of art according to theme, whether on cards as in, say, the Princeton Index of Christian Art or in codex form, often results in an overemphasis on details, a relativization of the important and unimportant. No one who works from firsthand experience of a major monument would equate a decorative detail with a major feature of the program. This is prone to happen, however, when one works from photographs. A minor detail can take on major proportions when it is reproduced to the same size as the major feature on the pages of a codex or projected on a slide screen. Goodenough had no sense of the limits of interpretation – not every grape or bird in a mosaic is meaningful. Having never visited Dura, and having visited Israel only during the early 1950s after his own ideas were fully formulated, Goodenough only knew what atomized photographs could yield about these monuments. In his analysis of "Jewish symbols," he juggled his visual sources and reorganized them according to predetermined categories, severing the ties, say, between a menorah in the floor at Beth Alpha with its archaeological locus, and even with the Land of Israel. Goodenough then applied universalizing interpretive principles drawn from his knowledge of Jewish diaspora sources in Greek and from psychology. Smith attributes Goodenough's focus on detail to his religious background. My own sense, however, is that it is based at least as much on an inability to judge proportional significance. Paul Veyne rightly refers to such explanations of art as "an excess of intellectualism."[82]

Jewish Symbols is ultimately a projection of Goodenough's own Christian theological questions onto Jews, redressed as a secularized "history of religions." Hypothetical Jews had served this function for Christian theology at least from the Gospel of John and Justin Martyr's *Conversation with Trypho* until modern times. Goodenough's colonization was genteel, in the best tradition of mid-century America, and it was surely not malicious in any way. Nevertheless, Goodenough's dislike for Orthodox "halakhic" Judaism (and his lack of understanding of it) is palpable throughout *Jewish Symbols*.

Thus, Goodenough's *Jewish Symbols in the Greco–Roman Period* should best be viewed as a transitional document. Its enduring scholarly significance rests in the way it set Jewish archaeology at the center of the scholarly agenda, particularly (although by no means exclusively) within Jewish circles. *Jewish Symbols* served as a goad for scholars to rethink the place of the rabbis in ancient Judaism, at a moment when elements within American Jewry were most receptive to such thinking. It is not surprising that Goodenough's critique was taken most seriously by Smith and by Conservative Jewish scholars and their students (including the present author). Historiographic and theological searching for the place of rabbis (ancient and modern) in Conservative Judaism was rife during the decades when *Jewish Symbols* appeared.

Goodenough's unique contribution to scholarship is found in the paradigm shift that his counterhistory generated. *Jewish Symbols* sparked two generations of scholars to actively seek out alternate voices in the extant sources, both archaeological and literary. This in itself is a major contribution. His most profound error, however, rests in his revaluation of the "classic" notion that Jews don't do art. Contrary to his British and American mentors, Goodenough knew that Jews *did* do art – and quite a lot of it. For Goodenough, mystical (read, ancient "Reform") Jews did indeed create art – just as modern Reform Jews did.[83] Ancient "Reform" Jews built the synagogues of Beth Alpha, Dura Europos, and Sardis – and buried their dead in lavishly decorated tomb complexes such as Beth She'arim and the Roman catacombs. He restricted the notion of Jewish artlessness to one group of Jews – the rabbis. Jews did do art, he argued – only rabbis didn't. Goodenough erred in believing that the Talmudic rabbis did not value the visual, maintaining that rabbinic "normative" Judaism, like the Methodism of his youth, was aniconic to the core.

Shortly after Goodenough's death, Smith likened Goodenough to Christopher Columbus. Concluding an important review essay in the *Journal of Biblical Literature*, Smith wrote: "Soit. Columbus failed too. But his failure revealed a new world, and so did Goodenough's. . . . Informed opinions of ancient Judaism can never, henceforth, be the same as they were before he published."[84] Smith's analogy reflects a long tradition of Columbian hyperbole. Goethe, for example, compared the legendary eighteenth-century scholar Johann Joachim Winckelmann to Columbus for supposedly having discovered Greek art.[85] The vision before Smith's eyes was Columbus the seeker of a path to India (in our case, mystical Judaism and the origins of Hellenistic Christianity) who inadvertently discovered "America" – for Smith, ancient Jewish art and nonrabbinic aspects of Judaism. Smith's "failed" Goodenough was the Columbus celebrated on the American civic holiday of Columbus Day – the hero commemorated in parades, public squares, and sculpture; in the "District of Columbia" and Columbus, the capital of Ohio; and, most importantly for Smith, his own Columbia University. Christopher Columbus is today often viewed quite differently. He is often looked upon as the person who opened the Western Hemisphere and its native inhabitants to centuries of colonial exploitation. If Goodenough – joined by Smith – is to be likened to Columbus, perhaps, we would do well to see in the work of these scholars curious and intriguing blends of both "Christopher Columbuses."

CHAPTER FOUR

ART HISTORY

TEXTBOOKS AND THE RHETORIC OF JEWISH ARTLESSNESS

Jewish Law actually forbade the making of images for fear of idolatry.

E. H. Gombrich, 1950[1]

. . . the most un-iconic (indeed anti-iconic) of religions.

Jaś Elsner, 1998[2]

WITH VERY FEW EXCEPTIONS, THE HISTORY OF WESTERN reflection on Jewish artistic creation is a history of exclusion. Not considered a "nation" in the sense meant by nineteenth-century nationalism, the Jews were excluded from the national categories upon which the history of art was constructed – and hence Judaism was intrinsically artless. The status of Jewish art (like the status of "Jewish literature," "Jewish philosophy," and "Jewish music") went to the core of the problem of Jewish identity in the modern world, where the nature of Judaism underwent almost constant renegotiation. Although the early-twentieth-century

German academy allowed Jews to enter the history of art (as opposed to many other areas of academic life), those Jews were often distant from Judaism and highly critical of it. Many of the greats of art history during this century – Abby Warburg, Adolph Goldschmidt, Erwin Panofsky, Meyer Schapiro, Richard Krautheimer, and E. H. Gombrich – were Jews, not to mention the baptized Bernard Berenson. Few Jewish scholars ever dealt explicitly with Jewish subjects. As my teacher, the Heidelberg-trained, German–Jewish art historian and founding director of New York's Jewish Museum, Stephen S. Kayser, once quipped: "Art History is what one Jew tells another Jew about *goyeshe* [that is, Christian] art." Kayser was not far from the truth. It should come as no surprise that even today, the best current scholarship on art and Judaism is carried out within Jewish academic contexts and not within general art history departments.

One might draw comfort from the fact that this treatment of Judaism by art history is not unique, even if it is extreme. Scholars of all art that falls outside the Western canon seem to have similar complaints. Robin Cormack testifies to this regarding the study of Byzantine art, and I have read similar comments regarding African, Islamic, and Indian art, and more recent categories such as women's art and African American art.[3] Cormack writes:[4]

. . . The study of Byzantine art has its own further obstacles. 'Medieval studies', it soon transpires, do not necessarily include Byzantium. While it may not actually be ostracized, Byzantine art can all too frequently be relegated to the margins. Although the art of Byzantium (as the Middle Ages in the 'Greek East') is sometimes given a walk-on part, more often than not it is seen as an entity apart, opportunely offering explanations for changes in western Medieval art: it becomes a 'source' or an 'influence.' The 'Byzantine Question' is conceived as the role of Byzantine art in the reconstruction of western European art at the beginning of the Italian Renaissance. . . .

The exclusion of Judaism is nonetheless different from other marginalized artistic traditions, for it involves the absolute denial of the existence of Jewish art and hence either the absolute superiority of Western (Christian) culture or, for some Protestants, the depravity of Western Christian (read, Catholic) art. Either way, this denial is a continuation and extension of traditional Christian supercessionism, albeit in a nationalistic and secular guise. Even for scholars who praised ancient Jewish art, be they the anti-Semitic Joseph Strzygowski or the positively inclined Kurt

Weitzmann and his student Herbert Kessler, Jewish art was only important as a background for Christian art. These attitudes – at times anti-Semitic, at others philo-Semitic, and at still others expressive of Jewish self-loathing and ambivalence – are addressed in detail in Catherine Soussloff's edited volume, *Jewish Identity in Modern Art History*, and to an even greater extent in Margaret Olin's *The Nation Without Art.*[5] I will not rehearse further the examples and conclusions of these volumes here. Instead, I turn to one specific body of evidence as a way of summarizing the established positions of the discipline. I look at ways that ancient Jewish art has been presented in the canonical treatments of art history: "Introduction to Art History" textbooks used throughout the English-speaking world by beginning students. More than even the most influential articles and monographs, introductory textbooks are often a good place to see what a discipline "really" thinks.

The long-lived "bibles" of modern English-language art history survey courses – namely, H. W. Janson's *History of Art*, E. H. Gombrich's *The Story of Art*, and *Gardner's Art through the Ages* – reflect this phenomenon. For most of the histories of these classics, Judaism is almost invisible. Selected Jews appear: Pissaro, Chagall, and Modigliani, for example, are all discussed in the first edition of Janson's classic work (1966). Chagall's work is exemplified by his image of the crucified Christ – an example of Jewish content curiously elided!

Dura appeared already in the first edition of E. H. Gombrich's *The Story of Art*, published in 1950. Gombrich chose to illustrate his discussion with a more distinctly Jewish image, "Moses striking water from the rock." After discussing the Hellenized Indian art of distant Gandhara (in modern Pakistan), Gombrich turns to the Dura synagogue. His evaluation did not change from edition to edition:[6]

Yet another oriental religion that learned to represent its sacred stories for the instruction of believers was the Jewish religion. Jewish Law actually forbade the making of images for fear of idolatry. Nevertheless, the Jewish colonies in eastern towns took to decorating the walls of their synagogue with stories from the Old Testament. One of these paintings was discovered fairly recently in a small Roman garrison in Mesopotamia called Dura-Europos. It is not a great work of art by any means, but it is an interesting document from the third century A.D. The very fact that the form seems clumsy and that the scheme looks rather flat and primitive is not without interest. . . . The artist was doubtless not very skillful, and that accounts for some of these features. But perhaps he was not really much concerned with drawing lifelike figures. The more lifelike they were the more they sinned against the Commandment forbidding images. His main intention was to remind the beholder of the occasions when God had manifested His power. The humble wall-painting from the Jewish synagogue is of interest to us, because similar considerations began to influence art when the Christian religion spread from the East and also took art into its service.

It is astonishing how many ways this art historian of Jewish origin found to describe the Dura synagogue and Judaism in general in negative terms. Gombrich removed Judaism beyond the Indus River in his evaluation, as far from Rome as possible. For him, being an "oriental religion" was no compliment!

Beginning with the second edition of his *History of Art* (1977), H. W. Janson, who was not Jewish, discussed the Dura Europos synagogue:[7]

It is characteristic of the melting-pot conditions described before [at Dura] that even Judaism should have been affected by them. Momentarily, at least, the age-old injunction against images was relaxed so that the walls of the assembly hall could be covered with a richly detailed visual account of the history of the Chosen People and their Covenant with the Lord. The new attitude seems to have been linked to a tendency to change Judaism from a national to a universal faith by missionary activity among the non-Jewish population, interestingly, some of the inscriptions on the murals (such as the name Aaron . . .) are in Greek. In any event, we may be sure that the artists who designed these pictures faced an unaccompanied task, just as painters who worked for the earliest Christian communities; they had to cast into visible form what had hitherto been expressed only in words . . . .

There is little in this description that even slightly resembles the situation of Roman-period Jewry, and specifically of the Dura Europos synagogue. The truth is that were the word synagogue removed, this might be a reasonable description of a Christian community. Janson shared the ubiquitous notion that Judaism is artless and begrudges the possibility that similar monuments might have existed in antiquity. For him – perhaps oddly enough, like Goodenough – only Jews seeking a "universal faith" (that is, ancient Classical Reform Jews) could possibly have created the Dura paintings. It was only owing to the "melting pot," a metaphor drawn from the American context, that Jews at Dura did art. Janson's choice of illustrations is again indicative of his approach. He did not choose an image of obvious Jewish content, nor one with a seemingly particularistic Jewish Aramaic inscription. Rather, Janson presented perhaps the most Greek-looking image, labeled with a Greek inscription. Even when showing a Jewish artifact, it is neutered of its Jewish content.

No other religious art suffers the deprecation that Judaism does in the introductory volumes by Jansen and Gombrich. It is no wonder that Roth introduced *Jewish Art* by acknowledging: "The conception of Jewish art may appear to some to be a contradiction in terms. . . ." In these textbooks we read what initiates to the history of art throughout the English-speaking world learn about "Jewish art." The significance of Gombrich's evaluation in the formation of young art historians should not be underestimated. A sticker affixed to the sixteenth edition, reprinted in 2000, proclaims proudly: "Over 6,000,000 sold. 'The World's Best Selling Art Book' – *US News and World Report.*" Within the acknowledged bearers of the art historical canon to generations of beginning art history students, Jewish art has been at best a sloppy appendage of Christian art – at worst a contradiction.

Recent years have seen a partial reevaluation of the place of Judaism in the history of art – even within derivative contexts. The 2001 edition of *History of Art*, prepared by Anthony F. Janson, expands on earlier editions, including greater discussion of the Dura synagogue paintings and comparison to late Roman monumental art.[8] This edition subtly slackens the "link" between these pictures and the alleged universalization of Judaism, by suggesting that they "have been linked" to these phenomena. The link, we recall, was forged by H. W. Janson himself in the 1977 edition! The Dura synagogue is the only artifact in the chapter on "Early Christian and Byzantine Art" to be derided as being "not very skillfully" executed. He explains this away with the comment that "even in the hands of a great artist . . . the shapes and colors would have been an imperfect embodiment of the spiritual truth they were meant to serve. That, surely, was the outlook of the authorities who controlled the program and execution of the mural cycle." In other words, the synagogue paintings are intentionally mediocre for religious reasons, enforced from above. Who these authorities were, I (a historian of ancient Judaism) do not know, and Janson does not elaborate. Janson concludes: "These pictures can no longer be understood in the framework of ancient art. They express an attitude that seems far closer to the Middle Ages." What he is getting at is beyond me. I think it is something like this: This art looks Christian, and so it is by definition medieval.

Thus, Janson pulls the synagogue out of its original late Roman historical context for the sake of his narrative of the origins of Christian art. Janson continues, suggesting that "To sum up their purpose, we may quote a famous dictum justifying pictorial representation of Christian themes: *Quod legentibus scriptura, hoc idiotis . . . pictura*. Translated freely it means 'painting conveys the Word of God to the unlettered.' " Quite a statement about a synagogue where Greek labels, Persian graffiti, Aramaic dedicatory inscriptions, and descriptive labels (including parallels to Aramaic Biblical paraphrases, *Targumim*) appear on the surfaces of the paintings and where a fragment of a Hebrew liturgical parchment was discovered nearby. In short, although the Dura synagogue is discussed in somewhat more detail in Janson's newest volume, the prejudice inherited from earlier editions – especially exclusive focus on this synagogue as an underdeveloped precursor of Christian art – is maintained. This is reinforced by the fact that Jewish art never reappears in this mammoth compendium.

The history of *Gardner's Art through the Ages* suggests similar approaches, as well as new ones that are only a bit more useful. The Dura synagogue appears late in the history of *Gardner's Art through the Ages*. It makes its debut in the tenth edition, published in 1996. *Gardner's Art through the Ages* reflects transitions in the art historical evaluation of Dura, as well as some vestiges of the previous paradigm. Introducing the chapter on "Early Christian Art," this city serves as a "microcosm" for the author of "the powerful religious crosscurrents of the world of late antiquity."[9] The synagogue is the first monument discussed and illustrated in this chapter, setting it as a forerunner for the discussion of Christian art to follow. The paintings of this Jewish precursor, we are told,

seem to be in defiance of the Second Commandment prohibiting graven images, and surprised scholars when they were first reported. But it is now apparent that while the Jews of the Roman Empire did not worship idols as did their pagan contemporaries, biblical stories not only were painted on the walls of synagogues like that at Dura-Europos but were also illustrated in painted manuscripts.[10]

The author is clearly more balanced than many earlier writers. "Surprise" at the existence of the paintings is set in the mouths of earlier interpreters and not taken at face value. The well-worn Second Commandment postulate is even hedged just a bit. The speculation on manuscript illustration, based on Kurt Weitzmann's work, is stated as fact – one that art historians have generally accepted with little criticism. Perhaps this may be excused in an introductory volume that uses the synagogue as a jumping-off place to discuss early Christian architecture, painting, and book illumination. "Pagans" with their "idols" (as opposed to, say, polytheists with their cult images) fare more poorly, betraying our author's implicitly Christian orientation. The Dura synagogue does not come off unscathed, however. Like "pagan" monuments that are listed, "the [Biblical] story is told through stylized gestures, and the figures, which have expressionless features and are lacking in both volume and are shallow, tend to stand in frontal rows." This characteristic, the rhetoric implicitly suggests, derives from the synagogue as well. Oddly, the quality of the paintings in the nearby Dura church is not discussed, except to suggest that they are "poorly preserved." While the synagogue paintings receive a negative evaluation of their artistic value, the artistic value of the technically inferior church paintings is passed over in silence. Surely an advance, *Gardner's* tenth edition continues the habits of the art historical discipline.

Virtually the same text and evaluation appear in the eleventh edition of *Gardner's Art through the Ages*, published in 2001.[11] The frame, however, has been completely changed. No longer introducing a chapter on "Early Christian Art," the Dura Europos synagogue now introduces "Pagans, Christians and Jews: The Art of Late Antiquity." This is indeed a step forward. In the rush to multicultural interpretation, however, the editors of *Gardner's* have made a binary and no less supercessionist error. A sidebar to their discussion of Christian iconography is called "Jewish Subjects in Christian Art." The text then describes Christian visual appropriation of "Old Testament" scenes, "Biblical tales of Jewish faith and salvation," in Christian wall paintings.[12] Here, then, Judaism is the religion of the Old Testament providing meaning for the superseding believers of the New Covenant. What is in fact described here is Christian visual exegesis of the Christian Old Testament – a book of the Christian canon that was accepted by the Church. Its component books are ordered to provide a seamless narrative of salvation through Christ stretching from Genesis to the book of Revelation, from creation to the apocalypse. The "Jewish faith" in its own right is nowhere discussed in *Gardner's,* even in regard to the synagogue. No other Jewish monument appears later in this volume – leaving the theologically imprinted impression that Christian art, like the Christian Bible, grew out of Judaism and superceded it.

The most recent addition to the canon of art history surveys is Marilyn Stokstad's 1995 work, *Art History.*[13] The Dura synagogue is among the first artifacts discussed in Stokstad's chapter on "Early Christian, Jewish and Byzantine Art." Based in a multicultural model, the treatment of the Dura synagogue in this chapter is short and accurate, focusing on the image of Pharoah's daughter rescuing baby Moses from the bulrush. Jewish painting in the Roman catacombs (illustrated by the famous Torah shrine image from the Villa Torlonia [Figure 50] and expanded in the 2000 edition)[14] and a brief discussion of synagogue mosaics also appear in this volume – a clear expansion of Jewish content over other surveys. Stokstad theologizes, writing that "the variety of placid animals (in one particular mosaic, from Maon [Nirim]), may represent the universal peace prophesized by Isaiah." The discussion of the mosaics is dropped from the 2000 edition (much of the context of this section appended to the discussion of catacomb art from Rome), apparently because discussion of these Byzantine-period floors breaks the flow to the baptistery at Dura and Christian art. Jewish mosaics do not reappear later. Stokstad's discussion of Jewish art of late antiquity is nevertheless reasonable, especially when read against the background of her predecessors. Her historical survey, however, needs improvement. Stokstad traces Jewish history from the Bible to the destruction of the Temple in 70 C.E., and then proceeds to discuss late antique Jewish monuments. This chapter once again leaves what is clearly the unintended (though in art history, default) impression that Judaism merely sets the stage for the triumph of Christianity. To the author's credit, selected monuments from later periods (including the Altneuschul in Prague) are illustrated, and the discussion of the Arch of Titus reliefs is excellent. Any imbalances in this volume are easily rectified. Stokstad's *Art History* is a major step away from the methodological dead end that art history had hit in its understanding of all things Jewish.

I conclude this chapter with an examination of the work of one particularly fascinating scholar, Oxford University's Jaś Elsner. Elsner's 1998 *Imperial Roman and Christian Triumph: The Art of the Roman Empire AD 100–450,* a book that would serve well as an American upper division college textbook, provides an extremely positive evaluation of the Dura synagogue, taking into account recent scholarship.[15] Yet, Elsner could not break himself from the habits of his discipline. He comments that "while it may seem strange that the most un-iconic (indeed anti-iconic) of religions should have resorted to the rich programme of narrative images we find in the Dura Synagogue . . . , in fact the Dura frescoes are not unique in the Judaism of their time." The truth is that the Dura paintings are unique in the history of ancient Judaism, although this is undoubtedly due only to the whimsy of survival and discovery. Elsner nevertheless considers the period when this structure was built to be unique in the history of Judaism. This is expressed in Elsner's characterization of Judaism as "the most un-iconic (indeed anti-iconic) of religions" – a characterization with no basis in fact, though much support in the history of the history of art. Still, Elsner's early discussion of the Dura synagogue was a step forward.

Between his 1998 volume and today, Elsner has thoroughly rethought his position vis-à-vis Judaism and art. In 2001, he wrote:

The Jews, whose brilliant efforts at stealing Graeco-Roman culture's visual vocabularies at Dura we have already seen, were to prove the most spectacularly adaptable of all the cults. They switched from resisting the Roman Empire's pagan environment to resisting Christianity's monotheistic hegemony with appetite, aplomb, and remarkable (if low-key) success.[16]

Elsner had still not completely broken with the assumption that Christianity was the central focus of Jewish art and the most important point from which to judge it. This is an error with a very long history in scholarship (even Blau accepted it unquestioningly). A Christocentric model has been repeated with increasing vigor in recent years by a small group of Jewish text scholars and historians who consciously break with classical Zionist historiography's search for alternative interpretations.[17] Elsner's use of the term "stealing" to describe Jewish participation in the art of the Roman empire is unfortunate, and suggests that Jewish participation in that art was somehow illegitimate.

In an article that appeared in 2003, Elsner had transformed further. He places Jewish art, together with Christian art and the art of other religious groups, squarely within the confines of Roman religion.[18] No longer assuming a

Christocentric approach, Elsner quite correctly sees the art of the Jews as part and parcel of "late ancient" art, just like "Christian art." Though formulated in differing ways, no Jewish interpreter of Jewish antiquities of whom I am aware (marginal as they were, and still are, to art history) has ever argued against this general proposition. Elsner's transformation is largely in response to the work of Wharton and Olin. Elsner develops a methodologically sophisticated statement of the relationship between Jewish and Christian artistic production. He rightly suggests that "it is in part because of my doubts about the validity of both terms (Jewish and Christian) when used in a strong and exclusive sense – especially in relation to the visual materials before the fifth century – that I have my doubts about the traditional art-historical focus on Jewish and Christian art in late antiquity to the exclusion of the parallel religious arts of the Graeco-Roman environment." Elsner is broadly correct.

In this transformation, Elsner follows on trends developed more than thirty years ago by historian Peter Brown, who sees Jewish, pagan, Christian, Sassanian, and early Islamic cultures within the context of a larger "late antique" culture.[19] With Elsner, I too find the scholarly construction of exclusive categories difficult, and in the first draft of this volume I used the term Jewish art only in quotation marks. I removed the quotation marks only because this term, like, say, American art, Kurdish art, Spanish art, African American art, or Mithraic art, is both conventional and useful to describe a community's experience with the visual – when it is not used in an overly determined manner. Elsner's work is the most profound example thus far of the ways that art history is changing.

CHAPTER FIVE

TOWARD A NEW JEWISH ARCHAEOLOGY

METHODOLOGICAL REFLECTIONS

The fable of the hatred entertained by the Synagogue against all manner of art in the middle ages and the new time should at last succumb to the evidence of facts. . . .

David Kaufmann, 1897[1]

THE "FABLE" THAT KAUFMANN DESCRIBES WAS APPLIED TO antiquity no less than to later periods. One hundred and eight years after Kaufmann published these words, his dream is just now being realized. The core assumption that Judaism is aniconic – held for so long by a powerful cultural elite – set the backdrop, if not the agenda, for all twentieth-century scholarship on "Jewish art." From the Frank Memorial Synagogue in Philadelphia to Slouschz at Hammath Tiberias and Sukenik at Beth Alpha to Goodenough's mystical Judaism and art history's virtual blindness to Jewish visual culture, this chapter presents ways that the art of ancient Judaism was constructed during the twentieth century. This was a century that witnessed phenomenal discoveries and often superb scholarship. A full appreciation of this material was at times impeded and at others prompted by negative attitudes that have little basis in historical fact. The "artless Jew," Bland's succinct coinage, is but one of the many legacies of what was arguably the single most difficult period in Jewish history since Titus destroyed the Jerusalem Temple in 70 C.E. Thanks to postmodern and multicultural perspectives, we are now in a position to contextualize the past, reveal destructive attitudes in earlier scholarship, and recognize the useful work that was done by twentieth-century scholars.

What may we take from the scholarship that I have surveyed into the project before us? First of all, the great discoveries of Jewish archaeology and art and the prodigious publication programs of Jewish texts during the twentieth century made an incredible body of evidence available for the first time. These were truly magnificent achievements. If for the twentieth century these discoveries were new and exciting, for us they are a natural part of the popular Jewish visual vocabulary and the landscape of texts studied by scholars (and even of undergraduates and rabbinical students). Academic publications, first among them Goodenough's catalog, set Jewish archaeological evidence within easy reach of every scholar. More recent discoveries have added to our knowledge, but have not radically changed the landscape blazed by mid-twentieth-century archaeologists and philologians.

Second, the sense that Jewish art is a normal part of world art will be treated as a given in this study. Catholic scholars and some Jews – notably for our period Kaufmann, Blau, and Sukenik – knew this to be the case. In wider academic circles, however, this simple assertion was often revolutionary and even heretical. Even the partial diminution of this paradigm that has occurred in recent scholarship is not to be taken lightly. My work will not be invested with either the need to overly praise Jewish attitudes or products or by a proclivity to neutralize them.

We have seen that archaeology was a crucial tool in studies on the question of rabbinic authority. The central role of the rabbis in Jewish life is assumed by Moore's "normative Judaism" and attacked by Goodenough, Smith, and their protégées – often presuming (if only tacitly) that the rabbis were particularly antagonistic toward art. According to this logic, the existence of art is thus evidence

for "nonrabbinic Jews." In my own work, I assert a careful balance that includes rabbis and magicians, peasants and patriarchs, Palestinians and diaspora Jews within a broad spectrum of Jewish practice and belief. There was indeed a single religious community, with a set of symbols, beliefs, and customs that was shared by Jewish communities across the Roman and Persian empires. Late in his life, Goodenough disparagingly called this "minimal Judaism," and, with Scholem and Smith, he focused on the esoteric. For some Smith students, a radical sense of ambiguity has allowed for the reading of increasingly ambiguous American Judaism into the ancient equation. Having experienced the Goodenough/Smith paradigm for nearly fifty years, a balance is developing between these positions. E. P. Sanders's strenuous assertion of the "common Judaism" of the latter Second Temple period is a reaction to this approach, as is my application of Sanders's approach to late antiquity. This study of the Greco-Roman Jewish *koiné* focuses on the consensus religion of Jews while accounting fully for regional, local, class, educational, and religious variety. It will also be attentive to the literary and interpretive context of each source in this attempt at cultural history. Still, to my mind, there is no longer reason to assert variety with the strenuousness that some late-twentieth-century scholars deemed necessary. The question is how to balance the various types of evidence and read them to elicit the multiple voices of Judaism during the Greco-Roman period – together with the shared voice.

A related dichotomy that must be laid to rest is that of Judaism versus Hellenism, reaching as it does to the roots of Jewish identity – and of western constructions of the Jew in the modern world. This unfortunate bifurcation has led scholars to spend inordinate amounts of energy assessing the relative levels of acculturation among ancient Jews to the Greco-Roman culture or projecting a modern synthesis onto the ancients. Instead, I suggest a more organic model, drawn from contemporary studies of identity. It is my sense that the Jews as a whole were full participants in the Greco-Roman world, just as most were full participants in the Jewish community. This minority identity was not merely a matter of acculturation, but was constantly under renegotiation and in most ways in confluence with the majority. The default culture for Jews came to be Greco-Roman, even as they set and reset their own ethnic boundaries within that culture.[2] The negotiation of this

Romano–Jewish (or is it Jewish–Romano?) identity was essential to their minority or "ethnic" status and is reflected in the art of ancient Judaism.

This approach does not suggest that antiquity was a happy period of multicultural understanding. Although emotionally appealing, this model was no more true of late antiquity than it is in describing Jewish history since World War II. There was much tension in antiquity, much fighting, and for Jews, often much to fear. Jewish reactions to non-Jewish art in Palestine were conditioned by the fact that Jews lived under colonial domination. The role of Christianity in the formation of late antique Jewish art will be taken seriously, although Christian influences were complex and not automatically decisive or determinative – particularly before the late fourth or fifth century.

The analysis I undertake must account for the distinctiveness of each source and each variety of sources that have come down to us, and requires that all be used – not so difficult for a period whose primary literary sources may be stored in one large bookcase (as they are in my home); most reside comfortably on a couple of compact disks. We are "rich" in the variety of sources available for late Second Temple Palestine. Archaeological discoveries during the twentieth century – including, most prominently, excavations throughout the Land of Israel and the uncovering of the Dead Sea Scrolls – added greatly to the literary sources preserved through the centuries by the Church. These literary sources include, most prominently, the books of the Apocrypha, of the so-called Pseudepigrapha, the Dead Sea Scrolls, the writings of Josephus Flavius, Philo of Alexandria, and comments by Greek and Roman authors. By contrast, our knowledge of the second and third centuries is almost completely dependent on rabbinic literature that continues to be read, copied, edited, and studied by the Jewish community – as is almost everything we know about Babylonian Jewry during late antiquity. To make matters more complex, what we know of Western diaspora communities after the first century is almost completely based on archaeological discoveries. The Byzantine period in Palestine is better represented, owing to twentieth-century archaeological discoveries for this rather wealthy period and also to the fact that Byzantine period documents continued to be used into the medieval period. Some of these were deposited in the attic of the Ben Ezra synagogue in old Cairo and hence preserved. Fortunately, the "Cairo Genizah" was discovered near the turn of the twentieth

century. Without this resource, the Jewish literary heritage of the Byzantine period would be slight indeed!

It is often forgotten that the preservation and discovery of ancient sources are as much a matter of historical caprice as of modern luck. Relative paucity or richness of source materials must be factored into our discussion at a most profound level. This reality requires a cautious modesty before the vast amounts that we cannot know. As Menahem Stern, the much-lamented scholar of the Second Temple period, once quipped in his Hebrew University Josephus seminar: "We have less than 10% of the sources for the Second Temple period." Then he looked up slyly: "And who would say that these are the best 10%?" Modern experience has shown how fleeting historical knowledge is and how thoroughly ideology has colored scholarship on the history of the Jewish relationship with art.[3] Although the goal of the historian is to bridge to the past using his or her methodologically tuned imaginative powers, I must admit my own inabilities and the limits of my discipline at the very start of this endeavor.

My goal in this volume is to move beyond twentieth-century paradigms of ancient Judaism and its relationship to art. Through the careful reading of sources and by asking questions that the sources can answer, much may be learned about the place of the visual within Jewish culture during the Greco–Roman period. This is not a book about sources, however, whether literary or archaeological, but ultimately about a religious community and the ways that its members lived within and constructed their visual environment. What did Jews mean when they made, used, enjoyed, ignored, and sometimes destroyed or discarded "art"? This question will be approached through a series of studies using models drawn from recent scholarship on identity, symbolism, and liturgy, all of which assert a much more multivalent interpretive schema than has previously been accepted. I draw on recent discussions of identity construction and on a holistic approach to religious art and architecture pioneered by scholars of early Christian art.

I call this approach a new "Jewish archaeology," drawing on the legacy of Catholic "Christian archaeology" rather than once-dominant German Protestant approaches. Ludwig Blau and E. L. Sukenik were the most important early scholars of Jewish archaeology. Blau pioneered Jewish archaeology by demonstrating a sophisticated reading of rabbinic texts to uncover Jewish participation in

Roman art even as his subject was ancient Jews and not literature. Sukenik fathered a discipline, discovering and interpreting archaeological remains within the broadest framework of Jewish literature. By appropriating the virtually discarded term "Jewish archaeology," I thus forge a link between my approach and the contributions of these great scholars. By adding the adjective "new," I integrate the achievements of the second half of the twentieth century into this study, even as I attempt to move the discussion forward.[4]

PART TWO

ART AND IDENTITY IN THE GRECO–ROMAN WORLD

I N 1960 HEINRICH STRAUSS, A GERMAN–JEWISH–ISRAELI ART HISTORIAN, published a programmatic essay for interpreting Jewish visual culture. He called it "Jewish Art as a Minority Problem."[1] In this exceptionally important (and generally forgotten) reflection, Strauss attempted to go beyond the nationalist preoccupations of his native Germany and of the new State of Israel. Strauss stressed and legitimized the proposition that Jewish art (like, he believed, German art) is the art of a minority. "They remained a cultural minority," Strauss wrote, "an island in a sea of ancient Oriental and later Hellenistic–Roman culture – even in times of political autonomy."[2] During the Greco–Roman period, this "minority art" functioned within the visual culture of the majority civilization. For Strauss, however, Jews nevertheless remained a distinct "island" distinguished from the main and its universal visual culture.

More recent studies of identity allow me to take Strauss's insights further. Jewish "minority art" was not so separated from broader cultural developments as Strauss imagined. Identity, we now know, is constructed; it is under constant renegotiation – both by individuals within a society and by the society as a whole. As Sylvia Barack Fishman suggests, paraphrasing Frederik Barth's important work on ethnic identity, "ethnicity functions as a kind of boundaried vessel, within which the enclosed culture is continually adjusted, with some elements being emphasized and others de-emphasized according to a shifting spectrum of influencing factors."[3] In discussing ethnic identity in ancient Greece, Jonathan Hall has gone still further. Hall questions whether ethnic identity "is primarily constructed by either genetic traits, language, religion or even common cultural forms." Hall's description of the constitutive elements of "ethnicity" is a useful summary statement of current approaches. It can serve as a starting point for our discussion.[4] According to Hall,

1. Ethnicity is a social rather than a biological phenomenon. It is defined by socially and discursively constructed criteria rather than by physical indicia.
2. Genetic, linguistic, religious, or common cultural features do not ultimately define the ethnic group. These are symbols that are manipulated according to subjectively constructed ascripted boundaries.
3. The ethnic group is distinguished from other social and associative groups by virtue of association with a specific territory and a shared myth of descent. The notion of descent is putative rather than actual, and judged by consensus.
4. Ethnic groups are frequently formed by the appropriation of resources by one section of the population, at the expense of another, as a result of long-term conquest or migration, or by the reaction against such appropriation.
5. Ethnic groups are not static or monolithic, but dynamic and fluid. Their boundaries are permeable to a degree, and they may be subject to processes of assimilation and differentiation.
6. Individuals need not always act in terms of their membership in an ethnic group. . . . Ethnicity gains varying degrees of salience at different times.
7. Such behavioral convergence and ethnic salience is more common among (though not exclusive to) dominated and excluded groups.
8. Ethnic identity can only be constructed by opposition to other ethnic identities.

As we shall see, these categories describe the Jewish situation during the Greco-Roman period. Jewish ethnicity was certainly "a social . . . phenomenon," tied to a specific territory and "myth of descent." Membership was attained both through birth and conversion – and in many cases maintained as an act of volition. In addition, Jewish identity was most often defined over and against that of both conquerors (for Palestinian Jews) and majority cultures (for diaspora communities and for some Palestinian Jews). Jewish identity was neither "static nor monolithic," but, as Hall suggests, "subject to processes of assimilation and differentiation." Hall's sense that individuals do not always "act in terms of their membership in an ethnic group. . . . Ethnicity gains varying degrees of salience at different times" is significant, for it highlights the differing roles assumed by individuals and the diachronic nature of this change. At the same time, Jews exhibited astonishing commonalities ("salience") between their various communities, all of which were "dominated" by general Greco-Roman culture in one way or the other.

Scholarship on ethnic identity has recently been applied by Kenneth Stow to the acculturation of the Jewish minority in medieval and early modern Rome.[5] Stow shows how a tightly bound Jewish minority selectively absorbed the majority culture, refracting it through their own Jewish–Roman cultural lenses, sometimes conservatively maintaining elements of earlier absorption long after the majority culture had abandoned them. Stow explains that ". . . however Jews understood the process of selective absorption, it must be appreciated as one of cultural creation, of converting the external into something Jewish, something part and parcel of normative Jewish practice."[6] Although his sense of ethnic boundaries and the degree of cognitive intention involved in their construction and maintenance is somewhat overly determined, Stow's insight is useful in interpreting the Jewish experience under Greece, Rome, and Byzantium. While the situation of Jewry pre-70 was quite different from that after the destruction of the Temple (and certainly from that of the microscopic medieval Roman Jewry), the transformation of the Jews into a Greco-Roman ethnic group – both in imperial Judaea and in often tiny diaspora communities – led to fascinating experiments with selective absorption and to the conservative adoption of elements of the majority culture. This process was accelerated during late antiquity, a period when Jews were both "in" in the sense, after 212 C.E., of being citizens of Rome and "out" in the sense that the Jewish *ethnos* in Palestine lived under a self-perceived Roman colonial regime – under the Byzantines, a supercessionist one at that. Jews outside of Palestinian centers lived as minority communities; some very small, some substantial in size, under Rome, Christian Rome, and under the Zoroastrian Persians.

I suggest that Jewish attitudes toward art exemplify this process. Jews fully participated in this visual culture – unreflectively treating it as the natural "default" way to make art. It is no different from the "default" among medieval and early modern Romans in their use of Italian art[7] or our own "default" use of contemporary art, architecture, and design forms – most of us doing so without ascribing particular meaning to them even in our more visually reflective age. The artistic values of the majority were generally also those of the Jewish minority and coalesced with an always-developing yet distinct Jewish sense of identity. This piece of the Jewish experience of Greco–Roman art is not discussed explicitly in texts, but is taken for granted. Where the default visual culture came into partial or full conflict with Jewish approaches (which themselves were under continual renegotiation), art became a boundary marker, a point of cultural contention and self-definition. Jews were part and parcel of the general visual culture, their distinctive art unself-consciously coalescing[8] with Greco–Roman traditions even while creating a subcategory of distinctly Jewish art and architecture.

In this section, I examine Jewish attitudes toward "art" over a very long expanse of time: the Greco–Roman period. I have chosen monuments to serve as a focal point in our investigation. We begin with the Hasmonean tombs at Modi'in for our study of art and Judaism in Second Temple period Judaea. This monument, no longer extant, provides an excellent vantage point for interpreting Jewish attitudes from the third century B.C.E. to the destruction of the Jerusalem Temple in 70 C.E. We then continue our study of art in ancient Palestine, focusing on the period between 70 and the eighth century – the period now referred to in Jewish historiography as "late antiquity" and as "the period of the Mishnah and Talmud." Here, our focal point will be a synagogue discovered in 1917 on a bluff overlooking the Jordan River, at a place called Na'aran in antiquity. Our last evidence from diaspora communities. I assess attitudes toward art in the far-flung Jewish communities of the Roman and Persian empires. In all of these contexts, we see how Jews negotiated distinctive identities as minorities in relation to the art of their general environment.

CHAPTER SIX

ART AND IDENTITY IN LATTER SECOND TEMPLE PERIOD JUDAISM

———————

THE HASMONEAN ROYAL TOMBS AT MODI'IN

I F WE WERE TO APPROACH A JEW OF LATTER SECOND TEMPLE period Palestine and ask for his or her opinions on art, we would most certainly be met with hollow stares. Art as a separate category of thought is a relatively recent invention, just as the "history of art" is among the youngest of the humanistic disciplines. Reformulating the question in terms that our Judaean might comprehend, we might ask what he thinks is beautiful or skillfully designed. Here we would be on firmer ground. Beauty and design, however, do not encompass all that the term "art" suggests. Were we to point to a table made by a well-known artisan, made of marble and ivory and gold, our Judaean might well express pleasure. If we were then to point to a sculpture of Zeus made of the same materials by the same artisan, however, our Judaean would most likely express disgust at the nude "idol." As one ancient author put it: "They are made by carpenters and goldsmiths; they can be nothing but what the craftsmen wish them to be."[1]

In this chapter, I survey the extant literary and archaeological sources to show that Hellenistic and then Roman art were well-received by Jews and fully accepted by them – so long as this art was not seen as containing anything that Jews considered "idolatrous." The shifting boundary between the acceptable and the unacceptable, between art and "idolatry," was reflective of shifting forces within the Jewish community and the ways that Jews situated themselves within Greco–Roman culture. This discussion focuses on the tombs of the Hasmonean royal family at Modi'in. This complex, which no longer exists, provides an excellent vantage point for assessing the changing relationship between art and Judaism from the Hasmonean period (beginning 166 B.C.E.) through the destruction of the Jerusalem Temple in 70 C.E. As a measure of these trends, I begin with the differing ways that 1 Maccabees and the Jewish historian Josephus Flavius describe the Hasmonean tombs and set these texts against the full light of the considerable extant literary and archaeological sources. Our next task is to broadly contextualize these traditions historically through an examination of Jewish participation in Greco–Roman art, focusing on the writings of Joshua Ben Sirah and Josephus Flavius. These two authors provide ample evidence for Jewish use of art forms that were common throughout the Greco–Roman world and for the fact that Jews held attitudes toward art that were shared across this expanse.

The upshot of this discussion will be that the Hasmonean tombs fit well with what we know of Jewish attitudes, fully participating in the art of the broader culture. I set the Hasmonean monuments within developing Jewish attitudes toward the idolatrous. This chapter then moves to the issues of art and idolatry, tracing Jewish approaches from the Hellenistic period through the Roman destruction of the Temple in 70 C.E. In conclusion, I summarize the trajectory of Jewish attitudes toward the visual in latter Second Temple Judaea, refracting the discussion through the Hasmonean tombs at Modi'in.

THE HASMONEAN ROYAL TOMBS: KEYS TO UNDERSTANDING LATTER SECOND TEMPLE PERIOD ATTITUDES TOWARD ART

The Hasmonean royal tombs in Modi'in, described in 1 Maccabees 13: 27–9, provide a lens through which to assess the complexities of Judaean attitudes toward Hellenistic art from the second century B.C.E. through the first Jewish revolt against Rome. This text, written toward the end of the second century B.C.E.,[2] exemplifies Hasmonean participation in general Hellenistic art at a very early stage in their dynastic rule:

And Simon built a monument over the tomb of his father and his brothers; he made it high that it might be seen, with polished stone at the front and back. He also erected seven pyramids, opposite one another, for his father and mother and four brothers. And for the pyramids he devised an elaborate setting, erecting about them great columns, and upon the columns he put[3] suits of armor[4] for a permanent memorial, and beside the suits of armor carved ships, so that they could be seen by all who sail the sea. This is the tomb which he built in Modi'in; it remains to this day.

Simon the Hasmonean ruled between 143 and 134 B.C.E. The tomb complex described here is thoroughly Hellenistic in conception. No distinctively Jewish iconography is evident in this text. None of the images that were later associated with Judaism, principally the menorah, existed as icons at this early date. Were such images present, the text would certainly have mentioned them. Were this complex discovered, say, in Syria or Egypt, no one would suspect that it was a Jewish tomb. Archaeological parallels to this tomb complex are common and can help us to interpret this ancient, and long-lost building. Parallels stem from later Hasmonean and Roman Judaea, as well as the general Greco–Roman context. Monuments topped with pyramids, for example, have been discovered throughout the Levant. Among these are the first-century B.C.E. Tomb of Hamrath at Suweida in Syria, where shields and other military implements appear among the decorations of the tomb – just as is described in 1 Maccabees – and the monumental tombs at Hermel and Kalat Fakra in Lebanon.[5] The famous mausoleum at Halacarnassus in Asia Minor, dating to the fourth century B.C.E., and the Belevi Monument located close by are important precursors.[6] Maximillian Kon suggests a reasonable reconstruction of the Hasmonean complex: "It was apparently a very high rectangular structure built from ashlars which served as a base for the upper story of the monument, consisting of seven base structures in the form of towers surrounded by pilasters and crowned by pyramidal or conical tops. The wall-surfaces between the pilasters were decorated with reliefs of weapons and ships."[7]

11. The Tomb of Jason, Jerusalem (courtesy of Holylandphotos.com).

Particularly important among Jerusalem parallels to the Hasmonian tombs are the Tomb of Jason[8] in western Jerusalem (Figure 11) and the Tomb of Zechariah in the Kidron Valley (Figure 12). Near the Tomb of Zechariah is the slightly later so-called Tomb of Absalom, which is crowned with a conical "pyramid" (Figure 13).[9] Like the Hasmonean family tombs and perhaps in some ways following their lead, each of these single monuments was topped with a pyramid. Funerary monuments crowned with pyramids are well known from Herodian Jerusalem as well.[10] The so-called Tombs of the Kings, the sepulcher of the royal house of Adiabene, is particularly relevant (Figure 14). Josephus describes three pyramids above this complex, which has been confirmed by the modern discovery of remains of conical "pyramids."[11] Similarly, the image of a monument crowned by three pyramids is inscribed on an ossuary in the Nelson and Helen Glueck Collection of the Cincinnati Art Museum (Figure 15).[12] The multiplication of pyramids above the entrance portal of the Tombs of the Kings and illustrated on the Cincinnati ossuary parallels the seven pyramids set above the Hasmonean tombs. The Hasmonean-period monument of the Benei Hezir tomb in the Kidron Valley, now largely lost, is called a *nefesh* in a Hebrew dedicatory inscription.[13] A large funerary monument is called a *nefesh* in Rabbinic Hebrew. Cognates appear in related Semitic languages.[14] In the Syriac version of 1 Maccabees, the Hasmonean monuments are described by the rare Syriac cognate *nafshan*.[15]

Military equipment of the type described in 1 Maccabees is extant in only one other Hasmonean artistic context. A crested helmet "of a Hellenistic type" appears on a double lepta (Hebrew: *perutah*, a small bronze coin) of John Hyrcanus I.[16] The "suits of armor" that were set atop the columns, with "carved ships" beside them, find numerous Hellenistic and Roman parallels.[17] The "suits of armor," or trophies, are a Hellenistic convention. Suits of armor set up on standards, like those described here, appear on coins of the Hellenistic period with some regularity.[18] In the tomb of Lyson and Kallikles, a Macedonian tomb, for example, a lunette on the southern wall of the burial chamber contains the image of a "Macedonian shield"

12. Tomb of Zechariah, Jerusalem (photograph by Steven Fine).

13. Tomb of Absalom, Jerusalem (photograph by Steven Fine).

Galleys appear on Herodian coinage, and anchors are found for the first time in Jewish coinage on a small bronze coin (*lepta*) of the Hasmonean Alexander Jannaeus.[22] Yaakov Meshorer believes that the Jannaeus anchor coins were "apparently struck after the conquest of the coastal cities (with the exception of Ashkelon) in 95 B.C.E. The anchor probably publicized the annexation of these areas by the Hasmonean ruler, even as Hasmonean numismatic iconography maintained considerable continuity with Seleucid coinage."[23] Significantly, the image of two ships seemingly pursued by a warship was drawn on the wall of the entrance chamber of Jason's Tomb, providing yet another concrete parallel to the Hasmonean tombs from an archaeological context (Figure 16).[24] Rahmani goes so far as to suggest regarding Jason's Tomb that "the original occupant of the tomb (and the probable founder of the family) was in some way connected with the naval exploits of the coast of Palestine in the years 100–64 B.C., the most probable period of the drawings."[25] If this is accurate, then this tomb participates in a visual tradition first evidenced among Jews in the Hasmonean royal tombs. It seems that the armor and ships at the Hasmonean tombs were meant to project Hasmonean power by sea and land. Located in the home territory of the Hasmoneans at Modi'in, on the boundary between the Judaean heartland and the conquered (or soon to be conquered) coastal plain and the somewhat distant Mediterranean Sea (approximately 27 kilometers to the west as the crow flies),[26] this typically Hellenistic monument presents Hasmonean military accomplishments and objectives in a concrete form that was easily understood by Jew and Greek alike. From such a distance, it is likely that the monument could not be seen at sea.[27] More important for Hasmoneans looking to expand westward from their traditional habitations, however, is the fact that on a clear day the Mediterranean can certainly be seen from the hills of Modi'in. Apparently recognizing the geographic

flanked by helmet-topped corslets and hanging swords toward the corners.[19] Stella G. Miller suggests that the array of armor painted within this tomb represents either trophies or – more likely – is "a symbolic array of typical gear worn by members of the military class buried here."[20] I would suggest the same for the coin of Hyrcanus and the Hasmonean tombs. Representation of weapons within funerary settings, as well as in public places such as gateways and balustrades, bouleuteria, and theaters, and on trophies, has a long history throughout the Mediterranean world – although not among Jews in Palestine (with the exception of Herod's theater in Jerusalem, as we shall see).[21]

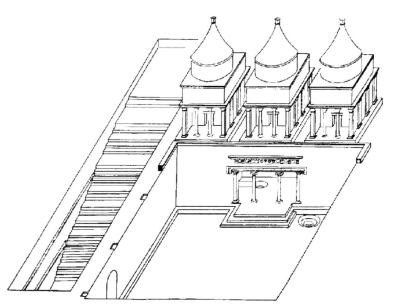

14. Tomb of the Kings, Jerusalem, reconstruction drawing (after B. Mazar, *The Mountain of the Lord* [Garden City: Doubleday, 1975], 231).

15. Tomb topped with three pyramids, inscribed on an ossuary in the Nelson and Helen Glueck Collection, Cincinnati Art Museum (courtesy of Steven Fine).

difficulties inherent in the 1 Maccabees description, Josephus later dropped it from his restatement of this tradition.

Of particular interest is the image of a pyramidal monument topped with an anchor on a Herodian ossuary in the Israel State Collection. L. Y. Rahmani notes the parallel between this anchor and anchors depicted on Hasmonean and Herodian coins, credibly suggesting that "such ornaments may have been used locally to replace statues found at the base and apex of tomb monuments

abroad . . ." (Figures 17, 18).[28] The anchor atop this monument, undoubtedly based on architectural models, parallels the nautical symbolism of the Hasmonian tombs. We might further suggest that the lack of an extensive sculptural program at Modiʿin reflects the type of Jewish sensitivities to which Rahmani alludes. Simon was willing to exhibit armor, which is very close to the human form itself, but unwilling to cross that threshold and decorate the royal tombs with unambiguously human imagery. This careful balancing is also known from Hasmonean coins. Although the models for Hasmonean coinage were clearly Seleucid, use of human imagery was not adopted from Seleucid coinage. This difference, like the constraints on decorating the Hasmonean tombs, reflects ways that Jews balanced their local concerns with full participation in "universal" Hellenistic visual culture.[29]

Josephus's reworking of the 1 Maccabees tradition of the Hasmonean tombs around 90 C.E. reflects changing attitudes toward the visual at the end of the Second Temple period. Basing his depiction on 1 Maccabees,[30] Josephus describes the tombs in *Antiquities* 13.211–13, as follows:

And Simon also built for his father and brothers a very great monument of polished white marble, and raising it to a great and conspicuous height, made porticoes around it, and erected monolithic pillars, wonderful thing to see. In addition to these he built for his parents and his brothers seven pyramids, one for each, so made as to excite wonder by their size and beauty; and these have been preserved to this day. Such was the zeal which we know to have been shown by Simon in burying Jonathan and building monuments to his family.[31]

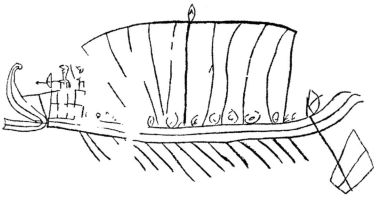

16. Graffito of a ship, Tomb of Jason, Jerusalem (after L. Y. Rahmani, "Jason's Tomb," *Israel Exploration Journal* 17 (1967), 71. Courtesy of the Israel Exploration Society).

17. Anchor on a lepton of Herod the Great (from the Alan I. Casden Collection of Ancient Jewish Coins, as represented in C. W. Samuels, P. Rynearson, Y. Meshorer, eds., *The Numismatic Legacy of the Jews as Depicted by a Distinguished American Collection* [New York: Stack's Publications, Numismatic Review, 2000], coin 48, reverse).

This depiction suggests Josephus's generally positive attitude toward elegant architecture, and particularly toward elegant royal tombs.[32] The Hasmonean tombs "excite

18. Image of a funerary monument on an ossuary (after L. Y. Rahmani, "Jerusalem's Tomb Monuments on Jewish Ossuaries," *Israel Exploration Journal* 18 (1968), 221. Courtesy of the Israel Exploration Society).

wonder by their size and beauty." They are a "wonderful thing to see," he wrote. What is more fascinating, however, is what he does not say. There is no mention here of "suits of armor," nor of "carved ships." What is the reason for this deletion? Were the armor and ships gone by Josephus's time? His erasure would then be nothing more than contemporization. The addition or removal of iconography from monuments is not unusual in human history, the meaning of the monument changing with ideology and the times. Alternately, did Josephus "erase" these images from the Hasmonean tombs through literary device? Literary sources suggest that this may be the case. In this way, the Hasmonean tombs could be made to conform with Josephus's leitmotif, whereby Jews are fundamentally antagonistic toward images. Although we will probably never know for sure, we may determine the contexts for the 1 Maccabees and Josephus descriptions within the literature and archaeology of latter Second Temple Judaea. To this task we now turn.

JEWISH PARTICIPATION IN GRECO–ROMAN ART: THE EVIDENCE OF BEN SIRAH AND JOSEPHUS FLAVIUS

Literary and archaeological evidence for the latter Second Temple period suggests that Jews, like their subaltern neighbors, had made the Greco–Roman artistic tradition their own. This confluence is exemplified in the Hasmonean tombs, as it is throughout the extant literary and visual sources. The most extensive discussions of the visual appear in the *Wisdom of Ben Sirah* around 175 B.C.E. and the writings of Josephus Flavius during the latter part of the first century C.E. Ben Sirah and Josephus thus frame our period near its beginning and near its end, providing important windows into the development of Jewish attitudes toward "art" during the latter Second Temple period.

Joshua son of Sirah, a second-century B.C.E. priest and wisdom-writer who preceded the Hasmonean revolt by only a decade or two,[33] reveals a keen interest in the visual. Ben Sirah shows a special interest in Aaron's priestly garment.[34] He concludes an extensive panegyric on Aaron's garments with a discussion of his crown:[35]

with a gold crown upon his turban,
inscribed like a signet with "Holiness,"

a distinction to be prized, the work of an expert,
the delight of the eyes, richly adorned.
Before his time there never were such beautiful things.
No outsider ever put them on,
but only his sons
and his descendants perpetually.

Describing the Biblical priestly garments,[36] this panegyric revels in the vestments of Aaron the Priest and of his contemporary descendent, the high priest Simon II (c. 219–196 B.C.E.). Ben Sirah's appreciation of art and architecture is expressed in his lavish description of Simon. Simon is presented by Ben Sirah as the culmination and high point of a list of Biblical heroes (Chapters 41–50) reaching back to Enoch, through the Patriarchs, the Davidic kings, the Prophets, the return to Zion, and finally to Simon:[37]

The leader of his brethren and pride of his people
was Simon the high priest, son of Onias,
who in his life repaired the house,[38]
and in his time fortified the Temple.
He laid the foundations of the high double walls,
the high retaining walls for the Temple enclosure.
In his days a cistern for water was quarried out,
a reservoir like the sea in circumference.
He considered how to save his people from ruin,
and fortified the city to withstand a siege.

Simon II, high priest, is here set in the mold of Biblical builders, of Solomon, who was given by God "rest on every side, that he might build a house for His name and prepare a sanctuary to stand forever"[39]; of Zerubbabel and Jeshua the son of Jozadak, who "in their days . . . built the house and raised the Temple, holy to the Lord, prepared for everlasting glory"; and of Nehemiah, who "raised for us the walls that had fallen, and set up the gates and bars and rebuilt our ruined houses."[40] While Simon is presented as following in the path of these Biblical predecessors, his construction projects may also be understood in terms of standard Hellenistic euergetism: public benefaction.[41] As Ben Sirah said in Chapter 41, verse 19, "Children and the building of a city establish a man's name."

Modern scholars connect Ben Sirah's description of Simon's projects with a document preserved in Josephus's *Antiquities of the Jews*. There we learn that upon his capture of Palestine from the Ptolemies, Antiochus III wrote a letter intending "to restore their city (Jerusalem) which

has been destroyed by the hazards of war." The relevant section reads:[42]

And it is my will that these things be made over to them as I have ordered, and that the work on the Temple be completed, including the porticoes and any other part that it may be necessary to build. The timber, moreover, shall be brought from Judaea itself and from other nations and Lebanon without the imposition of a toll-charge. The like shall be done with the other materials needed for making the restoration of the Temple more splendid.

Victor Tcherikover argued that "it is impossible not to perceive a certain connection between the work of Simon the Just [*sic*] and the building program in 'Antiochus' declaration, as Simon was a contemporary of Antiochus III. . . . Simon the Just carried out what Antiochus had promised the Jews in his manifesto."[43] For Ben Sirah, these projects were carried out by Simon alone with Divine assistance and based on Biblical models. Antiochus is of no theological importance, and any munificence on his part would have been lost in Ben Sirah's panegyric on Simon the High Priest. If Tchernikover is correct, then Simon's reconstruction clearly fits with the way that local rulers and their Hellenistic patrons behaved in the Hellenistic world – the Jews adding a local twist to a general cultural bent.

Ben Sirah well-appreciated the work of skilled artisans, considering them to be a basic part of a well-ordered city. As is typical of Greeks of Ben Sirah's social status, however, he disparaged artisanship as being inferior to "wisdom":[44]

The wisdom of the scribe depends on the opportunity of
    leisure;
and he who has little business may become wise.
How can he become wise who handles the plow,
and who glories in the shaft of a goad,
who drives oxen and is occupied with their work,
and whose talk is about bulls?
He sets his heart on plowing furrows,
and he is careful about fodder for the heifers.
So too is every craftsman and master workman
who labors by night as well as by day;
those who cut the signets of seals,
each is diligent in making a great variety;
he sets his heart on painting a lifelike image,
and he is careful to finish his work.
So too is the smith sitting by the anvil,
intent upon his handiwork in iron;
the breath of the fire melts his flesh,
and he wastes away in the heat of the furnace;

he inclines his ear to the sound of the hammer,
and his eyes are on the pattern of the object.
He sets his heart on finishing his handiwork,
and he is careful to complete its decoration.
So too is the potter sitting at his work
and turning the wheel with his feet;
he is always deeply concerned over his work,
and all his output is by number.
He moulds the clay with his arm
and makes it pliable with his feet;
he sets his heart to finish the glazing,
and he is careful to clean the furnace.
All these rely upon their hands,
and each is skilful in his own work.
Without them a city cannot be established,
and men can neither sojourn nor live there.
Yet they are not sought out for the council of the people,
nor do they attain eminence in the public assembly.
They do not sit in the judge's seat,
nor do they understand the sentence of judgment;
they cannot expound discipline or judgment,
and they are not found using proverbs.
But they keep stable the fabric of the world,
and their prayer is in the practice of their trade.

Ben Sirah's sense of the education and status of artisans "in the public assembly" reflects a widespread attitude toward craftsmen during the Greco–Roman period, particularly among philosophers and other men of letters. As Alison Burford notes, "No matter how useful or how beautiful the object, how essential to the physical or spiritual needs of the individual or community for whom it was made – be it hunting-knife, defense tower, or gold and ivory cult statue – the maker was in no way admirable."[45]

If we jump ahead more than two centuries, the lower social status of artisans is expressed in a document that straddles Jewish and non-Jewish realms. Jesus of Nazareth is described as a carpenter in the Gospel of Mark and as a carpenter's son in the Gospel of Matthew.[46] The Gospels register the surprise of the Nazareth villagers after Jesus, a local craftsmen, had spoken impressively in the local synagogue. His speech was apparently not of the sort expected from a mere craftsman – both in Jewish and general Roman circles. For the Christian authors, this bucking of caste is a sign of Jesus's godliness.

Although Josephus described the construction of the Second Temple in great detail, no contemporaneous artisan is mentioned in his writings. Josephus does, however, mention the artisans of the Biblical Tabernacle and of

Solomon's Temple. "Bezalel the son of Uri, son of Hur, of the tribe of Judah" (Exodus 31: 2) and with "him Oholiab, the son of Ahisamach, of the tribe of Dan" (Exodus 31: 6), are discussed in glowing terms, even as Josephus reflects his age's ambivalence to artisans per se. The honor afforded the artisans by Scripture seems unusual to Josephus, who wrote of Moses that[47]

he appointed architects for the works, in accordance with the commandment of God, yet those whom the people too would have chosen had they been empowered to do so. Their names – for these are recorded also in the holy books – were Basael son of Uri, of the tribe of Judah, grandson of Mariamme, the sister of the chief, and Elibaz, son of Isamach, of the tribe of Dan.

Josephus suggests that unusual attention to the "architects" is owing to their popularity – a detail unknown from Scripture,[48] and perhaps more significantly, to the fact that their names are "recorded also in the holy books." Josephus lavishes great attention upon the construction and beauty of Solomon's Temple. Following the Biblical record, he mentions a craftsman from Tyre:[49]

And Solomon summoned from Tyre, from Eiromos's[50] court, a craftsman named Cheiromos, who was of Naphthalite descent on his mother's side – for she was of that tribe – and whose father was Urias, and Israelite by race. This man was skilled in all kinds of work, but was especially expert in working gold, silver and bronze, and it was he who constructed all the things about the Temple, in accordance with the king's will. . . .

The skill of this artisan follows the account in 2 Chronicles 2: 12–13, where Huram-abi (as he is called in 2 Chronicles) is far more skilled than in the earlier parallel account in 1 Kings 7: 13–14. There, he is identified only as a copper worker. Most fascinating in Josephus's retelling is the reformulated genealogy of Hiram the craftsman. In 2 Chronicles, he is referred to as "the son of a woman of the daughters of Dan, and his father was a man of Tyre," whereas in 1 Kings "He was the son of a widow of the tribe of Naphtali, and his father was a man of Tyre." Josephus has given this temple artisan Jewish lineage on both sides, not only on that of his mother![51] In the Biblical text, Hiram-abi is a kind of transitional figure – the son of an Israelite mother and a Tyrian father who bridges the cultures and brings to Solomon the Tyrian technical skills.[52] Josephus (and later the rabbis)[53] thoroughly Judaizes Hiram. Josephus apparently held that only a pure Jew could

19. Reconstruction drawing of Herod's Temple by Balage Balogh (courtesy of Eilat Mazar).

fabricate the most important artifacts of the Temple. In his own day, the rule was even stricter. Josephus reports that Herod trained a cohort of priests as stonecutters and carpenters specifically to build his Temple in the style of the age of Augustus.[54] Heir to a Biblical tradition of tabernacle and temple builders, Josephus emphasizes the skills and credentials of the stellar tabernacle/temple artisans of the past. In contrast, architects and artisans of Herod's Temple go unnamed – seemingly dwarfed by Herod's proprietary ownership of the project.[55] Only Herod, the benefactor, is worthy of mention. An ossuary discovered in Jerusalem nevertheless offers us a glimpse at those involved in the construction of Herod's Temple. An Aramaic inscription on this ossuary proudly proclaims this to be the final resting place of "Simon the Temple Builder".[56]

Although Ben Sirah maintained the scholar's deprecation for those who work with their hands, he had a keen sense of craftsmanship and beauty – which he at times equated with costliness, size, or wealth. He draws metaphors from architecture, for example, when he writes that "a mind settled on an intelligent thought is like the stucco decoration on the wall of a colonnade."[57] Similarly, Ben Sirah contrasts

". . . the man who sits on a splendid throne" and "the man who wears purple and a crown" to the impoverished.[58] There does not seem to have been a lack of fine architecture in Ben Sirah's Judaea. The pleasure palace of Hyrcanus the Tobiad in Iraq El-Emir, 17 kilometers west of modern Amman and dating after 180 B.C.E., may bear witness to the monumental architecture of pre-Hasmonean Judaea.[59] Surrounded by a huge reflecting pool, the palace was decorated with massive relief friezes of lions and eagles. Particularly noteworthy is a fine lioness fountain, "a provincial Greek work," that was discovered facing toward the corner in the lowest course of blocks on the east side toward the north end of the crowning lion frieze.[60] Uncharacteristic in his lack of criticism (as we shall see), Josephus described the fortress, called *Tyros*, writing that Hyrcanus the Tobiad ". . . built a strong fortress which was constructed entirely of white marble up to the very roof, and had beasts of gigantic size carved on it, and he enclosed it with a wide and deep moat."[61]

Josephus Flavius shared Ben Sirah's respect for physical objects, pairing beauty and costliness in his descriptions. He assumed that his non-Jewish audience shared these values,

68

which was indeed the case. Josephus's descriptions of the Tabernacle and his two descriptions of the Second Temple are only the most extensive examples. Discussing the Tabernacle, Josephus built on the Biblical descriptions. Of the Biblical Ark of the Covenant, for example, Josephus wrote:[62]

Furthermore there was made for God an ark of stout timber of a nature that could not rot; the ark is called *eron* in our tongue, and its construction was on this wise. It had a length of five spans, and a breadth and height of three spans alike; both within and without it was all encased in gold, so as to conceal the woodwork, and it had a cover united to it by golden pivots with marvelous art, so even was the surface at every point, with no protuberance anywhere to mar the perfect adjustment. . . .

Josephus described Herod's Temple on two occasions.[63] In *The Jewish War* 1.401, he wrote that "the expenditure devoted to his work was incalculable, its magnificence never surpassed." The Temple, its platform, and its porticos are typical of Roman architecture in the age of Augustus.[64] This architectural fact in no way diminishes Josephus's adulation. This appreciation for the costly, well-produced, and large, I would argue, was typical of attitudes held by Jews in latter Second Temple Palestine, as it was among non-Jews during the same period.[65] Roman authors acknowledged this about Herodian Jerusalem. Cassius Dio (c. 160–230 C.E.) called the Temple "extremely large and beautiful."[66] Even Tacitus (c. 56–120 C.E.), no friend of the Jews, described the Temple as having been built "with more care and effort than any of the rest [of Jerusalem]; the very colonnades around the Temple made a splendid defense."[67] In short, Jews fully participated in art in ways that were wholly consonant with the general trends of the latter Greco–Roman period.

THE LIMITS OF "ART": "IDOLATRY" IN THE HELLENISTIC PERIOD

Although Jews were fully a part of the visual culture of the Greco–Roman world, distain of idolatry was a dynamic and developing marker of Jewish identity throughout this period. Biblical malice toward "idols" – that is, toward the religious representations of the Other – was a central marker of the "common Judaism" of the Hellenistic and Roman periods.[68] This focus has deep roots in Biblical literature, where self-definition in response to the "polluting" cultic art of the Other is a basic principle.[69] The best-known statement of this approach is the Second Commandment of the Decalogue. In Exodus 20: 4–6, we read:[70]

You shall not make for yourself a graven image, or any likeness of anything that is in heaven above, or that is in the earth beneath, or that is in the water under the earth; you shall not bow down to them or serve them; for I the Lord your God am a jealous God, visiting the iniquity of the fathers upon the children to the third and the fourth generation of those who hate me, but showing steadfast love to thousands of those who love me and keep my commandments.

From the Decalogue's ban on idolatrous imagery to the scorn of the Prophets and Psalmists, enmity for the religious iconography of the Other was essential to Israelite self-definition. As Yehezkel Kaufmann has noted, the Biblical narrative polemicizes against "idols" as "fetishes" and does not respond to them theologically. He asserts on the basis of this insight that Israelites were monotheistic and hence far removed from idolatry. Kaufmann hit on an important rhetorical point but erred in his interpretation of this phenomenon. Biblical rhetoric erases idolatry by calling it names. For the Biblical authors, the cult images of the Other ". . . have mouths, but do not speak; eyes, but do not see. They have ears, but do not hear; noses, but do not smell. They have hands, but do not feel; feet, but do not walk and they do not make a sound in their throat" (Psalm 115: 4–8).[71] They are idolatrous and therefore not worthy of engagement. Clearly, the authors must have considered this a reliable tactic in their war against Israelite attraction to "idolatry."

Jews were not against imagery per se: Witness the numerous Biblical, Second Temple, and rabbinic descriptions and discussions of the Tabernacle, the Temple(s) of Jerusalem, and their vessels,[72] not to mention the allegiance of Greco–Roman period Jews to the central "icon" of the synagogue – the Torah scroll.[73] What Jews did not like was the religious imagery of peoples whom they considered to be idolaters.

Scholars usually describe the Jewish approach to art as "aniconic." Often used to denote the absence of images,[74] aniconism more correctly refers "to simple material symbols of a deity, as a pillar or block, not shaped into an image of human form; also to the worship connected with these."[75] Aniconism, "iconoclasm" – the desire to destroy images – and even "iconophobia" – the fear of images (as if Jews have some sort of aesthetic malady!) – have all been used to describe the Jewish position.[76] The truth is, the English language has no term that adequately represents the nuances of the Jewish attitude. The Jewish approach, which is specific in its dislike of the religious iconography of "idolaters" but is positive toward specifically Jewish imagery, might be most correctly called "anti-idolic."[77]

Aniconism in the sense of a "simple material image of a deity" was, however, practiced by the Nabateans during the Hellenistic period. Taken together with the "anti-idolism" of the Jews and the other Israelite people, the Samaritans[78] (and eventually of the Judaized Iturians and Idumeans as well), this contiguity of territories meant that broad swatches of Palestine were devoid of figurative "idols." It is not beyond credulity to suggest that one could travel from the Lower Galilee through Samaria, Judaea, and south into Nabatea and not encounter a single figurative "idol."[79]

Idolatry was an important factor in Jewish perceptions of the Greco–Roman world from early in the Hellenistic period. This is expressed already, in the *Letter of Jeremiah*. This fourth-century B.C.E. Palestinian document is preserved in Greek in the Apocrypha and in Greek fragments that were discovered at Qumran. It was composed in Hebrew.[80] Appended to the Biblical Book of Jeremiah at Chapter six, the Second Temple period homilist extends Jeremiah's derisive attitude toward the religious paraphernalia of polytheism and turns this derision against Greek cult objects. As Charles J. Ball suggested long ago, "the idolatry that he denounces is no imaginary picture, but the reality of his own environment."[81] Projecting his attitudes toward "idols" into the Babylonian exile, the author of this document is intent on convincing Jews to stay away from idolatry in their midst. In his own words,[82]

Now in Babylon you will see gods made of silver and gold and wood, which are carried on men's shoulders and inspire fear in the heathen. So take care not to become at all like the foreigners or to let fear for these gods possess you, when you see the multitude before and behind them worshiping them. But say in your heart, "It is thou, O Lord, whom we must worship."

The *Letter of Jeremiah* is quite thorough in its derision of idolatry. Missing from this polemic, however, is any explicit sense of fear or of impending violence that appears in later sources.

The fact that Jews did not maintain cult images of their god was widely discussed by both Greek and Roman authors.[83] Some writers, early and late, showed disdain for the Jewish approach; others, a more positive evaluation. The Roman author Varro (116–27 B.C.E.) used the example of the Jews in support of his desire that fellow Romans might return to their ancient imageless religion.[84] If the earlier Roman practice had continued, Varro wrote, "our worship of the gods would be more devout." Strabo of Amaseia's description of the Jewish cult betrays considerable respect for the Jewish position, at least in its origins. Strabo (64 B.C.E. to the 20s of the first century C.E.) wrote that Moses was an Egyptian priest who "held a part of Lower Egypt" and

went away from there to Judaea, since he was displeased with the state of affairs there, and was accompanied by many people who worshiped the Divine Being. For he said and taught that the Egyptians were mistaken in representing the Divine Being by the images of beasts and cattle, as were the Libyans; and that the Greeks were also wrong in modeling gods in human form; for, according to him, God is the one thing alone that encompasses us all and encompasses land and sea. . . . What man, then, if he has sense, could be bold enough to fabricate an image of God resembling any creature amongst us? Nay, people should leave off all image-carving, and setting apart a sacred precinct and a worthy sanctuary, should worship God without an image. . . . Now Moses, saying things of this kind, persuaded not a few thoughtful men and led them away to this place where the settlement of Jerusalem now is. . . .[85]

Such positive evaluations of the Jewish attitude toward cult images must certainly have eased Jewish social integration and participation in the Greco–Roman world.

In differing ways, depending on their social contexts, Jews sought to strike a balance between distinctly Jewish concerns and participation in the broader culture. 2 Maccabees 4: 18–20 narrates one such attempt.[86] This text describes participants in the Jerusalem gymnasium taking part in games in honor of Melqart/Hercules in Tyre (the same god whose imagery appears on Tyrian sheqels used in the Temple (Figure 20). The high priest, Jason, an extreme "Hellenizer," is said to have sent along "three hundred drachmas of silver for the sacrifice of Heracles. The very bearers, however, judged that the money ought not to be spent on a sacrifice, but devoted to some other purpose, and, thanks to them, it went to fit out the *triremes* (ships)." Though participating in the games, these "Hellenizers" avoided the customary donation of funds to support sacrifices to Hercules that Jason had intended, and instead equipped ships for Tyre. As Martha Himmelfarb correctly

20. Tyrian sheqel (after T. E. Mionnet, *Description de médailles antiques, grecques et romaines avec leur degré de rareté et leur estimation* [Paris: Testu, 1806–13], 8, pl. 17, no. 4).

noted, "The hellenizing Jews who made up the delegation could apparently participate in the games in good conscience; they would surely have pointed out that the Torah does not forbid such activities. But they surely knew well that Torah does not permit idolatry, so they took pains to avoid even the *pro forma* idolatry of the entrance fee to games."[87] The exclusion of "pagan" cult was a central feature of Jewish boundary construction that these "Hellenizers" did not dare traverse. No one seems to have gone so far as to bring images into the Temple. If they had, we might expect to hear of it from the books of Maccabees, Daniel, or from the Greek and Roman authors![88] The "anti-idolic" element of Jewish culture gained new prominence, I suggest, when the kind of balance that Jews developed under tolerant Ptolemaic and Seleucid rule was lost under Antiochus IV Epiphanes. Attention to idolatry grew and become increasingly more intense throughout the remainder of the Second Temple period.

Beginning with the Hasmonean Revolt, "idolatry" shifted to the front burner of Jewish identity formation – its

flame turned high. 1 Maccabees suggests that Antiochus IV Epiphanes required that Jews, on pain of death, "build altars and sacred precincts and shrines for idols."[89] Worse still, even earlier "many even from Israel gladly adopted his religion; they sacrificed to idols and profaned the Sabbath."[90] 1 Maccabees locates the first shot of the revolt, and hence subsequent Hasmonean legitimacy, in Mattathias's zealous slaughter of a Jew who chose to obey the king's command to sacrifice.[91] Idolatry is also central to Daniel, Chapter 3, a text thought to reflect the persecutions of Judaism under Antiochus IV Epiphanes.[92] Judaean contempt and fear of government-sponsored idolatry are expressed in terms of the sculpture of Baalshazar: "King Nebuchadnezzar made an image of gold, whose height was sixty cubits and its breadth six cubits."[93] The king, we are told, decreed that all must "fall down and worship" his statue, and that "whoever does not fall down and worship shall immediately be cast into a burning fiery furnace."[94] Intercommunal tensions are reflected in the claim that "certain Chaldeans came forward and maliciously accused the Jews"[95] of nonparticipation, a situation which we are led to believe would have gone unnoticed without their intervention. Four youthful representatives of the Jews are indeed cast into the furnace for refusing the king's command and emerge unharmed through Divine intervention.[96] In the end, Nebuchadnezzar recognizes the greatness of the Jewish God and declares Judaism a licit religion.

With Hasmonean victory, Judaean antipathy and activism against Hellenistic "idolatry" increased in significance. This activism is imbedded in the *Book of Jubilees*, a rewritten Bible of sectarian origins thought by most scholars to have been written in Hasmonean Judaea between 170–150 B.C.E.[97] Imagining the prelude to Abraham's momentous departure to Caanan in Genesis 12:1, *Jubilees* projects contemporary attitudes and behaviors onto the Biblical narrative:[98]

During the sixth week, in its seventh year, Abram said to his father Terah: "My father." He said: "Yes, my son?" He said: "What help and advantage do we get from these idols before which you worship and prostrate yourself? For there is no spirit in them because they are dumb. They are an error of the mind. Do not worship them. Worship the God of heaven who makes the rain and dew fall on the earth and makes everything on the earth. He created everything by his word; and all life (comes) from his presence. Why do you worship those things which have no spirit in them? For they are made by hands and you carry them on your shoulders. You receive no help from them, but instead they are a great shame for those who make them and an error of the mind for those who worship them. Do not worship them." Then he said to him: "I, too, know (this), my son. What shall I do with the people who have ordered me to serve in their presence? If I tell them what is right, they will kill me because they themselves are attached to them so that they worship and praise them. Be quiet, my son, so that they do not kill you." When he told these things to his two brothers and they became angry at him, he remained silent. . . . In the sixtieth year of Abram's life (which was the fourth week, in its fourth year), Abram got up at night and burned the temple of the idols. He burned everything in the temple but no one knew (about it). They got up at night and wanted to save their gods from the fire. Haran dashed in to save them, but the fire raged over him. He was burned in the fire and died in Ur of the Chaldeans before his father Terah. They buried him in Ur of the Chaldeans. Then Terah left Ur of the Chaldeans – he and his sons – to go to the land of Lebanon and the land of Canaan. He settled in Haran, and Abram lived with his father in Haran for two weeks of years.

This text preserves a veritable script for the proselyzation and Judaization of Gentiles – through force and persuasion. Although Abram seems to have fled Ur for his life, the Hasmoneans could act against "idolatry" with considerable impunity.

Abram's burning of the temple fits well with later Hasmonean treatment of non-Jewish cult sites. As early as 1 Maccabees 2:45, "Mattathias and his friends went about and tore down the altars." His son Judah burned the local temple (témenos) at Karnain, together with all who had sought refuge within it.[99] He "turned aside to Ashdod, to the land of the Philistines, pulled down their altars, burned up the carved images of their gods, plundered the cities, and then returned to the Land of Judah."[100] His brother Jonathan returned to Ashdod, destroying the Temple of Dagon.[101] Simon the Maccabee (the builder of the Hasmonean tombs) banished the original inhabitants of Gaza, resettling the coastal city with law-observing Jews, but only after having "purified their houses where there were idols." In a sort of rededication rite, he then "entered it [the city] with hymns and songs of praise."[102]

Particularly relevant is John Hyrcanus I's[103] conversion of the Idumeans, Aristobulus I's conversion of the Ituraeans, and the destruction of temples within the expanding boundaries of Hasmonean Judaea.[104] The Idumeans and

Ituraeans, like *Jubilees'* Terah, were expected to give up ancestral idolatry and adhere to the religion of Abraham (whose traditional tomb, not incidentally, is located in Idumean territory, in Hebron).[105] *Jubilees* projects this activism against polytheism back to the first Jew, even as the Hasmoneans constructed an idolatry exclusion zone in Judaea. This zone expanded with each convert and each destroyed altar.

"Idol" worship, when forced upon Jews, occasionally adopted by Jews, or in any way in proximity to Jews or to Jewish territory, was fundamentally at odds with the Jewish *koiné* of the Second Temple period. Anti-idolatry became a particularly powerful symbol of group identity for Hellenistic-period Jews, a community that came to exemplify its uniqueness through the ritual recitation of the Ten Commandments paired with Deuteronomy 6:4, "Hear O Israel, the Lord our God, the Lord is One."[106] This liturgical choice, made by at least some Jews during the first centuries B.C.E., reinforced through repetition a commitment to the "one temple to the one God,"[107] as well as reinforcing antagonism toward polytheism. The importance of this boundary marker intensified as Palestine was increasingly Hellenized and Judaea was ever more exposed to the physical manifestations of Hellenistic religion.[108] The Hasmonean program in Judaea regarding the visual, I would suggest, was intended to restore the Land of Israel to a strongly ideological and activist "anti-idolism" as Biblical ideal[109] – something well beyond restoration of the equilibrium that existed before the radical breach described in the books of Maccabees. The intrinsic political instability of the early Hasmonean era – with the Ptolemies and Seleucids distant and Rome just on the horizon – allowed the Hasmoneans a free hand to (re)construct a greater Judaea free of "idols" and "idolatry." The result was a heightened awareness of "idols" and active antagonism against idolatry.

I emphasize that the Hasmoneans did not object to all aspects of Hellenistic art in equal measure, as the Hasmonean tombs and Hasmonean coinage demonstrate. Their concern was with idolatrous imagery only. The bubble of "anti-idolism" that they stretched over their Hellenistic kingdom was nevertheless porous. One example of tolerated imagery is, as previously mentioned, the Tyrian sheqel – the official coinage of the Temple, with its imagery of Melqart (identified with Hercules) and a Tyrian eagle.[110] Unlike the situation during the later revolts against Rome, there is no evidence of an attempt by the Hasmoneans to replace this foreign coinage with their own silver issues. Until its destruction, good and pious Jews paid their Temple dues in the Tyrian sheqel, a coin preserving the high silver content of the Ptolemaic standard.[111] These coins bore imagery that in some other context might be thought to be in conflict with God and His Temple![112] There is no positive evidence that any Jews responded negatively to this imagery during the Hellenistic period. As with all areas of ancient history, however, a paucity of sources does not necessarily constitute evidence.[113]

"IDOLATRY" AND IDENTITY IN ROMAN PALESTINE: THE EVIDENCE OF JOSEPHUS

The ships and trophies of the Hasmonean royal tombs were "erased" by Josephus's time – either by iconoclasts or, perhaps in a literary sense, by Josephus himself.[114] The breadth of Palestinian Jewish attitudes toward offending idolatrous images might well support either possibility. In this section, I survey Josephus's descriptive rhetoric of "anti-idolism" and set it in the broader context of contemporaneous Jewish art and literature. I thereby clarify the forces at work in his reformulated description of the Hasmonean tombs.

Josephus's approach to idolatry is expressed in his portrayals of the removal of the eagle from the Jerusalem Temple in 5 B.C.E.[115]

There were in the capital two teachers with a reputation as profound experts in the laws of their country, who consequently enjoyed the highest esteem of the whole nation; their names were Judas, son of Sepphoraeus, and Matthias, son of Margalus. Their lectures on the laws were attended by a large youthful audience, and day after day they drew together quite an army of men in their prime. Hearing now that the king was gradually sinking under despondency and disease, these teachers threw out hints to their friends that this was the fitting moment to avenge God's honor and to pull down these structures which had been erected in defiance of their father's laws. It was, in fact, unlawful to place in the Temple either images or busts or any representation whatsoever of a living creature; notwithstanding this, the king had erected over the great gate a golden eagle. This is it which these teachers now exhorted their disciples to cut down, telling them that, even if the action proved hazardous, it was a noble deed to die for the law of one's country; for the souls of these who came to such an end attained immortality and an eternally abiding sense of felicity; it was only the ignoble, uninitiated in their philosophy, who clung in their ignorance to life and preferred death on a sick-bed to that of a hero.

While they were discoursing in this strain, a rumor spread that the king was dying; the news caused the young men to throw themselves more boldly into the enterprise. At mid-day, accordingly, when numbers of people were perambulating the Temple, they let themselves down from the roof by stout cords and began chopping off the golden eagle with hatchets. The king's captain, to whom the matter was immediately reported, hastened to the scene with a considerable force, arrested about forty of the young men and conducted them to the king. Herod first asked them whether they had dared to cut down the golden eagle; they admitted it. "Who ordered you to do so?" he continued. "The law of our fathers." "And why so exultant, when you will shortly be put to death?" "Because, after our death, we shall enjoy greater felicity."

These proceedings provoked the king to such fury that he forgot his disease and had himself carried to a public assembly, where at great length he denounced the men as sacrilegious persons who, under the pretext of zeal for the Law, had some more ambitious aim in view, and demanded that they should be punished for impiety. . . .

The eagle was seemingly placed in the Temple complex long before this episode took place.[116] It was apparently a festering sore that was excised by an extreme element of Jerusalem society near the end of Herod's life. Scholars have tried with little success to locate the eagle more specifically within the Temple,[117] many placing it on the main facade of the Temple. Duane W. Roller recently placed it "over the main gate, essentially a pediment sculpture."[118] This decision fits well with other temples of this period; the image of the eagle was often placed on the facades of temples in Rome and Syria.[119] One might mention that the image of an eagle with broad spread wings was the symbol for the god Baal Shamin (witness the large spread-wing eagles that appear on lintels of the Temple of Baal Shamin in Palmyra).[120] Similarly, the eagle destroying the snake appears on the coins and in the monumental sculpture of the nearby Nabatean kingdom.[121] Peter Richardson attempts to locate the Temple eagle more specifically, taking into account his assumption that placing the eagle over the main doors would be "an offence almost too great to contemplate for most pious Jews." He therefore places it more discreetly "over the gate above what is now called Wilson's arch, the bridge leading to the upper city."[122] Wherever it was, Herod's eagle was close enough at hand to have been a goad to Judas, son of Sepphoraeus, and Matthias, son of Margalus, and their followers.

21. Eagle on a lepton of Herod the Great (after F. Madden, *History of Jewish Coinage* [London: B. Quaritch, 1864], 112).

Herod also used eagle imagery in his Judaean coinage. A rampart eagle appears on one face of a bronze lepton of Herod and a cornucopia on the other (Figure 21).[123] Yaakov Meshorer notes that this issue was in circulation for some time, and is not at all rare in contemporary numismatic collections.[124] Herod seems to have been particularly attracted to the eagle as a symbol, perhaps because of its local and Roman resonances, and it is the only animal to appear on Herod's Judaean coinage. It provides a parallel in local bronze coinage to the silver Tyrian sheqel with its eagle imagery – the "official" currency of the Temple. But whereas the Roman eagle is generally shown with spread wings, the eagle on Herod's coin has closed wings. This follows Hellenistic tradition and is related to the eagle on Tyrian sheqels. The eagle on the Temple facade paralleled, then, the eagles that appeared on Judaean currency. These coins were presumably carried in the change purses of Judaeans along with Tyrian sheqels. Herod's use of the eagle is certainly owing to the fact that this creature was the symbol of Rome. The use of the eagle on coinage and sparingly in the Temple is a good example of Herod's attempt to balance Jewish sensibilities with the interests of his Roman patrons.

The removal of the eagle seems to be an act of zealousness occasioned by the opportunity provided by Herod's physical decline. It is likely that the eagle stood above the Temple, and could well have been viewed by perhaps hundreds of thousands of visitors before it was removed in guerrilla fashion by the young students of Judas and Matthias. Other, less extreme sorts of resistance to such offensive imagery were undoubtedly practiced by some Jews. One is reminded of the practice among the circle of Rabbi Johanan in third-century Tiberias to avert their gaze rather than look upon idols on the Sabbath[125] (or for that matter, by many Eastern European Jews, who, following ancient

precedent, would cross the street and spit each time they walked past a church). Imagery that was clearly tolerated by the majority (or minimally, to which the majority had reconciled itself) found no quarter among the religiously energized sectarians.

In a similar way, one is reminded of the near riot in Jerusalem when Jerusalemites first saw trophies of armor adorning Herod's theater in Jerusalem, a building that Josephus described as "spectacularly lavish but foreign to Jewish custom."[126] He reports that "all around the theater were inscriptions concerning Caesar and trophies of the nations which he had won in war, all of them made for Herod of pure gold and silver."[127]

When the practice began of involving them (wild beasts) in combat with one another or setting condemned men to fight against them, foreigners were astonished at the expense and at the same time entertained by the dangerous spectacle, but to the natives it meant an open break with the customs held in honor by them. For it seemed glaring impiety to throw men to wild beasts for the pleasure of other men as spectators, and it seemed a further impiety to change their established ways for foreign practices. But more than all else it was the trophies that irked them, for in the belief that these were images surrounded by weapons, which it was against their national custom to worship, they grew exceedingly angry. That the Jews were highly disturbed did not escape Herod's notice, and since he thought it inopportune to use force against them, he spoke to some of them reassuringly in an attempt to remove their religious scruples. He did not, however, succeed, for in their displeasure at the offences of which they thought him guilty, they cried out with one voice that although everything else might be endured, they would not let images of men being brought into the city – meaning the trophies –, for this was against their national custom. Herod, therefore, seeing how disturbed they were and that they could not easily be brought around if they did not get some reassurance, summoned the most eminent among them and leading them to the theatre, showed them the trophies and asked just what they thought these things were. When they cried out "Images of men," he gave orders for the removal of the ornaments which covered them and showed the people the bare wood. So soon as the trophies were stripped, they became a cause of laughter; and what contributed most to the confusion of these men was the fact that up to this point they had themselves regarded the arrangement as a disguise for images.

These trophies could not have been so different in form from the armor at Modi'in. Only when the self-selected Jerusalemite theatergoers realized that Herod had erected faux trophies did they relent. Faux trophies were apparently just within the realm of the acceptable, where a step over the boundary to displaying trophies was not. Herod knew this, and apparently his workmen and eventually the theatergoers (whom one might imagine would have been more inclined to participate in the delights of Roman theater than many other Judaeans) did as well. The presence of trophies must have been a particularly sore spot for Judaeans. The coins minted in honor of the governor of Syria, Caius Sosius, in 34 B.C.E. bear the image of a Roman trophy flanked by a male and a female captive.[128] Caius Sosius is here celebrated for the final victory over the Hasmoneans that brought Herod to power, a siege that included the sacking of the Temple courts and the Upper City and the butchering of Jerusalem's inhabitants.[129] Herod's faux trophies were placed in the theater to celebrate his victories in typical Roman fashion.[130] Jewish disdain of trophies (and of Herod's in particular) was so intense that this consideration was given precedence over the blatantly "pagan" bloodthirstiness of the games themselves – which the Jerusalem audience was somehow willing to overlook! This seeming reversal of values reflects just how potent "anti-idolism" had become for Jewish identity formation in Roman Palestine.

The incidents of the eagle and the theater trophies were directed against Herod's iconic violations in the public domain in the holy city. Although not all Jews were agitated by this imagery, at least not to the point of revolting against Rome, radicalized groups certainly were. One could imagine this attitude spreading as tensions with Rome increased. Hellenistic imagery that smacked of Roman paganism, like the eagle and the trophy, were highly suspect. Pontius Pilate's decision to bring "busts of the emperor that were attached to military standards" into Jerusalem and then to quickly remove them in the face of solid Jewish opposition was an example not only of foolish governance, but also of the Realpolitik of ruling the Jews in their own land during the first century C.E.[131] Previous procurators had entered Jerusalem using only "standards that had no ornaments," thus maintaining the delicate balance between the Jewish right to practice their ancestral religion, the need for Jewish allegiance to Rome, and Jewish aversion to participation in the imperial cult.[132]

The issue of standards was such a point of strife between Judaeans and the Roman armies that with the defeat of Judaea in 70 and capture of the Temple, the Romans "carried their standards into the Temple court and, setting them up opposite the eastern gate, there sacrificed to them, and with rousing acclamations hailed Titus as imperator."[133] Standards were also set in the towers of the Temple by the victorious Romans.[134] As Mary Smallwood notes, sacrifice to Roman standards in the Temple itself was "the ultimate desecration of the Jewish sanctuary."[135] Jewish dislike of standards, whether decorated or not, was even projected into Biblical prophecy by the Dead Sea sect, commenting (pesher) on the Biblical book of Habbakuk:

And what it says: "For this he sacrifices to his net and burns incense to his seine. . . ." (Habbakuk 1:16a)

Its interpretation: They offer sacrifices to their standards and their weapons are the object of their worship.[136]

Josephus relates that Pilate brought his iconic standards into Jerusalem at night and set them up. Attempting to silence Jewish protesters in Caesarea, Pilate threatened them with death if they did not relent. In the end, however, he was the one who relented, "astonished at the strength of their devotion to the laws."

For Josephus, Roman iconography represents not only political domination, but also an unambiguous religious abomination. The continuing tensions focused on pagan religion reached a low point in Caligula's attempt to enforce Jewish worship of the imperial cult in Temple in 40 C.E. – complete with the intention to place a sculpture of the "divine" emperor and transforming the Jerusalem Temple into a shrine to his honor.[137] This provocation exasperated a broad swatch of the Jewish population throughout the Empire, certainly increasing the receptivity among Jews of a more radical anti-iconic tendency. In fact, the very position of the Jews everywhere was jeopardized – and ultimately protected only with Caligula's fortuitous death on January 24, 41 C.E. and Claudius's subsequent reaffirmation of Jewish rights.[138]

Philo of Alexandria discusses the Caligula episode in the bleakest terms. He was part of a delegation of Jews who traveled to Rome to dissuade the emperor from enforcing the emperor cult among Jews. Philo places this concern into the mouth of Agrippa I, writing in his *Embassy to Gaius*, line 290:[139]

My Lord Gaius, this Temple has never from the beginning admitted any man-made image, because it is the dwelling-place of the true God. The works of painters and sculptors are representations of gods perceived by the senses. But the making of any picture or sculpture of the invisible God was considered by our forefathers to be blasphemous.

In contexts where Jewish idolatry was not at stake, Philo was far more accepting of Greco–Roman iconography.[140] Another Egyptian text of this period is the apocryphal *Wisdom of Solomon*.[141] David Winston believes that this text makes reference to the reign of Caligula. The *Wisdom of Solomon* provides an extended diatribe against "idols" and those who serve them.[142] To cite just one example:[143]

But the idol made with hands is accursed, and so is he who made it; because he did the work, and the perishable thing was named a god. For equally hateful to God are the ungodly man and his ungodliness, for what was done will be punished together with him who did it. Therefore there will be a visitation also upon the heathen idols, because, though part of what God created, they became an abomination, and became traps for the souls of men and a snare to the feet of the foolish. For the idea of making idols was the beginning of fornication, and the invention of them was the corruption of life for neither have they existed from the beginning nor will they exist for ever. For through the vanity of men they entered the world, and therefore their speedy end has been planned. For a father, consumed with grief at an untimely bereavement, made an image of his child, who had been suddenly taken from him; and he now honored as a god what was once a dead human being, and handed on to his dependents secret rites and initiations. Then the ungodly custom, grown strong with time, was kept as a law, and at the command of monarchs graven images were worshiped. When men could not honor monarchs in their presence, since they lived at a distance, they imagined their appearance far away, and made a visible image of the king whom they honored, so that by their zeal they might flatter the absent one as though present. Then the ambition of the craftsman impelled even those who did not know the king to intensify their worship. For he, perhaps wishing to please his ruler, skilfully forced the likeness to take more beautiful form, and the multitude, attracted by the charm of his work, now regarded as an object of worship the one whom shortly before they had honored as a man. And this became a hidden trap for mankind, because men, in bondage to misfortune or to royal authority, bestowed on objects of stone or wood the name that ought not to be shared. Afterward it was not enough for them to err about the knowledge of God, but they live in great strife due to ignorance, and they call such great evils peace. For whether they kill children in their initiations, or celebrate secret mysteries, or hold frenzied revels with strange customs, they no longer keep either their lives or their marriages pure, but they either treacherously kill one another, or grieve one another by adultery, and all is a raging riot of blood and murder, theft and deceit, corruption, faithlessness, tumult, perjury, confusion over what is good, forgetfulness of favors, pollution of souls, sex perversion, disorder in marriage, adultery, and debauchery. For the worship of idols not to be named is the beginning and cause and end of every evil. For their worshipers either rave in exultation, or prophesy lies, or live unrighteously, or readily commit perjury; for because they trust in lifeless idols they swear wicked oaths and expect to suffer no harm. But just penalties will overtake them on two counts: because they thought wickedly of God in devoting themselves to idols, and because in deceit they swore unrighteously through contempt for holiness. For it is not the power of the things by which men swear, but the just penalty for those who sin, that always pursues the transgression of the unrighteous.

This text suggests not the detachment of the *Letter of Jeremiah*, but rather a deep loathing for idols and those who serve them.

Tensions regarding Roman imagery, as well as a general complacency toward it by large numbers of Palestinian Jews, are expressed in the Gospels' discussion of imperial imagery on coinage. In Mark 12:13–17, we read:[144]

And they sent to him some of the Pharisees and some of the Herodians, to entrap him in his talk. And they came and said to him, "Teacher, we know that you are true, and care for no man; for you do not regard the position of men, but truly teach the way of God. Is it lawful to pay taxes to Caesar, or not? Should we pay them, or should we not?" But knowing their hypocrisy, he said to them, "Why put me to the test? Bring me a coin, and let me look at it." And they brought one. And he said to them, "Whose likeness and inscription is this?" They said to him, "Caesar's." Jesus said to them, "Render to Caesar the things that are Caesar's, and to God the things that are God's." And they were amazed at him.

The early Christian storyteller, it seems, considered active disparagement of Roman imperial coinage to be a sign of Jewish radicalism and not a mainstream act. The New Testament author was probably also correct that the adversaries of this sort of active disparagement included Jews with a vested interest in the *Pax Romana*, including "Pharisees," "Herodians," and at some point the early Jesus community as well (if not Jesus himself).[145] It is significant that the copper coins minted by the Roman governors of Judaea bore no human imagery at all, undoubtedly in an attempt to placate the Jewish population. Silver, however, was not minted locally. Numerous coins were found at Qumran as well as a hoard of Tyrian sheqels.[146] Although utterly opposed to the symbols of Greco–Roman idolatry, the Qumran sectarians, like most other Jews, traded in the coin of the realm.

22. Silver denarius of Vespasian, *Judaea Capta* series, minted in Rome, c. 69–71 (from the Alan I. Casden Collection of Ancient Jewish Coins, 144 rev.).

Our New Testament author well understood Jewish dislike of imperial numismatic iconography. In the numismatic propaganda war with Rome, images derived from the Temple cult and the flora of Palestine were minted on Jewish coins of both revolts and set opposite images of "pagan" temples, gods, and of the emperor himself. This acceptable Jewish imagery, itself drawing upon traditions in Roman numismatics, would stand in stark contrast to *Judaea Capta* coins minted by Rome in bronze, silver, and gold denominations (Figures 22, 55). Roman minters decorated these coins with iconography that was well known from Flavian imperial sculpture: busts of Vespasian, Titus, or Domitian on one side of the flange, often with images of Judaea despondently seated beneath nothing less than the potent symbol of the Roman trophy (sometimes transformed into a Judaean palm tree trophy) planted in Jewish Judaea.[147]

Josephus was no mere chronicler of past "anti-idolism," but also a player in enforcing it in his day. He relates that in 66 C.E. he was sent as an emissary of the Jerusalem assembly (*sanhedrin*) to the Galilee with the goal of removing idolatrous imagery that decorated Herod Antipas's palace in Tiberias. Josephus's mission is framed as a religious one. Speaking to a group of local dignitaries,[148]

I told them that I and my associates had been commissioned by the Jerusalem assembly to press for the demolition of the palace erected by Herod the tetrarch, which contained representations of animals – such a style of architecture being forbidden by the laws – and I requested their permission to proceed at once with the work. Capella and the other leaders for a long while refused this, but were finally overruled by us and assented. We were, however, anticipated in our task by Jesus, son of Sapphias, the ringleader, as already stated, of the party of the sailors and the destitute class. Joined by some Galilaeans he set the whole palace on fire, expecting, after seeing that the roof was partly of gold, to obtain from it large spoils. There was much looting, contrary to our intention; for we, after our conference with Capella and the leading men of Tiberias, had left Bethmaus for Upper Galilee. Jesus and his followers then massacred all the Greek residents in Tiberias and any others who, before the outbreak of hostilities, had been their enemies.

One can only imagine what types of images decorated the palace of Antipas. Was there an eagle, perhaps signifying to Josephus and the "Jerusalem assembly" the power of Rome? The palace of the Tobiads, with its friezes of carved lions, lionesses, panthers, and eagles is a useful parallel, but that parallel is two centuries earlier than Antipas's palace. Architecture that served polytheistic communities in this region used images of animals to decorate public buildings, as was the practice throughout the Empire. Antagonism toward such imagery reflects a new resistance to animal images – one not shared by the Tobiads, by those who preserved their palace, or, it seems, by the Tiberian elite whom Josephus describes as having no interest in destroying Antipas's palace.

Archaeological remains from Jerusalem and Judaea shed some light on the issue of imagery in the holy city during the first century. Geometric forms predominate on floor mosaics, stone furniture, and in funerary contexts.[149] Images that Josephus might have considered illicit have nonetheless been discovered. The earliest extant animal image is of a resting stag drawn on a wall of the outer chamber of Jason's Tomb.[150] Fragments of fresco containing images of birds "on a stylized architectural – floral background of trees, wreaths, buildings and the like" were uncovered by Magen Broshi near the "House of Caiaphas" on today's Mt. Zion.[151] A fish carved in relief on the side of a table top, a bronze fitting for a table leg in the shape of an animal paw, and a bone gaming disk bearing the image of a human hand were discovered by Nahman Avigad in what is now the Jewish Quarter.[152] A table top bearing the image of a bird was also discovered, and two birds appear on a small stone labeled in Hebrew *qorban*, "sacrifice," that was uncovered in Benjamin Mazar's excavations near the Temple Mount.[153] In addition, cast stucco moldings from residential buildings discovered by Mazar bear images of various animals against a naturalistic background in a repeating pattern. These include a lion, a lioness, an antelope, a rabbit, and apparently also a pig.[154] The decoration on the tomb and stone sarcophagi of the royal house of Adiabene (the "Tombs of the Kings") is floral and architectonic in the fashion of monumental art in Jerusalem. A fragment of a lead Sidonian sarcophagus found there is decorated with images of a sphinx and a dolphin.[155] The base of the Temple menorah, as presented on the Arch of Titus (Figure 59), may also belong to this group.

Daniel Sperber has recently reasserted his belief that the various images on the menorah base were placed there during Herod's reign.[156] Kon, by contrast, dates the base to the Hasmonean period.[157] Both authors agree that the base resembles column bases discovered in the Hellenistic Temple of Apollo at Didyma in Asia Minor. The exception is that at Didyma human mythological figures appear, whereas on the menorah base we find only animals (eagles; sea monsters with fishtails; a dragon; and two-winged, bird-headed dragons). Both Sperber and Kon see this as a bow to Jewish sensibilities. In light of Herod's eagles and the Hasmonean tombs, neither position is to be rejected outright, although the evidence is hardly conclusive. Some scholars have even suggested that the base was added only once the menorah was taken to Rome.[158] Whether or not the Arch of Titus menorah base is an accurate reflection of the art of Second Temple Jerusalem, the mere possibility is indicative of the ambiguities inherent in extant literary and archaeological sources. The limited number of animal images discovered in Jerusalem support, at least in part, a statement ascribed to an early rabbi: "Rabbi Eleazar son of Jacob says: All sorts of faces (*kol ha-partsufot*) were in Jerusalem, except for the face of man."[159]

Visual conservatism in the public realm nevertheless finds important, if somewhat opaque, verification in the excavated remains of the Temple. The interior vaults of Hulda's Gates, at the southern side of the Temple Mount, are decorated in geometric patterns that are highly reminiscent of sarcophagus and tomb facade decoration (Figure 23). No animal or human imagery is present in either context. Similarly, a composite capital of Corinthian and Ionic elements discovered near the Western Wall reflects both full participation in Roman art and a level of local conservatism.[160] The image of a wreath appears on

23. Fragment of the interior vault of Hulda's Gate (photograph by Steven Fine).

two opposite faces – certainly a Greco–Roman icon. On the other set of faces, we find a pomegranate. Pomegranates are rich in literary associations, and their image appears in ancient Jewish numismatics.[161] Their use is consistent with the lack of human or animal imagery of Hasmonean and most Roman coinage in Judaea. These artifacts support Josephus's comment in *War* 5.191 regarding the magnificent columns of the Temple porticos. There, he emphasizes that the columns were built "without adventitious embellishment of painting or sculpture."

Josephus reflects on Herod's construction and the king's propensity to walk a very narrow line between what was acceptable and unacceptable in his Judaean building projects:[162]

. . . But because of his ambition in this direction and the flattering attention which he gave to Caesar and the most influential Romans, he was forced to depart from the customs (of the Jews) and to alter many of their regulations, for in his ambitious spending he founded cities and erected temples – not in Jewish territory, for the Jews would not have put up with this, since we are forbidden such things, including the honoring of statues and sculptured forms in the manner of the Greeks, – but these he built in foreign and surrounding territory. To the Jews he made the excuse that he was doing these things not of his own account but by command and order, while he sought to please Caesar and the Romans by saying that he was less intent upon observing the customs of his own nation than upon honoring them. On the whole, however, he was intent upon his own interests or was also ambitious to leave behind to posterity still greater monuments of his reign. It was for this reason that he was keenly interested in the reconstruction of cities and spent very great sums on this work.

Josephus did not believe for an instant that Herod's "transgressions" were imposed from without. He was fully aware that Herod's own inclinations caused him to engage in a building program that paralleled that of his patron, Augustus. He even suggests that Herod "apologized" to his subjects for his indiscretions. Be that as it may, Josephus fully recognized the boundaries maintained by Herod in Judaea, limits that the king tested severely but did not overstep. Thus, he built temples and made Jewishly illicit images only "in foreign and surrounding territories."[163] Most interesting is a unique fragment of a wash basin from Herod's bathhouse in his palace at Herodion, south of Jerusalem. Ehud Netzer discovered there a terra-cotta fragment bearing the sculpted image of a bearded head, identified by the excavator as the moon god Selinos.[164] This small bit of evidence may suffice to suggest Herod's use of "pagan" imagery within his private domain. Josephus describes sculptures of his daughters that Agrippa I placed in his palaces at Caesarea Maritima and Sebaste (although apparently not in Jerusalem or the Galilee). He makes no explicitly negative comment on the existence of these images. Nevertheless, his graphic descriptions of the rude ways that these statues were treated by the non-Jews of those cities may reflect an implicit judgment:[165]

. . . and all who were there on military service – and they were a considerable number – went off to their homes, and seizing the images of the king's daughters carried them with one accord to the brothels, where they set them up on the roofs and offered them every possible sort of insult, doing things too indecent to be reported.

On a more public level, Agrippas I minted coins bearing his own image, that of his son Agrippas II, and those of their Roman patrons. His coins minted in Jerusalem, however, were decidedly anti-idolic. Agrippas I and II both minted the image of the goddess Nike, and Agrippas II also minted the images of his patrons. Agrippas II did not, however, mint coins bearing his own image.[166]

For Josephus, Jewish attitudes were the constant; Herod and those who came after him deviant. I would nuance Josephus's monochromatic apology, suggesting that a somewhat narrow range of attitudes existed in latter Second Temple Judaea. This "non-idolic" stance was generally taken for granted by Jews. Attitudes became increasingly politicized during the last centuries before the Temple's destruction, in response to political, social, and religious complexities caused by Greco–Roman domination. This increasing strictness, often expressed as an ideology of "anti-idolism," undoubtedly affected different groups within society in differing ways. Josephus presents his Roman readers with a strict response to Roman visual culture as a whole in his apologetics for Judaism. In light of his part in the destruction of Antipas's palace, his attitude was no doubt heartfelt.

Let us return to the Hasmonean tombs. Were the sculptures of armor and ships intentionally removed from these tombs sometime before Josephus's day by Jews who came to consider them "too" Hellenistic? One can imagine a situation where the isolated and less politically sensitive imagery at Modi'in could be removed in accord with stiffening Judaean resistance to Greco–Roman iconography – whether by local authorities or even by zealots, who could act in Modi'in in ways that would be impossible in Roman Jerusalem. Increased exposure to, and sophistication regarding, the broader Greco–Roman world brought on by Herod's building projects and increased Roman presence in Judaea certainly might have encouraged a hardening of some Jewish attitudes. This scenario would reflect an intensifying stance against idolatrous imagery among elements of Judaean society. Just as Josephus erased the seemingly errant reference to viewing the monument from the sea, he could well have removed reference to no longer extant sculpture.

Alternatively, did Josephus "erase" the Hasmonean ships and armor himself? Josephus's oeuvre as a whole emphasizes to the Roman audience the wholesale incompatibility of "idolatrous" imagery with Judaism. This subnarrative begins with the theater and eagle incidents in *War* and *Antiquities*, continues throughout his retelling of the Biblical narrative in *Antiquities*, his account of the palace of Antipas incident in the *Life,* and with discussion of the Decalogue in his last work, *Against Apion*. Writing with obvious reference to images of Roman deities (particularly of the emperor), Josephus asserts in *Against Apion* that "no materials, however costly, are fit to make an image of Him; no art has skill to conceive and represent it; the like of Him we have never seen, we do not imagine, and it is impious to conjecture."[167] Elsewhere in *Apion,* Josephus adds that God "forbade the making of images, alike of any living creature, and much more of God."[168]

The consistency of Josephus's approach led him to condemn even King Solomon. Regarding the brazen laver of the Temple and the decoration of Solomon's throne, Josephus wrote:[169]

As he advanced in age, and his reason became in time too feeble to oppose to these the memory of his own country's practices, he showed still greater disrespect for his own God and continued to honor those whom his wives had introduced. But even before this there had been an occasion on which he sinned and went astray in respect of the observance of the laws, namely when he made the images of the bronze bulls underneath the sea which he had set up as an offering, and those of the lions around his own throne, for in making them he committed an impious act.

In Scripture, Solomon's throne and the brazen laver are reported with great pride and no tinge of a negative evaluation.[170] For Josephus, however, the sin of illicit imagery is the ultimate offense of Solomon's old age. Significantly, in the Biblical account Solomon's sin was not iconographic, but rested in the construction of idolatrous high places for the Moabite god Chemosh and for Molech, the Ammonite god. Louis Feldman argues that Josephus used the charge of illicit imagery as a cover, protecting "the wisest of all men" from the far more abhorrent charge of out-and-out idolatry.[171]

Josephus screens imagery in Solomon's Temple that might be construed to be illicit. Regarding the cherubim, the Biblically ordained winged creatures that hovered over the Ark of the Covenant, he wrote evasively: "as for the Cherubim themselves, no one can say or imagine what they looked like."[172] Josephus's description of the Temple veil is similarly apologetic, although the apology is less apparent. Following the Septuagint to 2 Chronicles 3: 14, he writes that the veil was ". . . a cloth brightly colored in hyacinth blue and purple and scarlet, which, was, moreover, made of the most gleaming soft linen."[173] Josephus fails to mention the cherubim decorating the veil that, according to the Biblical text, Solomon "wove on it." This ellipsis is not a matter of divergent Biblical versions, but rather an inten-

tional reworking of the Biblical description. It is consistent with Josephus's description of the veil of the Biblical Tabernacle. There he wrote: "But before the gates, extending to a length of twenty cubits and a height of five, was a tapestry of blue and crimson, interwoven with blue and fine linen and beautified with many and diverse designs, but with nothing representing the forms of animals."[174] Josephus's elimination of the cherubim from the veil of Solomon's Temple is a good parallel to the trophies and ships of the Hasmonean tombs. It is possible he used the same method in both contexts – erasing a secondary element that contradicts the broader "anti-iconism" of his narrative.

The evidence that speaks most loudly for this interpretation is Josephus's own silence over the golden calf incident in his retelling of Biblical history in *Antiquities*:[175] The golden calf does not exist in Josephus's rewritten Bible. No degree of reinterpretation (the path taken by Philo, Pseudo-Philo, and later by the rabbis), it seems, could have undone the devastation that the image of Jews serving the golden calf on Moses' watch might have done to Josephus's apologetics! Did Josephus himself "erase" the armor and ships through his rewriting of Maccabees, just as he erased the incident of the golden calf, the sphinxes from the veil of Solomon's Temple, and had earlier come to Galilee to physically "erase" the sculpted animal imagery from Antipas's palace? This was certainly not beyond the powers of our author.

CONCLUSION

The hypothetical late Second Temple period Judaean with whom we began this discussion would have been stymied if asked for his opinions regarding "art." Even still, our Judaean would certainly have known what he found visually pleasing when he saw it. Much of the Greco–Roman visual heritage would have been known and perhaps appreciated by him. The glories of Jerusalem, the beauty of the Hasmonean tombs, and the fine craftsmanship of well-made household vessels might all have been within his experience. At the same time, our Judaean would have had definite limits regarding acceptable visual imagery. "Idolatrous" foreign iconography was forbidden, at least in principle. With the Hasmonean revolt, the exclusion of idolatry became an active (and at times activist) feature of communal identity, although Hellenistic art per se was not problematic. The Hasmonean tombs, architectural structures that fully reflect the visual vocabulary of their time, are a fine example of Hasmonean participation in Hellenistic art. I would argue that the intensification of "anti-idolism" beginning with the Hasmoneans was a neoconservative attempt to restore an imagined situation that existed before the traumatizing rule of Antiochus IV Epiphanes. Over the almost two centuries between the construction of the Hasmonian tombs and Josephus Flavius's depiction of these monuments, the attitudes of many Jews toward Greco–Roman visual culture became increasingly strident. This stringent approach may simultaneously reflect both greater integration into that culture and a desire by some to restrict connections with it through the construction of social boundaries. This transformation is well reflected in Josephus's writings and in other latter Second Temple period sources. This process is exemplified in the construction and subsequent transformation of the Hasmonean royal tombs at Modi'in.

CHAPTER SEVEN

ART AND IDENTITY IN LATE ANTIQUE PALESTINE

THE NA'ARAN SYNAGOGUE

J EWISH ADMIRATION FOR GRECO—ROMAN ART CONTINUED unabated during the late Roman and Byzantine periods. Late antique Palestinian Jews, like their Second Temple period ancestors, often appreciated the well made and the expensive. A well-crafted table, a golden tiara, or a well-constructed building were likely to have been prized by members of this community.[1] With time, even human images were thought by some to be acceptable, both among those who built synagogues and those who wrote rabbinic tracts. When it came to the religiously charged art of gentiles, however, the Jewish evaluation would invariably turn negative. A religious artifact – a statue, carving, or relief of a god (or later, a Christian icon) – was to be avoided. Jews, among them the rabbis, were not innately "aniconic," "iconoclastic," or "iconophobic."[2] They were, however, "anti-idolic." As during the Second Temple period, Jewish animus was directed against art that was considered to be idolatrous, although there were differing ways that Jews approached this term.

With the destruction of the Temple in 70 C.E. and the debacle of the Bar Kokhba Revolt of 132–135 C.E., Jewish understandings of art and its place in society changed in important ways. The destruction of Jerusalem, migrations of Jews to outlying areas, and the influx of polytheistic and later Christian colonists into previously Jewish areas had a profound impact on Jewish society and the place of art within it. Soon a minority in a land no longer called Judaea but "Palestine,"[3] Jews lived under what appeared to them a relentless imperialist and colonial regime. The visual continued to provide important markers for interpreting the construction of Jewish identity between the late first century and the eighth century – that is, between the destruction of Jerusalem and beginning of Islamic rule under the Fatamid Caliphate. In this chapter, I trace the vast changes that took place in the art of the Jews in "Palestine" during this period of almost 800 years.

Issues related to idolatry have stood at the forefront of most scholarly discussion of art during this period, particularly in relation to the religion of the ancient rabbis. This focus is natural. The subject of idolatry was a major concern of the rabbis, being the subject of an entire tractate of the Mishnah, Tosefta, Jerusalem, and Babylonian Talmuds – and discussions in other contexts throughout the rabbinic corpus. Positive attitudes toward "art" not construed as idolatrous, by contrast, were not a point of distinction between Jews and their neighbors, and hence appear sparingly. A number of studies appeared during the twentieth century that explored Jewish attitudes toward idolatry and idolatrous artifacts. The most important textual studies were those penned by Saul Lieberman, Ephraim E. Urbach, Gerald J. Blidstein, Joseph Baumgarten, and recently, by Robert Goldenberg, Moshe Halberthal, Avishai Margalit, Sacha Stern, and Yaron Z. Eliav.[4] Ludwig Blau was revolutionary as he was successful in his balancing of rabbinic concern for idolatry with positive rabbinic statements about art. His work profoundly influenced both Blidstein's study and my own.

In this chapter, I explore late antique Jewish attitudes toward art, both in terms of positive attitudes toward the positive "default" art of Greco–Roman Palestine and the anti-idolic attitude. In this way, I seek out a more balanced and realistic view of Jewish attitudes toward art in late antique Palestine. I begin, pointedly, by focusing on the archaeological record (and not with a commentary on the rabbinic literature model of all earlier interpreters). By studying this rather complex body of material in relative isolation, I focus on the dialectic between inculturation of Roman art on the one hand and anti-idolism on the other. From there, we move to the rabbinic corpus. We will find that these corpora are in surprising agreement in regard to attitudes over the *longue durée* of late antiquity. In both sets of sources, a distinct conservatism in the earliest periods loosened in some respects during the later Roman and Byzantine periods. I begin this survey of rabbinic responses to "art" with examples of positive discussions of the Roman visual heritage, of rabbinic participation in the art of the majority, and ways that the rabbis incorporated Greco–Roman art into their imaginations and projections of the Biblical past, the geographically distant, and the messianic future. I then turn to rabbinic attitudes toward artisans, locating the artist within rabbinic thought. Here, I turn to the builder of the Biblical Tabernacle – Bezalel – as a focal point for evaluating rabbinic attitudes toward artisans.

The next section deals with the notion of *hiddur mitz-vah*, the beautification of ritual objects and criterion for beautification. In the last section, I approach the question of idolatry. The first part deals with issues related to living in a world surrounded by idols and how the rabbis dealt with the problems inherent in surviving with integrity in such an environment. Rabbinic attitudes toward "idolatry" will be discussed, relying heavily on the scholarship of my predecessors. Sources from the last stages of our period assert a renewed conservatism. In the final part of this chapter, I discuss the reasons for this swing during the 700-year chunk of time we call late antiquity.

THE NA'ARAN SYNAGOGUE: A TOUCHSTONE FOR INTERPRETING CHANGING ATTITUDES TOWARD ART DURING LATE ANTIQUITY

The mosaic pavement of the synagogue at Na'aran (Na'arah) was discovered in 1917, when a shell fired by an Austrian artillery unit against British positions exploded on a bluff at Ayn al-Duq – a spring 7 kilometers north of Jericho.[5] The site was known from literary sources: In about 324 C.E., the Church father Eusebius of Caesarea referred to it as "Noorath, a village of Jews 5 milestones from Jericho."[6] Rabbinic sources suggest a thorny relationship

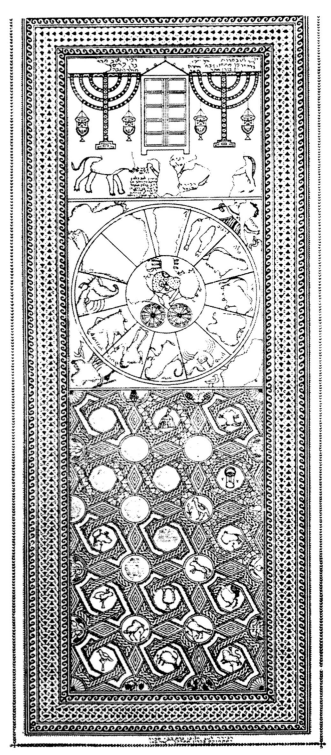

24. Drawing of the Na'aran Synagogue mosaic (courtesy of the E. L. Sukenik Archive, Institute of Archaeology, Hebrew University of Jerusalem).

between the Jewish town of Na'aran and the non-Jewish city of Jericho.[7] The Austrian shell revealed a decorated mosaic pavement, which was investigated by British archaeologists and excavated by French archaeologists of the École Biblique in Jerusalem in 1919. The archaeologists discovered a mosaic in the nave and side aisles of this rather typical Byzantine basilica of the late fifth or sixth centuries (Figure 24). The mosaic (22 × 15 meters) included at its center a panel containing a zodiac wheel. In the corners of the panel are personifications of the seasons. At the center of the wheel is the image of Helios driving his quadriga (chariot drawn by four horses) across the heavens. Before the spot where the ancient Torah shrine stood was a mosaic depicting a Torah ark flanked by two menorahs, with a panel showing Daniel in the lions' den just below. Geometric patterns and images of animals fill out the mosaic, in which Aramaic dedicatory inscriptions abound (there are eight in all). A beautifully abstract menorah, with twelve flames aglow, was laid before the main entrance to the hall. Numerous inscriptions were discovered within the mosaic. Hebrew inscriptions label "Daniel," each sign of the zodiac, and the seasons. Aramaic inscriptions honor donors, who refer to the synagogue four times as a "holy place."[8]

Sometime during the eighth or ninth centuries, near the beginning of Islamic rule in Palestine, human and some animal images were carefully and systematically removed from the mosaic. The extensive and extremely careful iconoclastic behavior at Na'aran was almost certainly carried out by Jews. Virgo, for example, is easily recognizable, although only the outline of her torso remains. Similarly, the legs of the scorpion, Scorpio, remain even as his body is no more. The signs of the seasons, Helios on his chariot, and Daniel in the lions' den were treated similarly. Significantly, the inscriptions as well as images of menorahs and the Torah shrine were, as far as we can tell, avoided by the iconoclasts.[9] Two gazelles and two birds – images without apparent symbolic meaning – were also untouched. Once the mosaic was defaced, the religious life of the community seemingly continued as usual.[10]

The mosaic of the Na'aran synagogue could not have been anticipated. Nothing in the previously uncovered remains of synagogues – neither the Galilean-type synagogues at Capernaum and elsewhere nor the few fragments of mosaics that had turned up[11] – could have predicted this discovery. No zodiac wheel or Biblical scene had

25. The zodiac panel of the Na'aran Synagogue mosaic (courtesy of the E. L. Sukenik Archive, Institute of Archaeology, Hebrew University of Jerusalem).

ever before been discovered within an ancient synagogue. Alhough this should have startled some scholars, the truth is that in the years after World War I this site was ignored, except, of course, by Slouschz and Sukenik.[12] L. H. Vincent wrote up the results of his excavation, but his report sat in a file at the École Biblique et Archéologique Française in Jerusalem until P. Benoit finally published it in 1961.[13] Sukenik wrote in 1949 that "apart from the inscriptions they did not publish the results of their excavation of the synagogue at Na'aran. The complete material was kindly entrusted to me by Pere L. H. Vincent."[14] The synagogue formed a major part of Sukenik's dissertation. He also collected mosaic fragments left behind by the French on behalf of the Hebrew University of Jerusalem. Still, at the time of its discovery, this mosaic did not provoke great interest, either among Jews or non-Jews. Slouschz's theatrical excavations at Hammath Tiberias dwarfed this site among Zionists, and both discoveries were totally eclipsed by Sukenik's more theatrical excavation of the Beth Alpha synagogue in 1929.

The Na'aran mosaic was altered during the early Islamic period, apparently by its own religious community. We will see that a less iconic aesthetic set in with the coming of Islam that was more akin to that of the first century than to the fifth-sixth-century community that commissioned the floor. Sukenik clearly understood the significance of this find for Jewish studies, writing in 1949 that "although they had been deliberately defaced by Jewish

iconoclasts, the significance of this discovery can hardly be over-estimated. Until that time, scholars had believed that mosaic floors containing figures were forbidden by Jewish law."[15] It is exactly the fact that this permitted synagogue mosaic later became unacceptable that is of interest to us here.

What factors led to the creation of this floor, followed centuries later by its iconoclastic transformation? It is this process of transforming the interior décor of a religious space that draws me back again and again to Na'aran. In this chapter, I trace the history of Jewish attitudes toward art in the Land of Israel from the destruction of the Temple through the rise of Islam in Palestine. The touchstone for our discussion is the synagogue at Na'aran, a building that reflects both the rise of a more "iconic" stance in Byzantine Palestine and its demise during the early Islamic period. The extant literary and archaeological sources for this process are large in number and quite varied. We begin with archaeological evidence, looking for ways that Jewish art coalesced with general artistic trends in late antiquity and that Jews asserted their distinctive ethnic identity visually. This process will lead up to the construction of the Na'aran synagogue under Christian Rome, and continue with the development of the new less iconic approach under the followers of Mohammed. We then turn to the only extant literary sources of late antique Palestinian Jewry: rabbinic literature. This section begins by describing coalescence between rabbinic attitudes and the art of the majority. It then moves to the limits that the rabbis placed on Jewish participation in this visual culture on account of perceived idolatry. This "anti-idolic" approach is pervasive in rabbinic thought as it was subject to interpretation and refinement. Finally, I suggest that rabbinic sources themselves reflect conflict regarding the acceptability of decorated mosaics within synagogues and study houses. This conflict appears as early as Amoraic literature of the third century, but is more clearly expressed in Targum Pseudo-Jonathan, a Biblical paraphrase that dates to the early Islamic period – precisely the time when the defacement of the Na'aran and other mosaics took place and Jewish aesthetics turned less iconic. I conclude with a discussion of the historical factors that led to the changing face of Jewish art during the 700 years this chapter covers.

THE ARCHAEOLOGICAL EVIDENCE

Like evidence for the Second Temple period, archaeological evidence from the late first through the mid-third centuries of the Common Era did not presage the discovery of the Na'aran synagogue. The Judaean materials continue well-established latter Second Temple period themes, a continuity apparent in a group of ossuaries and terra-cotta oil lamps that were made between the destruction of the Temple and the Bar Kokhba Revolt of 132–135. Scholars refer to these lamps as "Darom" ("southern") lamps, because they stem from southern Judaea. Botanical forms, the occasional menorah, the *lulav* and *ethrog*, rosettes,[16] and even funerary monuments and a Herodian coin appear as decorations on these oil lamps.[17] Other forms that appear include earrings,[18] bronze keys,[19] and a boat.[20] Within this broad repertoire of imagery, it is significant that no animals or people appear. This fits well with pre-70 mores in Judaea. Particularly significant is a lead weight that bears the name of "Simeon son of Kosba [that is, Bar Kokhba], *Nasi* (sometimes translated "Prince") of Israel . . ." in square Hebrew script. Discovered near Beth Guvrin in the Judaean Shephalah, the weight is decorated on each side with a large rosette.[21] If these few examples are any indication, artistic traditions from before 70 continued in southern Palestine during the conclusion of the Bar Kokhba War of 132–135 C.E.

The coins of the Bar Kokhba Revolt reflect only a general continuity with Second Temple coinage. Like their predecessors, these coins are decorated with images drawn from the Temple, its implements, *lulav* bunches, the fruits of Palestine, and paleo-Hebrew script. No human or animal likenesses appear. There is no direct iconographic continuity, however. This is somewhat surprising because First Revolt coins would certainly have been known at this time. The general themes of Bar Kokhba's coins – sacred architecture, cult objects, and agriculture – are well known from Roman numismatics. Of particular interest are images of the Temple facade and the Table of Showbread (Figure 26), which do not appear in First Revolt coins. Bar Kokhba coins are prime examples of the ways that Jews adopted standard Roman imagery and adapted it to their "anti-idolic" stance – even in the midst of a revolt against the "evil" empire.

Remains from late Roman and Byzantine Palestine show no continuation of the artistic tradition of latter Second

26. Silver tetradrachm of the Bar Kokhba Revolt, year 2, 132/134 C.E. (from the Alan I. Casden Collection of Ancient Jewish Coins, 105).

Temple Jerusalem or of the Bar Kokhba revolt. In fact, they reflect a radical disjunction that might be expected of art that is more than a century later than Bar Kokhba, and within a Palestine transformed by Roman and then Christian Roman colonization. These later discoveries generally coalesce with art forms current during late antiquity, and just as interestingly, with the contemporary literary record preserved in rabbinic literature of the late Roman and Byzantine period. This new attitude, which reached its final stage in synagogue mosaics of the late fifth and sixth centuries (which include Na'aran), is first evidenced in the third- or fourth-century necropolis of Beth She'arim in the Lower Galilee. The construction and planning of this necropolis is typically Roman.[22] Were the distinctly Jewish inscriptions and large quantity of Jewish symbols removed (principally the menorah, Torah shrines, the *lulav* and *ethrog*, and Hebrew/Aramaic script), one would be hard-pressed to identify this as a Jewish site. As in Second Temple Judaean burials, the tombs of Beth She'arim were built in the manner of their age.[23]

The Beth She'arim catacombs provide evidence for a range of attitudes toward art during this period. The presence of "art" within the caves in which rabbis were buried is illuminating because we know so much already about these internees from their preserved literature. The tombs

27. The Leda sarcophagus, Beth She'arim (photograph by Steven Fine).

of rabbis are clustered together. It is perhaps significant that catacomb 14 – the apparent burial place of Rabbi Judah the Prince, rabbinic leader par excellence and editor of the Mishnah – bears no images of humans or of animals, although decorative motifs and costly sarcophagi abound.[24] This is in marked contrast with other tomb complexes in this necropolis, where images of humans (on occasion winged humans, and one man with a menorah on his head) and particularly of animals are reasonably common. Some Jews painted images of ships – apparently to steer them across the river Styx – on the walls of their tombs (just as was done in latter Second Temple Jerusalem).[25] An image of Leda being penetrated by Zeus in his guise as a swan on a sarcophagus discovered in cave 11 at Beth She'arim, is especially striking (Figure 27).[26] Well attested in general contexts, this is the only example of Leda and the Swan that has been identified in a Jewish context. This imported sarcophagus (as well as other imported sarcophagi decorated with the image of a mounted combatant, human figures with togas, and the head of an Amazon) was procured for burial in this Jewish necropolis, and no one removed them.[27] We might postulate that other Jews visiting this catacomb could not stomach the presence of this blatantly sexual and mythological three-dimensional representation and took the hammer to the Leda sarcophagus.[28] The fact that it was intentionally defaced in antiquity confirms the sense that a broad spectrum of attitudes toward appropriate and inappropriate imagery existed among late antique

Jews, although a broad consensus chose a more conservative attitude.

Catacomb 20 contains a number of rabbinic figures and their families among its internees, including "Rabbi Joshua" and his family; "Miriam, the daughter of Rabbi Jonathan"; and ". . . Gamaliel son of Rabbi Eliezer." The sarcophagus of ". . . Gamaliel son of Rabbi Eliezer," called the "shell sarcophagus" by the excavator, was decorated with "both floral and animal designs, as well as architectural and geometric elements." Moshe Fischer noted that the "greatest percentage of marble sarcophagi used in Beth She'arim" were found here. "It seems," Fischer suggests, "that this was the most elaborated funerary monument of the site."[29] Sarcophagi carved with images of an eagle, bulls' heads, and, as previously mentioned, fragments of an an Amazon were also found there. In death as in life, rabbinic attitudes toward visual images spanned a broad spectrum.[30] More than that, the rabbis did not desist from burial at Beth She'arim because of possibly offensive imagery, and nonrabbis did not stay away because the apparent burial place of Rabbi Judah the Prince was "too" rabbinic.[31] Animal imagery appears in a public context at Beth She'arim, decorating a large mausoleum adjoining catacomb 11.[32] Here, images of hunting lions, an eagle, and wolves are carved in bas relief within the decorative arch of the entrance portal.[33] What is significant about this structure is that the animal imagery is not buried deep in the ground, as in the catacombs, but was in full sight of all passersby. These animals, typical of their period, suggest the broad range of possibilities at Beth She'arim.

SYNAGOGUE ARCHITECTURE AND JEWISH ATTITUDES TOWARD ART

Although archaeological evidence for synagogues that dates between the destruction of the Temple and the fourth century is scarce, literary sources suggest that synagogues could be found throughout Jewish Palestine. Jewish public buildings existed in Lod, Tiberias, and elsewhere. The majority of synagogues, I would imagine, were not terribly impressive affairs. They were "house synagogues," the archaeological identity of which would be hard, if not impossible, to discover (just as modern house-synagogues, *steblach*,[34] disappear into the urban landscape as American Jews abandon neighborhoods and move further into the suburbs). In constructing synagogues, Jews throughout this period used the same architecture, the same furnishings, and mostly the same imagery used by the majority culture. Not surprisingly, Jews who lived in the Upper Galilee built synagogues that drew their inspiration from the nearby churches of Lebanon and Syria, whereas those in the Lower Galilee and throughout the rest of Palestine built buildings that were contiguous with Christian longhouse basilicas.[35] This required some adjustments. For example, the focal point of Galilean-type basilicas – at Capernaum, Kefar Baram, Gush Ḥalav, and Meiron – was apparently the Torah shrine, which in at least some cases was set between the portals of the synagogue on the wall facing southward toward Jerusalem. This peculiarity was remedied at Arbel, where because of the geographical context a southern entrance was not possible. This synagogue was entered from the east, and a niche for the Torah shrine was constructed on the southern side of the building.

The Torah shrine areas of longhouse basilicas also expanded from the fourth to sixth centuries, with the addition of apses and screens. A good example is the synagogue at Ma'oz Ḥayyim in the Beth Shean Valley. At Ma'oz Ḥayyim, a Torah shrine on the Jerusalem wall in the first phase (c. fourth century at the latest) was replaced by a shrine set within an apse in the second phase (c. mid-fourth century). A raised platform enclosed by a screen appeared in the third phase (c. fifth century).[36] The fourth- and fifth-century adaptations were derived directly from churches, although they coalesced nicely with Jewish attitudes toward the sanctity of the Torah scroll, its ark, and immediate surroundings. The same craftsmen worked on both church and synagogue decorations. Long ago, Avi-Yonah showed that the synagogue and church mosaics decorated with scrolls inhabited with various animals in the Gaza region were produced by the same workshops. The only Jewish imagery in the synagogue at Maon (Nirim) is a menorah before the apse containing the Torah shrine and an Aramaic inscription set before the apse by an artisan who was not skilled in Aramaic or Jewish script.[37] Synagogue screens and Christian chancel screens in the Beth Shean region were also made by the same workshops.[38]

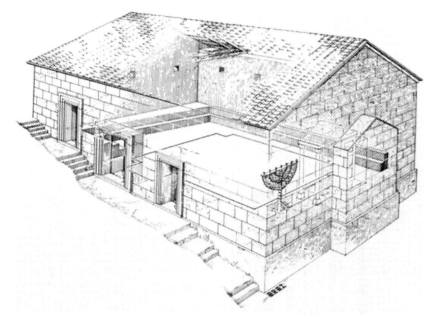

28. The synagogue of Maon in Judaea, phase 1, reconstruction drawing (after D. Amit and Z. Ilan, "The Ancient Synagogue of Ma'on in Judah," *Qadmoniot* 23, nos. 3–4 [1990], 118, Hebrew. Courtesy of the Israel Exploration Society).

Unique Jewish adaptations of Christian architecture did, however, occur. The synagogues at Khirbet Shema in the Upper Galilee, Horvat Rimmon 1 in the southern Shephalah,[39] at Eshtemoa, and Khirbet Susiya in southern Judaea (the Mount Hebron region)[40] were built as broadhouses and not as longhouse basilicas. In these buildings, the basilica form is turned on its side, and the focal point of the synagogue is the wide wall of the hall. Benches were built around the interior walls of these synagogues, focusing attention on the center of the room. This architecture is a continuation of the house-synagogues that literary sources suggest existed from the second and third centuries. The fifth-century study house (synagogue?) discovered at Beth Shean is also a continuation of this tradition.[41] There, a Torah shrine was added on one wall of a rather intimate square hall and benches placed against each wall. The synagogue of Dura Europos, completed in 244/5 C.E., reflects this sort of adaptation. A long room within a private home was reconstructed as an assembly hall (Figure 71). A large Torah shrine was added on the wide western wall of the meeting room, and benches added against each of the walls. The same was the case at Priene in Asia Minor. Khirbet Shema and the broadhouses of Mt. Hebron reflect a distinctive Jewish adaptation of the longhouse basilica to Jewish use. The architecture of the basilica was literally turned on its

29. The mosaic of the synagogue of Hammath Tiberias IIa (after M. Dothan, *Hammath Tiberias: Early Synagogues* [Jerusalem: Israel Exploration Society, 1983], pl. 26, courtesy of the Israel Exploration Society).

side and a Torah shrine placed on the wide wall, facing Jerusalem.

The earliest iconographic "ancestor" of the Na'aran synagogue is the well-preserved synagogue mosaic of the late-fourth-century synagogue at Hammath Tiberias (Figures 29, 30). It is one of the earliest and most interesting examples of coalescence between Palestinian synagogues and Roman art.[42] According to dedicatory inscriptions, this structure, built south of Tiberias on the shore of the Sea of Galilee, served the aristocratic circle of the patriarch.[43] A longhouse with two broad side aisles on the eastern side, it is not clear whether this building was entered from the east or from the north. The mosaic is aligned with a platform for the Torah shrine at the southern

end of the hall. There was no apse in this basilical synagogue, in this way similar to the church built by Paulinus in Tyre that is described by Eusebius.[44] These buildings do not suggest influence from one community to the other, but parallel appropriation of standard Roman basilical architecture.

One would assume, as the excavator did, that the hall at Hammath Tiberias was entered from the north. The inscription of the side aisles, however, are oriented to be read by a visitor entering from the west. This has led one investigator to identify Hammath Tiberias as a broadhouse, entered from the eastern side.[45] It seems to me more likely that the synagogue at Hammath Tiberias had two entrances – a dual focus dictated not by topography, but

During the fourth century, however, this imagery was well-established, and even used on the coins and other imperial iconography of the first Christian emperor, Constantine.[46] Zodiac imagery was taken over in its entirety from a non-Jewish source, including the sun god and an image of Libra, nude and uncircumcised. The dedicatory inscriptions, which mention twice one "Severos student of the illustrious patriarch," provided Joseph Baumgarten with a key for interpreting this piece.[47] Not reflective of some Jewish "mystery religion" as Goodenough thought, Baumgarten points out that in rabbinic literature members of the patriarchal community are presented as increasingly distant from the rabbinic community. Roman sources suggest that by the 380s, the patriarch had "attained a prominent role in Roman aristocratic circles."[48] Baumgarten suggests that patricians in the patriarch's circle, proud of his Roman credentials (as is evidenced in Severos's inscription), might have been amenable to Roman art. Helios was taken over by fourth-century Christians as well, who interpreted it in Christian terms. It is likely that Jews developed their own interpretations.[49] For the Roman Christian, this was a traditional iconography, reflecting continuity with the art used in Roman contexts before the rise of Christianity. The premiere example is the image called today "Christ as Helios" in Mausoleum M (of the Julii) beneath St. Peter's Basilica.[50] Still, I will show in detail later that the presence of the zodiac fit (or came to fit) well with Jewish conceptions as we know them from late antiquity – even as it was discouraged by Christians. The interior décor of the synagogue contained images of animals in bas relief. Just one example is extant: a Corinthian capitol ornamented with a bull motif in place of the middle calyx between the volutes.[51] Animal motifs become common fare within later synagogues.

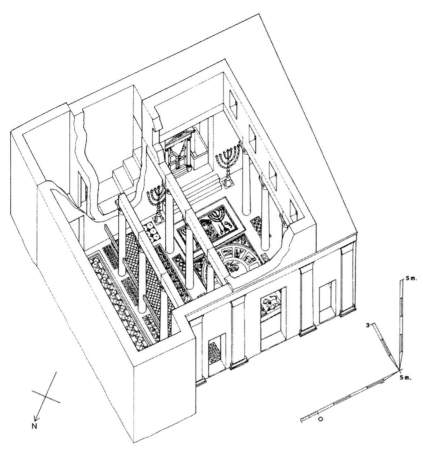

30. The synagogue of Hammath Tiberias IIa, reconstruction (after Dothan, *Hammath Tiberias: Early Synagogues*, 63, courtesy of the Israel Exploration Society).

by other considerations. It may reflect a kind of hybrid between the longhouse and broadhouse forms, at a time when Jews were just emerging from house synagogues toward more monumental architecture during the better economic times of the late third and fourth centuries.

The mosaic at Hammath Tiberias is of particular interest as it is the first time that Jews are known to have adopted the zodiac for synagogue decoration. The zodiac at Hammath Tiberias is set within a square frame. A large ring, divided equally into twelve parts, contains one sign of the zodiac and is labeled as such in Hebrew. In the corners are female personifications of the seasons, each of which are also labeled. At the center, the god Helios rides through the heavens on a chariot drawn by four horses (a *quadriga*). Helios is the only element of the composition that is unlabeled, perhaps signaling some discomfort with this element of the borrowed iconography. As we shall discuss in Chapter 12, zodiac mosaics were taken over by Jews and maintained over a long period – even after Christians virtually ended their use in other architectural contexts.

The panel closest to the ancient Torah shrine contained the image of a cabinet flanked by lighted menorahs. This imagery became emblematic as late antiquity progressed – appearing no less than three times in the more or less contemporary Beth She'arim catacombs. Details of the menorah agree with descriptions of the Tabernacle menorah in

31. Zodiac panel of the Sepphoris Synagogue mosaic (after Z. Weiss and E. Netzer, *Promise and Redemption: A Synagogue Mosaic from Sepphoris* [Jerusalem: Israel Museum, 1996], 27, courtesy of Ze'ev Weiss).

rabbinic sources. In two of the inscriptions, the synagogue is called a "holy place"; once in Greek, the other time in Aramaic. The notion of synagogue sanctity had a long history even before Hammath Tiberias was built, and this notion developed further in the following centuries.[52]

The Jews who constructed the synagogue of Hammath Tiberias used the architecture and art of the day to create what they considered to be their "holy place." This Jewish "holy place" coalesces with general late antique forms – in its use of the basilical form, the mosaic, and even the imagery of the zodiac, the shape of the Torah shrine, and the use of dedicatory inscriptions. The donors called themselves by Greek names. All the dedicatory inscriptions are in Greek – save one very general inscription in Aramaic.

"Pagan" imagery like that in the Hammath Tiberias zodiac wheel was apparently too much for the designers (or sources) of the fifth-century Sepphoris synagogue mosaic. A zodiac wheel is at the center of the floor (Figures 31, 76). This zodiac brings together two visual traditions: one that illustrates the labors of the months, the other the signs of the zodiac. Although the community at Sepphoris was

more than willing to allow human imagery – both of the monthly labors and of Biblical personalities – to appear in their mosaic, the sun god is replaced by a sun disk and the symbols for the months are fully clothed.[53] Sepphoris contains a complex collection of images drawn from Biblical tradition. These include the angelic meal in Genesis 18, the binding of Isaac (Genesis 22), and the image of Aaron sacrificing in the Tabernacle as well as other Temple themes.

Moving to the sixth through the eighth centuries, we continue to find a broad range of attitudes toward visual imagery. Among the sixth-century synagogues discovered in the Beth Shean region, two have been particularly important: Beth Alpha and Reḥov. Discovered in 1929 by Sukenik, Beth Alpha, with its depictions of a Torah ark flanked by lions and menorahs, of a zodiac wheel, and of the binding of Isaac, has served as a litmus test for methodological approaches since its discovery (Figures 10, 32, 80, 85).[54] Little of the walls is preserved. For Goodenough and his successors, Beth Alpha is proof for a nonrabbinic Judaism. Today, it is often contrasted to the nearby

32. Zodiac panel of the Beth Alpha Synagogue mosaic (after Sukenik, *The Ancient Synagogue of Beth Alpha*, pl. 10).

Reḥov synagogue (Figure 33). There, a twenty-nine-line inscription from rabbinic literature covered the floor of the narthex. This is the earliest extant physical text of rabbinic literature, the earliest manuscripts dating at least two centuries later.[55] It is quite an astonishing and unique artifact, reflecting the high level of Jewish textuality in Byzantine Palestine. No Christian inscription of such a length is extant from Palestine. The nave mosaic is not preserved, although some yet unpublished wall inscriptions were discovered.[56] The truth is, there is no reason to consider Beth Alpha any less "rabbinic" than Reḥov. The zodiac and the binding of Isaac were important themes in Byzantine-period Jewish literature (particularly in liturgical texts), and complex animal and even zodiac imagery is described in Byzantine-period literature. What if the Reḥov inscription had been discovered painted on a wall of the Beth Alpha synagogue, as a version was at Reḥov itself? Alternately, what if a zodiac and Biblical scene once graced the now-destroyed nave mosaic or even the wall paintings at Reḥov?[57] A lintel fragment bearing a bas relief of a lion head was discovered there,[58] so it is clear that this community was not as "aniconic" as it is often portrayed. We simply do not have enough of either building to make blanket statements – that

is, to turn the villagers of Beth Alpha into ancient Reform or Conservative Jews, and the synagogue at Reḥov into an ancient Orthodox community – a sixth-century "Young Israel" Orthodox congregation![59] This is especially true in agricultural settings like these, which tend to be both more traditional and less ideological.

Differences in iconography were at times very local, almost on a micro level, with little blatant ideology attached. Within a single building complex at Beth Shean, for example, seemingly incongruous attitudes toward art were coexistent. Opening onto a large Byzantine-period courtyard in Beth Shean, we find a public room known as the "House of Kyrios Leontis" and a second room that served as either a rabbinic study house or a synagogue.[60] The mosaic of the House of Kyrios Leontis contains two scenes from Homer's *Odyssey* and an image of the Nile god, while the synagogue/study house is paved in an inhabited scroll pattern (Figure 34). Animal images and a menorah appear in the study house/synagogue, but there is no mythological imagery. We have no idea how the hall containing the *Odyssey* was utilized by the community. It is likely that the choice of less iconic imagery for the study house/synagogue is indicative of differing attitudes within a more-or-less homogeneous group of donors regarding which imagery was appropriate within synagogues/study houses, and which was appropriate imagery for other public contexts.[61]

Remains of synagogues of the so-called Galilean type and the related Golan Heights type (Figures 5, 35) are related architecturally to the churches of Lebanon and Syria.[62] They date from the fourth to the seventh centuries. Their finely carved surfaces sometimes yield a broad range of visual images. At Chorazin numerous images of animals, wine making, an armed soldier, and even a Medusa, an eagle, and a three-dimensional lion are extant – and were probably brightly painted (Figure 36)[63] – but at Qasrin, in the Golan Heights, by contrast, no such images are extant. Images of winged victories were carved on lintels at Capernaum, as well as lions.[64] At Baram, fragments of three-dimensional lions were found, as well as a frieze containing a variety of animals and perhaps humans, and winged victories. The gable of the Gush Ḥalav synagogue was adorned with an eagle, and animals in bas relief, perhaps

33. The Reḥov Synagogue inscription (courtesy of the Israel Exploration Society).

34. Mosaic from the House of Leontis, Beth Shean (photograph by Steven Fine).

representing the zodiac, were found at Meroth. The aedicula of a Torah shrine at Nabratein is decorated with two rampart lions in bas relief (Figures 78). At En Samsum in the Golan, an element of a Torah shrine was discovered, with a large three-dimensional lion and Daniel in the lions' den carved in bas relief (Figures 37, 38).

Moving southward, we return to the Na'aran mosaic, with its images of the zodiac wheel and the Torah shrine flanked by menorahs. Na'aran and Beth Alpha are very different in tone from the Ein Gedi pavement with its list of the months and zodiac signs without any iconographic imagery.[65] Whether this list represents an attitude that was antagonistic toward images of the zodiac or merely an alternate artistic convention, we cannot know. Birds appear in the mosaic, however, which suggests that an absolute antagonism toward images was not at play here. What is clear is that Na'aran and Beth Alpha are among the last of the strongly iconic synagogue mosaics.

The new, less figurative approach is exemplified by the eighth-century Jericho synagogue, one of the latest synagogue mosaics discovered (Figure 39).[66] The Jericho synagogue pavement is lacking in human and animal imagery. Instead, we find only a stylized Torah shrine and a roundel containing a menorah flanked by a *lulav*, *etrog*, and shofar, below which is the inscription "Peace unto Israel (Psalm 125:5 and parallels)." This is in contrast to the nearby Khirbet al Mafjar (Hisham's Palace), where Jews were apparently counted among the workmen and such imagery predominates.[67] One might suggest that in the Jericho synagogue, Jews have consciously chosen not to

93

35. The Chorazin Synagogue (photograph by Steven Fine).

use the broad palate of imagery in favor of the geometric. A contemporaneous synagogue in Tiberias was also paved with a mosaic containing images of *lulavim*. No images of fauna or human beings adorned this floor.[68] The synagogue of Hammath Tiberias B well reflects the transitions that I have suggested occurred. When the synagogue of Severos was destroyed, according to the excavator between 396 and 422,[69] a larger apsidal basilica was built in its stead. Little of the decoration of this structure survives, the

36. Fragment of a sculpted lion, Chorazin Synagogue (courtesy of the E. L. Sukenik Archive, Institute of Archaeology, Hebrew University of Jerusalem).

extant mosaics being a typical late Roman inhabited scroll. The mid-eighth-century basilical synagogue, however, was decorated in the spirit of the new age. Its mosaic seems to have been essentially geometric, the only factor distinguishing it as Jewish the images of a menorah and perhaps a Torah shrine.[70] By the eighth century, the "anti-idolic" aesthetic had taken hold within synagogues, displacing the human and animal images that once had decorated many a synagogue pavement.

Iconoclastic behavior at Na'aran represents the transition from the old to the new aesthetic. There are many parallels throughout the Land of Israel. Floors and carved architectural members that did not conform to the new aesthetic began to be altered to fit newer aesthetic conceptions. Synagogue iconoclasm took place during the years following the Islamic conquest of Palestine. Robert Schick has shown that church and apparently synagogue iconoclasm occurred "within a few hundred years of the Islamic conquest."[71] The laying of the Jericho and Tiberias mosaics occurred while this iconoclastic period was well under way and directly parallels it.

It seems a characteristic of Jewish iconoclastic behavior that just enough of the image

37. Torah shrine base, En Samsum (photograph by Steven Fine).

dealing with art that was no longer acceptable, not with art made for "idolatrous" purposes. The result, however, is the same: Imagery that was not acceptable was removed in order to allow use of an artifact. Moving from north to south, I will survey some of the most poignant examples. At Meroth in the Upper Galilee, the eyes of a mosaic showing a Roman soldier (whom Y. Yadin identified as "David") have been carefully removed (Figure 40).[73] The removal of eyes is a well-known iconoclastic behavior. Also at Meroth, other mosaics were destroyed and two relief eagles flanking a wreath on a lintel suffered iconoclastic damage, with all of their distinguishing characteristics systematically destroyed.[74] When exactly this careful iconoclasm was undertaken is unclear, especially because according to the excavators the synagogue continued in use until the time of the First Crusade. At Kefar Baram and Capernaum, where iconoclastic activity was particularly intense, Nikes flanking a wreath once graced the main entrance portal of the buildings. In all three synagogue buildings, the wreaths were untouched, although the Nikes that flanked them have been carefully removed.[75] When the Nikes were removed is difficult to determine. At Kefar Baram, this could have taken place at any time over the past 1,500 years, by Jews, Muslims, or even Christians who bore a destructive (though perhaps not theological) impulse. This building has been exposed from antiquity until modern times.[76]

While the situation at Meroth, Capernaum, Na'aran, and particularly Baram is somewhat problematic, at Khirbet Susiya in the Hebron hills the evidence is conclusive. At Khirbet Susiya, we find that objectionable imagery was removed both from the mosaic and from the screens surrounding the main bema. In the fifth-century mosaic, a wheel – most likely a zodiac wheel – was replaced with a much cruder geometric pavement.[77] Only the side of

was removed so as to render it acceptable, and no more. The careful removal of images, as opposed to haphazard destruction, may often be taken as a sign of Jewish iconoclasm within synagogues rather than disfigurement carried out by others.[72] This is formally related to the rabbinic notion of the "nullification" of idolatry. In this case, however, we are

38. Torah shrine base, En Samsum, image of Daniel in the lions' den (photograph by Steven Fine).

39. Mosaic of the Jericho Synagogue (photograph by Steven Fine).

this wheel was left undisturbed by the somewhat imprecise artisans. An image of a figure in an *orans* stance flanked by lions, certainly identified as Daniel in the lions' den, was essentially removed from the mosaics and only scant elements of this scene are preserved. The final Hebrew letters of the name "Daniel" (*alef* and *lamed*) are all that

40. Image of a soldier from the Meroth Synagogue mosaic (photograph by Steven Fine).

is left of the inscription that once identified this Biblical hero. One wonders whether there was some religious reticence among the iconoclasts about removing these letters, inasmuch as they spell out the Divine name *El*. In no instance does an explicit Divine name appear in any Jewish synagogue inscription, perhaps supporting this conjecture. Images of deer or rams flanking a Torah shrine in the mosaic were left untouched, as the gazelle were at Na'aran. The new aesthetic at Khirbet Susiya falls in line with the choice not to portray Helios in his chariot at Sepphoris and the figurative mosaics at Ein Gedi (both phases), Tiberias, and Jericho. At Khirbet Susiya, as perhaps at Na'aran, the community was then able to continue using its synagogue for centuries afterward without being disturbed by the now-forbidden images. It is not clear from the excavators' preliminary report when this refurbishing of the Khirbet Susiya mosaic took place, except for their rather cryptic statement that it occurred "already at a relatively early phase of this floor." In any event, it certainly predated the transformation of the building into a mosque during the tenth century.[78]

The screens surrounding the main bema at Susiya are of considerable interest in that, like the mosaic, they too were subjected to intense iconoclastic activity. Images of animals were partially or completely removed from these panels, although Jewish symbols such as the menorah were left intact.[79] Carving on the surface of two panels suggests that human figures were removed as well. Birds were removed from a screen (apparently from a synagogue) that was discovered in Tiberias (Figure 41).[80] Flanking the image of a menorah on this screen are images of two birds. The heads of the birds have been carefully removed. One might imagine the efficiency of the iconoclast in removing images from the synagogue where this piece once stood if he went so far as to remove even this rather insignificant bird image. The menorah was left intact, just as the menorah was on the Susiya screen. Iconoclastic behavior within synagogues was indeed very common, having been discovered throughout Jewish Palestine. This iconoclasm, I believe, was in many cases occasioned by a desire to keep using a synagogue mosaic or appurtenance after the communal aesthetic changed from one of

41. Synagogue screen from Tiberias (photograph by Steven Fine).

tolerance for images to one of lessened tolerance or even hostility.

To sum up: Archaeological remains dating from the second century through the eighth reflect differing attitudes toward "art." The Na'aran synagogue exemplifies this process. Built in the fifth or sixth century, the pavement of the building includes extensive and colorful imagery drawn from the general milieu. It also includes distinctly Jewish imagery. The archaeological record shows that Jews used the art and architecture of their times, adapting it to their specific needs.

ATTITUDES TOWARD "ART" IN RABBINIC LITERATURE

Literary sources from late antiquity reflect a process similar to that which we have seen in archaeological sources. Amoraic sources suggest that by the third century Jews were using, or at least imagining, the use of figurative art. Sources dating to the Byzantine period reflect both this trend and a trend toward visual conservatism. We begin by exploring coalescence between rabbinic and general attitudes toward art, followed by discussions of the points of "disconnect." As has become clear, this "disconnect" is related directly to issues of idolatry.

Points of Coalescence between Late Antique Art and the Rabbinic Community[81]

The rabbis, like all ancients, did not conceive of "art" in the modern sense. There was no distinctive word for "art"

in the Hebrew language until the early twentieth century. Chaim Nahman Bialik used the term "pure art" (*omanut tehorah*) to refer to the fine arts, as did others in mandatory Palestine.[82] Eliezer Ben Yehuda referred to the introduction of the noun *omanut* to refer to "art" in his monumental lexicon: "This word (*omanut*) was recently coined (*nithadesh ba-zeman ha-aharon*), and its usage has spread in the newspapers and in speech."[83] Linguistically, the term *omanut* is derived from the Rabbinic Hebrew term *umanut*, which bears the sense of handicraft or skill.[84] It hearkens back to Song of Songs 7:2, "the work of a master's hand (*oman*)."[85] *Umanut* (*umanuta* in Palestinian Jewish Aramaic) is a term that late antique Jews would well have understood: *Umanut* is the work of an *uman*, a craftsman. An Aramaic inscription from a study house (or perhaps a synagogue) in Beth Shean (Scythopolis) includes Aramaic terms for both the artisan and his product: "Remembered for good, the artisan (*umana*) who made this work (*avidata*)."[86] The pairing of "craftsman" and "work" is reminiscent of the Targumic translation of the Biblical *melekhet makhshevet*, "work in every skilled craft" (Exodus 36:33) that describes the making of the Tabernacle.[87] *Targum Neofiti*, which dates to the fifth century, translates *melekhet makhshevet* as *avidat be-umanut*, "[to do every] work with craftsmanship."[88] To go one step further: The term *umanut* parallels the Greek *tékhnē*, "craft."[89] In a Greek dedicatory inscription from the Beth Alpha synagogue mosaic, the artisans are referred to as the *tekhnîte*, the word from which the English "technicians" derives.[90] This philological exercise emphasizes that "art" in the sense intended in our post-Renaissance lexicon (with all of its associated pieties) would have been unknown to the rabbis.

Rabbinic literature of the second to eighth centuries reflects a love of the expensive and well-made that fits well with the Greco–Roman patterns. The women of this community, for example, wore all sorts of Greco–Roman finery. Rabbi Aqiva is said to have given his wife a "city of gold" – a common type of tiara also worn by the goddess Tyche and by Esther in the Dura Europos synagogue paintings."[91] In Amoraic literature, it was called as a "Jerusalem of gold," giving this artifact distinctive Jewish content.[92] The women of the rabbinic community were governed by such questions as "[wearing] what jewelry may a woman go out on the Sabbath?" The list provided in response might fit in the jewelry cabinet of any well-dressed Roman lady:[93] "Nor [may she go out] with a [tiara in the shape of a] city of gold, a necklace, nose rings, a ring lacking a seal or a needle lacking a hole." Another list of metal jewelry included a golden city; a necklace with beads made of metal, precious stones, pearls, or glass; ear and finger rings; a ring with or without a seal; and a nose ring.[94] Rabbinic sources assumed that women wore such jewelry, and so the rabbis controlled the circumstances under which it might be worn in ways consistent with their principles. As part of the *Sotah* ritual, the Biblical "trial of the bitter waters (Numbers 5:11–31)," the trial court was told, for example, that "[if] she had on gold jewelry, necklaces, nose rings and finger rings, they take them away from her to put her to shame."[95] During the Byzantine period, Jewish women in Palestine adopted the practice of wearing marriage rings from the ambient culture.[96]

By the third century, Jews who were in close contact with Tiberias's rabbinic elite had painted walls and mosaic floors decorated with "images" – standard decorative options in late Roman times. This is expressed most clearly in a Genizah fragment of Jerusalem Talmud, *Avodah Zarah* 3:3, 42d:[97]

In the days of Rabbi Johanan they permitted (or, began to make) images (ציורין) on the walls, and he did not stop them. In the days of Rabbi Abun they permitted (or, began to make) images on mosaics, and he did not stop them.

It is generally assumed that this text refers to synagogue art. This text could just as well refer to bathhouses, other public buildings, or perhaps even the decoration of private homes.[98]

The desire of some Jews to build lavish synagogues, a rabbinic center, and ostentatious funerary monuments are evidenced in this literature. Within the rabbinic community of the third century, some tension existed regarding the use of funds for large communal building projects, reflecting both the greater wealth of the period and the move from more modest house-synagogues and house-study houses to monumental architecture. As expressed in the *Jerusalem Talmud*, tractate *Sheqalim* 5:7, 49b,[99]

Rabbi Ḥamma son of Ḥanina and Rabbi Hoshaya were walking among the synagogues of Lod.
Rabbi Ḥamma son of Ḥanina said to Rabbi Hoshaya: "How much money my fathers invested here!"
He replied to him: "How many souls have your fathers invested here? Were there no people to study Torah?"

In this tradition, a presumably mature Rabbi Ḥamma son of Ḥanina, a younger contemporary of Rabbi Hoshaya,[100] shows off the euergetism of his family in the Judaean city Lod – an important rabbinic center during the second century.[101] Synagogue inscriptions from the fourth century onward demonstrate that Palestinian and diaspora Jews were fully involved in euergetism similar to that of the Lod congregation of which Rabbi Ḥamma's family was a part. As Claudine Dauphin aptly suggests regarding the Byzantine period, "Landowners and rich citizens, both Christians and Jews, vied with each other for attention from the church or the synagogue, and God."[102] In his startlingly sharp comment, the senior scholar, Rabbi Hoshaya, negates this popular value in favor of popular support of rabbinic study.

The *Jerusalem Talmud* continues with a second, paired discussion of rabbinic euergetism within the rabbinic community itself:

Rabbi Abun[103] was passing the gates of the *Sidra Rabba* ["great study house/synagogue"][104] when Rabbi Mani came toward him.
He [Abun] said to him: "Look what I have made."
He [Mani] said: "Israel has forgotten its maker and built shrines (*hekhalot*, Hosea 8:14).
Were there no people to study Torah?

Rabbi Mani here denigrates benefaction by the head of the Tiberias academy. The gates that Rabbi Abun donated must have been "monumental" – or they would not be worthy of comment.[105] A communal building in the city of Tiberias, the *Sidra Rabba* was probably an academy, although it may have been a synagogue.[106] The *Sidra Rabba* seems to have been some sort of landmark in Tiberias for members of the rabbinic community (and perhaps for others).[107] Is it too much to conjecture that through his very visible donation of the gates to the *Sidra Rabba* (in what seems to have been a typical subscription-type building project), Rabbi Abun, the head of the academy, was not just asserting his personal status among the rabbis but rabbinic position in urban Tiberias as well? That Rabbi Hoshaya and Rabbi Mani compare these public buildings to Hosea's illicit "shrines" is more pointed than it seems: It was clearly the ultimate taunt to compare synagogues and study houses to idolatrous temples. Further, the synagogue of Lod and the *Sidra Rabba* were undoubtedly built in the vernacular public architecture of their times, the archetypical examples of which were Roman temples and basilicas. The use of architecture to assert communal position is made by the rabbis in their determination that synagogues must be built, like the Temple, "at the high point of the city," and in the Byzantine-period acknowledgment that synagogues (like churches and other public buildings) were built in the town center.[108] Rabbi Hoshaya and Rabbi Mani (and perhaps the editor[s] who paired, formulated, and preserved their comments) reflect a negative attitude toward the use of resources for the construction of architecturally significant structures, preferring that Jewish euergetism be directed toward the maintenance of scholars.

This attitude toward conspicuous building in the Roman mode is found in a Tannaitic tradition preserved in *y. Sheqalim* 2:7, 47a: "Rabbi Simeon son of Gamaliel says: Monuments (נפשות) are not built for the righteous. Their words are their memorial."[109] Read against the background of the necropolis of Beth She'arim with its lavishly carved tombs and large concentration of rabbis (including, apparently, Rabbi Simeon son of Gamaliel's grandson, Rabbi Judah the Prince), this text reflects a continuing dialogue within the rabbinic community about appropriate and inappropriate uses of funds that pits Torah study against monumental architecture. What these traditions suggest is that within the rabbinic community of the late second or third century, there were conflicting voices. Some, especially local and some rabbinic leaders, were positively inclined toward the construction of Jewish monumental buildings in the Roman style; others were clearly not. This was an obvious tension within the rabbinic community, for Jews increasingly constructed public buildings in the Roman mode as life improved, the pain of the two Jewish revolts faded into memory, and Palestine became an increasingly Roman place.

ARTISANS IN RABBINIC LITERATURE

A good vantage point from which to assess rabbinic attitudes toward art is from their thinking about artisans. The rabbis were generally positive toward craftsmen, with little of the explicit condescension seen in Ben Sirah and in the Greco–Roman context.[110] Nevertheless, they were very ambivalent in their evaluation of the powers of artisans when their creations seemed to infringe on Divine prerogatives. This ambivalence is expressed in traditions in the *Mekhilta of Rabbi Simeon Bar Yoḥai* that both treat human portraiture as normal and suggest an ambivalence toward

the work of the artisan. The midrash comments on Exodus 15:11: "Who is like thee, O Lord, among the gods? Who is like thee, majestic in holiness, terrible in glorious deeds, doing wonders?":[111]

". . . doing wonders" (Exodus 15:11).
The attributes of flesh and blood are not like the attributes of the Omnipresent.
Flesh and blood, when he creates an image (צר צורה) begins from its head or its foot or from one of its limbs.
But the Omnipresent, blessed be He, when he creates an image, creates it all at once.
For it is said: "for he is the former (יוצר) of all things" (Jeremiah 10:16).
And says: "there is no artisan (צור) like our God" (1 Samuel 2:2), there is no artisan like God.

Another example:

"Who does wonders" (Exodus 15:11).
The attributes of flesh and blood are not like the attributes of God.
Flesh and blood goes to a maker of images (צלמים) and says to him: Make me a likeness of my father.
He (the craftsman) says to him: Bring me your father and place him before me, or bring me his picture (דיוקנו) and I will make one like it (כצורתה).
But He who spoke and the world was created is not so.
He gives this man a son resembling his father from a drop of water (semen).

The starting place of this tradition, Exodus 15:11, sets up the comparison between man and God. Citation of Jeremiah 10:16 deepens the polemical underpinnings of the *Mekhilta* here. Jeremiah 10:14b–15 contrasts God as creator to the maker of idols:

. . . every founder is put to shame by his idols; for his images are false, and there is no breath in them. They are worthless, a work of delusion; at the time of their punishment they shall perish. Not like these is he who is the portion of Jacob, for he is the former of all things, and Israel is the tribe of his inheritance; the Lord of hosts is his name.

Still, the *Mekhilta* does not portray the artisan as an idolater or his craft as idolatry, but merely as a craftsman whose inferiority to the Divine requires reiteration. Portraits of family members were not uncommon in the Roman world; examples have been discovered in Egypt.[112] From our *Mekhilta of Rabbi Simeon Bar Yoḥai* tradition, it is clear that the rabbis clearly knew of the existence of such domestic portraiture, perhaps also to be found among the

Jews. Our traditions do not hint that they are dealing with a gentile context – but rather with the limitations of an artist – whether Jew or gentile. A version in *b. Berakhot* 10a explicitly discusses human figures drawn on walls.[113] We have seen that Jews who were close to the Tiberian rabbis in third-century Palestine had figurative wall paintings and mosaics.[114]

Rabbinic attitudes toward artisans are refracted through the image of Bezalel son of Uri. With Josephus, the rabbis praise Bezalel and Oholiab, the builders of the Biblical Tabernacle, for their artistry.[115] The personality of Bezalel is not well developed in Tannaitic and classical *midrashim*. In fact, his name appears nowhere in the Mishnah, Tosefta, or Tannaitic midrashim (including the two Mekhiltas on Exodus). Palestinian midrashim from the Byzantine period, perhaps coincidentally the period when major synagogue construction projects were being undertaken throughout Palestine, explore this character more fully. They focus on the ambiguous relationship between Bezalel and Moses that is set out in Scripture.

In Exodus 31:1–6 and 35:30–6, God Himself presents Bezalel as His choice to be the principal builder of the Divinely designed Tabernacle.[116] In Exodus 31:3 and 35:31, Bezalel is described as having been "filled with the Spirit of God, with ability and intelligence, with knowledge and all craftsmanship, to devise artistic designs, to work in gold, silver, and bronze, in cutting stones for setting, and in carving wood, for work in every craft." Indicative of his status, his name – Bezalel son of Uri – translates as "in the shadow of God, son of Light" (Exodus 31:2, 35:30). Together with his assistant Oholiab, the son of Ahisamach, of the tribe of Dan" (Exodus 31:6) Bezalel "made" of the Tabernacle appurtenances.[117] Bezalel's workmanship fulfills a series of Divine commands to Moses to make the vessels. Exodus 25:9, 25:40, and 26:30 and Numbers 8:4 all treat Moses as the earthly patron of the Tabernacle. In Exodus 25:40, Moses is commanded: "And see (*ur'eh*) and make (*ve-aseh*) them after the pattern which is being shown you (*asher atah mareh*) on the mountain." Moses was commanded to fabricate the Tabernacle according to the Divinely ordained plan; the actual craftsmanship was carried out by Bezalel. This relationship is emphasized throughout the Exodus narrative, particularly in the description of the finished Tabernacle in Exodus 39–40. In 39:43, Moses receives the completed Tabernacle: "And Moses saw all the work, and behold, they had done it; as the Lord had commanded, so had they done it. And

Moses blessed them." From this point on, Moses' role in the Tabernacle is central, as he assembled and dedicated it.

The issue of who "made" the Tabernacle is complicated in the Books of Chronicles. In 1 Chronicles 21:29 and 2 Chronicles 1:3, we hear of ". . . the Tabernacle [2 Chron.: "of witness"] of the Lord, which Moses [2 Chron.: the servant of the Lord] had made (*asah*) in the wilderness." 2 Chronicles describes Bezalel's craftsmanship in similar terms. 2 Chronicles 1:5 mentions that "the bronze altar that Bezalel the son of Uri, son of Hur, had made (*asah*)" was in the Tent of Meeting in Jerusalem. Through the use of this verb, Moses' role in the construction of the Tabernacle is also subtly compared to that of Solomon in building the Temple (and vice versa). We read in 2 Chronicles 5: 1: "Thus all the work that Solomon did (*asah*) for the house of the Lord was finished."[118]

Classical rabbinic literature explored roles of Bezalel and Moses as the "makers" of the Tabernacle and its vessels in a number of ways. In the *Baraita de-Melekhet ha-Mishkan*, the locus for rabbinic discussion of the construction of the Tabernacle, Bezalel's name appears only two times. Still, the overlapping roles of Moses and Bezalel are treated without any sense of competition.[119] This is expressed in the tradition's discussion of the menorah. Chapter nine opens, "The menorah that Moses made in the desert was wrought from hammered gold. . . ." The next chapter opens unproblematically with the question: "How did Bezalel make the menorah?" *Seder Olam Rabba* brings the two phrases from Chronicles together. This Tannaitic chronology recalls ". . . the tabernacle that Moses made in the desert, and the bronze altar that Bezalel made. . . ."[120] Similarly, classical midrashim suggest no difficulties with Bezalel's status as builder of the Tabernacle.[121]

That Bezalel actually fulfilled Moses' oft-repeated Divine charge to "make" the Tabernacle and that Chronicles attributes the altar to Bezalel (and not to Moses) set up a kind of competition between the two figures in Byzantine period midrashim. Dissonance is created between the towering image of Moses as the recipient of God's command and the Divinely gifted artisan, Bezalel (titled *Bezalel umana*, "Bezalel the artisan," in the targum to Song of Songs 7:2), who was filled with the "spirit of God."[122] This perceived dissonance is in line with Greco–Roman attitudes toward craftsmen, as we have seen in our discussion of artisans (including Bezalel) in Second Temple period literature.[123] Although some particularly famous Greek and Roman artisans and architects are known by name, these are clearly the exception. Bezalel was a similar exception, for he was chosen by God for the project.

Several traditions preserved in Byzantine-period collections suggest that tradents were discomforted by Bezalel's prominent role. A tradition in *Midrash Tanḥuma* intentionally spawns ambiguity in the Biblical description of Bezalel's divine gifts. In Exodus 35:30–1, we read: "And Moses said to the people of Israel, 'See, the Lord has called by name Bezalel the son of Uri, son of Hur, of the tribe of Judah; and he has filled him with the Spirit of God, with ability, with intelligence, with knowledge, and with all craftsmanship. . . .'" Interpreting these verses, which are explicit as to Bezalel's gifts, the midrash suggests that Bezalel really was not as special as one might think – "rather, everyone who was occupied in the fabrication of the Tabernacle was given by God understanding, wisdom and understanding, as it says: 'And all the wise of heart among the workmen made the tabernacle with ten curtains. . . .' But of all of them only Bezalel is made known by name."[124] By arguing that others were "wise," this text not only increases the specialness of all involved in the Tabernacle process, but also not so subtly lowers the status of Bezalel. The *Exodus Rabba* version of this tradition goes so far as to include wise animals in the process, before mentioning that Bezalel is simply the only recipient of this gift who is mentioned by name.[125] Another tradition in *Midrash Tanḥuma* attempts to resolve the dilemma of Bezalel's status, arguing that Moses really did "make" the menorah.[126] According to this tradition, after having failed to create a menorah based on a pattern shown him by God, Moses threw an ingot of gold into the fire. Through Divine intervention, a fully formed menorah came out. Moses' assumed artistic lacking provides a rationale for the Biblically ordained role of Bezalel as artisan of the Tabernacle and its implements. Thus, we read in *Midrash Tanḥuma* (and parallels):[127]

R. Levi son of Rabbi says: A pure menorah came down from heaven. For the Holy One, blessed be He, said to Moses, "And you will make a menorah of pure gold" (Exodus 25:31).
Moses said to Him: 'How shall we make it?'
He said to him: "Of beaten work [shall the menorah be made]" (ibid.).
Nevertheless, Moses still found difficulty with it, and when he came down he forgot its construction.
He went up and said: "Master of the Universe, I have forgotten how to make it!"

The Holy One, blessed be He, showed Moses again, but he still had difficulty.
He [God] said to him: Look and make (it), and finally He took a coin of gold and showed him its construction.
Still, he [Moses] found its construction difficult.
So He said to him: "See it and make it" (Exodus 25:40) and finally He took a menorah of fire and showed him its construction.
Yet, in spite of all this, it caused Moses difficulty.
Said the Holy One, blessed be He, to him: "Go to Bezalel and he will make it."
He went down to Bezalel, and the latter immediately constructed it.
Immediately Moses began to wonder, saying: "To me it was shown many times by the Holy One, blessed be He, yet I found it hard to make, and you who did not see it constructed it with your own intelligence! Bezalel, you stood in the shadow of God (*betsel El*) when the Holy One, blessed be He, showed me its construction! . . .

This midrash solves the dilemma of Bezalel's artistic acuity and seeming superiority over Moses through interpretation of his name. Bezalel is subservient to Moses, this midrash suggests, because he stood in God's shadow when God showed Moses the fiery menorah. Bezalel's special skills are set in the shadow of Moses' revelation.

Moses' difficulty in constructing the vessels is based in another issue of Biblical exegesis. Anyone who has tried to draw or fabricate the Tabernacle artifacts based solely on the Biblical descriptions, as my students and I oftentimes try to do, knows that the Biblical text assumes that the reader can visualize the object described based on preexisting knowledge. These word pictures are in no way complete, but rather are schematic verbal renderings. The descriptions must have been clear to the original audience, who could visualize the artifacts in terms of their own material culture(s).[128] For later generations, however, this context was lost and the text became opaque. This opacity was acknowledged by the rabbis when they imagined that God needed to show Moses a fiery model of the menorah drawn by the Divine finger as a guide.

Dissatisfied with any sense of parity between Bezalel and Moses, *Exodus Rabba* 35:3 sets up an explicit hierarchical relationship between Moses' position and that of Bezalel:

. . . did Moses make the Tabernacle?
Behold, it is written: Bezalel and Oholiab and every able man in whose mind the Lord had put ability made [the Tabernacle] (Exodus 36:1).
Rather, Moses taught, and Bezalel acted.

Moses "made" the Tabernacle as its patron, while Bezalel was in essence his employee. This lexical distinction is fortified by the fact that in late antiquity, the Hebrew *asah* and the Aramaic cognate *avad* bore the sense of both benefaction and active "making" (as does the Greek cognate *poiéō*). Yannai, a sixth-century synagogue poet, articulates this relationship in a poem on the construction of the Tabernacle in which Bezalel is never mentioned:[129]

> Happy is the faithful [servant *ne'eman*, Moses], who is
>   truly the artisan (*ha-oman*),
>   To hear and to see, to cause to be done and to do.
> Understanding of all the work of the structure He
>   (God) provided, and He agreed to all that was done.
> You commanded him, and make the Tabernacle,
>   And he supported and caused it to be done, just as he
>   did every deed.
> Know that anyone who supports something, it is named
>   after him; all that he supported is called after him.
> The Tabernacle is called the Tabernacle that Moses
>   made. . . .

The attitude described by Yannai is paralleled in dedicatory inscriptions from Palestinian synagogues. Of the more than 100 extant inscriptions, only three artisans appear. Marianos and his son Hanina appear in two mosaics, as the artisans of the Beth Alpha synagogue mosaics and a second synagogue mosaic (perhaps Samaritan) in neighboring Beth Shean.[130] The Beth Alpha inscription reads:

May the craftsmen who carried out this work, Marianos and his son Ḥanina, be held in remembrance.

In the Aramaic inscription from Beth Shean that I discussed in the introduction to this chapter, the artisans are praised anonymously; and a Greek inscription, probably a dedicatory text, appears on the pilaster capital from Tiberias: "The Gracious God, be with Abraham the marble worker."[131] Significantly, in every other Jewish dedicatory inscription from Eretz Israel – whether in Hebrew, Aramaic, or Greek – the focus is on the donor who "made" the gift or "strengthened" the synagogue. Like Moses in Yannai's poem, it is the local donors who "made" the synagogue – not the workmen. Bezalel, like the local artisans who constructed most of the anonymous synagogues, study houses, and other communal structures in Byzantine Palestine, is merely the artisan. Thus, this rabbinic image of Bezalel resolves the status of the Biblical builder vis-à-vis that of the patron in ways that are consistent with the mores of most synagogue communities in the Land of Israel during the Byzantine period.

IMAGINING THE IMPOSSIBLE, PROJECTING THE POSSIBLE

Rabbinic literature is rich in projections of rabbinic ideals back to Biblical days and forward to messianic times. This projection outward from *zeman ha-zeh* – literally, "this time" – provides us with a rich vision of the contours of the rabbinic imagination. Similarly, rabbis projected distant diaspora communities in their own images, the only limits on their projection often being the limits of their culture-specific imaginations.[132] These sources are important because they tell us much about rabbinic attitudes that are unrestricted by political, economic, or other considerations. They show just how deeply the rabbis were inculcated with the art and architecture of their time and place, and how fully they imagined themselves and their followers participating in it.

Rabbis often fantasized about the expensive, unique, and beautiful – and imagined that it existed beyond their reach in time and space. Just as significantly, they assumed that visual imagery drawn from their daily lives exists in the imaginable distance. Two particularly interesting rabbinic traditions imagine Jewish wealth in the diaspora. In its own way, each of these traditions gives its own view of the diaspora in a way that is strikingly evocative of America – the *goldineh medineh*, the "golden land." In the imaginations of Eastern European Jews at the turn of the twentieth century, the very streets of American cities were paved with gold. So too, the Western diaspora for second- and third-century rabbis.

Tosefta Sukkah 4: 6 (and parallels) is a fine example. This text describes the great synagogue of Alexandria:[133]

Said Rabbi Judah: Whosoever has never seen the double colonnade of Alexandria[134] of Egypt has never seen the great glory of Israel in his entire life.
It was a kind of large basilica, one colonnade within another. Sometimes twice as many as those who went out of Egypt were within it.
There were seventy-one thrones there, one for each of the seventy-one elders, each one made of twenty-five talents, with a wooden platform in the center.
The leader of the assembly stands upon it at its horn, with flags in his hand.

When one begins to read [a section from a biblical scroll], the other would wave flags so [the people] would answer "amen" for each and every blessing.

Then that one would wave the flags and they would answer "amen."

They did not sit in a jumble, but the goldsmiths sit by themselves, the silversmiths by themselves, the common weavers by themselves, the Tarsian (that is, fine) weavers[135] by themselves, and the blacksmiths by themselves. . . .[136]

For the rabbinic storyteller, the structure of this synagogue hearkens to the Temple itself. Both the Alexandrian synagogue and the Temple Mount were described as being constructed as a "stoa within a stoa."[137] In the *Babylonian Talmud*, the descriptions of both buildings are ascribed to the second-century Palestinian sage, Rabbi Judah son of Ilai.[138] Such buildings were rare in the Roman world. The Forum of Trajan and the Forum of Julia in Rome were such buildings. The golden thrones find parallels in Roman contexts. Plutarch, for example, relates that Marc Antony assembled within the gymnasium of Alexandria a large number of people, and placed "on a tribunal (*bámatos*) of silver two thrones of gold, one for himself, and the other for Cleopatra. . . ."[139] The *Jerusalem Talmud* adds that the synagogue thrones were "covered with fine stones and pearls." Such thrones are known to have existed in the Roman world and are illustrated in later church mosaics.[140] Non-Jews too would have been impressed by the description of this "basilica," which fits well with the architecture and conspicuous wealth that was so prized.

Beauty associated with the supposed conspicuous wealth of diaspora Jews is explored in *Genesis Rabba* 11:4.[141] This text seeks an answer for the seeming paradox of Jewish material success while living in "exile." The midrash opens, "by what merit do they exist?," and answers:

. . . by the merit of their honoring the Sabbaths and festivals. Rabbi Ḥiyya son of Abba said: I was once invited by a man in Laodicea.[142] He brought before us a golden table borne on sixteen silver staves,[143] and on it was [the food] of everything created during the six days of creation.

A child sat in its middle [of the table] proclaiming, "The earth is the Lord's, and the fullness thereof" (Psalm 24:1). . . .

In the *Babylonian Talmud* version, the grandness of the place settings is amplified. The table was "borne by sixteen men and sixteen silver chains were attached to it and bowls and cups and ladles and flasks were set upon it and every sort of food and delicacies and spices."[144] Like the synagogue of Alexandria, the cart in Laodicea projects rabbinic

fantasies regarding wealth into the "touchable" distance, just as other traditions project lavishness into the Biblical past, supernal realm, and the messianic future.

PROJECTION INTO THE BIBLICAL PAST

Occasionally, midrashic sources project the art of the Roman period directly into the Biblical reality. Projection of contemporary art into the Biblical arena is well known in the wall paintings at Dura Europos and in later mosaics, where Greco–Roman garb, furniture, architecture, poses, and even gods are projected into the Biblical story. I will deal with three groups of traditions. I begin by discussing the projection of Roman coins into Biblical times, moving from there to Roman road markers that "led" to the Biblically ordained cities of refuge, and finally to Solomon's Throne as imagined by *Targum Sheni* to Esther.

Coins were invented during the seventh century B.C.E. in western Asia Minor.[145] Rabbinic traditions suggest, however, that coins were used by Biblical figures beginning with Abraham. The rabbis considered minted coins with visual imagery struck onto their faces to be so obvious that they projected its existence back to Biblical times. Many of these coins were decorated, we are told, with images. Thus, we read in an apparently Tannaitic tradition in *b. Baba Qama* 97b:

Our Rabbis taught:
What is the coin of Jerusalem?
David and Solomon on one side,
And Jerusalem the holy city on the other.[146]
What is the coin of Abraham?[147]
An old man and an old woman on one side,
And a young man and a young woman on the other.

The authors of this tradition imagined that the Biblical ancestors minted their own coins as a reflection of their sovereignty.[148] Abraham is mentioned as a military leader by Josephus, a tradition that continued through rabbinic sources.[149] As on our rabbinic coins, Roman coin types sometimes bore images of more than one individual on a single face. Images of both two males and a male with a female side-by-side appear.[150] On a bronze minted in Aelia Capitolina, for example, the busts of Septimus Severus and his wife Julia appear on one side, standing portraits of the caesar and his wife clasping hands on the other.[151] The legend "Jerusalem the Holy" appears on First Revolt coins, and the facade of the Temple with the legend "for the redemption of Zion" appears on Bar Kokhba coins (which continued, like First Revolt coins, to be known to the rabbis for a considerable period after the war).[152] They projected the existence of Jerusalem coins back to the ideal kingship of David and Solomon. This projection may respond to 1 Chronicles 29:7, which anachronistically projects a coin of the Persian period to the reign of Solomon. This text suggests that among the free-will offerings given for the construction of Solomon's temple were 10,000 אדרכונים, a loan word derived from the Persian "daric."[153] The term דרכון (darkon) was used by the rabbis to refer to Persian gold or silver coins, so an association of the Biblical term with an actual currency might have been very natural.[154]

The use of human images on Davidic coins was imagined with none of the discomfort that the minters of the Jewish revolts had with "graven images." In the Biblical golden age, the ideal coins of David and Solomon and of Father Abraham – like the broadly circulated currency of their own day – unproblematically bear the images of the ruler.[155] This projection is applied to Mordecai and Esther in *Esther Rabba* 10:12. This text explicitly compares Biblical currency to the Roman currency that it ultimately imitates: "Just as the currency of a king goes out throughout the land, the currency of Mordecai goes out. And what was his currency? Mordecai on one side, and Esther on the other."[156]

Genesis Rabba 39:11 contains an extensive discussion of "Biblical" currency, based on Biblical references, with a wider selection of coins:[157]

[And I will make you a great nation and I will bless you and I will make your name great . . . (Genesis 12:2)]
Rabbi Berekhiah said in the name of Rabbi Ḥelbo: [It means that] his currency (מוניטא) went out.
There were four whose currency went out in the world:
Abraham: [as it is written], "And I will make you a great nation and I will bless you and I will make your name great. . . ." (Genesis 12:2).
His currency went out.
What is it?
An old man and an old woman on one side, and a youth and a young woman on the other.
Joshua: [as it is written], "So the Lord was with Joshua, and his fame was in all the land" (Joshua 6:27).
His currency went out in the world.
What is it?
An ox on one side and a wild-ox on the other, corresponding to, "His firstling bullock, majesty is his, and his horns are the horns of a wild-ox" (Deuteronomy 33:17).[158]

David: [as it is written] "And the fame of David went out into all the lands" (1 Chronicles 14:17).
His currency went out to every land.
What is it?
A staff and a sack on one side, and a tower on the other, corresponding to, "Thy neck is like the tower of David, built with turrets [on which hang a thousand bucklers, shields of mighty men]" (Song of Songs 4:4).
Mordecai, [as it is written] "For Mordecai was great in the king's house, and his fame went forth throughout all the provinces" (Esther 9:4).
His currency went out.
What is it? Sackcloth and ashes on one side and a golden wreath on the other.[159]

The name of Abraham will be "made great" by spreading it through currency, *moneta* (a Latin loan word).[160] Similarly, the fame of Joshua, David, and Mordecai, this midrash tells us, was spread. Aside from the imagery of Abraham, which, like that described in *b. Baba Qama* 97b, is derived directly from Roman coins, the imagery of the others is derived midrashically from Biblical texts. That said, all of these images except "sackcloth" appear with regularity on Roman coin types. Wreaths and palm fronds appear, for example, on Hasmonian issues,[161] and the ox plowing a furrow at the foundation of Aelia Capitolina appears on coinage of that city that seems to have been known to the Tannaitic rabbis.[162] David's tower hung with shields clearly parallels both Roman trophies (like those that appear on the *Judaea Capta* series) and images of towers.[163] A coin of Trajan (104–111 C.E.), for example, shows an ornamental triumphal arch topped with trophies bearing shields.[164] The use of "sackcloth" was clearly dictated by the significance of garments in expressing the central theme of the Book of Esther. Where in Esther 4:1, Mordecai "rent his clothes, and put on sackcloth with ashes and went in to the midst of the city, and cried a loud and bitter cry," in 8:15, after defeating the evil Haman, "Mordecai went out from the presence of the king in royal apparel of blue and white and a great wreath of gold, and with a wrap of fine linen and purple, and the city of Shushan rejoiced and was glad."

The rabbis' "Biblical" currency, read through the filter of Biblical texts, clearly reflects the numismatic context in which they lived. Significantly, the coins of Abraham – the only coin types not derived from verses – represent human images. This tradition, like the *b. Baba Qama* and *Esther Rabba* sources that we have discussed, is independent of Scriptural warrant. The coins of Joshua, says *Genesis Rabba*, contained representations of animals; the other coins described are decorated with inanimate objects. It is possible that these Biblically derived icons represent more strict attitudes by the author of the exegetical traditions in *Genesis Rabba*. It is more likely, however, that the author was focused on providing Biblical precedent without any particular bias regarding human or animal forms.

One tradition imagines Jews setting up mile markers that differed little from sculpted Roman mile markers.[165] The midrashic context for this discussion is the Biblical city of refuge.[166] According to a Byzantine-period collection, *Midrash Tehillim*,[167] those who committed unintentional homicide were guided to the city with the help of sculpted markers – "Said Rabbi Abin:[168] At each and every mile there was a structure (*burgan*),[169] and atop each structure a statue (*tselem*) with its hand pointing in the direction of the city of refuge."[170] The version in *y. Makkot* 2:5, 31d, is more tentative, reading in place of "a statue with its hand pointing" simply "a kind of hand (*ka-min yad*) would show them the way." "A kind of hand" is elsewhere used in Amoraic literature to avoid anthropomorphism.[171] Images of the Divine hand appear in the Dura Europos synagogue wall paintings, and later in the Beth Alpha synagogue mosaic, and in relief on a marble synagogue screen from Khirbet Susiya.[172] While rabbis discuss in negative (or at least, belligerently tolerant) terms the presence of "idolatrous" sculpture in their midst, including in the principally Jewish city of Tiberias,[173] the *Midrash Tehillim* text actually assumes that sculpture in the round was set up under (proto-) rabbinic auspices in compliance with a Biblical commandment.

The most lavish projection into the Biblical past appears in a Byzantine period midrash in Aramaic, *Targum Sheni* to Esther.[174] This text describes the throne of Ahasveros in considerable detail. This throne, the Targum tells us, was constructed by Solomon, taken by Nebuchadnezzar to Babylonia, and inherited by the Persian king:[175]

. . . This is Solomon, the great king, who made his great royal throne covered with fine gold from Ophir, overlaid with beryl stones, inlayed with marble, it was overlaid with samargel, carbuncle, diamonds and pearls and all kinds of precious ones. For no king was one made like it, or were any of the kings able to produce one similar to it. Now this was the workmanship of his throne: twelve lions of gold stood upon it, and opposite them were twelve eagles of gold, a lion opposite an

eagle and an eagle opposite a lion, they were arranged opposite each other. The right paw of the golden lion. The sum of all the lions was seventy two. Now the top of the throne where the king's seat was located, was round. It had six steps, for it is written: then the king made a great throne of ivory, the throne had six steps" (I Kings 10:18). Thus on the first step lay a golden ox and opposite it lay a golden lamb. On the third step lay a golden panther and opposite it lay a golden suckling kid. On the fourth step lay a golden eagle and opposite it a golden peacock. On the fifth step lay a golden cat and opposite it a golden hen. On the sixth step lay a golden hawk and opposite it a golden bird. Now on the top of the throne stood a golden dove, grasping a golden hawk in its claw. So likewise will all the nations and (speakers of all) languages in the future be delivered into the hand of Israel. Now at the top of the throne was located a golden lampstand set in proper order in its arrangement of its lamps (and) with pomegranates, (and) with its ornaments, (and) with its snuffers/ashpans (and) with its cups and with its lilies. Now at one side of the lampstand were standing seven golden branches, upon which were portrayed the seven Patriarchs of the world, and these are their names: Adam, Noah and the great Shem, Abraham, Isaac and Jacob and Job among them. Now at the other side of the lampstand were standing seven other branches, upon which were portrayed the seven pious ones of the world and these are their names: Levi, Qehat, Amram, Moses, Aaron (and) Eldad and Medad, as well as the prophet Haggai among them. Now at the top of the lampstand was a golden vessel filled with pure olive oil, whose light supplied the lights of the lampstand, and upon it were portrayed the high priest. From the large basin proceeded two golden clusters, upon which were depicted the two sons of Eli – Hophni and Pinchas. Now within the two golden clusters there proceeded from the large basin upon which were portrayed the two sons of Aaron – Nadav and Abihu – as well as two golden seats, one for the high priest and one for the deputy high priest. Towards the top of the throne were set seventy golden thrones, upon which sat the seventy (members of the) Sanhedrin, dispensing justice before King Solomon. Now two dolphins were on either side of King Solomon's two ears in order that he should not become frightened. Above the top of the throne were set twenty-four golden vines, which provided shade for King Solomon. . . .

This amazing tradition builds upon Biblical descriptions of Solomon's throne – themselves quite fantastic. In 1 Kings 10:18–20 and 2 Chronicles 9:17–19, the throne is described. In the 1 Kings text, we read:

The king also made a great ivory throne, and overlaid it with the finest gold. The throne had six steps, and at the back of the throne was a calf's head, and on each side of the seat were arm rests and two lions standing beside the arm rests, while twelve lions stood there, one on each end of a step on the six steps. The like of it was never made in any kingdom.

As the first expansion of this tradition, 2 Chronicles 9:18 adds a golden footstool. The process of expansion continued up to and beyond our *Targum Sheni* text. The ever-more-ornate throne epitomizes the Biblical notion that "the like of it was never made in any kingdom." In the words of the Targum,[176]

Now when kings heard about the fame of the king's throne, they assembled themselves and all of them came together, prostrating themselves and throwing themselves before him, they said: "Such a throne was never made for any king, and no nation or people could design one like it." Now when the kings beheld the excellence of the throne, they paid respect to the One who created the whole world.

Into the Biblical frame, traditions drawn from classical rabbinic literature are added. The thrones of the Sanhedrin, for example, are taken from *t. Sukkah* 4:6. Similarly, the lampstand is reminiscent of rabbinic and visual interpretations of the menorah (Figures 64, 68). The Targum continues to describe how the throne moved from place to place, as well as the astonishing movements of each of the animals on the throne:[177]

the oxen lowed, the lions roared, the bears growled, the lambs bleated, the panthers screamed, the owls hooted, the cats mewed, the peacocks shrieked, the roosters crowed, the hawks screamed and the birds chirped. . . . The lions would sprinkle spices whenever King Solomon would ascend to sit on the king's throne.

This is a superb example of Byzantine automata, of mechanized moving contrivances meant to enthrall the viewer. Actual working "thrones of Solomon" are known to have existed at the Byzantine court.[178] The rambling style of this Targumic presentation is not intended, I believe, to suggest the actual structure of the throne, but rather through accretion of traditions and compulsive overstatement to affirm its Biblically proclaimed glory.

This literary depiction of Solomon's throne finds an important parallel in the Dura Europos synagogue, where a

42. Ahasveros on his throne with Esther crowned with a "city of gold" to the upper right. Dura Europos Synagogue (photograph by Fred Anderegg, after Goodenough, *Jewish Symbols* 11, pl. vi).

throne labeled as Solomon's is depicted with alternating eagles and lions resting on the sides of each step.[179] Significantly, the throne of Ahasveros, of which far more has survived, is depicted in a similar way (Figure 42).[180] Thus, at Dura, Solomon and Ahasveros sit on thrones of similar design. Is this intended to suggest that they sat on the same throne? Based on Targumic traditions, this interpretation is certainly possible.

The portrayal of Biblical heroes and animals is significant, although it is not revolutionary. No fewer than nineteen Biblical figures are said to be portrayed on Solomon's throne. The *Targum Sheni's* portraits expand upon a motif that is found already in classical midrashim and in early targumim.[181] These sources describe the Divine throne as having been decorated with the image of the patriarch Jacob. In *Genesis Rabba* 82:2, for example, God lauds "Jacob, whose image (אי׳קונין) is carved (חקוקה) on my throne." The *Targum Sheni's* interest in animals is preceded by the *Pesikta de-Rav Kahana*, another classical Amoraic

43. Bas relief of a soldier and vintners from the Chorazin Synagogue (courtesy of the E. L. Sukenik Archive, Institute of Archaeology, Hebrew University of Jerusalem).

midrash. There, the throne is described: "a golden scepter was suspended behind it, and a dove was at its top. A golden wreath was in the dove's mouth, and when he [Solomon] sat under it on the seat [of the throne] the wreath would touch but not quite touch his head."[182] This scepter is clearly drawn from Roman imperial iconography, where the emperor's scepter is topped with an eagle. In *Targum Sheni*, this wreath is automated: "When the king ascended and sat down upon the royal throne, the great eagle would go around and take the royal wreath and place the wreath upon King Solomon's head. . . ."[183]

The visual themes of this midrash, as well as that of *Targum Sheni*, mesh well with imagery within late antique public contexts and provide a *Sitz im Leben* for these texts. Bas reliefs of animals appear often in the Beth She'arim catacomb complex, including, as we have seen, those where the tombs of rabbis are present.[184] The same is true of Byzantine-period synagogues, where, as in church decoration, all sorts of animals are to be found. Lions sculpted in the round and lions and birds as decorative elements of Torah shrines are particularly evocative.[185]

The broad range of imagery at Chorazin provides a unique set of parallels to our text. Animals appear quite commonly, including hunting scenes, a centaur, and a lioness suckling her young. Among the discoveries were a throne, apparently with reliefs of animals carved on the forward finials of its armrests; a large sculpted lion; fragments of a lioness; and apparently another lion and a panther (Figures 36, 43).[186] Ze'ev Yeivin proposes that the chair at Chorazin rested on a raised platform that was enclosed within an aedicula supported by two columns.[187] Lions and birds appear in the Torah shrine panel of the Beth Alpha mosaic (Figure 78); lions crown the Nabratein Torah shrine aedicula (Figure 79) and appear on the Torah shrine base from the synagogue of En Samsam in the Golan Heights

44. Bas relief of Medusa from the Chorazin Synagogue (photograph by Steven Fine).

(Figures 37–38).[188] The eschatological image of predators and domesticated animals dwelling in peace not only influenced the Targum's depiction of Solomon's throne, but also the floor mosaic of the Meroth synagogue. There a sheep and a wolf face toward a footed fountain filled with drinking water. This rather standard iconography was Judaized through the addition of Isaiah 65:25: "the wolf and the lamb will graze together."[189]

Unlike our *Targum Sheni* tradition, human figures are not noted in classical rabbinic descriptions of Solomon's throne. One is nonetheless reminded of the numerous Biblical figures at Dura Europos and, more to the point, the images of Noah, his sons, Abraham, Sarah, Isaac, Aaron, and Daniel in various Palestinian synagogue settings from Byzantine Palestine – not to mention the repetitive presence of images of Biblical heroes in church contexts. The decoration of book bindings, service vessels, wall mosaics, and church domes with repetitive human figures (be they Prophets or saints) is ubiquitous in Christian settings.[190] Human imagery in the synagogue at Chorazin is extensive.

This includes hunting and prey scenes, wine production, Medusa (Figure 44), Eros, Zeus–Serapis, and the Rape of Ganymede, although I doubt that by this late date Jews were particularly cognizant of the sources of this imagery (any more than most contemporary Christians were aware of origins when they used similar imagery, or most Americans [particularly Jews] are aware, say, that a dove holding an olive branch in his mouth represents Noah's dove as the "Holy Spirit" of Christian tradition).[191]

Wreaths were very common among the decorations of Byzantine-period synagogues and churches. The wreath had been adopted by Jews as early as the Hasmonean period.[192] At Qasrin, for example, it appears on the lintel of the synagogue's main portal, and at Chorazin wreaths appear eight times.[193] Wreaths are mentioned in Jewish liturgical texts with some frequency. Although the zodiac does not appear in *Targum Sheni*, a Hebrew description of the throne has it that fine stones and pearls were set above Solomon's head to correspond to the signs of the zodiac.[194] The zodiac is a major theme, as we have seen, in synagogue mosaics.[195] These parallels are *not* to suggest that the Targumic traditions of Solomon's throne necessarily influenced the synagogue art or that the art necessarily influenced the Targum. My only claim is that the Targum, a product of the late antique synagogue and study house,[196] and ancient synagogue art share important themes and motifs.

Unlike Josephus, who scorned Solomon's use of animal sculpture,[197] the *Targum Sheni* follows on Biblical and rabbinic literature (and paralleling archaeological discoveries), delighting in this imagery. One wonders whether the opulence of the Targum is more than just a response to the richness of the Biblical narrative and the rabbinic tendency to expansive fantasy in imagining the heroic past. Perhaps this adaptation of Byzantine automata includes within it a response or reaction to Byzantine "thrones of Solomon" and to the general lavishness of Christian art with which Jews would certainly have been familiar in Christian Palestine.[198] The famous comment ascribed to Justinian at the dedication of the Hagia Sophia in Constantinople rings in my ears: "Solomon, I have outdone you."[199]

HIDDUR MITZVAH AND ITS LIMITATIONS

Rabbinic literature shows considerable concern that artifacts used in ritual contexts be particularly fine. In medieval sources, these traditions were the generative source of a

legal category known as *hiddur mitzvah*, literally "beautification of the commandment." It refers to the desire to go "beyond the call of duty" in acquiring and preparing the implements necessary to fulfill Divine commandments.[200] The exegetical locus for this notion is Exodus 15:2, the magnificent "Song at the Sea." Exodus 15:2 is translated by the New Jewish Publication Society (*NJPS*) version as "this is my God, and I will enshrine (or, alternatively, 'glorify') him, my father's God, and I will exalt him." The word translated "enshrine" or "glorify," *ve-anvehu* (ואנוהו), appears only once in the Bible; hence, its interpretation is quite opaque and open to interpretation.[201] With our homilists, *NJPS* assumed that the root is *naeh*, "glory or beauty."[202] The first place where this approach appears is a Tannaitic midrash on Exodus, the *Mekhilta of Rabbi Ishmael*. There, we read:[203]

"I will glorify him" (Exodus 15:2).
Says Rabbi Ishmael: And is it possible for flesh and blood to glorify his creator?
Rather, I will glorify him through commandments (*mitsvot*). I will make before him a beautiful (*naeh*) lulav, a beautiful *sukkah*, beautiful fringes and beautiful phylacteries. . . .

The list of artifacts is adjusted to various circumstances in the rabbinic corpus. In *b. Shabbat* 133b, the *shofar* is added to the list, as is the writing of a Torah scroll "with fine (*naeh*) ink and a fine pen by a skilled scribe, and he should wrap it in beautiful silks."[204] Other Tannaitic sources suggest that scrolls were wrapped in fine embroidered cloths[205] adorned with bells that "make noise."[206]

Although *hiddur mitzvah* was a positive value in rabbinic sources, this as yet unarticulated category did not supercede other values that were considered to be more essential. Thus, a Torah scroll should be made of the finest materials by the best scribe available. Its wrappings could be beautified as well. A tradition preserved in Byzantine-period collections has it that when the Jews of Alexandria attempted to beautify the manuscript of their scrolls by writing the Tetragrammaton in golden letters, the rabbis are said to have disallowed the innovation.[207] One is reminded of the practice found in the Qumran library of writing the Tetragrammaton in paleo-Hebrew script in places where the remainder of the manuscript was written in Hebrew square script.[208] The rabbis considered each Torah scroll to be a facsimile of the scroll received by Moses,[209] and therefore any diversion from standard production and writing procedures was unacceptable.

Gold and silver plating of ram's horns (*shofar*) was permitted, provided the gold did not affect the sound (which was, of course, the essential function of this ritual appurtenance).[210] For the Tannaim, *lulav* bunches could not be bound with materials not derived from the palm, although the rabbis did discuss the possibility that bunches bound with gold bands existed in Second Temple times.[211] According to *m. Megillah* 4:8, *tefillin* may not be made round, nor may they be plated with gold. Later traditions consider the form and color of the *tefillin* to be "laws from Moses at Sinai."[212] The mishnah explains that the avoidance of golden *tefillin* was a response to the heretical practice of donning golden phylacteries.[213] The maintenance of black *tefillin* was thus perceived as a boundary marker within the Jewish community.

The *Mekhilta* further explores the meaning of *ve-anvehu*, pairing the notion of beautifying God with a common rabbinic identification of the Temple as God's *naveh* (נוה), "His habitation."[214] The two possibilities offered by *NJPS* are assumed by the rabbis:

Rabbi Jose the son of the Damascene says: I will make before him a beautiful Temple, for *naveh* denotes the Temple. . . .

The rabbis remembered the beauty of the Temple as a developing phenomenon, a memory that accords with reality. With no concern for the direct inspiration of Roman public architecture, a Tannaitic tradition preserved in *b. Sukkah* 51b could claim that "whoever did not see Jerusalem in its glory never saw a beautiful city. Whoever has never seen the Temple as it stood (בבנינו) never saw a beautiful building"; and another in *b. Baba Batra* 4a could state: "whoever has never seen the Temple of Herod has never seen a beautiful building." (Figure 45).[215] Although unarticulated, appreciation of the Temple's physical splendor is implicit in the glowing Tannaitic presentations of the Temple's architecture.[216] It squares nicely with the massive remains of Herod's Temple, Josephus's descriptions,[217] and positive evaluations by a number of

45. The Temple of Jerusalem, model at the Holyland Hotel, Jerusalem. The "Gates of Nicanor" are in the middle-ground (photograph by Steven Fine).

Roman authors. These include Pliny the Elder, who called Jerusalem "the most famous city of the east."[218]

Rabbinic sources contain a number of descriptions of golden vessels donated by individuals to the Temple. These include a golden vine and lamp that were suspended above the entrance to the shrine and a golden tablet inscribed with the trial by bitter waters of the accused wife (said to have reflected sparks of sunlight) given by Queen Helena of Adiabene.[219] They also describe gold-covered horns of wreathed oxen that *m. Bikkurim* 3:3 recalls pulled wagons of first fruits to Jerusalem, perhaps carrying silver and gold baskets brought by the wealthy and donated together with the fruits.[220] Donation by individuals is well attested. Donors included a certain Ben Gamla who replaced the two wooden lots used in the scapegoat ceremony of Yom Kippur with golden lots.[221] *Mishnah Yoma* 3:10 provides a list of donors to the Temple. These are Ben Qatin, who made twelve spigots for the brazen laver and other improvements; Queen Helene of Adiabene and her son King Monobases, who gave gold handles for the vessels of Yom Kippur; and Nicanor of Alexandria, who gave doors of Corinthian bronze that shone as brightly as gold.[222] These donations were typical of Roman euergetism, of individuals benefacting the community and thus gaining communal position. *Mishnah Yoma* 3:10 makes this euergetic impulse clear in reference to the donors listed: "they were remembered with praise."[223] An ossuary discovered in a tomb on Jerusalem's Mt. Scopus in 1902 contains the following Greek inscription: "bones of the sons of Nicanor the Alexandrian, who made the doors."[224] Nicanor's euergetism was so greatly esteemed that its influence continued at least a generation beyond his lifetime – to be remembered and embellished by the rabbis centuries later.

The continual upgrading of the Temple furnishings throughout the Second Temple period is a theme that appears a number of times in rabbinic sources. The gates of the Temple, excluding Nicanor's bronze gate, were at some point replaced with golden ones, as were the scapegoat lots and the handles of the Yom Kippur vessels.[225] Similarly, in *b. Menaḥot* 28b (and parallels), we are presented with a sense of the Temple vessels being upgraded as time went on:[226]

Rabbi Jose son of Rabbi Judah says: One may not make [the menorah] of wood as the Hasmonean dynasty did.
They said to him: Is this proof?
They had iron rods (שיפודים), and they covered them with tin.
They became more wealthy, and made them of silver.
They became even more wealthy, and made them of gold.

At the same time, the *Mekhilta of Rabbi Ishmael* and other sources were alert to Deuteronomic prohibitions against Jews building alternative temples to the Temple of Jerusalem, the Samaritan temple on Mt. Gerizim[227] and the temple of Onias in Egypt being the prime examples in recent memory.[228] The *Mekhilta*, commenting on Exodus 20:20, "gods of silver and gold do not make for yourselves," forbids the placement of cherubs like those in the Tabernacle and in Solomon's Temple in "synagogues and study houses."[229] Other texts forbid the construction of whole buildings modeled on the Temple.[230] An apparently

Tannaitic tradition preserved in *b. Rosh ha-Shanah* 24a–b (and parallels) makes this point:[231]

Our Rabbis taught: No one may make a building in the form of the Shrine, an exedra[232] in place of the entrance hall, a courtyard in place of the court,
a table in place of the table of the showbread,
a menorah in place of the menorah,
but one may make (a menorah) with five, six or eight lamps[233]. Even of other metals you shall not make a menorah.

The concern of these traditions is to maintain the uniqueness of the Temple, particularly as the increasingly holy synagogue was ascribed with Temple-like qualities. The balance between the synagogue as a beautiful "holy place" or "small temple" and overstepping the Deuteronomic prohibition against alternate temples was well understood by the rabbis.

ART AND "ANTI-IDOLISM" IN RABBINIC LITERATURE: IDOLATRY IN THE PUBLIC REALM

Even the most accepting of rabbinic sources on the visual dimension reflect disdain for "art" serving idolatrous purposes. This rabbinic "anti-idolism" is based on negative Biblical attitudes toward idolatrous or potentially idolatrous images. Such texts as the Second Commandment of the Decalogue (Exodus 20:4–6; Deuteronomy 5:7–10) and many lesser-known sources set the tone for Jewish attitudes. Whereas Biblical sources leave little leeway in regard to idolatrous images, the rabbis were equivocal – reflecting the ambiguities of acting upon Biblical ideals in what for them was the less than ideal world of late antiquity. Rabbinic sources oscillate between stringency and leniency in a way that exemplifies the difficulties involved in evoking either extreme in a world where Jews were a minority living under a strongly visual (and "idolatrous") imperial domination.[234] Rabbinic attitudes divide into two distinct categories. The first refers to attitudes toward the religious art of the Other within public contexts where the rabbis had little control or influence. The second is the distinctly Jewish realm, where rabbinic influence was stronger.

LIVING WITH IDOLATRY: PUBLIC CONTEXTS

The rabbis well understood the complexities of living in the Roman cities of late antique Palestine. These were intensely visual environments, with "idolatrous" sculpture on almost every street corner. The rabbis were a deeply urban community, thriving in the growing cities of Roman Palestine. Their vision of the Roman city began with the local. They called the cities where they lived by historic Hebrew names, not sharing this element of the geography with their imperialist neighbors. Rabbis lived in Lod, while Romans (with, no doubt, some Jews) built up the self-same city of Lydda (after 200 CE Diospolis). They lived in Beth Guvrin, called in Greek, Eleutheropolis, in Sepphoris, known to others as Diocaesarea, and in the Biblical city of Beth Shean, called Scythopolis – all of which were cities of *Eretz Israel*. Like their co-religionists in the cities and backwaters of Palestine, Jews were in constant contact with Roman "idolatry." Where the Psalmist once could lament, "How shall we sing the Lord's song in a foreign land?" (Psalm 137:4), the rabbis now were confronted with this question in their own increasingly colonized land.

A major center of the rabbinic community during the third and fourth centuries was Tiberias, on the western shore of the Sea of Galilee. Named for Emperor Tiberias, the city was built by Herod Antipas and inaugurated in 18 C.E. While little of Roman Tiberias has been excavated, we have some evidence for its architecture. Josephus describes Herod Antipas's palace and mentions baths and a stadium in first-century Tiberias. The discovery of a Roman-period stadium was recently announced.[235] Remains of Roman period baths, a roofed marketplace, a basilica, the cardo, and the south gate of the city have also been uncovered.[236] Coins minted under the Antonine emperors portray a temple with four columns and a triangular pediment. Seated within the temple is the image of a god who may be Zeus.[237] Nicole Belayche cautiously identifies this building with the *Hadrianeum*, a temple dedicated to Hadrian, which the emperor himself decided to have built in Tiberias when he visited Palestine in 119/20. During the third century, the church father Epiphanius writes that "there was a very large temple in the city already. I think they may have called it the *Hadrianeum*. The citizens may have been trying to restore the *Hadrianeum*, which was standing unfinished, for a public bath."[238] These slight remains of a once-great Roman city correlate well with rabbinic descriptions of life in this typical Roman provincial city.

Living within this environment, Jews of the rabbinic community (and undoubtedly others as well) developed numerous survival tactics, including avoiding certain places, detours beyond the usual path, spitting at idols, and the simple aversion of eyes. These were an internal way of navigating a difficult terrain, a "hidden transcript" that might have been obvious to other Jews even as it was unrecognized by the Romans.[239] Toleration of "idols" was usually less a matter of "liberality" (a term often used to describe some rabbinic positions) than a necessary survival skill. Stringency was a matter of exceptional piety and had real implications for the course of daily life. Within the Romanized environment of late antique Palestine, the rabbis understood the need to reach a *modus vivendi* with pagan religious artifacts in public contexts such as baths, streets, and fountains – contexts over which they had little or no control and whose use was of great communal value – if not a necessity. *Tosefta Avodah Zarah* 6:6, for example, provides an excellent example of a slightly altered behavior as a "hidden transcript" in response to the threat of being religiously compromised through contact with idolatry. This text permits drinking from public aqueducts "that bring water to cities." The aqueducts in question are said to have had nozzles decorated with "idolatrous" sculpture. Jews could drink from these nozzles, the Tosefta suggests, as long as their lips did not touch the nozzle. Touching the nozzle, the rabbis conjectured, could be misconstrued as a pious act of "kissing idolatry." Instead, the Tosefta suggests that he "receive [water] in his hands and drink. . . ." Hand drinking is set out as an appropriate response, mediating between Jewish discomfort with idolatrous imagery and a need for water. Another member of the rabbinic community would understand and presumably appreciate the "hidden transcript" involved in hand drinking in this way. However, the gesture would likely go right past a Roman observer![240] What the Tosefta does not suggest is that Jews refrain from drinking water from fountains bearing forbidden imagery.

The complexities involved in negotiating the urban environment are expressed in the famous story of Rabban Gamaliel II in the baths of Aphrodite.[241] This text is often taken as representing the crux of the Jewish–Roman cultural dilemma. According to *m. Avodah Zarah* 3:4, Rabban Gamaliel visited the baths of Aphrodite while in Akko, a Phoenician port known in Greek as Ptolemais and to us as Acre. Here in this ancient "city of the sea," Rabban Gamaliel explains his actions to a questioner identified as "Peroqlos son of Peloslos":[242]

Peroqlos son of Peloslos asked Rabban Gamaliel in Akko, when he was bathing in the bathhouse of Aphrodite. He said to him, "It is written in your Torah, And there shall cleave nothing of a devoted thing to your hand" (Deuteranomy 13:8). How is it that you are bathing in the bathhouse of Aphrodite? He said to him: One does not answer in a bathhouse.

When he came out, he said to him: I did not come into her domain. She came into mine. They do not say, "let us make a bathhouse as an ornament (noy) to Aphrodite." But they say: "Let us make Aphrodite as an ornament to the bathhouse."

Whether this conversation occurred or not and whether Peroqlos was Jewish or not is not really significant. This story served as a vehicle for the rabbinic author to question the limits of participation in the general idolatrous culture through discussion of Rabban Gamaliel's behavior.[243] Finding himself in nearby yet foreign territory, speaking to an individual whose name and whose father's name were Greek (whether gentile or Jew), this leader of the early Tannaitic community explains that Aphrodite was but a decoration and not the subject of cult in baths.[244] Peroqlos does not question Jewish use of the baths per se. Jews had used them for centuries, and rabbis were often to be found in these public facilities. The issue was the Jewishly illicit sculpture. Rabbis were well aware that some statues were worshiped and others not – a factor they used legally to gain some leeway with which to interact with the idolatrous environment in which they struggled to live.[245] The Mishnah adds support to Rabban Gamaliel's position:

If you were given much money, you would not enter before your idol naked, or suffering a flux, nor would you urinate before it.
Yet this (idol) stands beside the gutter and all the people urinate in front of her.
It is said only "[. . .] you shall hew down the graven images of] their gods," (Deuteronomy 12:3) – that which is treated as a god is prohibited, but that which is not treated as a god is permitted.

The balance between tolerable and forbidden imagery was thus context-specific and clearly precarious. By positing (or acknowledging) the fact that some images were worshiped while others were not, the rabbis were able to create a very complex cultural space in which to navigate.[246] Complex discussion of the status of a statue based on context allowed Jews to participate in the non-Jewish public domain while maintaining a sense of their own propriety. Yaron Z. Eliav notes that "the writer's use of the Hebrew term noy corresponds to the Latin ornamen-

tum – which, for many in the Roman world, signified a statue that had not been transformed in the formal process of consecratio into a sacred artifact (res sacra). In the mind of the ancients, these procedures instilled the statue with the 'holy spirit' – pneuma (or its Latin equivalent the numen, i.e., the divine power, presence, and will) – of one of the gods or, alternatively, the numen or genius of one of the emperors."[247] The approach ascribed to Rabban Gamaliel is both cognizant of Roman categories and uses them in order to facilitate Jewish presence in the Bath of Aphrodite. It should be remembered that others in Ptolemais clearly thought differently of Aphrodite – or at least of some sculptures of Aphrodite. Coins minted in Ptolemais under the emperor Gallen (ruled 253–68) express the local significance of this goddess. There, the image of Aphrodite is shown rising from the bath and standing within a niche.[248]

Mishnah Avodah Zarah 1:7 imagines Jews building bathhouses in cooperation with their non-Jewish neighbors, with the stipulation that "when they arrive to the vault (or, niche), and set the idol within it, it is forbidden [to Jews] to build." The presence of an idolatrous statue within a bathhouse used by Jews and gentiles together is taken here to be de rigueur. The Mishnah does not question whether Jews may participate in building a bathhouse, an institution that was accepted by Palestinian Jews. The question was only at what point must Jews desist from building for fear that they might be implicated in the idolatry of their neighbors. Participation in building a bathhouse containing an "idol" is much more serious, of course, than casually bathing in the "Bathhouse of Aphrodite" in a mainly pagan city like Acre.

About a century and a half after Rabban Gamaliel, the Tiberian sage and pivotal rabbinic leader Rabbi Johanan son of Napha allowed followers to use what seems to have been a water installation (a nymphaeum, or perhaps a bath) in the southern Syrian city of Bostra:[249]

Rabbi Simeon son of Laqish was in Bostra.
He saw them (Jews?) sprinkling (water) to this Aphrodite
(מזלפין להדא אפרודיטי).[250]
He said to them: Is it not forbidden?
He came and asked Rabbi Johanan.
Rabbi Johanan said to him, in the name of Rabbi Simeon son of Jehozedek:
That which is public property is not forbidden.

Rabbi Johanan overruled his compatriot, Rabbi Simeon son of Laqish. Rabbi Simeon's concern seems to have been not so much the sculpture, but possibly illicit Jewish reverence toward it. Unfortunately, we cannot know what kind of behavior Rabbi Simeon son of Laqish saw, or even who he saw. It was clearly not serious enough to raise Rabbi Johanan's ire and to cause him to take the serious step of forbidding Jewish use of this water source.

The significance of Rabban Gamaliel's and Rabbi Johanan's responses should not to be underestimated. These leaders allowed Jews to participate in the life of the public institutions of the Roman city over the objections of rabbinic contemporaries. The voices of Peroqlos son of Peloslos and Rabbi Simeon son of Laqish speak for more conservative rabbinic opinions – opinion that functioned somewhere between extreme pietism and the pragmaticism of the titular rabbinic leaders of their days, Rabban Gamaliel and Rabbi Johanan. On a practical level, these traditions suggest that Jews associated with the rabbis maintained a kind of internal "map" of idolatrous space in their cities, and responded to the ever-present sculpture with an almost ritualized response that was expressed through scorn, spitting, and avoidance – but also through real knowledge of the religious landscape in which they lived.

This mapping process is well expressed in the Amoraic presentation of a first-generation amora, Rabbi Nahum son of Simai, known as "Rabbi Nahum of the Holy of Holies." Nahum, who flourished near the beginning of the third century, appears three times as the representative of the most extreme acceptable position toward idolatry within the rabbinic community. In the *Jerusalem Talmud*, tractate *Avodah Zarah* 3: 1, 42b–c, we read:

Asyan the carpenter in the name of Rabbi Johanan: "Likenesses[251] (האיקוניות): why are they prohibited?"
"Because they (that is, gentiles) offer up incense before them at the time that they are setup."
Said Rabbi Johanan: It is permitted to look upon them at the time that they fall.
What is the reason?
"You will look upon the destruction of the wicked (Psalm 37:34)."
It is written: "He who walks below images (הצורות) or likenesses – One does not look upon them on the Sabbath."
More than that, even on weekdays one must not look at likenesses.
What is the reason?
"Do not turn toward the idols (Leviticus 19:4)" – do not turn to serve them.
Rabbi Judah says: Do not turn to look at them at all (ממש).

When Rabbi Nahum son of Simai died, they covered up the likenesses with mats.
They said: "Just as he did not look at them when he was alive, he should not look at them after his death."

Averting eyes, particularly on the Sabbath, was a subtle form of cultural resistance. Only an insider might be cognizant of this "hidden transcript." It is significant that Asyan is a carpenter, as tradesmen were likely to come in contact with idolatry in the course of their work and so in need of specific guidance.[252] Discussions of whether Jews were permitted to build "pagan" structures and precisely what parts they might construct reflect the ambiguities of earning one's living in a religious and architectural environment to which the rabbis could only react.[253]

Rabbinic sources suggest that Nahum achieved his title because "he never looked upon the image on a coin." His behavior is reminiscent of pietists during the Second Temple period, who apparently avoided idolatrous imagery on coins as well.[254] From statuary to simple coinage, Nahum is said to have averted his eyes from potentially idolatrous Roman imagery. This is presented as an act of virtuoso piety, indicative of his "holiness."

A somewhat less passive response to Roman idolatry in the public domain appears in *y. Avodah Zarah* 3:13, 43b. Again, Nahum is used to represent the extremes of rabbinic piety:[255]

Gamaliel Zuga supported himself on Rabbi Simeon son of Laqish [as they walked].
When they reached an image (תבניתא),[256] he (Gamaliel Zuga) said to him:
"Should we pass before it?"
He (Rabbi Simeon son of Laqish) said: "Pass before it and put its eyes out."

Rabbi Isaac son of Matnah supported himself on Rabbi Johanan.
When they reached the statue at the *boule* (the council building צלמא דבולי), he (Rabbi Isaac son of Matnah) said to him:
Should we pass before it?
He (Rabbi Johanan) said: "Pass before it and put its eyes out."

Rabbi Jacob son of Idi supported himself on Rabbi Joshua son of Levi.
They reached the image of *aduri* (or alternately, they came behind an image).[257]
He (Rabbi Joshua son of Levi) said to him:
"Nahum of the Holy of Holies would pass, and you, you do not [wish to] pass? "Pass before it and put its eyes out. . . ."

It is not clear what is meant by "put its eyes out." Perhaps reflecting Jewish practice in his own day, Lithuanian commentator Moses son of Simeon Margoliot (d. 1781) writes: "do not be concerned to pass before it. *And blind its eyes*: That is to say, are you embarrassed to pass before it? Pass, and let it be humiliated because you treat it as a short cut" (a form of humiliation that the rabbis did not countenance on the Temple Mount or even in a destroyed synagogue)."[258] This is a wonderfully inside-focused response, the "transcript" of which would certainly have been lost on both a Roman and a modern-day observer! Blidstein conjectures that the rabbis spit in the eyes of the statues, and Peter Schäfer revises it to read: Shut your [own] eyes.[259] Whatever the case – and each of the scenarios fits rabbinic culture – this scorn somehow permitted these rabbinic leaders to use the public roads despite the presence of unacceptable sculpture. Spitting is surely a less "hidden" form of derision, although that depends on how it is carried out. I am reminded of contemporary Hassidim who at the point where the uncensored version of the *Alenu* prayer reads, "for they bow down to emptiness and to nothingness (*riq*), and pray to a god who will not save," spit on the floor (*riq* is also Hebrew for spit). While some are indecorous, others are quite subtle at this point.[260] This response was truly a counterpoint to pagan treatment of divine images. Peter Brown writes graphically of the types of pious expression with which polytheists treated their gods:[261]

Bowing, of course, was never enough when it came to the gods. Pagans would blow kisses to their idols. They would lift little children up to kiss their faces. They would sit and gossip with them, placing food, even letters, at their feet. They wished to sleep with them. . . .

Nahum's behavior is taken as the paragon of rabbinic virtue, against which any other piety is to be judged. Through recourse to his virtuoso piety, pietistic behavior that is even more restrictive is blocked. Nahum's approach is used in a similar way in *b. Avodah Zarah* 50a:[262]

The palace of King Yannai (בי ינאי מלכא) was in ruins.
Gentiles came and set up a Mercury there (and worshipped it).[263]
Other Gentiles who did not worship Mercury came and removed them, and paved the roads and streets with them.
Some sages refrained [from walking on them], and there are some sages who did not refrain [from walking on them].
Said Rabbi Johanan: The son of the holy ones walks on them, shall we abstain?

Belayche notes that "Mercuries" were not covered under imperial legislation that protected public religious buildings and tombs, *loci religiosi*. She argues that this lack of legal status may set the context for the destruction of the Tiberian Mercuries.[264] The ambiguous status of the stones of Mercuries in Roman law and practice thus facilitated leniency in rabbinic thought. For Nahum, a first-generation Amora, the reused stones of Mercuries were sufficiently removed from idolatrous worship ("nullified" in rabbinic parlance), that they might be walked on. This is a fascinating case where the stones maintain their possibly idolatrous status even after they have visually disappeared into the pavement of the street and their previous use forgotten by the general populace. By the third Amoraic generation, near mid-century, members of the rabbinic community still remembered the Mercury stones. These rabbis questioned whether this leniency was sanctioned by Jewish law and attempted to move stringently beyond it. Rabbi Johanan, who clearly wanted to maintain access to the public thoroughfare that had been paved with Mercury stones, used the example of Nahum in order to stave off increasing stringency. Remembrance of Nahum's piety was thus to serve a mimetic effect within the rabbinic community, as a barrier against further seclusion of the rabbis and their followers. As Nahum was honored for his piety in life, in death the seemingly unusual step of covering the statues was taken, we are told, so that he would not be exposed to impious sculpture. If this is the case, then the holy man seems to have been venerated beyond the inner circle of rabbis, perhaps even beyond the Jewish community (or minimally, rabbis imagined that this type of reverence was possible).[265]

The strictness of Nahum – and the even more limiting approaches against which our traditions argue – would have the effect of highly restricting Jewish participation in the Greco–Roman urban environment. Certain well-traveled areas, it seems, would have been off-limits. This was precisely the path taken by some Christian pietists. Unlike many Christian holy men, rabbinic holy men generally engaged with urban society and did not generally develop communities of separatist pietists. Evidence for Jewish pietism that has eschewed the urban context may be found in the writings of the church father Hippolytus of Rome (third century). Hippolytus ascribes almost ascetic piety to the first-century "Essenes." It seems to me quite likely that Hippolytus's "Essenes" are a projection of later practice of Jews or Christians on to the Essenes of Second Temple period Judaea.[266] According to Hippolytus, some of them discipline themselves more than is requisite, so that they would not handle even a current coin, saying that they ought not either to carry, or behold, or fashion an image; wherefore no one of those goes into a city, lest he should enter through a gate at which statues are erected, regarding it a violation of the law to pass beneath images.[267]

While avoidance of coins is a behavior dating to the Second Temple period, the decoration of city gates with sculpture was not a feature of Second Temple period Judaean architecture. The position ascribed to "Essenes" by Hippolytus represents the position against which our traditions of Nahum respond. Even if Hippolytus's comments are mere fantasy or are drawn from the behaviors of Christian pietists, the scenario he suggests is only a step or two beyond the most extreme known member of the third-century Palestinian rabbinic community, Nahum of the Holy of Holies.

The rabbis were well aware that some Jews were attracted to Roman religion and that the temptation could readily be satiated. Hence, the well-known midrash of Rebecca walking by the way, carrying Jacob and Esau in her womb. When she passed a synagogue or study house, Jacob clamored to get out, but Esau (a rabbinic cipher for Rome) wanted out when she passed "a place of idolatry."[268] The point, for our purposes, is that the rabbis could imagine the matriarch Rebecca passing a "house of idolatry" at all – a common occurrence for Jewish men and women in Rome-dominated "Palestine." Similarly, in their search for reasons why Elisha son of Abuyah went bad, one explanation among many given by the rabbis is that "his mother, when she was pregnant with him, passed by houses of idolatry and smelled 'that kind' (a circumlocution, it seems, for incense) and the odor penetrated her body like the venom of a snake."[269] The mere act of passing too close was enough to destine her baby to no good! Later versions imagine a much more serious infraction: The problem was not merely the odor encountered in the public arena, but that "Mrs. Abuyah" was given some sort of food in the "houses of idolatry," which she ate.[270] Either way, this text expresses a clear warning to pregnant mothers and to their families! The possibility of idolatrous behavior by Jews is discussed in rabbinic literature, although most of these discussions seem to be more theoretical than actual.[271] *Jerusalem Talmud Avodah Zarah* 4:4, 43d, suggests a case of Jewish idolatry and a possible rabbinic response:

Rabbi Johanan said to Bar Drosai: Go and break those images in the bath house.

He went down and broke all but one.
Said Rabbi Jose son of Rabbi Bun: An Israelite was suspected to have burned incense upon it.

This is the only anecdotal description of what appears to be the destruction of specific sculpture under rabbinic auspices. It illustrates Mishnah *Avodah Zarah* 4:4, which sets out that an idol worshipped by a Jew cannot be "nullified" (rendered religiously neutral) by a non-Jew. Shamma Friedman suggests that Bar Drosai was a non-Jew of Semitic origins with ties to the rabbinic community.[272] Legendary for his strength (and his appetite), Friedman suggests that Bar Drosai worked on behalf of the rabbis. As a non-Jew, Bar Drosai was capable of removing the religious potentiality of those images – something that the rabbis believed a Jew was incapable of doing. In keeping with *m. Avodah Zarah* 4:4, he left one statue still standing. We cannot, of course, be sure of this reconstruction or of Rabbi Johanan's intention. Rabbi Jose son of Rabbi Bun's explanation, however, suggests that the extralegal scenario posited by Friedman would have been wholly believable to third- and fourth-century rabbis. Urbach suggests that the suspicion that a Jew had worshipped a statue in the bathhouse was a rare one, "as indeed the whole tone of the story indicates."[273] He is probably right.

Generally, responses within the rabbinic community to "pagan" imagery were more passive – like that of Asyan the carpenter with which I began this section. We have seen that "when Rabbi Nahum son of Simai died, they covered up the likenesses with mats."[274] The *Jerusalem Talmud* believed that the rabbis of the third century had been sufficiently powerful to cover the sculpture for the limited duration of a funeral. They had no power, it seems, to rid their surroundings of statuary of which they disapproved on a permanent basis (nor could they imagine such power). For this, they waited for the sort of miracle that one could expect in the earthquake-prone Jordan Rift Valley:

When Rabbi Ḥanan died, the statues (אנדרטיא) were overturned.
When Rabbi Johanan died, the images (איקונייא) were overturned.
When Rabbi Hoshaya died the column of Tiberias (קלון דטיבריא) fell.[275]

Adding complexity to our picture, the Yerushalmi suggests that the images were overturned for Rabbi Johanan in homage to his physical beauty – not due to idolatry at all! When Jewish idolatry was at stake, however, the rabbis could contemplate the kinds of tactics apparently perpetrated by Bar Drosai on their behalf.

We really do not know how widespread Jewish participation in Roman cult was in late antiquity, although if rabbinic literature is any measure, it was limited. I am nonetheless reminded of a temple built at Qasion on the border of Phoenicia in the Upper Galilee, to which Jews donated a monumental inscribed lintel. The Greek inscription, which appears within a conventional Herculean knot, bespeaks a closeness to the Severan dynasty that is also represented in rabbinic sources:[276]

For the salvation of our masters the rulers, the Caesars,
L[ucius] Sept[imius] Severus Pius
Pert[inax] Aug[ustus], and M[arcus]
Aur[elius] A[nton]inus and L[ucius]
Sept[imius] G]eta, their sons, by a
vow of the Jews.

This Greek inscription describes Jewish eugeterism, although not necessarily mass Jewish participation in the local cult. As Antoninus, a legendary member of the Roman emperor and reputed friend of Rabbi Judah the Prince, is said to have donated a lamp to a synagogue,[277] so "the Jews" gave to a temple dedicated to the Severan imperial cult. The fact that the donation fulfills "a vow of the Jews" suggest that this was indeed a pagan site, to which an amorphous group of "Jews" donated a lintel (just as Rabbi Abun would do for the *Sidra Rabba* in Tiberias). Urbach has suggested that the rabbis focused their attention on the emperor cult.[278] Whether this was so or not is still open for discussion.[279] The evidence at Qasion certainly points in that direction, supporting Urbach's contention.

Lieberman and Urbach are probably correct that Jewish participation in Roman cults was not widespread. Lieberman notes in support just how few refutations of idolatry are scattered through rabbinic literature when compared with the ubiquities of Christian polemics.[280] Urbach makes similar claims, writing that "the consensus of opinion amongst the Rabbis in the third century was that all idolatrous impulses had been eradicated from amongst the people of Israel as early as the beginning of the Second Temple."[281] Both argue that in the rabbinic evaluation, the Jewish "taste for idolatry" had been conquered. Lieberman notes that ridicule of idols (ליצנותא דעבודה זרה) does exist in rabbinic literature, but it is limited. He is correct in distinguishing the situation of the rabbis from that of

the Christians. Christians wrote whole tracts on this subject, whereas Jews, it seems, were satisfied with a relatively few quips and anecdotes. This difference between Jews and Christians is dictated by the very different purposes and situations of the rabbis and the churchmen. While the rabbis were intent on shielding Jews from ever-more-present Roman idolatry (whether polytheistic or, later, Christian), the early Church was intent on destroying Roman religion and superceding it with its own.[282] The Church's goal was to convince (and later, to compel) "idolators" to take up Christian beliefs – and not to revert to their ancestral practice. Rabbinic sources, by contrast, suggest careful boundary construction through law and ridicule of pagan religion – but no panic over mass alienation from Judaism. This is expressed in the very term used to describe non-Jewish cult – *Avodah Zarah*, "alien (or 'foreign') worship."

The degree of disinterest in idolatry expressed in rabbinic literature has much to do with the nature of our sources. An instructive parallel may be drawn from Biblical studies. We have seen that the Biblical authors avoided engagement with the religious art of non-Jewish neighbors by treating it as so many fetishes. The rabbis, who saw their world through the prism of Scripture, seldom engaged with "pagans" (and later Christians) in apologetics – and certainly granted their gods no reality. Following upon a Biblical model, idolatry was not frontally engaged, but ridiculed – only when necessary was it grudgingly acknowledged.

The response to the threat of "idolatry" should not be underestimated, however. As in earlier generations, twice daily pious Jews were "inoculated" against idolatry through the liturgical recitation of Divine unity inherent in Deuteronomy 6:5, "Hear O Israel, the Lord our God, the Lord is one." Many other liturgical contexts made this point as well, for example, the repetition of texts like Psalm 115 in the *Hallel* on new moons and festivals. The rabbinic "cheer" upon seeing a destroyed "place of idolatry" – "Blessed is he who uprooted idolatry from our land"[283] – is of a piece with the very serious discussions of how to live with Roman "idolatry" on a daily basis. The *Tosefta* adds a short prayer: "May it be Your will, Lord our God, to uproot idolatry from all the places of Israel, and to return the heart of your servants to serve you."[284]

For the rabbis, the Roman world was a place where "we" Jews had no choice but to interact with "those" gentiles who practiced their "foreign cult." Jews who engaged in "foreign cult practices," whether polytheistic or Christian, were clearly beyond the norms of the common Judaism of this period. These individuals might eventually wash out of the Jewish community, allowing those who remained to maintain the rhetorical stance of Jewish unity and distance from idolatry.[285]

Art was an important boundary marker in Jewish definition of what was acceptable for "us" in "our" encounter with "them." Polemics against idols become much more pointed in Byzantine period sources than in rabbinic literature of late Roman times. This reflects the heightened religious danger of these Bible-reading though supercessionist pagans – whose religious buildings were architecturally and artistically almost indistinguishable from synagogues. In fact, the greatest church poet of the sixth century Romanos the Melodist, is said to have been a convert from Judaism,[286] and both Jews and Christians recited litugical poetry (*piyyut* in Hebrew, from the Greek *poiātas*) in their houses of worship (which were sometimes built and decorated by the same artisans). *Piyyutim* from the Byzantine era attack Christian "idols" face on and with great vehemence. This vehemence in itself is a form of boundary construction intended to keep Jews firmly within the fold and away from Christians. Anger toward Christian images was expressed within the Rabbinic community as early as Yannai's sixth-century liturgical poem against Christians and their cult.[287] Yannai rails against the Christians,

Who say to nothingness, save [*shoa*]![288]
    Who chose the disgustingly repulsive,
Who rejoice in statues of human figures
    Who cleave to the dead over the living,
Who become excited and turn aside to lies
    The experienced in evil, to do evil,
The polluted with sacrifices of the dead
    Who dispute Your commandments,
Who hide in the darkness their deeds
    Who . . . to the death of their god,
Who prostrate and pray to a bush and are prostrated
    Who passionately follow the error of their own
       creation,
Who believe in . . . to suffer
    Who are saddened on account of their idols,
Who burn those who see their mystery
    Who arrange a sacrifice [*minḥah*] of pig's blood,
Who, by their very nature, explode with illegitimate
    children
    Who fast and afflict themselves for emptiness,
Who acquire assemblages of bone
    Who moan to them on their festivals,

Who guard the emptiness of nothingness
    Who seize the world with their lies.

Note particularly Yannai's complaint that they "rejoice in statues of human figures," "prostrate and pray to a bush" (that is, the cross), are "saddened on account of their idols," and, most telling, pray to relics ("assemblages of bone") at their festivals. Yannai knew quite a lot about Christian images and cult, and let this knowledge be known in his poem. He assumed that his synagogue audience knew them and should despise them as well. This text well expresses the close proximity of Jews to Christians – a closeness that did not exist with Roman polytheists, whose religions were far more distant from Judaism. This is due not only to the vehemence of Christian imperial supercessionism, but also to the very proximity between Judaism and Christianity occasioned by Christian veneration of the Old Testament, their liturgical practice, and their attachment to the Holy Land. It was a closeness (both religious and geographic) that clearly bred active contempt. Jews expressed their side of this unequal relationship liturgically within the comfort and safety of the synagogue, in Hebrew – a language that few Christians understood. This was a "hidden transcript," an internal conversation, shielded from the ears of the Christian empire.

Another poetic example was published by Michael Sokoloff and Joseph Yahalom, a Byzantine-period Aramaic *piyyut* that explicitly refers to Christian icons. In this *piyyut*, the Jewish author portrays Jesus as the last in a long list of enemies of the Jews to engage in dialogue with Haman of the Esther story. Attempting to prove that his lot was worse than the hanged (that is, crucified) Haman, Jesus complains that he was[289]

Nailed on the wood [the cross, *qis*]
And my image in the church [*ba-Merqoles*][290]
Is painted on wood [*qis*].

Related to these texts is a somewhat earlier law, promulgated by Theodosius II in his name and in the name of Honorius on May 29, 408, according to which Jews were reprimanded for burning images of Jesus in effigy on the Feast of Esther.[291] Disdain for Christian religious art was an important element of Jewish self-understanding in Byzantine Palestine, a cultural barrier between the tightening colonialism of the Church and the Jewish minority. Although Halakhic discourses on idolatry from this period is scarce, those that do exist suggest the permeability of boundaries. A legal text known as *Sefer ha-Ma'asim le-Venei*

Eretz Yisrael, a work that preserves many practices from the later Byzantine period, suggests a case of boundary permeability in which Jewish male society watches out for "its" womenfolk from gentiles: "It is forbidden for a woman to decorate her daughter and take her out into the marketplace, because she endangers her life. A woman who perfumes herself (that is, carefully prepares herself) and goes to the houses of idolatry [churches], she is given lashes and her hair is shaved. It is forbidden for a woman to put earrings in her daughter's ears."[292] We have already seen what Byzantine period rabbinic sources imagined happened to the son of "Mrs. Abuyah" when she came too close to a place of "idolatry." This concern for boundaries is given credence from the other side of the relationship by a Christian of the last third of the sixth century. The Piacenza Pilgrim, aware that he was crossing a cultural boundary, describes his own encounter with the Jewish women of Nazareth even as he interpreted it within distinctly Christian categories:[293]

The Jewesses (*mulierum Hebraeis*) of that city are better looking than any other Jewesses in the whole country. They declare that this is Saint Mary's gift to them, for they also say that she was a relation of theirs. Though there is no love lost between Jews and Christians, these women are full of kindness (*caritate plenae*).

ROMAN IMAGERY WITHIN RABBINIC CONTROL

We have seen that rabbinic literature presents Jews participating fully in the art of late antiquity, so long as that art was not "idolatrous." If the public arena was so fully steeped in "pagan" art over which the rabbis had no real control, what about possibly idolatrous imagery within contexts where rabbis did have some influence? What did they allow/disallow among their own? The possibilities were extremely broad. The rabbis developed two separate categories: possibly illicit images that were owned by Jews, but not made by them, and art made specifically for Jewish contexts. One penetrating text describes an artifact with what some might have construed as idolatrous imagery that was kept by one sage, son of a sage:[294]

Rabbi Ḥiyya son of Rabbi Abba had a cup with the image of Tyche (Fortuna) of Rome drawn (צירה) on it.
He came and asked the sages [whether it was permitted].
They said: Since water runs down over it (the image), this is a form of nullification [and so permitted].

A bowl engraved with the image of Tyche affords a fine sense of the type of vessel intended by this *Jerusalem Talmud* tradition. Now in the Louvre, the bowl is said to have been discovered in Caesarea Maritima.[295] The image of Tyche is "nullified" through the use of this bowl, allowing a Jew who followed the opinions of the rabbis to keep it. When it was useful for Jews to own apparently idolatrous artifacts, a way was found to effect the procurement. According to Yigael Yadin, seeming "nullification," a kind of controlled destruction and rehabilitation of otherwise forbidden artifacts, is to be found beyond the rabbinic corpus.[296] Among Yadin's discoveries of the Bar Kokhba Revolt in the "Cave of Letters" was a group of bronze cooking pots and an incense shovel.[297] Many of these typically Roman artifacts originally bore images of human faces and a patera bears mythological imagery. These images were filed off of the vessels and kept by Bar Kokhba's followers. The medallion on the patera portrays: "Thetis, Achilles' mother, rides on a sea-centaur bringing weapons to her son." Yadin reports that the faces have been "rubbed and intentionally erased till there remains little more than the eye sockets. On Thetis' bosom, too, there are signs of rubbing."[298] The issue of nudity was clearly less vexing than the faces themselves.[299] "Nullification," in rabbinic law by a non-Jew, allowed for the use of artifacts drawn from the broader society – and their Judaization. The "nullification" required for Rabbi Ḥiyya son of Rabbi Abba's bowl was indeed minimalist. It is a subtle and impermanent boundary statement that allowed Rabbi Ḥiyya to maintain this otherwise forbidden imagery in his home.

The rabbis discussed in detail what constituted forbidden imagery within contexts controlled by Jews, and definitions were elastic. For example, the mere fact of being formed like an animal or even a human being did not automatically qualify an artifact as an idol (as it would have for Josephus and his fellow travelers). The question for the rabbis was limited to whether or not it was worshipped. Hence, a sculpture holding "a staff, bird or sphere," "a hand or a foot," "a sword, a wreath, a ring, an image or a snake," "a seal ring bearing the image of an idol," and numerous other artifacts had to be disposed of or "nullified" by a non-Jew because they were presumed to be worshipped or used for idolatrous purposes. Some rabbis softened the stringencies of these prohibitions, especially in regard to smaller artifacts that Jews were likely to own. *Tosefta Avodah*

Zarah 5:2 states, "If the seal was incised, it is prohibited for use as a seal, because an image is made thereby. If it projects, it is permitted to make a seal with it." Historical support is even brought in favor of these leniencies:

Rabbi Ḥanina son of Gamaliel says: "Those of father's household would seal with [seals bearing images of] faces."
Rabbi Lazar son of Rabbi Simeon says: "All sorts of faces were in Jerusalem, except for that of man."

Based on the scant archaeological evidence from first-century Jerusalem, I have suggested above that Rabbi Lazar son of Rabbi Simeon's comments may well reflect reality.[300] Taken together with firsthand testimony from Rabbi Ḥanina son of Gamaliel, in our context, Rabbi Lazar son of Rabbi Simeon's comment is used to legitimate what appears to be a leniency. This text dovetails nicely with the statement in *m. Rosh ha-Shanah* 2:8 that Rabban Gamaliel, the father of Rabbi Ḥanina, kept a tablet in his chamber with images of the faces of the moon that was used to test witnesses to the appearance of the new moon.[301] Similarly, the cup with an image of Tyche, a decorative three-legged table known as a "Delphic table" (seemingly the same furnishing used by Josephus to describe the table of showbread),[302] and even a drinking vessel supported by the image of a dragon (as opposed to a dragon supported by a cup) were permissible.[303]

For the rabbis, the only real issue regarding imagery was whether a particular object was worshipped, and thus patently idolatrous – or not. If the object was worshipped, the rabbis provided little leeway in setting boundaries. If not, then they felt free to exempt or remove the artifact from the category of idolatry. A general trend toward leniency suggests how complex the problem of living in a polytheistic environment was for the rabbis and their followers.

What about art made by Jews for specifically Jewish contexts? Here too, we find a range of interpretations. The most extreme position appears in the *Mekhilta of Rabbi Ishmael*, *ba-Ḥodesh* 6, commenting on Exodus 20:4–5: "You shall not make for yourself a graven image, or any likeness of anything that is in heaven above, or that is in the earth beneath, or that is in the water under the earth; you shall not bow down to them or serve them. . . ." The *Mekhilta* sets out a stringent rule for art made by Jews, apparently for Jews. A selection from the beginning and the conclusion of this long tradition exemplifies the point:

"You shall not make a sculptured image" (Exodus 20:4). One should not make one that is engraved, but perhaps one may make one that is solid?
Scripture says: "Nor any likeness" (ibid). One should not make a solid one, but perhaps one may plant something?
Scripture says: "You shall not plant an *asherah*" (Deuteronomy 16:12).
One should not plant something, but perhaps one may make it (an image) of wood?
Scripture says: "Any kind of wood" (ibid.).
One should not make it of wood, but perhaps one may make it of stone?
Scripture says: "And a figured stone" (Leviticus 26:1).
One should not make it of stone, perhaps one may make it of silver?
Scripture says: "Gods of silver" (Exodus 20:20). . . .

. . . If in the heavens [is intended] perhaps one may make an image of the sun, moon, stars and planets?
Scripture says: "above" (Exodus 20:4) – neither the images of angels nor of cherubs, nor of heavenly creatures.
One may not make an image of any of these, but perhaps one may make an image of the abyss, darkness and the deep darkness?
Scripture says: "And that which is under the earth" (ibid.).
"or in the waters under the earth" (ibid).
This comes to include the reflected image, according to Rabbi Aqiva.
Others say it comes to include the *shavriri* (the spirit who causes blindness).
Scripture goes to such great lengths in pursuit of the evil inclination so as not to leave any room for allowing it.

This is a unique source and appears to be a uniquely strident position among the Tannaim.[304] It is reminiscent of Josephus's position throughout his work, as stated in *Against Apion*, to the effect that God "forbade the making of images, alike of any living creature, and much more of God."[305] A close reading of this *Mekhilta* text, however, suggests that it is not as stringent it seems. Blau, followed by Blidstein and Sacha Stern, has argued that each of the restrictions set out in this long tradition are a midrashic process whereby Biblical proof are called upon to outlaw idolatry.[306] The *Mekhilta* here is a polemic against potentially idolatrous images – not against "art" as a general category.

As we have seen, the most influential rabbi of the Amoraic period in Palestine, Rabbi Johanan, and his successor as leader of the Tiberias academy, Rabbi Abun, reacted with a sort of diffidence ("he did not stop them") to the use of wall paintings and mosaics by Palestinian Jews during the third and early fourth century C.E.[307] Ambivalence toward wall paintings, we have seen, relates to issues of Divine prerogatives as the creator, and not to idolatry per se.

Mosaics are a good place to judge how rabbis from differing locales and backgrounds, and those who followed in their footsteps, dealt with the question of art. In dealing with mosaic floors, rabbis were concerned with decorated stone pavement as a potential violation of Leviticus 26:1, "and figured stone you shall not place in your land to bow down upon it":[308]

Rav commanded the house of Rabbi Aḥa and Rabbi Ami commanded his own household not to bow down as is customary when they go [to the synagogue?] on a fast day.
Rabbi Jonah bowed sideways, as did Rabbi Aḥa.
Rabbi Samuel said: "I saw Rabbi Abbahu bow as usual."
Rabbi Jose said: "I asked Rabbi Abbahu: Is it not written, 'and figured stone [you shall not place in your land to bow down upon it]' (Leviticus 26:1)?"
It should be solved [by applying this verse to the situation] where one has a fixed place for bowing. . . .

Here, mosaics were used to pave what appears to be a Jewish public building. Rav clearly did not approve of them. Mosaic pavements were prevalent in Palestine from the latter Second Temple period onward. During the third century, highly decorated mosaics existed in Palestine, as witnessed by the third-century triclinium (reception and banquet hall) mosaic from Sepphoris.[309] Mosaic floors, both figurative and not, certainly existed in Caesarea Maritima, home of Rabbi Abbahu — and no doubt in Tiberias as well. The question of Rabbi Jose, and Rabbi Abbahu's response, would have us believe that difficulty resided in the application of Leviticus 26:1. This verse was understood by the Tannaim to restrict prostration on stone flooring anywhere other than the Temple. Thus, we read in Sifra be-Har 6:

"and figured stone you shall not place in your land to bow down upon it" (Leviticus 26:1): In your land you shall not prostrate yourselves upon the stones, but you shall prostrate yourselves on the stones of the Temple.

"Figured stone" in this verse was applied by rabbis to mosaics, an art form that did not exist in Biblical Israel but is thought to have existed to a limited extent in Herod's Temple.[310] Mishnah Middot 1:6 suggests that dividers between various sections of the Temple compound were laid with mosaics, "the tops of pesifasin."[311]

There is no explicit reference in our Jerusalem Talmud tradition to the problem of images on mosaics. Nevertheless, it has been suggested that that Rabbi Abbahu's "tolerant" attitude toward bowing on mosaics must have been influenced by the Greco-Roman social and artistic environment in which he lived.[312] It has even been suggested that Rabbi Abbahu had a greater degree of "Hellenistic acculturation" than his colleagues, which assumes a rather static approach to cultural integration.[313] Assuming that this contextual approach is correct, it seems likely that the other rabbis were just as cognizant of mosaic floors and may have been just as cosmopolitan as Rabbi Abbahu. Rav, Rabbi Aḥa, and Rabbi Ami all flourished — at least for a time — in Tiberias, certainly no backwater. Their positions may also have been conditioned by a deep understanding of the Roman world. One need only recall that modern neo-orthodoxies in Judaism, Islam, and Hinduism are often highly sophisticated urban phenomena, and not products of the periphery.[314] Those who chose against bowing on mosaics (over whose existence they had no control) seem to have made decisions reflective of their own senses of propriety. Leviticus 26:1 loomed large, at least in our texts' presentation of Rabbi Abbahu. Even for this "tolerant" rabbi, however, a set place for prostration on a mosaic was necessary in order to resolve any conflict with this Biblical commandment.

The propriety of synagogue mosaics with figurative imagery was a hotly debated issue in early Islamic Palestine. This does not represent a generalized questioning of "art," I hasten to note. Rather, it is a continuation of the conversation regarding mosaics and the interpretation of Leviticus 26:1. This is made clear in Targum Pseudo-Jonathan's translation of this verse:[315]

. . . but a pavement[316] figured with images and likenesses you may make on the floor of miqdasheikhon. And do not bow down to it, for I am the Lord your God.

This Pseudo-Jonathan text can be regarded as a defense of decorated synagogue mosaics at about the time when disfigurement of synagogue mosaics, most prominently the Na'aran mosaic, is thought to have occurred. The element of this text most significant for our discussion is the mention of mosaics "figured with images and likenesses." Some scholars interpret this text as referring directly to synagogues, but the midrashic process is much more complex. The problem resides in the noun *miqdasheikhon* and its second-person plural suffix. It might legitimately be translated as "your temples" or "your temple." Those twentieth-century scholars who have read *miqdasheikhon* in the plural suggest that this term refers to synagogues.[317] This approach is evident in Tannaitic sources such as *m. Megillah* 3:1 that interpret *miqdasheikhem* in Leviticus 26:31, "and I will make your sanctuaries desolate," as a plural noun that refers to synagogues.[318] The motivations behind this explanation are Tannaitic interpretations of Leviticus 26:31, the increasing use of Temple language in the sanctification of synagogues, Amoraic and post-Amoraic relaxation of Tannaitic strictures against prostration on mosaics, and, most importantly, the discovery of mosaic pavements in ancient synagogues.[319] The major problem that argues against this interpretation is that "temple" or "small temple" is never used in rabbinic literature to refer to synagogues without being paired explicitly with the word "synagogue."

Other commentators have justifiably read *miqdasheikhon* in the singular and understand it to refer to the Jerusalem Temple.[320] This interpretation follows the Tannaitic interpretation of Leviticus 26:1 that we have seen in *Sifra be-Har* 6,[321] which suggests that while idolatrous "figured stones" are not permissible in "your land," they are permitted in "your Temple." *Mishnah Middot* 1:6 made later rabbis aware that the Temple platform was laid with at least some mosaics – although none of the figurative type.[322] It is my contention that carpet mosaics, a popular type of pavement in public buildings (including synagogues, churches, mosques, and palaces) during the Byzantine and early Islamic periods, are retrojected by our Targumic tradition to the *pesifasin* of the Temple.[323] If I am correct, the permissible figured carpet mosaics thought to have existed in the Temple were used as a precedent by the author of the Pseudo-Jonathan text to legitimize the use of illustrated carpet mosaics in the synagogue, an institution that was increasingly seen as being a "small temple" (*miqdash me'at*),[324] "second only to the [Jerusalem] Temple."[325] A loop is thus formed between the mosaics of the Temple and late antique synagogue mosaics.[326] This exegesis might have provided a powerful argument in support of mosaics against opinions that were predisposed to forbid and perhaps destroy them. Just as mosaics "figured with images and likenesses" were permissible in the Temple (*miqdash*), the defense seems to suggest, they now legitimately exist within the "small temple" (*miqdash me'at*), the synagogue.

WHAT ACCOUNTS FOR CHANGES IN JEWISH ATTITUDES TOWARD ART IN LATE ANTIQUE PALESTINE?

Jewish attitudes toward the visual during late antiquity reflect broad changes and divergences of attitude. By the third century, Jews were using imagery that was previously unknown. Animal, human, and celestial imagery abounded for centuries, borrowed directly from the art of the majority culture. By the eighth century, Jews were again using a very restricted visual vocabulary. What happened? Michael Avi-Yonah's disappointment with the return of Jewish conservatives is clearly evident:[327]

The figurative efflorescence of Jewish Art, which began in the third century, did not last beyond the sixth. As the times became more difficult and the Byzantine laws directed against the Jews more oppressive, aniconic orthodoxy resumed its sway, even before similar trends prevailed in Islam and in the iconoclastic tendency at Byzantium. . . . The old fear of the human image returned again, as in Hellenistic times. . . .

Avi-Yonah here projected his own Jewish secularist antagonisms against Jewish orthodoxy in his own period into the Greco–Roman past. Jewish art, he believed, was a popular phenomenon, developed during a respite from rabbinic dominance. For Avi-Yonah – like Goodenough – it was the reemergence of those big-bad-iconophobic rabbis that led to the "decline" of Jewish art. The problem with this is that, as we have seen, there is no evidence that a unified community of rabbi iconophobes ever really existed. More to the point, we know precious little about rabbinic attitudes in Byzantine period, most named rabbis having flourished at least a century earlier. The real question is, What led to the dramatic difference between the art of the Second Temple period and that of the late Roman/Byzantine period? For Goodenough and Avi-Yonah it was the decline of rabbinic power with the destruction of the Temple that allowed for this bubble of iconism. Urbach, responding to Goodenough, believed that this situation was the result of rabbinic decision. According to Urbach, the rabbis determined that the surrounding non-Jews were essentially no longer pagans – that they did not believe in their gods any longer, and so their art was not really idolatrous.[328] That being the case, Jews were "allowed" to participate in this art. Urbach's theological interpretation may be correct regarding rabbinic reflection on Roman art – but that position would be merely a post-facto argument to legitimize the fact that

Jews of all sorts were using such imagery. It is clear that by the third or fourth century, Jews in Palestine were making and using art quite similar to that of their neighbors. Sometimes they integrated Jewish themes; at other times, they simply avoided (and even destroyed) certain elements of Roman religious iconography.

This transformation reflects the fact that by the third century, art was a less focal element of Jewish self-identity that it had been in latter Second Temple Judaea. We have seen that during the latter Second Temple period, "anti-idolism" snowballed in Judaea, with antagonism toward Greco–Roman imagery growing and intensifying among elements of society that eventually dominated and revolted against Rome. During the second and third centuries, in the wake of the Jewish defeat in two wars against Rome and the resulting economic and social dislocations, we find relatively little art in Jewish contexts – although we hear from rabbinic sources that rabbis were far from adverse to such creativity, as long as it was not "idolatrous." Beginning during the third century, we start to find archaeological evidence of Jews participating in the visual culture of the Roman world and using visual imagery that was not widely used before the destruction of the Temple.

Why the transformation? The loss of the First Revolt and then of Judaea itself after Bar Kokhba surely caused an almost unfathomable degree of dislocation. The fact that Jews became a numerical minority in most regions of Palestine surely had something to do with it. Of necessity, Jews became accustomed to seeing Roman art on a much more constant basis, and for the first time no segment of the population was sheltered (or could shelter itself) from intense contact with Roman visuality. The fact that rabbis identified ultimate pietism (exemplified in Nahum of the Holy of Holies) with lack of willingness to look upon Roman religious/political iconography well expresses this notion. The Romanization of Palestine had a secondary effect. Where for the period before the Hasmoneans the most important contacts were with local Semites, under Rome – particularly after 70 – Palestine assumed an essentially Roman identity and receded from its previous identity as the most westerly area of Mesopotamia. As among the Nabateans centuries earlier, less figurative Jewish visual traditions faded as integration into the Greco–Roman world accelerated. Jewish integration in this respect was even greater than among the Samaritans. While the Samaritans adopted Roman architecture and the art of the mosaic pavement, there is no evidence that they made

images of anything "in the heavens above, or in the earth below."[329] The Samaritan case parallels Jewish approaches during the later Second Temple period, and shows that had Jews wished, similar "aniconism" could have been maintained. One wonders whether this Samaritan approach reflects a minority response to the Jewish minority – differentiation from Judaism through strenuous maintenance of Biblical image taboos.

Unlike the period from the Hasmonians through 70, however, when idolatrous imagery became a serious issue of communal identity, most late antique Jews do not seem to have publicly raised the banner of "anti-idolism" in relations with Rome. With the Temple gone, and with it political independence and even their majority status in most of Palestine in the balance, most Jews chose a different mode. The politicization of images lost much of its vigor once the battle was lost. A sense of acquiescence (if not tolerance) toward images that is described disparagingly by Josephus and hinted at by the archaeological record before and immediately after 70 came to dominate. This adaptation, which is nascent in rabbinic sources, is fully expressed for the first time in an archaeological context at Beth She'arim during the latter third century. Jews increasingly used imagery drawn from the general Roman context with less concern for the ideological ramifications – even the images of Helios and the Roman eagle, which by the Byzantine period were widespread among synagogue decorations. The adoption of Greco–Roman imagery by Jews came at a time when the use of Jewish imagery was increasingly an internal matter within the communities of a Roman minority and, unlike the latter Second Temple period, of no concern to the Romans. In a sense, Roman disinterest facilitated Jewish adoption.

Jews developed imagery that was distinctly their own, adapting a template that was distinctly Greco–Roman. This utilization of Roman imagery was a reflection of their acculturation to living in a fully Romanized Palestine, where boundary issues were considerably more complex than they had been in semiautonomous Judaea. The wholesale development of the menorah as a Jewish symbol was, as we will discuss later, a part of this process. Jewish visual culture became thoroughly Romanized – keeping only the most religiously focused imagery beyond the Jewish purview. This is particularly true in Byzantine Palestine, where archaeological evidence shows that some Jews used iconography drawn from the general context quite widely. The wealth of Byzantine Palestine afforded Jews the luxury to build monumental structures, which they naturally constructed in the style of their age. More than ever before, the menorah and other "symbols" – including Hebrew/Aramaic script itself – served as visual markers of Jewish identity.

What accounts for the decline of figurative art among the Jews during the early Islamic period? Following upon J. B. Frey's influential essay "La question des images chez les Juifs a la lumière des récentes découvertes,"[330] Ernst Kitzinger suggested in 1954 that

There was evidently a rather sudden return to rigorism on the part of the Jews [during the latter 6th and 7th centuries]. Could this have been caused by the spectacle of vastly increased image worship among the Christians, which the Jews could hope to exploit more effectively for polemic purposes if they themselves could claim to be strict observers of Biblical Law?[331]

Kitzinger connected this supposed "sudden turn" to increasing use of icons under Justin II, which accompany supposedly Jewish polemics against "Christian idolatry" that "started not long after that time." Kitzinger's approach was recently taken up by Charles Barber, who expands on it and argues based on analysis of the Na'aran synagogue and Patristic sources that "under attack from imperial Christianity Judaism attempted to reconstruct an identity that differed from the materialism of Christian religious culture."[332]

The approach adopted by Kitzinger and Barber has a number of difficulties. The archaeological sources available today reflect, as we have seen, a gradual, and by no means lock-stepped, movement toward a less figurative approach among Jewish communities – particularly after the sixth century. They do not suggest a "sudden return to rigorism." It is not impossible or even unlikely that Jews were influenced by Christian "idolatry" to avoid certain images in the decoration of their synagogues – although my guess is that most Jews could distinguish a floor that was trod upon from the icons that Christians regularly paraded through the streets of Palestinian cities. Even within the Christian community in Syria–Palestine, there were communities that were ambivalent regarding images, even before the fall of Byzantine Palestine.[333] Jewish discomfort with images may have been strengthened by both

of these trends, Jewish communities choosing a path of heightened "anti-idolism" or even iconoclasm. This response would not reflect anything as grand or unnecessary as an attempt to "reconstruct" an identity, as Barber would have it, but rather a response to blatant or at least noticeable "idolatry" by the Bible-reading colonial power. The poems we have cited are the response of the colonized to the colonists, the "hidden transcript" which they said to one another of their neighbors when Jewish communities came together and knew that the Christians were not listening.[334]

More significant, however, was the rise of Islam. Schick has argued that iconoclasm within churches and apparently synagogues occurred during the early Islamic period.[335] From the first, Islam eschewed images within religious settings. Islamic aesthetics must have been particularly influential among Jews. The Muslim rulers of Palestine were greeted much more positively by Palestinian Jews, and Islam was not subjected to the same level of scorn that Jews felt (and continued to feel) toward Christianity.[336] Islamic attitudes toward images in religious contexts would have been supportive of Jews who advocated a more strict approach. In a sense, it gave the Jews "one up" over the Christians and the appearance of being closer in attitude to the Muslims in this multicultural though increasingly Islamic culture.[337] The intrinsic ambivalence of rabbinic tradition toward religious images certainly provided ready ground for this shift, leading to the iconographic transformation of synagogue floors. We might assume that Palestinian Jews would have had no particular interest in continuing to use a now-passé art form. Jews simply adopted and adapted the aesthetics of the new colonial power. According to this scenario, the close of antiquity and the rise of Islam reinforced the "anti-idolic" impulse that had existed in Jewish thought in the Land of Israel throughout the Greco–Roman period. Jewish "anti-idolism" and iconoclasm reflect the transition from a visual vocabulary that some Jewish communities found to their liking in the Byzantine Holy Land to a decreasingly figurative approach. In the end, the most significant non-Jewish influences were the artistic and religious mores of Islamic Palestine. Once again, the colonial power's interest in the visual affected Jewish approaches in the development of their "minority art."

CHAPTER EIGHT

ART AND IDENTITY IN DIASPORA COMMUNITIES IN LATE ANTIQUITY

FROM ROME TO NEHARDEA

O UR KNOWLEDGE OF THE FAR-FLUNG JEWISH COMMUNITIES of the Roman and Persian diasporas is spotty at best. Often a single inscription, fragment of a menorah, or a chance mention in the writings of a Church father is all that we really know of an entire Jewish community in the Roman Empire. What we know of Jewish culture in Babylonia is almost exclusively based on the insular and highly redacted texts of the Babylonian Talmud. Nevertheless, the evidence that has come down to us suggests that diaspora communities participated in a "common Judaism." Although sometimes geographically distant from one another, Jews in all of these places understood their religion to be "Judaism" and assumed that it was related to the "Judaism" of every other community. This rather loose late antique religious *koiné* was expressed architecturally through the construction of synagogues with shrines to house Torah scrolls; a focus on Scripture and its interpretation through the use of Temple-related symbolism (especially the menorah) and ritual or symbolic use of the

46. The mosaic of the synagogue at Ḥamman Lif (Naro), Tunisia (after R. Wischnitzer, *Symbole und Gestalten der jüdischen Kunst* [Berlin-Schoneberg: S. Scholem, 1935], 60).

Hebrew language (however limited that may have been in some communities); and other ritual acts such as ritual circumcision, dietary laws, and sabbath observance.[1] Literary sources and archaeological remains suggest that the notion the synagogue was a "holy place" was widely held.[2]

The degree of relationship between the various communities must not be overstated, however. Shared symbols, customs, and beliefs notwithstanding, each community was first and foremost a part of the local, linguistic, and social contexts in which it functioned. Jewish residents of Sardis in Asia Minor, Ilici in Spain, or Sura in Babylonia had much in common with their immediate non-Jewish neighbors. This is certainly true in regards to art. The Sardis synagogue, the Dura Europos synagogue, and the Roman catacombs, for example, were built and decorated according to the conventions and realities of each locality. No Jewish diaspora architectural style existed in antiquity that stretched across the entire "diaspora." Each community (or regional group of communities) must therefore be approached as an essentially autonomous unit.[3]

ROMAN DIASPORA COMMUNITIES

The art of Jewish tombs and synagogues has been collected and analyzed by E. R. Goodenough[4] and, more

recently, by Rachel Hachlili.[5] Inscriptions were made readily available by Jean-Baptiste Frey, Harry Leon, Baruch Lifschitz, William Horbury, David Noy, Lea Roth-Gerson, and others.[6] With all of this scattered evidence literally at one's fingertips, it is possible with little strain to know quite a bit about the religion of Jews in the western diaspora – at least in the public realm of the synagogue and in burial contexts. Still, the local context of each source is sometimes lost through the decision to bundle Jewish materials together in compact volumes rather than integrate them into local studies. Of course, this is a perennial issue in the formulation of Judaic studies as a self-contained discipline. Site reports suggest that Jewish materials generally coalesced with the remains of each town, city, or region in which the Jews lived. Thus, for example, in Ḥamman Lif (Naro), near Carthage in North Africa, the sixth-century synagogue was paved with a lavish mosaic containing an inhabited scroll as well as aquatic and garden scenes typical of North African mosaics of this place and time (Figure 46).[7] The only marker that indicates any Jewish connection is a Latin inscription that mentions the place as "the holy synagogue" (*sancta sunagoga*), flanked by two lozenges containing small stylized menorahs. Scholars have interpreted the mosaic as representing "creation" and as an escathological scene.[8] For Goodenough, it is "a series of signs of heaven and salvation."[9] Katherine Dunbabin and Rachel

47. The Sardis Synagogue, looking eastward (photograph by Steven Fine).

Hachlili are completely correct in eschewing such interpretations. They see the Ḥamman Lif synagogue mosaic as a rather conventional example of the art of North African mosaic craft. Without the inscription and the menorahs, there is no reason to identify this floor with Judaism – especially because we have little sense of how the room was furnished and none of how the walls were decorated. The same can be said of the synagogue at Apamea.[10] The beautiful floor of this fourth-century synagogue is paved in mosaics set in a geometric pattern. Only the content of the mosaic inscriptions and an occasional menorah set into the geometric design identify this site as a synagogue.

The relationship between local practice and "common Judaism" is well-expressed in the synagogue at Sardis in Asia Minor (Figures 47, 48). The Sardis synagogue is the largest and the grandest synagogue yet discovered, its main hall measuring 54 × 18 meters.[11] It has been estimated that the synagogue could accommodate a thousand people. This impressive building was part of the municipal center of Sardis and taken over by the Jewish community and remodeled as a synagogue during the fourth century. It formed the southern side of the civic center of Sardis. The remodeling included the installation of two aediculae on the eastern wall of the synagogue and the construction of a podium in the center of the hall. The significance of these aediculae is made clear both by their prominence and by an inscription

found near them that reads, "Find, open, read, observe." Another Greek inscription refers to the Torah shrine as the *nomophulákion*, "the place that protects the Torah." A molding from the synagogue contains an inscribed menorah and the image of a Torah shrine with its doors open to show scrolls stacked horizontally within it.[12] The mosaic pavement is largely geometric, with a golden urn flanked by two peacocks in the mosaic of the synagogue apse. If the floor, minus its inscriptions, were all that was left of this synagogue, the Jewishness of this site might even be open to discussion.[13] A large table flanked by free-standing lions was placed near the western side of the nave. Eighty donor inscriptions, most in Greek and some with particular Jewish content, have been discovered. The Hebrew word "shalom" appears once in extant inscriptions.[14] Finally, a large fragment of a free-standing seven-branched marble menorah, a dedicatory plaque for a menorah, a small bronze menorah, and a large stone plaque bearing an incised menorah were found.[15]

Menorahs were clearly pivotal in the definition of this building as a Jewish space. The bases of the large table are decorated with bas reliefs of eagles, and the flanking lions are reused. All of these "archaic or classical" elements were reused in the synagogue.[16] The lower portions of the walls were decorated with inlaid marble in "geometric, floral and animal designs (including pomegranates, fish and birds)."[17]

48. The Sardis Synagogue, looking westward (photograph by Steven Fine).

A Corinthean capital found in the synagogue was carved with the image of a male lion.[18] The peacocks flanking the urn of the synagogue apse mosaic were "destroyed in antiquity."[19] We do not know who destroyed the peacocks nor the reason for their removal, as other animal imagery at Sardis was left untouched. It is clear that the Jews of Sardis appreciated fine Roman architecture and that, in general, they had no aversion to animal imagery. No human imagery has been discovered. The addition of Torah shrines in the form of aediculae is typical of synagogues in Palestine and elsewhere in the Empire, as are images of Torah shrines and menorahs to decorate (and to illuminate) their synagogue. Were all of this Jewish material removed from the Sardis hall – a relatively easy task – it would be just another large Roman basilica. With the addition of Jewish artifacts, this basilica became a synagogue.

We have more information regarding the city of Rome and its environs – the construction and decoration of the catacombs used by Jews from the late second to the early fifth centuries C.E. was similar to those used by their polytheistic and Christian neighbors. Very few painted surfaces survive. Most bear decorative motifs that are the same as those used by the non-Jewish majority. In one case, in a ceiling painting in the Vigna Randanini catacomb, the goddess Fortuna (Tyche) appears. An extremely limited repertoire of Jewish imagery was used in the wall paintings and

49. Jewish gold glass from Rome (after Wischnitzer, *Symbole und Gestalten der jüdischen Kunst*, 90).

Jewish gold glasses (Figure 49). Images of menorahs and of Torah shrines in close proximity to menorahs are very common. The latter appears on six of the thirteen extant Jewish gold glasses, in five inscriptions, and in a large wall painting from the Villa Torlonia catacomb (Figure 50).[20] This

50. Villa Torlonia catacomb, Rome (after A. Reifenberg, *Denkmäler der jüdischen Antike* [Berlin: Schocken, 1937], pl. 53).

painting is particularly significant iconographically, because above the shrine, which is flanked by two menorahs, the images of the sun and the moon appear. The meaning of this astral imagery is not clear, although my sense is that it asserts a sort of timelessness to the imagery – certainly an appropriate theme within a cemetery! This interpretation may be strengthened by a burial inscription from the Monteverde catacomb. The inscription opens: *oikos aiónios*, "eternal home."[21] Immediately to the right of this phrase is the image of a Torah shrine, its doors open to reveal the scrolls within. The inscription goes on to memorialize a "twice-archon," a synagogue leader named Eupsychus.

It seems to me likely that the "eternal home" and the Torah shrine image are related, helping to explain some of what at least one synagogue-focused Jewish family saw when they looked upon the image of a Torah shrine. An apparently Jewish gold glass discovered in the Christian cemetery of Saints Peter and Marcellinus shows a Torah shrine in the form of a temple (or is it a temple in the form of a Torah shrine?).[22] This shrine is called a "house of peace" (*oíkos irá[na]s*). A Latin inscription from the synagogue at Ostia makes this point as well, commemorating one who "set up the ark (*keibōtòn*) of the Holy Torah (*nómō hagíō*)".[23] One unique image in the Villa Torlonia

catacomb asserts the centrality of Scripture once again. A lozenge representing a Biblical scroll serves as a decorative motif.[24] To top it off, inscriptions often reflect the significance of the synagogue within the lives of the interned. Images of the menorah abound.

The synagogue of Ostia, the port of Rome, is iconographically contiguous with the remains from the catacombs. There is nothing in the third-century synagogue that might tip off an excavator that this public building served Jews except for the Latin dedicatory inscription.[25] During the fifth century, the synagogue hall was remodeled and a large Torah shrine installed on the eastern side of the building. Shrines like this one served as models for the various visual representations found in Rome and for the image of a shrine on oil lamps uncovered in Ostia. Also found within the synagogue is a small stucco fragment of a lion's mane. Again, lion imagery is very common on gold glasses from Rome. Thus, there is real continuity between the port of Rome above ground and Jewish *Roma Sotterranea*.

Perhaps the most interesting thing about Jewish remains from Rome is the imagery that does not appear. While Christians were painting elaborate Biblical and other scenes on the walls of their tombs, Jews stuck to a very conservative and limited repertoire. Paul Corby Finney compares the paintings of the Jewish catacombs to "journeymen wall painters" who in Christian contexts "struggled to bring forth plausible figural subjects,"[26]

whereas at Randanini and Torlonia, no doubt in conformity with demands set by Jewish patrons, these same (or similar) *parietarii* were spared the embarrassment of displaying their incompetence as figure painters.

In other words, the Jewish catacombs were decorated by mediocre painters, whose technical skill matched the requirements set by the community that commissioned their

51. Seasons sarcophagus, Rome (after Reifenberg, *Denkmäler der jüdischen Antike*, pl. 55).

work. This question of quality is important, because it bespeaks the differing needs of Jews and Christians and the ways that catacomb painters responded to each community. Jewish gold glasses were made in the same workshops as Christian and polytheistic glasses, yet Jews distanced themselves from human imagery in all extant exemplars.[27] The exception to this rule are Painted Rooms I–II in the Vigna Randanini catacomb. Although the construction history of this catacomb cannot yet be written, and full excavation is a desideratum, some comments can still be ventured.[28] In room "I" the image of Fortuna and in room "II" other mythological images appear, and no Jewish imagery or inscriptions. Leonard Rutgers rightly notes that it is "impossible to determine if rooms I and II were originally commissioned by Jews."[29] If they were, then this is evidence of Jews participating fully in the visual vocabulary of their age. If not, and if these rooms housed Jewish burials, then this is apparently evidence that Jews tolerated such imagery and did not destroy it. Specifically, Jewish imagery appears only one time in the Vigna Randanini wall paintings, although menorahs appear in memorial inscriptions. A menorah is painted above the acrosolium facing the entrance, and objects that Rutgers suggests "appear to be ethrogim" decorate the white ceiling.[30]

A wider variety of images appear on sarcophagi. The problem with sarcophagi is that due to the vissicitudes of the catacombs, it is often impossible to know where a sarcophagus found in or near a Jewish catacomb actually originated.[31] The few sarcophagi that can be securely identified nevertheless present themes that are unknown from wall decorations. Among my favorites is a sarcophagus fragment decorated with three well-carved theater masks.

It also contains a rather primitive Greek inscription and images of a menorah flanked by a horn on the left, a palm frond to the right, and the Hebrew word *Shalom* farther to the right.[32] The Seasons Sarcophagus is perhaps the best example, with its *clipeus* (medallion) containing a menorah and supported by two Victories (Figure 51). The four seasons are represented by winged nude males. Beneath the medallion are three *amorini* treading grapes in a vat with spouts in the shape of lions' heads. Beneath the personification of Autumn, "two other amorini are shown riding, one on a hare, the other on a dog, which is leaping towards the slain animal held by winter."[33] Franz Cumont, followed by Goodenough,[34] interpreted this iconography as representing life after death – a rather predictable application of the salvation motif that has been roundly refuted by George Hanfmann and Harry Leon.[35] Some distinction based on the remains of each catacomb may be possible, although the remains within each catacomb have been so thoroughly disturbed that this approach is not particularly enlightening. What is clear is that specifically Jewish imagery was extremely conservative. Sarcophagi, which were seemingly bought on the general market by individual families, suggest a far broader selection of Roman iconography. I would not be surprised if this distinction reflects a more rigorous religious scruple (or perhaps, a lower level of Roman artistic acuity) on the part of those who controlled the catacombs and their decoration as compared with some of the interned and their bereaved. I have suggested a similar scenario at Beth She'arim, where the Leda sarcophagus was defaced and her nude body (shown in the act of copulation with Zeus in his guise as a swan) turned against the wall (Figure 27).

52. The Ark of the Covenant in the Temple of Dagon, Dura Europos Synagogue (photograph by Fred Anderegg, after Goodenough, *Jewish Symbols* 11, pl. xiii).

The Dura Europos synagogue is the earliest diaspora synagogue we will discuss. Its paintings were completed in 244/45 C.E. and the structure destroyed around 256. A veritable feast for the eyes, the synagogue paintings are among the finest paintings discovered at Dura, a site where numer temples, a church, and private dwellings were decorated with lush wall paintings. Each of its four walls was covered with lush images drawn from the Biblical narrative and interpreted through the prism of *aggadic* tradition. Sixty percent of the paintings are thought to be extant. The paintings in no way suggest any ambivalence about depicting Biblical heroes, animals, God's hand, or even nudes. An eye (labeled "IAO") attacked by snakes and three daggers appears on one of the ceiling tiles.[36] Were this building our only evidence for ancient Judaism (as mithraea are, essentially, for Mithraism), no one would have even considered the possibility that this community was "aniconic" or "iconophobic." Nevertheless, an "anti-idolic" attitude may be discerned. The paintings describe graphically Elijah's vanquishing of the priests of Ba'al on Mt. Carmel in 1 Kings 18:30–8. While Elijah's sacrifice is successfully set ablaze, the priests of Ba'al were not so lucky. Their altar contains a small cubicle. Within it stands an equally diminutive man, about to light the fire beneath the sacrifice upon command.

Such theatrics were, of course, common in Roman religious drama. His cheat (or if you will, ritual performance) is thwarted, however, by a Divinely sent snake, which bites the man.[37] The image of the Ark of the Covenant before the Temple of Dagon in Ashdod is especially graphic (Figure 52).[38] According to 1 Samuel 2–4,

. . . the Philistines took the ark of God and brought it into the house of Dagon and set it up beside Dagon. And when the people of Ashdod rose early the next day, behold, Dagon had fallen face downward on the ground before the ark of the Lord. So they took Dagon and put him back in his place. But when they rose early on the next morning, behold, Dagon had fallen face downward on the ground before the ark of the Lord, and the head of Dagon and both his hands were lying cut off upon the threshold; only the trunk of Dagon was left to him.

In illustrating this scene, prominent among a group of images of the Ark of the Covenant, the artists painted a plethora of images of Dagon's broken body parts and cult utensils. Dagon is portrayed as none other than a Palmyrene god – exactly the divinities worshipped in nearby temples. Although the designers of the Dura synagogue were obviously comfortable with intense visuality, idolatry was another matter altogether. They went out of their way to show contemporary pagan gods broken into pieces.

Once completed, graffiti in Middle Persian was added to the paintings. In addition, the eyes of various figures were gouged out. Goodenough ascribes this iconoclasm to "some of the less influential Jews." According to his scenario,[39]

The Jews who did not like the paintings seems to have been impotent to stop their being put up on the walls, but we seem to have clear evidence of their dissent. For on figure after figure in the lower registers the eyes have carefully been scratched out. . . . It seems quite likely, then, that the eyeless figures in the synagogue attest secret visits by members who did not care or dare to demolish the building or ruthlessly to disfigure it, but who reached up with knives, and, by taking out the eyes annulled the threat of such creations. In the gloom of the place their act may long have gone undetected, so that it would have been difficult to establish their guilt. But only such protest seems to me to account for these slight but deeply significant defacements. Perhaps those people represented a very considerable part of the congregation, or perhaps a single recalcitrant member gouged out all the eyes.

Goodenough truly let his imagination run wild in suggesting how this protest might have been carried out! He cites rabbinic and patristic support for the removal of eyes as a way of rendering art unobjectionable. Lurking behind his impassioned description are, once again, obscurantist Jews. Kraeling has quite a different take on the gouged eyes, though it is no less imaginative. Without providing support, he suggests that in the course of filling the synagogue with soil as part of the embankment wall that was to support the northern wall of Dura against Persian attack around 256 the eyes were gouged. He goes still farther, suggesting that "those who introduced into the Synagogue's House of Assembly the masses of earth needed to hold its walls in place were by no means friendly to toward the owners and worshipers. In the course of their work they took occasion to gouge out the eyes of such painted figures as came within their reach."[40] Recently Christopher Pierce Kelley took up Kraeling's position, arguing that the gouging was carried out by Romans and not Jews.[41] I find it hard to support either position, owing to the real lack of evidence. It does not seem beyond reason that Jews did gouge the eyes, just as they did in later periods in Palestine. It is quite possible that some Jews intensely disliked the paintings, which is probably the simplest explanation for the iconoclasm at Dura. At the same time, mutilation by Romans also is not beyond credulity – although there is no evidence to support anything of the sort.

THE BABYLONIAN DIASPORA

No substantive evidence of Jewish art from Babylonia has been found. The *Babylonian Talmud* is the single literary compilation of the rabbis in Sassanian Persia. A large and masterful document, traditions preserved therein tell us principally about attitudes within the rabbinic community. We know that some Babylonian rabbis signed documents with drawings rather than signatures: "Rav drew a beehive and Rabbi Ḥanina a palm branch . . . and Rabba son of Rav Huna would draw a boat."[42] Babylonian synagogues frequented by rabbis were furnished in ways similar to Palestinian synagogues; some rabbis preferred that synagogues be built taller than any other building in the area.[43]

Much of the Babylonian rabbinic discussion of "art" is in the form of commentary upon Palestinian Tannaitic and Amoraic traditions. These comments are particularly significant because they mediate between the received Tannaitic tradition and the realities of Sassanian Persia. The rabbinic discussion interprets the experience of the Tannaim under Rome into a wholly other, Zoroastrian context. A block of tradition (*sugya* or, pericope) preserved in *Babylonian Talmud Rosh ha-Shanah* 24a–b (repeated in *Avodah Zarah* 43a–b) provides a window into rabbinic reflection on Tannaitic traditions against the backdrop of rabbinic realities in third- and fourth-century Babylonia. We have come across many of these texts in our study of the Tannaitic reality. Here, however, these texts are engaged as part of a thoroughgoing examination of what is permissible in the contemporary Babylonian context. This elegant *sugya* begins with discussion of a tablet that the late-first- and early-second-century patriarch, Rabban Gamaliel II, is said to have used to test witnesses to the appearance of the new moon. I cite the *sugya* in its entirety, highlighting Tannaitic traditions in italics:[44]

An image of the phases of the moon (דמות צורות הלבנה) did Rabban Gamaliel have on a tablet (בטבלה)[45] on the wall of his upper chamber, which he would show to the ordinary people (ההדיוטות) and ask them: Did it look like this or this? (m. Rosh ha-Shanah 2:8)

Is this permissible? Is it not written:
"You shall not make with me [gods of silver, and gods of gold you shall not make for yourselves] (Exodus 20:20)? You shall not make according to the likeness of my attendants who serve before me."

Said Abaye: The Torah only forbids the making of attendants that can be reproduced in facsimile, for we learn:

"No one may make a building in the form of the Shrine, an exedra in place of the entrance hall, a court in place of the court,
a table in place of the table [of showbread],
a menorah in place of the menorah,
but one may make [a menorah] with five, six or eight [lamps].
Even of other metals [you shall not make a menorah]."
Rabbi Jose son of Rabbi Judah says: One may not make [the menorah] of wood as the Hasmonean dynasty did.
They said to him: Is this proof?
They had iron rods (שיפודים), and they covered them with tin.
They became more wealthy, and made them of silver.
They became even more wealthy, and made them of gold.
They [the compatriots of Rabbi Jose son of Rabbi Judah] said to him:
Is this proof? It consisted of iron rods overlaid with tin.
When they [the Hasmoneans] grew rich they made them of silver and when they grew richer, they made them of gold.

Are his attendants who cannot be reproduced in facsimile permitted? Is it not taught:

"You shall not make with me"? You shall not make according to the likeness of my attendants who serve before me.

Said Abaye: The Torah only prohibited the making of the likeness of the four faces opposite one another [of the chariot vision of Ezekiel 1:10].

Accordingly, the face of man by itself is permitted.

Is that so? Do we not learn:

"All sorts of faces (kol ha-partsufot) are permitted[46] except for the face of man."

Said Rav Huna son of Rav Joshua:[47]

From the words of Abaye[48] I have learned:

"You shall not make with me (אתי) [should be repunctuated to read] "You shall not make me (אותי)" – but the other attendants are permitted.

Are the other attendants indeed permitted? Is it not taught:

"You shall not make with me" – Do not make according to the likeness of my attendants who serve before me in the heavens, like the Ophannim, Seraphim, Holy Creatures, and Ministering Angels?

Said Abaye: "The Torah only forbade the attendants in the highest level [of heaven]."

And [those in] the lowest level (the sun and moon and constellations), are they allowed?

Is it not taught:

"That is in heaven" (Exodus 20:4) – this includes the sun, moon, stars and constellations?

"above" – this includes the Ministering Angels.

That *baraita* (Tannaitic tradition) refers to serving them [in an idolatrous fashion].

If they are made to be served [idolatrously], even [the image of] a tiny worm [is forbidden].

Certainly this is so, and this is derived from the continuation of the verse:

As we learn:

"that is on the earth" – To include the seas, rivers, mountains and hills.

"beneath": To include a tiny worm."

Is the mere making [of them] permitted?

Is it not written:

"You shall not make with me" (Exodus 20:20)? You shall not make according to the likeness of my attendants who serve before me in the heavens. For example: the sun and the moon and the stars and the constellations?

Rabban Gamaliel is different [and hence exempt from this prohibition], because others (non-Jews) made it for him [and he did not make the tablet himself].

And similarly in the case of [the seal ring of] Rav Judah, that others made it for him.

Said Samuel to Rav Judah: "You big toothed guy (a term of endearment)! Blind the eyes of this [image]!"

[This refers to a] seal that is carved in positive relief and because of suspicion [of idolatry],

As we learn:

A ring with a seal that is carved in positive relief, it is forbidden to wear, but it is permitted to seal with it. [A seal that is carved in] negative relief, it is permitted to wear it, but not seal with it.

Are we really concerned [that it will be worshipped]?

For in the synagogue of Shaf ve-Yatev in Nehardea there is a statue (אנדרטא), and the father of Samuel and Levi would come there and pray there, and they were not concerned [that the statue might be idolatrous].

– Public property is different. Rabban Gamaliel's tablet was private property.

Since he was the patriarch, many persons were always present with him.

One might answer that the tablet was in sections (and hence it was permissible), or one might answer that he made it for educational purposes, and hence permissible.

For we learn: *"You shall not learn to do [the abominable practices of those nations]"* (Deuteronomy 18:9), but you may learn in order to understand and to teach.

The purported purpose of this *sugya* is to judge the acceptability of Rabban Gamaliel's lunar tablet. It does this by setting two sorts of sources into dialectical opposition. On the one side is a strict interpretation of the Second Commandment (Exodus 20:3–6) and of Exodus 20:20 that appears in the *Mekhilta of Rabbi Ishmael*. On the other side are more lenient stances by Babylonian Amoraim, the most significant among them being the fourth-generation rabbi

Abaye. The final conclusion of the anonymous editor of this *sugya* is a kind of grudging acquiescence to the tablet. The Talmud legitimizes Rabban Gamaliel's tablet in two ways. The first is a highly technical issue of ritual purity (by describing the tablet as having been made in parts, no "whole" exists that might violate a Biblical prohibition). The second is an educational imperative, which seems to be the preferred approach. In either case, the stature of the patriarch and his public role are important issues that mitigate against what otherwise would be considered unacceptable.

The earliest Amoraic tradition assembled in this *sugya* describes proto-Amoraim, the father of the first-generation Amora Samuel and his compatriot, Levi, in the synagogue of Shaf ve-Yatev in Nehardea. They are described as praying in the presence of an *andarta* (a Greek loan word, denoting a statue).[49] By Islamic times, praying in the presence of a statue was out of the question. The Babylonian Gaon, Hai son of Sherira (939–1038) removes any sense of Jewish culpability, arguing that "there was an image (צלם) and the Persians were serving it. . . . By decree of the king they raised it against the will of Israel, and when the edict was revoked they removed it, and the monarchy (מלכות) itself nullified it."[50] This solves any problem of Jewish culpability using the (rather standard) persecution defense.[51] The Talmud itself belies this interpretation, however, asserting that the statue was Jewish public property. The form of the statue is unknown. The Babylonian Gaon Ḥananel son of Ḥushi'el (d. 1055/6) thought the statue was in the "form of a man" (צורת איש), and Rashi posits that it is an image in the "form of a king" (צלם דמות מלך). The Babylonian response to the *andarta* is strikingly different from Palestinian attitudes toward imperial Roman sculpture that we have surveyed – especially if Rashi is correct. The statue and the rabbinic response to it were apparently unusual even for the redactor, who chose to preserve this episode.

This event is highlighted further by the fact that it occurred in the Shaf ve-Yatev synagogue – one of the two "extra-holy" synagogues of Babylonia. Gaonic tradition has it that at the start of the Babylonian captivity, Jehoiachin, King of Judea, founded this synagogue and included in its foundation earth and stones from the first Temple.[52]

A tradition preserved in *b. Megillah* 29a places the father of Samuel and Levi praying in this synagogue. The Divine presence was considered to be particularly strong in Shaf ve-Yatev. So, for example,

The father of Samuel and Levi were sitting in the synagogue of *Shaf ve-Yatev* in Nehardea.
The Divine Presence (*Shekhinah*) came, they heard the tumult and they rose and left.

The reputation of this synagogue continued long after Nehardea itself was destroyed by the Palmyrenes in 259 C.E.[53]

Samuel appears later in our *sugya*, this time demanding that his student, Rav Judah, nullify a seal ring by "blinding" the sculpted image. This suggests that Jews used such rings, with images, in Babylonia. Samuel reacted quite differently to the ring of his student than his father did to the sculpture in the synagogue. Perhaps the reason is as the Talmud suggests: a distinction between the public and private realms. It is also possible that it rests in the sense that the sculpture (whatever it depicted) was not an object that Samuel's father could control, whereas the ring of his student was within his purview.

Abaye of our *sugya* was of the opinion that only images of the heavenly attendants that can actually be made in facsimile are forbidden. This leaves room for a broad artistic repertoire. This *sugya* suggests that at the very heart of the Babylonian rabbinic community, an extremely liberal attitude toward making nonidolatrous art was well established. This difference is clearly related to the different visual environments in which Palestinian and Babylonian rabbis existed. In Babylonia, Sassanians did not worship human sculpture and there was no cult of the emperor.[54] Jews there do not seem to have felt besieged by Persian idolatry in the same way that Palestinians did. Babylonian Jews, living in an ancient diaspora community yet still outside the bounds of the religiously hypercharged Land of Israel, never experienced the traumas that Palestinians experienced – most notably, the paganization of their land and the events surrounding Caligula's statues. They lived in relative security, their rabbis (beginning with Samuel) asserting that "the law of the land is the law."[55] Whatever they thought of Persian worship, the response to idolatry was not an issue of mortal concern.

CONCLUSION

Throughout the Greco–Roman period, Jewish art was, as Heinrich Strauss taught, a "minority art." Jewish use of the visual was but one factor of the life of the Jewish *ethnos* in the Greco–Roman world. Jews participated fully in the visual culture of their times, even as they continued to safeguard that they need not participate in idolatry. What it meant to participate in "idolatry," however, was expressed in differing ways throughout this period. This boundary construction was sometime erratic as it was often subtle or even personal, as Jews struggled to live as a minority in what was once their own land and which they still believed to be so, surrounded by idolators (whether polytheists or Christians). Focusing on the Hasmonean tombs at Modi'in and the synagogue of Na'aran in the Land of Israel, and offering a more diffuse interpretation of diaspora communities, I have traced attitudes toward art held Jewish communities of the Greco–Roman period.

PART THREE

JEWISH "SYMBOLS" IN THE GRECO–ROMAN WORLD

ERSHOM SCHOLEM, LIKE OTHER MEMBERS OF THE ERANOS GROUP, displayed a profound interest in "symbols."[1] In fact, one of his most important monographs is entitled *On the Kabbalah and Its Symbolism.*[2] This concern was turned to the purposes of state building when, in 1949, Scholem set out to explain the historical meaning of the Shield of David – a "symbol" that had served as the centerpiece of the Zionist flag since its inception, and of the Israeli flag beginning on May 15, 1948. The results of Scholem's research were not intended exclusively, or even mainly, for scholars. They were published in an annual distributed to subscribers of the liberal daily *Haaretz*, known as *Luaḥ Haaretz* (the *Haaretz Almanac*) – without footnotes. This essay was later expanded and translated into German and English for scholarly audiences, and reformulated further as popular articles in English and French.[3] The urgency to develop national symbols experienced in those days is expressed in the cover illustration chosen by editor Gershon Schocken for *Luaḥ Haaretz* 1948/9, where the stylized image of a menorah derived from an ancient Jewish oil lamp is illustrated. This menorah was part of a series, for the 1949/50 issue is decorated with a stylized version of a menorah discovered at Priene in Asia Minor. These book bindings, like some of the advertising icons within *Luaḥ Haaretz*, drove home the sense of the "Old–New Land."

"The Star of David: History of a Symbol" was intended to set the *Magen David* firmly within this symbolic framework. Methodologically, this article reflects Scholem's own internal tensions as both a "phenomenologist" and a philologist. Among the Eranos scholars, Scholem has been described as "the most independent-spirited," rejecting "the conceptual terminology of psychoanalysis" and particularly Jung's "theory of archetypes."[4] This said, Scholem's enthusiasm for symbols was shared with his Eranos compatriots. In a spirit that would be well received by his Eranos friends, Scholem waxed poetic on the nature of the symbol. He wrote in "The Star of David: History of a Symbol":

Symbols arise and grow out of the fruitful soil of human emotion. When a man's world possesses spiritual meaning for him, when all of his relations to the world around him are conditioned by the living content of this meaning – then, and only then, does this meaning crystallize and manifest itself in symbols. A reality without tension, a reality which in the eye of the beholder contains no specific intent, cannot address him in the language of symbols. It remains, mute, uninformed matter. Certainly a very high degree of tension is required in order to crystallize the variegated phenomena of this world into simple, unitary and characteristic forms. Something of the secret of man is poured into his symbols; his very being demands concrete expression. The great symbols serve to express the unity of his world.

If this is true of the individual, it is true to an even greater extent for the symbols used by a group, a community, or a people. . . . The community lays hold of some detail of its world, apprehends the totality in it, and derives from it and through it that totality and its contents. The more such a detail contains within it of the specific character of that community's world, the more is it suited in the eyes of the community to become a symbol. . . .

Scholem continues his pangyric for another page, although this selection provides a sense of his approach. "Symbols" have considerable pride of place in Scholem's thought, serving as visual shorthand for the worldviews of the communities responsible for them.

The main body of Scholem's essay is a historical discussion of the history of the *Magen David* in Jewish history that is sensitive to place, time, and social group. In this section, Scholem describes the Star of David before Zionism as a "hollow" symbol, invested with meaning differently by Jews of varying allegiances. Reflecting his own biography and subsequent conversion to Zionism, Scholem writes harshly that "just at the time of its greatest dissemination in the nineteenth century the Shield of David served as the empty symbol of Judaism which itself was more and more falling into meaningless."[5] With Zionism, he adds, "This fault became a virtue: rather than calling to mind past glory, it addressed hopes for the future, for redemption."[6]

Unfortunately for Scholem the "phenomenologist," his historical evaluation of the Star of David does not reveal a historical symbol that reaches the theoretical lofty heights with which he began his article. Instead, it symbolizes a period of religious decadence, an "exile" (to use his terminology in other contexts) that was followed by a Zionist "redemption." This model is further spelled out in Scholem's discussion of the *Magen David* during the Holocaust and in the State of Israel. Here, Scholem the mythmaker reaches a crescendo, remythologizing the *Magen David* fully in terms of his own historiosophical categories of exile and redemption. Scholem writes:[7]

But far more than the Zionists have done to provide the Shield of David with the sanctity of a genuine symbol has been done by those who made it for millions into a mark of shame and degradation. The yellow Jewish star, as a sign of exclusion and ultimately annihilation, has accompanied the Jews on their path of humiliation and horror, of battle and heroic resistance. Under this sign they were murdered, and under this sign they came to Israel. If there is a soil of historical experience from which symbols draw their meaning, it would seem to be given here. Some have been of the opinion that the sign which marked the way to annihilation and to the gas chambers should be replaced with a sign of life. But it is possible to think quite the opposite: the sign which in our own days has been sanctified by suffering and dread has become worthy of illuminating the path to life and reconstruction. Before ascending, the path led down into the abyss; there the symbol received its ultimate humiliation and there it won its greatness.

In reading "The Star of David: History of a Symbol," I find myself taken with the dichotomy within Scholem, and drawn to Scholem the philologically based historian over Scholem the phenomenologist. The historical survey is a model of how scholarship on symbols is to be conducted. But what Scholem saw as a detriment in the history of the *Magen David*, I see as a virtue. What allowed nineteenth-century Jews of varying approaches to identify with this symbol was its flexibility, a conceptual hollowness that allowed Jewish communities and individuals to see themselves in the *Magen David* even when their worldviews had little else in common.

An important theoretical model for a less determined approach to symbols is Anthony P. Cohen's *The Symbolic Construction of Community*. Cohen suggests that symbols (visual and otherwise), essential for the maintenance of communal boundaries, are of necessity shells for varying imparted meanings, and not signifiers of unchanging ideas. Cohen spells out his approach in regard to the peace symbol, so meaningful in 1960s America:[8]

On any demonstration or procession at which this symbol is prominently displayed, sympathizers could all comfortably associate themselves with it and, indeed, find it an adequate expression of their position for the purpose of a certain kind of discourse. Yet, were they to debate among themselves the merits of unilateralism as opposed to multilateralism; the advisability of one kind of campaigning strategy as opposed to another; their attitude towards NATO or to the Soviet Bloc; the importance of Christianity, pacifism or socialism to their support for nuclear disarmament, the symbol would become revealed as an effective, but very superficial gloss upon an enormity of variety of opinion, much of it hostile rather than merely opposed. This is not just to say that any great social movement is invariably a coalition of interests. It also demonstrates the versatility of symbols: people of radically opposed views can find their own meanings in what nevertheless remain common symbols.

The discomfort that Scholem found with the modern Star of David would simply be de rigueur for Cohen in his interpretation of the multivaliancy of symbols. In dealing with ancient history, the range of meanings of a particular visual symbol are especially hard to extract from the sources. We know only the interpretations that were written down by literary elites, and of those, we have at our disposal only the interpretations that have been preserved. Images that were used over broad chronological periods, in diverse cities and towns – by speakers of Persian, Greek, Aramaic, Hebrew, and Latin in two empires and on three continents – must certainly have meant differing things in different contexts. It was the very elastic nonverbality of the symbol that made it meaningful for diverse Jewish communities, providing an agreed language of commonality within their differences. When the same symbol was used by non-Jews in reference to

Jews, the breadth of meaning became even broader – even more so when colonized Jews and imperialist Romans used the same imagery to denote Jews and Judaea. Symbols hide as much as they reveal, providing a focal point for social communication and for community building. They are not unequivocally "concrete embodiments of ideas," as Clifford Geertz would have it[9] and Goodenough and Scholem would accede to be true. More than being static signifiers, symbols are focal receptors of meaning that serve diverse living communities. Some personal examples follow.

THE SAMARITAN MENORAH

A few years ago, I was a guest in Neve Marqeh, the Samaritan section of the Tel Aviv suburb of Holon. As part of my tour, Benyamim Tsedaka, editor of *News of the Samaritans*, brought me into a number of private homes. On the walls were various framed pictures of Biblical scenes, glossed with Biblical verses in Samaritan script (Figure 53). The imagery in one house was of particular interest. There, I saw a large framed image on textile of the seal of the State of Israel, but with one difference: The word "Israel" was written in Samaritan script, not in the modern Hebrew "Jewish" font of the original seal.

53. A Samaritan symbol of the State of Israel, Holon (photograph by Steven Fine).

The sorts of "syncretism" that a historian might find in this image are too good to pass up. Rachel Hachlili offers a more-or-less standard Israeli explanation of the seal:[10]

The emblem of the State of Israel has this symbolic meaning: the depiction of the menorah from the Arch of Titus is meant to express the return of the menorah from Rome to the Land of Israel, and the end of the Exile, and the close connection of the people's history to their land. The olive branches express the peaceful aims of the state, with the inscribed Hebrew name of the new state, Israel. The ancient symbol of Judaism, the menorah, was rightly chosen to express and represent the continuity and creation of the old-new state of Israel.

If this explanation is the standard one, does the seal in the home of the Samaritan family suggest complete identification with the Jewish national myth? Is this what they meant? What about the olive branches, which are drawn from standard European heraldry, and associated elsewhere with the prophet Zechariah's vision of the menorah?[11] Does this mean that the Samaritans now accept post-Pentateuch literature? Because their menorah was not exiled to Rome, does identification with the seal mean they have been completely assimilated into the civil religion of Israeli Jews? It is clear, of course, that Samaritans accept the Torah, in their own version – and no other "Biblical" literature. The placement of the seal of the state on the wall of a private home suggests how thoroughly the Holon Samaritans have integrated into modern Israel. In fact, many of the women of the community are Jewish, Samaritan children in Holon study in Israeli secular schools (and in their own supplemental afternoon school), and they serve in the Israel Defense Forces. When I visited, close to Israel Independence Day, the synagogue was draped with blue-and-white flags bearing the Star of David (David was a Jewish hero, and certainly not a Samaritan one). Except for the Samaritan script of the signage on the gate of the synagogue, one could easily mistake this synagogue for a typical Jewish synagogue in Israel. Comparison of the Holon community with Samaritans who reside on the Samaritan holy mountain Mt. Gerizim or in neighboring Nablus suggests how much more "Israelicized" the Holon Samaritans are. In Nablus a large group of Samaritans live within the Palestinian ethos; many speak Arabic as their primary language. Significantly, I saw no symbols of Israeli patriotism on Mt. Gerizim. The display of Israeli symbols is clearly as much an internal Samaritan conversation as one directed to the broader Israeli culture.[12]

This Samaritan example suggests how complex the interpretation of symbols may be – in the present, as in the past (where our access to sources is definitionally less). My guess is that the individuals who created this image and displayed it proudly in their home had no cognizance of the complex historical and art historical issues I have raised. Their goal in displaying this menorah was to assert their "Israelite" patriotism in a way that is transformed by their minority subculture. The use of Samaritan script absorbs the symbol of the state into the sacred history of their community, and their community into the state.

THE CARPET OF SIMON THE RIGHTEOUS

In 1978, I found myself wandering from the Old City of Jerusalem toward Mt. Scopus. Walking through the Sheikh Jarrah neighborhood, I came upon a sign pointing toward the *Qever Shimon ha-Tsadiq*, "The Tomb of Simon the Just." Not being one to pass up the opportunity to visit such a place (especially as my Hebrew name is Shimon), I turned in. The Second Temple tomb chamber had been completely refurbished to house "the Just one," and the large sarcophagus stood to the side. Upon it were a number of textiles. My eye was caught by one textile in particular – a large red rug bearing a pointed arch, a lamp suspended from its pinnacle, in the lower register. The smaller, upper register was divided into two squares. To the left was the image of the mosque at Medina; to the right, the Kaaba in Mecca. Intrigued by the incongruity, I turned to the only other person in the shrine: a Hasidic man. I asked him, curiously, what the image to the right illustrates. He responded, without missing a beat: "This is the Temple Mount." I then turned to the image of Medina to the left. His response: "This is the repulsive thing (*sheqets*) that the Arabs have built on the Temple Mount." Thanking my informant profusely, I took my leave and continued on my way to Mt. Scopus.

Recently, I encountered this mass-produced carpet once again. This time, I was in the tomb of Nebi Shu'eib – the founder of the Druze religion – above the Sea of Galilee. The Druze minority in Israel has greatly expanded and rebuilt this once distant shrine, adding a broad parking lot and even gift shops. Removing my shoes, I entered the domed shrine of Nebi Shu'eib. There on a wall separating the tomb from the prayer hall, I saw the carpet hanging! The attendant was a bit taken aback by my focus on a mere decoration. Nevertheless, he gladly answered my questions. I pointed to each of the buildings in the upper register and inquired in Hebrew regarding their identities. My informant knew that these were Muslim mosques. This did not seem to bother him, perhaps because Druze participate in the same architectural tradition. The attendant explained that the mosques did not represent any particular buildings, but rather are just a general impression. He was seemingly unaware that before him were the holy places of Islam.

The most recent place where I saw this carpet was in Nazareth, where dozens like it, in three or four colors, were stretched out on a parking lot next to the Church of the Nativity. Others were for sale at a nearby kiosk. In 2001, this parking lot served as a makeshift mosque for Islamists determined to force the Israeli government to allow construction of a mosque taller than the church. Here our carpet was used to symbolize a militant strain of Islam, to turn the lot next to the largest church in the Holy Land into a Muslim holy place as it claims Nazareth for politicized Islam.

When I revisited the Tomb of Simon the Just in 2001, the carpet was gone. I can imagine numerous scenarios: Perhaps it wore out during the intervening quarter-century. Or, perhaps, during the more recent renovations of the tomb, someone decided that this object was inappropriate in the holy place. In the symbolically hypercharged atmosphere of contemporary Israel, this does not seem to me far-fetched. Whatever the case, the same rug, whether found at the Tomb of Simon the Just, at Nebi Shu'ab, or in the makeshift Nazareth protest mosque, bears a locally specific charge – even as it expresses the notion of "holy place" for each community.

I tell these stories in order to illustrate a number of points. First, iconographic boundaries and definitions that are "obvious" to scholars may be unknown to our subjects or only vaguely understood by them. Visual details that do not fit our rarified definitions of religious communities need not necessarily reflect heterodox beliefs or practices. Second, and similarly, members of human communities have differing levels of visual acumen and understanding. Art historians, we should remember, are a self-selecting group of visually literate individuals. Not everyone, throughout history, saw with the same specificity that we do.[13] Nor did they have the files of comparative information that we have at our disposal. No artisan in ancient Palestine, after all, had access to the hundreds of thousands of cards that make up the Princeton Index of Christian Art! The development and choice of imagery were often much more mundane than moderns (with their rarified senses of art, "national spirits," or religious pluralism) would sometimes like to admit. Although the seemingly incongruous reflects religious "variety" in some cases, the use of archaeology to express this interpretation must be treated with considerable circumspection. Third, and most importantly, context matters. Where an image appears is significant for its interpretation. Our examples of the Samaritan menorah and the carpet of Simon the Righteous are not only significant for the history of the Seal of Israel or of Muslim carpets and religion, but also for the way that they – and their imagery – cross (or do not cross) boundaries.

In the following chapters, I will focus on two symbols: the palm tree as it appears in Roman and Jewish contexts and the menorah as used by Jews from the Hasmonian period through the Arab conquest of Palestine. Although visually related by the fact that both are designed as parallel rounded branches that bisect a central stalk, these symbols could not be more different. The palm was never a distinctly Jewish symbol, though for a short time it served as a cipher for Jews and Judaism in imperial art and to a lesser extent among Jews as well. The menorah is the Jewish symbol par excellence, derived from Scripture and signifying Jews and Judaism from the Roman period until the present.

CHAPTER NINE

BETWEEN ROME AND JERUSALEM

THE DATE PALM AS 'JEWISH SYMBOL'

THE PALM MOTIF IS AN EXCELLENT IMAGE THROUGH WHICH to demonstrate how literature and archaeology may be used in tandem in the interpretation of an ancient "symbol." In this chapter, I trace the development of the date palm (*phoenix dactylifera*)[1] as it appears on coins related to Eretz Israel and the Jews from the period of the Roman governors through the Bar Kokhba Revolt, some 129 years. Visual and literary sources stem from a number of independent contexts – Greek and Latin authors, Jewish literary sources, and Roman and Jewish coinage. This variety of sources is unusual for ancient Jewish symbols. The use of date palm iconography on coins minted by both Romans and Jews reflects a complex series of relationships. The question before us is what a date palm meant to the minting authorities who issued these coins and to the populations who used them.

The date palm coin type seems to have appeared for the first time between 480 and 445 B.C.E. in Carystus on the Aegean island of Euboea.[2] During the fourth century, the palm – one of several symbols used extensively in Phoenicia – was particularly popular in the Punic colonies of North Africa.[3] From the end of the third century B.C.E. until the second century C.E., the palm, laden with two clumps of dates, was a particularly important coin type of the Phoenician coastal city of Tyre.[4] Five-, seven-, and nine-branched palms are represented, although seven-fronded date palms predominate.[5] This choice of seven surely reflects formal considerations: The image of a date palm with less than seven fronds is difficult to identify as a date palm (or at least as a hearty date palm suitable to represent a fruitful land). Heavily laden with two clusters of dates hanging beneath a large comb of fronds, the date palm served as a symbol for the fecundity of Tyre and its environs. More than that, the date palm on Phoenician and Punic coins was a shorthand pun for Phoenicia itself – in Greek, *phoînix* means both palm tree and Phoenician.[6] Of the 128 palm tree types cataloged by Leo Anson in his *Numismata Graeca: Greek Coin Types*, sixty-nine derive from Phoenicia or the Punic colonies.[7]

The date palm appears on only one Hasmonian coin, not coincidentally a Tyrian lepton of 98 B.C.E. whose reverse was restruck under Alexander Yannai (103–76 B.C.E.).[8] It appears on Roman coinage minted in Palestine four times between 6 and 59 C.E.: on a lepton of the Roman governor Coponius in 6 C.E.,[9] a lepton of the governor Ambibulus between 9 and 12 C.E.,[10] a series struck by Herod Antipas in 38/9 C.E.,[11] and a lepton of governor Antonius Felix between 52 and 59 C.E.[12] The palm types usually appear with seven branches, as in the Tyrian examples. "Neither distinguished in design or execution,"[13] it is likely that the Roman minters simply borrowed the date palm type from Tyrian issues as a matter of convenience. Tyre exerted considerable economic influence on Roman Palestine. The Tyrian sheqel, which maintained the Ptolemaic standard even through later Roman devaluations, was the standard currency for the sheqel tax paid by Jews to support the Jerusalem Temple.[14] This reality is expressed most vividly by the relatively large number of Tyrian sheqel hoards discovered in first-century Judaea. Furthermore, both the silver standard and the legends of Tyrian tetradrachms served as models for Jewish tetradrachms of the First Revolt. Where Tyrian issues are labeled "Tyre the Holy," the Jewish coins are labeled "Jerusalem the Holy."

The date palm would have been an expedient choice for the Roman minters in designing coins to be used by Palestinian Jews. As we shall see, the date palm type reflected much about the economic life of first-century Palestine. In addition, Jews might raise no objection to the date palm as a "graven image" in violation of their traditions of "anti-idolism." Jews used date palms in their own artistic and literary creations, where it often held an important position. In this regard, an interesting example is a bulla published by Nahman Avigad in 1975. This piece shows a date palm with an inscription in paleo-Hebrew script that reads "King Jonathan." Avigad ascribes the bulla to Alexander Jannaeus (103–76 B.C.E.), noting that the Hasmonean king borrowed the symbols for his coins (anchor, cornucopia, and flower) from current Seleucid coinage, and similarly may have drawn a symbol for his seal from the same sources. Avigad cites small bronze Tyrian coins in support of this contention, noting that this type enjoyed a wide currency in the second century."[15] Why did Jannaeus choose the date palm to adorn his seal? Perhaps he thought that it represented his kingdom both to his Jewish subjects and to the outside world. Incised date palms flank a rosette on two basalt lintels discovered in Gamla. One of these was the main lintel of the synagogue.[16] Palm trees were apparently used as a decorative motif in private contexts as well. Numerous ossuaries for example, bear images of palm trees.[17] The use of date palms represents, therefore, an attempt at accommodation between Rome and its Judaean subjects. Consideration of Jewish discomfort toward human and cultic representations was consistently shown by Roman minters in pre-70 Jewish Palestine – although such concerns were not addressed regarding silver and gold coins, which were minted at regional mints such as Antioch and Alexandria and used in Palestine.

The best-known Biblical reference to the date palm is Psalm 92:13, "the righteous will flourish like a date palm. . . ." This Biblical description of the date palm's fecundity foreshadows the apocryphal book of Ben Sirah 24:14: ". . . I grow tall like the date palm in Ein Gedi, like rose plants in Jericho" – as well as the description of the tree of life in 1 Enoch 24:3–25:6, a book of the Pseudepigrapha. The fruit of this tree is "beautiful, and resembling the clustered fruits of a palm tree. . . ."[18]

Keys to interpreting date palms on Palestinian coins are provided by a series of three nominations issued by Herod Antipas in 38/9 C.E. The reverse of each denomination bears one element of the date palm. Like the lepta of the Roman governors and the coins of nearby Tyre, Antipas's largest denomination bears a fruit-laden palm. The middle denomination bears a palm frond, a common type used throughout the Greco–Roman world as well as by the Hasmonians, Herod, and Antipas himself.[19] This palm frond is generally taken to represent victory, as palm fronds were borne in victory parades. It metamorphosed into a *lulav* in the coins of the First Revolt against Rome. The *lulav* represents the festival of Sukkot, and often was thought to represent victory in early literature.

Antipas's series concluded with the smallest denomination, a coin bearing a cluster of dates.[20] This cluster seems to have been Antipas's innovation, as it appears on no other ancient coins of which I am aware. Why did Antipas place such emphasis on the date palm? Neither close economic relations with Tyre nor the earlier gubernatorial coins can explain this phenomenon. The answer to this riddle lies in the smallest of Antipas's coins, the lepton with its cluster of dates. It is the dates that made Judaea famous in the Empire, which is why Antipas placed such emphasis on them. The significance of Judean dates becomes clear in the writings of Greek and Roman authors who described Judaea and its principle agricultural product: the date.

Theophrastus (372–288/7 B.C.E.) was the first Greek author to discuss Palestinian dates, in the context of the date plantations of Coele-Syria, which Menachem Stern has identified in the Jordan Rift Valley.[21] Like the authors who followed him, Theophrastus was impressed by the palm groves, but even more so by the product of the trees: the dates.[22] In describing the Mediterranean coast, Lucanus (35–65 C.E.) intones poetically the date plantations of Idumea – that is, Judaea[23] – and compares it with neighboring cities:

Idume, rich in palm-plantations, tottering Tyre and Sidon precious for its purple.

Sources suggest that Judaean dates had a considerable following beyond the borders of the Holy Land and that these dates were even the object of intrigue. Josephus notes that Herod's lucrative plantations at Jericho (also in the Jordan Rift Valley) were much coveted by Cleopatra, who procured them through the help of Marc Antony in 31 C.E. In the autumn of 30, after Cleopatra's death, Herod regained them through the intervention of Augustus.[24] Anecdotes regarding Judaean dates and their use in international diplomacy survive in the writings of Athenaeus[25] and Plutarch.[26] According to both authors, Nicholas of Damascus, court historian of Herod the Great, sent dates to Augustus in order to further Herod's relationship with the emperor. Athenaeus notes that Augustus therefore called

them "nicholas dates" in honor of the historian. Plutarch tells a slightly different story: Herod conferred Nicholas's name upon the dates because Nicholas resembled them in sweetness, slenderness, and ruddiness. By the fourth century C.E., the rabbis did not know why this variety was called "nicholas dates," although the name was preserved.[27] The most extensive treatment of Judaean dates occurs in the writings of Pliny the Elder (23/4 C.E.) and bears extensive citation:[28]

But Judaea is even more famous for its palm trees, the nature of which will now be described. It is true that there are palms in Europe, and they are common in Italy, but these are barren. In the coastal regions of Spain they do bear fruit, but it does not ripen, and in Africa the fruit is sweet, but will not keep for any time. On the other hand, in the east the palm supplies the native races with wine and some of them with bread, while a very large number rely on it for cattle fodder. For this reason we are justified in describing the palms of foreign countries. . . . Next to these the most famous [variety of dates] is caryotae, which supply a great deal of food but also of juice, and from them the principle wines of the East are made. But not only are these trees abundant and bear largely in Judaea, but also the most famous are found there, and not in the whole country, but especially in Jericho, though those growing in the valleys of Archaelais and Phaselis and Livias in the same country spoken of. Their outstanding property is the unctuous juice which they exude and an extremely sweet sort of wine-flavor like honey. The nicholas date, belonging to this class, is not so juicy but exceptionally large in size, four put end to end making a length of eighteen inches. The date that comes next in sweetness is less attractive to look at, but in flavor is the sister of caryotae and consequently it is called in Greek the sister date. . . . Of the many drier dates the finger-date forms a class of its own: it is a very long slender date, sometimes of a curved shape. The variety of this class which we offer to honor the gods is called chydaeus by the Jews, a race remarkable for their contempt of the divine powers.

Date palms of rich clusters – or in Antipas's case simply a single date cluster – were used by the numismatic artists to denote both the impressive palms of Palestine and, perhaps more important, the fruit.

Linguistically, the relationship between the dates and the date palm is clear. The Biblical Hebrew *tamar*,[29] Tannaitic Hebrew *deqel* and *temara*,[30] Palestinan and Babylonian Jewish Aramaic *deqla*,[31] Greek *phoînix* and *dakulta*,[32] and the Latin *palma*[33] all denote both the tree and its fruit. The linguistic conflation of the palm and the date parallels the visual conflation I have suggested. Antipas's attempt to

54. Bronze coin of the First Jewish Revolt, year 4, 69/70 C.E. (from the Alan I. Casden Collection of Ancient Jewish Coins, no. 91).

show the dates without the palm was ultimately unsuccessful and was never repeated. The great numismatist and keeper of the British Museum collection, Frederick Madden, even mistook this coin type for a "a fig tree or an orange-tree laden with fruit."[34]

As we have seen, the Greek and Roman authors were vocal in their praise of Palestinian dates and impressiveness of the local palm plantations. Together with any possible Tyrian influence, this fact explains credibly the presence of date palms on Roman coins in Palestine. Any Jewish input into the choice of this numismatic symbol cannot be measured, although the date palm certainly was a popular theme among Jews in Second Temple Palestine. This is reflected in the bulla and coins of King Jonathan and on the lintel of the Gamla synagogue.

Jewish interest in the date palm coin type is clearly reflected in the coinage of the First and Second Revolts against Rome. In the year 70 C.E., year 4 of the First Jewish Revolt, a tetradrachm was issued by the Jewish minting authorities (who themselves are anonymous) that is of particular interest (Figure 54).[35] On the reverse side of this coin appear two lulav bundles flanking an *ethrog* (citron), clearly representing the festival of Sukkot. On the other side is the image of a date palm, flanked by two baskets of fruit. Paul Romanoff identified this palm tree with its baskets as the first fruits that were brought to the Temple on the festival of Shavuot, Pentecost.[36] He suggests that the reverse represents Sukkot, the obverse Shavuot. Whether the festival connection for the palm tree with its baskets is accepted or not, however, Meshorer is clearly correct that the baskets "provide an excellent artistic expression for the fertility of the land."[37] In regard to the first fruit offering, the second-century patriarch Rabban Simeon son of Gamaliel is cited in *t. Bikkurim* 1:5 as saying: "First fruits of dates are not brought except from the date

palms that are in Jericho." The quality of Jericho dates, attested to by Greco–Roman sources, is thus confirmed by an early rabbinic source. For the first time since the Hasmoneans, the date palm had become a "Jewish numismatic type."

Romans continued to use the date palm to symbolize Judaea and the Jews throughout the first century. The *Judaea Capta* series is the most famous usage. This series appeared between 71 and 82 C.E. in bronze, silver, and gold at mints throughout the Empire (including Caesarea Maritima).[38] The *Judaea Capta* type is apparently modeled on the victory coin of Herod and Sosius over Mattathias Antigonos in 37 B.C.E.[39] There, a large trophy is flanked by two seated and bound prisoners. The *Judaea Capta* series appeared in numerous variations, but we will focus here on two representative types. The earliest *Judaea Capta* issue shows a large trophy to the left, a personification of Judaea seated and bound to the right (Figure 22). Later images show the trophy transformed into a date palm. From a formal standpoint, the narrow stalk supporting the heavy upper part of the trophy is transformed into a date palm and vice versa: The date palm is transformed into a sort of a trophy (Figure 55). This iconography follows sculptural models;[40] it appeared on the facade of the "Temple of Peace" constructed by Vespasian in Rome to commemorate the victory of Judaea as well as on Titus's armor in sculptural representations. This palm trophy is tailored specifically to represent Judaea, the newly "captured" nation. This image of the destruction of Judaea, symbolized no less by the date palm than by her personification, is not principally directed toward the Jews. Minted throughout the Empire, the *Judaea Capta* series is a warning to all other groups within the Empire not to follow suit, so it can be seen as a propagandistic assertion of the greatness of the Flavians and the Flavian peace.

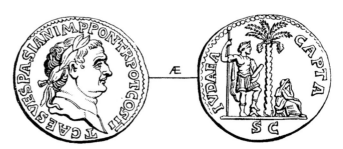

55. Bronze *Judaea Capta* coin of Vespasian, 72 C.E. (after F. Madden, *History of Jewish Coinage* [London: B. Quaritch, 1864], 191, no. 1).

56. Bronze coin of the Bar Kokhba Revolt, year 3, 134/135 C.E. (from the Alan I. Casden Collection of Ancient Jewish Coins, no. 133).

A seven-branched date palm appeared on Roman coins for a period of six years during the decade after the conclusion of the First Jewish Revolt. Its use as a regional type was clearly resumed after the war. In the Roman capital of Palestine, Caesarea Maritima, a series bearing the date palm on the reverse and the image of Domitian on the obverse appeared between 80 and 86.[41] These coins echo the Caesarea coins of Domitian. The date palm appeared three other times in Palestine between 81 and the Second Jewish Revolt. In all three issues, the bust of the emperor appears on the obverse, the palm on the reverse. In the pagan city of Neapolis, the bust of Domitian appears on the obverse, the palm on the reverse.[42] Under the Jewish king Agrippa II, Domitian again appeared in 85–6;[43] and between 98 and 117 the emperor Trajan appeared, with the palm tree on the reverse, in the predominantly Jewish city of Sepphoris.[44] These coins do not reflect any particular "Jewish" or "Jewish–Samaritan" iconography.[45] Rather, a regional type had developed that reflects the fecundity of Palestine as well as the significance of the regional mint at Caesarea. The connection between Domitian and the palm could have been lost on few iconographically interested viewers, who were certainly aware of the coins of *Judaea Capta*. Agrippa II and Sepphoris used the same imagery as Neapolis and Caesarea. This attempt to dispel any appearance of ambivalence might explain the decisions by these Jews to include portraits of the emperor on their coins. The latter first century was no time for the Jews who had sided with Rome through the revolt to distinguish themselves in a way that might be interpreted nationalistically or appear anything but fully loyal.

In 96 C.E., the emperor Nerva issued still another Roman coin bearing the image of the palm tree[46] – a bronze sestertii commemorating his decision to relieve the abuses perpetrated in the collection of the *fiscus Judaici*. The

obverse contains the image of the emperor, and a seven-branched date palm appears on the reverse. The legend reads: *Fisci Judaici Calumnia Sublata*. The date palm of Nerva's issue represents a subtle resignification of this symbol. Jews throughout the Empire were subjected to the Jewish tax, not just those of Judaea.[47] The date palm here represents the Jewish minority group within the Empire, both Palestinian and diaspora Jewry. Meshorer makes a similar point, stating that "this design came to symbolize both Judaea and Jewish affairs."[48] To the nations under Roman subjugation, perhaps more than the Jews, this was a reminder of the way that Rome had handled a rebellious province as well as its diaspora population. Behind the surface focus on mitigating the ill-effects of the tax, this coin, which was circulated widely throughout the Empire, both warns others not to revolt and at the same time asserts the beneficence of the Roman state.

The final usage of the palm tree in Palestinian coinage took place on a bronze denomination of the Bar Kokhba Revolt of 132–135 C.E. (Figure 56). H. St. Hart suggests that "the frequency of the palm tree on the coins of the

57. Lozenge of a palm tree, Capernaum synagogue (photograph by Steven Fine).

Second Revolt is a deliberate rejection of the Roman yoke, a deliberate echo of an answer to the Flavian issue of long ago."[49] One might also suggest that it is a reaction to the Nerva coins and the Jewish tax. Whether all of this is true, however, is hard to tell. Ancients, after all, did not have the benefit of extensive illustrated catalogs and large collections to draw on, as we do now (although they certainly had longer memories than we sometimes do). If the polemical point was so clearly intended, one might have expected the date palm to have appeared on a silver denomination. It is always possible that the date palm, which in truth does not occur terribly frequently in the coin types of either revolt, appeared during the Second Revolt on bronze coins, the reverse of which is the image of a clump of grapes simply to reflect the fecundity of the Holy Land.

Numismatists and archaeologists have often interpreted the seven branches of many of the palm trees on Jewish coins as a hidden code for the menorah and its seven branches. In 1916, Heinrich Kohl and Carl Watzinger suggested a connection between the numismatic representation of the date palm and date palms that appear carved on two consoles from the synagogue at Capernaum and in Jewish funerary reliefs.[50] One of the consoles is illustrated, the palm indeed sporting seven fronds. Following on Kohl and Watzinger, Leo Kadman implicitly claimed continuity between the seven-branched image on Bar Kokhba coins and the same consoles.[51] This connection might have seemed more plausible in those days, when Capernaum was still dated to the second century, and not the fourth or fifth as it is today. Leo Mildenberg strongly identifies the seven-branched date palm with the menorah:[52]

Noteworthy, however, on Bar Kokhba pieces – and on one rare Herodian bronze coin . . . and a stone architectural fragment from the Capernaum synagogue is the fact that the tree always has seven branches – which can hardly be interpreted as anything but a reference to the menorah.

The problem is, however, that the second console at Capernaum, generally not shown in early publications, does not display a palm with seven branches (Figure 57). It has eleven! This alleged connection between the menorah and the seven-branched palm is an outstanding example of eisegesis and overinterpretation by people who for whatever contemporary reasons miss not finding the menorah in Jewish numismatics of antiquity.[53]

We have seen that the image of the date palm on Judaean coins is relatively easy to trace and its "meaning" well attested in ancient sources. For Jews and Romans alike, the date palm represented the fecundity of Palestine. For Greeks and Romans, however, the meaning was considerably more stable: The date palm represented Judaea and its most famous product, its dates.

CHAPTER TEN

"THE LAMPS OF ISRAEL"

THE MENORAH AS A JEWISH SYMBOL

T HE ARCH OF TITUS, CONSTRUCTED ON THE ROMAN FORUM
in 81 C.E., memorializes the ultimate subjugation of Judaea by the
Roman general Titus, son of the emperor Vespasian, in the Jewish
War of 66–74 C.E. (Figure 58). The bas reliefs within the arch stand tribute to
the glorious victory parade staged in Rome in celebration. On one side of
the arch's interior, Titus is shown riding a chariot drawn by four horses, the
winged goddess Nike hovering above and crowning the victorious warrior.
On the opposite wall, the spoils of the Jerusalem Temple are portrayed
(Figure 59).[1] Trumpets made of fine metals are shown as well as a tablelike
structure, apparently the golden Table of the Showbread. The table is set to
the right of the seven-branched menorah and enters Rome at the front of
the procession. The artist has set the Showbread Table in the middle ground,
thus highlighting the lampstand in the foreground. Above are placards that
once bore inscriptions. These identified and explained the glorious displays of

58. The Arch of Titus, Rome (photograph by Steven Fine).

Titus's procession to those who witnessed it – and to anyone who passed under the Arch of Titus in future generations.[2]

The central focus of the composition is the golden seven-branched Temple menorah. The Temple artifacts are borne into the city by Roman soldiers crowned with wreaths that bespeak their victory over the Jews. In book seven, lines 148–52, of *The Jewish War*, Josephus Flavius describes this event in great detail. He too stresses the menorah:

The spoils in general were borne in promiscuous heaps; but conspicuous above all stood those captured in the temple at Jerusalem. These consisted of a golden table, many talents in weight, and a lampstand, likewise made of gold, but constructed on a different pattern than those which we use in ordinary life. Affixed to a pedestal was a central shaft, from which there extended slender branches, arranged in the shape of a trident-fashion,[3] a wrought lamp being attached to the extremity of each branch, of these there were seven, indicating the honor paid to that number among the Jews. After these, and last of all the spoils, was carried a copy of the Jewish Law. They followed a large party carrying images of victory, all made of ivory and gold. Behind them drove Vespasian, followed by Titus; while Domitian rode beside them, in magnificent apparel and mounted on a steed that was in itself a sight.

Following the same order portrayed in the Arch of Titus, Josephus places the table before the menorah. This order follows Biblical precedent as well, the table being described in Exodus 25:23–7 and the lampstand in Exodus 25:31–9.[4] Josephus also follows this order in his descriptions of the wilderness Tabernacle[5] and in his description of Pompey's viewing of the Temple vessels during his conquest of Jerusalem in 63 B.C.E., when Pompey illicitly entered the shrine. Josephus writes that when Pompey entered ". . . the golden table was there and the sacred lampstand and the libation vessels and a great quantity of spices. . . ."[6] Only in Josephus's description of the Maccabean revolt does he deviate from this sequence, there under the influence of 1 Maccabees – a text that consistently, although subtly, emphasizes the menorah.[7]

In describing the booty of the Second Temple taken to Rome, Josephus assumed that his readers needed no description of the golden table or of the scroll of the Torah. Objects of this sort were well known. In fact, in describing the Tabernacle Table of Showbread, Josephus tells his readers only that it looked like "those at Delphi."[8] It was not visually descript – either in his writings or the Arch of Titus reliefs. The menorah was different; its form was so unique as to require Josephus to describe it. For lack of a comparative artifact, Josephus likens the menorah to a trident. Focusing on the visually unique and evocative, the artist of the bas relief stressed the seven-branched lampstand of the Jerusalem Temple. Its structure made the menorah the ideal image to evoke the "captive" vessels of the Jerusalem Temple and the glory that their capture (and eventual public display) brought to Flavian Rome.

Roman taste for the costly and interesting is expressed in Josephus's description of Vespasian's intention in collecting and displaying great art in his Temple of Peace and in his palace:[9]

ancient masterworks of painting and sculpture; indeed, into that shrine were accumulated and stored all objects for the sight of which men had once wandered over the whole world, eager to see them severally while they lay in various countries. Here, too, he laid up the vessels of gold from the temple of the Jews, on which he prided himself; but the Law and the purple hangings of the sanctuary he ordered to be deposited and kept in the palace.

The Temple of Peace, completed in 75 C.E., was close to the (somewhat later) Arch of Titus in the Roman Forum. The Arch of Titus relief literally portrays the ceremonial delivery of the golden Temple artifacts to Rome, objects that the visitor (including, during the second century, perhaps

59. The sacred objects of the Jerusalem Temple, Arch of Titus, Rome (photograph by Steven Fine).

including rabbis) could then view among Vespasian's treasures.[10] If "the opulence and variety of the furnishings [within this temple] stood as a symbol for Rome as the center of the world," as Paul Zanker suggests,[11] then the Temple menorah must have been one of the most visually interesting (and costly) specimens.

Josephus and the designer of the Arch of Titus relief both focused on the menorah's unique design. This uniqueness is an important part of the reason why the menorah has continued to serve as a Jewish symbol for more than two millennia. Its distinctive physical structure, derived from Scripture and then from the Temple, made the menorah an ideal symbol. The distinctiveness of the menorah is well spoken by the fact that the most fragmentary carving of a menorah preserved from antiquity is often enough to make a positive identification. No other Jewish symbol has this instant recognition value – not the date palm in antiquity and not the "Star of David" in modern times. This uniqueness stands behind the rabbinic notion that God showed Moses the menorah drawn in fire by the Divine finger.[12] Still, visual singularity is not enough to explain the use of menorah imagery during the latter Second Temple period and on into late antiquity. Unlike the Star of David for modern Jews, whose greatest asset from the beginning was its very opaqueness, the menorah originates in Biblical

texts and had stood ablaze in the Temple of Jerusalem. Parallel to this deep Scriptural and cultic significance among Jews, the menorah was well known within non-Jewish circles, thanks to the Arch of Titus relief and its presence in the Temple of Peace. This was even more the case under Christian Rome, where the Scriptural references to the menorah were familiar beyond the Jewish community. In this chapter, I explore the ways that this symbol was both represented visually and interpreted by Jews in antiquity.[13] We begin with a discussion of the Second Temple period, the second to fourth centuries, and continue through the Byzantine period.

THE MENORAH DURING THE SECOND TEMPLE PERIOD

Images of the menorah from the Second Temple period are exceedingly rare. The first appears on a lepton of the last Hasmonean king, Mattathias Antigonos, minted in 39 B.C.E. The menorah, together with a Greek legend that reads "Antigonos the king," appears on one side; the Table of Showbread, with an inscription in paleo-Hebrew script that reads "Mattathias the king," on the other (Figure 60). This is the only time that the menorah appears in

60. Lepton (*Perutah*) of Mattathias Antigonos (from the Alan I. Casden Collection of Ancient Jewish Coins, no. 45).

ancient Jewish coinage. Its use by Mattathias Antigonos was context-specific, as numismatist Yaakov Meshorer explains:

> . . . Herod, aided by Roman troops, attempted to conquer Jerusalem. Antigonos was engaged in a struggle for survival, but he was not without support. The Jewish king was backed by families of the priestly rank and by those who desired to preserve the nationalistic Hasmonean heritage from the hands of Herod. . . . Therefore, Antigonos may have depicted the menorah and the table on his coins both to encourage his supporters, and to remind the people of their duty to preserve the sanctity of the Temple (and its priests) from foreigners.[14]

This is an unimpressive bronze coin, smaller than an American penny. The die was clearly designed to be stamped on a larger flange. Antigonos used this unique Jewish coinage as a rallying point – his battle cry (or swan song) in the face of a formidable enemy.[15] All of the numerous "nonidolic" images employed by the Hasmonians before Antigonos were drawn directly from Seleucid coin types. The cultic specificity of Antigonos's coins was developed just at the time when the Hasmonean kingdom was about to be replaced with the Roman client Herod.

Five seven-branched menorahs are inscribed on the walls of the entry hall of Jason's Tomb in western Jerusalem.[16] A seven-branched menorah incised on a sundial was found at the foot of the southwest corner of the Temple Mount that was discovered during the Western Wall excavations.[17] Another menorah, of somewhat finer workmanship than the others, was discovered incised on a piece of plaster from a house uncovered in the Jewish Quarter excavations (Figure 61).[18] Three ossuaries have been discovered as well that bear incised images of menorahs. Rahmani has published an ossuary with five branches on its side, and another with a seven-branched menorah on its lid.[19] In all, a small but significant collection of menorah images exist from latter Second Temple period Jerusalem or its environs.

61. Menorah graffito, Jerusalem (photograph by Zev Radovan, courtesy of the Hebrew University of Jerusalem Photo Archive).

A wide variety of menorah bases are portrayed. This is not surprising, even in a context where the lampstand as a whole might be commonly viewed. Scripture provides no sense of the base of the menorah, and, as we have seen, the menorah base portrayed on the Arch of Titus is problematic. Apparently, the base that did exist must not have been particularly unusual or worthy of note; otherwise, more uniformity might have been expected. Clearly, some Jews in Jerusalem used images of the menorah within a wide variety of contexts – likely many more than this limited sample suggests. This sample does not suggest, however, that the menorah was used in the overwhelming numbers that are known from late antique contexts.

Images of the menorah in latter Second Temple Jerusalem carry a deeper resonance than the same imagery might have in another place at the same time, or in subsequent centuries. Bezalel Narkiss goes so far as to suggest that the "Jewish Quarter" menorah graffito served a functional purpose. He argues that the object to the menorah's right is apparently the Table for the Showbread and perhaps the incense altar. To his mind, the fragment "could therefore be a schematic plan of the sanctuary . . . [that] combines a birds' eye view of the entire area with the frontal display of the objects contained in it."[20] Narkiss is overly concrete in his inference from medieval manuscript illustration that this image "may have been used as a means to instruct young children of the priestly families in the intricate layout of the Temple area; or to instruct young priests in their complicated and responsible future tasks."[21] Jews who drew or engraved menorahs in their tombs, on their sundials, and in their homes had the opportunity to see this Temple vessel. Priests and Levites might view it regularly during the Temple service. According to Mishnah Ḥagigah 3:8, "the table [of showbread] and the menorah" required purification through immersion after the pilgrimage festivals. Uncontrolled contact with pilgrims, it seems, might defile the holy vessels, necessitating their purification through immersion:[22]

How do they undertake the purification of the Temple court? They immerse the utensils which were in the Sanctuary, and say to them [the pilgrims]:
"Be careful not to touch the table and the menorah!"

The Table for the Showbread and the menorah are paired here, following the Biblical sequence. Evidence for popular viewing of the Temple vessels comes from a second, somewhat unexpected, source – a papyrus fragment of a noncanonical gospel found in Oxyrhynchus in Egypt. A "high priest" addresses Jesus and his disciples in a manner highly reminiscent of our m.:[23]

And he took them [the disciples] with him into the place of purification itself and walked about in the Temple court, and a Pharisee chief priest, Levi (?) by name, fell upon them and s[aid] to the Saviour:
Who gave you leave to [trea]d this place of purification and to look upon [the]se holy vessels without having bathed thyself and even without the other disciples having [wa]shed their f[eet]? On the contrary, being defi[led] thou hast trodden in the Temple court, this clean pl[ace], although no [one who] has [not] first bathed [himself] or [chang]ed his clot[hes] may tread it and [venture] to vi[ew] [these] holy utensils!
Forthwith [the Saviour] s[tood] still with h[is] disciples and [answered]: "How stands it [then] with thee, thou art forsooth (also) here in the Temple court. Art thou clean?"
He [the priest] said to him: "I am clean. For I have bathed myself in the pool of David and have gone down by the one

stair and come up by the other and have put on white and clean clothes, and [only] then have I come hither and have viewed these holy vessels. . . ."

The continuation of this tradition, in which Jesus reprimands the priest's sense of piety, need not detain us. *Miqva'ot* (ritual baths) discovered in proximity to the Temple Mount suggest that the priest's description of having "gone down by the one stair and come up by the other" fits the procedures for ascent of the Temple. His process of cleaning, dressing in white clean clothes, and then entering the Temple and viewing the utensils is quite believable – and was apparently standard practice.[24] Taken together with our *Ḥagigah* tradition, this text reinforces the sense that the Temple vessels were seen by large numbers of Jews in first-century Judaea. Their forms were far from being esoteric knowledge.

The coins of both the first and second Jewish revolts portray vessels of the Temple. Images on coins of the First Revolt include horns, and perhaps the brazen laver. Significantly, neither the menorah nor the Table for Showbread is portrayed, although I have no idea what the significance of this decision was. Second Revolt tetradrachms portray the Temple's facade (Figure 26). Between the columns of the tetrapylon and within the shrine is seen an artifact whose identify was in question. Scholars spent much of the twentieth century attempting to identify this object, positing that it is an entrance or door, the Ark of the Covenant, or the synagogue Torah ark. Only in 1987 did Dan Barag correctly identify the Table for Showbread, based upon portrayals on rare Bar Kokhba issues.[25] The long period of uncertainly reflects the visual truth of the Table for Showbread. It is visually nondescript. For this reason, I believe, it dropped out of the Jewish visual repertoire after Bar Kokhba. On Bar Kokhba issues, the table is set in the position where non-Jewish coins often portray sculptural cult figures. The placement of the table in this position suggests, as we have seen, that the cult objects served as Jewish replacements for images of the god, the viewing of the Temple appurtenances being parallel to the viewing of sculptural cult objects in pagan temples. The image of the table on Bar Kokhba coins represents an important parallel to rabbinic and early Christian literary descriptions of the Temple vessels viewed in the Temple. This coin may be seen as a visual presentation of viewing the Temple vessels within the shrine, a practice that the minters hoped would resume once Bar Kokhba rebuilt the Temple.

How did latter Second Temple period Jews relate to the Temple menorah? Its pairing with the table on the Mattathias Antigonos coin and perhaps on the Jewish Quarter graffito is no coincidence. It follows upon the order in Exodus 25:31–40 and 37:17–24, which provides extensive descriptions of both artifacts. Exodus 40:24 relates that once the Tabernacle was completed, Moses "put the lampstand in the tent of meeting, opposite the table on the south side of the tabernacle." The Biblical narrative clearly invests both artifacts with considerable significance – although the Exodus narrative tells us nothing explicit of the symbolism of either.[26] The prophet Zechariah's vision of the menorah builds on the Pentateuchal tradition of a single menorah in the Temple, rather than the ten "menorahs" that are said to have illuminated the more recent Solomonic temple.[27] Thus, the menorah of the Second Temple was connected to the increasingly significant sacred story of the Divinely ordained Tabernacle. Zechariah provides a conceptual understanding of the lamps of the menorah, suggesting that they represent the eyes of the omnipresent God: "These seven are the eyes of the Lord, which range (משוטטים) through the whole earth" (Zechariah 4:10).[28] The notion of God's far-ranging eyes seems to have had some currency during the Persian period and continued through late antiquity.[29] 2 Chronicles 16:9 includes the same verse almost verbatim, with a significant addition: "For the eyes of the Lord range (משוטטות) through the whole earth, to strengthen those whose hearts are blameless toward him."

In the vision of Zechariah, each lamp of the menorah had seven spouts, increasing the light of the menorah exponentially to forty-nine wicks.[30] Zechariah's description of the menorah does not focus on arboreal aspects of the lampstand, as the Exodus descriptions of the lampstand do. Rather, with Numbers 8:1–3, it focuses on the lamps themselves. Eric Meyers and Carol Meyers reasonably suggest that the menorah of the Persian period was a bridge between the Tabernacle menorah and menorahs of the Greco–Roman period.[31] The writings of this sixth-century B.C.E. prophet were certainly known in first-century Judaea, part of the conceptual "toolbox" Jews drew upon for inspiration. Zechariah's vision is also significant in that it focuses on the menorah as emblematic of the Temple. This builds upon notions of the menorah's specialness that are already present in Exodus. Twice the menorah is referred to as the "pure menorah," the only artifact of the Tabernacle so singled out.[32] In Zechariah's vision, the lampstand is not paired with the table but stands on its own. His focus on the menorah is important, for it presages the images of the lampstand that do not set it with the Table of the Showbread that appeared during latter Second Temple times, and then in late antiquity.

Philo of Alexandria, writing during the first third of the first century C.E., returns to the menorah three times. He treats the lampstand in celestial terms. In his *Questions and Answers on Exodus*, Philo discusses the menorah in some detail,[33] his theme the direct correspondence between the menorah and the heavens. Not coincidentally, Philo provides seven questions and answers about the menorah. I cite two examples here:

Question 73: Why is the lampstand "turned (and) of pure gold" (Exodus 25:30a, according to the Septuagint version)?

The lampstand is a symbol of the purest substance, (namely) of heaven. For this reason it is said later that it was made of one (piece of) gold. For the other parts of the world were wholly made through the four elements, earth, water, air and fire, but the heaven of (only) one, (this being) a superior form, which the moders call "the quintessence." And rightly has (heaven) been likened to the lampstand in so far as it is altogether full of light-bearing stars. And rightly has He described it as "turned," for the heaven was made and illuminated by a certain turner's art in accordance with periodic cycles each of which is accurately and clearly turned and the natures of the stars are all described by divine skill.

Question 75: What were the six branches which went out from either side, three equally (Exodus 26:31, according to the Septuagint version)?

Since it is not in a straight line but opaquely that the zodiac lies over and glancingly comes near the summer and winter solstices, He says that the approach to them is from the side (and) the middle place is that of the sun. But to the other (planets) He distributed three positions on the two sides; in the superior (group) are Saturn, Jupiter and Mars, while in the inner (group) are Mercury, Venus and the moon.

We need not linger over the specifics of Philo's cosmology. The point is that this prolific thinker conceived of the menorah as a projection of the heavens. Philo states this most clearly in *On Moses* 2.102–3, where he described the arrangement of the holy vessels within the Tabernacle:

The candlestick he placed at the south, figuring thereby the movements for the luminaries above; for the sun and the moon and the others run their courses in the south far away from the north. And therefore six branches, three on each side, issue form the central candlestick, bringing the number up to seven, and on all these are set seven lamps and candlebearers symbols of what the men of science call planets. For the sun, like the candlestick, has the fourth place in the middle of the six and gives light to the three above and the three below it, so turning to harmony an instrument of music truly divine.[34]

Philo even interprets the menorah metaphorically, comparing Sarah's virtue to the light emanating from the central shaft of the menorah, "which is the brightest of all and geared to God's eyes."[35] In fact, Philo's comparison of a virtuous woman to the menorah is reminiscent of Ben Sirah 26:16–17:[36]

The sun shines in the heights of God,
and the beauty of a good woman adorns the home.
A lamp shines on the holy lampstand,
and a beautiful face on an upright figure.

The lamps and the height of the menorah stand behind Ben Sirah's simile. The use of the menorah to epitomize cultural values far removed from the Temple cult continued into early rabbinic times. *Genesis Rabba* 91: 38 relates that "when a person spoke correctly before Rabbi Tarfon, he would say: bulb and flower (*kaftor u-ferah*). . . ."[37] In Rabbi Tarfon's seemingly idiosyncratic metaphor, the beauty of well-spoken teachings is expressed through reference to the beautiful "bulbs and flowers" of the menorah.[38]

Josephus puts considerable emphasis on the menorah, tracing it back from its ignoble (from a Jewish perspective) placement in Vespasian's Temple of Peace in the Roman Forum at the conclusion of Titus's victory celebration in his *Jewish War* to its Biblical origins in *Antiquities of the Jews*. Josephus loosely paraphrased the Exodus description of the menorah, adding that the various ornaments of the lamp "numbered seventy in all." Hachlili has convincingly argued that the Tabernacle "menorah indeed consisted of seventy parts," and enumerates her calculations.[39] In Scripture, the number seven (and thus, seventy) signifies totality or completeness. Significantly, in *Antiquities* Josephus does not suggest the "trident" analogy of *War*; rather, he describes the menorah in detail:

. . . It was made up of globules and lilies, along with pomegranates and little bowls, numbering seventy in all; of these it was composed from a single base right up to the top, having been made to consist of as many portions as are assigned to the planets with the sun. It terminated in seven branches regularly disposed in a row. Each branch bore one lamp recalling the number of planets. . . .[40]

The celestial significance of the menorah was apparently known to the Sadducees as well – if a tradition in *Tosefta*

Ḥagigah 3:35 indeed reflects their position accurately. According to this text, "It happened that they (the Pharisees) immersed the menorah on the Sabbath day. The Sadducees said: 'Look, the Pharisees are immersing [something as clean as] the light of the moon!'"[41] A parallel in y. Ḥagigah 3:8, 79d, is far more evocative: "Look, the Pharisees are immersing the orb of the sun!" Sources that reflect attitudes of first-century Jews, with or without these rabbinic sources, are vocal in describing the cosmological significance of the menorah. One wonders whether its use on the sundial is related to this cosmological interest. With our fragmentary knowledge, to assert such a connection would be to overinterpret the evidence.[42]

To sum up: The menorah appears with some frequency in the art of first-century Jerusalem. It appeared in the decoration of a patrician house, on a sundial, and within funerary contexts. The few extant examples point to a wider usage of this symbol, although the menorah was not nearly as widely used during this period as it was during late antiquity. That this imagery was utilized literally in the shadow of the Temple menorah is significant, for it suggests the broadening of temple imagery beyond the specifically cultic environment. This process began with the coin of Antigonos Mattathias, who used the menorah and Table of Showbread as rallying cries during the last days of Hasmonean rule. The comparison of virtuous women to the menorah by both Ben Sirah and Philo also suggests that the image of the menorah had wide currency in the imaginations of latter Second Temple-period Jews – and that this interest both preceded the Hasmonean revolt and was known in the Greek-speaking Egyptian diaspora of the first century. Overwhelming evidence – from Philo, Josephus, and perhaps even the rabbis – suggests that the menorah was widely associated with the celestial bodies. This connection is first found in the writings of the prophet Zechariah, who flourished during the sixth century B.C.E. We have no evidence that images of the menorah were used for symbolic purposes beyond Jerusalem and its environs. This was to change, however, in the centuries that followed.

THE MENORAH DURING LATE ANTIQUITY

The great counter-Reformation "Christian archaeologist," Antonio Bosio, explored Jewish catacombs along Rome's Via Portuense on December 14, 1602. Bosio describes his impressions in great detail in his monumental *Roma Sotterrannea*. He writes that the tomb

. . . is very crudely and roughly constructed, containing only two private chambers and even these are very small and mean, as is the entire cemetery, since not even a fragment of marble can be seen there nor any painting nor any mark of Christianity. One sees only, on practically every grave, the seven-branched candelabrum, either painted in red or imprinted in stucco, a practice peculiar to Jews and even persisting to our own time . . . Notably, at the head of a dead-end corridor there can be seen a large candelabrum painted in graves in the following manner:

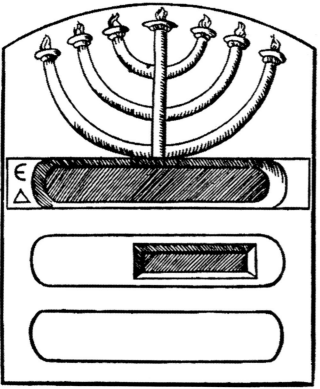

62. A menorah from the Roman catacombs (after A. Bosio, *Roma Sotterranea* [Rome: G. Facciotti, 1632], 1: 141–3).

Bosio goes on to describe – and illustrate – oil lamps bearing images of the menorah. All of this in addition to a Greek inscription bearing the word "synagogue" led Bosio to tentatively identify the cemetery as a Jewish catacomb, although as he notes: "We are, however, ready to yield to any saner and better judgment." Thus, Bosio ends the "second book." It is not insignificant that in the space below, Christ is shown flanked by angels and holding a large cross.[43]

In describing the catacombs at Beth She'arim, E. R. Goodenough makes a similar comment: "the interiors present a great collection of menorahs . . . the menorah was at this time of the greatest importance for Jews to have on their graves."[44] The Roman catacombs and the Beth She'arim catacombs are roughly contemporaneous, both dating to the third and fourth centuries C.E. In both burial contexts, the most strikingly Jewish thing about the catacomb was the preponderance of menorahs. What this means is that Jews from both Palestine and its vicinity and Jews in Rome marked their tombs with the same symbol. This may also be said of Jews in Venosa, Italy and Spain.[45] The menorah had amazingly wide range in burial contexts and beyond.

During the period between the Jewish wars, 74–132 C.E., we find images of menorahs among the numerous symbols used on so-called Darom type lamps from southern Judaea. They appear nowhere else, although admittedly the sample of Jewish art and iconography from this period is small. Of the six "Darom" lamps with images of menorahs, all but one of the menorahs has more than seven branches.[46]

Scholars have suggested that that the presence of menorahs with less or more than seven branches in this small sample reflects a religious scruple against representing seven-branched menorahs.[47] While possible in some cases, it is just as likely that this phenomenon is an example of artistic license, sometimes occasioned by a need to fill a predetermined space. These representations can be quite sloppy – in one case, the image of a lamp has ten branches with eleven lamps upon it![48] An apparently Tannaitic tradition in the *Babylonian Talmud* (which problematically, appears in no Palestinian collection) is errantly cited as evidence for this religious scruple.[49] This tradition is specific in its focus. As we have seen, it forbids three-dimensional functional menorahs with seven branches "even of other metals" than gold that could be used in violation of the centralization of cult in Jerusalem.[50] This tradition does not address symbolic representations of the seven-branched menorah that were not free-standing and potentially functional within a sacral context.

Menorahs predominate as the most important Jewish symbol from the third century onward. Rachel Hachlili recently cataloged each and every occurrence, and there is no need to repeat her findings here. Still, I note that menorahs appeared as decorations within both tombs and synagogues – carved in relief, set down as mosaics, and as decorations on oil lamps and ritual objects. A large open-work marble menorah was discovered within the Sardis synagogue. Judging by the inscription, which appears on both sides of the crossbar that connects the branches at the top, the lampstand could be viewed from both sides. A small

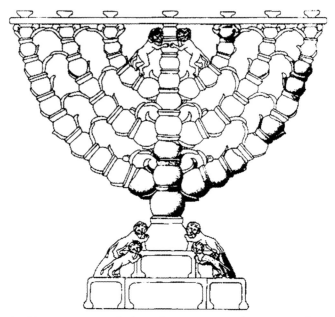

63. Limestone menorah from the Synagogue of Maon in Judaea, reconstruction drawing (after D. Amit and Z. Ilan, "The Ancient Synagogue of Ma'on in Judah," *Qadmoniot* 23, nos. 3–4 [1990], 118, Hebrew, courtesy of the Israel Exploration Society).

fragment of a small bronze menorah was also uncovered. A fragment of dedicatory inscription was found there.[51] The inscription reads:

Aurelios Hermogenes, citizen of Sardis, God-Fearer, from his gifts of Providence, I made [i.e., donated?] the seven-branched lampstand (*heptamuxion*).

Rabbinic sources describe the donation of a lamp to a synagogue by another "godfearer," the legendary "Antoninus Caesar." We cannot know what variety of lamp the storyteller envisions. It is called a *menorah* (and the Aramaic equivalent, *menarta*), a term that represents a broad range of lamps that includes seven-branched lampstands.[52] I entertain the possibility that this lamp (or at least, the lamp imagined by the storyteller) was a branched menorah because so many such lamps are known from late antiquity. An inscription mentioning two menorahs derives from a synagogue in Side in Pamphylia.[53] Remains of free-standing menorahs were found in Nahum Slouschz's Hammath Tiberias synagogue; in the southern Judaean synagogues of Susiya, Maon, and Eshtemoa[54]; and perhaps at Ḥorvat Qoshet in the Western Galilee (Figure 63).[55] During late antiquity, the menorah was by far the most important Jewish symbol.

Execution of menorahs varied widely. Most images portray three legs, and many portray a crosspiece across the top that would have maintained stability on a three-dimensional lamp. The stone lamps from Sardis, Maon, and a small bronze menorah from Ein Gedi all have this crosspiece. In Asia Minor, curls were added beneath the lowest branches. This too is illustrated in numerous images, and is extant in the bronze fragment from Sardis.[56] The Hammath Tiberias limestone portrays the bulbs and calyxes of Scripture as pomegranates – a relationship known from Josephus, although not from any midrashic source before *Targum Sheni*'s depiction of the menorah on Solomon's throne (Figure 64, 68). In others, the segments of the branches are undifferentiated or, as in an image from the Villa Torlonia in Rome, highly floral. Menorahs appear in jewelry from both Palestine and the diaspora, and on amulets as well.[57] In short, the menorah was ubiquitous.

In 1985, Bruce Zuckerman and I treated the menorah as a minority symbol – the symbol of the Jewish minority (*ethnos*) in the Empire.[58] Whether in Palestine or the western diaspora (we have no evidence for Babylonia), Jews commonly marked off their visual space with images of the menorah. It is the very uniqueness of this symbol and its reducible simplicity that made its use advantageous – even with the Temple menorah captive, and for all intent and purposes, lost. Of course, Roman Jews and visitors from abroad (as described in rabbinic sources)[59] could visit the menorah in the Temple of Peace – and this continuity between the actual artifact, the Arch of Titus menorah, and the catacombs and, perhaps, the synagogues of Rome must have been obvious to all.

The increasing sanctity of the synagogue during late antiquity and the articulation of this sanctity in terms of Temple categories led communities in Palestine and beyond to place free-standing, seven-branched lampstands in their synagogues.[60] These lamps did, of course, serve a practical function: providing lighting for the reading of Scripture and to emphasize the Torah shrine within synagogues. Once the Torah shrine – called until the third century merely a chest, a *teva* – became an ark (*aron*) and its curtain a *parokhta* after the Temple veil, the addition of menorahs naturally followed. While Jews were restricted from placing showbread tables or golden altars in their synagogues, light was an essential element of the synagogue service. In Palestine, two menorahs often flanked the shrines, and lamps were suspended from the lower branches

64. Menorah in the mosaic of the Hammath Tiberias IIa Synagogue, juxtaposed to a ripe pomegranate (photograph by Steven Fine).

of some so as to provide even more light. The menorah was at times a utilitarian object and symbol simultaneously, a memorial to the lost menorahs of the Tabernacle and the Solomonic and Herodian temples, and a living symbol in the lives (and deaths) of many members of late antique Jewry.

Jewish development of the menorah as a symbol fit well with Roman modes of thought, where the identification of groups or localities through adaptation of imagery from their cult had long been commonplace. As Richard Brilliant notes suggestively about late antiquity,[61]

The recollection of things, pasts, precious symbols of a better time, maintained the traditions of Greco-Roman culture among those for whom the act of recollection itself served to reaffirm their connection to the classical world.

For Jews, the centrality of recollection was that much stronger, having been "hot-wired" to the core of religious experience reaching back to Scripture itself.[62] Jews in both diaspora communities and in Palestine – an increasingly non-Jewish environment as late antiquity progressed – surrounded themselves with the image of the menorah and other cult objects in order to create visual separation/distinction from the general environment. The menorah became the marker of Jewish religious space, Jewish bread, Jewish tombs, occasionally Jewish homes, and – when worn as jewelry – Jewish bodies. This practice continued from late antiquity through the Middle Ages and into modern times, when its position was in many ways usurped by the Star of David.

Scholars have recently stressed the notion that increased use of menorahs during late antiquity was a response to Christianity.[63] During the fifth and sixth centuries, the menorah was indeed used in ways drawn from the larger Christian context. Mosaics and screens that in a church context might be decorated with a cross were adorned with menorahs in synagogues – and were often made by the same artisans for both religions.[64] The menorah and cross were thus twinned symbols, both serving their communities as markers separating them from one another. This appeared on oil lamps regularly, where Jews increasingly decorated their lamps with menorahs and Christians with the cross.

Overreliance upon the Christian influence model is not convincing, however. Before the rise of exclusivist Christian power in Palestine and throughout the Empire, Jews used the menorah widely for their own purposes – as we have seen at Beth She'arim and in the Jewish catacombs at Rome. At Rome, as in Palestine, three groups were serviced by the same craftsmen during the third and fourth centuries: Jews, Christians, and polytheists.[65] An oil lamp factory discovered at Beit Netophah in Judaea is a good example. Found there were oil lamps "containing the remains of lamps engraved with the emblem of the menorah and shofar, and beside them images of horsemen and nude women."[66] Similarly, in Rome, Jewish gold glasses were made in the same workshops as non-Jewish glass. The glass was sometimes decorated with menorahs and other Jewish symbols, sometimes with Christian imagery, and sometimes with pagan images. Inscriptions are often the same as well.[67] The same is true of sarcophagi in Rome and lead coffins from Phoenicia.[68] Once Christians put an end to polytheism (or at least to its public manifestations), the art of the Christian majority became the main influence on Jewish art and architecture. The essential pattern of symbols was established before the influence of Christian art and architecture had set in.

The success of the menorah as a Jewish symbol is expressed in the fact that it was used broadly by Samaritans and apparently by Christians as well – although the Christian case is far more complex. On occasion, images of the menorah appear in Christian contexts. This makes internal Christian "sense," because Christians had adopted the Jewish Bible and with it the symbolism of the menorah. Since the time of Eusebius of Caesarea (260–339 C.E.), churches and their architecture had been conceived in terms of Solomon's Temple.[69] One could easily suggest that this association was derived from Judaism, as Jewish association of the synagogue with the Temple preceded Eusebius by centuries. It is just as possible, however, that this was an internal Christian development. The Church father Procopius suggests that the menorah of the Second Temple was taken to Constantanople under the emperor Justinian (527–565 C.E.). Procopius suggests that Justinian sent it on to a church in Jerusalem.[70] The presence of menorahs within Christian contexts would work to drive home the connection. The earliest known free-standing Christian menorahs are seven-branched candelabra that are recorded to have stood in churches at Fulda (in Hessen) and Aniane (in southern France) during the reign of Charlemagne (c. 800 C.E.).[71] According to the emperor Constantine Porphyrogenitus (905–59), a seven-branched lampstand (*heptaluxnos*) was lit and used in religious processions. In addition, the imperial palace in Constantinople is said to have included a "Dome of the Seven-Branch Candelabrum."[72]

The archaeological record suggests that images of the menorah were used on a very limited basis by Christians. No menorah imagery has been discovered, for example, in church floors or wall mosaics. A menorah with angular branches flanked by two crosses appears on the tombstone of the "blessed Germanos," an artifact discovered in a sixth-century church at Avdat in the Negev (Figure 65).[73] A similar tombstone was discovered in Syracuse in Sicily. This piece contains the image of a menorah with a tripod base and more than seven branches, apparently an ethrog and a Christian Chi-Ro above and between the

65. Christian grave marker, Avdat (photograph by Steven Fine).

two "Jewish" symbols.[74] Combinations of the menorah and the cross appear in the Golan Heights, and a menorah appears on one side of a church chancel screen from Pella in Jordan.[75] On the other side of the screen is a cross. A seven-branched menorah appears next to a cross enclosed in a medallion on an architectural fragment from Catania in Sicily.[76] Menorahs appear together with Christian imagery on oil lamps from North Africa. A particularly evocative lamp shows an enthroned figure, perhaps Christ, holding a cross. An inverted menorah is at his feet.[77]

A bread stamp, apparently from Egypt or Palestine, shows on one face a large menorah with a crossbar in the center.[78] To the right of the menorah is a cross, and perhaps a very stylized shofar and a palm frond. The Greek name *Probou*, apparently the name of the owner, also appears on the face. Were it not for the cross, there would be no reason not to identify this iconography as Jewish – and rather standard Jewish imagery at that! We have seen that the crossbar may suggest a Jewish model. The presence of a stylized shofar and palm frond is stereotypical. The body of the stamp is in the form of a bull's head (*bucranium*). Such imagery is not unknown in Jewish circles. It appears in bas relief on a Beth She'arim sarcophagus and on a capital from Hammath Tiberias B, stratum IIb.[79] The second face of the stamp is less well preserved; nevertheless, the Greek inscription clearly begins with a Christian cross. What is most fascinating about this stamp is that without the presence of crosses, it would immediately be identified as Jewish. This is precisely the point: Sometime during the (probably later) Byzantine period, Christians occasionally adopted Jewish iconography for their own purposes. I do not believe that this iconography should immediately be taken as evidence for alleged Jewish–Christians, but rather for Christian interest in Judaism and Jewish interpretations of Scripture.[80] The notion of Christian innovation and passive Jewish reception that some have suggested is clearly too simplistic. The relationship must be understood in a more dynamic manner.

Glass pilgrim flasks from Jerusalem reflect a similar liminality. It is unclear whether they were made for Jews, for Christians, or both. Glass pilgrim flasks from Jerusalem bear images, alternately, of crosses or menorahs. Dan Barag dates these vessels to 578–629 C.E., although these dates may be a bit too exacting.[81] They were apparently made in the same workshop.[82] The fact that no flask mixes the imagery may support the notion that the flasks were made to serve the separate communities.

Christians evidently used the bottles to carry holy oil from Jerusalem.[83] It is less clear what Jews might have done with them. Scholars have connected them with a comment by the fourth-century Bordeaux pilgrim[84] that describes Jews ascending to the Temple Mount on the Ninth of Av to rend their garments and anoint a rock with oil. According to this approach, the oil would be collected and transported home – just as Christians are known to have done with oil that had anointed their relics.[85] No Jewish source provides any context for these bottles. The truth is that we do not know why menorah bottles were created – perhaps that is the most interesting thing about them! In one case described by Barag, the menorah is topped with a crossbar, which may suggest that this iconography derives from a Jewish context.[86] The crossbar, I would argue, reflects the practical need to stabilize the upper branches of actual three-dimensional menorahs – and thus perhaps a Jewish iconographic source. Actual lamps that have been recovered from Ein Gedi, Maon (Figure 63), and Sardis

all have crossbars for precisely this purpose.[87] Images of the shofar, incense shovel, and *lulav* beneath the lowest branches of some of the three-legged menorahs of the glasses also suggest internal Jewish iconography. This is not, however, a foolproof sign. Barag posits that the hexagonal shape of the bottles was adopted from hexagonal vaulted canopies (*ciboria*) that stood above the Holy Sepulcher and the cross of Golgotha. This innocuous detail, he creditably argues, would have been taken over by Jews with no cognizance of its origins.[88] Whether produced for Jews, or perhaps for Christians who liked menorah flasks, these bottles suggest close proximity and interaction between Jews and Christian pilgrimage art in late-Byzantine-period Jerusalem.

Christian use of the menorah, limited as it was in visual terms during late antiquity, had deep roots in Christian theology and notions of sacred space. This usage suggests close proximity to Jews and broad Jewish use of the menorah as a symbol during late antiquity. At some level, it is impossible at times to determine the *limus* – the border – where we might state with absolute certainty that this menorah was used by Christians and that menorah by Jews. Context is everything. It is my contention, however, that Christian representation of the menorah during late antiquity was a response to Jewish usage, although Christian interest may have strengthened Jewish attachment to this symbol.

The Samaritan case is particularly interesting in light of important discoveries toward the end of the twentieth century. From the fourth to seventh centuries, the Samaritans used menorahs often within a variety of contexts – on amulets, oil lamps, tombs, millstones, and in synagogue decoration.[89] In fact, the mere discovery of an object with the image of a menorah should not de facto lead to its identification as Jewish – particularly within Samaria or mixed regions like the coastal plain. Other factors – such as the use of Samaritan script, the content of inscriptions, and orientation of buildings (Samaritan synagogues are aligned with Mt. Gerizim) – need to be taken into account. Samaritan menorahs are often highly evocative of the Exodus description of the menorah, with bulbs and calyxes strongly pronounced in mosaics and bas reliefs. The menorah is often set in the context of the Tabernacle/Temple and its appurtenances, as in the mosaic from el-Ḥirbeh in Samaria – where to the left of the menorah is a table of food (the Table of Showbread?), and beyond that a shrine (Figures 66, 67). It is not unlikely that the Samaritans borrowed

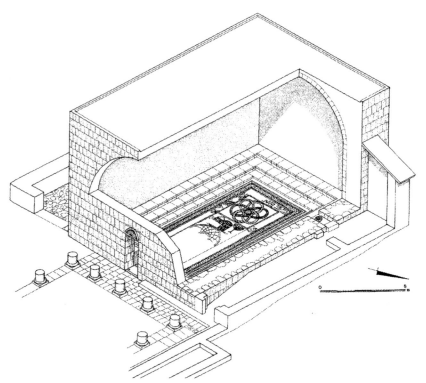

66. The Samaritan synagogue of el-Ḥirbeh, reconstruction drawing (after I. Magen, "Samaritan Synagogues," *Qadmoniot* 25, nos. 3–4 [1992], 68, in Hebrew, courtesy of the Israel Exploration Society).

mosaic from Beth Shean A.[90] The central image, before the podium, shows a Torah shrine flanked by two menorahs. It was laid by the same artisans who fabricated the mosaic of the Beth Alpha synagogue: Marianos and his son Ḥanina. The only explicit indication that the mosaic might be Samaritan is an inscription in Samaritan script in a side room of the synagogue. On secondary examination, however, the lack of a *lulav* bunch in the decoration of the floor seems to support the Samaritan designation.[91] – Samaritans do not use such bunches in their ritual. The Beth Shean A mosaic is an excellent example of the porousness of Jewish and Samaritan imagery in late antiquity – a time of general rapprochement between Jews and Samaritans. Samaritan adoption and use of imagery that was more commonly used by Jews reflects the religious and social closeness between the two communities.

the menorah as a religious symbol from the Jews, as Jewish usage predates Samaritan usage by centuries. It is always possible, however, that Samaritan menorahs were a parallel development, responding to similar late Roman stimuli.

Another suggestively liminal exemplar, this time straddling the Jewish and Samaritan modes, is the synagogue

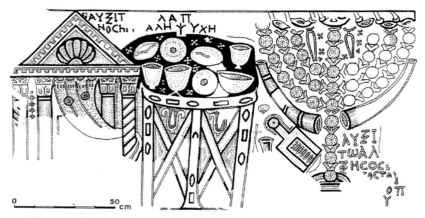

67. The menorah with other sacred objects, mosaic of the Samaritan synagogue of el-Ḥirbeh (after Magen, "Samaritan Synagogues," 68, courtesy of the Israel Exploration Society).

"THE" MEANING OF THE MENORAH AMONG JEWS DURING LATE ANTIQUITY

How did late antique Jews think about the menorah? Scholars have focused on the menorah as a messianic symbol, interpreting it as a symbol of redemption.[92] There is some value in this approach, but it is far from the entire story.

The truth is, this question is beyond what the available evidence can answer, for we have no literary sources from western diaspora communities at our disposal. There is considerably more to say about the Land of Israel – at least within the rabbinic community.

Even among the rabbis, the meanings of the menorah are hard to pin down. No Tannaitic and few Amoraic sources discuss the broader implications of the menorah. It is treated as a Tabernacle/Temple artifact revealed by God. The menorah was to be revered and its details studied in detail, the more so because its form was hard to conceptualize. It was a beautiful golden artifact.

We have seen that the rabbis were aware that some Jews ascribed celestial meaning to the menorah, although early sources do not tell us whether rabbis held this view as well. In one rare early case, in b. Baba Batra 25b, the third-century Palestinian sage Rabbi Joshua son of Levi explains the menorah as a symbolic representation of Torah.[93]

We have seen that the rabbis considered the design of the menorah to be so unique that Moses understood its Biblical description only after God drew it out in fire.[94] From the Temple Scroll of the Dead Sea sect[95] through rabbinic literature,[96] the vast majority of discussion of the menorah was in the form of commentary on the Biblical description of the lampstand. Rabbinic scholars were greatly concerned with imagining what the menorah looked like, to construing for themselves what Moses had seen when God showed him the fiery prototype. This discussion takes its lead from the description of the menorah in Exodus 25 and 37, and forms a chain of continuity with the Biblical appurtenance.[97] It should be remembered that the rabbis never gave up on the rebuilding of the Temple, even as they oriented Judaism to a difficult and "unredeemed" era when sacrifices were "temporarily" suspended. They called this period by the descriptive term zeman ha-zeh, "this time," in contradistinction to sha'at (or, zeman) ha-Miqdash – "the time of the Temple," which existed before 70 C.E. and will resume with the coming of the Messiah.[98] Discussions of the vessels were as practical as they were ideological. Just as Jews studied (and some still study) the sacrifices to prepare themselves for their tasks in the restored Temple, the reflection on the fabrication of the vessels was (and is) often of vital interest.[99] This possibility was never distant. Permission by Emperor Julian "the Apostate" to rebuild the Temple was apparently met with concrete action.[100]

During the mid-second century, one rabbi is said to have viewed and studied the Second Temple menorah in Rome, possibly in Vespasian's Temple of Peace.[101] Sources as early as 2 Maccabees and continuing through rabbinic literature were well aware that the menorah of the Second Temple was not the one created by Bezalel. Both books of Maccabees mention the fabrication of a menorah for use in the rededicated Temple.[102] We have seen that the rabbis imagined that the Hasmonean menorah was constructed of iron rods (שיפודים) plated with tin, which was eventually replaced with a silver lampstand and finally with a golden one.[103] Beginning with 2 Maccabees 2:5–8 and continuing through rabbinic literature, a tradition developed which suggests that the Ark of the Covenant and other elements of the Tabernacle were hidden in Jerusalem when Nebuchadnezzer destroyed the Solomonic Temple in 586 B.C.E. and will be revealed in the apocalyptic future. During the Byzantine period, the Tabernacle menorah was explicitly added to this group. This notion is expressed, for example, in a treatise known as "Tractate Kelim" (which is not to be confused with the Mishnaic tractate of the same name).[104]

Sources from the Byzantine period are far more talkative about the significance of the menorah. The rabbis attach a number of interpretations to the lampstand, ranging from the inherited cosmic interpretation to the notion that the menorah symbolized all of Judaism, the Jews, and their sages. A fine focal point for this discussion is a poem by the Palestinian synagogue poet Yannai (sixth century). Yannai touches on the menorah a number of times in his oeuvre. His is the most extensive preserved reflection on the meaning of the menorah from late antiquity, especially useful because it is the work of a single author (unlike other genres of rabbinic literature, which are composite, and often multigenerational works). Yannai wrote two entire compositions (qedushta'ot) that focus on the menorah, one for the Sabbath morning (shaḥarit) that falls during Hanukkah and an even more focused one for Shabbat be-Ha'alotkha (Numbers 8:1–4). I will translate and comment upon much of Yannai's composition (qedushta) for Shabbat be-Ha'alotkha, in order to gain a sense of how one Byzantine-period Jew – a virtuoso to be sure – presented the menorah to his audience. Although there is little markedly new in Yannai's conception that could not be gleaned elsewhere in rabbinic sources, the beauty of his unified composition (which can only be glimpsed in translation) is striking and affords a congenial locus for surveying rabbinic conceptions.

As we shall see, Yannai presents both a discussion of the physical structure of the menorah and broader conceptions of the menorah as a cosmic symbol for immutable Divine oversight and as a symbol for the Jewish people and its fortunes under foreign domination (particularly under Christian Rome). The menorah, like the trisagion ("Holy, holy, holy is the Lord of hosts; the whole earth is full of his glory," Isaiah 6:3) that is the high point of this poem, is a cosmic bridge between the eternal and the difficulties of Jewish life in the current unredeemed and sometimes dangerous epoch (zeman ha-zeh):[105]

By day we grope like the blind, and by night we feel about like the sightless.

And we say, the Lord is my light, a lamp to the path of my feet.
They were broken in anger, the branches of the menorah.
And the city that was a light to all, is now more ugly than all others.
Search Jerusalem with lamps, and we will see ten menorahs, which were arranged within it, and set near the menorah of the faithful one (Moses).
They will see its strength, those who hear the vision of her greatness
She is entirely pure gold, and on her head a bowl.

As it is written:

"And he said to me, "What do you see?" I said, "I see, and behold, a lampstand all of gold, with a bowl on the top of it, and seven lamps on it, with seven lips on each of the lamps which are on the top of it." (Zechariah 4:2).

א Light that shows and makes seen, and of action and deed
  You gave wisdom to the humble one (Moses), and his eyes were aglow.
ב By your finger you showed him, and by your mouth you instructed him
  And in your household you trusted him, and as an artisan you taught him.
ג . . . hammered, it was hard [to work],
  His hand was unwilling, and he found making it difficult.
ד Its parts were not welded together, but made from a [single] ingot,
  The weight of a talent, of recognized value.
ה Decorated with almond blossoms, [the lamps] inclined [toward the central lamp] and of beaten work,
  It was eighteen handbreadths tall in measure.
ו There were forty-two vessels on it, and all of them were drawn out of it.
ז One gold was as in the vision, and the image of three [different] golds was seen.
ח The calyxes were formed (חרוץ) in green gold,[106] the bulbs in red and the flowers in white.
ט The shape of the calyxes was like cups,
  According to the vision it was created and made.
י The bulbs were made like apples,
  And the beautiful flowers, like capitals (עמודים).

א The lamps of Edom strengthened and increased
ב The lamps of Zion were swallowed up and destroyed.
ג The lamps of Edom prevailed and glittered
ד The lamps of Zion were crushed and extinguished.
ה The lamps of Edom prance over every pitfall (?).[107]
ו The lamps of Zion receded.

ז The lamps of Edom their brightness shines.
ח The lamps of Zion were darker than soot.
ט The lamps of Edom were filled and they dripped [oil].
י The lamps of Zion were lowered and broken.
כ The lamps of Edom were honored and adorned.
ל The lamps of Zion were seized and turned asunder.
מ The lamps of Edom shine over the dead.[108]
נ The lamps of Zion are forgotten like the dead . . . .

While the next section of the poem is fragmentary, one extant line suggests that "the beauty of their lamps will shine" before entering into an acrostic pang to light.[109] Fragmentary, each line of the acrostic ends with the Hebrew word *or*, light. The poet then presents a reverse acrostic. In this text, he moves from the light of the mystically charged heavenly chariot of Ezekiel's vision to the light of the sun, moon, and stars. Yannai masterfully ties together his composition in the last preserved line: "and all of these lamps in the heavens, and You [God] wished to light lamps on earth, according to . . . the vision of the tent in heaven, made according to the pattern of. . . ." Paralleling traditions that were well known in Second Temple period literature – although not prominent in classical rabbinic sources – this conception of the cosmic menorah appears elsewhere in Yannai's oeuvre. In his poem for Hanukkah, Yannai writes:

The seven lamps of the menorah below
Are like the seven constellations [planets] above.[110]

This equation of the menorah with the "seven constellations" builds on Zechariah 4:10 with its seven heavenly "eyes of the Lord." The climax of Yannai's *qedushta'ot*, invariably the recitation of Isaiah 6:3, was a liturgical recitation intended to connect the earthly synagogue community with the supernal realm. Yannai's *piyyutim* conclude dramatically with a poetic interpretation of each repetition of "holy" in terms of the themes of the poem. Unfortunately, this most powerful moment of the liturgical performance has not survived. Within the synagogue context, this poem would next be followed with the Torah reading from Numbers 8, the prophetic reading (*haftarah*) of Zechariah's menorah vision. The Tabernacle menorah, the menorah(s) of the Second Temple, and the heavenly menorah were thus subsumed within a synthesizing rabbinic exegetical and liturgical rhetoric. The effect of reciting this poem in a synagogue decorated with images of menorahs (as most extant synagogues show evidence of having been the case), or even where lighted menorahs stood beside the ark (apparently not a rare occurrence), would have been quite striking even for those with a less thorough knowledge of Hebrew. Yannai's poems balance harmoniously between sections that are linguistically esoteric (heavenly?) in their language and those that are more accessible to the less learned, though Biblically and rabbinically knowledgeable, ear.[111] Thus, the visual and aural, the Biblical, rabbinic and contemporary, would have merged into a marvelously unified and aesthetic liturgical performance.

As a symbol both of Israel and the lights of the firmament that represent Divine oversight, Yannai's menorah brings together the theme of the menorah's loss with its unique form. His sense that the menorah was "broken in anger" and not taken into captivity is unique among extant sources. It emphasizes the real sense that "the lamp of Israel is extinguished."[112] Yannai alludes to the difficulties of conceptualization that the rabbis ascribed to Moses, who is the maker of the menorah. He also resolves the disparity between the one menorah of the Tabernacle and the ten of Solomon's Temple, a theme in other rabbinic sources.

This *piyyut* describes the calyxes of the menorah as having been made of green gold, the bulbs of red gold, and the flowers of white gold. With Yannai, *Midrash Tanḥuma* describes the menorah projected by God to help Moses conceptualize the lamp as having been quite colorful. According to this midrash, Moses was shown the menorah in white fire, red fire, black fire, and green fire.[113] The ascription of colors to specific parts of the menorah is known only from this poem. This variety of colors occurs in an artifact that Scripture emphatically demands be made of "pure gold" (Exodus 25:31, 36, 38, 39). Yannai describes the menorah as having come "from a [single] ingot." His text takes full advantage of the range of hues possible in gold during this period. Colored gold was well within the capacities of Yannai's day. A fine example is a Greek papyrus from Egypt, dating from the third to fourth centuries C.E., that contains explicit directions for the coloration of gold and other metals.[114] None of the extant menorah images from Palestine reflect such a broad color range. It seems to me likely that brilliant colors were applied to any of the now-bare stone bas reliefs that have been uncovered – and even to the now-bare limestone menorahs from Ḥammath Tiberias A, Maon, and elsewhere (Figure 68). I would not be surprised if multiple colors were applied to these menorahs. The notion that parts of the menorah were of different colors was known to artisans in medieval Ashkenaz and Italy and continued in synagogue art into the modern period.

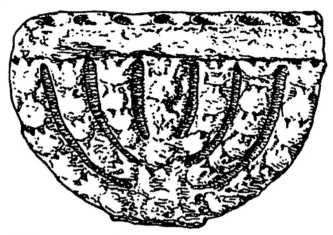

68. Limestone menorah from Hammath Tiberias A (courtesy of the Israel Exploration Society).

An early example is a Bavarian pentateuch from Regensberg in Bavaria, which dates circa 1300. There, the bulbs are red and blue and flowers gold, green, and blue.[115]

Yannai's composition argues strenuously that although the menorah itself is lost, God's heavenly menorah – symbol of Divine love for Israel and of Israel herself – is built into the natural realm and is brightly ablaze. For our purposes, this composition is an excellent example of how one late antique Jew conceived of the menorah and presented his conception to a contemporary Palestinian audience.

Other sources present differing visions of the menorah. The seventh-century poet Yehuda focuses on the menorah in his *piyyut* for Hanukkah. This *piyyut*, which is somewhat fragmentary, discusses the menorah in terms of the seven heavens, seven stars, and the seven clouds of glory that were said to surround the Children of Israel during the desert wanderings. I cite the first stanza only, which is the most complete:

Indeed, He placed seven canopies around the fathers and their flocks,
Corresponding to the seven stars and to the seven lamps of the menorah did he arrange them.
From the beginning, the first canopy corresponds to the sun, and to the first lamp [of the menorah] and to their array.
"And the pillar of cloud moved from before them and stood behind them (Ex. 14:19)."

One of the most expansive rabbinic discourses on the menorah is preserved in a homily that seems to be for Hanukkah in a midrashic collection called *Pesiqta Rabbati*. The most recent editor of *Pesiqta Rabbati* suggests that "the core material" of this midrashic collection "probably dates from the fifth or sixth century."[116] The starting point was Zephaniah 1:12, "And it will come to pass at that time that I will search Jerusalem with lamps," which may have been the prophetic reading (*haftarah*) for the Sabbath of Hanukkah.[117] *Pesiqta Rabbati* contains an explicit messianic interpretation of the menorah:

The Holy One, blessed be He, said: Just as these seven lamps [were][118] kindled in my holy house, in the future I will do the same when I build Jerusalem.

Pesiqta Rabbati's longest reflection on the menorah begins with this verse suggesting that the lamps with which God will search Jerusalem are not ordinary lamps, but the lamps of the menorah. The midrash, whose focus is the light of Zephaniah's words, engages in sustained explication of Zechariah's vision:[119]

. . . [the lamps to be used to fulfill Zephaniah's prophesy] are like those that I showed Zechariah.
As it is written: "and behold, a lampstand all of gold" (Zechariah 4:2).
"You are fair, my love" (Song of Songs 4:7).
And thusly was it shown to Moses, "And you shall make a menorah of pure gold" (Exodus 25:31).
This is the congregation of Israel:
"And you shall make the menorah of pure gold; of hammered work shall you make the menorah, its base and its shaft, its cups, its bulbs, and its flowers shall be of one piece with it" (ibid.).
What is "its base"? This is the patriarch.
"and its shaft"?[120] This is the head of the court.
"[its] cup[s]"? These are the sages.
"its bulbs"? These are the students.
"and its flowers"? These are the young children who study at school.
[All of these] "shall be of one piece with it."
[Hence], "Thou art all fair, my love."
"I see, and behold, a lampstand all of gold, with a bowl on the top of it" (Zechariah 4:2).

This tradition imports Song of Songs 4:7 to identify the entire "community of Israel" with the menorah, and then specifies the parts of the menorah in terms of the social/educational system of the rabbinic leadership. *Pesiqta Rabbati* continues with exposition of Zechariah's vision, comparing the seven lamps to seven commandments of the Torah: the priestly gifts, tithing, sabbatical years, the jubilee, circumcision, honoring parents, and Torah study – which "is greater than them all." *Pesiqta Rabbati* concludes this section with numerical calculations of the menorah's parts that are contrived to add up to seventy (precisely the number of completeness mentioned half a millennium earlier by Josephus):

Behold, "seven" appears three times (in Zechariah 4:2): "seven lamps on it, seven, with seven nozzles – a total of twenty-one. And "seven" [nozzles] times seven [branches] is forty-nine, plus [the previously mentioned] twenty-one, corresponds to the seventy elders.[121]

Other late antique interpretations could be mentioned. I have cited enough, however, to represent the breadth of ways that rabbinic culture during the very long period between the second and eighth centuries approached the menorah. Yannai sees the menorah as a symbol of the Tabernacle/Temple, of Divine oversight, of Torah, and of the people of Israel itself. The lost menorah lived on in the attempt to imagine its structure and discuss its significance. This loss was temporary. For some sources, the menorah and other Tabernacle vessels will reemerge in messianic times. This deep theological connection to the menorah, coupled with its unique physical form, made it an exemplary "symbol" in late antique Palestine. With that, I do not contend that any particular menorah image was always and exclusively interpreted in the ways that the earlier rabbinic sources, Yannai, Yehuda, or *Pesiqta Rabbati* did. These are texts belonging to the rabbis and do not necessarily reflect broader circles within Jewish culture. We do not know how Jews who were less steeped in rabbinic tradition might have approached the symbolism of the menorah. We do have some sense, however, of how the rabbis verbalized their understanding of this artifact.

CONCLUSION

Today, the menorah is the second most important Jewish symbol, after the Star of David. From the third century through the nineteenth, however, this was not the case. The menorah was the premier Jewish symbol. Beginning with the last of the Maccabees and building through first-century Jerusalem, Flavian Rome, and ultimately throughout the Roman world in the centuries after the destruction of the Temple, the menorah's popularity grew. This popularity stems, first and foremost, from the menorah's unique form. It became the Jewish "trademark" par excellence. During late antiquity, the menorah served to mark off Jewish space, Jewish bread, and even Jewish bodies. It served as a visual marker of a minority people. With the rise of a clear and consistent Christian icon – the cross – the menorah became ever more important. This was an intensification of usage, however, and not an innovation inspired by Christian symbolism. From the earliest Second Temple period onward, we know that the lamps of the menorah were given meanings that were both cosmic and expressive of Divine oversight. During the Second Temple period, its height was even used as a social metaphor. We do not know what most Jews during late antiquity thought of the menorah. No evidence is extant for Greek- and Latin-speaking Jews of the West, or even of nonacademic Jewish within Palestine. We do know that they all used the menorah symbol quite liberally. In rabbinic literature – the only intensive literary tradition that does survive – cosmic and providential meanings were further developed. The rabbis associated the menorah with Torah in its broadest sense, with the Jewish people as a whole: its glorious past, ignoble present, and future messianic greatness.

PART FOUR

READING HOLISTICALLY

ART AND THE LITURGY OF LATE ANTIQUE SYNAGOGUES

It was for the performance of liturgy that, for example, a medieval community took upon itself the burden of erecting a cathedral, and it was for the performance of liturgy that any church was ever built.

Soren Sindling-Larson, 1984[1]

All the world's a stage. . . .

William Shakespeare, *As You Like It*, 2, 7

IN ANNO DOMINI 395, PAULINUS, LATER KNOWN AS SAINT Paulinus of Nola, settled in the city of Nola in the fertile Sarnus Valley in southern Italy.[2] There, Paulinus dedicated himself to the veneration of Saint Felix, who had formerly served as a priest in Nola and was known for the miracles and exorcisms he had performed there. Paulinus expressed his veneration of Felix by restoring his grave and having a new church and compound built. He wrote extensively about his work in the church; about the architecture, the paintings, and the ritual objects; providing a commentary to the entire structure that is unique in the writings of late antique Christianity. I cite one passage of Paulinus's description to give a sense of how he planned and then interpreted the decoration of the edifice:

Now I desire thee to see the paintings on the porticos decorated with a long series and to make the slight trouble of bending thy neck backwards, taking stock of everything with head thrown back. He who on seeing this recognizes Truth from the idle figures, feeds his faithful spirit with a by no means idle image. For the painting contains in faithful order everything that ancient Moses wrote in five books, what Joshua did, marked by the name of the Lord, under whose guidance the Jordan stayed with its current in its momentum, the waves remaining fixed and fell back before the continence of the divine Ark. An unknown force divided the river, a part stopped because of the water having flowed back and a part of the river, gliding on, rushed seawards and left the bed dry, and at the side where the river with powerful current poured forth from its source, it had held fast and piled high the waves and as a quivering mass a water mountain hung menacing, seeing beneath it that feet were crossing a dry bottom and that in the middle of the river-bed dusty human soles were speeding over hard mud without the feet getting wet. Now run tense eyes over the portraiture of Ruth, who separates periods by a booklet, the end of the time of Judges and the beginning of Kings. This seems to be a short history, but it points to the mysteries of a great war that two sisters part from each other for different regions. Ruth follows her holy relative, whom Orpah leaves; one daughter-in-law gives proof of faithlessness, the other of faithfulness. The one places God above her country; the other, her country above life. Does not, I ask, this discord remain in the whole world, as a part follow God and a part rush through the world? And if only the part of death and salvation were equal, but the wide road takes many and irrevocable error sweeps down those who slip.

It may be asked how we arrived at this decision, to paint, a rare custom, images of living beings in the holy houses. Hark, and I will attempt to briefly expound the causes. What crowds of the glory of St. Felix drives hither, is unknown to none; the majority of the crowd here, however, are peasant people, not devoid of religion but not able to read. These people, for long accustomed to profane cults, in which their belly was their God, are at last converted into proselytes for Christ while they admire the works of the saints in Christ open to everybody's gaze.[3]

Paulinus was the patron, a member of the clergy, and the interpreter of the church at Nola (a building that no longer exists). He provides us with a unique vision of the churches of this period. Paulinus himself might well have provided differing interpretations for the recently converted "crowds" or to priests who clearly shared his love of the visual and hence had no need for apologetic.[4] Theological in tone, his approach is highly selective. Paulinus reports that the church portico was decorated with images stretching from the Pentateuch through Kings and Ruth. One could imagine a long wall illustrated with images from Genesis through Kings that was viewed in succession as one passed through the portico. Paulinus chooses to focus, however, on only two scenes: the images of Joshua's crossing of the Jordan and the moral implications of Ruth's decision to stay with Naomi – images with obvious allegorical relevance to contemporaneous conversions of polytheists to Christianity. The interpretation offered here required special effort to comprehend, for the visitor was asked "to make the slight trouble of bending thy neck backwards, taking stock of everything with head thrown back." One could imagine that at another season of the year, a different audience or even a change of mood would suggest to Paulinus starkly different interpretations. The central organizing principle of these paintings is Biblical chronology. Over time, interpretations of the architecture and paintings (and the architecture and paintings themselves, for that matter) would certainly have changed in accordance with changing customs, beliefs, and the visual acumen of the interpreter. Paulinus's text is the "official" narrative that our author set down in writing. The process of writing narratives about art is never neutral. It is itself a form of translation from the visual realm to the verbal. Discussing Byzantine art, Ruth Webb correctly notes that

Any description necessitates the selection and ordering of details according to the rules of language. . . . In this sense one can argue that all descriptions, and not just those by Byzantine authors, are mirrors that must in some way "distort" their subjects. At the same time, by the very act of selecting, ordering and presenting material they can act as a sort of commentary on their subjects.[5]

Modern commentaries on the art of ancient synagogues have "distorted" their subjects in similarly profound ways, often by providing a linear discussion of the extant remains that attempts to draw together all of the disparate elements of the artifact into consecutive story lines. Narratives that forefront redemptive themes,[6] the Jewish response to Christianity and Jewish forerunners to Christian art, neo-Platonic projection of the Jerusalem Temple onto the Beth Alpha synagogue,[7] the admixture of Hellenistic Jewish sources with Jungian psychology to create the mystically nonrabbinic Judaism of *Jewish Symbols*, and the search for the less (or the more) rabbinic are among the many themes that have been attempted. These modern "narratives" often explore important and interesting questions. None of them, however, truly focuses on the meaning of the art within its most immediate, local contexts, but rather, uses the art to ask larger historiographic questions. All of these approaches share certain characteristics of reading. Each begins with a conception that is not drawn from the artifacts themselves, but to greater and lesser degrees superimposes these conceptions upon the material culture. A synagogue, for example, is not a synagogue, but a series of disembodied iconographic opportunities for interpretation. By imposing external categories, these scholars impose their own senses of order and value on the materials in ways that would be unrecognizable to the communities that built them and lived their liturgical lives within them.

Narratives pursued by scholars in recent decades have tended to disconnect the artifacts from their original contexts and renarrativize them in terms of new consecutive narratives that are often exclusive of other modes of interpretation. They determine ways of seeing that would have been unknown to the ancients. In the case of a carpet mosaic, they determine which is the "top" and which is the "bottom" – treating the mosaic as a painting hanging on the wall of the Museum of Fine Arts of any city or as a photograph carefully fit into the pages of a codex and often dissected into detail shots – and not as a floor for walking upon within a "living" building. We seldom view these floors from the perspective of the ancients – under foot along the once well-worn paths from the heavy doors inward. The details of mosaics that have been reset in museums and reproduced in codices are "unencumbered" by furniture, textiles suspended before the doors of a Torah shrine or perhaps between the columns of the nave, mats and of course, the presence of ancient Jews. These details take on vital importance as photographers wet the mosaics to bring out otherwise opaque colors that were only seen by ancient custodians on washing day. This common approach is reinforced (if not dictated) to

a large extent by the codex-based technology with which scholars have worked and the modes of exhibition they have practiced. Marshall McLuhan was correct in claiming that "the media is the message" – whether for modern scholars, contemporary "lay" viewers, or ancient synagogue communities.[8]

A recent example of the practice of interpreting an art object in terms of a preconceived consecutive narrative is Ze'ev Weiss and Ehud Netzer's preliminary presentation of the Sepphoris synagogue mosaic. This museum catalog accompanied an exhibition of the mosaic at the Israel Museum in 1996. The floor was later exhibited at New York's Jewish Museum and elsewhere. The title of the catalog tips off the theme; it is called *Promise and Redemption: A Synagogue Mosaic from Sepphoris*. Weiss and Netzer interpret the mosaic beginning with the "bottom" and continuing to the "top" as a consecutive movement from Divine promise to messianic redemption. The authors sum up their approach as follows:[9]

When the mosaic is read as a whole, as a single structured scheme, the significance of each of its foci in the overall message becomes clear: the Angels' Visit to Abraham and Sarah and the Binding of Isaac symbolize the promise; the zodiac expresses God's centrality in creation, in his promise, and in redemption; and the architectural facade and other symbols associated with the Tabernacle and Temple represent the future redemption.

For Weiss and Netzer, this is apparently the only possible interpretation. They see the floor as an intensely theological document. Weiss and Netzer have constructed a modern-day homily in order to explain the apparently singular meaning of the Sepphoris mosaic. They have meticulously interwoven rabbinic sources – traditions that fit the theme were chosen, and others discarded. The visual homily is not constructed according to a single unifying theme or cluster of Biblical verses, as rabbinic homilies are, but through reference to the mosaic and the inextricable movement *From Promise to Redemption*. In describing the mosaic, Weiss and Netzer move from one end of the mosaic to the other, carefully interpreting each image. Not coincidentally, their movement was projected into the realm of hermeneutics as they argued that the floor's "meaning" moves progressively. This homily removes the mosaic from the clutter of having been the floor pavement of a communal building and turns it into an object of veneration, which the modern visitor is to reverentially circumambulate. This is reinforced in the reconstruction drawing of the synagogue exhibited in the mosaic's permanent pavilion in Sepphoris National Park.[10] Ancient Jews are shown seated neatly in the side aisle of the synagogue, and not on the floor of the nave (as modern visitors do when they visit the site pavilion). In the reconstruction, Jews are not shown walking or sitting upon this otherwise unfurnished modern masterpiece of Jewish theology.

Weiss and Netzer's consecutive interpretation is the result of the training that until recently all aspiring art historians received. As students, we were taught to organize our thoughts and evidence on index cards that organize our materials (and to think) in progressive succession. The Princeton Index of Christian Art is the grand example of this approach, every artifact carefully described and dissected into its most miniscule iconographic parts on thousands upon thousands of cards. Whether working from cards or from codices, we were trained to work consecutively and to order our vision toward the iconographic detail rather than to the broader "picture."[11] The ways that data were stored made large artifacts often seem small, while small artifacts or details were often printed in large format on the page. As I have already mentioned in regard to Goodenough's work, the atomization of visual elements in standard-sized book plates (where the relative sizes and importance of artifacts can be lost) and the general loss of context are serious impediments to interpretation.

In a Windows-based computer technology, of the sort I used to write this book and store my images, the monotonous and continuous movement from page one to two, from two to three, and so on to the end of the volume is only one of many options for organizing data. Further, three-dimensional viewing technology is already widely available – and will surely improve with time. Within the *Microsoft Encarta Encyclopedia*, for example, it is already possible to study the interior of the Capernaum synagogue "in the round."[12] That means that artifacts may be viewed in something approaching their full three-dimensional context while one is sitting in front of a computer screen. This is an experience that I cannot reproduce within the codex that you are now reading, no matter how hard I might try! With recent technological developments, it is no longer necessary to restrict our three-dimensional viewing and thinking to the structures of linear, two-dimensional codices. Similarly, it is no longer necessary to store our data

within the straitjacket of consecutive index cards or codex pages. New configurations are now imaginable.[13]

The approach I am suggesting is not merely a response to technological developments: I am arguing for a more roundly holistic interpretation that sets the community that built a liturgical space at the center of the project, not at the periphery. It is an *anthropos*-centered approach. By focusing on the flesh-and-blood community and its religion, rather than upon narratives that atomize and then reconstitute the buildings and texts into broad consecutive theories, I hope to better understand the art of ancient synagogues (and of public space in general). To use a theater metaphor, in this section I will treat the remains of ancient synagogue buildings for what they are: "stages" constructed for the purpose of housing Jewish liturgy. Like all theater sets, these "stages" were constructed to fit the needs of the ever-changing ritual "plays" acted out by communities. In this approach, the members of the religious community stand at the center of the discussion – not the texts, and not the artifacts. It is the ancient "actor" I hope to understand by studying the "stage" that he and his community constructed (and constantly reconstructed).

The *anthropos*-centered approach that I am applying to Jewish remains was first developed among scholars of late antique Christianity, each of whom studies art in order to better understand religious experience (and not for its "own sake"). In differing ways, Thomas Mathews and Peter Brown have interpreted the late antique church as the backdrop for the liturgical life of a community.[14] This approach challenges the monist scholarship that is so well-entrenched in the study of art, architecture, and religion during the twentieth century. It is rooted in Catholic rethinking of church architecture and worship in the wake of the Second Vatican Council's charge to revitalize Catholic worship by (re)focusing attention on the community and its spiritual needs.[15]

A stark comparison might be drawn from within the symposium volume that accompanied Kurt Weitzmannn's monumental exhibition, *The Age of Spirituality: Late Antique and Early Christian Art, Third to Seventh Century*.[16] Penned by the most important art historians of the 1970s, many of the articles are mainly iconographic studies, interested in the broad history of visual transmission. The contribution of historian Peter Brown was of a different order altogether.[17] Brown, a cultural historian associated with the French *Annales* tradition of historical interpretation, argued through demonstration for a holistic approach to the literature and artifacts, one in which art is set in the full context of the religious life of the communities that made them. Brown writes in response to the title of the exhibition that[18]

In many ways, Late Antique Christianity was not "otherworldly" in the rarefied sense that is usually associated with the period. For the "otherworld" was not abstraction; it was a precise place, paradise. The solemn liturgy, blaze of lights, the shimmering mosaics, and the brightly colored curtains of a Late Antique church were there to be appreciated in their entirety. As with imperial ceremonials, these trappings should not be detached from one another. Taken together, they provided a glimpse of paradise. . . . The representational elements would have been swamped in the overwhelming impression conveyed by the building, its overall decoration, and its liturgy. In the Late Antique church, the processional movements, the heavy silver of the sacred vessels, and the bindings of the Gospel books as they flashed by on their way to the altar, the mysterious opacity of the curtains shrouding the entrance (even if the curtain itself might have been woven with frankly secular scenes), these things in themselves were the visual "triggers" of a Late Antique worshiper's sense of majesty.[19]

Beginning with his 1971 dissertation volume, *The Early Churches of Constantinople: Architecture and Liturgy*, art historian Thomas Mathews also has been committed to a holistic approach to early church art and architecture.[20] Mathews recently provided a clear formulation of his approach in discussing Orthodox churches:[21]

Their tightly woven programs of images are so wedded to the architectural vessel as to constitute a single unit, an environmental work of art. Together with the ritual that they contained, they constitute a single symbolic matrix. The church, beyond being a container for iconography, is a container for religious experience, to which the imagery must constantly be referred.

In describing Orthodox churches, Mathews was forced to resort to the language of contemporary art: "an environmental work of art." In a sense, Mathews has translated his liturgical conception into a language that might be familiar to art historians, many of whom were firmly attached to object-focused diachronic and nonlocalized iconographic and "iconological" interpretation of individual art objects, often irregardless of their liturgical contexts. No such language is available to him from medieval

scholarship. Mathews continues in a tone that reflects the intense opposition of many toward liturgical interpretation:

Religious experience may seem an extremely nebulous referent for an historical enquiry, but the manner of worship, that is the liturgy, is extremely well documented in Byzantium, and has been the subject of exhaustive scientific research in recent years. What the Byzantines did in church and how they understood what they were experiencing is not mere speculation. Furthermore, historical sources witness the depth of the emotional impact of the experience.[22]

The most extreme proponent of the liturgical interpretation of Christian art is the Norwegian scholar Soren Sinding-Larsen. Sinding-Larsen has correctly suggested that the art of late antique and medieval churches actually took on different meanings depending on the liturgy pronounced before, within, or upon it. That is to say, "Liturgy determines specific modes of relationship in action and idea between the onlooker or congregation and the subject illustrated in the liturgical iconography."[23] Sinding-Larsen sees the meaning of church art changing according to the progress within a given liturgy. He makes his position clear in his discussion of the apse of the church of San Clemente in Rome: "The figure of Christ [in the apse at San Clemente] obtains a complete sense only when evaluated in its functional context, which is that of the altar, and the point is that this meaning is changing, consisting as it does of multiple elements in varying relations to one another – rather like molecules in reaction."[24] According to Sinding-Larsen, the art and architecture of churches are a backdrop for the liturgical life of its community, as the "set" in which the priests and the rest of the community were the "actors." Like every good stage set, of course, the architecture and art of the church were a reflection, reaction, and complement to the variety of performances that took place there.

It is easier to apply a liturgical approach to churches than to ancient synagogues. Owing to the vicissitudes of history and the generally small scale of Jewish construction in antiquity (as is fitting for a small minority like the Jews), ancient synagogue remains are far less rich than the often still-functioning monumental churches of Byzantine Rome, Ravenna, and Constantanople. The extant remains of synagogues are mere hints of what once existed, and so the types of historical "imagining" that are possible in synagogues are limited in comparison to the experience of churches. In the best-preserved synagogue, at Dura Europos, 60 percent of the structure survives – though none of the furnishings and little of its liturgy remain. The reconstruction in the Damascus Museum provides some sense of the synagogue that once was – without benefit of the dim light provided by flickering oil lamps, the textiles, and holy books that once graced the synagogue space.

Synagogue mosaics in Palestine are often well-preserved, although the walls of the buildings and the furnishing are generally not.[25] We have little sense of what was painted on the walls. We simply do not know if buildings that have less figurative imagery on their floors possessed beautifully painted walls or even painted ceilings. Such a scenario would certainly change our views of the synagogues at Ein Gedi and Reḥov. I have already asked what we would say if the walls of the synagogues at Hammath Tiberias B, Sepphoris, or Beth Alpha were covered with Halakhic texts, like those which appear on the floor and columns at Reḥov? Or, what if the carved images of Medusa, of a she-wolf, and of vintners at Chorazin were brightly painted (as is likely), and the flagstone floors covered with beautifully decorated carpets or mats? Allow me one further example: What if the synagogue at Dura had been leveled in antiquity (as so many synagogues were), and all that remained of it were a few ceiling tiles, the lower tier of benches, and the base of the Torah shrine? Our knowledge of ancient synagogues and their furnishings is partial, to say the least – knowledge that is vital if we are to understand the liturgical functions that these structures served. Models of ancient synagogues – be they three-dimensional or computer-generated – can give us the sense of what these buildings looked like, but we are still looking at sacred spaces into which we (not to mention a breathing liturgical community) cannot enter (Figure 69).

Finally, still-active ancient (or at least medieval) churches offer a glimpse into the workings of ancient Palestinian synagogues. In order to imagine the lives of ancient synagogues, I decided to examine the "living" continuation of late antique tradition, Christian liturgy as performed in early medieval churches. I spent considerable time in Jerusalem's twelfth-century Monastery of the Cross, studying (with the help of some modern studies) the

69. Model of the Beth Alpha Synagogue, Yeshiva University Museum (photograph by Steven Fine).

iconography of its mosaic floors, wall paintings, its iconostasis, and other sacred vessels.[26] This experience did not prepare me, however, for the moment one Easter Sunday when I observed the morning liturgy. Suddenly, the paintings, mosaics, lamps, the naves, and side aisles with which I was so familiar faded away before the image of priests with incense (whose facial expressions seemed to mirror the painted icons), lighted candles before the icons, processions, and the facial expressions of the men and women, many dressed in black and seated separately on each side of the church. At that moment, I realized just how limiting my historian's focus on each image was, and just how profoundly the church served as the set for this amazing ritual. This excursion out of the comfort of my own deeply embedded sense of the synagogue and its ritual jolted me to "reimagine" the synagogue – both modern and ancient.

This section includes two main sections. The first deals with the art of Dura Europos and the second with Palestinian synagogue mosaics, with a focus on the Sepphoris mosaic. We conclude with a discussion of the zodiac and its meaning in Palestinian synagogues and a discussion of synagogue art and synagogue sanctity.

CHAPTER ELEVEN

LITURGY AND THE ART OF THE DURA EUROPOS SYNAGOGUE

The synagogue had quite as radical implications for our knowledge of Judaism as the Dead Sea Scrolls, if not far deeper. . . .

E. R. Goodenough, 1956[1]

There is great danger in letting our eyes be blinded to, or by, the novelty of the material and thus of losing perspective either upon the paintings themselves or upon the picture of ancient Judaism as it has been developed from the study of other types of evidence by scholars of the last hundred years.

Carl Kraeling, 1956[2]

. . . the pictures were an integral part of the house of worship, related to the order of prayer or readings and perhaps used as "illustrative" material for sermons.

Stephen S. Kayser, 1953[3]

N O JEWISH PAULINUS WROTE ABOUT THE DURA Europos synagogue – or at least, no ancient writings on the meaning of the Dura paintings have survived. We know little about how ancient Jews experienced this space, what it was like when the liturgical life of this community pulsed within these walls. What was the religious experience of Dura when Torah was read, Jews sat on the benches (whether attentively or bored), and lamps illuminated the brilliant paintings, enveloping the hall in ever-changing shadows?

The Dura synagogue paintings have not been interpreted as decorative elements of a building produced by a local Jewish community as a context for its liturgical life. Nevertheless, the Dura Europos synagogue has been the subject of numerous important studies during the almost seventy years since its discovery. The best of these interpretations have focused on identifying the various images within the synagogue paintings, and identifying literary and iconographic parallels to each and every individual image. The most significant of these were carried out by E. L. Sukenik, whose Hebrew volume appeared in 1947, and more exhaustively by Carl Kraeling, whose final report on the synagogue appeared in 1956.[4] Attempts at the theoretical or global interpretation of these images have been less successful, with art historians and historians alike imposing templates upon the material that have had the net effect of limiting interpretation.

We have already seen that historians of ancient Judaism, beginning with Goodenough, have often treated the Dura paintings as a vehicle for uncovering nonrabbinic Judaism in antiquity. Art historians, particularly those influenced by Kurt Weitzmann, have most often viewed the Dura paintings as a backdrop for the history of Christian art, and assigned significance to them on the basis of their relationship to what followed centuries later in the Christian West. Most important for our purposes is Annabelle Wharton's analysis of the Dura Europos synagogue. Wharton criticizes earlier scholarship for ignoring the religious aspect of synagogue decoration and asserts a holistic approach to the Dura synagogue paintings. Wharton recognized that the Dura synagogue images and rabbinic literature are interwoven in ways far more complex than previous scholars have noted. Her approach stresses the similarities in mind-set that she posits between the creators of the paintings and rabbis of Palestine and Babylonia of the third century. While scholars such as Kraeling, Sukenik, and later Jewish art historian Joseph Gutmann could find parallels between rabbinic literature and the individual images within the synagogue, Wharton has posited a shared "midrashic" mind-set with the rabbis.[5] I will argue for similar correspondences within Palestinian synagogues, which is methodologically easier owing to the geographic and chronological proximity between rabbinic literature of the Byzantine period and archaeological sources of the same period.[6]

Relations between rabbinic mind-sets and those of the synagogue painters/donors/members in Dura are harder to assert. No known rabbis lived in Dura, and in any event this border city is somewhat distant from rabbinic centers in the Galilee and Babylonia (modern Iraq). Scholars have noted the many parallels between rabbinic midrash and the paintings, a search that parallels the modern search for exegetical proximity between the rabbis and the Church fathers. Thankfully, parchment fragments containing a Hebrew liturgical text were discovered at Dura. This text, virtually overlooked by art historians and scholars of Jewish liturgy, sheds considerable light on the relationship between Dura and the rabbis. This document provides a key to the question of conceptual contiguousness with the rabbis. More importantly, it provides an important, if narrow, window into the liturgical life of the Jews of Dura and their synagogue.

How did the Dura synagogue function as a religious space? In this chapter, I suggest some answers to this question. My interpretation is refracted through the focusing lens of a fragmentary Hebrew prayer parchment. After carefully analyzing this text from a philological perspective, I apply the insights gained from it to the interpretation of the Dura synagogue's inscriptions and iconography. These small parchment fragments have broad implications for the interpretation of the Dura Europos synagogue and its paintings, providing textual legitimization for the use of rabbinic materials to interpret the paintings. They also suggest that the mind-sets of the community members who commissioned the paintings and lived with them paralleled in many ways those of the rabbis. I do not suggest a continuous narrative to explain the art of the Dura synagogue, nor will I go beyond the iconographic analyses suggested by my predecessors. Instead, I focus on how the "set" – including inscriptions and graffiti – might have served its community liturgically. I illustrate this interpretation by paralleling the themes of the paintings with those of the central rabbinic prayer, the *Tefillah*. By using all of the extant evidence – architectural, artistic, paleographic, and literary – I will suggest an interpretation that treats the Dura Europos synagogue as the liturgical setting for the life of the local Jewish community that built it and played out its communal life there.

THE DURA LITURGICAL PARCHMENT

The Dura Europos liturgical fragments have been all but forgotten by scholars. In concluding his extensive discussion of the Dura Europos synagogue, Goodenough wrote: "Just how worship was conducted in the room we have no way whatever of knowing, except as we transport over to it the information about synagogue worship which survives in rabbinical writings."[7] Joseph Gutmann, who hazarded the most extensive discussion of liturgy at Dura, wrote similarly that "we have no evidence of Jewish literature from such Syrian cities as Dura. . . ."[8] Astonishingly, neither Goodenough nor Gutmann seems to have been aware of the Dura parchment and its implications. Scholars of Jewish liturgy did not know of the Dura fragments either; none of the major monographs or surveys of the history of Jewish prayer makes reference to them. This is quite perplexing, as the Dura prayer parchment is the earliest extant archaeological evidence of Hebrew prayer from post-Temple times, dating perhaps a century before the earliest Aramaic and Hebrew Palestinian synagogue inscriptions that were influenced by liturgy[9] and five centuries before the earliest Cairo Genizah documents. Although the existence of written liturgical texts is evidenced in rabbinic sources, the Dura parchments are the earliest physical evidence for Jewish prayer manuscripts during this period.[10]

The Dura Europos Hebrew liturgical fragments were discovered on the narrow street to the west side of the synagogue (designated "Wall Street" by the excavators). The Dura parchment was buried when Wall Street, the synagogue, and all buildings in its environs were filled with earth to create an embankment wall.[11] It was discovered on December 17, 1932. This embankment was built in the failed attempt to support the exposed western wall of Dura in preparation for the final Persian siege of Dura in about 256 C.E.[12] In the frenzy of that moment, the parchment was covered with a huge mound of soil. Texts from within the synagogue were apparently cleared away in the last days of Dura Europos (none were uncovered there), but the liturgical parchment was lost – only to be recovered by modern scholars.[13]

The early and prompt publication of the Dura fragments made this artifact widely accessible. Scholars who studied the Dura Europos preliminary or final reports could gain easy access to them. This document was first published by Charles Torrey in 1936 in the preliminary report of the Dura synagogue excavation (and restated by Kraeling in the final report of the synagogue in 1956).[14] Torrey's reading was improved upon by Robert de Mesnil du Buisson in 1939[15] and by E. L. Sukenik in 1947.[16] The editors of the final report on the manuscripts at Dura accept Du Mesnil du Buisson's readings, adding little to the discussion.

Unlike their peers in related disciplines, academic Talmudists were attentive to the implications of the parchment from a very early date, undoubtedly because this document fit well within their general frame of reference. The publication of medieval manuscripts and Cairo Genizah fragments was, and still is, a major preoccupation of academic Talmud scholars. Based on Du Mesnil du Buisson's edition of the Dura parchment, the two greatest Talmudists of the twentieth century – Saul Lieberman and Louis Ginzberg – each independently offered some brief comments on rabbinic parallels to the parchment. Lieberman's findings were presented in a brief appendix to a 1940 Hebrew pamphlet published in Jerusalem, *A Lecture on the Yemenite Midrashim, Their Character and Value*. Ginzberg discussed the parchment in the course of his Hebrew *Commentary on the Palestinian Talmud*, published in New York in 1942.[17] The comments of Lieberman, Ginzberg, and later of archaeologist Sukenik (who had originally brought the parchment to Lieberman's attention)[18] are virtually unknown beyond the Hebrew-speaking academy. In the intervening years, J. L. Teicher published an idiosyncratic article in which he claimed that the parchment is a Jewish–Christian prayer.[19] The most important study to discuss the parchment since Sukenik's was published in 1997 by Israeli art historian Shulamit Laderman, who built upon Lieberman's discussion of the relationship between the Dura parchment and later liturgical poetry (*piyyut*). Laderman used the Dura parchment as a jumping-off point for interpreting the Dura paintings in terms of themes developed in *piyyut* literature.[20]

Three fragments of this animal skin parchment are extant. The largest and most complete, fragment "A," is 5.5 × 5 cm. Fragment "B," which is much less complete, is 5 × 3.5 cm.; and the third piece, called a "tiny scrap" in the final report, is only 1.3 × 0.8 cm. Du Mesnil du Buisson suggested that fragments "A" and "B" are not contiguous (contra Torrey), which is clearly correct. The alignment

dedicatory inscriptions.[23] There is evidence of scoring on the surface of the parchment, which parallels line markings on the ceiling tiles.[24] Eight lines of fragment "A" and the very top of line nine are extant. Seven lines of fragment "B" are extant. The preserved sections of the text are reasonably clear, particularly when enhanced through computer imaging. The last two lines of fragment "B," as well as details of both fragments, were deciphered thanks to these technological advancements (Figure 70).

Fragment "A":

Blessed is X king of the world/eternity	ברוך X מלך העלם	1.
apportioned food, provided sustenance	חלק מזון התקין מ[חיה]	2.
sons of flesh cattle to . . .	בני בשר בהמה ל . . .	3.
created man to eat of . . .	יצר אדם לאכול מ . . .	4.
many bodies of . . .	גויות רבאות ממ . . .	5.
to bless all cattle	לברך כלם בהמות	6.
	. . . ה . . מ . . .	7.
. . . prepared . . .	ל תקן . . .	8.
	ק . . . ל	9.

Fragment "B":

for	כי	1.
pure (animals) to (eat?)	[ט]הרות לא[כל]	2.
provides sustenance	מכלכל	3.
small and large	קטנות עם גדו[לות]	4.
all the animals of the field . . .	כל חית השדה	5.
. . . feed their young	ל מאכל טפם . . .	6.
and sing and bless	ושיר וברך	7.

Even in this fragmentary state, the document provides ample evidence for the liturgical life of Jews at Dura. The language is rich in phraseology that closely parallels rabbinic and Cairo Genizah documents. In fact, were this text discovered in Tiberias, in the ancient Babylonian city of Pumbedita, or some other rabbinic center, no one would question that it is a rabbinic document. If it had been discovered in the Cairo Genizah, the Byzantine-period provenance of the text (although not the script) would not be doubted. For the sake of illustration, I will present some of the most glaring literary parallels.

The formula with which the prayer opens, "Blessed is X king of the world/eternity . . ." (line A-1), directly parallels the rabbinic introductory blessing formula, "Blessed are you, Lord our God, king of the world/eternity."[25] This formula does not appear in Biblical or Second Temple period sources. Reuven Kimelman notes that this formula

70. The Dura Europos Hebrew liturgical parchment (courtesy of the Beinecke Rare Book and Manuscript Library, Yale University).

suggested by Du Mesnil du Buisson (with which I concur) is based on the arc of a curved scratch that appears on both fragments. In the final report of manuscripts discovered at Dura, C. Bradford Welles correctly notes that "the upper fragment [fragment 'A'] contains the top margin of the original sheet, and the lower fragment contains the bottom margin, probably."[21] The fragments are written by the same, rather pedestrian hand. They are written in Jewish square script, called by the rabbis *ktav ashurit*, "Assyrian script."[22] The letter forms, written in black ink, are consistent with those that were used in Aramaic inscriptions within the synagogue, particularly those written in ink on two preserved ceiling tiles bearing Aramaic first appears in rabbinic literature during the mid-third century.[26] The use of the sign X as a circumlocution for the Divine name appears in a palimpsest that predates the eighth century, now in Munich. There, the sign X is used as an abbreviation for the Divine name *Elohim*. Early Cairo Genizah documents often substitute the letter aleph for *Elohim* (and its derivative forms).[27]

The phrase "apportioned food" (חלק מזון) in line A-2 parallels the rabbinic "apportions food" (מחלק מזון) that appears first in *m. Shevi'it* 9:8 and later in *Midrash Tehillim* 136: ". . . the Holy One, blessed be He, sits at the heights of the universe and apportions food (מחלק מזון) to all living things."[28] Lieberman notes that the formula "apportioned food" appears in Genizah fragments of the blessing after meals.[29] This text praises God, who "apportioned sustaining food for all that He created."[30] Line A-4 also hints at an interesting rabbinic parallel. It refers, apparently to God, as the one who "created man to eat of. . . ." "Created man" (יצר אדם) is a common phrase in rabbinic liturgy. "Who created man in wisdom" (אשר יצר האדם בחכמה), appears, for example, in the blessing after meals as preserved in *y. Berakhot* 9:4, 14b. In *b. Ketubot* 8a, this phrase appears as part of the marriage blessings:

Blessed are you, Lord our God, king of the universe creator of man (יוצר האדם).

Blessed are you, Lord our God, king of the universe who created man (יצר את האדם), in his image a likeness of his form [woman], and established (התקין) it for him as an eternal structure.

Blessed are you, Lord, who creator of man (יוצר האדם).

The appearance of the phrases "creator of man" and "established" in such close proximity in the intermediate blessing parallels the language of the Dura fragment, where "established" (התקין) appears in line 2 and apparently in line 8.[31] This proximity does not seem to relate to function, however, as much as to shared liturgical vocabulary.

Fragment "B" is less complete, although considerable information may be gleaned from it – especially using computer imaging. "Provides sustenance" (מכלכל) in line B-3 parallels the phrase "provides sustenance for the living with love" (מכלכל חיים בחסד) in the *Tefillah* prayer. "The small and large" (קטנות עם גדולות) in line B-4 is drawn from Psalm 104:25, "Yonder is the sea, great and wide, which teems with things innumerable, living things both small and large." Line B-5, "All the animals of the field" is a phrase that appears with some regularity in Scripture,

appearing for the first time in Genesis 2:19: "So out of the ground the Lord God formed every beast of the field and every bird of the air. . . ."[32] Line B-6, ". . . feed their young" (. . . ל מאכל מפם . . .), is based on Biblical idiom. In Genesis 47:24, we read: "and for food for your young" (ולאכל לטפכם). Line B-7, "and sing and bless" (ושיר וברך), is part of a group of prayer terms often brought together in liturgical texts. So, for example, in the *Qaddish* prayer, God is praised as being "beyond all blessing and song (ברכתא ושירתא), praise and consolation that is uttered in the world."[33]

There are more examples. These are sufficient, however, to support my assertion that the Dura parchment is related in language, form, and content to rabbinic prayer texts from late antiquity. The text of this parchment is, like rabbinic prayer, a conglomeration of rabbinic and Biblical formulae,[34] although ancient Jews certainly did not distinguish the two as clearly as modern academic scholars tend to do. This linguistic reality parallels the Dura paintings themselves, where Biblical and legendary themes are freely intertwined. The use of the Hebrew language on the parchment is significant, for it is the only evidence of a Hebrew text from Dura. All of the inscriptions in or near the synagogue are in Aramaic, Greek, or Persian; the only other document that appears to be Jewish, a parchment whose text has not yet been fully interpreted, is in Aramaic.[35] The letter script of this document suggests that it was copied at Dura or within a community with ties to Dura Europos.

What kind of prayer is this? Following Du Mesnil du Buisson, who conferred with Chief Rabbi of France and professor of Talmud, Israel Levi, scholars of Judaic studies agree that this text is somehow related to the rabbinic grace after meals, *Birkat ha-Mazon*. Carl Kraeling took a different tack.[36] He argued that the parchment should be seen neither as a prayer nor as a liturgical document:

The document seems to be concerned only with the eating of animal food, and to set forth in concise terms both the fact and the authority of the Jewish practice . . . It may be suggested that the time and place were perhaps likely to bring forth a tract of this nature. In Persia, on the other hand, the vegetarian doctrine had its able champion among the Greeks; it was in this same generation that Porphyry composed his treatise on abstaining from animal food.[37] Perhaps we have a text prepared for use in the Jewish school in Dura.

Kraeling was clearly uncomfortable with the notion of separating the parchment from the synagogue and locating it within some "school" for which we have no archaeological evidence. He posits that "if so, it may have belonged to the materials used in the Synagogue, though kept in the Elder's residence [another place that has never been discovered!] or the school room."[38] In a brief comment, Jacob Neusner takes Kraeling's approach in a slightly different direction. While accepting that our fragment is related to the grace after meals, he suggests tentatively that "this may be an anti-Mithraistic polemical 'blessing' condemning taurobolium."[39] This is apparently based on the fact that a mithraeum is close by in Dura.[40] The predilection of some scholars to see polemic under every rabbinic tradition is not useful for understanding our text, however.[41] Only a pagan philosophical elite doubted the acceptability of meat consumption.[42]

Du Mesnil du Buisson went so far as to identify a kosher restaurant in the synagogue precinct, on the supposition that "it seems to us certain that Jewish travelers who found lodging in the Synagogue were able to get there suitable food, together with the ritual formulas to recite after the meal. Such is the explanation of the liturgical parchment that was found there."[43] Drawn apparently from the structures of modern Jewish communities and modern blessing booklets, Du Mesnil du Buisson's suggestion is less far-fetched than it sounds. A kitchen was discovered adjacent to the Ostia synagogue.[44] Meals were eaten within Palestinian synagogues at least from the third century onward.[45] Although the exact context is unclear, the Dura liturgical parchment may suggest that Jews participated in meals where some form of grace was enacted either within or in close proximity to the Dura synagogue.

Lieberman conjectures that the Dura parchment is a poetic rendition of the grace after meals for a special occasion. He assumes without discussion that the Dura parchment may be interpreted unproblematically in terms of Genizah documents that were copied centuries later (and likely composed in later centuries as well). Parallels are obvious, but analogous social performance of our text cannot be assumed. Sukenik apparently recognized this, simply and correctly asserting that the fragments are "without a doubt part of a prayer text that is related to the blessing after meals" (my translation).[46]

Thus, this parchment is very important evidence that the Dura Jewish community participated in a Jewish *koiné* that, as early as the third century, used liturgical forms that are known to have been central to the rabbis. This parallels the evidence of the images found in the synagogue, where lore

that is preserved in rabbinic sources and was well known to Jews beyond the close-knit rabbinic community found visual expression. The Dura parchment provides external support for those scholars – notably Kraeling, Sukenik, and Gutmann – who interpreted the Dura Europos synagogue paintings in light of rabbinic sources. Both the liturgical text (as much as we have of it) and the decoration of the synagogue reflect an amazing closeness to the world of the ancient rabbis.

LITURGY AND THE REMAINS OF THE DURA SYNAGOGUE BUILDING

The scholars who have written about the synagogue of Dura Europos are completely correct in their claim that the building does not explicitly tell us very much about the liturgy that took place there. The paintings nevertheless provide hints of the liturgical practice of this community, and inscriptions provide even more information. The Dura parchment is an important element of this tapestry, suggesting the possibility that parallels to rabbinic prayer and rabbinic ways of thinking might be fruitfully applied to the interpretation of this liturgical space. After a survey of liturgical themes that may be drawn from the remains of the synagogue proper, I will suggest some broader parallels to the themes and concerns of rabbinic prayer.

Within the space of the synagogue hall, the large aedicula dominates the center of the western wall of the synagogue (Figure 71). It is the focal point of the hall and keystone of the wall paintings. The presence of Scripture is celebrated through this massive ark, which the excavators believe was draped in an ornate curtain. Scripture as refracted through Jewish lore is projected out onto the walls of the synagogue, pointing to its centrality in the ritual life of the community. The shrine is called a *beit arona* in one of the Aramaic dedicatory inscriptions that were somewhat haphazardly painted on its facade.[47] The Aramaic inscription reads:

[I . . .] donated (or, made) the *beit arona* (literally, house of the ark).
Joseph son of Abba. . . .

The term *beit arona* to describe the shrine is significant, as it draws a connection between the Dura "ark" and the Ark of the Covenant.[48] The Ark of the Covenant, formed as a Torah shrine, appears prominently in the wall paintings. We see it in west wall panel 8, set within the Tabernacle, with Aaron the priest standing to its right. The rounded

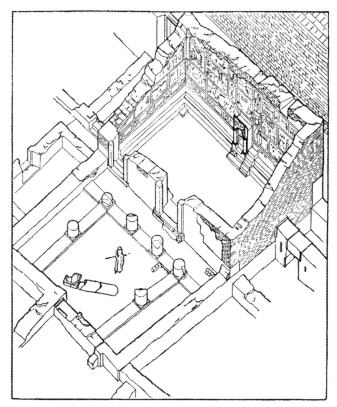

71. Drawing of the Dura Europos Synagogue (courtesy of the E. L. Sukenik Archive, Institute of Archaeology, Hebrew University of Jerusalem).

gable of this ark contains the image of a menorah. The ark is also shown vanquishing the Temple of Dagon in Ashdod (Figure 52),[49] and on the north wall, the defeat of the Israelites at Eben-Ezer.[50] This sort of correspondence between the synagogue shrine and the Ark of the Covenant is expressed in rabbinic literature as well, as in the comment of Rabbi Huna the Elder of Sepphoris, who is said to have lamented on the occasion of a public fast that:

Our fathers covered it (the Ark of the Covenant) with gold, and we cover it (the Torah ark) with ashes.[51]

The iconographic correspondence between the Torah shrine at Dura and the image of the Temple is also seen in the entrance portal of the Temple illustrated on the face of the Torah ark. Like the Torah shrine, it is crowned with a large conch shell.[52]

The paintings at the center of the western wall were arrayed to highlight the centrality of the Torah shrine. Two rectangular panels containing portraits of standing men, one above the other, were placed on either side of a central panel above the ark, a symmetry not found elsewhere

in the synagogue. Each faces frontally, "looking" outward from his panel. These images are more iconic than narrative, making the identification of these Biblical characters difficult for modern scholars. One image is of particular relevance to us: Above and to the right of the Torah shrine, the image of a man holding a Biblical scroll emphasizes the significance of Scripture within the synagogue (Figure 72). The intimate knowledge of the community with Biblical scrolls is made clear in this image. The text of Scripture is shown bleeding through the back of the parchment, a phenomenon that is common with modern Biblical scrolls

72. Moses with a scroll, Dura Europos Synagogue (photograph by Fred Anderegg, after Goodenough, *Jewish Symbols* 11, pl. v).

as well.[53] By showing this detail, the artist emphasizes the words on the scroll even as its text is turned toward the reader. The animal skin upon which the liturgical parchment was copied is important evidence for the types of holy books used at Dura and sheds light upon the material of the Biblical scroll illustrated here. Similarly, this illustration teaches us about the size of the Dura scrolls.[54] Extant Jewish and non-Jewish scrolls from this period did not exceed 39 cm. in height, as is the case of the scroll in proportion to the man's forearm. The intimate knowledge of the community with Biblical scrolls is made clear in this image.

Garments that are very similar to those illustrated in the synagogue (and throughout Dura Europos) were uncovered at Dura.[55] The man is illustrated with fringes at the right corner of his four-cornered mantle, in keeping with Numbers 15:37–41. Elsewhere in the Dura synagogue paintings, we also find fringes on the corners of the garments of Moses as he leads the Israelites through the Red Sea (western Wall, register A).[56] This is not, of course, a prayer shawl in the sense of the later Jewish ritual garment – there was no such distinctive Jewish costume during antiquity.[57] Nevertheless, the visible fringe is a rather quiet insider reference to Jewish practice that might easily be missed by those not cognizant of Jewish practice. Mantles that bear great affinity to those illustrated at Dura were uncovered among the remains of the Bar Kokhba-era rebels at Wadi Murrabat in the Judaean Desert, although no ritual fringes were attached to these mantles. Also discovered was a bundle of wool dyed purple that Y. Yadin identifies as ritual fringes that were being prepared for attachment to garments.[58] The garments illustrated at Dura thus find an important parallel in the material culture of late antique Jewish Palestine. Similarly, the man's hairstyle is consistent with hairstyles illustrated throughout Dura Europos and the Roman East.[59] This is truly a man of his place and time.

Who is the man holding the scroll? Scholars have posited every possible identification – pretty well any Biblical character who at any time carried a scroll.[60] One scholar went so far as to suggest that the man is Rabbi Judah the Prince, proclaiming the Oral Torah.[61] Every narrative image in the synagogue illustrates a Biblical character, so it is reasonable to suggest that the man with a scroll is a Biblical character as well. Kraeling debated whether to identify this image as Moses or as Ezra – Moses on the basis of Exodus 20 and its later interpretations; Ezra on the basis of Nehemiah 8. He eventually chose Ezra, mainly

because no Biblical text explicitly describes Moses reading the Torah![62] I suggest that this image should be identified as none other than Moses, the archetypal sage in Second Temple and rabbinic times. The rabbinic notion of transmission holds that "Moses received Torah from Sinai, and passed it on to Joshua, and Joshua to the Elders," through the prophets to the earliest proto-Rabbis (the "Men of the Great Assembly") and continuing unbroken to rabbis in our own day.[63] The revelation of Torah at Sinai through Moses is expressed in Nehemiah 8, where the public reading of Scripture on the first day of the seventh month is led by Ezra, the "priest and the scribe." This event is clearly modeled on the Sinaitic prototype and derives its authority from the "book of Moses."[64] From Tannaitic times onward, the public reading of Torah has been modeled on Nehemiah 8, and numerous sources beginning with Josephus and the *Acts of the Apostles* attribute the institution of public Torah reading to Moses himself.[65] The "man with the scroll" at Dura may be, then, both Moses and derivatively a Torah reader who in some way carries the authority of Moses by virtue of his public reading and/or interpretation of Scripture in third-century Dura Europos. The Jews of Dura projected their physical appearance onto Moses and the other Biblical characters in a visual manner, just as Second Temple and rabbinic lore assumed continuity between the mores and material culture of their own world and that of their Biblical ancestors.[66]

This image of Moses is the visual equivalent of rabbinic texts where Moses is consistently presented in contemporizing terms, even as a sage in Roman garb. A superb example of the latter appears in an early liturgical poem:

Moses was pleased with the gift that you bestowed upon him,
For you called him a faithful servant.
A wreath of glory[67] you placed on his head,
As he stood before you on Mt. Sinai. . . .[68]

Here, Moses is praised as God presents him with a wreath as a sign of his Divinely ordained calling. The use of wreaths is well known from the Greco–Roman world.[69] The poet asks us to imagine Moses with a wreath upon his head, which parallels very nicely our image of the Lawgiver in his Roman garments at Dura.

The assumption at Dura that Biblical characters wore ritual fringes is paralleled in rabbinic sources. Among the most piquant, *b. Baba Batra* 73b–74a describes

73. Wilderness encampment and the miraculous well of Be'er, Dura Europos Synagogue (photograph by Fred Anderegg, after Goodenough, *Jewish Symbols* 11, pl. xii).

one Rabba bar bar Ḥanna who viewed "those who died in the desert" and tried, unsuccessfully, to take a bit of the blue string from their ritual fringes.[70] In short, the images at Dura, and particularly that of Moses with the Torah scroll, suggest a strong parallel with rabbinic assumptions and patterns of behavior in matters of dress and performance with the dress of local Dura Jews, as well as a local Jewish performance of the Biblical commandment of ritual fringes in a manner that well parallels rabbinic assumptions and patterns of behavior. This has implications for the performance of other commandments as well.[71]

Because the parchment establishes that at least some Dura Jews prayed in Hebrew, it seems reasonable to suggest they may also have recited Scripture in that language. The longer Aramaic labels on some of the synagogue's images hint that an Aramaic translation or paraphrase may also have been recited at Dura – whether together with the Hebrew, as was rabbinic practice in both Palestine and in Babylonia, or perhaps (less likely) on its own. Between the legs of Moses in the Exodus scene we read: משה כד נפק מן מצרים ובזע יאמא, that is, "Moses when he went out of Egypt and split the sea."[72] Above his head later in this scene, we find:

משה כד ב[ז]ע יאמא, "Moses when he split the sea."[73] This language is very close to the known Aramaic paraphrases of the Torah. *Targum Neofiti*, the only complete Palestinian paraphrase to the Torah, comments on Exodus 14:16: "Raise your staff and incline your hand over the sea and split it (ובזע יתה)."[74] Targum Onkelos, which was essentially Babylonian, preserves a similar reading.[75] Comparing the language mix in the synagogue to the languages used in documents recovered throughout Dura Europos, George D. Kilpatrick finds that "it is remarkable that the largest number of texts is in Aramaic."[76] Aramaic was a significant language among the Jews of this community, which, like the liturgical use of Hebrew, distinguished them from their neighbors.

The Dura paintings also seem to illustrate prayer postures that were known, and perhaps practiced, by Jews at Dura. In the image of "the wilderness encampment and the miraculous well of Be'er," we find; personifications of each of the twelve tribes within their tents, their arms raised in an *orans* position posture with their hands lifted upward toward heaven, as water flows from the well to each tribe (Figure 73). Similarly, in the Ezekiel panel, the reviviated "dry bones" of the Ezekiel panel also stand in an *orans* posture. Is this indicative of a prayer stance used by the Dura Jews or simply a visual convention? It is well known that Christians assumed this stance; in the Dura church, this stance is illustrated in the image of Jesus walking on water.[77] Did Jews employ this gesture as well?[78] Rabbinic literature of this period does not mention the *orans* as a prayer stance, although silence is not always evidence of historical fact.[79] Synagogue art from Palestine indicates that the *orans* position may have been used by Jews during the fifth or sixth century. Was this prayer stance assumed by Jews at Dura as well?

Alternatively, the image identified by Kraeling as Abraham in wing panel 4 stands with his hands clasped under his robe.[80] This clasping of hands was a prayer stance in the Babylonian diaspora. *b. Shabbat* 10a relates the practice of two Babylonian Amoraim:

When Rabba prayed, he removed his cloak, folded his hands and prayed, saying '[I pray] like a slave before his master.' Said Rav Ashi: I saw Rav Kahana, when there was trouble in the world, he removed his cloak, folded his hands and prayed, saying '[I pray] like a slave before his master.'"[81]

Did Jews at Dura stand with hands folded in prayer, or did they assume the *orans* posture? Perhaps neither, and perhaps both, depending on their understanding of the meaning of the gestures. Perhaps both approaches were taken, just as three languages were spoken by Jews who frequented the synagogue. Perhaps some members of the community assumed one stance; other members, the other. Being a border city, Dura certainly had a diverse Jewish population, and that population must have had varied customs.

The Dura paintings have long served as a focal point for testing modern identities and scholarly approaches (including, of course, my own). As with the Sepphoris synagogue mosaic intricate all-encompassing approaches are more indicative of Renaissance sensibilities and of modern scholarly modes of thought than ancient Jewish ones.[82] The fact that only the western wall is fully preserved, slices of the side walls, and virtually none of the back wall, is complicated by problems of identifying some of the less complete images. The extant Dura synagogue paintings do not seem to reflect a carefully structured consecutive order, on the pattern of a modern comic book or art history survey (or the final report of the Dura synagogue), where image number one leads to image number two and so on. It is my sense that once the Torah shrine paintings,

the panel above it, and the four flanking images of men were in place, the designer(s) and perhaps the "building committee" listed on the dedicatory ceiling tiles arranged groups of somewhat related images on the walls. Some images, like those detailing the movements of the Ark of the Covenant, were grouped together, and others stand alone. That the image of Moses with the scroll, the crossing of the sea, and Pharaoh's daughter rescuing baby Moses are grouped on the same wall to the right of the Torah shrine does not seem haphazard to me.

The second band of the western wall is unified by the fact that each scene contains a gabled image of the Tabernacle or the Temple, with the gabled Temple of Dagon to the far right. The placement of Samuel anointing David above the chair where the synagogue leader, Samuel, seems to have sat may have had local political implications (Figure 74); as would images of local Dura gods destroyed in the Temple of Dagon and of the unsuccessful sacrifice by the priests of Baal (temples to the Palmyrene gods, including Bel and Zeus-Kyrios-Baalshamin, existed at Dura, Figure 52).[83] These discredited deities are set in opposition to images from the Biblical cult, from Elijah's successful sacrifice to Aaron at the Tabernacle and the averted sacrifice of Isaac, and images of the Temple and menorah on the face of the Torah shrine. Unfortunately, the central panel of the western wall, just above the Torah shrine, was repainted so often that it is hard to know what was originally there. The fact that the area was reworked evidences just how important this area of the paintings was to the community. Of particular interest is the image of David playing his harp – an important connection to the themes of David as psalmist, king, and messiah. The artistically adept might have recognized formal similarities between David and Orpheus, although others probably did not take notice. That certain paintings were particularly popular is reflected in the Persian graffiti preserved on them. Not surprisingly, these panels were within easy reach because they were in the lowest register. Were they popular because they were low on the wall, or were they in the bottom register because the themes were popular? This we shall never know, just as we shall never know what treasures existed on the 40 or 50 percent of the walls that did not survive.

There is no overarching, global theme to the paintings – as much as many modern scholars would like to find one. One might imagine a preacher within the synagogue turning to the images and using them to homiletic effect – and to different effects according to the content of his homily.

74. Samuel anointing David, Dura Europos (photograph by Fred Anderegg, after Goodenough, *Jewish Symbols* 11, pl. vii).

The assembled community would focus on different images according to their interests, concerns, and visual facility.[84] The use of synagogue decorations as "props" by homilists is known from rabbinic sources, as is a similar process within somewhat later church contexts.[85] There was no one exclusive meaning for each image, but rather a range of interconnected interpretations were possible.[86] The preacher likely interpreted the images differently depending on the lesson he was teaching, the audience, the liturgical calendar, and the particular text being explicated. The vast quantity of images at Dura certainly facilitate an astonishingly wide variety of possibilities!

This approach fits well with the midrashic approach to Scripture itself. Wharton associates this with chaos theories in modern literary scholarship, although the model proposed here fits better with the "organic thinking" that Max Kadushin and Isaak Heinemann[87] in somewhat different ways suggested was operative in rabbinic thought. This hypothesis would be reasonable as interpretations of

the synagogue without the Dura parchments. Once again, the Dura liturgical parchment, containing prayer formulae so close to the world of the ancient rabbis, warrants a more sustained interpretation and strengthens the hand of those who interpret the synagogue in light of rabbinic literature.

The Dura synagogue served not only as a setting for study and exegesis, but also for liturgical prayer in the more specific sense of the word. This, it seems to me, is one of the lessons of the Dura parchment: that at least some Jews in Dura prayed in forms that we know from rabbinic circles. What did they "pray"? It is likely that we shall never know. For strictly heuristic purposes, however, let us imagine that the Dura Jewish community prayed the most central rabbinic prayer, the *Tefillah* – or something like it.[88] With the weight I have given here to the Dura parchment, this is not as outlandish as it might sound – especially because the *Tefillah* so well encapsulates the central themes of Rabbinic theology. How would the Dura wall paintings function for a community that, say, recited the weekday *Tefillah* prayer together within this synagogue?[89]

The language of the *Tefillah* would have been quite recognizable to at least portions of the Dura community. The formulae and language of the Dura parchment are closely related to those of rabbinic prayer, as we have seen. As to the content, the power of the Divine is expressed throughout this text, as it is in our images. The references to Abraham, Isaac, and Jacob in the *Tefillah* would find resonance in the paintings, where the binding of Isaac, Abraham, and Jacob's ladder all appear. This focus on Biblical ancestors of heroic stature as the backdrop for contemporary religion is found in both the paintings and the *Tefillah*. Similarly, David the messiah and the rebuilding of the Temple are central to both.[90] The focus on knowledge and Torah finds parallels in the project as a whole, particularly in the image of "Moses" with the scroll. Hope for health and the resurrection of the dead are expressed in the images of Elijah revivifying the dead child and the literal resurrection illustrated in Ezekiel's vision of the dry bones. This theme was emphasized by one of the Persian graffiti. Above Elijah's right thigh, we read: "Praise to God, praise! For life, life eternally he gives (. . .?).[91] The curse against slanderers and the wicked, in some Cairo Genizah versions, against the "*notsrim* and the *minim*," the Christians and heretics"[92] might be directed against Jews who behaved poorly (none of whom, "obviously" appear on the walls). It might equally apply to the evil Haman, the dead Egyptians at the Sea, against the "idolatrous" Palmyrenes and worshippers of Baal, and Mithraites (the vanquished Dagon being "coincidentally" represented by deities of polytheistic communities at Dura). There is no direct reference to Christians, who may simply be ignored (as they generally were by third-century rabbis as well).[93] The notion that the Bible projected through the prism of midrashic tradition was a distinctly Jewish possession, a leitmotif of these images, might to some degree suggest a very opaque response to this neighboring group.[94]

The "righteous and godly" are, of course, illustrated on every wall. The "righteous" include all of the Biblical heroes and their exploits. Finally, this prayer would be recited facing toward Jerusalem, and publicly within the synagogue context, while facing in the direction of the Torah shrine that at Dura stood on the western Jerusalem-aligned wall of the synagogue.[95] On the face of this shrine is the image of the Temple, the menorah, and the *aqedah*, the intended sacrifice of Isaac (which 2 Chronicles 3:1 and later Jewish tradition place on the Temple Mount). Referring to the restoration of the Temple and its cult, the *Tefillah* says, using a visual metaphor that fits well with our Dura shrine, "May our eyes behold your return in mercy to Zion." In short, there are few images in the Dura paintings that could not somehow relate to the themes of this prayer – which itself was not recited without a frame of still other liturgical compositions (including Biblical texts) and, on specific occasions, Scriptural reading and translation.

Again, I am not suggesting that the Jews at Dura necessarily recited the rabbinic *Tefillah*, nor am I suggesting that the text of the *Tefillah* was intentionally encoded into these paintings – even in part. Rather, strong thematic parallels may be drawn between these two "documents" of late antique synagogue liturgy. The themes of the *Tefillah* are the basic building blocks of rabbinic prayer. Jews in the frontier city of Dura Europos participated with the rabbis in a kind of Jewish *koiné* – a shared or common religion that included theological, midrashic, and liturgical components not inconsistent with these themes.

To conclude – the Dura Europos liturgical parchment provides a powerful key for the interpretation of the Dura synagogue and its paintings. This fragment firmly anchors the community at Dura within a religious world that was shared by the rabbis of Babylonia and Palestine – a point that was hotly debated during the past century. The proximity of this fragment to the world of the rabbis is paralleled in the content of the paintings themselves, particularly as regards liturgical issues. In comparing the paintings to the central rabbinic prayer, the *Tefillah*, I have attempted to show the close conceptual proximity between the themes inherent in that text and the Dura synagogue paintings. It is my firm belief that the remains of prayer texts at Dura and the "set" for the liturgical drama – the synagogue – form a holistic whole: "a single symbolic matrix" for religious experience.

CHAPTER TWELVE

SYNAGOGUE MOSAICS AND LITURGY IN THE LAND OF ISRAEL

Multiple explanations of symbols are common in Jewish art of all ages: Zodiac and Helios, often represented in Palestinian synagogues during the Byzantine period, are perfect examples of symbols with diverse interpretations.

Leila Avrin, 1994[1]

I F AT DURA THE EXTANT ARCHAEOLOGICAL EVIDENCE IS RICH AND the literary remains miniscule, in the Land of Israel the situation is far more complex. In Palestine, we find numerous "shards" of evidence: here an isolated rabbinic or Genizah text, there a Torah shrine aedicula, at another site a "chancel" screen, and still another a fragmentary mosaic floor. If in Israel the evidence for the Byzantine period is abundant, it is also frustratingly fragmentary. In this chapter, I attempt to reconstruct some of what we might say about the relationship between synagogue remains and the liturgical life of the synagogue. In the process, I look to Christian parallels to provide additional resources for interpreting the Jewish remains.

This approach makes particular sense in an environment where the large Palestinian Jewish community lived as a minority in the ever-expanding and intensifying Christian Holy Land. As a minority, Jews were receivers of the art of the majority. They seamlessly inculturated the visual culture in which they lived. Although Jews rejected some elements, as we have seen, the basic structures of late Roman and Byzantine visual culture were digested and made their own. This has been the case of synagogue art and architecture since.

We will focus on a group of synagogues that once bore carpet mosaics. These mosaics are particularly rich in imagery and inscriptions, which makes them an ideal focus for this discussion – as opposed to, for example, Galilean-type synagogues, which provide few clues. The late-fourth-century synagogue of Hammath Tiberias B, the fifth-century synagogue of Sepphoris, and the sixth-century synagogues of Na'aran and Beth Alpha are particularly evocative. These mosaics form a definite group, bearing very similar and extensive iconography. This regional type is unique in ancient Jewish artistic production. In cities of the diaspora, no specific Jewish iconography may be found in floor mosaics, synagogue mosaics being representative of local techniques and having no relationship with one another. In the Land of Israel, on the other hand, a regional type existed for more than 200 years. What unifies these floors is that each bears the image of a zodiac wheel in the center, and a Torah shrine on the floor immediately before the podium (in Beth Alpha and probably Na'aran, the apse) where an actual Torah shrine stood.

In this chapter, I will assert close proximity between the remains of ancient synagogues and the vast numbers of Jewish liturgical texts and related literature that are extant. Some of these sources have been preserved in canonical texts such as the Talmudim, midrashic collections, and prayer books. Many others have come down to us because of the discovery of a great repository of books from Old Cairo, known to us as the Cairo Genizah. This assertion of proximity between these documents and extant inscriptions is legitimized, first of all, by comparison of the more than 100 inscriptions in Aramaic (with a few in Hebrew) from Palestinian synagogues from the fourth through the seventh centuries. Written in the same characters and languages as preserved documents in Palestinian Jewish Aramaic[2] and "Rabbinic" Hebrew, these inscriptions preserve numerous formulae in common with preserved liturgical texts. Gideon Foerster has cataloged

dozens of parallels between inscriptions and liturgical texts, and there is no need to repeat the similarities here.[3] The use of the Biblicized phrase "amen sela" (and similar forms) in inscriptions, liturgy, and amulets; the designation of the synagogue as a "holy place"; and focus on the Biblically ordained priestly courses are just three of the many examples of continuity.[4] The most profound example of continuity comes from the eighth-century Jericho synagogue.[5] This Aramaic inscription translates:

Remembered for good, may their memory be for good, all of the holy community, the elders and the youths, whom the eternal King helped and who donated and made the mosaic. He who knows their names and the names of their sons and the people of their households will inscribe them in the book of life with the righteous.
All of Israel are interconnected (haverim). Peace [Amen].

This inscription closely parallels versions of the *Qaddish* prayer that is preserved in a number of liturgies, including that of Aleppo in neighboring Syria. In a manuscript dated 1410, we find the following prayer:[6]

Remembered for good, may your memory be for good, for a good name, all of this holy community, your elders and your youths.
He who knows your names will inscribe them in the book of life with the righteous.

Other versions of this prayer preserve the third person used in the inscription, and include the phrase "all of Israel is interconnected, amen."[7] The hope in the inscription and the prayer that God "inscribe" the donors "in the book of life [with all] the righteous" is the inverse of a version of the "blessing" against heretics of the *Tefillah* preserved in a Genizah fragment that we have mentioned.[8] The close philological relationship between synagogue inscriptions and liturgical texts provides the first anchor for mooring this liturgical interpretation of the art.

As we shall see, parallels are not limited to liturgical formulae, but are expressed in the themes that occur in both synagogue art and in extant liturgical texts. This chapter is divided into two main parts. In order to assert the sense that despite the fragmentary nature of the extant evidence, we are dealing with complex spaces and not just with objects that may be explained through linear interpretation or as disconnected icons, I begin by focusing on the mosaic that bears the most extensive iconographic program, that of the Sepphoris synagogue. After describing the mosaic in terms of other extant pavements, I suggest one particularly illuminating parallel in late antique Palestinian Jewish literature that ties together many of the themes of this floor. I will exemplify a holistic reading of this floor that can then be applied to the rest of the corpus. In the remainder of the section, I turn to two specific iconographic themes in the synagogue mosaics and what they might mean in liturgical terms: "The Torah, Its Shrine, and the Decoration of Late Antique Palestinian Synagogues" and "The Zodiac." Finally, I return to the notion of synagogue sanctity, a concept that provides an important rubric for understanding the art of ancient synagogues liturgically.

THE SEPPHORIS SYNAGOGUE: A LITURGICAL INTERPRETATION

The discovery of a synagogue mosaic during the construction of a parking lot at Sepphoris National Park in 1993 created immediate excitement among scholars. Little wonder, for no discovery of Jewish narrative art in Israel has matched this one since Kibbutz members digging a water channel uncovered the Beth Alpha synagogue mosaic and brought it to the attention of Eleazar Lipa Sukenik in late 1928. The Sepphoris mosaic contains unique images of not only a Torah shrine and zodiac wheel (Figure 31), but also of the visit to Abraham by the Divine messengers, the binding of Isaac (Figure 82), Aaron in the Tabernacle, and images drawn from the sacrificial cult itself (Figures 75, 76).

The general characteristics of the Sepphoris synagogue mosaic fit well with the synagogue discoveries that preceded it. As in the fourth-century mosaic of Ḥammath Tiberias and the floors at Beth Alpha and Na'aran, the center of the nave is dominated by a large zodiac wheel (Figures 24, 25). Close to the *bimot* of these synagogues was the image of a Torah shrine flanked by two seven-branched menorahs. This imagery appeared at times outside of the synagogue context, occurring first in graffiti from the Beth She'arim catacombs and later on a mirror plaque that some hold to have magical significance.[9] The image of the binding of Isaac at Sepphoris was not unheralded, a less refined version from about a century later having been discovered at Beth Alpha (Figures 10, 82).[10] The rest of the Biblical scenes, while unique and exciting, fall into well-established categories. Biblical narrative scenes were discovered at a number of sites: Noah's ark was uncovered at Gerasa (Figure 77), Daniel in the lions' den at Na'aran (Figure 24) and probably at Khirbet Susiya, and David the Sweet Singer

75. Drawing of the Sepphoris Synagogue mosaic (after Z. Weiss and E. Netzer, *Promise and Redemption: A Synagogue Mosaic from Sepphoris*, 14, courtesy of Ze'ev Weiss).

76. Basket of first fruits, Sepphoris Synagogue mosaic (photograph by Steven Fine).

Christian parallels – except, as we shall see, the zodiac. Ze'ev Weiss and Ehud Netzer, the excavators, have shown important parallels to the binding of Isaac in the Ravenna wall mosaics, and close parallels can be found as well for the Showbread Table,[12] the image of Aaron before the Tabernacle,[13] and the zodiac.[14] The image of Aaron before the Tabernacle strangely reaches into the register below. While the images within the upper scene are spatially well planned, the panel below bears no sign of perspective. It seems likely that the image of Aaron – which has parallels with the Dura panel of Aaron at the Tabernacle – was borrowed from a Christian or general Greco–Roman pattern book and cultic imagery added in the lower register to make the image more distinctively sacrificial and Jewish. Images of priests sacrificing before shrines are common in Roman art,[15] and it is only natural that, as at Dura, Aaron would be depicted before the Tabernacle. The designer of this mosaic then added even more sacrificial content as well as a connecting Biblical verse. The rather pedestrian stature of the local mosaicist (be he a Jew or non-Jew) or the poor quality of his model probably also limited his iconographic options.[16]

The floors at Hammath Tiberias, Beth Alpha, Na'aran, Ḥorvat Susiya, and Sepphoris reflect the creativity of both the local artisans and the communities they served through the organization of the various panels. While the large zodiac was always placed at the center and the ark near the bema in synagogue mosaics, the Biblical scenes were set out in a number of different arrangements. At Beth Alpha, the binding of Isaac appears near the northern entrance to the basilica and at Na'aran Daniel is situated immediately before the ark in an *orans* position that may be reminiscent of a late antique synagogue prayer position.[17] At Susiya, the organization is entirely different because the hall is a broadhouse and not a basilica. The organizing principle at Sepphoris, it seems to me, is, first and foremost, the placement of the zodiac near the center of the long nave, and the image of Torah shrine image near (though not adjacent to) the ark. The Abraham narrative was then grouped together below the zodiac, and the Temple/Tabernacle above the zodiac and below the Torah shrine due to the architectural resonances shared with the synagogue ark.

of Israel at Gaza.[11] This is without mentioning the geographically and chronologically distant wall paintings at Dura Europos, which were destroyed around 256 C.E.

Significantly, the only distinctively Jewish contents that can be identified in the Sepphoris mosaic are the Torah shrine and images of vessels from the Temple cult. All of the imagery in Jewish narrative art from Palestine has clear

77. The Gerasa Synagogue mosaic (after E. L. Sukenik, *The Ancient Synagogue of Beth Alpha*, pl. 26).

Still, what does all this "mean"? The answer is difficult, specifically because I am not willing to construct a singular metanarrative beyond the thesis that the enactment of Scripture within a liturgical structure is the unifying glue of the composition. I would imagine that the imagery of the binding of Isaac would have a different meaning at Rosh Hashanah than it might at other times, just as the Temple imagery would be seen differently at Passover than on *Tishah be-Av*, the anniversary of the destruction of the Jerusalem Temples. Fortunately, literary sources provide some relief. Large quantities of more or less contemporaneous local literature are extant, much of it discovered in the Cairo Genizah, through which to interpret this floor. Many examples are cited by Weiss and Netzer. The rich literature of late antique Palestinian Judaism ranges from homiletical midrashic collections to liturgical texts to Aramaic paraphrases of Scripture, the *targumim*.[18] While it is useful to draw parallels from throughout the rabbinic corpus to interpret individual images, this practice creates a kind of textual free-for-all when one attempts to construct an all-encompassing consecutive narrative. Fortunately, the large number of extant liturgical poems (*piyyutim*) provide a kind of control.

Reading through one poet's corpus of work, as we did in our discussion of the menorah during late antiquity, one can observe how a single Jew in late antique Palestine formulated and reformulated tradition within the synagogues of his day. I again draw on the work of Yannai the Paytan, because his 165 published poems cover the entire Pentateuch and festival cycle, were written just a century or so after Sepphoris mosaic was laid, and are the work of a single author. The striking fact is that all of the issues that appear in the Sepphoris mosaic are dealt with by Yannai, from the binding of Isaac to Aaron in the Tabernacle to the Table for the Showbread to the first fruits, the menorah, and the zodiac.[19] By reading how this author understands these subjects, it is possible to imagine how one particularly learned and creative Jew who well could have visited the Sepphoris synagogue might have understood the themes that were set in stone by the mosaicist.

I will cite one acrostic poem by Yannai that within just a few lines utilizes many of the themes represented in the Sepphoris floor. The poem was recited on Rosh Hashanah eve. This extended poem reflects upon the liturgical themes of the day as it poetically embellishes the themes of the central *Tefillah* prayer that it celebrates. I am in no way

suggesting that this particular poem influenced the floor, only that the selection and arrangement of themes to decorate the Sepphoris mosaic and the selection and arrangement of themes by the liturgical poet both reflect how Jews constructed the synagogue environment through image and word at nearly the same time. The literary and the visual artists each assembled similar building blocks in constructing their own unique presentation for a synagogue setting. The section of Yannai's poem that concerns us translates as follows:[20]

א Then the shofar will be blown for the Complete [One] (לשלם),
The hope that the complete [shofar blasts] be received like peace offerings (שלמים) [in the Temple].

ב Hence any shofar that has a crack (בקיעה),
Is not fit, for it interrupts the sounding (התקיעה).

ג Come forth with a broken soul (שבורה) and not with a broken horn (שבורה),
With a broken heart and not with a broken shofar (שבור).

ד Lovers (דודים) drawn after Him, and like the girdle cleave (דבוקים),
They will sound a long shofar that has no [impermissible] adhesions (דבקים).[21]

ה For from the ram come the horns (הקרנות),
To remember the merit of the ram stuck by its horns (בקרנות) [at the binding of Isaac].

ו Sound, O sons of God (בני אלים), sound to the God of gods (אל אלים),
Who covers over and removes (ומעלים) from them all sins (מעלים).

ז A time of concealment when the moon is concealed (לבנה),
To conceal sins well, just as the moon [is concealed] (כלבנה).[22]

ח The sun, how can it bear witness [to the new month] alone (בעידות)?
When one witness is not enough [for a court] to inflict the death penalty (למות).

ט The [heavenly] array of the seventh month, its constellation is Libra (מאזנים),
For sin and righteousness God will lay upon the scales (במואזנים).

י His hand will remove sin and the day we will proclaim with the shofar (נריע),
To the scale of utter righteousness He will incline (יכריע).

Themes of the shofar; the binding of Isaac; and the sun, moon, and zodiac are among the building blocks for Yannai's Rosh Hashanah liturgy. It is important to note, however, that the binding of Isaac (representing the doctrine of "merits of the ancestors,")[23] the zodiac (representing to Yannai both the heavens and the Jewish solar–lunar calendar), and the sacrificial system are extremely common throughout Yannai's corpus, because of their centrality to the *Tefillah* prayer upon which our author artistically expands. Reflecting upon the Scriptural readings of Rosh Hashanah, upon the ceremonies of that day, and upon the calendrical cycle, Yannai brought together imagery that gives texture to his liturgical creation.

That all of this imagery appears in the Sepphoris floor is no accident. These themes were central to Jewish liturgical life during this period. Elsewhere in his corpus, Yannai weaves these themes and many others together in other ways depending on the reading for the day and the festival context. At other seasons, Yannai stresses different subjects, many of which are expressed in the synagogue mosaics. We have seen that the menorah is the subject of Yannai's Hanukkah and liturgical poems for Numbers 8. At *Tisha be-Av*, the Tabernacle/Temple is dealt with differently than on *Sukkot*, and so on. One might even conjecture that on various occasions the synagogue was furnished in different ways. We know that this was the case in contemporary churches.[24] In Gaonic Babylonia, for example, women's jewelry was placed on Torah crowns for the festival of *Simhat Torah*. These crowns, apparently used throughout the year, were made of silver, gold, and myrtle.[25] Since medieval times, it has been customary to dress the synagogue and congregation in fine (white) textiles for Yom Kippur (and more generally for the fall festivals),[26] and in Ashkenaz to adorn the synagogue in greenery and flowers for *Shavuot* (Pentecost).[27] It seems likely that ancient Jews had their own distinctive ways of decorating their synagogues in accord with the liturgical cycle. The various elements of the synagogue, the visual, the textual, and the human actors, were as so many molecules, interacting with one another in different ways at different seasons and in different contexts. The art and the liturgy of the synagogue are cut from a single cloth, reflecting differing but always interwoven aspects of the synagogue religiosity in Byzantine Palestine.

To conclude: The Sepphoris floor, like all synagogue appurtenances, is preeminently a liturgical object. Its iconography, drawing from a tradition of synagogue art that was highly influenced by the iconographic possibilities of late antique Christian art, was organized so as to complement and give visual expression to the Biblically infused prayers, Scriptural reading, and homiletics of the synagogue. I suspect that the elements of the floor were chosen on a consensus basis based on convention, availability of models, the preferences of the community as a whole, and those of the patron whose name appears prominently at the top of each panel.[28] What unified the composition was the Biblical text that stood within the ark at the focal point of the hall, which, through the refractive lenses of the literature of the synagogue, was projected onto the synagogue pavement.

In the end, it is important to remember that this pavement is just a floor. The images of Aaron, the sacrificial cult, Abraham, Sarah, Isaac, the angels, and even citations of Biblical verses were regularly trodden upon by the Jews of Sepphoris.[29] Imagine if the walls, the ark, the menorahs, and the other lamps that illuminated this synagogue were extant.[30] We would barely notice the pavement below, covered with furniture and perhaps with reed mats.[31] Walls painted with images like those of the Dura Europos synagogue or covered with mosaics like the churches of Ravenna and Bethlehem would require of us a completely different attitude toward the Sepphoris floor mosaic and toward its ultimate "meaning" – both as an art object and as testimony to the rich liturgical life of late antique Palestinian synagogues.

THE TORAH, ITS SHRINE, AND THE DECORATION OF LATE ANTIQUE PALESTINIAN SYNAGOGUES

. . . liturgy, art and preaching worked together to mediate an experience of worship. Biblical motifs, if not always particular biblical narratives, richly inform all three.

Wayne A. Meeks and Martha F. Meeks, describing early church mosaics, 2002[32]

Raising our eyes from the mosaic pavement of the Sepphoris synagogue and looking down the nave, we are likely to have seen a Torah shrine, perhaps flanked with lighted menorahs. This was not an unusual feature, for the focal point of the synagogue was the Torah. The placement of the Torah cabinet against the Jerusalem-aligned wall of the synagogue goes back to Tannaitic times, if not before. While this Jerusalem alignment was not immutable (the Sepphoris synagogue is aligned to the west), it was ubiquitous.[33] Where in churches an apse at the far end of the hall would be taken up with the Eucharist table, in synagogues the focal point was the Torah shrine. This cabinet stood on a large platform, by the late fifth and sixth centuries constructed within an apse.[34]

The image that I have suggested emerges from the Torah shrine panels in our mosaics. A large shrine, crowned with an aedicula, in some cases with a lamp suspended from its apex, stood at the focal point of the synagogue. In fact, all of the elements of such a Torah compound have been discovered at one site or another.[35] The most interesting preserved aedicula was uncovered in the synagogue of Nabratein in the Upper Galilee (Figure 78).[36] This gabled structure is topped with rampart lions, with a suspension hole at its apex for a lamp. This shrine is markedly similar to the shrine illustrated at Beth Alpha, although at Beth Alpha birds appear rather than lions (Figure 79).[37] Cloths like those illustrated before mosaic images of synagogue Torah shrine, called in rabbinic parlance a *vilon* or *parokhta* (reminiscent of the veil of the Biblical Tabernacle and later the temples, the *parokhet*),[38] are well known from extant Egyptian textiles and images in non-Jewish contexts (particularly church mosaics).[39] In some instances, the curtain is pulled back to reveal the shrine – a standard late antique convention.[40] Even sculptured three-dimensional lions like those illustrated flanking the Beth Alpha ark were found at Chorazin and Baram, and the base of a Torah shrine bearing large carved lions was found at En Samsam in the Golan Heights (Figures 36, 37, 38).[41] The Chorazin and Baram lions are among the only examples of three-dimensional sculpture in any ancient Jewish context. In short, the large artifacts that are illustrated were, to a large extent, what actually stood in the synagogue (Figure 80).

Seven-branched menorahs blazed on either side of a cabinet that by the third century was already being associated with the Ark of the Covenant, and was called an *arona*.[42] These lamps reflected a connection between the synagogue and the Temple.[43] On a practical level, they served to focus the eye of the visitor on the Torah shrine. The lamp suspended from the Torah shrine (which was later called an "eternal

78. Torah shrine aedicula from the Nabratein Synagogue (courtesy of Eric M. Meyers).

lamp") would have provided an additional spotlight for the true focal point of the synagogue: the Torah. At times, other lamps were crowded into the apse, hung from the menorahs and the ark itself. Lamps were sometimes suspended from the lowest branches of the menorahs, as is illustrated in the mosaics at Na'aran (Figure 24) and on tomb doors from Kefar Yasif and Khirbet Kishor.[44] In the study house/synagogue at Beth Shean, a lamp and an incense censer are illustrated in the mosaic, and two lamps (perhaps incense censers) appear on a screen from Khirbet Susiya.[45] Within churches, lamps were sometimes suspended from large crosses in a similar manner.[46] A pottery fragment from Nabratein shows a Torah shrine literally crowded with hanging lamps.[47] All of these lights together served an important practical function: They provided the light necessary for the reading of Scripture in otherwise dark (and in the winter, cold) halls. When later traditions publicly bless those who provide lamps for illumination, *ner le-maor*,[48] they reflect a true need within the synagogue

79. Torah shrine panel, Beth Alpha Synagogue mosaic (after Sukenik, *The Ancient Synagogue of Beth Alpha*, pl. 8).

80. Reconstruction drawing of the Beth Alpha Synagogue by Jacob Pinkersfield (after Sukenik, *The Ancient Synagogue of Beth Alpha*, pl. 7).

context and a real opportunity for participation in synagogue life that is somehow beyond those of us who live in a world changed forever by Mr. Edison. Anecdotally, participants in a recent reenactment of the 1866 dedication of Cincinnati's neo-moresque Plum Street Temple complained of the dimmed light that "almost put us to sleep!"[49] The brilliance of light at the focal point of the ancient synagogue must have been quite striking. Although no Jewish text describes this effect, Paulinus of Nola describes a similar construction at the tomb of St. Felix:[50]

Now the golden threshold is adorned with snow-white curtains, and the altars crowned with crowds of lanterns. The fragrant lamps burn with waxed wicks of paper, and are ablaze night and day, so that the night shines with the brightness of day, and the day, too, is bright with heavenly glory, gleaming the more since its light is redoubled by the countless lamps.

Paulinus elsewhere describes the total effect of precious metals, fine cloths, and lights within the church of St. Felix:[51]

I grant that others may outdo me with the costliness of their service in the precious gifts they bring, when they provide fine curtains, made of gleaming white linen or of material colored with bright shapes, for covering the doorways. Let some polish their smooth inscriptions on pliant silver, and cover the holy portals with the metal they affix there. Others may kindle light with colored candles, and attach lamps with many wicks to the vaulted ceilings, so that the hanging torches cast to and fro their flickering frames. . . .

Paulinus's description could well have been written about a Palestinian synagogue. Fine cloths are illustrated in synagogue mosaics and were most certainly suspended before Torah shrines and elsewhere in the meeting halls. Inscriptions too are common, and although gold and silver accoutrements have not been discovered from synagogues, the donation of precious metals is mentioned in a dedicatory inscription at Hammath Tiberias B:[52]

Remembered for good everyone who donates and contributes, or will (in the future) give in this holy place, whether gold, silver or anything else. Amen. Their portion is in this holy place. Amen.

Polished bronze was certainly common.[53] The bronze polycandelon now in the Musee de'Mariemont in Belgium that lit "the holy place of Kefar Ḥananyah" (be it a synagogue or a study house) is important in this context,

81. "Ancient Synagogue Apse" in the exhibition installation of *Sacred Realm: The Emergence of the Synagogue in the Ancient World*, Yeshiva University Museum, 1996. The displayed aedicula is from the Chorazin synagogue, screen fragments are from (left to right) Tiberias, Hammath Tiberias A, Tiberias, and Dalton. The menorahs are facsimilies of the Hammath Tiberias A menorah (photograph by Steven Fine).

as are a large bronze plate bearing the images of a menorah and a Torah shrine from Naanah in the Judean Shefelah (now in the Louvre),[54] a chalice and small menorah from Ein Gedi,[55] and a bronze incense censer decorated with images of animals from a Samaritan (?) synagogue in Beth Shean.[56] The image of a similarly fashioned censer (without animal imagery) appears suspended from the lowest branch of a menorah in a study house (or synagogue) mosaic from Beth Shean.[57] In the continuation of his text, Paulinus describes pilgrims who "eagerly pour spikenard on the martyr's burial place, and they withdraw the healing unguents from the hallowed tomb." This usage, of course, is unthinkable within synagogue settings. It is a real point of discontinuity between the Christian and the Jewish sacred spaces. Jews, by contrast, would wax midrashic that the synagogue, like the Temple, must be illuminated perpetually as a mark of its holiness.[58]

In curating Yeshiva University Museum's exhibition, *Sacred Realm: The Emergence of the Synagogue in the Ancient World*, I was given the opportunity to construct a full-scale model of a synagogue apse and furnish it with actual artifacts (Figure 81). A basalt aedicula from Chorazin was flanked by two reproductions of the limestone menorah from Hammath Tiberias A, with fragments of synagogue "chancel" screens from Dalton and Tiberias before the shrine.[59] On the floor before the model was a life-size photograph of a mosaic from a Beth Shean synagogue, created with a process that allowed visitors to walk on it. Represented on this mosaic were images of a Torah shrine flanked by menorahs. The sight was quite evocative, and expresses my sense of the interconnectedness of visual representations of the Torah shrine flanked by menorahs and the reality of synagogue furnishings during late antiquity.

Scholars have long asked why, if the furnishings illustrated actually existed, it was necessary to illustrate them on the floor. The answer is a simple one: The ark panels of our mosaics are reflections of the Torah shrine and menorahs of the synagogue. Christians used the same technique within churches, paralleling the ritual furnishings of the church in its wall and floor decorations. The best examples are the strikingly similar image of the Torah shrine at Susiya and its parallel in the Church of the Priest John on Mount Nebo.[60] Closer to the Jewish context, Samaritan synagogue communities seem to have used this approach as well. Mosaics discovered in the Samaritan synagogues of Khirbet Samara and El-Ḥirbeh all bear images of shrines. At El-Ḥirbeh the menorah and a table that represents a ritual meal of some sort appear (Figures 66, 67).[61] The mosaic that we used in the Yeshiva University Torah shrine model, from the synagogue at Beth Shean A, may also be Samaritan – if a Samaritan inscription in a side room of that synagogue is any indication.[62] This mosaic was fabricated by the same artisans who laid the Beth Alpha floor, Marianos and his son Hanina. These mosaics serve the same function that a reflecting pool does (and did) before a major public building:[63] These reflections add dignity to the shrine and to the Torah within it.

A second debate has been whether this imagery represents the synagogue furnishings or is a projection of the Jerusalem Temple, with all sorts of rationales offered for choosing one over the other. My own sense is that this choice is unnecessary, for from the third century on, the Torah shrine was conceived in terms of the Biblical Ark of the Covenant. We have seen this in the tradition attributed to Rabbi Ḥuna the Elder of Sepphoris,[64] who speaks of the local Torah cabinet as if it were the Ark of the Covenant. Throughout our period, the two are closely linked in rabbinic literature (as they were earlier at Dura), until in some midrashim the Biblical ark was treated as a Torah shrine and the Tabernacle itself as a big synagogue![65] An inscription from the Syrian Golan town of Nawa (Naveh) refers to the Torah shrine as the *beit arona*, the "house of the ark."[66] Still, late antique rabbis were not oblivious to the distinctions between their local arks and the Holy Ark. The Torah ark is not referred to as the "Ark of the Covenant" or the "Holy Ark" in Palestinian Amoraic or post-Amoraic literature or in inscriptions.[67] Drawing on a midrashic mind-set that is known well from the literature of this period, I posit that the potential to read the local ark in terms of the Biblical Ark, and vice versa, is the best explanation for this mosaic imagery and group of synagogue furnishings.

The mosaicist at Na'aran went a step further. Below the image of the Torah shrine at Na'aran, the artist set the image of Daniel in the lions' den (Figure 24). Daniel's hands are raised in an *orans* position in Christian art, called *nessiat kappayim*, the "raising of hands" in Biblical and rabbinic sources.[68] Elsewhere in this mosaic, we find other figures, both male and female, assuming this position. This image of Daniel is not unique. It appears on a Torah shrine base from En Samsam in the Golan (Figure 38) and apparently appeared in the synagogue mosaic at Susiya in Mount Hebron.[69] In fact, the *orans* position seems to have been a Jewish prayer stance in Byzantine-period Palestine. It is my suggestion that "Daniel" was placed before the ark so as to reflect another important feature of synagogue

"furnishings": the *sheliah tsibbur* (prayer leader) who stood before the ark during public liturgy, in the technical language of the period, *over* (or, *yored*) *lifne ha-teva*.[70] In a sense, the flesh-and-blood *sheliah tsibbur* fills the ritual space between the three-dimensional ark and the two-dimensional representation of the same ark. The actual image of Daniel, drawn from Christian art, was placed in a position in our mosaic that reflects an essential element of Jewish spirituality. Like the *sheliah tsibbur*, Daniel directs his prayers toward the ark – and through it – toward the Holy City of Jerusalem. Daniel here is illustrated acting out the verse in Daniel 6:10, which describes how he "went to his house where he had windows in his upper chamber open toward Jerusalem. . . ." Closing the loop, this text was taken by the rabbis to be the Biblical warrant for their own alignment toward Jerusalem in prayer.[71]

Another possible reflection of the *sheliah tsibbur* seems to occur at Sepphoris. Within the Tabernacle panel, immediately "below" the image of the Torah shrine is a horned altar. I would argue that the shape of the top of the horned altar, a kind of rhombus, visually parallels the image of the ark with which it is aligned and the three-dimensional ark of the synagogue towering above. When the prayer leader stood to lead the community in prayer, he would have essentially stood, de facto, in the position of Aaron. This would be particularly meaningful on the festivals, and even more so at the *musaf* liturgy on Yom Kippur morning, when to this day the prayer leader takes the persona of the high priest in the Temple. This reliving and revitalization of the priestly service is well reflected in *piyyut* literature. According to the internal logic of this liturgy, the prayer leader "is" the high priest, while the congregation in the synagogue imagines that they stand in the great plaza of the Temple on Yom Kippur morning as participant observers in the sacrificial liturgy. The images of the Tabernacle implements and sacrifices, some interpreted in accord with rabbinic prescriptions,[72] all provide the stage for this drama. Aaron at Sepphoris was dressed, as far as we can tell, in clothing that suits the Byzantine period, just as the youths are in the binding of Isaac panel and as Abraham and Isaac must have been as well. In a real sense, the *sheliah tsibbur* looked like Aaron, and Aaron looked like him. Michael Swartz's comment regarding the role of the prayer leader in the Yom Kippur liturgy must certainly have been true as the leader towered above mosaic representation of Aaron at Sepphoris: ". . . the poet – who, we must remember, was usually the performer – identified with the priest."[73]

82. The binding of Isaac, Sepphoris Synagogue mosaic (photograph by Steven Fine).

Though by our sins the Temple Mount is not ours, we do have the small sanctuary (the synagogue), and we are obligated to behave (towards it) in sanctity and awe. For it is written: "My Temple, fear" (Leviticus 19:30, 26:2). Therefore the ancients decreed in all synagogue courtyards that lavers of living water for the sanctification of the hands and feet [be set up]. If there was a delicate or sick person, unable to remove (his shoes), and he was careful as he walked [not to dirty them], he is not forced to remove [the shoes]. . . .

This passage suggests that piety toward the synagogue, and particularly ritual ablution of the feet and entry to the synagogue barefooted, was taken over from the Temple to the "small sanctuary." The notion that ritual purity was necessary for entrance into late antique synagogues first appears in post-Amoraic literature.[78] An interesting parallel to our text is the liturgy of Anan son of David (c. eighth century), who, on the model of the Temple, decreed that worshippers wash their hands and feet before entering into synagogues.[79] A washing installation (*gorna*) in the synagogue compound (forecourt?) is evidenced as early as the *Jerusalem Talmud*.[80] Evidence of ritual ablution is found in synagogue ruins from the Byzantine period. A particularly well-preserved washing installation was discovered in the narthex of the last stage of the Ein Gedi synagogue.[81] By placing the images of shoes near the entrance to the synagogue, the Sepphoris artist, inadvertently or not, suggests that like Abraham and Isaac on the Temple Mount, shoes are to be removed before entering the synagogue.

The binding of Isaac at Beth Alpha and the image of David, "sweet singer of Israel," also bespeak liturgical life. Avigdor Shinan has surveyed the ways that the binding of Isaac (Genesis 22) is presented in midrash, liturgy, and *Targum*.[82] This panel is unusual in late antique art specifically because Abraham, "the father of faith" in Christian contexts, is not the focal point of this composition. Rather, at the focal center of the panel is the Hand of God reaching down from the heavens, the ram caught in the thicket immediately below. The focal point is the redemptive moment, when God cries out, Don't do it! and the ram is revealed ready to serve as Isaac's substitute. This focus fits well with Jewish reflection on the binding of Isaac, where Abraham's faith is subsumed to God's eternal pledge to

Unique to the binding of Isaac scene at Sepphoris is the image of Abraham's and Isaac's shoes left at the base of Mount Moriah (Figure 82). This theme is known from Christian illustrations.[74] This detail is unknown, however, from Jewish art or literature. Nowhere do we hear in midrashic literature God ordering Abraham to "put off your shoes from your feet, for the place on which you are standing is holy," taken over from Moses' encounter with the Divine in Exodus 3:5. Whether the source of this detail was Christian, or whether by one of those circuitous paths of relationship by which Jewish sources made their way to Christian audiences, this detail reflects a notion that the rabbis and other synagogue goers in antiquity would have well understood. A hint of the need for clean feet within synagogue contexts may be found in *Genesis Rabba* 42. In this text, clean feet are clearly described as a virtue for one who was entering the synagogue context. According to this tradition, when Abraham and his men chased after the kings to rescue Lot in faraway Dan, miraculously, "their feet did not become dusty." They were "like he who walks from his home to the synagogue."[75] The necessity of removing shoes before going up to the Temple Mount appears in *m. Berakhot* 9:5, and the requirement of removing shoes (and washing feet) before entering synagogues is well-documented.[76] In a document preserved in the Cairo Genizah, this is stated explicitly:[77]

"And so the Sages said: One shall not enter the Temple Mount with his staff and shoes" (*m. Berakhot* 9:5).

83. Wall mosaic, Church of San Vitale, Ravenna (after G. Galassi, *Roma o Bisanzio* [Rome: La Livreria dello Stato, 1930], pl. 76).

redeem the children of Israel. The horn of the ram is much brighter than the rest of the creature and draws attention. My sense is that this is intentional. The ram's horn is emphasized specifically because of its enduring liturgical significance. Its blowing on Rosh Hashanah was considered to be a reminder of the Covenant, the binding of Isaac the fullest statement of *zekhut avot*, the protective and enduring "merit of the fathers." The notion of *zekhut avot*, so central to rabbinic theology and so often expressed in liturgy, provides ample reason for the presence of all images of the ancestors that appear in synagogue mosaics – from Noah and the ark at Gerasa to the visitation of Abraham, the binding of Isaac, and Aaron at Sepphoris to the list containing Abraham, Isaac, and Jacob, Hananyah, Misha'el, and Azariah in a synagogue mosaic from Ein Gedi.[83] David at Gaza is a particularly interesting case. For anyone versed in Greco–Roman lore, this image, like David in the Dura synagogue, is clearly Orpheus. However much Jews in late antique Palestine knew of Greco–Roman lore, the Hebrew label, "David," removes any chance of "error." There is no evidence that Jews played instruments in synagogues during this period, and the Gaza David is no help in this regard (any more than images of instruments in medieval and modern synagogues are evidence for this practice). This image was taken over in the synagogue, and into churches as well, to bespeak David's role as psalmist.

The use of Biblical characters to presage and reflect contemporary practice is a common feature of rabbinic sources, and is common in Christian sources as well. For example, in the wall mosaics of the Church of San Vitale in Ravenna (Figure 83), we find that[84]

All four scenes allude to the eucharist sacrifice. To make this significance plain, an altar is depicted between Abel and Melchizedek, on which are placed a chalice and two loaves of bread, identical in shape with that which Melchizedek offers and also with the eucharistic bread which the church used during the sixth century. The altar motif appears again in the opposite mosaic: Isaac is shown kneeling upon the altar, and even the table behind which the three angels are seated resembles the simple wooden altar of Christian antiquity. The three round cakes which Sarah has placed before the heavenly messengers are marked with the sign of the cross and recall again the eucharistic hosts of that time.

The art of the Church, so influential in so many ways upon the art of the synagogue, provides a reasonable parallel for interpreting Daniel at Na'aran, Aaron and the empty shoes of Abraham and Isaac at Sepphoris, and perhaps even the ram's horn at Beth Alpha. Like Melchizedek at San Vitale, these images legitimize contemporary practice and project it into the eternal present.

Not illustrated in the Torah shrine panels, but present in numerous sixth- and seventh-century synagogues, are partitions separating the bima from the nave. Extant examples are made of marble, and evidence of a wooden screen was uncovered in dry Ein Gedi.[85] This element was borrowed from the church context in its entirety, where it served as a screen between the laity and the chancel area that was reserved for priests. Synagogue and church screens were often made in the same workshops, as was the case of screens discovered in the Beth Shean region. In the Beth Shean examples, a wreath encircles either a cross or a menorah. At Susiya, however, we find a much more complex group of images, one of which is a narrative scene that includes the hand of God. Gideon Foerster ingeniously identifies this scene with the giving of the Torah.[86] The screen seems to have been fully integrated into Jewish ritual contexts together with the entire Byzantine building, an integration so complete that screens were taken to be "natural" elements of the environment. A fine example of this process is a text discovered in the Cairo Genizah that projects protective screens separating the places where Scripture is publicly read into the heavenly study house. In the Cairo *Genizah* version of *Pereq Meshiaḥ*, we read:[87]

84. The binding of Isaac, Beth Alpha Synagogue Mosaic (after Sukenik, *The Ancient Synagogue of Beth Alpha*, pl. 19).

R. Eliezer son of Jacob says: The great study house of the Holy One, Blessed be He, in the future will be eighteen thousand myriad parsangs (in size), for it is written: "Its circumference [will be] 18,000" (Ezekiel 48:35). The Holy One, Blessed be He, sits on the chair among them, and David sits before him, for it is said: "His chair is like the sun before me" (Psalm 89:37). All the teaching women who educate and pay so that their sons may be taught Torah, Scripture and Mishnah, manners, pious sincerity and honesty stand by (or, within) reed mats made as a partition for the *bima* (platform) and listen to the voice of Zerubabel son of Shaltiel when he stands as interpreter (*meturgeman*). . . .[88]

What is most distinctive about this text is the complete lack of self-consciousness with which Jews assimilated this church furnishing. It was undoubtedly assimilated to Jewish notions of spatial sanctity and modes of distinction that are represented in rabbinic sources. This inculturation is part and parcel of the process by which the entire basilical structure – with its three doors reminiscent to Christians of the Trinity and its narthex from which catechumens (proselytes in the process of conversion) could listen to the liturgy[89] was seamlessly taken over by Jews. This ritual space was Judaized, and constructed as a "holy place" (a Biblical term also used by Christians beginning during the fourth century), as a "set" where Torah could be enacted and celebrated through the choice of themes chosen to decorate the mosaics and the furnishings of the synagogue.

THE ZODIAC, SYNAGOGUE MOSAICS, AND JEWISH LITURGY

. . . few scholars realize that the zodiac signs, as well as other symbolic figures used as ornaments, cannot and should not

be treated as fixed ideograms, which, once deciphered, have always the same unchangeable connotations.

Isaiah Sonne, 1953–54[90]

Images of the zodiac appear in the mosaics of Byzantine-era synagogues discovered in many areas of Jewish habitation in the Land of Israel. They have been uncovered in Hammath Tiberias on the Sea of Galilee in the north, in Beth Alpha in the Jezreel Valley (Figure 32), westward to Sepphoris and Ḥuseifa in the Carmel Mountain range (Figure 85), and perhaps in Yafia, near Nazareth in the Lower Galilee. In the south, zodiac mosaics were found in Na'aran near the Dead Sea and probably at Susiya in the Hebron hills. The sheer quantity of zodiac mosaics, dating from the fourth

85. Fragment of the zodiac panel of the Ḥuseifa Synagogue mosaic (photograph by Steven Fine).

to sixth centuries, is startling. This assemblage is unique for the Byzantine period, a time when the zodiac was systematically suppressed within non-Jewish contexts by the Church. The zodiac in Palestinian synagogue floors is a highly complex example of the "inculturation" of non-Jewish imagery and its resulting Judaization.

The fact that Jews maintained this art form long after its diminution in the general culture is not unprecedented in Jewish history. Describing early modern Italy, Kenneth Stow discusses the Judaization and maintenance of culture traits even after their abandonment by the majority culture. Stow shows that Jews selectively absorbed the majority culture, refracting it through their own cultural lens – sometimes conservatively maintaining elements of earlier absorption long after the majority culture had abandoned them. It is my suggestion that Jews borrowed and maintained this image within synagogues long after they had been abandoned by the general culture because of the considerable and growing significance of cultural issues that the zodiac represented within late antique Palestinian Jewish culture. This significance is represented in the literary remains of the liturgical tradition. As the "sets" upon which liturgical texts were enacted, ancient synagogues with zodiac mosaics reflect a real continuity between the aural and visual aspects of the liturgical experience.

Archaeological and Art Historical Contexts

The stylistic and iconographic parallels between the extant synagogue mosaics have been amply discussed by Moshe Dothan, Rachel Hachlili, Ze'ev Weiss, and Ehud Netzer.[91] These authors have shown in intricate detail the common sources of these synagogue mosaics as well as the elements that distinguish each mosaic. Although there is much variation, each is designed as a large ring set within a square frame. At the center of the ring is a chariot pulled by four horses, in all but one case, at Sepphoris, driven by the sun god Helios. The ring is divided into twelve parts, each containing a sign of the zodiac, labeled as such in Hebrew. At Sepphoris, a personification of the labors of that month appears, and also is labeled. The corners of the squares contain personifications of the seasons, these too labeled in Hebrew. The zodiac panels are set at the center of each of the synagogue naves and serve to draw together the entire hall.

Writing in the prestigious American journal *Art Bulletin* in 1945, German–Jewish expatriate Karl Lehmann was the first classical art historian to integrate synagogue mosaics into general art historical research. In "The Dome of Heaven,"[92] Lehmann shows in exquisite detail how common the zodiac motif was in late antique art, arguing, by and by, that the synagogue mosaic at Beth Alpha is a projection of the heavenly dome onto the floor of the hall. Although Thomas F. Mathews has rightly shown Lehmann's dome to contain many conceptual "cracks,"[93] Lehmann's then-revolutionary sense that synagogue zodiacs fit within an overall pattern in Roman art has proven to be true. Lehmann could only provide parallels from the western Mediterranean, dating two or three centuries earlier than Beth Alpha. In 1972, Aaron G. Sternberg suggested close proximity between this mosaic and the Vatican *Ptolemy Handlists*.[94] This manuscript was copied in Constantinople during the reign of Emperor Leo V, between 813 and 820. Franz Boll calculated on the basis of the zodiac, however, that the original model dates to the mid-third century.[95] At the center of a series of three concentric bands is an image of Helios riding his quadriga; in the innermost band are nude representations of each month, in the middle band personifications of the months, and in the outer band the signs of the zodiac.[96] This distinctly "pagan" image was Christianized through the addition of a cross on Helios's chariot; the Greco–Roman god was thus transformed into Christ. This is similar to the neutralization of Helios in the Sepphoris mosaic, where the god is removed from his quadriga. A mid-third-century mosaic from Munster-Sarnsheim, Germany, contains a zodiac wheel with a large Helios riding his quadriga in its center, the corners of the panel decorated with amphora flanked by fish.[97] Another, the image of a zodiac wheel inhabited by Selene and Helios (without chariot), the four winds of heaven depicted in its corners, was found at Sparta and dates to the fourth century.[98] Neither, however, is an exact parallel to the Jewish mosaics. They are also considerably earlier than all but the fourth-century mosaic at Hammath Tiberias. Imagery of the zodiac wheel preserved in other media from throughout the Roman world are cataloged by Hans Georg Gundel in *Zodiakos: Tierkreisbilder im Altertum* (1992).

The lack of images of the zodiac that parallel precisely the synagogue mosaics allowed some scholars to consider the synagogue floors – or at least certain design elements, – to be distinctly Jewish. This search for elements to consider uniquely Jewish is of one piece with the general search for a uniquely "Jewish art," and so was given great significance

86. Zodiac panel, Tallaras Baths, Island of Astypalaea, Greece.

by some scholars (although notably, not by Sukenik). In her 2001 Israel Museum exhibition volume, *The Realm of the Stars*, Iris Fishoff wrote, for example, that "in synagogues an interesting change occurred [from the standard Roman zodiac]. The emphasis transferred from the images of the pagan gods in the center to the area of the zodiac signs."[99]

The assumed uniqueness of the Jewish zodiac was shown to be incorrect by an unexpected discovery. Visiting the isolated eastern Aegean island of Astypalaea, archaeologist Ruth Jacoby came upon a previously unnoticed fifth-century bathhouse mosaic whose overall composition closely parallels our synagogue mosaics.[100] The Tallaras Baths were first excavated by Italian archaeologists during the 1930s and have still not been properly published (Figure 86). They therefore went unnoticed. Like the synagogue mosaics, it is designed as a square panel. At its center is a proportional image of Helios holding both a globe and a staff (though not riding a chariot), and in the surrounding band are the signs of the zodiac. In the corners are personifications of each of the four seasons, each in an *orans* position. The signs of the zodiac are very similar to those presented in Jewish mosaics. No doubt, other such mosaics will come to our attention in the future. Jacoby has conclusively shown that there is no reason to consider Jewish zodiacs a unique manifestation of "Jewish art."

Perhaps even more interesting, however, are the features of synagogue mosaics that do not exist in the Vatican *Ptolemy* or at Astypalaea. In all of the extant synagogue mosaics, the signs of the zodiac and the seasons are labeled in Hebrew. In adopting zodiac iconography, Jews "Judaized" the standard form and made it their own by adding Hebrew designations. The use of Hebrew in the zodiacs and Biblical

illustrations in synagogue mosaics stands out because the dedicatory inscriptions are written in Aramaic and Greek. This is at least in part because Hebrew was a liturgical language, the "language of the holy house." This use of Hebrew connects the mosaics to a synagogue-based liturgical tradition.[101] The Hebrew designations were known beyond the liturgy. This is demonstrated by the fact that Epiphanius, the fourth-century churchman, knew them, and later Aramaic and even Jewish magical texts in Arabic still maintain the Hebrew designations.

The first evidence for this Jewish borrowing is the fourth century at Hammath Tiberias B synagogue (Figure 29). All of the signs of the zodiac, as well as the seasons, are labeled in Hebrew in this fine mosaic. Oddly enough, Aquarius and Aries are written in mirror image. At the point where this imagery was adapted for the Jewish context, the Hebrew was added – although not without error.[102] The Judaization of the zodiac pattern was still fresh at this date. In later mosaics, no such mirror imaging takes place. Other examples of the transfer of the zodiac from the general context to Hammath Tiberias are the images of Aquarius and Libra, which are nude. Libra and Gemini are uncircumcised – a minor detail clearly taken from a non-Jewish source (that led the excavator, Moshe Dothan, to suggest that the mosaic may have been made by gentile workmen).[103] In later floors, all of the images are dressed. Finally, I note that at Sepphoris the image of Helios, the personification of the sun, has been removed from his chariot and replaced with a radiating sun disk. Sixth-century mosaics contain Helios, by that time a "dead" god. It should be remembered that by this time mythological gods appear even in Orthodox Church contexts![104] The type of borrowing that I have described is the norm in the design of Jewish architecture and ritual objects, where forms taken from the general culture are taken over by this minority community and "Judaized." The Sepphoris floor is transitional in another way (Figure 31). It includes both the signs of the zodiac and the works of each month. Both the zodiac symbol and the human laborer are labeled. So, for example, the first month is labeled both Taurus (*shor*) and Nisan. In this, it is like the Vatican *Ptolemy*, with the exception that the *Ptolemy* presents the works and the zodiac in separate concentric circles. It is also like the Ein Gedi synagogue mosaic, which includes lists of both the months and the zodiac signs.[105] Christian sites use the works exclusively, as at the Monastery of Lady Mary in Beth Shean.[106] The sixth-century mosaic at Beth Alpha seems to be modeled on a source that was in many ways akin to the mosaic at Hammath Tiberias.

Jews maintained the zodiac as an art form long after the general culture, by now dominated by Christianity, had discarded it. The Astypalaea mosaic is the rare example for the continuance of this iconography that proves the rule. Gundel cites strikingly few sources beyond the third century. The decline of the zodiac in public architecture relates directly to the rise of Christian ecclesiastical influence. An excellent example of this is Epiphanius, Bishop of Salamis, a fourth-century Church father who lived in Beth Guvrin, known to the Romans as Eleutheropolis. Epiphanius's intent was to chastise Jewish attachment to the zodiac. He does this by tarring the Jews with the brush of "paganism":

Also fate and astrology were quite popular notions with them. For instance, the Greek names from the astrology of those gone astray were translated by them into Hebrew names, such as the sun being called *hema* and *semes*, and the moon *ieree* and *albana*, whence it is also called *mene* (for the month is called *ieree*, the moon *mene*, just as it is by the Greeks because of the month). Mars is called *cocheb okbol*, Mercury *cocheb ochomod*, Jupiter *cocheb baal*, Venus *zeroua* or *loueth*, and Saturn *chocheb sabeth* (they also call him other names, but I could not explain their nomenclature exactly). In addition the names vainly adopted by those gone astray accord with the number of the elements, and which [the pagans who?] lawlessly seduced the world to impiety called the "Zodiac," they translate into Hebrew as follows: *tela, sor, thomim, saratan, ari, bethula, moznae[m], akrab, keset, gadi, dalli, deggim*. They, I mean the Pharisees, vainly following the pagans, convert the names into Hebrew ones thus: Aries they call *tela*, Taurus, *sor*, Gemini, *thomim*, Cancer *saratan*, Leo *ari*, Virgo *bethula*, Libra, *moznae[um]*, Scorpio *akrab*, Saggitarius *keshet*, Capricorn *gadi*, Aquarius *dalli*, and Pisces *deggim*.

Whether Epiphanius knew of Jewish astrology, as he claims, or simply knew that Jews set great store in the zodiac signs, we do not know. For Epiphanius, the Jews of Jesus's time (and hence of his own time) were no better than the pagans from whom they learned astrology. By "blaming" Jewish astrology on the pagans, Epiphanius redeems Biblical Israel for the Church, while damning Israel of the flesh. The Church's campaign against the zodiac was but a piece of its campaign to destroy the religious content of Roman art. In place of the zodiac, Orthodox Christian imagery was installed in the heavens. Mathews notes:[107]

The fact that the planets and the signs of the zodiac have no role in Early Christian imagery is not accidental. They were deliberately excluded. The celestial divinities of Roman art (and they were fairly common in many areas outside of ceilings) were not innocent decoration. They were astrological and the refutation of astrology was a theme of universal concern of the Fathers of the Church, whether one looks at authors from Syria, Alexandria, Cappadocia or the Latin West. . . .

Gazing at night at the heavens, the Christian beheld a different universe from his pagan neighbor. To Tatian (c. 160) the planets and the signs of the zodiac were demons introduced to men by the fallen angels. . . . Hence when the Lamb is set in the heavens in S. Vitalis, it is against a background of "fixed" stars. So too, the splendid crosses that appear in the starry sky at the Mausoleum of Galla Placidia and the apse of Saint Apollinaris in Classe. The old divinities have fallen out of the skies; the heaven to which Christ ascended is above and beyond the erratic movements of planets.

The continued use of the zodiac as a decorative feature by Jews should be seen against this background. Jews borrowed this iconography by the fourth century C.E. They continued using it during the following centuries, even as this motif was being dropped by Christians. The zodiac was not used in religious buildings by Christian designers (who did, however, portray the labors of the months). The Jews, however, kept using the zodiac — specifically, as we shall see, because the zodiac fit so well with their own religious conceptions. The use of this imagery was untouched by the Church, even as it was disdained.

Interpretations of Synagogue Zodiac Mosaics

Why did Jews continue to use this Judaized iconography in the decoration of their synagogues? While Lehmann saw in synagogue zodiac mosaics a manifestation of a generalized Greco–Roman "dome of heaven," Judaica specialists have sought out a singularly convincing Jewish interpretation. Armed with the notion that Jewish mosaics were somehow unique, most have assumed, with Rachel Hachlili, that ancient Jews "were seeking a design that could be used to express a certain concept or idea."[108] In their own ways, individual scholars set about to figure out what that singular, unitary, and unchanging idea was. As usual, E. R. Goodenough offered the most provocative theory. He, and after him certain other modern scholars, have seen in the zodiac mosaics visual evidence of a nonrabbinic Judaism that has left behind few literary texts. Convinced that the rabbis were anti-art, anti-zodiac, and, for Goodenough, otherwise puritanical, these scholars located Jewish zodiac mosaics, with their images of Helios, at the very center of the debate on the role of the Talmudic rabbis in ancient Judaism. Together with the Dura Europos paintings, synagogue zodiac wheels were seen by Goodenough to be the most unrabbinic archaeological evidence yet uncovered. As I have argued, however, Goodenough's view of rabbinic attitudes toward art was skewed.

Responding to Goodenough, in 1964 Michael Avi-Yonah suggested an interpretation that was diametrically opposed:[109]

Without trying, therefore, to look for esoteric meaning in the zodiacal representations, which would imply serious deviations for the synagogue authorities (and those supervising them) from the rules of the *halakhah*, we can regard the zodiac panel as a reminder of the duties toward God implied in a fixed calendar and of God's bounties given in return (in the representation of the seasons accompanying it).

It is not clear to me who saw a fixed calendar as "a reminder of the duties toward God" or of his "bounties given in return." Still, Avi-Yonah's association of the zodiac with the calendar was common among scholars of Jewish art during his day.[110] Returning to the subject of the synagogue zodiacs in 1973, Avi-Yonah suggested a variant of his original interpretation. Again responding to Goodenough, he argued that[111]

. . . the signs of the Zodiac with Helios in the center and the seasons in the corners were divested of all idolatrous associations. Instead they were given specifically Jewish significance, so that the Zodiac itself, for instance, stood for the ordering of the Temple services throughout the year . . .

Avi-Yonah does not explain explicitly why the zodiac mosaics stood for the Temple service, except that he was aware of texts of the priestly courses discovered in various synagogues (including one that he found in Caesarea Maritima)[112] and was attempting to connect these two time-based systems. Crossing the boundary from archaeologist to religion scholar, Avi-Yonah was less successful. His specific interpretations of the mosaics are not supported by extant evidence. The general connection between the zodiac and the Jewish calendar, however, is correct.

Avi-Yonah's students, Hachlili and Gideon Foerster, focused on different parts of this interpretation in their own work.[113] For Hachlili, the zodiac is preeminently a calendar, whereas Foerster stresses the zodiac as symbol of Divine cosmic order. Building on Foerster's insight, Ehud Netzer

(who also studied with Avi-Yonah) and Netzer's student Ze'ev Weiss have set a variant of the Avi-Yonah/Foerster approach within a global interpretation of the Sepphoris synagogue mosaic. For them, the Sepphoris zodiac is a representation of "God's centrality in creation."[114] Why the zodiac is given the seemingly exclusive charge of expressing either the covenant or God's strength is unclear to me.

Avi-Yonah is almost certainly correct that synagogue mosaics of the zodiac emphasize the Jewish year. This is expressed most clearly through the Hebrew inscriptions that label each sign, and in Sepphoris each sign and symbol for the monthly works. Avi-Yonah is also correct that calendrical issues were important to Jews. Living by what amounted to a separatist calendar, by their own months and ways, Jews asserted their distinctiveness. The significance of the calendar for Jewish self-definition, both internally and in terms of how Jews perceived non-Jewish reactions to the calendar, is expressed in a tradition preserved in *b. Shabbat* 75a:

Said Rabbi Samuel son of Naḥmani said Rabbi Johanan: Whence is it a commandment for a person to calculate the seasons and the constellations?
For it is said: "Keep them and do them; for that will be your wisdom and your understanding in the sight of the peoples" (Deuteronomy 4:6).
What is referred to by "your wisdom and your understanding in the sight of the peoples"?
Let us say: This is the calculation of seasons and constellations.

Jewish attachment to the calendar was indeed an important element of Jewish identity during this period. Jewish literature beginning during the Second Temple period and particularly after the destruction of the Temple shows extreme concern with proper calculation of the years, and hence with the dates of the festivals.[115] From the early Roman period on, the distinctly Jewish lunar–solar calendar was an important marker of Jewish identity – particularly as the Roman solar calendar spread throughout the Levant during the first century C.E. Often based on local observation of the new moons and intercalation of the year by individual communities (including the rabbis), the establishment of Jewish dates was an essential communal task throughout late antiquity. Although experts proposed standardized calendrical systems, such a unified approach did not predominate until the ninth or tenth centuries.[116]

Calendrical calculations in sixth-century Zoar, an isolated village to the south of the Dead Sea, reflect the type of concern for the calendar that existed even in areas far distant from Jewish urban concentrations. Evidence of the calendar used at Zoar is preserved in numerous extant tombstones. As Sacha Stern has pointed out, the calendar of this community was based on firsthand observation of the moon. It is nonetheless quite different from what we might expect based on rabbinic approaches. Stern notes that this distinction may be related to the high mountains surrounding Zoar that preclude precise observation of the waning and new moons.[117] For our purposes, what is most interesting is the care this local center took to get the calendar "right."

The relationship between the dates of Easter and Passover made Jewish calendrical calculations of much broader concern, particularly for eastern churches that continued to associate these holidays long after the Orthodox Church disassociated them at Nicaea in 325.[118] An Armenian Monophysite chronicle, for example, asserts that a Tiberian Jew by the name of Phineas participated in a Christian conclave consisting of thirty-six experts to determine the correct date of Easter.[119] The connection between the mosaics and the calendar should not be overstated, however, nor should these representations of the Jewish year be treated in some functional manner.

In recent years, liturgist Joseph Yahalom has resurrected a way of looking at the zodiacs in ancient synagogues that was first considered by E. L. Sukenik.[120] Sukenik was well-aware that the theme of the zodiac is expressed throughout the corpus of late antique liturgical poetry (*piyyut*). Sukenik also knew of the relationship between these poems and visual representations of the zodiac found in medieval Ashkenazi manuscripts, where images of the zodiac are quite common and *piyyutim* for rain and dew by Qalir are often accompanied by images of the zodiac. Sukenik applied this relationship to the art of ancient synagogues. In its use of *piyyutim* and in many other liturgical and religious areas, medieval Ashkenaz was the inheritor of the Palestinian tradition. While it is doubtful that a continuity of Jewish art existed, the impulse to illustrate synagogue floors and later liturgical, magical, and astrological texts (not to mention ceremonial objects and synagogue walls) with zodiac themes that were common to the liturgy

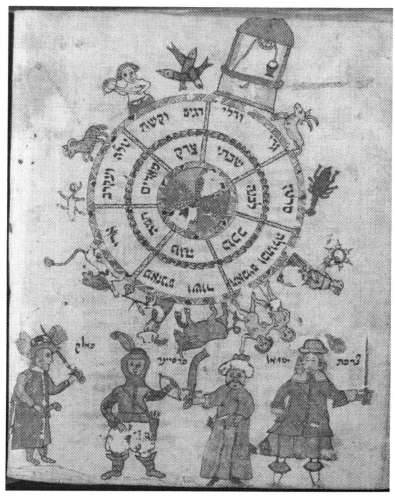

87. Illustration of the Zodiac and the heavens in *Sefer ha-Evronot*, Germany, seventeeth century (Klau Library, Cincinnati, of the Hebrew Union College–Jewish Institute of Religion, HUC Ms. 906, 73v).

seem to be phenomenologically related (Figure 87).[121] Yahalom has emphasized that references to the zodiac in liturgical poetry point toward the significance of the Jewish year for late antique Jews. Somewhat romantically, Yahalom envisions the *Sitze im Leben* of these poems: "we may conjecture that these poems, based on lists of the signs of the zodiac, were recited while the community was gathered on the floor around a zodiac mosaic, a common feature of ancient Palestinian synagogues."[122]

To their credit, Sukenik and Yahalom deal with the *Sitze im Leben* of the mosaics and do not posit any singular interpretation. Liturgy, midrash, and targum, as well as the *Talmudim* often reference the heavens in general and the zodiac signs in particular. Michael Klein has shown, for example, the large number of Targumic texts that focus on zodiac issues.[123] The theme of the zodiac is extremely important in midrashic literature as well.[124] Thus, in the translation of Scripture, in its homiletic explication, and in liturgy that was closely aligned with the liturgical cycle – the three most important facets of the liturgical lives of synagogue communities – we find real interest in the zodiac. This seems to me sufficient to explain why Jews took over and preferred to use zodiac themes in synagogue decoration over a very long period. The art fits the general themes of their theology as expressed in the liturgical life of the synagogue, and over time, may even have increased focus on this theme through the mere presence of zodiacs in the synagogue.

To begin to explain the parameters of what Jews thought when they placed zodiac mosaics on the floors of their synagogues and kept them there, I will focus on liturgical texts, both standard prose texts and *piyyutim*. I argue that issues of time were indeed central to Jewish liturgy, and that the calendar was a part of that – particularly because the Jewish calendar was separatist. The zodiac was more than a calendar, however. That only one zodiac panel, at Sepphoris, is explicitly labeled with both zodiac and calendrical terms suggests that more is going on than issues of calendration. It was a projection of the "dome of heaven," the place of the Divine court that is beseeched in prayer. These themes provide enough justification for the presence of the zodiac on floors and in liturgy. All of these themes might have been sensed by at least some late antique Jews in their synagogues.

Jewish attachment to the zodiac and its relation to the calendar is expressed in numerous Hebrew and Aramaic synagogue poems that are roughly contemporaneous with the mosaics. We have already seen one usage in a *piyyut* of Yannai.[125] The most famous zodiac *piyyut*, written by Eleazar ha-Qallir, is recited to this day by Ashkenazim on *Tishah be-Av* eve:[126]

> Because of our sins, the Temple was destroyed.
>> Because of our crimes, the Sanctuary was burned.
> In the city that was once bound firmly together,
>> Lamentations were heard,
> And the host of heaven
>> Sounded a dirge . . .
> Aries, first of all the constellations
>> Wept bitterly, for his sheep
>> Were led to slaughter.
> Taurus howled on high for the horns of the firstling bull
>> Were brought low. . . .

Different in tone is a recently published Aramaic *piyyut* from the Genizah, apparently recited at the "sanctification"

of the month of Nisan in the spring. This delightfully playful text presents Nisan vehemently defending its right to be the first month of the Jewish liturgical year. In supporting its claim, Nisan plays between the historical events of each month and its zodiac sign:[127]

א All the months (ירחייה) gathered together (each month and its zodiac sign),[128]
> Because of Nisan, which is called the Redeemer.

ב Violence we scream before Nisan.
> We are eleven and he beats us (נצח לן)?

ג Bellowed Nisan with all his heart and thus said to them:
> Receive from me all that I say to you.

ד Do not say another word, Nisan said to Iyyar.
> You are compared to an Ox. You shall not redeem!

ה You should know that the [golden] calf that was made was a heifer and you are like him.

ו And what of you Sivan, bellow and come,
> for Sinai is your accomplice.[129] You shall not redeem!

ז Muzzle your mouth, do not speak, said Nisan to Tammuz.
> You are a water crab. You shall not redeem!

ח Look and do not speak another word.
> The tablets that you broke[130] are claimed from you.

ט Av became dull (טפש) and did not know. Said Nisan to Av:
> You are all laments and all songs,

י Can you redeem the sons of the lion (Israel)?
> I [Av] am destined to raise up the lion (Nebuchadnezzar) to Ariel (that is, to destroy Jerusalem).

כ Shut your mouth, said Nisan to Elul.
> . . . to the virgin, to cover yourself.

ל Don't say another word, said Nisan to Tishri.
> . . . . the scales

מ They beseech within you in fasts and prayers.
> I [Nisan] am accustomed to eating roasted [meat] and matzot.

נ Guard yourself, do not speak, said Nisan to Marḥeshvan.
> You are ruled by the scorpion. You shall not redeem!

ס Do not hold your anger, said Nisan to Kislev.
> There is no reason to ask you to go to war.[131]

ע Responded Nisan and said to Tevet:
> You watch your kids, and I [will watch] my lambs.

פ Do not enlarge your mouth said Nisan to Shevat,
> for the cold and the snow enslave you. . . .[132]

ש I rule, and am head of all of you.
    I am compared to a [Pascal] lamb, and in me a lamb
      is distributed to each household.
ת The Rock (God) made me redeemer of his people,
    And within me He in the future will redeem them
      (Israel).

The identification of the zodiac with the calendar is well documented. This is made explicit in a variant to the first line of this poem, which has both each month (moon) and its zodiac sign assembling. I would suggest, however, that it is an expression of a more generalized Jewish interest in time. Time, as calibrated through the heavenly cycles, is central to all of Jewish liturgy and identity, on an hour-by-hour basis, and not just on a weekly, monthly, and yearly cycle. Abraham Joshua Heschel was not off the mark when he wrote poetically that

Judaism is a *religion of time* aiming at the *sanctification* of time. . . . Jewish ritual may be characterized as the art of significant forms in time, as *architecture of time*. Most of its observances – the Sabbath, the New Moon, the festivals, the Sabbatical and the Jubilee year – depend upon a certain hour of the day or season of the year. It is, for example, the evening, morning or afternoon that brings with it the call to prayer.[133]

As Tamar Rudavsky suggests, "the marking of time assumes overwhelming significance in the rabbinic period."[134] Much of rabbinic literature is dedicated to the articulation of sacred and regular time, the Mishnah itself opening with "from what time do we recite *Shema* in the evening?"[135] A fine example of this focus on time appears in the statutory evening prayers. For the sake of convenience, I cite the contemporary Ashkenazi version:[136]

Blessed are you, Lord our God, King of the universe, who by His word brings on evenings, with wisdom opens gates, with understanding alters periods, changes the seasons and orders the stars in their heavenly constellations according to His will. He creates day and night, rolling back light before darkness and darkness before light. He causes day to pass and brings night, and separates between day and night, the Lord of Hosts is His name. May the living and enduring God always reign over us, for all eternity. Blessed are you, Lord, who brings on evenings.

Ancient versions of this text are particularly important because this blessing, and the parallel formulation in the morning prayers, was recited on a daily basis. Thus, it is reflective of a central and recurring concern in synagogue liturgy. This consciousness of time affords meaning to the zodiac mosaic in broad strokes, placing the cycles of day, night, week, month, and ultimately the entire Jewish year graphically within sight of the community. The zodiac mosaics are in part emblematic of Judaism's strong focus on time. The presence of the zodiac within synagogues thus participated in the Divinely mandated construction of time, and hence the Jewish (counter-) reality in late antique Palestine.

The Zodiac and the Dome of Heaven

Lehmann was right in calling the zodiac the "dome of heaven." In Jewish thought, and particularly liturgy, the separation between the heavenly and earthly realms was quite small. The heavenly realm is invoked at every turn. This closeness is expressed throughout rabbinic literature, and with greater complexity in liturgical and mystical sources from late antiquity. During the sixth century, for example, the synagogue poet Yannai explicitly asserted the closeness of the synagogue community to the heavenly host in regard to the recitation of the *Shema* prayer (Deuteronomy 6:4):[137]

The nation is called Jews (*Yehudim*)
    Because they thank the name of God (*Yah modim*).
In truth, they are called one
    Because they constantly unify the One.
Rejoice in fear and trembling
    Serve him with awe and quivering.
Come forth with praise and thanks
    Call out to Torah and to testimony.
The multitudes will not say "Holy" above
    Until the believers say "Blessed" below.
And when they stand and whisper in their mouths
    below
    Standing, [the angels] will slacken their wings above
      [and recite . . .].

In fact, the *Yotser* prayers recited as an introduction to the *Shema* and the *Qedushah*, recited in public repetition of the *Tefillah*, stress closeness to the Divine realm together with a sense of praying with the angels. Bridging the chasm between the heavenly court and the synagogue community is essential to these prayers, which are close in interest and language to liturgically charged professional mystical literature of this period.[138] I would suggest that the synagogue zodiacs are well suited to this vertical orientation, bringing the dome of heaven into the realm of the prayer hall.

This closeness to the Divine realm is not merely that of humans reaching upward, but also of God and the angels reaching downward. The signs of the zodiac were thought by some Palestinian Jews to influence human behavior (we have no idea what percentage of them, but I would guess that this was a broadly held belief). This too is reflected in liturgy, although it appears most profoundly in professional magical literature. Such speculation has a very long history in the Near East, and was reinforced and possibly invigorated by Greco–Roman astrological concerns. An Aramaic liturgical poem points to the calendrical significance of the zodiac as well as prognostication based on the appearance of the moon. This poem, recited at the monthly "sanctification" of the new month, encompasses the entire yearly cycle. I cite several sections in order to give a sense of the poem:[139]

א The moon (זהרה) was chosen for the sanctification of
   the months (ירחין)
   For festivals and fixed times and for pleasant
     [sacrificial] scents (ולריח נ:[י]חוחין).

ב In it are signs and also omens;
   when it rises experts study it (חכימין מיתבוננין).

ג Uncover your eyes and tell the observer
   to raise his eyes and to look at the moon.
ד If when it rises, its horns are of equal size,
   the world is in danger.

ה If you saw the moon straight up pointing southward,
   and its other horn pointing downward toward the
     north,
ו that will be a sign for you: beware of evil,
   for from the north distress comes forth.

ז If the moon is seen straight up, pointing to the north,
   and its other horn pointing towards the south,
ח there will be great rejoicing for the entire royal court;
   there will be low prices and abundance in the world.

ט The sign is good (טב) if it is pointed downward to the
   south,
   for the year will be fruitful and there will be
     abundance in the world.
י If its face is yellow-green (ירק) on the north side,
   high prices and famine will be in the world.

כ If it is eclipsed in the middle of Nisan,
   a great man (אנש רב) will fall from the Sanhedrin.
ל This will always be to you a trustworthy sign
   For in it are eaten pure cattle (בעירה דכיה) [for the
     pascal sacrifice]. . . .[140]

מ If it is eclipsed in the month of Adar,
   there will be pestilence and mice will multiply.[141]

נ These are the signs of the lunar calculations
   For all the signs (or, sanctifications)[142] of the months
     of the year.

Jonas C. Greenfield and Michael Sokoloff have discussed this poem in relation to omen texts from the ancient Near East. Other omen texts are known from the Genizah, and these too are related to omen texts that were prevalent in late antiquity. What is fascinating about this tradition is its liturgical setting. Unlike other extant traditions, which seem to be guidebooks for professional omen readers, this text was recited on the new moon of the month of Nisan, apparently within synagogues. Thus, the boundaries between "astronomy" and "astrology" and between professional literature and public liturgy were seemingly breached in the performance of this *piyyut*.

To conclude: Zodiac mosaics were not unique to Jews during the fourth century. Jews did, however, adopt and adapt this iconography for their synagogues and keep using it long after their neighbors had abandoned it. The zodiac became at some level emblematic of their unique culture. This absorption from the general culture was successful because it fit well with the beliefs and concerns of local Jewish communities. Over time, the zodiac became a "traditional" synagogue decoration – a position that it kept until modern times in Western Europe and continues in some Jewish communities to this day. Only when the notion that the zodiac is antithetical to Judaism took hold in very recent times did this iconography cease to be used by Western Jews.

It is my suggestion that the zodiac within ancient synagogues was indeed related to the calendar. It was more than a calendar, however. The zodiac panels in the floors of ancient synagogues represented distinctly Jewish notions of time, notions that were especially Jewish as they were separatist in the Roman and Byzantine world. Zodiac images were projections of the "dome of heaven" into the synagogue building. This dome contained within it a plethora of associations and meanings. Some were related to the proximity between the Divine and human realms that is expressed in prayer, others to astrological prognostication, others to the calendar, and still others to the generic significance of time within Jewish culture. These conceptions existed in Jewish liturgy of the Byzantine period. There is no reason for us to give priority to one of these aspects over the others, for they were coexistent as they were interwoven. All appear in extant liturgical texts, and all were at play at different times and perhaps among differing audiences within the late antique Jewish population. By focusing on liturgical texts to the virtual exclusion of other forms of Jewish sources, I have suggested a control that pushes to the sidelines both academic rabbinic discussions and the literature of professional magicians and mystics. The synagogues were the province neither of academics nor of magicians – but rather of local communities. To the best of our knowledge, extant liturgical sources are the closest we have to "their" sources.

CHAPTER THIRTEEN

SANCTITY AND THE ART OF ANCIENT SYNAGOGUES

M Y 1997 VOLUME, *THIS HOLY PLACE: ON THE SANCTITY of the Synagogue During the Greco-Roman Period*, traced the notion of synagogue sanctity as it developed in Second Temple period and late antique literary and archaeological sources. I sought out definitions of this concept, beginning with the synagogue inscriptions of the Hammath Tiberias B synagogue (Figures 29 and 30) and working backward and forward through the various genres of sources. Referring to the inscriptions at Hammath Tiberias, I asked then: "The community that tread upon this mosaic pavement thought of their synagogue as a 'holy place.' What did they mean?"[1] I reached the conclusion that Jews in antiquity understood synagogue sanctity within two specific categories: the sanctity of the Torah scroll and the use of Temple imagery to provide metaphors for sanctity. Here is what I wrote in the conclusion, which sums up the entire study:[2]

In this study we have traced the process by which late antique synagogues came to be considered "holy places." Beginning with the earliest synagogues during the Second Temple period, the cult object of the synagogue was the "Sacred Scripture" that was studied and probably stored there. The development of the synagogue was related to the increasing mobility of religion in Greco-Roman period away from temples and in the direction of smaller religious communities. While others focused upon the holy person, Jews set their attention upon their own cult objects, the scroll of the "Sacred Scriptures."

We have argued that the synagogue in the Land of Israel became the primary institutional locus for the Rabbinic revitalization of Judaism after the destruction of the Jerusalem Temple. Throughout their development Rabbinic sources show a tension between the mobility of the synagogue and the desire to root the synagogue in a more permanent manner. The conception that synagogues were "holy" was the ideological underpinning for this process, providing the essential rubric for the conceptual development of this institution throughout the Greco-Roman world. For the Rabbinic sages the synagogue became the sacred institution of *zeman ha-zeh*, the time between the Temple's destruction and its ultimate messianic reconstruction. The synagogue was so successful that it itself was projected into sacred time. The notion of synagogue sanctity was embraced by Jews of various social groupings in late antique Palestine, as well as communities throughout the Greco-Roman and Babylonian diasporas. It is striking evidence of the "common Judaism" shared by Jewish communities the world over.

This is not to say that various communities did not have their own specific ways of expressing synagogue sanctity during late antiquity. We have discussed, for example, the "extra-holy" synagogues of Babylonia, the human bones deposited in the foundations of the Dura-Europos synagogue, and the exclusion of menstruating women from some synagogues in Palestine. Throughout the inhabited world (*oikomenê*), however, two factors predominated in the sanctification of synagogues: the sanctity of the biblical scrolls that were publicly read (and often stored) in synagogues and the application of imagery derived from the Jerusalem Temple.

While hints of these factors exist in sources of the latter Second Temple period, they were first developed in a systematic way by the Tannaitic Sages. From Tannaitic literature onward the synagogue environment was differentiated from other settings as a realm of Torah. The reading of Scripture in the "holy tongue," the sounds of bells dangling from richly colored textiles in which the "holy writings" were wrapped, and the provisioning of other fine furnishings surely differentiated the Tannaitic period synagogue. One Tannaitic tradition suggests that the community aligned itself toward the chest, which was the focal point of the synagogue interior. This alignment is expressed with ever greater profundity in Amoraic, post-Amoraic, and archaeological sources from Palestine, where the Torah shrine and its compound were made increasingly larger and more ornate. The sanctity of the synagogue scrolls was acknowledged by Christians as well. John Chrysostom polemicized against Christian veneration of the synagogue scrolls in fourth-century Antioch. Jewish literary sources from Babylonia and archaeological sources from the Greco-Roman Diaspora reflect a situation similar to that which appears in Palestinian literature.

We have called the application of forms derived from the Jerusalem Temple to synagogues *imitatio templi*. This notion seems to appear in nascent form in a source from Qumran, though it is otherwise unknown in sources from the Second Temple period. *Imitatio templi* appears in Tannaitic sources in both subtle and less subtle ways. The notion of "ascent in holiness" with the Torah scroll at the pinnacle, for example, is apparently derived from the Temple context. Many of the rules of proper synagogue decorum described in Tannaitic sources are presented elsewhere as having been in effect in the Temple. Similarly, the great Alexandrian synagogue is described as having looked and functioned something like the Jerusalem Temple. Seven-branched menorahs may have illuminated second-century Palestinian synagogues. According to one text synagogues were to be built at the high point of the town, doors open to the east like those of the Temple. The interior was to be aligned through the Torah cabinet toward Jerusalem. While communal prayer modeled upon the Temple service is evidenced in Second Temple period contexts, it seems to have been restricted to fringe groups like the Qumran community and the Masada rebels. After 70, however, such prayer was developed by the Tannaim and came to be localized in synagogues. On the model of the Temple, synagogues became places where through liturgy Jews could encounter the Divine.

In Amoraic and post-Amoraic literature synagogues were increasingly conceptualized in terms of the Temple. Synagogues and study houses are called "small temples" in one representative tradition. The Torah shrine was transformed into an "ark," a curtain named for the Temple *parokket* suspended before it. In post-Amoraic Palestinian literature additional Temple forms and notions were applied to synagogues, including the burning of incense and the taboo against menstruating women entering sacred domain. Archaeological evidence from both Palestine and the Greco-Roman Diaspora parallel Palestinian literary sources. The large majority of the synagogues that have been excavated had Torah shrines that were aligned toward Jerusalem, and many were illuminated with seven-branched menorahs.

Despite these developments, the application of Temple forms to synagogues never constituted more than a conceptual veneer. In an age when temple culture was the dominant form of religion, the Tannaim applied Temple language and concepts to synagogues. They were careful, however, that synagogues not become temples in their own right. Such safeguards do not appear in Amoraic or post-Amoraic literature. This may be attributable to a perception that temple culture was in decline, to the success of the Rabbinic movement, and to the increasingly distant and mythic Temple. By the close of Tannaitic literature the form of the synagogue was essentially set, and there was little concern that synagogues might become replacements for the Temple. As in Tannaitic literature, the application of Temple concepts and forms to synagogues legitimized contemporary practice. Temple categories provided the terminology through which holiness was expressed. The long-standing scholarly hypothesis that saw the synagogue as a "replacement" for the Temple has been shown to overly stress the importance of Temple imagery in the ideological formation of this institution. The transformation of synagogues into places where communities would assemble to encounter the Divine was often articulated in terms derived from the Temple. The sanctity of this institution was dependent in the most profound sense, however, upon the community and its sacred scrolls. With this we have concluded our study of the sanctity of the synagogue in the Greco-Roman world: how it became a holy place and the factors that lead to this development. Over the thirteen hundred or so years since the close of antiquity the synagogue and notions of synagogue sanctity have matured in ever new and always fascinating ways. Subsequent development of this institution has its roots in the rich soil of ancient Judaism and takes its nourishment from the sources that we have assembled and analyzed here. The Rabbinic sources that we have discussed were central to the development of the synagogue throughout the millennia. It is my hope that this discussion will prove useful to contemporary communities of every allegiance as they reenergize their sacred spaces and resanctify their sanctuaries. Whether constructed in medieval Prague, eighteenth century Baghdad or twentieth century Baltimore, medieval and modern synagogues are in truth the spiritual descendants of the late antique synagogue. They are the progeny of those long lost meeting houses that were first called *hadain atra qadisha*, "this holy place."

Completing *This Holy Place*, I was left with the overwhelming sense that something was missing – that there was more to say, yet I did not know how to say it. This becomes painfully clear in my discussion of zodiac mosaics, where I frankly admitted that "I can think of no reason why this image in itself is holy. . . ."[3] A decade after I penned these words, I look back on them with the horror of a (more) mature scholar reading the work of a doctoral student. In defining synagogue sanctity, my approach was far too tied to the ways that late antique Jews might have verbalized this notion (that is, to "philology") and not focused enough upon the broader phenomenon. The zodiac and all the other imagery within synagogues did indeed form a single matrix, often expressed in the notion of "holy place." Together with the Torah shrine, Temple imagery, inscriptions that often only Jews could read that praise donors through liturgically based formulae (and at Reḥov, instructed Jews how to live a sacred life), and the blatantly secular motifs decorating virtually all synagogue remains, the zodiac was (or at least, became) a projection of conceptions that were central to the "holy people" and its "holy Torah" – particularly in a "Holy Land" increasingly populated and controlled by Bible-reading colonialists. The synagogue was the place where this content was expressed and acted out, where the value concept (to borrow a term from Max Kadushin[4]) of *qedushah*, holiness, a central organizing principle of Jewish practice and belief, was given liturgical life. Every element of this "set" worked with every other to facilitate the notion of a synagogue as a "holy place" – an alternate and distinctly Jewish space. This is a sloppy definition, one for which earlier scholarship on the synagogue – and my own training – were ill prepared. It is, however, a most human definition. Constructed in three and not two dimensions, my current approach does not assume a consecutive and authoritative narrative but a flowing notion of sanctity that flexed across categories and was never static – even as it coagulated in different ways within the bounds of the generally shared common Judaism as it developed through the very long period covered in this study. Kadushin's somewhat fluid notion of the value concept well-describes the many themes and impulses that led to the construction, decoration, and maintenance of distinctly Jewish "holy places" throughout the Roman and Sassanian Empires.

To conclude: The liturgical perspective is the natural lens through which to view the art of ancient synagogues. In this final section, I have focused on two particularly rich contexts: the Dura Europos synagogue and Palestinian synagogue mosaics. In discussing Dura, I engaged in careful philological reading of an almost forgotten liturgical text found there, and explored the implications of this text for the interpretation of the synagogue.

The situation in Palestine was more complex. There, I brought together a broad range of artifacts and texts to construct a liturgical, "holistic" interpretation. I focused on the Sepphoris synagogue as a liturgical space, Scripture in the life of the synagogue, and, finally, the adoption and adaptation of the zodiac to the artistic repertoire of the synagogue. In both Dura and the Land of Israel, I showed how Jews inculturated the art of the general society and used it to define and furnish their liturgical spaces. These liturgical contexts – and many others throughout the Roman world were conceived by many as "holy places."

EPILOGUE

IN THIS STUDY, I HAVE DISCUSSED A VAST QUANTITY OF EVIDENCE spanning a thousand years of creativity and reflection. These sources are widely dispersed geographically, separated into five distinct languages – and created according to the aesthetic canons of the Greco–Roman period. They stem from Rome in the west to Iraq in the east and are preserved in Hebrew, Aramaic, Greek, Latin, and Persian. Some of the sources are the huge hulks of once-glorious buildings; others are artifacts as small as a penny or a single sliver of marble – or a torn manuscript page with ink that has all but faded away. I have argued that "art" served as a kind of litmus test for Jewish participation in the greater Greco–Roman culture. The first section of this volume set the methodological "stage" for the rest. In "The '*Most Unmonumental People*' of the World: Modern Constructions of Ancient Jewish Art," I focused on four contexts that represent the ways that issues of Jewish art were grappled with by twentieth-century scholars and community leaders.

I began with the Henry S. Frank Memorial Synagogue in Philadelphia, a building modeled loosely on the Galilean synagogues of Kefar Baram, and its architect, Arnold Brunner. This synagogue provides a prism through which to view Jewish responses to the nineteenth-century commonplace that the Jews are an "artless" people – and thus not a "real" people. The Frank Synagogue exemplifies the growing recognition among Jewish culturalists (including Zionists) of a vibrant Jewish art in antiquity – and in later periods as well. I then turned to the Zionist context, which was in fact intertwined with American and European interests. Here, I focused on Ludwig Blau's call for a new "science" of Jewish archaeology; on the first Zionist excavation, conducted by Nahum Slouschz in Hammath Tiberias in 1921; and on the career of the true father of "Jewish archaeology," the intrepid E. L. Sukenik. I examined both the nationalistic aspects of this scholarship and the fact that beyond a strongly positive attitude toward Jewish remains, Zionist archaeology followed then-current international standards in trying to separate scholarship from ideology. The contribution of early "Jewish archaeology" was the sustained use of rabbinic texts to interpret archaeological remains and, on occasion, to make sense of ancient Jewish literature. These scholars, like their American and European fellow travelers, assumed continuity between ancient Jewish texts and artifacts. To a considerable degree, they were correct.

I then turned to the American context, where E. R. Goodenough and Morton Smith (again, following upon Blau) asserted a distance and sometimes a discontinuity between the literature of the rabbis and archaeology. Their counterhistory paralleled trends in Protestant scholarship of early Christianity and Gershom Scholem's focus on the primacy of mystical literature for the interpretation of the Jewish past. Goodenough knew that Jews had made art in antiquity. He was convinced, however, that the Jews who made art were not rabbis, nor were they under rabbinic influence. He called the religion shared by Jews of various approaches "minimal Judaism," focusing instead on the esoteric. Smith built on and nuanced this approach, teaching it to a cadre of Jewish students, many of them Conservative rabbis. These scholars explored the parameters of rabbinic Judaism and developed approaches to "non-rabbinic Judaism," or "Judaisms," some using archaeology as a key informant for uncovering this supposedly suppressed religious expression.

Finally, I looked at attitudes toward Jewish art within the field of art history as exemplified in undergraduate textbooks. The assumption that Jews are "the nation without art" is still widespread in this literature. When Jewish materials do appear, they have served merely as a precursor to Christian art. Happily, these attitudes are changing, and the need for apologetic by scholars of Judaism is also dissipating.

The substance of the book is devoted to studies of specific issues in the relationship between ancient Judaism and art. In all of these studies, I have set texts and artifacts in conversation with one another, in the hopes of learning more from each when they are read together. My focus has been more than these artifacts of the Jewish past, however. My hope has been to somehow imagine the ways that ancient Jews functioned within their visual environment over a very long period and across broad distances. In surveying the extant evidence, I found that no clear-cut dichotomy between texts and artifacts existed in antiquity. Rather, there was a broad Jewish *koiné* during each period and in each locale that is represented in both forms of evidence. Within this "common Judaism," various approaches to the shared religion are apparent. There is no reason to imagine a negatively defined counterreligion. In this study, I have steered a path that seeks out the shared Judaism of the Greco–Roman period, at the same time being particularly attentive to the range of Jewish possibilities that existed within and beyond the rabbinic community.

The second major division of this volume, "Art and Identity in the Greco–Roman World," focused on the ways that art served in the construction of Jewish identity (-ies) during the long period between the Hasmonean Revolt and the rise of Islam. Jews sometimes defined themselves in contradistinction to those majority cultures with whom they lived, though even this separatist self-definition was limited to specific visual forms. Those specific points where Jews chose paths different from the majority were an essential feature of their "minority" or "ethnic" art. At the forefront of Jewish issues was the question of idolatry and the problems that its presence created. The notion of "anti-idolism," a term that I have coined, expresses the Jewish approach over the thousand years that we have studied – and far beyond into medieval and modern times. That said, Jews had no qualms about art that was not taken to be "idolatrous" and made full use of it. Definitions of what was acceptable clearly changed over time, from the latter Second Temple period when few pictorial images appear to the Byzantine period – where Jews made use of a wide range of Byzantine art. I have argued that beginning with the Hasmonean Revolt and building steam through the destruction of Jerusalem in 70 C.E., "anti-idolism" became a vitally important marker of Jewish identity. The Hasmonean royal tombs at Modi'in and their literary portrayal served as the focal point for this discussion.

Jewish "anti-idolism" became more intense as the conflict with the Seleucids and then the Romans reached crisis levels. While before the Hasmoneans "anti-idolism" was clearly on the books, during the Hasmonean Revolt and again in the years building to the Jewish War, it became an important marker of distinction – well known to Jews and non-Jews alike. By the third century C.E., art had lost some of its potency as a marker of Jewish identity, as Jews accustomed themselves to their new reality as a minority in their conquered land. While there was distinct opposition to idols, definitions of art that could be conceived as neutral when made or owned by Jews expanded. Increased wealth in Byzantine Palestine led to a flurry of synagogue construction, the buildings designed and decorated in the spirit of the age. Although Jews fully participated in the art of their period, the "anti-idolism" question remained significant. This is clear, for example, in the fifth-century Sepphoris synagogue mosaic – where the "usual" image of Helios at the center of a zodiac mosaic was transformed into a more neutral image. Toward the end of this period, synagogue art again changed, with the development of a less figurative aesthetic and the iconoclastic transformation of many Byzantine period synagogues. Here, too, Jewish art was influenced by the art of the majority – now the less figurative and avidly anti-idolic Muslims.

Diaspora communities during late antiquity reflect their own very local aesthetic approaches, even as they share much in common with each other and with Palestinian communities. The third-century Dura Europos synagogue, unique as it is, was painted with imagery that fits nicely within the Jewish *koiné* of its period and shows real continuities with rabbinic literature. Roman Jewry is particularly significant, specifically for the very limited visual vocabulary that they chose to use at precisely the point when Christians were developing their own very extensive iconography. Jewish art, a minority art during the Greco-Roman period – even in Palestine – reacted to the art of the majority, taking on and transforming that art in ways that fit changing Jewish identities during this very long period.

The next section dealt with "Jewish 'Symbols' in the Greco-Roman World." Here, I argued for an open-ended interpretation of symbols, one that assumes that the "meaning" of symbols changed with changing contexts. We have seen that "Jewish symbols," derived from the visual vocabulary of Greco-Roman imagery, served important functions in boundary construction, helping to both expand and inhibit participation in the broader Roman culture. I focused on two symbols: the date palm and the menorah. The former is an image drawn from the general Greco-Roman visual vocabulary, used to refer to Judaea and to the Jews by both Romans and Jews. The latter, the menorah, is a specifically Jewish symbol. I have shown both how the menorah was used by Jews (and by Samaritans and Christians) in antiquity and some of the ways that Jews might have interpreted this symbol. Rabbinic literature has been important in this discussion, especially late antique liturgical poetry, *piyyut*. Liturgical poetry is unique in its single authorship and relatively secure dating, providing an important control for this study. My interpretation of symbols is open-ended, assuming that many different possibilities existed and that "meanings" were fluid.

Finally, I approached the interrelationship between "art" and liturgy, between Jewish religious praxis and the "set" upon which it was played out – the synagogue. My test cases in "Reading Holistically: Art and the Liturgy of Late Antique Synagogues" were the synagogue of Dura Europos and mosaic pavements from Byzantine Palestine. Interpreting Dura, I used all available evidence, visual as well as literary, to assess some of the ways that this fascinating community projected its sacred stories and beliefs onto the walls of the synagogue. I focused on the Dura liturgical parchment as a kind of control for imagining the liturgical life of the community that prayed between these walls. In dealing with synagogue mosaics in the Land of Israel, I used contemporaneous sources to discuss both specific imagery, such as the binding of Isaac and the zodiac, and the web of relationships created when these images were used in the decoration of a synagogue interior. Again, *piyyut* was important to this discussion. I suggested specific ways that Jews might have understood this imagery and why, once adopted, Jews continued to use images such as the zodiac long after this iconography was abandoned by the majority culture. The "glue" connecting all of the imagery, I argued, was the liturgy that was enacted within ancient synagogues. Through the nuanced discussion of the archaeological and literary records, I have demonstrated the interrelatedness of ancient Jewish literary and archaeological remains, and the interconnectedness of rabbinic literature and ancient Jewish art and archaeology. I have suggested that the notion of the synagogue as a "holy place" was important to the meaning of this religious space. It is this search for the interconnectedness of ancient Jewish writings and the archaeological record – without the imposition of heavy-handed external agendas – for which I reengage the antiquated, yet strikingly relevant, term developed by Blau and Sukenik, "Jewish archaeology."

In the preface to this volume, I referred to the very long germination period of this interdisciplinary project. It first began while I was a high school student and continued as I studied the history of religions, art history, and rabbinic literature and finally integrated these approaches under the rubric of Jewish history. Looking back, I sometimes imagine myself a sojourner between rival "sects," empathizing with Josephus Flavius's claim to have spent time with all of the Jewish "philosophies" of his day. My path took me from the disciples of Mircea Eliade and E. R. Goodenough to those of Kurt Weitzmann and E. L. Sukenik, from traditional yeshiva culture to the philological precision of J. N. Epstein and Saul Lieberman, and finally, in an almost "back to the future" scenario, to the historiography of the Morton Smith school – and out again. It has been a riveting path, one that I retraced in my examination of contemporary treatment of ancient "Jewish archaeology."

There have been many surprises along the way. As a student, I was taught to disembody the scholarly theories that I read. The individual's background was "unimportant," I was told; only the "ideas" mattered. This emphasis, we now know, was a conceit – itself a rhetoric that deflected attention from the ideological and personal perspectives of modern scholars. In this study, by contrast, I adopted the more recent notion that the biography of the scholar and the content of the scholarship are integrally linked. Plowing through archives and interviewing former students, I "met" the authors of my scholarly discourse face-to-face. Not surprisingly, their unique personalities emerged with each new letter in an archive and each change in handwriting! I found myself developing deep sympathy for some. Nahum Slouschz, for example, forgotten and superceded within years of his Hammath Tiberias excavations, lived to the stately age of ninety-five. For many years, Slouschz lived in relative obscurity, spending his last days alone in an old age home near Tel Aviv. Six months before his ninety-fifth

birthday, Slouschz wrote a letter to the president of the Hebrew University and to his cousin-in-law, Rahel Yanait Ben Zvi (widow of the second president of Israel who had long looked after Slouschz's affairs) complaining that he had no facilities to write, no archive for his papers, and no one to talk to. He threatened suicide. A newspaper reporter, Itzhak Nimtzovich, took up Slouschz's plight. Soon, a festive meal was organized, a volume of Slouschz's studies promised, and an archive found for his papers.[1] The first professor of modern Hebrew literature, first Jewish ethnographer, and first "Hebrew archaeologist" died shortly thereafter.

Sukenik was another story. His scholarly work and archived letters reflect both a dogged scholar worthy of far more respect than he is afforded in some contemporary circles and a somewhat difficult personality. I could go on, but the point is made. The scholars who shaped "Jewish archaeology," and those who came after them during the second half of the twentieth century, were and are people – each of whom wrote the story of the Jewish past through his (and increasingly, her) own lens and unique palette of colors. This does not mean that I do not consider some interpretations to be more objectively "correct" or "plausible" than others – as the reader already knows. What I am suggesting is that knowing who is interpreting and the assumptions and personal motivations that lay behind the printed page can serve as yet another control for evaluating previous work and moving scholarship forward.

My personal scholarly "journey" has reluctantly taken me from a very comfortable modernist perspective to this far more ambiguous and cautiously "postmodern" one. Just as I set out to "embody" my scholarly ancestors and predecessors, I have attempted here to "embody" the Jews who made and lived with art in the Greco–Roman world, working under a rubric of the new "Jewish archaeology." My goal has been, first and foremost, to try to get into their "heads" and "bodies," to explore the complexities of Jewish identity in antiquity among Jews who were every bit as "Greco–Roman" as they were "Jewish." In this sense, I too am projecting my own reality as a "native-born" American Jew (or is it Jewish–American?) from the suburbs of San Diego onto my long-dead "ancestors." Both "Greek" and "Jew" myself, I find myself attracted to a nonrevolutionary synthesis of the two in antiquity that is as "traditionalist" as it is "contemporary" and whose boundaries are both stable and yet in motion. In constructing this portrait of the past, I have anchored myself in a strong foundation of philology and the coterminous groundwork necessary for interpreting any physical object. Interpretations that are overly positivistic in their use of sources or, alternatively, are overly suspicious or ideologically driven do not attract me. Maintaining an artifact and text focus throughout, I have tried to build bridges between the ancient Jewish objects and buildings that we can "see" and "touch" and preserved Aramaic, Greek, Latin, Persian, and Hebrew "voices" that we can both read and, with some imagination, hear. I have engaged the various methodological perspectives developed during our own much-vaunted fin-de-siècle, "end of the century" (or, as we called it, Y2K). At the same time, I am chastened by the knowledge that the next Jewish century is still thirty-five years away – and that the seventh Jewish millenium will not dawn for another 200 years after that.

NOTES

PREFACE

1. Berkeley: University of California Press, 1999.

2. Omaha: University of Nebraska Press, 2002.

3. Chapter 1, "Building an Ancient Synagogue on the Delaware: Philadelphia's Henry S. Frank Memorial Synagogue and Constructions of Jewish Art at the Turn of the Twentieth Century" is a revised version of "Arnold Brunner's Henry S. Frank Memorial Synagogue and the Emergence of 'Jewish Art' in Early Twentieth-Century America," *American Jewish Archives Journal*, 54, no. 2 (2003), 47–70. The discussion of E. L. Sukenik in Chapter 2, "The Old–New Land: 'Jewish Archaeology'" and the Zionist Narrative," is revised from "E. L. Sukenik, Ancient Synagogues, and the Birth of 'Jewish Archaeology,'" E. L. Sukenik, *The Beth Alpha Synagogue* (Piscataway, N.J.: Gorgias Press, 2003), v*–ix*.

An earlier version of Chapter 6 was published as *Art and Identity in Latter Second Temple Period Judaea: The Hasmonean Royal Tombs at Modi'in, The Twenty-fourth Annual Rabbi Louis Feinberg Memorial Lecture in Judaic Studies* (Cincinnati: University of Cincinnati, Department of Judaic Studies, 2002).

Earlier versions of sections of Chapter 7, "Art and Identity in Late Antique Palestine: The Na'aran Synagogue," appeared as "Art in Midrash," *Encyclopedia of Biblical Interpretation in Formative Judaism*, eds. J. Neusner and A. Avery-Peck (Leiden: E. J. Brill, 2004), 1–19, "Iconoclasm and the Art of Late Antique Palestinian Synagogues," *FDS*, 182–93.

An earlier version of Chapter 9, "Between Rome and Jerusalem: The Date Palm as a 'Jewish Symbol,'" appeared as "On the Development of a Visual Symbol: The Date Palm in Roman Palestine and the Jews," *Journal for the Study of the Pseudepigrapha*, 4 (1989), 105–18.

A more technical version of Chapter 11, "Liturgy and the Art of the Dura Europos Synagogue," appears in *Liturgy in the Life of the Synagogue: Studies in the History of Jewish Public Prayer*, eds. S. Fine and R. Langer (Winona Lake, Ind.: Eisenbrauns, 2005).

4. A. J. Heschel, "Symbolism and the Jewish Faith," *Religious Symbolism*, ed. F. E. Johnson (New York and London: Institute for Religious and Social Studies. Distributed by Harper, 1955), 59–62.

INTRODUCTION

1. On "art" in the English language, see *The Oxford English Dictionary* (Oxford: Clarendon Press, 1989), 1: 657–9.

2. E. P. Sanders, *Judaism: Practice and Belief 63 BCE–66 CE* (London and Philadelphia: Trinity International, 1992), ix, 47–51; idem, *Paul and Palestinian Judaism* (London and Philadelphia: Fortress Press, 1977), especially 419–28. A similar approach is suggested by L. Schiffman, *From Text to Tradition: A History of the Second Temple and Rabbinic Judaism* (Hoboken, N.J.: Ktav, 1991), 4–5, and J. Burtchaell, *From Synagogue to Church: Public Services and Offices in the Earliest Christian Communities* (Cambridge: Cambridge University Press, 1992), xiii–xv. On semantic difficulties surrounding the term "Judaism," in antiquity, see J. Pasto, "The Origin, Expansion and Impact of the Hasmoneans in Light of Comparative Ethnographic Studies (and outside of its Nineteenth – Century Context)," eds. P. R. Davies, J. M. Halligan. *Second Temple Studies III: Studies in Politics, Class and Maternal Culture* (Sheffield: Sheffield Academic Press, 2002), 172–7.

3. P. Brown, *Society and the Holy in Late Antiquity* (Berkeley and Los Angeles: University of California Press, 1989), 173, 179–81, 189–93; S. Fine, *This Holy Place: On the Sanctity of the Synagogue During the Greco–Roman Period* (Notre Dame: Notre Dame University Press, 1997), 9.

PART 1: "THE '*MOST UNMONUMENTAL PEOPLE*' OF THE WORLD"

1. L. Blau, "Early Christian Archaeology from a Jewish Point of View," *Hebrew Union College Annual*, 3 (1926), 158.

2. See note 14 below.

3. Hachlili, *AJAALI*, xxi.

4. S. Gilman, *The Jew's Body* (New York and London: Routledge, 1991).

5. M. Davis, *Jews Fight Too!* (New York: Jordon Publishing Co., 1945).

6. For an important parallel, see N. Kleeblatt, "The Body of Alfred Dreyfus: A Site for France's Displaced Anxieties of Masculinity, Homosexuality and Power," *Diaspora and Visual Culture: Representing Africans and Jews*, ed. N. Mirzoeff (London: Routledge, 2000), 76–91.

7. D. Boyarin, *The Rise of Heterosexuality and the Invention of the Jewish Man* (Berkeley: University of California, 1997), especially 271–312.

8. For an astonishing example of Jewish apologetic regarding nose size, see J. D. Brutzkus, "The Anthropology of the Jewish People," *The Jewish People Past and Present* (New York: Jewish Encyclopedic Handbooks, Central Yiddish Culture Organization, 1946), 1: 19–20. On the body in Zionist and Israeli contexts, see M. Berkowitz, *Western Jewry and the Zionist Project, 1914–1933* (Cambridge: Cambridge University Press, 1997), 7–25; M. Weiss, *The Chosen Body: The Politics of the Body in Israeli Society* (Stanford: Stanford University Press, 2002).

9. J. W. Joselit notes: "Just as immigrants as a whole were pointedly enjoined to change their personal behavior to conform to that of Western norms, so too were their religious and social institutions if they were to take root in the new world." See her "Of Manners, Morals and Orthodox Judaism: Decorum Within the Orthodox Synagogue," *Ramaz: School, Community, Scholarship and Orthodoxy*, ed. J. S. Gurock (Hoboken, N.J.: Ktav, 1989), 25.

10. P. C. Finney, *The Invisible God: The Earliest Christians on Art* (New York and Oxford: Oxford University Press, 1994). See also M. Charles Murray, "Art and the Early Church," *Journal of Theological Studies*, new series 28, no. 2 (1977) 304–45.

11. See S. Heschel, *Abraham Geiger and the Jewish Jesus* (Chicago: University of Chicago Press, 1998), 75.

12. It is striking that the early monographs on Jewish art were almost all authored by non-Jews, often with Jewish support. These include H. Kohl and C. Watzinger's *Antike Synagogen in Galilaea* (Leipzig: Hinrichs, 1916); in the field of Hebrew illuminated manuscripts, Jewish scholar D. H. Müller collaborated with J. von Schlosser on *Die Haggadah von Sarajevo. Eine spanisch-judische Bilderhandschrift des Mittelalters* (Vienna: A. Hölder, 1898); H. Frauberger on ceremonial art: *Ueber Alte Kuntusgegenstände in Synagoge und Haus* (Frankfort: Gesellschaft zur Erforschung Jüdischer Kunstdenkmäler, 1903).

13. See A. Julius, *Idolizing Pictures: Idolatry, Iconoclasm and Jewish Art* (London: Thames & Hudson, 2000), 99.

14. *ha-Omanut ha-Yehudit*, eds. Z. Ephron and C. Roth (Tel Aviv: Masadah, 1956/7), 19, Hebrew; in English under the title *Jewish Art: An Illustrated History*, under the sole editorship of Roth in 1961 (New York: McGraw-Hill), 11. This volume was slightly revised by Bezalel Narkiss in 1971 (London: Vallentine, Mitchell). See my discussion in "Review of Gabrielle Sed-Rajna, *Jewish Art*, *H-Judaic* (August, 1999), *http://www2.h-net.msu.edu/reviews/showrev.cgi?path=1172935681955*. As early as 1952, Roth also considered publishing an America-focused "Menorah Book of Jewish Art." See A. Pappas, "The Picture at *Menorah Journal*: Making 'Jewish Art,'" *American Jewish History*, 90, no. 3 (2002), 237–8.

15. Hachlili, *AJAALI*, xxi. Note Hachlili's somewhat more nuanced comments in her foreward to the 1998 companion volume, *Ancient Jewish Art and Archaeology in the Diaspora* (Leiden: E. J. Brill, 1998), xxx.

16. "Good and Bad Images from the Synagogue of Dura Europos: Contexts, Subtexts, Intertexts," *Art History*, 17, no. 1 (1994), 1–25; idem, *Refiguring the Post Classical City: Dura Europos, Jerash, Jerusalem, and Ravenna* (Cambridge: Cambridge University Press, 1995), 15–23. See also R. I. Cohen, *Jewish Icons: Art and Society in Modern Europe* (Berkeley: University of California, 1998); E. Mendelsohn, *Painting a People: Maurycy Gottlieb and Jewish Art* (Hanover: University Press of New England for Brandeis University Press, 2002). This current rethinking is being fueled mainly by scholars outside the "Jewish Art" establishment. The exception is V. Mann, ed., *Jewish Texts on the Visual Arts* (Cambridge: Cambridge University Press, 2000).

17. Princeton: Princeton University Press, 2000.

18. See especially p. 100.

19. London and Portland: Littman Library of Jewish Civilization, 1997.

20. Tel Aviv: Zmora-Bitan and Haifa: University of Haifa, 1999, in Hebrew.

21. Tel Aviv: Am Oved, 2000, in Hebrew.

22. N. Mirzoeff, "Introduction: The Multiple Viewpoint: Diasporic Visual Cultures," *Diaspora and Visual Culture: Representing Africans and Jews*, ed. N. Mirzoeff (London: Routledge, 2000), 2–3.

23. See the recent review of Bland's volume by J. Blidstein, "Art and the Jew," *Torah U-Madda Journal*, 10 (2001), 163–72 and S. Wolitz's review of Olin's volume, to appear in *Jewish Culture and History*. Many thanks to Professor Wolitz for sharing his review with me prior to publication.

24. E. R. Goodenough, *Jewish Symbols in the Greco–Roman Period* (New York: Pantheon, 1953–68).

CHAPTER 1: BUILDING AN ANCIENT SYNAGOGUE ON THE DELAWARE

1. Today, the Albert Einstein Medical Center.

2. L. K. White, *The Henry S. Frank Memorial Synagogue: Rekindling the Ner Tamid* (Baltimore: Baltimore Hebrew University, unpublished seminar paper, 2000), 12.

3. S. D. Temkin, "Hackenburg, William Bowers," *EJ* 7, 1037–8.

4. Jewish Hospital Association of Philadelphia, *Thirty-Sixth Annual Report for the Year Ending April 1901* (Philadelphia: Jewish Hospital Association of Philadelphia, 1901), 16, cited by White, *The Henry S. Frank Memorial Synagogue*, 10.

5. On Palestine Exploration Fund exploration of ancient synagogues, see F. Vitto, "Synagogues in Cupboards," *Eretz Magazine*, 52 (1997), 36–42.

6. *JE*, 11: 621.

7. J. Naveh, *On Mosaic and Stone: The Aramaic and Hebrew Inscriptions from Ancient Synagogues* (Israel: Maariv, 1978), 19–20, in Hebrew.

8. R. Wischnitzer, *Synagogue Architecture in the United States* (Philadelphia: Jewish Publication Society, 1955), 98. R. Tabak, *The Frank Memorial Synagogue: Structure and Symbol* (Philadelphia: Albert Einstein Healthcare Network, 2001), 7. Candlesticks loosely fashioned after the Arch of Titus menorah had a wide distribution in both Europe and America.

9. *JE* 2: 107, 108.

10. See J. Kestenbaum, "Arnold W. Brunner and His Jewish Milieu," forthcoming. In the meantime: Wischnitzer, *Synagogue Architecture in the United States* 7, 8, 86, 89, 95, 96, 101, 104, 106, 110, 120. Wischnitzer was the first to recognize the significance of ancient synagogue architecture in the formulation of Brunner's neoclassicism. See also D. Kaufman, *Shul with a Pool: The "Synagogue Center" in American Jewish History* (Hanover, N.H.: Brandeis University Press and University Press of New England, 1999), 70, 104, 186, 260; "Arnold Brunner," *American Jewish Year Book*, eds. C. Adler and H. Szold (Philadelphia: Jewish Publication Society, 1904), 71–2; F. N. Levy, "Arnold W. Brunner," *American Art Magazine*, 16 (1925), 253–9; C. Adler, "Brunner, Arnold William," *JE*, 3, 404. F. M. Warburg, "Arnold W. Brunner," *Proceedings of the American Jewish Historical Society*, 31 (1928), 253–5.

11. This apt designation is credited to Daniel Elazar. See M. Freedman, "Introduction: The Philadelphia Group – A Collective Spirit," *When Philadelphia Was the Capital of Jewish America*, ed. M. Friedman (Philadelphia: Balch Institute Press, London and Toronto: Associated University Presses, 1993), 9–21. See J. D. Sarna, "The Making of an American Jewish Culture," idem, 144–55.

12. Warburg, "Arnold W. Brunner," 253–4.

13. See L. S. Lerner, "Narrating the Architecture of Emancipation," *Jewish Social Studies*, 6.3 (2000), especially 9–10.

14. On neoclassicism in American synagogue architecture, including earlier buildings of Shearith Israel Congregation, see S. Gruber, *American Synagogues: A Century of Architecture and Jewish Community* (New York: Rizzoli, October 2003), 29.

15. A. W. Brunner and J. Jacobs, "Synagogue Architecture," *JE*, 11: 630–40. On the *Jewish Encyclopedia*, see S. R. Schwartz, *Emergence of Jewish Scholarship in America: The Publication of the Jewish Encyclopedia* (Cincinnati: Hebrew Union College Press, 1991).

16. Brunner and Jacobs, "Synagogue Architecture," 632.

17. Brunner and Jacobs, "Synagogue Architecture," 636.

18. A. W. Brunner, "Synagogue Architecture," *The Brickbuilder: Devoted to the Interests of Architecture in Materials of Clay*, 16, no. 2–3 (1907), 20.

19. See C. W. Wilson and H. H. Kitchener, "Synagogues," *Survey of Ancient Palestine Special Papers on Topography, Archaeology, Manners and Customs, Etc.* (London: Committee of the Palestine Exploration Fund, 1881), 294.

20. Ibid., 14.

21. Wilson and Kitchener, "Synagogues," 299, describe the interior dimensions of the

large Baram synagogue as 60 ft., 6 in. by 46 ft., 6 in.

22. Brunner, "Synagogue Architecture," 20.

23. J. Gaudet. *Elements et Theorie de l'Architecture* (Paris: Librairie de la Construction Moderne, 1905), 3: 608.

24. Ibid.

25. Ibid.

26. Ibid. Brunner, apparently following Viollet-Le-Duc, attributes all of this to Solomon's Temple, with no mention of Herod, undoubtedly in the service of his polemical objective.

27. Ibid., 24.

28. Ibid., 21.

29. Ibid.

30. E.-E. Viollet-le-Duc, *Entretiens sur l'architecture* (Paris: A. Morel, 1863–72), translated as *Lectures on Architecture*, tr. B. Bucknall (London: S. Low, Marston, Searle and Rivington, 1877–81).

31. Ibid., 24. See A. Hertzberg, *The French Enlightenment and the Jews* (New York, Columbia University Press, 1968), 303–4.

32. Ibid., 213.

33. Ibid., 213–14.

34. Ibid., 224–5.

35. Wischnitzer, *Synagogue Architecture in the United States*, 7, 8, 86, 89, 95, 96, 101, 104, 106, 110, 120.

36. J. W. Joselit, "By Design: Building the Campus of the Jewish Theological Seminary," *Tradition Renewed: A History of the Jewish Theological Seminary of America*, ed. J. Wertheimer (New York: Jewish Theological Seminary, 1997), 1:274.

37. Kaufmann, *Shul*, 260–1.

38. D. G. Dalin, "The Patriarch: The Life and Legacy of Mayer Sulzberger," *When Philadelphia Was the Capital of Jewish America*, ed. M. Friedman (Philadelphia: Balch Institute Press, London and Toronto: Associated University Presses, 1993), 58–74.

39. This was preempted by illness.

40. Adolph Lewisohn. See *EJ*, 11:177–8. Adler's letter is cited by G. C. Grossman, *Judaica at the Smithsonian: Cultural Politics as Cultural Model*, dissertation (Los Angeles: Hebrew Union College–Jewish Institute of Religion, 1994), 180–1.

41. Hebrew University Archives, "Institute of Archaeology," file 144. Warburg insisted upon the inclusion of the newly founded Hebrew University of Jerusalem in the dig, though not as a full partner.

42. Sarna, "The Making of an American Jewish Culture," 152.

43. S. Schechter, *Aspects of Rabbinic Theology* (New York: Macmillan, 1909).

44. G. F. Moore, *Judaism in the First Centuries of the Christian Era: The Age of the Tannaim* (Cambridge: Harvard University Press, 1927–30).

45. Olin, *The Nation Without Art*, 73–98.

46. Leipzig: G. Fock, 1910–12.

47. "Grain Mills and Those Who Work with Them," *Tarbiz* 50 (1981), 128, in Hebrew, my translation. D. Sperber, *Material Culture in Eretz-Israel during the Talmudic Period* (Jerusalem: Yad Izhak Ben-Zvi Press and Ramat Gan: Bar Ilan University Press, 1993), 3–23, in Hebrew, surveys recent scholarship.

48. See my "The Redemption of Ancient Synagogues: The Hebrew University of Jerusalem, American Jewry and the Creation of 'Jewish Archaeology'," *Archaeology and Religion in Modern Israel*, eds. Z. Shiloni and M. Feige (forthcoming), in Hebrew.

49. Wischnitzer, *Synagogue Architecture in the United States*, 125. Today, this floor is covered with a carpet. University officials with whom I spoke describe the carpet as a protection against slippage. One wonders whether this covering of the zodiac is also part of a trend toward greater stridency in the Orthodox community (parallel to the larger *mezuzot* that in recent years have replaced the original smaller ones in this building).

50. I find no evidence of European funding in the interwar years, which is certainly a function of the economic situation following World War I and to a smaller extent to Magnes's personal connections in the United States.

51. L. Blau, "Early Christian Epigraphy," 225.

52. See T. Rajak, "Jews and Greeks: The Invention and Exploitation of Polarities in the Nineteenth Century," *The Uses and Abuses of Antiquity* eds. M. Biddiss and M. Wyke (Bern: Peter Lang, 1999), 57–77.

53. A literary parallel to the Frank Synagogue is the *Jewish Encyclopedia*. Roughly the same elite, reflecting the entire spectrum of Jewish opinion on religion, participated in the production of the *Jewish Encyclopedia* itself. On similar themes in exhibition design, including exhibitions organized by Cyrus Adler, see B. Kirshenblatt-Gimblett, *Destination Culture: Tourism, Museums, and Heritage* (Berkeley: University of California Press, 1998), 79–128. A significant predecessor of the Frank Synagogue is Moses Jacob Ezekiel's sculpture, *Religious Liberty*, sponsored by the Independent Order Benai Berith for the Centennial Exhibition in Philadephia in 1876. Also constructed in a neoclassical style, this sculpture bespeaks a more assimilationist attitude. Kirshenblatt-Gimblett (p. 88) notes: "One of six American ethnic and religious groups to erect monuments on the fairgrounds, Jews were the only group to make no explicit reference to their own history and historical figures."

54. H. H. Kitchener, "Synagogues of Galilee," *Palestine Exploration Fund Quarterly Statement* (1878), 128. See also E. L. Sukenik, *Ancient Synagogues in Palestine and Greece* (London: H. Milford, Oxford University Press, 1934), 62–3.

55. Wilson and Kitchner, "Synagogue," 304. See Bland, *The Artless Jew*, 26–7.

56. C. H. Krinsky, *Synagogues of Europe* (New York: The Architectural History Foundation and Cambridge, Mass: MIT Press, 1985), 72. See also 48, 73. This approach is rejected by E. L. Sukenik, *Ancient Synagogues in Palestine and Greece*, 61–3. Wischnitzer, *The Architecture of European Synagogues*, 159–60.

57. Krinsky, *Synagogues in Europe*, ibid.

58. Olin, *The Nation Without Art*; Bland, *The Artless Jew*, 13–70.

59. Bland, *The Artless Jew*, ibid.

60. S. J. Solomon, "Art and Judaism," *Jewish Quarterly Review*, old series, 13 (1901), 560.

61. Solomon, *Art*, 564. See Bland, *The Artless Jew*, 36–7.

62. H. Belting, *The Germans and their Art: A Troublesome Relationship*, tr. S. Kleager (New Haven: Yale University Press, 1998), 10–11.

63. *JE*, 2: 141. On Benzinger, see M. Avi-Yonah, "Benzinger, Immanuel," *EJ*, 4: 574.

64. *JE*, 2: 142, and the bibliography of nineteenth-century studies cited there. On the later history of this rhetoric in America, see Pappas, "The Picture at *Menorah Journal*," 225–38.

65. *JE*, 1: xvii.

66. This approach was not solely the purview of the Western Jews. A. Holtzman has recently shown how thoroughly this critique influenced, for example, Hebrew authors throughout Eastern Europe and how slowly it gave way. See Holtzman, *Aesthetics and National Revival*, especially 11–92.

67. Viollet-Le-Duc, *Lectures on Architecture*, 224.

68. See Hertzberg, *The French Enlightenment and the Jews*, 4, 255–6, 280–313, espcially 303–4.

69. Cited by Hertzberg, *The French Enlightenment and the Jews*, 304. Compare Bland's conclusions in *The Artless Jew*, 68. Bland, note 40, surveys Voltaire's various statements on this subject.

70. While Brunner's interest in Jewish neo-classicism is idiosyncratic among published documents, Judah L. Magnes too was interested in this approach. In a manuscript entitled "The Hebrew University Search for Antiquities in Palestine" (Hebrew University Archives, Institute of Archaeology file, 1934), he adopts a similar stance. After describing Palestinian synagogue discoveries, Magnes writes:

It is therefore a mistake to think that Synagogue architecture must necessarily be Arabesque and

Moorish. Some of the ancient wooden Synagogues of Poland and Russia look somewhat like pagodas at first sight. The Roman tradition of Synagogue interior construction is continued in part – consciously or not, I do not know – in the Synagogue, – now a church – at Toledo, Spain, and in the Spanish-Portuguese Synagogue at New York. There is the ark at the one end with seats at the sides of the building, and a broad space down the center from one end to the other. In the Roman basilica structure great columns lined both sides of this central space, dividing the ground floor into three parts. In the Capernaum synagogue separate steps to the women's gallery have been found, and there is here also an outer court with steps leading down to the street. The pavement of the synagogue here is intact in many places, as are some of the seats and a portion of one of the outer walls . . . .

Magnes's comment that continuities between the Spanish-Portuguese Synagogue (that is, Shearith Israel) and ancient synagogues may have occurred "consciously" suggests, perhaps, that he had no firsthand knowledge of Brunner's work. Magnes's membership in the American Jewish elite, including Louis Marshall and Cyrus Adler, probably accounts for his knowledge of the approach suggested by Brunner.

CHAPTER 2: THE OLD–NEW LAND

1. American Jewish Archives, Manuscript collection #19 3/12-JIR, letter from S. S. Wise to L. Blau dated December 11, 1924: "During the years 1923–1924 this allowance amounted, as you know, to $1000. per year for each of the five institutions [that is, the Jewish seminaries in Germany and its allies]."

2. See, most recently, M. Feige, "Identity, Ritual and Pilgrimage: The Meetings of the Israel Exploration Society," *Divergent Jewish Cultures in Israel and America*, eds. D. D. Moore and S. I. Troen (New Haven: Yale University Press, 2001), 87–106; N. Abu El-Haj, *Facts on the Ground: Archaeological Practice and Territorial Self-Fashioning in Israeli Society* (Chicago: University of Chicago Press, 2001).

3. T. Herzl, *Altneuland: Roman* (Leipzig: Nachfolger, 1902).

4. A. Brawer, "From the Earliest Days of the Palestine Exploration Society," *Western Galilee and the Coast of Galilee*, ed. J. Aviram (Jerusalem: Israel Exploration Society, 1965), 228–36, especially 231, 233, 236, in Hebrew.

5. Brawer, "The Early Years," 230.

6. A full-scale biography of this scholar is a desideratum. In the meantime, see *"Sha'ah be-meḥitzat ha-Prof. Dr. Nahum Slouschz,"* Les Cahiers de l'Alliance Israélite Universelle 5, nos.

10–12 (1956), 174–5, in Hebrew; *Nahum Slouschz (Nahum ben-David Slouschz)*, ed. Y. Churgin (Tel Aviv: Sifriat Rishonim, 1947), in Hebrew; "Slouschz, Nahum," *EJ*, 14: 1677–8.

7. N. Slousch, "Recent Discoveries in Palestine," *The Menorah Journal* 8, no. 6 (1922), 331.

8. "The Phenomenon of Israeli Archaeology," *Near Eastern Archaeology in the Twentieth Century: Essays in Honor of Nelson Glueck*, ed. J. A. Sanders (Garden City: Doubleday, 1970), 58.

9. On Ben Dov, see H. Tryster, *Israel Before Israel: Silent Cinema in the Holy Land* (Jerusalem: Steven Spielberg Jewish Film Archive, 1995), 24–47.

10. N. Slousch, "Hamath-by-Tiberias," *Recueil Publié par Société Hébraïque d'Exploration et d'Archéologie Palestiniennes*, 1 (1921), 32, in Hebrew.

11. N. Slouschz, "The Excavations in Hammath of Tiberias (General Survey)," *Hashiloach*, 38 (1921), 546–7, in Hebrew. See also his "Recent Discoveries in Palestine," 336–37.

12. Slouschz refers to Jacob Schiff, who financed the Samaria excavation of 1908–10 and Baron Edmond de Rothchild, who provided funds for Raymond Weill's excavation of the City of David in Jerusalem. See his "Recent Discoveries in Palestine," 333.

13. On the post-World War I period, see Abu El-Haj, *Facts on the Ground*, 75–82. Abu El-Haj does not recognize the distinctly "Jewish" aspects of early Zionist archaeology.

14. Slouschz, "The Excavations in Hammath of Tiberias (General Survey)," 548. Compare A. Elon, *Israelis: Fathers and Sons* (New York: Holt, Rinehart and Winston, 1971), 284.

15. Slouschz, "The Excavations in Hammath of Tiberias (General Survey)," 549.

16. The traditional tomb of the second-century Tanna Rabbi Meir is located at Hammath Tiberias, south of the excavation site. See Slouschz, "The Excavations in Hammath of Tiberias (General Survey)," 547.

17. See the documents collected in *Tsaakat Yeshene Afar: "Mada" Oh Zeváah: Sekirat Dugmaot ve-Leket Teudot al Heres ve-Ḥilul Qivre ha-Qadmonim be-Eretz Yisrael*, ed. Y. R. Salomon (Israel: Y. R. Salomon, 1982/3), in Hebrew. See also El-Haj, *Facts on the Ground*, 258–76.

18. Slouschz, "The Excavations in Hammath of Tiberias (General Survey)," 550.

19. Slouschz's contract of employment is preserved in Genazim: The Archives of the Hebrew Writers' Association in Israel, file 28780א. A. Rakeffet-Rothkoff, "The Semi-Centennial Celebrations of Yeshiva and Yeshiva College," *Ramaz: School, Community, Scholarship and Orthodoxy*, ed. J. S. Gurock (Hoboken: Ktav, 1989), 5.

20. Shimon Rubinstein, archivist of Yad Izhak Ben Zvi, tells me that Slouschz was a relative of Ben Zvi through Ben Zvi's father.

21. This focus on science is an important part of Zionist rhetoric regarding archaeology.

22. I. Ben Zvi, "Le-yovel ha-shishim shel Prof. Nahum Slouschz," *Journal of the Jewish Palestine Exploration Society*, 3 (1934), 1, in Hebrew.

23. Abu El-Haj, *Facts on the Ground*, passim.

24. Cited by N. Silberman, *A Prophet Amongst You: The Life of Yigael Yadin: Soldier, Scholar and Mythmaker of Modern Israel* (Reading, Mass.: Addison-Wesley, 1993), 23. Sukenik's career is described rather uncharitably by Silberman, 8–40.

25. Silberman, *A Prophet Among You*, 20.

26. On Magnes, see W. M. Brinner and M. Rischin, eds. *Like All the Nations?: The Life and Legacy of Judah L. Magnes* (Albany: State University of New York Press, 1987). As early as 1921 Magnes was a member of the JPES, one of only eight members listed as residing in New York. See *Recueil Publié par Société Hébraïque d'Exploration et d'Archéologie Palestiniennes*, 1 (1921), 96 and the errata page.

27. *Dropsie College Faculty Minutes*, (1926), 321–2. The Dropsie report was written and signed by noted Biblicist, semiticist, and avid Zionist Max L. Margolis and approved by historian Abraham Neuman and by Solomon L. Scoss (or Skoss), an expert in Judeo–Arabic philology. Seth Jerchower of the Center for Advanced Judaic Studies Library of the University of Pennsylvania informs me that "E. L. Sukenik received his Ph. D. from Dropsie College in 1926 (the information is found both in the *Dropsie College Register* for 1926–27, as well as in the *Dropsie College Faculty Minutes*)." Silberman, *A Prophet Amongst You*, 23, calls this work a "modest dissertation," writing that "For this he was awarded a quick – not to say unprecedented – doctor of philosophy degree." There is no suggestion of such a negative value judgment in the Dropsie records.

28. Hebrew University Archives, "Institute of Archaelogy," file 144.

29. For the history of excavation of the Arbel synagogue, see Z. Ilan and A. Izdarechet, "Arbel," *New Encyclopedia of Archaeological Excavations in the Holy Land*, ed. E. Stern (Jerusalem: Israel Exploration Society and Carta, 1993), 1: 87–9.

30. Letters to Magnes from Sukenik, received December 12, 1926, and August 14, 1927.

31. For photographs of Capernaum in the 1920s, see P. G. Orfali, *Capharnaüm et ses Ruines* (Paris: Auguste Picard, 1922), 20, 23.

32. See my "The Redemption of Ancient Synagogues," Berkowitz, *Western Jewry and the Zionist Project*, 137–8, 142.

33. See Hebrew University Archives, "Institute of Archaeology," file 144. This suggestion was not acted upon. On Congregation Emanu-El, see Wischnitzer, *Synagogue Architecture in the United States*, 125–30; C. Grossman, *A Temple Treasury: The Judaica Collection of Congregation Emanu-El of The City of New York* (New York: Hudson Hills Press, 1989), especially 17–23.

34. "Jewish Antiquities Museum to be Opened Today," *Jerusalem Post*, April 3, 1941.

35. E. L. Sukenik and L. A. Mayer, *The Third Wall of Jerusalem. An Account of Excavations* (Jerusalem: Hebrew University and London: Oxford University Press, 1930).

36. Letter from Sukenik to Magnes, received January 29, 1928.

37. Letter from Sukenik to Magnes, February 29, 1928.

38. T. Wiegand and H. Schrader, *Priene: Ergebnisse der Ausgrabungen und Untersuchungen in den Jahren 1895–1898* (Berlin: G. Reimer, 1904), 481.

39. The Beth Alpha excavations were followed by the synagogue at Hammat Gader in 1932. See Sukenik's *The Ancient Synagogue of El-Hammeh (Hammath-by-Gadera)* (Jerusalem: R. Mass, 1935).

40. E. L. Sukenik, *The Ancient Synagogue of Beth Alpha* (Jerusalem: Hebrew University, 1932).

41. E. L. Sukenik, "Ancient Synagogues in Palestine," *Rimon: A Hebrew Magazine of Art and Letters*, 5 (1923), 19, in Hebrew.

42. *Ancient Synagogues in Palestine and Greece*, 78.

43. E. L. Sukenik, "The Present State of Synagogue Studies," *Louis M. Rabinowitz Fund for the Exploration of Ancient Synagogues*, 1 (1949), 12–13.

44. E. L. Sukenik, *The Synagogue of Dura-Europos and its Frescoes* (Jerusalem: Mosad Bialik, 1947), in Hebrew. See also his "The Mosaic Inscriptions in the Synagogue at Apamea on the Orontes," *Hebrew Union College Annual*, 23, part 2 (1950/1), 541–51.

45. *Aufstieg und Niedergang der Römische Welt* (Berlin and New York: Walther de Gruyter, 1979) II 19(1): 479–510.

46. See M. Berkowitz, "Art in Zionist Popular Culture and Jewish National Self-Consciousness, 1897–1914," *Art and Its Uses: The Visual Image and Modern Jewish Society, Studies in Contemporary Jewry*, 6 (1990), ed. E. Mendelsohn (New York and Oxford: Oxford University Press), 9–42.

47. Y. Arkin, *Banknotes and Coins of Israel* (Jerusalem: Or v'Tseva, 1998), 32.

48. See, for example, a Bezalel carpet from the early 1930s designed in imitation of a geometric carpet mosaic from Beth Alpha. This mosaic also served to decorate the Israeli 50 mil

note in 1952. See A. Fenton, *Jewish Carpets: A History and Guide* (Woodbridge, Suffolk: Antique Collectors Club, 1997), 115.

49. Mishory, *Lo and Behold*, 277, especially 250–2. With his subjects, Mishory mistakenly identifies Bar Kohkba-era coinage as Hasmonean coins, an identification with a long history in Palestinian numismatics. He makes the same error on 307–8.

50. See, for example, P. Romanoff, *Jewish Symbols on Ancient Jewish Coins* (Philadelphia: Dropsie College, 1944); Y. Meshorer, *Ancient Jewish Coinage* (Dix Hills: Amphora, 1982); idem, *A Treasury of Jewish Coins from the Persian Period to Bar-Kochba* (Jerusalem: Yad Izhak Ben-Zvi Press, 1997), in Hebrew. This is more pronounced in Meshorer's popular volume *TestiMoney* (Jerusalem: Israel Museum, 2000).

51. See especially R. Wischnitzer, *Symbole und Gestalten der judischen Kunst* (Berlin-Schoneberg: S. Scholem, 1935); idem, *The Messianic Theme in the Paintings of the Dura Synagogue* (Chicago: University of Chicago, 1948). For this approach in more recent scholarship: A. St. Clair, "God's House of Peace in Paradise: The Feast of Tabernacles on a Jewish Gold Glass," *Jewish Art* 11 (1985), 6–15; E. Revel-Neher, "L'Alliance et la Promesse: Le symbolism d'Eretz Israël dans l'iconography juive du moyan âge," *Jewish Art*, 12–13 (1986–7), 135–46; L. Roussin, "The Beit Leontis Mosaic: An Escathological Interpretation," *Jewish Art*, 8 (1981), 6–19; Z. Weiss and E. Netzer, *Promise and Redemption: A Synagogue Mosaic from Sepphoris*, (Jerusalem: Israel Museum, 1996), 38; Y. Englard, "The Escathological Significance of the Zodiac Panels in the Mosaic Pavements of Ancient Synagogues," *Cathedra* 98 (2000), 33–48, in Hebrew; J. A. Goldstein, *The Judaism of the Synagogues (Focusing on the Synagogue of Dura-Europos): Judaism in Late Antiquity*, ed. J. Neusner (Leiden: E. J. Brill, 1995), Pt. 2, 109–58. Goldstein goes so far as to suggest Jewish duplicitousness in hiding real messianic hopes: "Great as was their discretion in concealing the full import of the paintings by labels and by other means, we can be astonished by the audacity they showed in displaying such perilous topics" (154). Against this approach at Dura, see P. V. M. Flesher, "Rereading the Reredos: David, Orpheus, and Messianism in the Dura Europos Synagogue," in *ASHAAD*, 2: 346–66. Flesher in turn underestimates the messianic content of the Dura Europos synagogue wall paintings. See also my "Art and the Liturgical Context of the Sepphoris Synagogue Mosaic," *Galilee: Confluence of Cultures: Proceedings of the Second International Conference on the Galilee*, ed. E. M. Meyers (Winona Lake, Ind.: Eisenbrauns, 1999), 227–37. On the use of these images in Zionist iconography, see Mishory, *Lo*

and Behold, 102, 139–222, 240–54, 307–8. See also A. Elon, "Politics and Archaeology," *The Archaeology of Israel: Constructing the Past, Interpreting the Present*, eds. A. Silberman and D. Small (Sheffield: Sheffield Academic Press, 1997), 34–47; Y. Shavit, "Archaeology, Political Culture and Culture in Israel," *The Archaeology of Israel: Constructing the Past, Interpreting the Present*, 48–61, especially 58–60.

52. For a specific context, see my "A Note on Ossuary Burial and the Resurrection of the Dead in First Century Jerusalem," *Journal of Jewish Studies*, 51 (2000), 69–76.

53. D. N. Myers, *Re-inventing the Jewish Past: European Jewish Intellectuals and the Zionist Return to History* (New York: Oxford University Press, 1995).

54. Mishory, *Lo and Behold*, 138–64, especially 143–7.

55. G. Scholem, "The Star of David: History of a Symbol," *Luah Haaretz* (1949), 148–63, in Hebrew; tr. and expanded, *The Messianic Idea in Judaism and Other Essays on Jewish Spirituality* (New York: Schocken, 1978), 257–81.

56. A typical example of attempts to maintain a distinction between scholarly and non-scholarly activities appeared in the *Jerusalem Post* on September 23, 1942, describing the organization of "Jewish Antiquities Week": "While the organization of 'Antiquities Week' is in the hands of well-known archaeologists guaranteeing its strictly scientific character, it is meant primarily for the general public." Elon is correct that Israeli archaeologists "may have been prejudiced in their choice of study but not, in most cases, in their analysis of the results" ("Politics and Archaeology," 38–9). See also Feige, "Identity, Ritual and Pilgrimage," 101. S. L. Marchand, *Down from Olympus: Archaeology and Philhellenism in Germany, 1750–1970* (Princeton: Princeton University Press, 1996), 22–3, 39, 83, 226, discusses the rhetoric of "disinterested scholarship" in German scholarship.

57. Sukenik, *Beth Alpha*, 6–8.

58. Sukenik, *The Synagogue of Dura-Europos*; M. Kon, *The Tombs of the Kings* (Tel Aviv: Dvir, 1947), 73–9, in Hebrew; N. Avigad, *Ancient Monuments in the Kidron Valley* (Jerusalem: Mosad Bialik, 1954), in Hebrew; M. Narkiss, *Coins of Palestine* (Jerusalem: Beney Bezalel, 1938), in Hebrew.

59. This is in marked contrast with the first generation of Jewish university professors of art history, for whom "objectivity and distance were seen as the means to avoid anti-Semitic prejudice." See K. Michels, "Art History, German Jewish Identity, and the Emigration of Iconology," *Jewish Identity in Modern Art History*, ed. C. Soussloff (Berkeley and Los Angeles: University of California Press, 1999), 168.

60. The same impulse may be suggested in M. Narkiss's beautifully produced *The*

Hanukkah Lamp (Jerusalem: Beney Bezalel, 1939), in Hebrew.

61. J. Strzygowski, *Orient oder Rom: Beitrage zur Geschichte der Spatantiken und Fruhchristlichen Kunst* (Leipzig: J. C. Hinrichs'sche Buchhandlung, 1901).

62. J. Elsner, "Archaeologies and Agendas: Reflections on Late Ancient Jewish Art and Early Christian Art," *The Journal of Roman Studies*, 93 (2003), 120.

63. Ibid. See idem, "The Birth of Late Antiquity: Riegl and Strzygowski in 1901," *Art History*, 25, no. 3 (2002), 371–4.

64. Olin, *The Nation Without Art*, 18–24, 135–9, 151–3, though this attention to Strzygowski was not "posthumous" as Olin suggests. As early as 1926, Blau, *Early Christian Archaeology*, 160, claimed that "in recent times all archaeologists agree with the view of Joseph Strsygowski that not Rome, but the Orient, was the principal creator of the early Christian art (p. 45 ff.). Consequently Jewish influence is to be assumed *a priori*."

65. Sukenik, *Synagogues of Palestine and Greece*, 67. By contrast, M. Avi-Yonah's approach, still followed by some of his students, builds upon Strzygowski's models, while ignoring the anti-Semitic element. See now Elsner, "Archaeologies and Agendas," 122, especially note 62. Avi-Yonah's attempt to set Jewish art in its "Oriental" context is part of a larger Zionist program to localize Jewish culture. See his *Oriental Art in Roman Palestine* (Rome: Centro di Studi Semitici of the Istituto di Studi del Vicino Oriente, 1961), Rpt. *Art in Ancient Palestine*, eds. H. Katzenstein and Y. Tsafrir (Jerusalem, Magnes, 1981).

66. K. Weitzmann, *Sailing with Byzantium from Europe to America: The Memoirs of an Art Historian* (Munich: Editio Maris, 1994), 345, 397, 437, 442, 474; idem, "The Illustration of the Septuagint"; "The Question of the Influence of Jewish Pictorial Sources on Old Testament Illustration." Both articles appear in *No Graven Images: Studies in Art and the Hebrew Bible*, ed. J. Gutmann (New York: Ktav, 1971), 201–31, 309–28. This approach is refuted persuasively by J. Gutmann, "The Illustrated Jewish Manuscript in Antiquity: The Present State of the Question," *No Graven Images: Studies in Art and the Hebrew Bible*, ed. J. Gutmann (New York: Ktav, 1971), 232–48; idem, "The Illustrated Midrash in the Dura Europos Synagogue Paintings: A New Dimension for the Study of Judaism," *Proceedings of the American Academy for Jewish Research*, 50 (1983), 100–4. See also Wharton, *Refiguring the Post Classical City*, 21–3; R. Jensen, "The Dura Europos Synagogue, Early Christian Art, and Religious Life in Dura Europos," *JCP*, 174–89; Olin, *The Nation without Art*, 127–54; idem, "The Road to Dura-Europos," *Budapest Review of Books*, 12,

nos. 1–2 (2002), 2–5; Elsner, "The Birth of Late Antiquity," 373–4; idem, "Archaeologies and Agendas," 120–2.

67. Berlin: R. C. Schmidt, 1927.

68. Berlin: Schocken, 1937.

69. Jerusalem: Reuven Mass, 1947.

70. A. Reifenberg, *Ancient Hebrew Arts* (New York: Schocken, 1950), 10–11; idem, *Denkmäler der jüdischen Antike*, 9–63. See A. D. Skinner, "German-Jewish Identity and the 'Schocken Bücherei,'" *Arche Noah: de Ideeden Kultur im deutsch-jüdischen Diskurs*, eds. B. Greiner, C. Schmidt (Freiburg im Breisgau: Rombach Verlag, 2002), 289–303.

71. Mirzoeff, "Introduction," 2–3.

72. On Kaufmann, see Olin, *The Nation Without Art*, 73–98.

73. For the varying uses of Beth Alpha, see Silberman, *A Prophet Amongst You*, 26–27. Perhaps paradigmatic of the religious Zionist approaches is E. E. Urbach, "The Rabbinical Laws of Idolatry in the Second and Third Centuries in Light of Archaeological and Historical Facts," *Eretz Israel*, 5 (1958), 189–205, in Hebrew. Translated and abridged in the *Israel Exploration Journal*, 9, nos. 3–4 (1959), 149–65, 229–45. Unless stipulated, the abridged English translation is cited. For a secularist approach, see the work of Michael Avi-Yonah. While Avi-Yonah assumes rabbinic dominance, his scholarly and personal proclivities reflect a distinct ambivalence toward the ancient rabbis. See, for example, his *Oriental Art in Roman Palestine*, 159. Many thanks to Bezalel Narkiss for discussing this aspect of Avi-Yonah's work with me.

CHAPTER 3: ARCHAEOLOGY AND THE SEARCH FOR NONRABBINIC JUDAISM

1. This chapter has been enriched by interviews with Albert Baumgarten, Shaye J. D. Cohen, Israel Francus, Robin Jensen, Lee I. Levine, Alan Mendelson, Jacob Neusner, Jonathan Seidel, and John T. Townsend – either in person or via e-mail.

2. I. Benoschofsky, "The Second Era," *The Rabbinical Seminary of Budapest 1877–1977: A Centennial Volume*, ed. M. Carmilly-Weinberger (New York: Sepher-Hermon Press, 1986), 76.

3. The context for Ginzberg's comments was the decoration of the new Congregation Emanu-El building in New York (L. Ginzberg, *The Responsa of Professor Louis Ginzberg*, ed. D. Golinkin [New York and Jerusalem: Jewish Theological Seminary of America, 1996], 159).

4. Letter from E. R. Goodenough to G. Scholem, April 27, 1937, Gershom Scholem Archive, Department of Manuscripts and

Archives, Jewish National and University Library, Correspondence files Arc. 4° 1599.

5. E. Yeshurun, "The Seminary, Zionism and Israel," *The Rabbinical Seminary of Budapest 1877–1977: A Centennial Volume*, ed. M. Carmilly-Weinberger (New York: Sepher-Hermon Press, 1986), 123.

6. D. S. Loewinger, *Zikhron Yehudah: Studies in Memory of L. Blau*, eds. S. Hevesi, M. Guttmann, and S. Loewinger (Budapest: s.n., 1938), 5–45, in Hebrew.

7. D. Kaufmann, "Etudes d'archéologie juive. 1. La synagogue de Hamman-Lif," *Revue Etudes Juives*, 13 (1886), 45–61, rpt. *Etudes d'archéologie juive et archéologie chretiénne* (Paris: Ernest Leroux, 1887). It does not seem insignificant that Kaufmann placed *"archéologie juive"* before *"archéologie chretiénne"* in this title or that this volume was published in France.

8. Paderborn, F. Schöningh, 1913.

9. Sperber, *Material Culture in Eretz-Israel during the Talmudic Period*, 3–23, surveys recent scholarship.

10. My use of the term "counterhistory" draws on the distinct loadings suggested by Amos Funkenstein (most recently in *Perceptions of Jewish History* [Berkeley and Los Angeles: University of California Press, 1993], 36) and by his student, David Biale (*Gershom Scholem: Kabbalah and Counter-History* [Cambridge: Harvard University Press, 197–9], 7). For Funkenstein, counterhistories are polemical. "Their aim is the distortion of the adversary's self-image, of his identity, through the deconstruction of his memory." Biale, by contrast, considers counterhistory to be "a type of revisionist historiography." The counter-historian "affirms the existence of a 'mainstream' or 'establishment' history, but believes that the vital force lies in a secret tradition." In our case, the work of Goodenough and, as we shall see, of Morton Smith are both polemical in dealing with contemporary religious communities and assertive of the central historical significance of "secret" or non-"mainstream" tradition. See most recently D. Biale, "Counter-history and Jewish Polemics Against Christianity; The 'Sefer Toldot Yeshu' and the 'Sefer Zerubavel,'" *Jewish Social Studies*, 6, no. 1 (1999), 130–45.

11. M. Smith, "Goodenough's 'Jewish Symbols' in Retrospect," *Journal of Biblical Literature*, 86 (1967), 63.

12. November 18, 1947, to John Bartlett of the Bollingen Foundation, cited by R. S. Eccles, *Erwin Ramsdell Goodenough: A Personal Pilgrimage* (Chino, Calif.: Scholars Press, 1985), 85–90.

13. Goodenough, *Jewish Symbols*, 12:3; S. Sandmel "An Appreciation," *Religions in Antiquity: Essays in Memory of Erwin Ramsdell Goodenough*, ed. J. Neusner (Leiden: E. J. Brill, 1970), 8, 10, 12.

14. *The Theology of Justin Martyr* (Jena: Frommann, 1923).

15. Sandmel, "An Appreciation," 4–5.

16. Goodenough, *Jewish Symbols*, 1, 27. Joseph Gutmann relates a similar story occurring at the Jewish Theological Seminary in 1952. In that case, it was Moshe Davis, vice president of that institution, who commented: "Mr. Gutmann, your studies do not come within the purview of Judaism. Maybe, forty years from now they will be." See J. Gutmann, *My Life of Jewish Learning: In Search of Jewish Art, the Forgotten Language; What Can Jewish History Learn from Christian and Jewish Art?* (New York: Hunter College Jewish Social Studies Program, Occasional Papers in Jewish History and Thought, 21, 2002), 1.

17. Goodenough, *Jewish Symbols* 1, 28.

18. Biale, *Gershom Scholem*, 11–12, 132.

19. Letter from Gershom Scholem to Jacob Neusner, January 5, 1965, Gershom Scholem Archive, Department of Manuscripts and Archives, Jewish National and University Library, Correspondence files Arc. 4° 1599.

20. Goodenough, *Jewish Symbols*, 1, 19–20; Biale, *Gershom Scholem*, ibid.

21. See the most interesting comments of W. McGuire (*Bollingen: An Adventure in Collecting the Past* [Princeton: Princeton University Press, 1982], 176–7) regarding Goodenough's personal relationship with C. G. Jung and the significance of these relations for Goodenough's scholarship.

22. Princeton: Princeton University Press, 1999.

23. A. Mendelson, "Memoir," *Religions in Antiquity: Essays in Memory of Erwin Ramsdell Goodenough*, ed. J. Neusner (Leiden: E. J. Brill, 1970), 18. In an e-mail dated October 1, 2003, Mendelson adds: "I don't think that the comment was ironic [my question to him – SF], because he ended up doing exactly what he said. Maybe it was half apologetic, and the other half humorous. He was, by the way, amusing and had a good sense of humor. . . . I would say that he had to have an ego. Otherwise how could he have convinced the people at Bollingen to produce 13 volumes of costly books. He had to have a strong belief in the rightness of his work. Modest, he wasn't. I for one am happy that he wasn't modest."

24. Wasserstrom, *Religion after Religion*, 239, 241.

25. Urbach, "The Rabbinical Laws of Idolatry"; J. Baumgarten, "Art in the Synagogue: Some Talmudic Views," *Judaism*, 19 (1970), 196–206. See also G. J. Blidstein, *Rabbinic Legislation on Idolatry – Tractate Abodah Zarah, Chapter I*, Ph.D. dissertation (New York: Yeshiva University, 1968), in Hebrew; idem, "The *Tannaim* and Plastic Art: Problems and Prospects," *Perspectives in Jewish Learning*, 5 (1973), 13–27; idem, "Prostration and Mosaics in Talmudic Law," *Bulletin of the Institute of Jewish Studies*, 2 (1974), 19–39; idem, "R. Johanan, Idolatry, and Public Privilege," *Journal for the Study of Judaism*, 5 (1974), 154–61; idem, Nullification of Idolatry in Rabbinic Law," *Proceedings of the American Academy for Jewish Research*, 41–2 (1975), 1–44.

26. Goodenough, *Jewish Symbols*, 1, ix.

27. Letter from Goodenough to Scholem, April 27, 1937.

28. M. Smith, "In Memoriam," *Religions in Antiquity: Essays in Memory of Erwin Ramsdell Goodenough*, ed. J. Neusner (Leiden: E. J. Brill, 1970), 2.

29. The classic statement of this ideology is W. Herberg's *Protestant, Catholic, Jew: An Essay in American Religious Sociology* (Garden City, N.Y.: Anchor Books, 1960).

30. The most significant exception being A. T. Kraabel, *Diaspora Jews and Judaism: Essays in Honor of, and in Dialogue with, A. Thomas Kraabel*, eds. A. J. Overman and R. S. MacLennan (Atlanta: Scholars Press, 1992).

31. Smith's second dissertation, *Judaism in Palestine. I: To the Maccabean Revolution*, was completed at the Harvard School of Divinity in 1957.

32. Letter from Smith to Scholem, January 22, 1947. See also May 9, 1947; September 26, 1948; as well as letters from Scholem to Smith dated March 23, 1947; November 25, 1948; March 8, 1949. Gershom Scholem Archive, Department of Manuscripts and Archives, Jewish National and University Library, Correspondence files Arc. 4° 1599. The growing affection and sense of collegiality between Smith and Scholem are evident throughout the correspondence.

33. New York: Jewish Theological Seminary of America, 1960.

34. S. J. D. Cohen, *In Memorium Morton Smith, Josephus and the History of the Greco-Roman Period*, eds. F. Parente and J. Sievers (Leiden: E. J. Brill, 1994), 7. Cohen, a Smith student and executor of Smith's literary estate, notes that his teacher piled scorn upon "pronouncements and opinions born of religious faith and confessional conviction but masquerading as 'objective scholarship.'" Later, he notes that "Smith never tired discomforting the faithful" (8). This scorn, it seems to me, bespeaks personal issues that reach the very essence of Smith's scholarship. A critical biography of this fascinating scholar is warranted.

35. M. Smith, "Moore, George Foot," *EJ* 12: 293–4. It was not the case that Moore "neglected" these elements. They certainly were not of interest to him. See also F. S. Lusby and S. Fine, "Moore, George Foot," *Encyclopedia of Religion*, 2nd edition, ed. L. Jones (New York: MacMillan, 2005), 9: 6176–7.

36. Cohen (*In Memorium*, 8) writes that Smith was "an ordained Episcopalian priest who left the church." Cohen's parenthetical comment is worth citing: "Whether Smith actually was an atheist or an Epicurean I do not know" (p. 8).

37. W. Bauer, *Reichtgläubigkeit und Ketzerie im ältesten Christentum* (Tübingen: Mohr Siebeck, 1934), tr. as *Orthodoxy and Heresy in Earliest Christianity*, tr. Philadelphia Seminar on Christian Origins, eds. R. A. Kraft and G. Krodel (Philadelphia: Fortress Press, 1971).

38. S. Cohen, *In Memorium*, 7.

39. S. Schwartz, *Imperialism and Jewish Society, 200 B.C.E.–640 CE* (Princeton: Princeton University Press, 2001), 6. See Schwartz's comments about Goodenough and Neusner, 7–8, and my review of this volume in *Biblical Archaeology Review*, 30, no. 2 (2004), 56-58. On the overly rigorous application of the "hermeneutics of suspicion" to Jewish studies, see J. Schorsch, "Losing What Would Be? A Response to Mitchell Hart," *Sh'ma*, 33 (December 2002), 3–5.

40. These interests continue to be of considerable concern to Levine and Cohen. Neusner's work has moved in more literary and theological directions.

41. J. D. Sarna, "Two Traditions of Seminary Scholarship," *Tradition Renewed: A History of the Jewish Theological Seminary of America*, ed. J. Wertheimer (New York: Jewish Theological Seminary, 1997), 74.

42. The exception was Cyrus Adler.

43. J. Wertheimer, "JTS and the Conservative Movement," *Tradition Renewed: A History of the Jewish Theological Seminary of America*, ed. J. Wertheimer (New York: Jewish Theological Seminary, 1997), 405–42, especially 405–6, 427–34; D. Ellenson, "The JTS Rabbinical Curriculum in Historical Perspective," *Tradition Renewed: A History of the Jewish Theological Seminary of America*, ed. J. Wertheimer (New York: Jewish Theological Seminary, 1997), 554–75.

44. L. H. Schiffman, "The Pharisees Revisited: Louis Finkelstein on the Second Temple Period," *Yakar le-Mordecai: Jubilee Volume in Honor of Rabbi Mordecai Waxman: Essays on Jewish Thought, American Judaism, and Jewish-Christian Relations*, ed. Z. Ginor (Hoboken: Ktav, Great Neck: Temple Israel, 1999), 85–101.

45. Abraham Ibn Daud, *A Critical Edition with Translation and Notes of The Book of Tradition (Sefer ha-Qabbalah)*, ed. and tr. G. Cohen (Philadelphia: Jewish Publication Society, 1967).

46. L. I. Levine. "E. Goodenough: Jewish Symbols in the Greco–Roman Period," *Qadmoniot* 5.2 (1972), 66, in Hebrew.

47. Ibid. Levine recently reaffirmed this estimation, writing that Goodenough "brought together a wealth of examples of Jewish art that few could have imagined beforehand. . . . " See his "Art, Architecture and Archaeology," *The Oxford Handbook of Jewish Studies*, ed. M. Goodman (Oxford and New York: Oxford University Press, 2002), 828.

48. Levine, *Judaism and Hellenism*, xi.

49. S. W. Baron, "Ghetto and Emancipation," *The Menorah Journal*, 14 (June, 1928), 515–26; idem, *A Social and Economic History of the Jews* (New York: Columbia University Press, 1958–83), passim. On the Baron's approach, see I. Schorsch, *From Text to Context: The Turn to History in Modern Judaism* (Hanover and London: Brandeis University Press, 1994), 376–88. Baron, followed by his students Cohen and Levine, saw historiography as a tool for evaluating and changing contemporary realities. See, for example, Baron's "The Effect of the War on Jewish Communal Life," Harry H. Glucksman Memorial Lecture at Columbia University, New York, 1942, 15; cited by M. B. Greenbaum, *Louis Finkelstein and the Conservative Movement: Conflict and Growth* (Binghamton, N.Y.: Global Publications, Binghamton University, 2001), 263.

50. R. Bonfil, *Jewish Life in Renaissance Italy* (Berkeley and Los Angeles, University of California Press, 1994), 1–3; and the comments of L. Rutgers, *The Hidden Heritage of Diaspora Judaism* (Leuven: Peeters, 1998), 22–4, 42.

51. Olin, *A Nation Without Art*, 127–54; idem, "The Road to Dura-Europos."

52. L. I. Levine, *The Synagogue: The First Thousand Years* (New Haven: Yale University Press, 2000), 277–8.

53. See, in particular, L. I. Levine, *The Rabbinic Class of Roman Palestine* (Jerusalem: Yad Izhak Ben-Zvi Press, 1989).

54. Y. Bronowski, "Yafet in the Tents of Shem," *Haaretz*, April 24, 2000, B–14, in Hebrew.

55. Letter to Scholem dated March 8, 1964, Gershom Scholem Archive, Department of Manuscripts and Archives, Jewish National and University Library, Correspondence files Arc. 4° 1599.

56. J. Neusner, "The Jewish Use of Pagan Symbols after 70 CE," *Journal of Religion*, 43 (1963), 287.

57. Goodenough, *Jewish Symbols*, 12: 9.

58. Ibid., 12: 8.

59. Goodenough, *Jewish Symbols*, 12, preface.

60. Letter from Scholem to Neusner dated March 3, 1964, Gershom Scholem Archive, Department of Manuscripts and Archives, Jewish National and University Library, Correspondence files Arc. 4° 1599.

61. See Urbach. "The Rabbinical Laws of Idolatry."

62. Neusner, "The Jewish Use of Pagan Symbols after 70 CE," 285–7.

63. In numerous essays, Jacob Neusner has maintained Goodenough's comparison between rabbinic literature and archaeology, arguing consistently that these varieties of evidence are incongruous. See, most recently, "The Iconography of Judaisms," *Approaches to Ancient Judaism*, New Series 13 (Atlanta: Scholars Press, 1998), 139–56.

64. E. R. Goodenough, *Jewish Symbols in the Greco–Roman Period*, abridged, edited, foreword, by J. Neusner (Princeton: Princeton University Press, 1988).

65. J. Wertheimer, "JTS and the Conservative Movement."

66. From e-mail conversations with Neusner, it is clear to me that he was not working consciously toward this agenda. For Levine, who has spent much of his professional life at the Hebrew University, this historiography has had specifically Israeli significance. It provided a powerful argument in his drive to establish Conservative Judaism in Israel and to distinguish the Conservative approach from legally established Orthodox Jewish religious practice and belief. Levine was a significant force in the establishment of the (Conservative-sponsored) Tali School system in Israel, and was founding president of the Israeli Conservative seminary now known as the Schechter Institute for Judaic Studies. See his "Masorti Judaism in Israel: Challenge, Vision and Program," *The Seminary at 100: Reflections on the Jewish Theological Seminary and the Conservative Movement*, eds. N. B. Cardin and D. W. Silverman (New York: The Rabbinical Assembly and the Jewish Theological Seminary of America, 1987), 381–9.

67. A good example of this use of history in the adjudication of Jewish law is D. Golinkin, "The *Meḥiza* in the Synagogue," *The Rabbinical Assembly of Israel Law Committee Responsa* (Jerusalem, 1987), especially p. 14. See D. Ellenson, "Conservative Halakha in Israel: A Review Essay," *Modern Judaism*, 13, no. 1 (1993), 191–204, especially 197–201; J. Roth, "Halakha and History," *The Seminary at 100: Reflections on the Jewish Theological Seminary and the Conservative Movement*, eds. N. B. Cardin and D. W. Silverman (New York: The Rabbinical Assembly and the Jewish Theological Seminary of America, 1987), 281–90; D. H. Gordis, "Positive-Historical Judaism Exhausted: Reflections on a Movement's Future," *Conservative Judaism*, 47, no. 1 (1994), 3–18. See especially the cautions of S. J. D. Cohen regarding the limits of historical scholarship for Conservative religious discourse: "Women in the Synagogues of Antiquity," *Conservative Judaism*, 34, no. 2 (1980), 23, 28.

68. See the documents edited by S. Greenberg, *The Ordination of Women as Rabbis: Studies and Responsa* (New York: Jewish Theological Seminary, 1988); P. S. Nadell, *Women Who Would be Rabbis: A History of Women's Ordination, 1889–1985* (Boston: Beacon Press, 1998), 119–214; B. S. Wenger, "The Politics of Women's Ordination: Jewish Law, Institutional Power, and the Debate over Women in the Rabbinate," *Tradition Renewed: A History of the Jewish Theological Seminary of America*, ed. J. Wertheimer (New York: Jewish Theological Seminary, 1997), 2: 485–523.

69. See A. Baumgarten's comments on Neusner's views of the Pharisees ("American Jewish Scholarship on the Pharisees," *Ramaz: School, Community, Scholarship and Orthodoxy*, ed. J. S. Gurock (Hoboken: Ktav, 1989), 131), where he points out that Neusner's interpretation of the Pharisees coincides with his then commitment to the Havurah movement in North America.

70. Goodenough had close relations with his student and Hebrew Union College faculty member Samuel Sandmel and with president Julian Morgenstern, who granted him an honorary doctorate in 1947.

71. Schwartz, *Imperialism and Jewish Society*, 12–14.

72. See the perceptive comments of A. Eden, "Debates on Gays Link Anglicans, Conservative Jews," *The Forward* (August 29, 2003), 1.

73. Letter to Scholem, April 27, 1937, p. 2.

74. See the recent exchange on these issues by J. Magness, E. M. Meyers, and J. Strange: J. Magness, "The Question of the Synagogue: The Problem of Typology," *Judaism in Late Antiquity, Part 3: Where We Stand: Issues and Debates in Ancient Judaism, Volume Four: The Special Problem of the Synagogue* (Leiden: E. J. Brill, 2001), 1–48, and the response of E. M. Meyers, "Dating of the Gush Halav Synagogue: A Response to Jodi Magness," idem, 49–63; J. F. Strange, "Synagogue Typology and Khirbet Shema: A Response to Jodi Magness," idem, 72–8; J. Magness, "A Response to Eric M. Meyers and James F. Strange," idem, 79–91. See also S. Loffreda, "Coins from the Synagogue of Capharnaum," *Liber Annus*, 47 (1997), 223–44; D. Chen, "Dating Synagogues in Galilee: The Evidence from Meroth and Capernaum," *Liber Annus*, 40 (1990), 349–55.

75. C. C. Torrey, "Fragments and Papyri," *The Excavations at Dura-Europos Conducted by Yale University and The French Academy of Inscriptions and Letters: Preliminary Report of the Sixth Season of Work*, eds. M. I. Rostovzeff, A. R. Bellinger, C. Hopkins (New Haven: Yale, London: H. Milford, Oxford University Press, 1936), 417–19.

76. "Un Parchemin Liturgique Juif et la Gargote se la Synagouge a Doura-Europos," *Syria*, 20 (1939), 23–6.

77. S. Lieberman, *Yemenite Midrashim: A Lecture on the Yemenite Midrashim, Their Character and Value* (Jerusalem: Bamberger and Wahrmann, 1940), 40–1, in Hebrew.

78. L. Ginzberg, *A Commentary on the Palestinian Talmud* (New York: Jewish Theological Seminary, 1941), 3: 355, in Hebrew.

79. Sukenik, *The Synagogue of Dura-Europos*, 157–9.

80. Smith, "Goodenough's 'Jewish Symbols,'" 63; A. D. Nock, "Review of Goodenough, *Jewish Symbols in the Greco–Roman Period*. Vols. 5–6," *Gnomen* 29 (1957), 571; idem, "Review of Goodenough, *Jewish Symbols in the Greco–Roman Period*. Vols. 7, 8," *Gnomen*, 32 (1960), 734.

81. Although an ordained Methodist minister, later in life he called himself an "ex-Christian" (Sandmel, "An Appreciation," 4).

82. P. Veyne, "Conduct Without Belief and Works of Art Without Viewers," *Diogenes*, 143 (1988), 13.

83. See, for example, the reflections of Rabbi Alfred Wolf on Wilshire Boulevard Temple's *Warner Murals* (completed by Hugo Balin in 1929). Wolf found a precedent in the Dura synagogue, going so far as to suggest that the leaders of the Dura community "must have reasoned similarly and drawn identical conclusions, almost seventeen hundred years earlier" in E. F. Magnin, *The Warner Murals in the Wilshire Boulevard Temple Los Angeles, California* (Los Angeles: Wilshire Boulevard Temple, 1974), introduction. See W. H. Kramer, "Hugo Ballin, Artist and Director," *A Crown For a King: Studies in Jewish Art, History and Archaeology in Memory of Professor Stephen S. Kayser*, eds. S. Sabar, S. Fine, and W. Kramer (Berkeley: Magnes Museum, Jerusalem: Gefen, 2000), 165–7. Kramer reports Magnin's happy response to the Dura paintings: "We have broken tradition to bring back tradition" (p. 166).

84. Smith, "Goodenough's 'Jewish Symbols,'" 66.

85. Marchand, *Down from Olympus*, 9. Winckelmann was not so much a discoverer as classical art's first great popularizer. Antonio Bosio has been called "the Columbus of the Catacombs." See H. J. Leon, *The Jews of Ancient Rome* (Philadelphia: Jewish Publication Society, 1960), 46.

CHAPTER 4: ART HISTORY

1. E. H. Gombrich. *The Story of Art* (New York: Phaidon, 1950), 87.

2. J. Elsner, *Imperial Roman and Christian Triumph: The Art of the Roman Empire AD 100–450* (Oxford: Oxford University Press, 1998), 215.

3. See, e.g., Z. S. Strother, *Inventing Masks: Agency and History in the Art of the Central Pende* (Chicago: University of Chicago Press, 1998), xiii–xvi. On African American art, see B. Hooks, *Art on My Mind: Visual Politics* (New York: The New Press, 1995), especially xii–xvi.

4. R. Cormack, *Painting the Soul: Icons, Death Masks and Shrouds* (London: Reaktion Books, 1997), 18.

5. See also Bland, *The Artless Jew*, 42–3.

6. Gombrich, *The Story of Art*, 87.

7. H. W. Janson, *History of Art: A Survey of the Major Visual Arts from the Dawn of History to the Present Day*, 2nd ed. (New York: Harry N. Abrams, 1977), 190–1.

8. H. W. Janson and Anthony F. Janson, *History of Art* (Upper Saddle River, N.J.: Prentice Hall and New York: Harry Abrams, 2001), 212–13.

9. H. de la Croix, R. G. Tansey, and D. Kirkpatrick, *Gardner's Art Through the Ages*, 10th ed. (Fort Worth: Hartcourt Brace Jovanovich, 1996), 258–9.

10. Ibid.

11. F. S. Kleiner, C. J. Mamiya, H. de la Croix, and R. G. Tansey, *Gardner's Art Through the Ages*, 11th ed. (Fort Worth: Hartcourt College Publishers, 2001), 302–3.

12. *Gardner's Art Through the Ages*, 11th ed., 305.

13. M. Stokstad, *Art History* (New York: Harry N. Abrams, 1995), 289–96.

14. M. Stokstad, *Art History*, 2nd ed. (New York: Harry N. Abrams, 2000), 289–96.

15. Elsner, *Imperial Roman and Christian Triumph*, 215.

16. J. Elsner, "Cultural Resistance and the Visual Image: The Case of Dura Europos," *Classical Philology*, 96, no. 3 (2001), 304.

17. See, for example, I. J. Yuval, *Two Nations in Your Womb: Perceptions of Jews and Christians* (Tel-Aviv: Alma and Am Oved, 2000, in Hebrew); D. Boyarin, *Dying for God, Martyrdom and the Making of Christianity and Judaism* (Stanford: Stanford University Press, 1999). For a discussion of this phenomenon, see my "A Cosmopolitan 'Student of the Sages': Jacob of Kefar Nevoraia in Rabbinic Literature," *New Views of Jewish and Christian Self-Definition: Studies in Honor of E. P. Sanders*, eds. M. Chaney, F. Udoh, G. Tatum, and S. Heschel (Notre Dame: Notre Dame University Press, forthcoming); S. Miller, *Sages and Commoners in Late Antique Erez Israel* (forthcoming), conclusion. Many thanks to Professor Miller for sharing his prepublication manuscript with me.

18. Elsner, "Archaeologies and Agendas," 114–28. Many thanks to Professor Elsner for sharing this article with me prior to publication.

CHAPTER 5: TOWARD A NEW JEWISH ARCHAEOLOGY

1. D. Kaufmann, "Art in the Synagogue" *Jewish Quarterly Review*, Old Series 9 (1897), 254.

2. M. Goodman, "The Roman Identity of Roman Jews," *The Jews in the Hellenistic-Roman World: Studies in Memory of Menahem Stern*, eds. I. M. Gafni, A. Oppenheimer, and D. R. Schwartz (Jerusalem: Zalman Shazar Center for Jewish History and The Historical Society of Israel, 1996), 85*–*99, is clearly moving in this direction.

3. A particularly illuminating example is a television project known as *The 1900 House: An Extraordinary Living Experiment* (London: Channel 4, 2000); M. McCrum and M. Sturgis, *The 1900 House: Featuring Extracts from the Personal Diaries of Joyce and Paul Bowler* (London: Channel 4 Books, 1999). Still (barely) within living memory, observing the family that entered this "time tunnel" and lived with 1900 technology for three months points up how difficult it is even to gain a sense of the near-past.

4. For a parallel development in Biblical archaeology, now referred to as the "New Biblical Archaeology," see S. Gitlin, "The House that Albright Built," *Near Eastern Archaeology*, 65, no. 1 (2002), especially 7–9.

PART 2: ART AND IDENTITY IN THE GRECO–ROMAN WORLD

1. H. Strauss, "Jewish Art as a Minority Problem," *Journal of Jewish Sociology*, 2 (1960), 147–71.

2. Ibid., 148. S. S. Kayser, "Defining Jewish Art," *Mordecai M. Kaplan Jubilee Volume* (New York: Jewish Theological Seminary of America, 1953), 457–67, another German-Jewish expatriate, reached similar conclusions, though clearly with a more religion-focused model. Kayser (p. 457) defines Jewish art as "art applied to Judaism."

3. S. B. Fishman, *Negotiating Both Sides of the Hyphen: Coalescence, Compartmentalization and American-Jewish Values* (Cincinnati: University of Cincinnati Judaic Studies Program, 1995), 42; F. Barth, *Ethnic Groups and Boundaries* (Boston: Little, Brown, 1969), 38.

4. J. Hall, *Ethnic Identity in Greek Antiquity* (Cambridge: Cambridge University Press. 1997), 32. The literature on "ethnicity" is vast. See pp. 17–33 for recent approaches. S. Stern (*Rabbinic Identity in Early Rabbinic Writings* [Leiden: E. J. Brill, 1994], xiv–xxii), A. Saldarini ("The Social World of Christian Jews and Jewish Christians," *Religious and Ethnic Communities in Later Roman Palestine*, ed. H. Lapin [College Park, Md.: University Press

of Maryland, 1998], 127–32), and M. Niehoff (*Philo on Jewish Identity and Culture* [Tübingen: Mohr Siebeck, 2001], 1–6) apply theories of ethnicity to ancient Judaism.

5. K. Stow, *Theater of Acculturation: The Roman Ghetto in the Sixteenth Century* (Seattle and London: University of Washington Press, 2001), especially 92–5.

6. Ibid., 93.

7. S. Sabar, *The Beginnings and Flourishing of 'Ketubbah' Illustration in Italy: A Study in Popular Imagery and Jewish Patronage during the Seventeenth and Eighteenth Centuries*, Ph.D. dissertation (Los Angeles: University of California, 1987).

8. This term is used by Fishman, *Negotiating Both Sides of the Hyphen*.

CHAPTER 6: ART AND IDENTITY IN LATTER SECOND TEMPLE PERIOD JUDAISM

1. *Letter of Jeremiah* 6:45. The version of the Septuagint consulted was edited by A. Rahlfs, *Septuaginta* (Stuttgart: Privilegierte württembergische Bibelanstalt, 1959).

2. T. Fischer, "Maccabees, Book of," tr. F. Cryer, *The Anchor Bible Dictionary*, ed. D. N. Freedman (New York: Doubleday, 1992), 4: 441.

3. The Greek reads simply *epoíesen*, "made." Translating, the Mosul edition of the Pshitta uses the verb *gelaf*, carved. See *Biblia Sacra: Pschitta* (Beirut: Typis Typographiae Catholicae, 1951).

4. *Panoplies.* See H. G. Liddell and R. Scott, *A Greek-English Lexicon* (Oxford: Clarendon, 1996), 1298.

5. See J. Fedak, *Monumental Tombs of the Hellenistic Age: A Study of Selected Tombs from the Pre-Classical to the Early Imperial Era* (Toronto: University of Toronto Press, 1990), 140–50. See now A. M. Berlin, "Power and its Afterlife: Tombs in Hellenistic Palestine," *Near Eastern Archaeology*, 65, no. 2 (2002), 141–7. Berlin refers derisively to Hasmonian "seduction by Hellenistic material culture" (145).

6. Berlin, Power and its Afterlife," 144–5.

7. M. Kon, "Jewish Art at the Time of the Second Temple," *Jewish Art*, ed. C. Roth (London: Vallentine, Mitchell, 1971), 53.

8. L. Y. Rahmani, "Jason's Tomb," *Israel Exploration Journal*, 17 (1967), 61–100.

9. Avigad, *Ancient Monuments in the Kidron Valley*, 73–132. On the Tomb of Zechariah, see D. Barag, "The 2000–2001 Exploration of the Tombs of Benei Hezir and Zechariah," *Israel Exploration Journal*, 53 (2003), 95–9.

10. See L. Y. Rahmani, "Jerusalem's Tomb Monuments on Jewish Ossuaries," *Israel Exploration Journal*, 18 (1968), 221: 220–5; idem, *A Catalogue of Jewish Ossuaries in the Collection of the State of Israel* (Jerusalem: The Israel Antiquities Authority, The Israel Academy of Sciences and Humanities, 1994), 31–4.

11. *Antiquities*, 20. 95; Kon, *The Tombs of the Kings*, 73–9.

12. See Fine, "Another View of Jerusalem's Necropolis During the First Century: A Decorated Ossuary from the Nelson and Helen Glueck Collection of the Cincinnati Art Museum," *Journal of Jewish Studies*, 54, no. 2 (2003), 233–1. A second ossuary in the Israel State Collection bears images of six free-standing pyramidal monuments on their sides and lid. Rahmani, *Catalogue*, no. 473. This piece is thought to derive from the Hebron hills.

13. This tomb was discussed most recently by Barag, "The 2000–2001 Exploration of the Tombs of Benei Hezir and Zechariah," 79–95.

14. E. Ben Yehuda, *A Complete Dictionary of Ancient and Modern Hebrew* (Jerusalem: Makor, 1980), 8: 3749, in Hebrew; M. Jastrow, *Dictionary of the Targumim*, 926; D. R. Hillers and E. Cussini, *Palmyrene Aramaic Texts* (Baltimore: Johns Hopkins University Press, 1995), 390.

15. *Biblia Sacra: Pschitta*, ad. loc.; C. Brockelmann, *Lexicon Syriacum* (Hildesheim, Zurich, New York: Georg Olms, 1982), 441; A. Kahana, *Ha-Sefarim ha-Hitsonim* (Tel Aviv: Hozaath M'qoroth, 1937), 2: 162.

16. C. W. Samuels, P. Rynearson, and Y. Meshorer, eds., *The Numismatic Legacy of the Jews as Depicted by a Distinguished American Collection*, ed. P. Rynearson (New York: Stack's Publications, Numismatic Review, 2000), no. 37; Meshorer, *Ancient Jewish Coinage*, 1: 66–7. Crested helmets also appear on the coins of Herod Archelaus. See 2: 32–3.

17. See J. Goldstein, *The Anchor Bible: I Maccabees* (Garden City: Doubleday, 1976), 474–5. On Roman trophies, see G. C. Picard, *Les trophées romains: Contribution à l'histoire de la religion et de l'art triomphal de Rome* (Paris: E. De Boccard, 1957), pl. viii, xi.

18. L. Anson, *Numismata Graeca: Greek Coin-Types* (London, L. Anson, 1911–1914), part 2, 106–12.

19. S. G. Miller, *The Tomb of Lyson and Kallikles, A Painted Macedonian Tomb* (Mainz am Rhein: Verlag Philipp von Zabern, 1993), 48–9.

20. Ibid., 49.

21. Ibid., 51.

22. Meshorer, *Ancient Jewish Coinage*, 1: 62, 2: 13, 18, 23, 28, 31–3, 79.

23. Ibid., 1: 62. See U. Rappaport, "On the 'Hellenization' of the Hasmoneans," *The Hasmonean State: The History of the Hasmoneans During the Hellenistic Period*, eds. U. Rappaport and I. Ronen (Jerusalem: Ben Zvi Institute, 1993), 87, in Hebrew; A. Kindler, "Hellenistic Influences on Hasmonean Coinage," *The Hasmonean State*, 113.

24. Rahmani, "Jason's Tomb," 69–72; R. Patai, *The Children of Noah: Jewish Seafaring in Ancient Times* (Princeton: Princeton University Press, 1998), 75, 147–8; N. Kashtan, "Seafaring and Jews in Graeco–Roman Palestine: Realistic and Symbolic Dimensions," *Mediterranean Historical Review*, 15, no. 1 (2000): 22–3.

25. Rahmani, "Jason's Tomb," 97.

26. Y. Aharoni and M. Avi-Yonah, *The Macmillan Bible Atlas*, 3rd ed. (New York: Macmillan, 1993), 206.

27. J. Goldstein believes this to be an ancient misreading of the text. See Goldstein, *The Anchor Bible: I Maccabees*, 471, 475.

28. Rahmani, *Catalogue*, 31; R. Hachlili, *Jewish Ornamented Ossuaries of the Late Second Temple Period* (Haifa: The Reuben and Edith Hecht Museum, University of Haifa, 1988), no. 11. Add to these the image of a monument on a "Darom-type" oil lamp published by V. Sussman, *Ornamented Jewish Oil Lamps* (Warminster: Aris & Philips, Jerusalem: Israel Exploration Society, 1982), 56–7, cat. no. 60 and a monument etched onto a stone found at Jotapata. See M. Aviam, "Jodefat/Jotapata: The Archaeology of the First Battle," *The First Revolt: Archaeology, History, and Ideology*, eds. A. M. Berlin and J. A. Overman (London and New York: Routledge, 2002), 132. Aviam's homiletical interpretation is not credible, however.

29. See Rappaport, "On the Hellenization," 87–8.

30. On Josephus's use of I Maccabees, see I. M. Gafni, "On the Use of I Maccabees by Josephus Flavius," *Zion*, 45, no. 2 (1980), 81–95, in Hebrew. Gafni notes that "Josephus felt free to rewrite major portions of his source" (English summary). Translated as "Josephus and One Maccabees," *Josephus, the Bible and History*, eds. L. H. Feldman and G. Hata (Detroit: Wayne State University Press, 1989), 116–31. L. H. Feldman, "Josephus' Portrayal of the Hasmoneans Compared with 1 Maccabees," *Josephus and the History of the Greco–Roman Period: Essays in Memory of Morton Smith*, eds. F. Parente and J. Sievers (Leiden: E. J. Brill, 1994), 41–68. For a comparison of the I Maccabees and Josephan passages, see Goldstein, *I Maccabees*, 475.

31. The edition and translation of Josephus used in this study is *Josephus Flavius, The Complete Works*, Loeb Classical Library, tr. H. St. J. Thackery, R. Marcus, A. Wikgren, and L. Feldman (Cambridge, Mass. and London: Harvard University Press, 1926–65).

32. As, for example, the royal family of Adiabene (discussed above). The most recent article on the Herodian royal tomb is J. Magness, "The Mausolea of Augustus, Alexander, and Herod

the Great," *Hesed ve-Emet: Studies in Honor of Ernest S. Frerichs*, eds. J. Magness and S. Gitin (Atlanta: Scholars Press, 1998), 213–30.

33. A. A. Di Lella, "Wisdom of Ben-Sira," *The Anchor Bible Dictionary*, ed. D. N. Freedman (New York: Doubleday, 1992), 1: 932. I have intentionally not discussed the Persian-period coins of Yehud, with their obvious Greek influence, since evidence external to them that might help in their interpretation is essentially lacking. See N. Kokkinos (*The Herodian Dynasty: Origins, Role in Society and Eclipse* (Sheffield: Sheffield Academic Press, 1998), 82. I hope to return to this problem in a future publication.

34. Sirah 45: 6–13. See also M. H. Segel, ed., *Sefer Ben Sira ha-Shalem* (Jerusalem: Mosad Bialik, 1953); Z. Ben-Hayyim, *The Book of Ben Sira: Text, Concordance and Analysis of the Vocabulary* (Jerusalem: Academy of the Hebrew Language and Shrine of the Book, 1977), in Hebrew.

35. Sirah 45:12–13.

36. See Exodus 28:2–42.

37. Sirah 50:1–5.

38. Referring to the Temple.

39. Sirah 47:13.

40. Sirah 49:12–13.

41. On this neologism, see A. J. S. Spawforth, "Euergetism," *The Oxford Classical Dictionary*, 3rd ed., eds. S. Hornblower and A. Spawforth (New York: Oxford University Press, 1996), 566.

42. *Antiquities* 12.141. V. Tcherikover, *Hellenistic Civilization and the Jews* (Philadelphia: Jewish Publication Society, 1959), 80–1.

43. Tcherikover, *Hellenistic Civilization*, 80–1.

44. Sirah 38:24–34.

45. A. Burford, *Craftsmen in Greek and Roman Society* (Ithaca: Cornell University Press, 1974), 13.

46. Matthew 13:53–8, Mark 6:1–6, Luke 4:16–30.

47. *Antiquities* 3.104–6.

48. *b. Berakhot* 55a makes a related comment, referring to Ex. 35:31. This unusual show of respect is unprecedented in the literature of the ancient Near East. Compare the texts discussed by C. Cohen, "Was the P Document Secret?," *The Journal of the Ancient Near Eastern Society*, 1, no. 2 (1968), 41–4.

49. *Antiquities* 8.76–8.

50. Hebrew: Ḥiram or Ḥuram.

51. Oddly, this text has not been noticed by scholars dealing with Jewish identity during this period.

52. W. Johnston, *1 & 2 Chronicles* (Sheffield: Sheffield Academic Press, 1997), 1: 310–11.

53. See L. Ginzberg, *Legends of the Jews* (Philadelphia: Jewish Publication Society, 1968), 6: 295, note 61.

54. *Antiquities* 15.390.

55. See *Antiquities* 15.380–425.

56. Rahmani, *Catalogue*, no. 200.

57. Sirah 22:17.

58. Sirah 40:3–4.

59. P. W. Lapp and N. I. Lapp, "Iraq El-Emir," *New Encyclopedia of Archaeological Excavations in the Holy Land*, ed. E. Stern (Jerusalem: Israel Exploration Society and Carta; New York: Simon & Schuster, 1993), 646–9. E. Netzer, "The Enchanted Palace Built by Hyrcanus the Tobiad in Transjordan," *Qadmoniot*, 36, no. 2 (1998), 117–22, in Hebrew; C. C. Ji, "A New Look at the Tobiads in 'Iraq El-Emir," *Liber Annuus*, 45 (1998), 417–440.

60. D. K. Hill, "The Animal Fountain of Iraq el-Amir," *Bulletin of the American School for Oriental Research*, 71 (1963), 45–55.

61. *Antiquities* 12.230.

62. *Antiquities* 3.134–5.

63. *Jewish War* 5.184–227; *Antiquities* 15. These texts were discussed most recently by L. I. Levine, "Josephus' Description of the Jerusalem Temple: War, Antiquities and Other Sources," *Josephus and the History of the Greco-Roman Period: Essays in Memory of Morton Smith*, eds. F. Parente and J. Sievers (Leiden: E. J. Brill, 1994), 233–46.

64. See most recently D. Jacobson, "Herod's Roman Temple," *Biblical Archaeology Review*, 28, no. 2 (2002), 18–27, 60–1.

65. See also the Greek Additions to Esther, 15:6 where Ahasuerus is described "seated on his royal throne, clad in all his magnificence, and covered with gold and precious stones; he was an awe-inspiring sight." See also Tobit 14:16–17; Revelation 21:21.

66. Cassius Dio, *Historia Romana* 15:2, *GLAJJ* 2: 350–1.

67. *Historiae* 5.12: 1 in *GLAJJ*, 2: 22, 30.

68. Sanders, *Judaism*, underplays the significance of dislike of idolatry.

69. For Biblical attitudes, see the most recent studies by T. N. D. Mettinger, *No Graven Image? Israelite Aniconism in its Ancient Near Eastern Context* (Stockholm: Almsquist and Wiksell International, 1995); "Israelite Aniconism: Developments and Origins," *The Image and the Book*, ed. K. van der Toorn (Leuven: Peeters, 1997), 173–204 and the bibliography cited there. R. Goldenberg, *The Nations That Know Thee Not: Ancient Jewish Attitudes Toward Other Religions* (New York: New York University Press, 1998), 9–27, surveys Biblical attitudes. For a broad discussion of Second Temple period attitudes, see pages 33–80.

70. Deuteronomy 5:8–10.

71. Y. Kaufmann, *The Religion of Israel: From Its Beginnings to the Babylonian Exile*, tr. M. Greenberg (Chicago: University of Chicago Press, 1960), 1–20. See M. Halbertal and A. Margalit, *Idolatry* (Cambridge, Mass.: Harvard

University Press, 1992), 77; Goldenberg, *The Nations That Know Thee Not*, 23.

72. This focus is emphasized by B. Wacholder, *Eupolemus: A Study in Judaeo-Greek Literature* (Cincinnati: Hebrew Union College Press, 1974), 173–4. On rabbinic discussion of the Tabernacle/Temple and its cult objects, see R. Kirschner's comments in his edition of the *Baraita de-Melekhet ha-Mishkan* (Cincinnati: Hebrew Union College, 1991), 80–3.

73. See my *This Holy Place*, passim.

74. Mettinger, *No Graven Image?*; idem, "Israelite Aniconism," 173.

75. The *Oxford English Dictionary*, 1: 172, defines aniconic as "Applied to simple material symbols of a deity, as a pillar or block, not shaped into an image of human form; also to the worship connected with these. Hence aniconism . . . , the use of, or worship connected with, such symbols." See also the entries for "iconic," "icon," and "iconism" (7: 608–9). Mettinger, "Israelite Aniconism," 199, attempts to finesse this definitional problem by describing the "cults where there is no iconic representation of the divine (anthropomorphic or theriomorphic) serving as the dominant or central cult symbol" as observing de facto aniconism, as opposed to Israelite "programmatic aniconism." See also idem, *No Graven Image?*, especially 16–27.

76. Mettinger, *No Graven Image?*, 17. See especially D. Freedberg's discussion of "the myth of aniconism" in his *The Power of Images: Studies in the History and Theory of Response* (Chicago: University of Chicago, 1989), 54–81; Bland, *The Artless Jew*, passim.

77. I construe "anti-idolic" to be a subset of the existing term "anti-idolatry." "Anti-idolic" focuses on the Jewishly objectionable visual aspects of non-Jewish religion, on objects that Jews construed as "idols." Many thanks to the staff of the *Oxford Dictionary of the English Language* for discussing with me the issues involved in coining this neologism. Ludwig Blau ("Early Christian Archaeology," 179) reached conclusions similar to my own, stating that "idols were not to be tolerated in the holy land, and yet from all this nothing can be gathered with reference to the attitude of the Jews towards images of a private character." See also C. Konikoff, *The Second Commandment and its Interpretation in the Art of Ancient Israel* (Geneva: Imprimerie du Journal de Genève, 1973), 57. M. A. Chancey, *The Myth of a Gentile Galilee* [Cambridge: Cambridge University Press, 2002], 6 suggests a similar distinction between Hellenism and paganism. See also B. Burrell, "Out Heroding Herod," *American Journal of Archaeology*, 106 (2002), 108.

78. A study of Samaritan attitudes is a desideratum. The consistency of "anti-idolic"

attitudes in the Samaritan Pentateuch, taken together with the lack of iconic elements from the Hellenistic-period Samaritan Temple on Mt. Gerizim and later synagogue art, support the notion that Samaritans, like Jews, were generally "anti-idolic." See I. Magen, "Mount Gerizim – A Temple City," *Qadmoniot*, 23, nos. 3–4 (1990), 70–96, in Hebrew; idem, "Samaritan Synagogues," *Qadmoniot*, 25, nos. 3–4 (1992), 66–90, in Hebrew; R. Pummer, "Samaritan Synagogues and Jewish Synagogues: Similarities and Differences," *JCP*, 143–4. Aniconism was practiced by the Nabateans into the first century. On the Nabateans: J. Patrich, *The Formation of Nabatean Art: Prohibition of a Graven Image Among the Nabateans* (Jerusalem: Magnes and Leiden: E. J. Brill, 1990); Mettinger, "Israelite Aniconism," 193–9.

79. For later periods, see Chancey, *Myth of a Gentile Galilee*, passim; N. Belayche, *Iudaea-Palaestina: The Pagan Cults in Roman Period (Second to Fourth Century)* (Tübingen: Mohr Siebeck, 2001), 14.

80. 7Q2 (7QpapEpJer gr). On the date of the *Letter of Jeremiah*, see C. A. Moore, *The Anchor Bible: Daniel, Esther and Jeremiah: The Additions* (Garden City: Doubleday, 1987), 326–7.

81. C. J. Ball, "Epistle of Jeremy," in *The Apocrypha and Pseudepigrapha of the Old Testament in English*, ed. R. H. Charles (Oxford: Clarendon Press, 1963), 1: 596.

82. *Letter of Jeremiah* 6:4–6.

83. Hecataeus of Abdera, in *GLAJJ*, 1: 26, 28, lines 3–4; Tacitus, *History*, 9:1 (*GLAJJ*, 2: 21, 28; Cassius Dio, *Historia Romana* 15:2 (in *GLAJJ*, 2: 349–51). See also Livy, in *GLAJJ*, 1: 330. Due to the brevity of his preserved statement, Livy's evaluation cannot be discerned. See the discussion by Bland, *The Artless Jew*, 60–2.

84. Varro, in *GLAJJ*, 1: 208.

85. Strabo of Amaseia, *Geography*, 16, 35, in *GLAJJ*, 1: 294, 299–300.

86. Perhaps significantly, derision of idols appears nowhere in Ben Sirah, perhaps suggesting that idolatry was a low-priority item for Jews of his time.

87. M. Himmelfarb, "Levi, Phinehas, and the Problem of Intermarriage at the Time of the Maccabean Revolt," *Jewish Studies Quarterly*, 6 (1999), 21–2. See also E. Bickerman, *The God of the Maccabees*, tr. H. R. Moehring (Leiden: E. J. Brill, 1979), 41; Tcherikover, *Hellenistic Civilization*, 166–7; D. Mendels, *The Land of Israel as Political Concept in Hasmonean Literature* (Tübingen: J. C. B. Mohr [Paul Siebeck], 1987), 141–2.

88. Elias Bickerman compares this silence to responses to later attempts to place images of Caligula and Nero in the Temple, deducing, quite reasonably, that no such idol was set up.

See Bickerman, *The God of the Maccabees*, 68. See also Himmelfarb, "Levi, Phinehas," 21.

89. *1 Maccabees* 1:46.

90. Ibid., 1:43.

91. Ibid., 2:15–28.

92. On the date of Daniel and of this tradition within Daniel, see L. F. Hartman, *The Book of Daniel* (Garden City: Doubleday, 1977), 9–18. Hartman (p. 159) interprets this tradition as a response to these persecutions.

93. Daniel 3:1. See also 2:31 ff.

94. Ibid., 3:6. See also *1 Maccabees* 2:15–28.

95. Ibid., 3:8.

96. Ibid., 3.

97. On the date of *Jubilees*, see *The Book of Jubilees*, tr. J. VanderKam (Louvaine: Peeters, 1989), v–vi.

98. *Jubilees* 12:1–15, tr. J. VanderKam.

99. *1 Maccabees* 5:43–4; *2 Maccabees* 12:26–7.

100. *1 Maccabees* 5:68. See the comments of S. Zeitlin, *The First Book of Maccabees: An English Translation*, tr. S. Tedesche, commentary by S. Zeitlin (New York: Harper and Brothers, 1950), ad. loc. For the chronology of these events, see Goldstein, *I Maccabees*, 161–74.

101. *1 Maccabees* 10:83–5.

102. *1 Maccabees* 13:47 and Zeitlin's comments. For further examples, see *1 Maccabees* 5:44, 10:84.

103. Ruled 135–104 B.C.E.

104. See S. L. Derfler, *The Hellenistic Temple at Beersheva, Israel*, Ph.D. dissertation (University of Minnesota, 1984), especially 86–92. Derfler suggests that after the destruction of a Hellenistic temple in Beer Sheva around 125 B.C.E. by Hyrcanus I, cult objects were "destroyed or buried" and the building was "modeled and resanctified in order to conform to traditional Yawistic practice." Derfler does not provide positive evidence for Judean usage or for other "Judean cults re-established by Hyrcanus" (ibid.). While the destruction of this structure by Hyrcanus seems reasonable, it seems just as reasonable to me that the local population rededicated the temple, and not Hasmoneans. On the destruction of the Samaritan temple on Mt. Gerizim, see Magen, "Mount Gerizim – A Temple City."

105. L. Feldman, *Jew and Gentile in the Ancient World* (Princeton: Princeton University Press, 1993), 324–6; S. J. D. Cohen, *The Beginnings of Jewishness: Boundaries, Varieties, Uncertainties* (Berkeley and Los Angeles, University of California Press, 1999), especially 109–39.

106. E. E. Urbach, "The Place of the Ten Commandments in Ritual and Prayer," *The Ten Commandments as Reflected in Tradition, and Literature Throughout the Ages* (Jerusalem: Magnes, 1985), 127–46, in Hebrew. On the question of the *Shema* in Jewish prayer of the Second Temple period focusing on Qumran, see D. K. Falk, *Daily, Sabbath and Festival Prayers in the Dead Sea*

Scrolls (Leiden: E. J. Brill, 1998), 47–54, 113–16, 248–50; R. S. Sarason, "The 'Intersections' of Qumran and Rabbinic Judaism: The Case of Prayer Texts and Liturgies," *Dead Sea Discoveries*, 8, no. 2 (2001), 179.

107. *Against Apion* 2.193.

108. Describing the cities of the seacoast, from Sidon and Tyre south to Ashkelon, the author of the Book of Judith (4:8) describes the armies of Holofernes who "demolished all their shrines and cut down their sacred groves."

109. W. D. Davies, *The Territorial Dimension of Judaism* (Berkeley and Los Angeles: University of California, 1982), 44–7.

110. Compare Sanders, *Judaism*, 243.

111. Kindler, "Hellenistic Influences," 103.

112. The rabbis were well aware that the Tyrian sheqel was in standard use in the Temple. See Meshorer, *Ancient Jewish Coinage*, 2:7–9; idem, "One Hundred Ninety Years of Tyrian Shekels," *Studies in Honor of Leo Mildenberg*, eds. A. Houghton, S. Hurter, P. E. Mottahedeh, and J. A. Scott (Wetteren, Belgium: Cultura, 1984), 171–9. Meshorer goes so far as to suggest that Tyrian sheqels were minted in Jerusalem under Herod after the closure of the Tyrian mint in 19 B.C.E.

113. See my "Review of Shaye J. D. Cohen, *The Beginnings of Jewishness: Boundaries, Varieties, Uncertainties*," *Archaeological Odyssey* (November/December 2000), 56, 58.

114. See Goldstein, *The Anchor Bible: I Maccabees*, 475.

115. Compare *Antiquities* 17.149–63. *War* 1. 684–54.

116. A. H. M. Jones, *The Herods of Judaea* (Oxford: Clarendon Press, 1938), 148. Compare Goodenough, *Jewish Symbols*, 8:123–4; Meshorer, *Ancient Jewish Coins*, 2:29; P. Richardson, *Herod: King of the Jews and Friend of Rome* (Columbia: University of South Carolina Press, 1996), 15–18.

117. This debate is mediated by Richardson, *Herod*, 16–17.

118. D. W. Roller, *The Building Program of Herod the Great* (Berkeley: University of California Press, 1998), 178.

119. M. Grant, *Herod the Great* (London: Weidenfeld and Nicolson, 1971), 207–9.

120. P. Collart and J. Vicari, *Le Sanctuaire de Baalshamin a Palmyre* (Rome: Institut Suisse, 1969), 2: xcvii.

121. Grant, *Herod the Great*, 208.

122. Richardson, *Herod*, 18.

123. Meshorer, *Ancient Jewish Coinage*, 2: 13, 29–30.

124. Ibid., 2: 29.

125. *y. Avodah Zarah* 3:1, 43b–c.

126. *Antiquities* 15.268.

127. *Antiquities* 15.272–9.

128. Picard, *Les Trophées Romains*, 243; Smallwood, *The Jews Under Roman Rule*, 57–9;

H. A. Grueber, *Coins of the Roman Republic in the British Museum* (London: British Museum, 1910), 2:506, no. 146; H. H. St. Hart, "Judaea and Rome: The Official Commentary," *Journal of Theological Studies*, new series 3 (1952), 180.

129. *Jewish War* 1.351–6; *Antiquities* 14.477–86.

130. See Picard, *Les Trophées Romains*, 283. Picard suggests that Herod's placement of triumphal trophies in a theater was inspired by the Forum of Pompei in Rome.

131. *Jewish War* 2.169–74, *Antiquities* 18.55–9; C. H. Kraeling, "The Episode of the Roman Standards in Jerusalem," *Harvard Theological Review* 35 (1942), 263–89; Smallwood, *The Jews Under Roman Rule*, 160–2, 165–6.

132. M. Pucci Ben Zeev, *Jewish Rights in the Roman World: The Greek and Latin Documents Quoted by Josephus Flavius* (Tübingen: Mohr Siebeck, 1998), 471–81.

133. *Jewish War* 6.316.

134. *Jewish War* 6.403.

135. Smallwood, *The Jews Under Roman Rule*, 324–5; Picard, *Les Trophées Romains*, 343.

136. *Pesher Habbakuk*, (1QpHab) col. 5, line 12 to 6, line 5. B. Nitzan, ed., *Pesher Habbabuk: A Scroll From the Wilderness of Judaea (1QpHab)* (Jerusalem: Bialik Institute, 1986), 169, in Hebrew. This translation follows F. García Martínez, *The Dead Sea Scrolls Translated: The Qumran Texts in English*, tr. W. G. E. Watson (Leiden: E. J. Brill, 1994), par. 1764–5.

137. *Antiquities* 18.257–309; Philo of Alexandria, *Embassy to Gaius*, tr. F. H. Colson (Cambridge, Mass.: Harvard University Press, 1971); Smallwood, *The Jews Under Roman Rule*, 239–45; idem, "Philo and Josephus as Historians of the Same Events," *Josephus, Judaism and Christianity*, eds. L. H. Feldman and G. Hata (Detroit: Wayne State University Press, 1987), 114–29; Niehoff, *Philo on Jewish Identity and Culture*, 80.

138. A. Kasher, *The Jews in Hellenistic and Roman Egypt* (Tübingen: J. C. B. Mohr, 1985), 22–3. Niehoff, *Philo on Jewish Identity and Culture*, 82, correctly writes that "aniconism may have played a considerable, yet hitherto overlooked role in this conflict."

139. This translation generally follows Niehoff, ibid. See Niehoff's discussion, p. 83.

140. E. R. Goodenough, *By Light, Light: The Mystic Gospel of Hellenistic Judaism* (New Haven: Yale University Press, 1935), 256–9; Niehoff, *Philo on Jewish Identity and Culture*, 30, 62, 65, 77, 108, 143.

141. *Wisdom of Solomon*, Ch. 13–15.

142. D. Winston, *The Anchor Bible: The Wisdom of Solomon, A New Translation* (New York: Doubleday, 1979), 23, 37.

143. *Wisdom of Solomon* 14:8–31.

144. See parallels in Matthew 22:15–22; Luke 20:20–6.

145. Finney, *The Invisible God*, 70–2, 84–5, reaches similar conclusions.

146. Y. Meshorer, "Numismatics," *Encyclopedia of the Dead Sea Scrolls*, eds. L. H. Schiffman and J. C. VanderKam (New York: Oxford University Press, 2000), 2: 619–20.

147. See Chapter 9 below.

148. *Life* 12.65–7. See, for example, *Jewish War* 5.262–4, where Josephus decries John of Gischala's destruction of gifts to the Temple by Augustus and other foreigners.

149. Cataloged by *AJAALI*, 9–127.

150. Rahmani, ("Jason's Tomb," 72–3, 97) does not discuss the date of this drawing, though it seems to date to the Hasmonean period.

151. M. Broshi, "Excavations in the House of Caiaphas, Mount Zion," *Jerusalem Revealed*, ed. Y. Yadin (Jerusalem: Israel Exploration Society, 1975), 58 and pl. 3.

152. N. Avigad, *Discovering Jerusalem* (Nashville: Thomas Nelson, 1980), 168–70, 193, 200.

153. M. Ben Dov, *In the Shadow of the Temple: The Discovery of Ancient Jerusalem* (Jerusalem: Keter, 1982), 160.

154. Ibid., 150–1. In a private communication, L. Feldman queried, "How do we know that the building was that of a Jew?" In this, he is completely correct. Nevertheless, the owner of this building does not seem to have had any scruples – religious, political, or otherwise – against maintaining this structure within meters of the Temple Mount.

155. Kon, *The Tombs of the Kings*, 71.

156. D. Sperber, "Between Jerusalem and Rome: The History of the Base of the Menorah as Depicted on the Arch of Titus," *In the Light of the Menorah: Story of a Symbol*, ed. Y. Yisraeli (Jerusalem: Israel Museum and Philadelphia: Jewish Publication Society, 1999), 50–3; idem, "The History of the Menorah," *Journal of Jewish Studies*, 16 (1965), 147–52.

157. M. Kon, "Jewish Art at the Time of the Second Temple," 54–5.

158. See H. Strauss, "The Date and Form of the Menorah of the Maccabees," *Eretz Israel*, 6 (1960), 122–9, in Hebrew.

159. t. *Avodah Zarah* 5:2. See Blidstein, "The Tannaim and Plastic Art," 18.

160. Israel Antiquities Authority IAA 1994-3643, published in J. Goodnick Westenholz, ed., *Sacred Bounty Sacred Land: The Seven Species of the Land of Israel* (Jerusalem: Bible Lands Museum, 1998), 130.

161. Meshorer, *Ancient Jewish Coinage* 1: 67, 88, 92, 2: 108–10; 2: 19, 20, 27, 100, 101, 103, 108–10. Westenholz, *Sacred Bounty*, 33–7, 150–4; N. Avigad, "Excavations in the Jewish Quarter of the Old City of Jerusalem, 1969/70 (Preliminary Report)," *Israel Exploration Journal* 20, 1–2 (1970), 3–5.

162. *Antiquities* 15.328–30.

163. D. M. Jacobson, "Herod the Great Shows His True Colors," *Near Eastern Archaeology*, 64, no. 3 (2001), 103, goes so far as to suggest that "at heart [Herod] was an 'unrepentant' pagan, who paid mere lip service to his adopted Jewish faith." See also Jacobson's "King Herod's Heroic Public Image," *Revue Biblique*, 95, no. 3 (1988), 386–403.

164. E. Netzer, *The Palaces of the Hasmoneans and Herod the Great* (Jerusalem: Ben Zvi Institute, 1999), 106, in Hebrew.

165. *Antiquities* 19.357. See also *Antiquities* 15.23–30, and compare J. Gutmann, "The Second Commandment and the Image in Judaism," *Beauty in Holiness: Studies in Jewish Customs and Ceremonial Art*, ed. J. Gutmann (New York: Ktav, 1970), 12.

166. Meshorer, *Ancient Jewish Coinage*, 74.

167. *Against Apion* 2.190.

168. *Against Apion* 2.75. Compare Blidstein's assessment of Josephus in "The Tannaim and Plastic Art," 15–16.

169. *Antiquities* 8.194–5, and note "a," ad. loc.

170. 1 Kings 10:18–20 and 2 Chron. 9: 17–19.

171. L. H. Feldman, "Josephus as an Apologist to the Greco–Roman World: His Portrait of Solomon," *Aspects of Religious Propaganda in Judaism and Early Christianity*, ed. E. Schüssler Fiorenza (Notre Dame: Notre Dame University Press, 1996), 77; idem, *Josephus' Interpretation of the Bible* (Berkeley and Los Angeles: University of California, 1998), 617–18; P. Spilsbury, *The Image of the Jew in Flavius Josephus' Paraphrase of the Bible* (Tübingen: Mohr Siebeck, 1998), 184–5; C. T. Begg, "Solomon's Apostasy (1 Kgs. 11, 11–13) According to Josephus," *Journal for the Study of Judaism*, 28, no. 3 (1997), 303–5.

172. *Antiquities* 3.137. On the cherubim, see Ginzberg, *Legends of the Jews*, 1: 81, 5: 104, n. 94; 3: 158–9, 6: 65, n. 333.

173. See note "a" to *Antiquities* 8, 72.

174. *Antiquities* 3.113. See also *Antiquities* 8, 145 and Feldman's comment in "Josephus as an Apologist," 77.

175. On Josephus's Aaron, see L. H. Feldman, *Studies in Josephus' Rewritten Bible* (Leiden: E. J. Brill, 1998), 55–73. On the golden calf incident in Josephus and other ancient Jewish writers, see 59–62.

CHAPTER 7: ART AND IDENTITY IN LATE ANTIQUE PALESTINE

1. See, e.g., t. *Sukkah* 4:6, and especially y. *Sheqalim* 5:7, 49b, y. *Peah* 8:9, 21b.

2. T. N. D. Mettinger, *No Graven Image? Israelite Aniconism in its Ancient Near Eastern*

Context, 17. See especially D. Freedberg's discussion of "the myth of aniconism" in his *The Power of Images: Studies in the History and Theory of Response* (Chicago: University of Chicago, 1989), 54–81.

3. See L. Feldman, *Studies in Hellenistic Judaism* (Leiden: E. J. Brill, 1996), 253–76.

4. S. Lieberman, *Hellenism in Jewish Palestine* (New York: Jewish Theological Seminary, 1950), 115–38; Urbach, "The Rabbinical Laws of Idolatry"; Blidstein, *Rabbinic Legislation on Idolatry*, "The *Tannaim* and Plastic Art"; idem, "Prostration and Mosaics in Talmudic Law"; idem, "R. Johanan, Idolatry, and Public Privilege"; idem, "Nullification of Idolatry in Rabbinic Law"; Baumgarten, "Art in the Synagogue: Some Talmudic Views"; Halbertal and Margalit, *Idolatry*; Goldenberg, *The Nations that Know Thee Not*; M. Halbertal, "Coexisting with the Enemy: Jews and Pagans in the Mishnah," *Tolerance and Intolerance in Early Judaism and Christianity*, eds. G. N. Stanton and G. S. Stroumsa (Cambridge: Cambridge University Press, 1998), 159–72; S. Stern, "Figurative Art and *Halakha* in the Midrashic–Talmudic Period," *Zion*, 61 (1996), 379–419, in Hebrew; idem, "Pagan Images in Late Antique Palestinian Synagogues," *Ethnicity and Culture in Late Antiquity*, eds. S. Mitchell and G. Greatrex (London: Duckworth and The Classical Press of Wales, 2000), 241–52; Y. Z. Eliav, "Visiting the Sculptural Environment: Shaping the Second Commandment," *Talmud Yerushalmi and Graeco–Roman Culture*, ed. P. Schäfer (Tübingen: Mohr Siebeck, 1998), 3: 411–33; idem, "The Roman Bath as a Jewish Institution; Another Look at the Encounter Between Judaism and the Greco–Roman Culture," *Journal for the Study of Judaism*, 31, no. 4 (2000), 416–54.

5. Sukenik, "The Present State of Synagogue Studies," 9.

6. Eusebius of Caesarea, *The Onomasticon: Palestine in the Fourth Century A.D.*, tr. G. S. P. Freeman-Grenville (Jerusalem: Carta, 2003), 76.

7. H. Eshel, "'Ki-gon . . . Yeriho le-Na'aran: Al ha-Yeshuv ha-Yehudi ba-Yeriho u-ve-Na'aran ba-Tequfah ha-Aravit ve-Tiarukh Beit ha-Knesset ba-Yeriho," *Lifne Efrayim u-Vinyamin u-Menasheh: Qovets Mehkarim ve-Tagliot be-Geografyah Historit*, ed. Z. H. Erlich (Jerusalem: ha-Moatsah ha-Ezorit Mateh Binyamin, 1985), 86.

8. Fine, *This Holy Place*, 100.

9. See M. Avi-Yonah, "Synagogue Architecture in the Late Classical Period," *Jewish Art*, ed. C. Roth, 2nd ed. rev. by B. Narkiss (London: Vallentine, Mitchell, 1971), 80; R. Schick, *The Christian Communities of Palestine from Byzantine to Islamic Rule: A Historical and Archaeological Study* (Princeton: Darwin Press, 1995), 203.

10. Schick, *Christian Communities*, 204, suggests that "although the fact that the iconoclasts did not damage Hebrew inscriptions at Na'arah suggests that they were Jews, it is conceivable that it was in fact later occupants who did the damage, and that only the area of the zodiac was still visible at the time."

11. For example, the mosaics from Sepphoris and Kefar Kana in the Lower Galilee. See M. J. S. Chiat, *A Handbook of Synagogue Architecture* (Chino: Scholars Press, 1982), 81–4.

12. N. Slouschz, "Quelques observations relative à l'inscription juive découverte à Ain Douk," 1 (1921) 33–35, 215, in Hebrew. See the discussion of Sukenik's dissertation, above, 28.

13. L. H. Vincent, "Un sanctuaire dans la region de Jericho, la synagogue de Na'arah," *Revue Biblique*, 68 (1961), 161–73; P. Benoit, "Note Additionnelle," *Revue Biblique*, 68 (1961), 174–7; M. Avi-Yonah, "Na'aran," (*Recueil Publié par Société Hebraïque d'Exploration et d'Archéologie Palestiniennes*) *NEAEHL*, 1075–6.

14. Sukenik, "The Present State of Synagogue Studies," 9.

15. Ibid., 10.

16. V. Sussman, *Ornamented Jewish Oil-Lamps: From the Destruction of the Second Temple Period through the Bar Kokhba Revolt* (Warminster: Aris & Phillips, Jerusalem: Israel Exploration Society, 1982), cat. nos. 104–17, 123,127–35.

17. Ibid., cat. no. 102.

18. Ibid., cat. nos. 86–91.

19. Ibid., cat. no. 92.

20. Ibid., cat. no. 231.

21. This object was discovered in a underground hiding complex of the Bar Kokhba Revolt at Horvat Alim, 2.5 km. north of Beth Guvrin in the Judean Shephelah. See A. Kloner, "Lead Weights of Bar Kochba's Administration," *Israel Exploration Journal*, 40 (1990), 58–67.

22. Y. Tsafrir, *Eretz Israel from the Destruction of the Second Temple to the Muslim Conquest, Art and Archaeology* (Jerusalem: Yad Izhak Ben-Zvi Press, 1984), 143–64, in Hebrew.

23. See Z. Weiss, *The Jewish Cemetery in the Galilee in the Period of the Mishnah and the Talmud: An Archaeological Investigation with the Aid of Talmudic Sources* (M.A. thesis, Jerusalem: Hebrew University, 1989), 5.

24. N. Avigad, *Beth She'arim* (New Brunswick: Rutgers University Press, 1976), 3: 42–65. See T. Rajak, "The Rabbinic Dead and the Diaspora Dead at Beth She'arim," *The Talmud Yerushalmi and Graeco–Roman Culture I*, ed. P. Schäfer (Tübingen: Mohr Siebeck, 1998), 349–66, for an excellent and strongly revisionist reassessment of scholarly interpretation of Beth She'arim.

25. Goodenough, *Jewish Symbols*, 1: 97–8; B. Mazar, *Beth She'arim* (New Brunswick: Rutgers University Press, 1973), 1: 52. Much of the most interesting material is assembled by D. Kraemer, *Meanings of Death in Rabbinic Judaism* (London: Routledge, 2000), 48–71.

26. On the Leda sarcophagus, see M. Avi-Yonah, "The Leda Sarcophagus from Beth She'arim," *Scripta Hierosolymitana*, 24 (1972), 9–21. According to Greek mythology, Leda subsequently produced an egg containing Helen (wife of Menelaus of Sparta, whose abduction led to the Trojan War) and Polydeuces. On Leda, see K. Dowden, "Leda," *OCD*, 837.

27. M. L. Fischer, *Marble Studies: Roman Palestine and the Marble Trade* (Konstanz: UVK, Universitätsverlag Konstanz, 1998), 206–7.

28. Avi-Yonah, "The Leda Sarcophagus," 21, suggests that the defacement of this piece was carried out by Muslims. The proof that he brings, that "harm was caused principally to the faces of the figures, and was carried out crudely," does not support his contention. He apparently ascribes "the careful hammering away of the offending parts in the Galilean synagogue reliefs" to Jews. This aesthetic criterion, in which the defacement of a sarcophagus is compared to the main portals of public buildings, has no basis.

29. Fischer, *Marble Studies*, 207.

30. Cf. Goodenough, *Jewish Symbols*, 1: 90; S. J. D. Cohen ("Epigraphical Rabbis," *Jewish Quarterly Review*, 72 [1981], 1–17); and Stuart Miller's critique of Cohen's approach ("The Rabbis and the Non-Existent Monolithic Synagogue," *JCP*, 61–4).

31. I borrow this locution from N. L. Kleebatt's exhibition catalog, *Too Jewish?: Challenging Traditional Identities* (New York: Jewish Museum; New Brunswick, N.J.: Rutgers University Press, 1996).

32. Sadly, this catacomb (like so many other important sites of the same period) has never been properly published. See Goodenough, *Jewish Symbols*, 1: 101; Avigad and Mazar, Beth She'arin, 244.

33. N. Avigad and B. Mazar, "Beth She'arim," *NEAEHL*, 1: 242–4.

34. See S. Miller, "The Rabbis and the Non-Existent Monolithic Synagogue," 64.

35. Hachlili, *AJAALI*, 161–6.

36. V. Tzaferis, "The Ancient Synagogue at Ma'oz Hayyim," *Israel Exploration Journal*, 32 (1982); Hachlili, *AJAALI*, 160.

37. M. Avi-Yonah, "Une École de Mosaïque à Gaza au sixième siècle," *La mosaïque gréco-romaine II: [actes du] IIe Colloque international pour l'étude de la mosaïque antique, Vienne, 30 août–4 septembre 1971*, eds. H. Stern and M. Le Glay (Paris: A. & J. Picard, 1975), 377–83; A. Ovadiah, "The Mosaic Workshop of Gaza

in Christian Antiquity," *ASHAAD*, 2: 367–72; Naveh, *On Stone and Mosaic*, 92–3.

38. G. Foerster, "Decorated Marble Chancel Screens in the Sixth Century Synagogues in Palestine and Their Relation to Christian Art and Architecture," *Actes du XIe Congres International d'Archeologie Chretienne* (Rome: Ecole Francaise, 1989), 2: 1809–20; J. Branham, "Sacred Space under Erasure in Ancient Synagogues and Churches," *Art Bulletin*, 74 (1992), 379.

39. A. Kloner, "The Synagogues of Horvat Rimmon," *Ancient Synagogues in Israel*, ed. R. Hachlili (London: BAR International, 1989), 44. On the broadhouse form, see E. M. Meyers, "The Ancient Synagogue of Khirbet Shema," *Perspectives in Jewish Literature*, 5 (1973), 33.

40. Note the comments of S. Gutman, Z. Yeivin, and E. Netzer, "Excavations in the Synagogue of Horvat Susiya," *ASR*, 124.

41. D. Bahat, "A Synagogue at Beth-Shean," *ASR* 82–5; Fine, *This Holy Place*, 100–1.

42. M. Dothan, *Hammath Tiberias: Early Synagogues* (Jerusalem: Israel Exploration Society, 1983).

43. This relationship was first suggested by Baumgarten, "Art in the Synagogue," 81. See Levine, *The Rabbinic Class of Roman Palestine*, 178; Goodman, "The Roman Identity of Roman Jews," *96.

44. See Eusebius's panegyric to Paulinus, Bishop of Tyre, in which he describes the newly built church of Tyre in c. 317 C.E. (*Historia Ecclesiastica* 10.4.36–46, in L. M. White, *The Social Origins of Christian Architecture* [Valley Forge, Penn.: Trinity Press International, 1997], 2: 94–9).

45. Z. Weiss, "The Synagogue at Hamat Tiberias (Stratum II)," *Eretz-Israel*, 23 (1992), 320–6, in Hebrew.

46. M. Dothan, "The Representation of Helios in the Mosaic of Hammath-Tiberias," *Atti del Convegno Internazionale sul Tema: Tardo Antico e Alto Medioevo. La Forma Artistica nel Passaggio dall'Antichità al Medioevo (Roma, 4–7 aprile 1967)* (Rome, Accademia nazionale dei Lincei, 1968), 99–104; idem, *Hammath Tiberias, Early Synagogues*, 41.

47. Baumgarten, "Art in the Synagogue," 80–1.

48. Goodman, "The Roman Identity of Roman Jews," *95.

49. Sukenik, *The Ancient Synagogue of Beth Alpha*, 36; S. Miller, "'Epigraphical' Rabbis, Helios, and Psalm 19: Were the Synagogues of Archaeology and the Synagogues of the Sages One and the Same," *Jewish Quarterly Review*, 94, no. 1 (2004), 27–76.

50. For a recent discussion of this iconography, see R. Jensen, *Understanding Early Christian Art* (London: Routledge, 2000), 41–4. In a turnabout that refers opaquely to scholarship

on the Hammath Tiberias zodiac, N. Hannestad ("How did Rising Christianity Cope with Pagan Sculpture?" *East and West: Modes of Communication. Proceedings of the First Plenary Conference at Merida*, eds. E. Chrysos and I. Wood [Leiden: E. J. Brill, 1999], 173, 179–80), wrote:

Most Christians . . . – and particularly for the upper class – seem to have had a rather relaxed attitude to the pagan past. Apparently many were even proud of their cultural heritage: the commissioned traditionally decorated silverware; their homes were embellished with pagan motifs. . . . In this respect they behaved no differently from their pagan fellow citizens – or Jews, when these belonged to the urban Hellenized society.

51. Dothan, *Hammath Tiberias: Early Synagogues*, 33, pl. 9. no. 2.

52. Fine, *This Holy Place*, 25–94.

53. Weiss and Netzer, *Promise and Redemption*, 26–9.

54. Sukenik, *The Ancient Synagogue of Beth Alpha*.

55. The earliest complete manuscript of the Mishnah, the Kaufmann manuscript, for example, was written "in the tenth or at the latest eleventh century." See M. Krupp, "Manuscripts of the Mishnah," *The Literature of the Sages, First Part*, ed. S. Safrai (Assen/Maastricht: Van Gorgum and Philadelphia: Fortress Press, 1987), 253, 266.

56. On Beth Alpha: Sukenik, *The Ancient Synagogue of Beth Alpha*. On Rehov: F. Vitto, "The Synagogue at Rehob." *ASR* 90–4; J. Sussman, "A Halakhic Inscription from the Beth-Shean Valley," *Tarbiz* 43 (1973–4), 88–158; 44 (1974–5), 193–5, in Hebrew. For a regional approach to these mosaics, see M. J. S. Chiat, "Synagogues and Churches in Byzantine Beit She'an," *Jewish Art*, 7 (1980), 6–24.

57. F. Vitto, "The Interior Decoration of Palestinian Churches and Synagogues," *Byzantinische Forschungen*, 21 (1995), 295. For evidence of wall painting at Rehov and in other Palestinian synagogues, see pp. 294–9. M. Avi-Yonah's assessment that ". . . mais il est peu probable qu'elles aient porté des images bibliques" is an argument from silence ("La Mosaïque juive et la Mosaïque classique," *Colloques internationaux: La Mosaïque gréco-romaine, Paris 1963* [Paris,1965], 330).

58. Hachlili, *AJAALI*, 325, Fig. 13.

59. L. I. Levine, "The Revolutionary Effects of Archaeology on the Study of Jewish History: The Case of the Ancient Synagogue," *The Archaeology of Israel: Constructing the Past, Interpreting the Present*, eds. N. A. Silberman and D. Small (Sheffield: Sheffield Academic Press, 1997), 186–9.

60. On the House of Leontis: N. Zori, "The House of Kyrios Leontis at Beth Shean," *Israel*

Exploration Journal, 16 (1973),123–34; Bahat, "A Synagogue at Beth-Shean"; Hachlili, *AJAALI*, 301, 312–14; Fine, *This Holy Place*, 101–2.

61. This, of course, was the case in early Islam, where mosque decoration tended to be noniconic at the same time that palace decoration was opulent. Good examples of this are the Mosque of Omar in Jerusalem and the so-called Hisham Palace (Khirbet al-Mafjar) near Jericho. Note M. W. Merrony's observation regarding the use of inhabited scrolls and mythological imagery in late antique Palestinian Christian mosaics ("The Reconciliation of Paganism and Christianity in the Early Byzantine Mosaic Pavements of Arabia and Palestine," *Liber Annuus*, 48 [1998], 442): "a significant trend . . . appears to be the dichotomy between *villae* on the one hand, which frequently exhibited mythological iconography, and ecclesiastical buildings on the other, which often contained inhabited vine rinceau pavements." Cf. Z. Safrai, "The House of Leontis," *The Image of The Judaeo-Christians in Ancient Jewish and Christian Literature,"* eds. P. J. Tomson and D. Lambers-Petry (Tübingen: Mohr Siebeck, 2003), 245–66.

62. Hachlili, *AJAALI*, 143–66.

63. See below, 106–107.

64. On lions in synagogue contexts, Hachlili, *AJAALI*, 321–8.

65. On the Ein Gedi synagogue, see D. Barag, Y. Porat, and E. Netzer, "The Synagogue at En-Gedi," *ASR*, 116–19; Tsafrir, *Eretz Israel from the Destruction of the Second Temple*, 431.

66. On the Jericho synagogue, see D.C. Baramki, "An Early Byzantine Synagogue near Tell es Sultan," *Quarterly of the Department of Antiquities of Palestine*, 6 (1936), 73–7; "The Synagogue at Tell Es-Sultan," *NEAEHL*, 2: 695–6.

67. H. Eshel, "'Ki-gon . . . Yeriho le-Na'aran," 84–5.

68. L. Roth-Gerson, *Greek Inscriptions in the Synagogues in Eretz-Israel* (Jerusalem: Yad Izhak Ben-Zvi, 1987), 61–4, in Hebrew.

69. Dothan, *Hammath Tiberias: Early Synagogues*, 67; idem, *Hammath Tiberias: Late Synagogues* (Jerusalem: Israel Exploration Society, 2000), 12.

70. Dothan, *Hammath Tiberias: Late Synagogues*, 41, 51, 147.

71. Schick, *Christian Communities*, 207; see also 202–4, 207–10. Sukenik, *The Ancient Synagogue of Beth Alpha*, 55, states without value judgment that the synagogue at Na'aran was "defaced by the Jews themselves." In note 1, he dates this defacement to "the close of the Byzantine period and perhaps even to the beginning of the Arab period." Sukenik maintains this approach in *Ancient Synagogues in Palestine and Greece*, 61–5, where he suggests that

... a contributing factor in the final banishment of human and animal motives from the synagogues of Palestine may have been the influence of Monophysite Christians of the Near East at about this time and which has likewise left traces in broken church mosaics; the conquest of the country by the Arabs, bearers of a religion unequivocally hostile to the representation of living beings, could only have intensified this environmental suggestion (p. 65).

72. See Avi-Yonah, *Oriental Art in Roman Palestine*, 42; Schick, *Christian Communities*, 193.

73. On Meroth: Z. Ilan and I. Damati, *Meroth: The Ancient Jewish Village* (Tel Aviv: Society for the Preservation of Nature in Israel, 1987), 53–8, in Hebrew; Z. Ilan, "The Synagogue and Study House at Meroth," *ASHAAD*, 1: 256–88.

74. Ilan and Damati, *Meroth*, 76. These authors tentatively suggest that bas reliefs on the round arch above the lintel of the main southern entrance of the building represent the signs of the zodiac. The state of preservation, however, makes this identification uncertain. The excavators identify evidence of iconographic defacement on these carvings (p. 47).

75. Hachlili, *AJAALI*, 206–16. The dating of the "Galilean-type" synagogues is again the subject of considerable scholarly discussion. See p. 222, n. 74 above.

76. On Baram: Avigad, "Bar'am," *NEAEHL*, 147–9; S. Fine, "Bar'am," *OENEA*, 1: 276. Nevertheless, Tsafrir, *Eretz Israel from the Destruction of the Second Temple*, 180, suggests that this iconoclasm at Baram "apparently dates to the end of the first quarter of the eighth century" (my translation).

77. Gutman, Yeivin, and Netzer, "The Synagogue at En-Gedi," 123, 126; S. Fine, "Susiya," *OENEA*, 5: 110–11.

78. Gutman, Yeivin, and Netzer, "The Synagogue at En-Gedi," 126, 128.

79. Z. Yeivin, "Khirbet Susiya, the Bima, and Synagogue Ornamentation," *Ancient Synagogues in Israel*, ed. R. Hachlili (London: BAR International, 1989), 93–100; Foerster, "Decorated Marble Chancel Screens," 2: 1818–20.

80. Hachlili, *AJAALI*, 187–8; S. Fine, ed., *Sacred Realm: The Emergence of the Synagogue* (New York: Oxford University Press and Yeshiva University Museum. 1996), 168, pl. xxxixb. On iconographic damage to church chancel screens, see Schick, *Christian Communities*, 201.

81. I use the phrase "rabbinic community" to refer to the rabbis, their immediate social circles, and those who took them and their religious approach into account. This is a broader term than "rabbinic class" used by L. I. Levine (*The Rabbinic Class*). J. Lightstone's "rabbinic guild" is difficult, as it resonates too closely with medieval guild structures. See J. Lightstone, *Mishnah and the Social Formation of the Early Rabbinic Guild: A Socio-Rhetorical Approach* (Waterloo, Ont.: Wilfrid Laurier University Press, 2000).

82. C. N. Bialik, *Kol Kitve C. N. Bialik* (Tel Aviv: Dvir, 1938), 258–60, in Hebrew.

83. E. Ben Yehuda, *A Complete Dictionary of Ancient and Modern Hebrew* (Jerusalem: Makor, 1980), 1: 286, in Hebrew.

84. Jastrow, *Dictionary of the Targumim*, 27.

85. *NJPS*. Note that popularly used printed editions of Targum Onkelos translate *u-ve-ḥaroshet even* in Exodus 31: 5 and punctuate it as *u-ve-omanut even*. Compare A. Sperber, ed., *The Bible in Aramaic* (Leiden: E. J. Brill, 1992), 1: 145, *u-ve-umanut*.

86. Naveh, *On Stone and Mosaic*, 78–9; Bahat, "A Synagogue at Beth-Shean." On the identification of this building as a study house, see Fine, *This Holy Place*, 100–1.

87. This term was used to describe fine craftsmanship in medieval Hebrew, and applied to fine arts during the nineteenth century. See Holtzman, *Aesthetics and National Revival*. This phrase is still occasionally used to describe fine craftsmanship. See, for example, Z. Yeivin, *The Synagogue of Korazim: The 1962–1964, 1980–1987 Excavations* (Jerusalem: Israel Antiquities Authority, 2000), 6, in Hebrew.

88. *Neophyti 1: Targum Palestinense Ms de la Biblioteca Vaticana*, ed. A. Díez Macho (Madrid and Barcelona: Consejo Superior de Investigaciones Cientificas, 1968).

89. J. J. Pollitt, "Art, Ancient Attitudes to," *The Oxford Classical Dictionary*, eds. S. Hornblower and A. Spawforth, 3rd ed. (New York: Oxford University Press, 1996), 178.

90. Roth-Gerson, *Greek Inscriptions in the Synagogues in Eretz-Israel*, 29–32, in Hebrew. On Jewish crafts in Greek inscriptions: 164–5.

91. See S. M. Paul, "Jerusalem – City of Gold," *Israel Exploration Journal*, 17 (1967), 257–63; idem, "Jerusalem of Gold – A Song and an Ancient Crown," *Biblical Archaeology Review* 3, no. 4 (1977), 38–40. See also S. Fine, "Archaeology and The interpretation of Rabbinic Literature: Some Thoughts," ed. M. Kraus, *How Should Late Antique Rabbinic Literature Be Read in The Modern World: Hermeneutical Limits and Possibilities*, forthcoming. On the use of Roman jewelry fashions in rabbinic culture, see U. Zevulun and Y. Olenik, *Form and Function in the Talmudic Period* (Tel Aviv: Haaretz Museum, 1979), 100–1, in Hebrew.

92. See *y. Shabbat* 6:1, 7d, *Sotah* 9:16, 24c; *b. Shabbat* 59a–b, *Nedarim* 50a.

93. *m. Shabbat* 6: 1. See Zevulun and Olenik, *Form and Function in the Talmudic Period*, 100–1.

94. *m. Kelim* 11:8.

95. *m. Sotah* 1:6. See also *b. Qiddushin* 48a.

96. M. D. Herr, "Hellenistic Influences in the Jewish City in Eretz Israel in the Fourth and Sixth Centuries C.E.," *Cathedra*, 8 (1978), 90–4, in Hebrew.

97. J. N. Epstein, "Additional Fragments of the Jerushalmi," *Tarbiz*, 3, no. 1 (1931), 20, in Hebrew.

98. See Baumgarten, "Art in the Synagogue," 76.

99. See also *y. Peah* 8: 9, 21b.

100. C. Albeck, *Introduction to the Talmud, Babli and Yerushalmi* (Jerusalem: Mosad Bialik and Tel Aviv: Dvir, 1969), 163–4, in Hebrew; J. Schwartz, *Lod (Lydda), Israel: From its Origins through the Byzantine Period, 5600 B.C.E.–640 C.E.* (Oxford: Tempus Reparatum, 1991), 118, n. 97.

101. B. Rosenfeld, *Lod and Its Sages in the Period of the Mishnah and the Talmud* (Jerusalem: Yad Izhak Ben-Zvi Press, 1997), in Hebrew.

102. C. Dauphin, "Mosaic Pavements as an Index of Prosperity and Fashion," *Levant*, 12 (1980), 125.

103. Albeck, *Introduction to the Talmud*, 384–5; Baumgarten, "Art in the Synagogue," 79.

104. Sokoloff, *A Dictionary of Jewish Palestinian Aramaic*, 369.

105. D. Urman, "The House of Assembly and the House of Study: Are They One and the Same?" *ASHAAD*, 1: 250.

106. On the *Sidra Rabba*, see most recently Y. Z. Eliav, *Sites, Institutions and Daily Life in Tiberias During the Talmudic Period* (Tiberias: Merkaz le-Ḥeker Teveria, 1995), 53–4, in Hebrew.

107. *y. Sanhedrin* 10: 1, 28a.

108. *Midrash Tanḥuma* (Warsaw: Lewin-Epstein, 1910) *be-Ḥukotai* 3, 4; ed. S. Buber (Vilna: Romm, 1913), *be-Ḥukotai* 2: 110; Fine, *This Holy Place*, 93.

109. See sources collected by Z. Weiss, *The Jewish Cemetery in the Galilee*, 62–4, 89, n. 185.

110. *Sirah* 11–12. On craftsmen in rabbinic literature, see M. Ayali, *Workers and Craftsmen: Their Labor and Their Status in Rabbinic Literature* (Israel: Yad la-Talmud, 1987), in Hebrew.

111. *Mekhilta of Rabbi Simeon Bar Yoḥai*, *be-Shalaḥ* 15: 11, eds. J. N. Epstein and E. Z. Melammed (Jerusalem: Hillel Press, 1955), 93–4; Urbach, "The Rabbinical Laws," 237.

112. Réunion des musées nationaux et le département des Antiquités égyptiennes du Musée du Louvre, *Portraits de l'Egypte romaine: Paris, Musée du Louvre, 5 octobre 1998–4 janvier 1999* (Paris: Réunion des musées nationaux, 1998).

113. See the parallel to this text in the *Mekilta de-Rabbi Ishmael, Shirata* 8, ed. J. Z. Lauterbach (Philadelphia: Jewish Publication Society,

1976), 2: 65 and Urbach, "The Rabbinical Laws," 237.

114. Epstein, "Additional Fragments of the Jerushalmi," 20.

115. *Antiquities* 3.104–6; idem, 8. 76–8.

116. C. Houtmann, *Exodus* (Leuven: Peeters, 1993), 3:323, 355.

117. See, e.g., Exodus 37:1.

118. See also 1 Kings 14:26; 2 Kings 24:13, 25:16; 1 Chronicles 18:8, 6:13, 7:7, 12:9.

119. *Baraita de-Melekhet ha-Mishkan*, Ch. 9–10, and the apparatus to 10:1.

120. *Seder Olam Rabba*, ed. B. Ratner (Jerusalem: H. Vagshal, 1988), 14, p. 61 and note 10.

121. See, e.g., *Genesis Rabba* 97:8 (eds. J. Theodor, Ch. Albeck [Jerusalem: Wahrmann, 1965], 1209), which mentions "Bezalel, who made the holy Tabernacle."

122. Sperber, *The Bible in Aramaic*, 4a: 136.

123. Pp 66–68 above.

124. *Tanḥuma*, va-Yaqhel 4–5; *Tanḥuma*, ed. Buber, va-Yaqhel 4, 2:121–3.

125. *Exodus Rabba*, va-Yaqhel 48, 3. See also *Yalkut Shemoni* (Warsaw: Y. Goldman, 1877), va-Yaqhel, no. 411.

126. be-Ha'alotkha 3; ed. Buber, be-Ha'alotkha 4; Houtman, *Exodus* 3: 403.

127. *Tanḥuma*, be-Ha'alotkha 6; *Tanḥuma*, ed. Buber, be-Ha'alotkha 11; *Numbers Rabba* 15: 10. On Bezalel in rabbinic sources, see L. Ginzberg, *Legends of the Jews*, 3: 154–61, especially note 338.

128. B. Jacob, *The Second Book of the Bible: Exodus*, tr. W. Jacob (Hoboken: Ktav, 1992), 763, 781, makes this point about the Pentateuchal descriptions of the Tabernacle. See C. Meyers, *The Tabernacle Menorah: A Synthetic Study of a Symbol from the Biblical Cult* (Missoula: Scholars Press, 1976) and compare to R. Hachlili, *The Menorah, The Ancient Seven-Armed Candelabrum: Origin, Form and Significance* (Leiden, Boston, Koln: E. J. Brill, 2001), 7–40.

129. *The Liturgical Poetry of Rabbi Yannai*, ed. Z. M. Rabinovitz (Jerusalem: Bialik Institute, 1985–87), 1:330. *Exodus Rabba* 35:3; *Midrash Tanḥuma Naso* 13, *Tanḥuma*, ed. Buber, Naso 20. See J. Yahalom, "Synagogue Inscriptions in Palestine-A Stylistic Classification," *Immanuel* 10 (1980), 53.

130. Roth-Gerson, *Greek Inscriptions*, 29–30, 33.

131. Ibid., 58–60.

132. See S. Safrai, "The Attitude of the Aggadah to the Halacha," *Dor Le-Dor: From the End of Biblical Times Up to the Redaction of the Talmud, Studies in Honor of Joshua Efron*, eds. A. Kasher and A. Oppenheimer (Jerusalem: Bialik Institute and Tel Aviv: Chaim Rosenberg School of Jewish Studies, 1995), 215–34, in Hebrew.

133. *t. Sukkah* 4:6.

134. Following the Erfurt manuscript.

135. See G. Alon, *Jews in Their Land, The Jews in Their Land in the Talmudic Age*, tr. G. Levi (Cambridge, Mass. and London: Harvard University Press, 1989), 170; Kasher, *Jews in Hellenistic and Roman Egypt*, 350, n. 28; Ayali, *Workers and Craftsmen*, 1987, 118.

136. See, *y. Sukkah* 5:1, 55a-b; S. Lieberman, *Tosefta Ki-fshutah: A Comprehensive Commentary on the Tosefta* (New York: Jewish Theological Seminary, 1955–88), 4: 889–92, in Hebrew. Kasher, *Jews in Hellenistic and Roman Egypt*, 350–1, compares the versions and scholarly discussion of this tradition.

137. *y. Ta'anit* 3:11, 66d; Josephus, *Jewish War*, 5.190; *Antiquities* 15.396, 411–16. On basilicas in rabbinic literature, see H. L. Gordon, "The Basilica and the Stoa in Early Rabbinical Literature," *Art Bulletin* 13 (1931), 353–75.

138. *b. Berakhot* 33b; *b. Pesaḥim* 13b.

139. *Plutarch's Lives*, Anthony 54, 3. See E. Honigmann, "Thrónos," *Paulys realencyclopädie der classischen Altertumswissenschaft*, 2nd series (Stuttgart: J. B. Metzler, 1936), 11: 613–18.

140. E.g., the Virgin on the throne in S. Apollinare Nuovo and the throne of the cross in the Arian Baptistry, both in Ravenna.

141. *Genesis Rabba*, eds. Theodor and Albeck 91.

142. A city on the Syrian coast. See P. Neaman, *Encyclopedia of Talmudical Geography* (Tel Aviv: Joshua Chachik Publishing House, 1971–2), 2: 92–6, in Hebrew; Roth-Gerson, *Greek Inscriptions*, 163–4.

143. I have intentionally chosen versions that mention gold and silver implements, which only serve to emphasize the notions of wealth implicit in this text. See the version cited by Theodor and Albeck to *Genesis Rabba* 11:4, p. 91.

144. *b. Shabbat* 119a. According to the Babylonian version, the sixteen servants sing the Biblical verse.

145. N. J. Richardson, "Coinage, Greek," *The Oxford Classical Dictionary*, 3rd ed., eds. S. Hornblower and A. Spawforth (New York: Oxford University Press, 1996), 356.

146. R. Rabbinowicz, *Diqduqei Sofrim* (New York: M. P. Press, 1976), ad. loc., note ב.

147. Ibid.

148. The most important discussions are M. A. Levy, *Geschichte der Jüdischen Münzen* (Leipzig: Nies'che Buchdruckerei [Carl B. Lorck], 1862), 160 and Blidstein, *Rabbinic Legislation on Idolatry*, 247. See now G. Bohak, "The Hellenization of Biblical History in Rabbinic Literature," *Talmud Yerushalmi and Graeco-Roman Culture*, ed. P. Schäfer (Tübingen: Mohr Siebeck, 1998), 3: 11–14, who reached conclusions similar to my own regarding these texts.

149. Cf. Feldman, *Josephus' Interpretation of the Bible*, 234–7, especially note 29.

150. Y. Meshorer, *Coins of Eretz-Israel and the Decapolis in the Roman Period* (Jerusalem: Israel Museum, 1985), nos. 172, 178, 201, 237, 243, 264, in Hebrew.

151. Meshorer, *City-Coins of Eretz-Israel*, no. 172.

152. *y. Maaser Sheni* 1:6, 52d; *b. Baba Qama* 97b. See D. Sperber, *Roman Palestine, 200–400: Money and Prices*, 2nd ed. (Ramat-Gan: Bar-Ilan University Press, 1991), 137.

153. This point is made by Bohak, "The Hellenization of Biblical History," 12, n. 35. See Ezra 2:69, Nehemiah 7:69–71. See F. Brown, S. R. Driver, and C. A. Briggs, *A Hebrew and English Lexicon of the Old Testament* (Oxford: Oxford University Press, 1972), 204. Projection of Roman-era coinage into Biblical times is common in rabbinic literature. *Targum Pseudo-Jonathan* to Genesis 24:22 projects this coin into another Biblical context, supporting Bohak's conjecture.

154. See *m. Sheqalim* 2:1; Jastrow, *Dictionary of the Targumim*, 324; Lieberman, *Tosefta Ki-fshutah* 4:679.

155. For a possible example of rabbinic cognizance of the iconography of Roman coins, see S. Stern, "Dissonance and Misunderstanding in Jewish–Roman Relations," *Jews and Greeks in the Roman World*, ed. M. Goodman (Oxford: Clarendon Press, 1998), 242–5.

156. See also *Targum Rishon* to Esther 9:4.

157. See the comments of Theodor and Albeck, 374–5.

158. This verse refers to Joseph, from whom Joshua, being of the tribe of Ephraim, was descended.

159. Esther 4:1, 8:15.

160. A. Kohut, *Aruch Completum* (New York: Pardes, 1955), 5: 175, in Hebrew.

161. Meshorer, *Ancient Jewish Coinage*, 1: 63–6.

162. Meshorer, *City–Coins*, no. 2; S. Stern, "Dissonance and Misunderstanding," 242–5.

163. M. Price and B. Trell, *Coins and Their Cities* (London: Vecci, 1977), Figs. 499–522.

164. Ibid., Fig. 506. See also Fig. 122.

165. See Blidstein, *Rabbinic Legislation on Idolatry*, 246–447; "The *Tannaim* and Plastic Art," 23.

166. Numbers 35:6–15.

167. Ed. Buber (New York: Om, 1947), Psalm 25.

168. For possible identifications of this Amora, see Albeck, *Introduction to the Talmud*, 352, 385, in Hebrew.

169. See Kohut, *Aruch Completum*, 2: 184–5.

170. G. Blidstein, "The Tannaim and Plastic Art," 23.

171. See, e.g., *Leviticus Rabba* 19. 6 (ed. M. Margulies [New York and Jerusalem: Jewish

Theological Seminary of America, 1993]), 1: 436; *y. Sheqalim* 6, 50a; *b. Ta'anit* 25a. For a related phenomenon, see H. Fox, "'As if with a Finger' — The Text History of an Expression Avoiding Anthropomorphism," *Tarbiz*, 49 (1980), 278–91, in Hebrew. According to *m. Avodah Zarah* 3: 2, possession of a sculpted hand should also be forbidden. This text may refer to a very specific artifact, however, and not to all hands.

172. See C. H. Kraeling, *The Synagogue*, with contributions by C. C. Torrey, C. B. Welles, and B. Geiger (New Haven: Yale University Press, 1956), 57; Sukenik, *The Ancient Synagogue of Beth Alpha*, 40–2; Foerster, "Decorated Marble Chancel Screens," 1818–20.

173. See, e.g., *y. Avodah Zarah* 3:1, 42b–c.

174. *The Two Targums of Esther*, ed. and tr. B. Grossfeld (Collegeville, Minn.: Liturgical Press, 1991), 19–21, 23–4, surveys scholarly opinion on the date of *Targum Sheni*. He suggests the early seventh century. See Blau, "Early Christian Archaeology," 188–9.

175. *The Targum Sheni to the Book of Esther: A Critical Edition Based on MS. Sassoon 282 with Critical Apparatus*, ed. B. Grossfeld (Brooklyn: Sepher-Herman, 1994), Ch. 1. My translation generally follows Grossfeld, *The Two Targums of Esther*, 107–11. See Ginzberg, *Legends of the Jews*, 4: 159ff; Kraeling, *The Synagogue*, 157–9.

176. Tr. Grossfeld, *The Two Targums of Esther*, 111.

177. Ibid., 112.

178. G. Brett, "The Automata in the Byzantine Throne of Solomon," *Speculum*, 29, no. 3 (1954), 477–87 and especially E. Ville-Patlagean, "Une Image de Salomon en Basileus Byzantin," *Revue des Études Juives*, 121 nos. 1–2 (1962), 9–33.

179. Kraeling, *The Synagogue*, 88–90.

180. Ibid., 158.

181. *Genesis Rabba* 68:12 and the discussion of Theodor and Albeck, 788; ibid, 82:2, p. 978; *b.* Hullin 91b; *Targum Neofiti, Fragment Targum, Targum Pseudo-Jonathan* to Genesis 28:12. See E. Wolfson, *Along the Path: Studies in Kabbalistic Myth, Symbolism, and Hermeneutics* (Albany: State University of New York Press, 1995), 4–6; S. Friedman, "Graven Images," *Graven Images: A Journal of Culture, Law and the Sacred*, 1 (1994), 233–4.

182. Ed. B. Mandelbaum (New York: Jewish Theological Seminary, 1962), 1: 6, 12.

183. Tr. Grossfeld, *The Two Targums of Esther*, 111.

184. N. Avigad and B. Mazar, "Beth She'arim," *NEAEHL*, 1: 236–48.

185. R. Hachlili, *AJAALI*, 1988; 278, 283, 321–40.

186. Z. Yeivin, *The Synagogue of Korazim*, 53–4, 56.

187. Z. Yeivin, "Reconstruction of the Southern Interior Wall of the Khorazin Synagogue," *Eretz-Israel* 18 (1985), 274–5; idem, "Ancient Chorazin Comes Back to Life," 32–3; idem, *The Synagogue of Korazim*, 62–3.

188. R. Hachlili, *AJAALI*, 294–5 and pl. 26.

189. Ilan and Damati, *Meroth: The Ancient Jewish Village*, 78–80.

190. K. Weitzmann, ed., *Age of Spirituality*, 396–669.

191. N. N. May, "The Decor of the Korazim Synagogue Reliefs," *The Synagogue of Korazim: The 1962–1964, 1980–1987 Excavations*, ed. Z. Yeivin (Jerusalem: Israel Antiquities Authority, 2000), 100–17 and English summary, *52–*53. I have conducted informal surveys of American Jews and Christians over many years, and my findings bear out.

192. Hachlili, *AJAALI*, 318.

193. Hachlili, *AJAALI*, 202; May, "The Decor of the Korazim Synagogue Reliefs," 129–30.

194. *Throne and Amphitheater of King Solomon*, ed. A. Jellenek, *Bet ha-Midrasch*, (Jerusalem: Wahrmann, 1967), 6: 34–9.

195. The excavators of the Meroth synagogue suggest that the arch above the main portal of the synagogue was decorated with the signs of the zodiac. See Ilan and Damati, *Meroth*, 47–8, and the discussion there.

196. A. D. York, "The Targum in the Synagogue and School," *Journal for the Study of Judaism*, 10, no. 1 (1979), 74–86; S. Fine, "'Their Faces Shine with the Brightness of the Firmament': Study Houses and Synagogues in the *Targumim* to the Pentateuch," ed. F. W. Knobloch, *Biblical Translation in Context* (Bethesda, Md.: University Press of Maryland, 2002), 63–92.

197. See *Antiquities* 8.194–5.

198. For a survey of Christian art in the Holy Land, see Y. Israeli and D. Mevorah, *Cradle of Christianity* (Jerusalem: Israel Museum, 2000).

199. In *Narratio de structura temple S. Sophiae* 27. R. J. Mainstone, *Hagia Sophia: Architecture, Structure, and Liturgy of Justinian's Great Church* (New York: Thames and Hudson, 1988), 147–8, notes that an inscription in the nave of the Church of St. Polyeuctos in Constantanople (built 523–527) makes a similar claim. A Jewish response to the Hagia Sophia from the reign of Basil I (867–886) is preserved in *Megillat Ahimaaz: The Chronicle of Ahimaaz with a Collection of Poems from Byzantine Southern Italy*, ed. B. Klar (Jerusalem: Sifrei Tarshish, 1974), in Hebrew, 18, lines 3–17, and Klar's comments, 143–4. See also *Targum Sheni* on Esther 9: 15.

200. *Talmudic Encyclopedia*, "Hiddur Mitsvah," ed. S. Y. Zevin (Jerusalem: Talmudic Encyclopedia Publishing, 1957), 8:271–84, in Hebrew.

201. See J. Goldin, *The Song at the Sea* (Philadephia: Jewish Publication Society, 1990), 113.

202. Jastrow, *Dictionary of the Targumim*, 865.

203. *Shirata* 3, ed. Lauterbach, 2:25.

204. *b. Nazir* 2b. See the discussion of versions and manuscript traditions in E. Z. Melamed, *Halachic Midrashim of the Tannaim in the Babylonian Talmud* (Jerusalem: Magnes Press, 1988), 110, no. 83, in Hebrew.

205. *m. Kelim* 28:4.

206. *t. Kelim, Baba Metsia* 1:13 and parallels.

207. *Sofrim* 1:8 and parallels discussed by J. P. Siegel, "The Alexandrians in Jerusalem and Their Torah Scroll with Gold Tetragrammata," *Israel Exploration Journal*, 22 (1972), 39.

208. E. Tov, *Textual Criticism of the Hebrew Bible* (Minneapolis: Fortress Press, Assen/Maastricht, Van Gorcum, 1992), 220.

209. S. Fine, "'The Torah that Moses Commanded Us': Scripture and Authority in Rabbinic Judaism," *Review & Expositor*, 95, no. 4 (1998), 523–32.

210. *m. Rosh ha-Shanah* 3:3–4; *t. Rosh ha-Shanah* 2: 4, and Lieberman, *Tosefta Ki-fshutah*, ad. loc.

211. *m. Sukkah* 3:8, *t. Sukkah* 2:10, and Lieberman, *Tosefta Ki-fshutah*, ad. loc.

212. *y. Megillah* 1:11, 71d; 4:1, 75c; *b. Shabbat* 28b, 62a, 79b; *b. Nedarim* 37b; *Menahot* 32a–b, 35a–b.

213. For discussion of *minim* and the relevant bibliography, see my "A Cosmopolitan 'Student of the Sages.'"

214. See Goldin, *The Song at the Sea*, 115; H. Orlinsky, ed., *Notes on the New Translation of the Torah* (Philadelphia: Jewish Publication Society of America, 1970), 170.

215. *b. Sukkah* 51b.

216. See, for example, the descriptions in *m. Middot*.

217. *Jewish War* 5.184–227; *Antiquities* 15. 380–425. These texts were discussed most recently by L. I. Levine, "Josephus' Description of the Jerusalem Temple: War, Antiquities and Other Sources," *Josephus and the History of the Greco–Roman Period: Essays in Memory of Morton Smith*, eds. F. Parente and J. Sievers (Leiden: E. J. Brill, 1994), 233–46.

218. Pliny, *Natural History* 5. 70 in M. Stern, ed. *GLAJJ*, 1: 469, 471; idem, "Jerusalem, the Most Famous of the Cities of the East (Pliny, *Natural History* V, 70), *Jerusalem in the Second Temple Period: Abraham Schalit Memorial Volume*, eds. A. Oppenheimer, U. Rappaport, and M. Stern (Jerusalem: Yad Izhak Ben-Zvi Press and Ministry of Defense, 1980), 257–70, in Hebrew.

219. Numbers 5:11–31. *m. Yoma* 3:9–10, *t. Kippurim* 2:3–4.

220. *m. Bikkurim* 3:8.

221. *m. Yoma* 3:9.

222. On Corinthian bronze, see D. M. Jacobson and M. P. Weitzman, "What Was Corinthian Bronze?" *American Journal of Archaeology*, 96, no. 2 (1992), 237–48.

223. Following the Kaufmann manuscript. See also *m. Middot* 1:4, 2:3, 6, *m. Sheqalim* 6:3, *m. Sotah* 1:5, *m. Nega'im* 14:8, *t. Kippurim* 2:4, and Lieberman, *Tosefta Ki-fshutah*, 4:760–1.

224. See L.I. Levine, *Jerusalem: Portrait of the City in the Second Temple Period (538 B.C.E.–70 C.E.)*, Philadelphia: Jewish Publication Society 2002), 210–11, 369–70.

225. *m. Yoma* 3:10, *t. Kippurim* 2:4.

226. *Rosh ha-Shanah* 24b, *Avodah Zarah* 43a; *Scolion to Megillat Taanit*, ms. Parma, Bibloteca Palatina, De Rossi 117, as cited by V. Noam, "The Miracle of the Cruse of Oil: Is it a Source for Clarifying the Attitude of the Sages to the Hasmoneans?," *Zion*, 67, no. 4 (2003), 385, 390–1, in Hebrew. See also *Pesiqta Rabbati* 2 (ed. R. Ulmer, *Pesiqta Rabbati: A Synoptic Edition of Pesiqta Rabbati Based Upon All Extant Manuscripts and the Editio Princeps* [Atlanta: Scholars Press, 1997], 13); D. Sperber, *Shipudei ha-Makabim: Mah Hem?*, Sinai, 54, nos. 4–5 (1968), 280–2.

227. See *b. Yoma* 69a; *Megillat Ta'anit, Versions, Interpretation, History*, ed. V. Noam (Jerusalem: Ben Zvi Institute Press, 2003), 46, 100–3, 262–5, in Hebrew.

228. *m. Menahot* 13:10; *y. Yoma* 6:3, 43c–d; *b. Menahot* 109a–110a; *Megillah* 10a.

229. *ba-Hodesh* 10, ed. Lauterbach 2:283.

230. Discussed in Fine, *This Holy Place*, 47–9.

231. Following the Vilna edition. See R. Rabbinowicz, *Diqduqei Sofrim*, ad loc.; *Avodah Zarah* 43a, *Menahot* 28b; *Midrash ha-Gadol to Exodus* 20:20, 2nd ed., ed. M. Margulies (Jerusalem: Mossad Harav Kook, 1967).

232. S. Krauss, *Griechische und lateinische Lehnwörter im Talmud, Midrasch und Targum* (Berlin: S. Calvary and Co., 1898–9), 44–5.

233. Following *b. Avodah Zarah*, Paris, Bibliotheque Nationale, Suppl. Heb. 1337.

234. Jewish attitudes have been discussed in some detail and with considerable nuance. My purpose here is simply to summarize attitudes toward idolatrous images among the rabbis, and not an exhaustive presentation of the sources.

235. On Antipas's palace, see above p. 114 stadium: *Jewish War* 2, 618; 3, 539; hot springs of Tiberias: *Jewish War* 2, 614; 4, 11; *Antiquities* 18, 36; *Life* 85. For an announcement of the discovery of the theater, see *Jerusalem Post*, "Roman Stadium Found in Tiberias," June 17, 2002, p. 4.

236. Hirschfeld, *A Guide to Antiquity Sites in Tiberias*, tr. E. Levin and I. Pommerantz (Jerusalem: Israel Antiquities Authority, 1992), 15–34.

237. Meshorer, *City Coins*, 34, no. 81.

238. *Panarion* 30.12, 2. See N. Belayche, *Iudaea-Palaestina: The Pagan Cults in Roman Palestine (Second to Fourth Century)* (Tübingen: Mohr Siebeck, 2001), 93. The evidence is surveyed by S. Schwartz, *Imperialism and Jewish Society*, 145–53.

239. On "hidden transcripts," see J. C. Scott, *Domination and the Arts of Resistance: Hidden Transcripts* (New Haven and London: Yale University Press, 1990). On the applicability of this model to Jews under Christian Rome, see S. Fine, "Non-Jews in the Synagogues of Palestine: Rabbinic and Archaeological Perspectives," *JCP*, 231–6.

240. I am reminded of the story of the Bar Kokhba Revolt preserved in *y. Hagigah* 2:1, 77b, in which two Jews carry a single load on the Sabbath in order to avoid a severe violation of the Sabbath. This circumlocution went right past the Romans, until the "hidden transcript" was revealed by their primary informant, Elisha son of Abuyah.

241. Which, interestingly, is not cited in support of Rabbi Johanan's position on the Botsra nymphaeum. See Blidstein, "R. Johanan, Idolatry, and Public Privilege," 156.

242. Following the Kaufmann Manuscript of the Mishnah. See D. Rosenthal, *Mishnah Aboda Zara – A Critical Edition (with Introduction)* (Jerusalem: Hebrew University of Jerusalem, 1980), 40–1, in Hebrew.

243. This text has been discussed in great detail by modern scholars. See most recently S. Schwartz, *Imperialism and Jewish Society*, 167–72, and the bibliography cited there.

244. Eliav, "The Roman Bath," 432.

245. See the discussion of this phenomenon by Eliav, "Visiting the Sculptural Environment."

246. This is highly reminiscent of discussions of the status of Christianity in medieval Ashkenaz that revolved around the wine trade and led to a recategorization of Christians. See now H. Soloveitchik, *Principles and Pressures: Jewish Trade in Gentile Wine in the Middle Ages* (Tel Aviv: Alma, Am Oved, 2003), in Hebrew.

247. Y. Z. Eliav, "The Matrix of Ancient Judaism: Review of S. Schwartz, *Imperialism and Jewish Society, 200 B.C.E. to 640 C.E.*," *Prooftext*, forthcoming. Many thanks to Professor Eliav for sharing this review with me prior to its publication.

248. Meshorer, *The City Coins of Eretz-Israel*, 14–15, no. 16; B. Trell, "The Cult-Image on Temple-Type Coins," *Numismatic Chronicle*, 4 (1964), 4: 241–6.

249. *y. Shevi'it* 8:11, 38b–c; *b. Avodah Zarah* 58b–59a. Lieberman, *Hellenism in Jewish Palestine*, 132–3, suggests that the Yerushalmi version refers to a bathhouse and the Bavli to a nymphaeum; see also Blidstein, *Rabbinic Legislation on Idolatry*, 276–319, especially 311–19;

1974, 155–6. D. Sperber, *The City in Roman Palestine* (New York and Oxford: Oxford University Press, 1998), 133–4 relies on the Bavli version in identifying the installation as a nymphaeum. See Schwartz's note (*Imperialism and Jewish Society*, 173, 24), which seems to me correct.

250. Cf. Lieberman, ibid.

251. I use "likenesses" throughout rather than "statues," which I see as a subcategory of "likenesses." See Sokoloff, *A Dictionary of Jewish Palestinian Aramaic*, 53–4. J. Neusner (*Tractate Avodah Zarah* [Atlanta: Scholars Press, 1991]), as well as P. Schäfer, "Jews and Gentiles in Yerushalmi *Avodah Zarah*," *Talmud Yerushalmi and Graeco–Roman Culture*, ed. P. Schäfer (Tübingen: Mohr Siebeck, 1998), 344, translate "icons," a usage that draws too close a conceptual connection to later Christian usage. Schwartz, *Imperialism and Jewish Society*, 173, writes regarding this and related traditions that "we may . . . wonder whether these stories were not retrospective creations of the later fourth century, when the Talmud was compiled, idealized projections made by Rabbis who no longer knew what it was like to live in a pagan city." Based on Byzantine-period documents discussed in this chapter, this comment seems to be an anachronism. There is no reason to assume that Jews viewed Christian Rome as any less idolatrous than polytheistic Rome.

252. Urbach, "The Rabbinical Laws of Idolatry," 158–62; Baumgarten, "Art in the Synagogue," 76–7.

253. *y. Avodah Zarah* 3:13, 43b.

254. Mark 12:13–17; Matthew 22:15–22; Luke 20:20–26.

255. See also *y. Berakhot* 2:1, 4b, and the comments of Blidstein, "R. Johanan, Idolatry, and Public Privilege," 158–9.

256. Sokoloff, *A Dictionary of Jewish Palestinian Aramaic*, 575.

257. The question is whether אדורי should be corrected to אחרי. If a deity, its name is unattested. See Sokoloff, *A Dictionary of Jewish Palestinian Aramaic*, 35. Schäfer, "Jews and Gentiles in Yerushalmi *Avodah Zarah*," 348, translates: "They came upon a procession where an idol was carried."

258. *m. Berakhot* 9:5, *Megillah* 3:3. See Fine, *This Holy Place*, 43.

259. Blidstein, *Rabbinic Legislation on Idolatry*, 158.

260. See Baer's comments to *Seder Avodat Israel*, ed. Z. Baer (Palestine: Schocken, 1937), 131.

261. P. Brown, "Images as a Substitute for Writing," *East and West: Modes of Communication. Proceedings of the First Plenary Conference at Merida*, eds. E. Chrysos and I. Wood (Leiden: E. J. Brill, 1999), 24–5.

262. See *y. Avodah Zarah* 3:10, 43d.

263. Following Ms. JTS Rab. 15.

264. Belayche, *Iudaea-Palaestina*, 31, 36. See also Schäfer, "Jews and Gentiles in Yerushalmi *Avodah Zarah*," 348–9.

265. On reverence for holy men beyond their own immediate circles, see P. Brown, *The Cult of the Saints* (Chicago: University of Chicago Press, 1981); idem, *Society and the Holy in Late Antiquity* (Berkeley and Los Angeles: University of California Press, 1982), 103–52. Schäfer, "Jews and Gentiles in Yerushalmi *Avodah Zarah*," 344, asks, "Indeed, would Gentiles have really allowed the Jews to cover their 'icons' in order not to offend rabbis?" The point of this story is that rabbis believed that the covering of images was possible in their world.

266. Hippolytus, *Refutation of All Heresies*, 9, 21, in *The Writings of Hippolytus, Bishop of Portus*, tr. J. H. Mac Mahon (Edinburgh: T & T Clark, 1870), as rev. by G. Vermes and M. Goodman, eds. *The Essenes According to the Classical Sources* (Oxford: Oxford Centre for Postgraduate Hebrew Studies and Sheffield: Jost Press, 1987), 70–71.

267. M. Black, "The Account of the Essenes in Hippolytus and Josephus," *The Background of the New Testament and its Eschatology: Studies in Honor of C. H. Dodd*, eds. W. D. Davies and D. Daube (Cambridge: Cambridge University Press, 1956), 172–82; Blidstein, *Rabbinic Legislation on Idolatry*, 331.

268. *Genesis Rabba* 63: 6, 683–4. On Esau in rabbinic thought, see G. D. Cohen, "Esau as Symbol in Early Medieval Thought," *Studies in the Variety of Rabbinic Culture* (Philadelphia: Jewish Publication Society, 1991), 242–50, and the bibliography cited there.

269. *y. Ḥagigah* 2:1, 77b.

270. *Ruth Rabba* (ed. Vilna), 6:4, ed. M. B. Lerner (*Aggadat Rut u-Midrash Rut Rabba*, Ph.D. dissertation [Jerusalem: Hebrew University, 1971]), 170; *Ecclesiastes Rabba* 7:1.

271. See, e.g., *m. Avodah Zarah* 4:4; *y. Avodah Zarah* 3:6, 43b–c; 4: 4, 43c.

272. S. Friedman, "Recovering the Historical ben D'rosai," *Sidra* 14 (1998), 88–9, in Hebrew; Urbach, "The Rabbinical Laws of Idolatry," 234, especially note 80; Schäfer, "Jews and Gentiles in Yerushalmi *Avodah Zarah*," 349–50. Again, Schäfer treats this story as "highly unlikely," without any substantive explanation. For the tradents who quote it, this story was clearly credible.

273. See Urbach, ibid.

274. *y. Avodah Zarah* 3:1, 42c, *b. Moed Qatan* 25b.

275. *y. Avodah Zarah* 3:1, 42c. Following S. Lieberman, "*Tiqqunei Yerushalmi* 1," *Tarbiz* 2: 113–14.

276. Roth-Gerson, *Greek Inscriptions*, 125–9, and the bibliography cited there; R. Hachlili

and A. Killebrew, "Ḥorbat Qazion," *Ḥadashot Arkheologiyot* 109 (1999), 8–10, in Hebrew; Fine, "Non-Jews in the Synagogues of Palestine: Rabbinic and Archaeological Perspectives," 227–9.

277. *y. Megillah*, 3:1–3, 73d–74a and parallels. Scholars have long discussed the identity of Antoninus. The various options are assembled by *GLAJJ*, 2: 626–7. L. Ginzberg, "Antoninus in the Talmud," *JE*, 1: 656–7, correctly considers these traditions to be legendary. See S. J. D. Cohen, "The Conversion of Antoninus," *The Talmud Yerushalmi and Graeco-Roman Culture*, ed. P. Schäfer (Tübingen: Mohr Siebeck, 1998), 1: 141–71; Fine, "Non-Jews in the Synagogues of Palestine," 229.

278. Urbach, "The Rabbinical Laws of Idolatry," 231.

279. M. Hadas-Lebel, "L'évolution de l'image de Rome auprès des Juifs en deux siècles de relations judéo-romaines, – 164 à +70," *Aufstieg und Niedergang der Römische Welt* (Berlin and New York: Walther de Gruyter, 1987), II 20.2: 715–856.

280. Lieberman, *Hellenism in Jewish Palestine*, 116–17.

281. Urbach, "The Rabbinical Laws of Idolatry," 154, cites mainly Babylonian Talmud sources in support of this claim, and no Palestinian sources that date earlier than the Byzantine period.

282. Lieberman, *Hellenism in Jewish Palestine*, 121.

283. *m. Berakhot* 9:1.

284. *t. Berakhot* 6:2. See Lieberman, *Tosefta Ki-fshutah*, ad. loc.

285. In a comment that bespeaks his own era, Lieberman (*Hellenism in Jewish Palestine*, 121) notes that "those few Jews who worshiped idols in order to identify themselves with the gentiles did it for lucrative reasons, and there was, of course, little hope of reclaiming this type of apostate with moral tracts."

286. E. Wellesz, *A History of Byzantine Music and Hymnography*, 2nd ed. (Oxford, Clarendon Press, 1961), 179–97.

287. Fine, "Non-Jews in the Synagogues of Palestine," 231–41.

288. *The Liturgical Poetry of Rabbi Yannai*, 2: 221–2. See 1: 45 and S. Lieberman, "*Ḥazzanut Yannai*" *Sinai* 2, no. 4 (1939), 224, rpt. *Studies in Palestinian Talmudic Literature*, ed. D. Rosenthal (Jerusalem: Magnes, 1991), 143–4, in Hebrew, 126. Lieberman, followed by Rabinovitz, suggests that *shoa* here may be a play on *Yeshua*, Jesus.

289. M. Sokoloff and J. Yahalom, *Jewish Palestinian Aramaic Poetry from Late Antiquity: Critical Edition with Introduction and Commentary* (Jerusalem: Israel Academy of Sciences and Humanities, 1999), 217; J. Yahalom, "The Angels Do Not Understand Aramaic: On the

Literary Use of Palestinian Jewish Aramaic in Late Antiquity," *Journal of Jewish Studies*, 47, no. 1 (1996), 43.

290. That is, Mercurius. Yahalom, ibid, note 39, suggests that while *Merqoles* generally denotes idolatry in rabbinic literature, "Here, apparently, it is a derogatory term for *ecclesia.*"

291. *Codex Theodosianus* 16.8.18, in A. Linder, ed., *The Jews in Roman Imperial Legislation* (Detroit: Wayne State University Press and Jerusalem: Israel Academy of Sciences and Humanities, 1987), 236–8. See E. Horowitz, "The Rite to Be Reckless: On the Perpetuation and Interpretation of Purim Violence," *Poetics Today* 15.1 (1994), especially note 44 and the bibliography cited there. A. S. Jacobs, (*The Remains of The Jews: The Holy Land and Christian Empire in Late Antiquity* [Stanford: Stanford University Press, 2004]), applies recent developments in Colonial Theory to Byzantine Palestine.

292. See "Sefer ha-Ma'asim le-Venei Eretz Yisrael," *Tarbiz* 1, no. 3 (1930), 12; Herr, "Hellenistic Influences in the Jewish City," 93.

293. *Antonini Placenti Itinerarium* 5 (*Corpus Christianorum Series Latina* 175, 130–1). Translated by J. Wilkinson, *Jerusalem Pilgrims before the Crusades* (Warminster: Aris & Philips, 1977), 79–80; Jacobs, *Remains of the Jews*, 127–28.

294. *y. Avodah Zarah* 4:1, Epstein, "Additional Fragments of the Jerushalmi," 19. See Lieberman, *Hellenism in Jewish Palestine*, 134; Urbach, "The Rabbinic Laws of Idolatry," 233.

295. E. Will, "La coup de Césarée de Palestine au Musée du Louvre," *Fondation Eugene Piot: Monuments et memories* 65 (1983), 1–24; K. G. Holum, R. L. Hohlfelder, and R. L. Vann, eds., *King Herod's Dream: Caesarea on the Sea* (New York: Norton, 1988), 13–15.

296. Blidstein, "Nullification of Idolatry in Rabbinic Law," discusses this phenomenon in depth.

297. Y. Yadin, *The Finds from the Bar Kokhba Period in the Cave of Letters* (Jerusalem: Israel Exploration Society, 1963), 42–83.

298. Ibid, 59–60.

299. I hope to return to issues of nudity in Jewish art in my *The Nude in Traditional Jewish Art*, in preparation.

300. See above, 78.

301. Cf. Levine, *The Ancient Synagogue*, 453, and his assessment of Rabban Gamaliel's activity.

302. *y. Avodah Zarah* 3:2, 42c; *Antiquities* 2.139.

303. *y. Avodah Zarah* 3:3, 42d. S. Stern reaches similar conclusions. See Stern, "Figurative Art and *Halakha*" and "Pagan Images in Late Antique Palestinian Synagogues."

304. This point was made early on by J. B. Soleveitchik in a private letter dated

December 6, 1950, relating to the construction of an interfaith chapel at Cornell University. On this letter in general, see my "Spirituality in the Art of the Ancient Synagogue," *Jewish Spirituality and Divine Law*, eds. A. Mintz, L. Schiffman, R. Hirt (Hobocken: Ktav, 2005).

305. *Apion* 2.75.

306. Blau, "Christian Archaeology," 179; Blidstein, *Rabbinic Legislation on Idolatry*, 210–16; S. Stern, "Figurative Art and *Halakha*," 408–9. Compare Urbach, "The Rabbinical Laws of Idolatry," 235; Levine, *The Ancient Synagogue*, 432.

307. See above, note 97.

308. *y. Avodah Zarah* 4:1, 43d; G. Blidstein, "Prostration and Mosaics," 59–65. Compare Levine, *The Ancient Synagogue*, 455.

309. C. L. Meyers, E. M. Meyers, E. Netzer, and Z. Weiss, "The Dionysos Mosaic," *Sepphoris of Galilee: Crosscurrents of Culture*, ed. R. Nagy (Raleigh, N.C.: North Carolina Museum of Art, 1996), 111–15.

310. *m. Middot* 1:6.

311. Krauss, *Griechische und lateinische Lehnwörter*, 2: 479–82; J. N. Epstein, *Introduction to the Mishnaic Text* (Jerusalem: Magnes, 2000), 2: 1235, in Hebrew.

312. L. I. Levine, "R. Abbahu of Caesarea," *Christianity, Judasm and Other Greco-Roman Cults: Studies for Morton Smith at Sixty*, ed. J. Neusner (Leiden: E. J. Brill, 1975), 4: 64; idem, *The Synagogue*, 455.

313. Levine, *The Ancient Synagogue*, 455.

314. Many thanks to Robert O. Freedman for this insight.

315. On the dating of this Targum, see Fine, "'Their Faces Shine with the Brightness of the Firmament,'" 65, note 6.

316. On the *stoa* in rabbinic literature, see H. L. Gordon, "The Basilica and the Stoa in Early Rabbinical Literature," *Art Bulletin*, 13 (1931), 366–74; S. Krauss, *Griechische und lateinische Lehnwörter*, 379.

317. See Blidstein, "Prostration and Mosaics in Talmudic Law," 39, note 2.

318. See also *Sifra, be-Har* 6 (ed. I. H. Weiss, *Sifra de-ve-Rav hu Sefer Torat Kohanim* [Vienna: Yaakov ha-Kohen Shlosberg, 1862]); *y. Avodah Zarah* 4:1, 43d; *b. Megillah* 22b. Cf. Blidstein, "Prostration and Mosaics," 28–39.

319. See Fine, *This Holy Place*, 35–94.

320. S. Z. Netter, "Commentary on Targum Jonathan," printed in *Miqra'ot Gedolot* (ed. Vienna, 1859, Rpt. Jerusalem: Eshkol, 1976) to Leviticus 26:1; S. Krauss, "Die Galilaeischen Synagogenruinen und die Halakha," *Monatsschrift für Geschichte und Wissenschaft des Judentums* 65 (1921), 218–19. See *Targum Neofiti* to Leviticus 26:19, 31; Pseudo-Jonathan to Leviticus 26:31. If Pseudo-Jonathan meant to say "synagogues," it had the resources to do so. See Exodus 18:20.

321. See note 318 above; *b. Megillah* 22b and Blidstein, "Prostration and Mosaics," 20, note 3.

322. Blidstein notes that "although the Temple area was paved with flagstones and mosaics, whatever decoration existed was purely geometric" (ibid.). See Hachlili, *AJAALI*, 66–7, and sources cited in note 311.

323. *m. Tamid* 3: 4 explicitly mentions prostration on the platform of the Temple Mount.

324. *b. Megillah* 29a. See discussion of this text and the relationship between synagogues and the Temple in Fine, *This Holy Place*, especially 81, 136.

325. *Targum Jonathan* to Ezekiel 11:16.

326. Other examples of this phenomenon are discussed in Fine, *This Holy Place*, 88–92.

327. Avi-Yonah, *Oriental Art in Roman Palestine*, 42. See the secularlized Christian statement of this as related to iconoclasm in Goodenough, *Jewish Symbols*, 2: 256–7. Regarding iconoclasm at Na'aran, Goodenough states: "again, we might suppose that the 'different type' of Judaism was rabbinic, halakhic Judaism at last coming to dominate Jewish standards and conceptions, at last becoming normative."

328. Urbach, *The Rabbinical Laws of Idolatry*, passim.

329. For a summary of the evidence, see Magen, "Samaritian Synagogues"; R. Pummer, "Samaritan Material Remains and Archaeology," *The Samaritans*, ed. A. D. Crown. (Tübingen: J. C. B. Mohr, 1989), 135–77; idem, "Samaritan Synagogues and Jewish Synagogues: Similarities and Differences."

330. *Biblia* 15 (1934), 265–300, especially 298.

331. "The Cult of Images in the Age before Iconoclasm," *Dumbarton Oaks Papers* 8 (1954), 130, note 204.

332. C. Barber, "The Truth in Painting: Iconoclasm and Identity in Early-Medieval Art," *Speculum* 72 (1997), 1035. This approach is close to that suggested by S. Schwartz, *Imperialism and Jewish Society*.

333. G. R. D. King, "Islam, Iconoclasm and the Declaration of Doctrine," *Bulletin of the School of Oriental and African Studies* 48, pt. 2 (1985), 275–7.

334. Fine, "Non-Jews in the Synagogues of Palestine," 231–41.

335. See note 71 above.

336. See R. Wilken, *The Land Called Holy: Palestine in Christian History and Thought* (New Haven: Yale University Press, 1992), 216–32; Fine, "Non-Jews in the Synagogues of Palestine," 231–41, and the bibliography cited there. On relations between Jews, Christians, and Muslims on the subject of Christian images, see King, "Islam, Iconoclasm"; S. H. Griffith, *Theodore Abu Qurrah, A Treatise on the Veneration of the Holy Icons* (Leuven: Peeters, 1997), especially 6–7.

337. See C. Roth's apologetic formulation: "Obviously Jews could not afford to be more tolerant in this matter than their Muslim neighbors" (*Jewish Art*, 521).

CHAPTER 8: ART AND IDENTITY IN DIASPORA COMMUNITIES IN LATE ANTIQUITY

1. See my *This Holy Place*, 127–57; idem, "'Peace Upon Israel': Synagogues in Spain During Late Antiquity," ed. J. Holo, *Los judíos españoles según las fuentes hebreas: Museu de Belles Arts de València, del 11 de abril al 9 de junio de 2002* (Valencia: Consorci de Museus de la Comunitat Valenciana, Generalitat Valenciana, Subsecretaria de Promocío Cultural, Museu de Belles Arts de Valencia, 2002), 146–50.

2. See Fine, *This Holy Place*, 127–57; A. T. Kraabel, "The Diaspora Synagogue: Archaeological and Epigraphic Evidence since Sukenik," *Aufstieg und Niedergang der Römische Welt* (Berlin and New York: Walther de Gruyter, 1979), II, 19.1: 479–510.

3. Archaeological evidence is conveniently collected by Hachlili, *AJAAD*. See my review of this volume, *Bulletin of the American Schools for Oriental Research*, 314 (1999), 88–9.

4. *Jewish Symbols*, especially vols. 2 and 3.

5. *AJAAD*, passim.

6. J. B. Frey, ed., *Corpus Inscriptionum Judaicarum* (Rome: Pontifico istituto di archeologia critiana, 1936), 1; Leon, *The Jews of Ancient Rome*; B. Lifshitz, *Donateurs et Fondateurs dans les Synagogues Juives* (Paris: J. Gabalda, 1967); W. Horbury and D. Noy, eds., *Jewish Inscriptions of Graeco–Roman Egypt* (Cambridge: Cambridge University Press, 1992); D. Noy, ed., *Jewish Inscriptions of Western Europe, 1: Italy (Excluding the City of Rome), Spain and Gaul, 2: The City of Rome* (Cambridge: Cambridge University Press, 1993, 1995); L. Roth-Gerson, *Jews of Syria as Reflected in the Greek Inscriptions* (Jerusalem: Merkaz Zalman Shazar, 2001), in Hebrew.

7. K. M. D. Dunbabin, *The Mosaics of Roman North Africa* (Oxford: Oxford University Press, 1978), 194–5; Hachlili, *AJAAD*, 209.

8. Hachlili, *AJAAD*, 208–9.

9. Goodenough, *Jewish Symbols*, 2: 95–9.

10. Hachlili, *AJAAD*, 32–4, 198–204.

11. The final report of the Sardis synagogue has yet to appear. In the meantime, the most recent synthesis of published evidence is Hachlili, *AJAAD*, 58–63. For a general survey of the synagogue, see A. R. Seager, "The Building History of the Sardis Synagogue," *American Journal of Archaeology*, 76 (1972), 425–35; idem, "The Synagogue at Sardis," *ASR* 178–84. The site and the artifacts, housed in the Archaeological Museum at Manisa, Turkey, were

investigated by the author, most recently in June 1998.

12. See Fine, *Sacred Realm*, 64–6, cat. nos. 21, 23, and the bibliography there.

13. See M. Goodman, "Jews and Judaism in the Mediterranean Diaspora in the Late-Roman Period; The Limitations of Evidence," *Journal of Mediterranean Studies*, 4, no. 2 (1994), 208–24.

14. F. M. Cross, "The Hebrew Inscriptions from Sardis," *Harvard Theological Review*, 95, no. 1 (2002), 3–19.

15. For a discussion of this and other menorahs from Asia Minor, see S. Fine and L. V. Rutgers, "New Light on Judaism in Asia Minor during Late Antiquity: Two Recently Identified Inscribed Menorahs," *Jewish Studies Quarterly*, 3, no. 1 (1996), 1–23.

16. Seager, "The Synagogue at Sardis," 181.

17. Ibid., 180.

18. Hachlili, *AJAAD*, 383–4.

19. Seager, "The Synagogue at Sardis," 180.

20. Discussed in Fine, *This Holy Place*, 150–6.

21. Noy, *Jewish Inscriptions of Western Europe*, 2: 130–1; Fine, *Sacred Realm*, no. 5.

22. See Noy, *Jewish Inscriptions of Western Europe*, 2: 471–3; Fine, *This Holy Place*, 154–5; Elsner, "Archaelogies and Agendas," 116–17.

23. Noy, *Jewish Inscriptions of Western Europe*, 1: 22; Fine, *Sacred Realm*, 158.

24. Goodenough, *Jewish Symbols*, 3: Fig. 810.

25. On the Ostia synagogue: A. Runesson, "The Synagogue at Ancient Ostia: The Building and Its History from the First to the Fifth Century," *The Synagogue of Ancient Ostia and the Jews of Rome: Interdisciplinary Studies, Skifter Utgivna av Svenska Institutet I Rome*, 4, LVII, eds. B. Olsson, D. Mitternacht, and O. Brandt (Stockholm: Paul Aströms, 2001), 29–100.

26. Finney, *The Invisible God*, 263.

27. Rutgers, *The Jews in Late Ancient Rome*, 83.

28. Finney, *The Invisible God*, 247. Finney, 247–63, presents the most recent survey of painting in the Jewish catacombs of Rome.

29. Rutgers, *The Jews in Late Ancient Rome*, 73–4. For the history of scholarship, see p. 44.

30. Ibid., 74.

31. These are cataloged by A. Konikoff, *Sarcophagi from the Jewish Catacombs of Ancient Rome: A Catalogue Raisonné* (Stuttgart: F. Steiner Verlag, 1988). See the review by L. H. Kant and L. V. Rutgers, *Gnomon*, 60 (1988), 376–8 and the astute comments of Leon, *The Jews of Ancient Rome*, 210–20.

32. Konikoff, *Sarcophagi from the Jewish Catacombs of Ancient Rome*, 46–9.

33. Ibid., 41–6, and the bibliography there.

34. F. Cumont, *Recherches sur le symbolisme funéraire des Romains* (Paris: P. Geuthner, 1942), 284–98; Goodenough, *Jewish Symbols*, 2: 25–7.

35. G. M. F. Hanfmann, *The Season Sarcophagus in Dumbarton Oaks* (Cambridge: Harvard University Press, 1951), 1: 195; Leon, *The Jews of Ancient Rome*, 211–12.

36. Goodenough, *Jewish Symbols*, 9: 54; Fine, *This Holy Place*, 145.

37. Kraeling, *The Synagogue*; Gutmann, "The Illustrated Midrash," 95–6.

38. Kraeling, *The Synagogue*, 99–105.

39. Goodenough, *Jewish Symbols*, 9: 23. See also 10: 179.

40. Kraeling, *The Synagogue*, 338.

41. C. P. Kelley, "Who Did the Iconoclasm in the Dura Synagogue?" *Bulletin of the American Schools for Oriental Research*, 295 (1994), 57–72.

42. *b. Gittin* 36a.

43. *b. Megillah* 26b, *Baba Batra* 3b. See Fine, *This Holy Place*, 130–3.

44. Translation follows the Vilna edition unless specified.

45. Following the Kaufmann manuscript.

46. See *Diqdukei Sofrim*, ad. loc.

47. Ibid.

48. Blidstein, *Rabbinic Legislation on Idolatry*, 265, note 145. See also *b. Avodah Zarah*, Paris, Bibliotheque Nationale, Suppl. Heb. 1337.

49. Krauss, *Griechische und lateinische Lehnwörter*, 65; Sokoloff, A *Dictionary of Jewish Babylonian Aramaic*, 144.

50. *Oẓar ha-Gaonim*, ed. B. M. Lewin (Jerusalem: H. Vagshal, 1984), 8: 44, no. 52. The Paris Manuscript of tractate *Avodah Zarah* suggests that the statue was "set up within it by gentiles (*goyim*)."

51. The classic discussion of this phenomenon is still J. Mann, "Changes in the Divine Service of the Synagogue due to Religious Persecutions," *Hebrew Union College Annual*, 4 (1927), 241–310.

52. *Iggeret Rav Sherira Gaon*, ed. B. M. Lewin (Haifa: s.n., 1921), 72–3. On this synagogue, J. N. Epstein, *Studies in Talmudic Literature and Semitic Languages*, ed. E. Z. Melamed, tr. Z. Epstein (Jerusalem: Magnes Press, 1983), 1: 40–1; A. Oppenheimer, *Babylonia Judaica in the Talmudic Period* (Wiesbaden: L. Reichert, 1983), 156–64, 276–93; idem, "Babylonian Synagogues with Historical Associations," *ASHAAD*, 1: 40–5; see Fine, *This Holy Place*, 134–7.

53. Oppenheimer, "Babylonian Synagogues," 41–3.

54. See M. Boyce, "Iconoclasm among the Zoroastrians," *Christianity, Judaism and Other Greco–Roman Cults: Studies for Morton Smith at Sixty*, ed. J. Neusner (Leiden: E. J. Brill, 1975), 4: 93–111. This *sugya* was discussed by R. Kalmin, "Idolatry in Late Antique Babylonia: The Evidence of the Babylonian Talmud," *The Sculptural Environment of the Roman Near East: Reflections on Culture, Ideology and Power, An International Conference Nov. 7–11, 2004*, University

of Michigan and the Toledo Museum of Art. Kalmin notes that the father of Samuel and Levi "flourished in Babylonia prior to the advent of the Sasanian dynasty," which he suggests might explain the presence of a statue of Shaf ve-Yatev.

55. This concept is invoked in very specific legal contexts in Talmudic literature. It nevertheless expresses a broader notion of comfort within the Babylonian milieu. See most recently I. Gafni, "Babylonian Rabbinic Culture," *Cultures of the Jews: A New History*, ed. D. Biale (New York: Schocken Books, 2002), 224–5.

PART 3: JEWISH "SYMBOLS" IN THE GRECO–ROMAN WORLD

1. For Scholem's definition of symbol and symbolism in Kabbalah, see Joseph Dan, *Gershom Scholem and the Mystical Dimension of Jewish History* (New York: New York University Press, 1987), 162–3.

2. *Zur Kabbala und ihrer Symbolik* (Zurich: Rhein-Verlag, 1960), tr. R. Manheim (London: Routledge and K. Paul, 1965).

3. *Luah Haaretz* 1949/50, 148–63; idem, "The Star of David: History of a Symbol," *The Messianic Idea in Judaism and Other Essays on Jewish Spirituality* (New York: Schocken, 1978), 257–81. For other versions, see L. A. Mayer, *Bibliography of Jewish Art* (Jerusalem: Magnes, 1967), nos. 2344–6.

4. W. McGuire, *Bollingen: An Adventure in Collecting the Past* (Princeton: Princeton University Press, 1982), 152–3.

5. "The Star of David: History of a Symbol," 280.

6. Ibid., 281.

7. Ibid.

8. A. P. Cohen, *The Symbolic Construction of Community* (Chichester: E. Horwood; London and New York: Tavistock Publications, 1985), 18.

9. C. Geertz, *The Interpretation of Cultures* (New York: Basic Books, 1973), 91.

10. R. Hachlili, *The Menorah*, 210. Mishory (*Lo and Behold*, 165–99) discusses the deliberations leading to the creation of the symbol of the State of Israel.

11. Mishory, ibid.

12. See S. Ireton, "Ethnicity, Nationalism and Identity with Specific Reference to Ethnographic Research on the Samaritan Communities of Holon in Israel and Kiryat Luza on Mount Gerizim," *A. B. – The Samaritan News*, nos. 848–50 (9/25/2003), 142–103.

13. This point is driven home by R. S. Nelson, "To Say and to See: Ekphrasis and Vision in Byzantium," *Visuality Before and Beyond the Renaissance: Seeing as Others Saw*, ed.

R. S. Nelson (Cambridge: Cambridge University Press, 2000), 143–68.

CHAPTER 9: BETWEEN ROME AND JERUSALEM

1. On the palm tree in the classical world, see H. F. Fracchia, *The Iconography of the Palm in Greek Art: Significance and Symbolism*, Ph.D. dissertation (Berkeley: University of California, 1979), 59–67 and the bibliography cited in note 279; I. Löw, *Aramäische Pflanzennamen* (Leipzig: W. Engelmann, 1881), 109–27; idem, *Die Flora die Juden* (Vienna and Leipzig: R. Löwit, 1924), 303–62.

2. Anson, *Numismata Graeca*, 3: 37–44, nos. 370–441.

3. Ibid., 3: 30–41, nos. 284–308, 364, 375–440.

4. G. F. Hill, *A Catalogue of the Greek Coins of Phoenicia in the British Museum* (London: Trustees of the British Museum, 1910), nos. 253–4, 258–9, 265–7.

5. E. Rogers, *The Second and Third Seleucid Coinage of Tyre* (New York: American Numismatic Society, 1927).

6. There is some discussion of the derivation of this word. *Phoinix* can refer to both the color purple and to the date palm. See the sources cited in note 1 above and S. Segert, *A Grammar of Phoenician and Punic* (Munich: C. H. Beck, 1976), 17–18; Y. Meshorer, *Ancient Jewish Coinage*, 1:145, note 218.

7. Anson, *Numismata Graeca*, 3:30–44.

8. Meshorer, *Ancient Jewish Coinage*, 1:79; idem, *A Treasury of Jewish Coins*, ך 23, p. 189.

9. Meshorer, *Ancient Jewish Coinage*, 2:281, nos. 1–2.

10. Meshorer, *Ancient Jewish Coinage*, 2:281, nos. 3–5a.

11. Meshorer, *Ancient Jewish Coinage*, 2:243, nos. 17–19.

12. Meshorer, *Ancient Jewish Coinage*, 2:284, nos. 29–31a. Caesarea issue: p. 286, nos. 7, 8.

13. C. Roth, "The Historical Implications of Ancient Jewish Coins," *Israel Exploration Journal*, 12 (1962), 24; H. St. Hart, "Judaea and Rome: The Official Commentary," *Journal of Theological Studies*, new series 3 (1952), 181, note 5.

14. t. *Ketubot* 12 (13): 6 and parallels. Compare Y. Meshorer, "One Hundred and Ninety Years of Tyrian Shekels," *Studies in Honor of Leo Mildenberg: Numismatics, Art History, Archaeology*, ed. A. Houghton (Wetteren, Belgium: Editions NR, 1984), 171–9; A. Ben David, *Jerusalem and Tyros* (Basel: Kyklos-Verlag; Tübingen: J. C. B. Mohr, 1969).

15. N. Avigad, "Two Bullae of Jonathan, King and High Priest, *Ancient Jerusalem Revealed*, ed. H. Geva (Jerusalem: Israel Exploration Society, 1994), 257–9.

16. Z. Ma'oz, "The Synagogue of Gamla and the Typology of Second-Temple Synagogues," *ASR*, 39; S. Gutman, *Gamla – A City in Rebellion* (Israel: Ministry of Defense, 1994), 125–6, in Hebrew.

17. Rahmani, *A Catalogue of Jewish Ossuaries*, 48–9.

18. Tr. E. Isaac in *The Old Testament Pseudepigrapha*, ed. J. H. Charlesworth (Garden City: Doubleday, 1983), 1:26.

19. Meshorer, *Ancient Jewish Coinage*, 2: 38–9, 242–3, nos. 13–16. Meshorer suggests that Antipas's usage may relate to the founding of Tiberias. See also vol. 1:147, 2:25.

20. Meshorer, *Ancient Jewish Coinage*, 2:243, nos. 16–19 and note 22.

21. *Historia Plantarum* 2.6.2–8, tr. A. Hort in *GLAJJ*, 1: 13–14 and note 2.

22. Greek and Latin authors who touch on these issues are collected by I. Taglicht, "Die Dattelpalme in Palästina," *Adolf Schwarz Festschrift*, eds. V. Aptowitzer and S. Krauss (Berlin: R. Löwit, 1917), 493–516; *GLAJJ*, 1: 494, note 26. On Palestinian trade during the Hellenistic period, see M. I. Rostovtzeff, *The Social and Economic History of the Hellenistic World* (Oxford: Oxford University Press, 1941), 1439, notes 148–9.

23. *GLAJJ*, 1:440.

24. *Jewish War* 1.396–7; *Antiquities* 15.217; Smallwood, *The Jews under Roman Rule*, 62, 70.

25. *The Delphosophists* 14.652.

26. *Quaestiones Convivales* 8.4.

27. S. Lieberman, "Palestine in the Third and Fourth Centuries," *Jewish Quarterly Review* 37 (1946–7), 51–2.

28. *Historia Naturalis* 13.26–46, tr. H. Rackham, in *GLAJJ*, 1:490–4; St. Hart, "Judaea and Rome."

29. F. Brown, S. R. Driver, and C. A. Briggs, *A Hebrew and English Lexicon of the Old Testament*, 1071.

30. Jastrow, *Dictionary of the Targumim*, 319, 1679.

31. Sokoloff, *A Dictionary of Jewish Palestinian Aramaic*, 154; *A Dictionary of Jewish Babylonian Aramaic*, 335.

32. H. Lewy, *Die semitischen Fremdwörter im Griechischen* (Berlin: R. Gaertner, 1895), 20–1.

33. C. H. Lewis and C. Short, *A Latin Dictionary* (Oxford: Clarendon Press, 1890), 1293.

34. F. W. Madden, "Rare or Unpublished Jewish Coins," *Numismatic Chronicle*, new series (1879), 19.

35. Meshorer, *Ancient Jewish Coinage*, 2: 269, no. 27.

36. Romanoff, *Symbols on Ancient Jewish Coins*, 19–20; Meshorer, *Ancient Jewish Coinage*, 2: 120–2 and note 75.

37. Meshorer, *Ancient Jewish Coinage*, 2: 121–2.

38. St. Hart, *Judaea and Rome*, 178–90, C. M. Kraay, "The Judaea Capta Sestertii of Vespasian," *Israel Numismatic Journal*, 3 (1963), 45–6; D. Barag, "The Palestinian 'Judaea Capta' Coins of Vespasian and Titus and the Era of the Coins of Agrippa II Minted Under the Flavians," *Numismatic Chronicle*, 138 (1978), 14–21.

39. St. Hart, *Judaea and Rome*, 164.

40. Ibid., 172–3, 180–1; A. Calò Levi, *Barbarians on Roman Imperial Coins and Sculpture* (New York: American Numismatic Society, 1952), 10.

41. Barag, *The Palestinian "Judaea Capta"*; Meshorer, *Ancient Jewish Coinage*, 2:194–7, 290–1, nos. 9, 9a, 9b.

42. Meshorer, *City-Coins of Eretz-Israel*, 48, no. 123.

43. Meshorer, *Ancient Jewish Coinage*, 2:254, nos. 28–9.

44. Meshorer, *City-Coins of Eretz-Israel*, 38, no. 88.

45. Cf. Meshorer, *City-Coins of Eretz-Israel*, 36, 48; idem, 1979.

46. St. Hart, *Judaea and Rome*, 190.

47. Smallwood, *The Jews under Roman Rule*, 371–8, 380, 385.

48. Meshorer, *Ancient Jewish Coinage*, 2:145.

49. St. Hart, *Judaea and Rome*, 185, note 2.

50. Ibid., 185–8.

51. L. Kadman, *Coins of the Jewish Revolt of 66–73 CE* (Tel Aviv: Schocken, 1960), 90. See also Romanoff, *Symbols on Ancient Jewish Coins*, 28–31; Meshorer, *Ancient Jewish Coinage*, 2:111, note 56.

52. L. Mildenberg, *The Coinage of the Bar Kokhba War* (Aarau: Verlag Sauerländer 1984), 48.

53. Already in 1944, Romanoff (*Symbols on Ancient Jewish Coins*, 28–30) argued against interpreting the seven-branched palm as a menorah, stating that "none of the symbols of this period suggest the Menorah."

CHAPTER 10: "THE LAMPS OF ISRAEL"

1. See M. Pfanner, *Der Titusbogen* (Mainz am Rhein: Philipp von Zabern, 1983); L. Yarden, *The Spoils of Jerusalem on the Arch of Titus: A Re-Investigation* (Stockholm: Svenska Institutet i Rom; Göteborg: P. Aströms, 1991).

2. See P. W. Holliday, "Roman Triumphal Painting: Its Function, Development, and Reception," *Art Bulletin* 79, no. 1 (1997), 146.

3. See Sperber, "The History of the Menorah," 158.

4. Exodus 35:13–14, 37:10–24.

5. *Antiquities* 3.139–46.

6. *Antiquities* 14.72.

7. See *1 Maccabees* 1:21–2 and 4:49 and compare *Antiquities* 12, 250, 318–19. See also *2 Maccabees* 1:8, 10:3.

8. *Antiquities* 2.139.

9. *War* 7.158.

10. See Fine, "'When I went to Rome, There I Saw the Menorah . . .': The Jerusalem Temple Implements between 70 C.E. and the Fall of Rome," *Festschrift for Eric Meyers*, ed. D. Edwards, forthcoming.

11. P. Zanker, "In Search of the Roman Viewer," *The Interpretation of Architectural Sculpture in Greece and Rome*, ed. D. Buitron-Oliver (Washington, D.C.: National Gallery of Art, 1997), 187.

12. Above, pp. 100–101.

13. The literature on the menorah during the Greco–Roman period is now quite extensive. See the recent survey by L. I. Levine, "The History and Significance of the Menorah in Antiquity," *FDS*, 131–53. See, in addition, bibliography cited by Hachlili, *The Menorah*, and my review of this work, Fine, "Review of R. Hachlili, *The Menorah, The Ancient Seven-Armed Candelabrum* (Leiden: E. J. Brill, 2001)," *Bulletin of the American Schools for Oriental Research*, 331 (2003), 87–8.

14. Meshorer, *Ancient Jewish Coinage*, 1: 94.

15. S. Fine and B. Zuckerman, "The Menorah as Symbol of Jewish Minority Status," *Fusion in the Hellenistic East*, ed. S. Fine (Los Angeles: University of Southern California Fisher Gallery, 1985), 24–5.

16. Rahmani, *Jason's Tomb*, 73–4.

17. B. Mazar, *The Mountain of the Lord* (Garden City: Doubleday, 1975), 143.

18. Avigad, "Excavations in the Jewish Quarter, 4–5; idem, *Discovering Jerusalem*, 147–9.

19. Rahmani, *A Catalogue of Jewish Ossuaries*, 51; nos. 815, 829. Rahmani notes that these artifacts are unprovenanced. In 1980, he ascribed these artifacts to "the area south or southwest of Jerusalem and to the period between 70 and 135 C.E.," although he provides no support for this attribution. Rahmani (*A Catalogue of Jewish Ossuaries*, 51; idem, "Depictions of Menorot on Ossuaries," "Representations of the Menorah on Ossuaries," *AJR*, 242) connects images of the menorah in Second Temple times and during the period before Bar Kokhba "with priests and their activities." No evidence to support or reject this hypothesis is provided.

20. B. Narkiss, "A Scheme of the Sanctuary from the Time of Herod the Great," *Journal of Jewish Art*, 1 (1974), 11. See also D. Barag, "The Temple Cult Objects Graffito from the Jewish Quarter Excavations at Jerusalem," *AJR*, 277–8.

21. B. Narkiss, *A Scheme of the Sanctuary*, 14.

22. *m. Ḥagigah* 3:8, following the Palestinian manuscript tradition as exemplified in the Kaufmann manuscript. See also *t. Ḥagigah* 3:35; *y. Ḥagigah* 3:8, 79d; *b. Ḥagigah* 26b, *Yoma* 21b, *Menaḥot* 29a, 96b; Lieberman, *Tosefta Ki-fshutah* ad. loc., especially notes 70, 72. On the historical context, see S. Zeitlin, *The Rise and Fall of the Judaean State* (Philadelphia: Jewish Publication Society, 1962), 1: 161; S. Safrai, *Pilgrimage at the Time of the Second Temple* (Jerusalem: Akadamon, 1965), 143–4, 179–81, Hebrew; D. R. Schwartz, "Viewing the Holy Utensils," *New Testament Studies*, 32 (1986), 158, note 29; I. Knohl, "Post-Biblical Sectarianism and the Priestly Schools of the Pentateuch: The Issue of Popular Participation in the Temple Cult on Festivals," *The Madrid Qumran Congress: Proceedings of the International Congress on the Dead Sea Scrolls, Madrid, 18–21 March, 1991*, eds. J. Trebolle Barrera and L. Vegas Montaner (Leiden: E. J. Brill; Madrid: Editorial Complutense, 1992), 2: 601–9; H. Maccoby, "Pharisee and Sadducee Interpretation of the Menorah as Tamid," *Journal of Progressive Judaism*, 3 (1994), 5–13.

23. P. Ox. V. 840, translation follows *New Testament Apocrypha*, ed. E. Schneemelcher, tr. R. McL. Wilson (Cambridge: James Clarke, Louisville: Westminster/John Knox, 1991), 1: 94–5.

24. See R. Reich, "Mishnah Sheqalim 8: 2 and the Archaeological Evidence," *Jerusalem in the Second Temple Period: Abraham Schalit Memorial Volume*, eds. A. Oppenheimer, U. Rappaport, and M. Stern (Jerusalem: Yad Izhak Ben-Zvi Press, 1980), in Hebrew, and the bibliography cited by D. R. Schwartz, "Viewing the Holy Utensils," note 3.

25. D. Barag, "The Showbread Table and the Facade of the Temple on Coins of the Bar-Kokhba Revolt," *Qadmoniot*, 20, nos. 1–2 (1987), 22–5, in Hebrew. Tr. *AJR*, 272–6.

26. There is no record that this interpretation was current during the Second Temple period or late antiquity.

27. See C. L. Meyers and E. M. Meyers, *The Anchor Bible: Haggai, Zechariah 1–8: A New Translation with Introduction and Commentary* (Garden City: Doubleday, 1987), 232.

28. Zechariah 4:10. See Meyers and Meyers, *The Anchor Bible: Haggai, Zechariah 1–8*, 254–5.

29. See, e.g., *Targum Neofiti* to Genesis 22:10 (and parallels). The Ein Gedi inscription, lines 13–14, is unique in its use of this phrase outside of the rabbinic corpus. See Naveh, *On Stone and Mosaic*, 106–7.

30. Meyers and Meyers, *The Anchor Bible: Haggai, Zechariah 1–8*, 237.

31. Ibid., 233–8.

32. Exodus 31:8, 39:37.

33. *Questions and Answers on Exodus*, 73–80, tr. R. Marcus, 122–31. On the menorah in Philo and Josephus, see Goodenough, *Jewish Symbols*, 4: 82–8.

34. *On Moses* 2.102–3, pp. 498–9.

35. *Preliminary Studies* 6–8. See also *Who is the Heir* 2.216.

36. Following Ed. Segel, *Sefer Ben Sira ha-Shalem*, 160, 163.

37. See the comments of Theodor and Albeck and parallels cited ad. loc.

38. See *Exodus Rabba* 15; Z. W. Einhorn, *Commentary of the Maharzu*, in *Midrash Rabba* (Vilna: Romm, 1884). This metaphorical usage is not evidenced elsewhere in rabbinic literature, although it appears in later Hebrew literature influenced by the *Genesis Rabba* tradition. See Ben Yehuda, *A Complete Dictionary of Ancient and Modern Hebrew*, 5: 2505–6.

39. Hachlili, *The Menorah*, 33–4 and bibliography there.

40. *Antiquities* 3.144–6.

41. The Tosefta version is difficult to translate. See Lieberman, *Tosefta Ki-fshutah* ad loc; J. Baumgarten, "The Pharisaic–Sadducean Controversies about Purity and the Qumran Texts," *Journal of Jewish Studies*, 31, no. 2 (1980), 165–6 and Knohl, "Post-Biblical Sectarianism," 603–4. See also *b. Ḥagigah* 26b.

42. Cf. M. Smith, "Helios in Palestine," *Eretz-Israel*, 20 (1982): 199*–214*.

43. A. Bosio, *Roma Sotterranea* (Rome: G. Facciotti, 1632), 1: 141–3. Translated by H. J. Leon, *The Jews of Ancient Rome*, 50–1.

44. Goodenough, *Jewish Symbols*, 1: 92.

45. On Venosa: D. Noy, "The Jewish Communities of Leontopolis and Venosa," *Studies in Early Jewish Epigraphy*, eds. J. W. van Henten and P. W. van der Horst (Leiden: E. J. Brill, 1994), 172–82. On Spain, see Fine, "'Peace Upon Israel': Synagogues in Spain During Late Antiquity," and the bibliographies cited by Noy and by Fine.

46. V. Sussman, *Ornamented Jewish Oil-Lamps*, nos. 1 (nine branches), 2 (eight branches), 3 (eight branches), 4 (two menorahs, one with twelve branches though no stalk and a second with ten branches with eleven "lamps" on top), 5 (eleven branches, no central stalk), and 6 (seven straight branches stemming from a horizontal bar). The phenomenon of menorahs with more or less than seven branches returns in late antiquity. See Hachlili, *The Menorah*, 200–2.

47. Rahmani, "Depictions of Menorot on Ossuaries"; Levine, "The History and Significance of the Menorah in Antiquity," 143.

48. V. Sussman, *Ornamented Jewish Oil-Lamps*, no. 4.

49. *b. Rosh ha-Shanah* 24a–b; *Avodah Zarah* 43a, *Menaḥot* 28b; *Midrash ha-Gadol* to Exodus 20:20 (ed. M. Margulies), 440–1. See Goodenough, *Jewish Symbols*, 4: 70; Rahmani, "Depictions of Menorot on Ossuaries," 242;

Levine, "The History and Significance of the Menorah in Antiquity," 143 goes so far as to suggest that "this baraita reflects the proclivity among some (many?) 2nd-century Jews to avoid depicting anything associated with the Temple." Cf. D. Kaufmann, *Etudes d'archéologie juive et archéologie chretiénne*, 9: "Naturellement, il s'agit ici d'une menorah employee comme objet d'usage journalier: on n'y parle pas d'une reproduction figurée peinture au fresque, sont en relief sont à plat."

50. A similar point was made by V. Klagsbald, "The Menorah as Symbol: Its Meaning and Origin in Early Jewish Art," *Jewish Art*, 12–13 (1986–7), 129. For later halakhic discussion of this tradition in light of actual menorahs in seventeenth–eighteenth-century Ashkenazi synagogues, see D. Sperber, *Minhagei Yisrael* (Jerusalem: Mossad Harav Kook, 1998), 6: 183–91, in Hebrew.

51. G. M. A. Hanfmann, "The Ninth Campaign at Sardis (1966)," *Bulletin of the American Schools of Oriental Research*, 187 (1967), 27. L. Seager, "The Synagogue at Sardis," 181–2; Fine, *This Holy Place*, 43, 160, no. 22; Fine, *Sacred Realm*, cat no. 22. Fine and Rutgers, "New Light on Judaism in Asia Minor during Late Antiquity," 11–12.

52. J. Brand, *Ceramics in Talmudic Literature* (Jerusalem: Mossad Harav Kook, 1953), 296–314, in Hebrew.

53. B. Lifshitz, *Donateurs et Fondateurs dans les Synagogues Juives* (Paris: J. Gabalda, 1967), no. 36; Fine and Rutgers, "New Light on Judaism in Asia Minor," 11–12.

54. Archaeological evidence for freestanding menorahs is surveyed by Hachlili, *The Menorah*, 51–8.

55. Hachlili, *The Menorah*, 51–2; Y. Israeli, *In the Light of the Menorah: Story of a Symbol* (Jerusalem: Israel Museum and Philadelphia: Jewish Publication Society, 1999), 101.

56. Fine and Rutgers, "New Light on Judaism in Asia Minor," 12–21.

57. Goodenough, *Jewish Symbols*, 4: 79 is correct that "the menorah would not appear upon amulets so often if it had not carried some idea of a direct potency." The potency of the menorah in later Jewish magic is well known. See: Y. Israeli, ed. *In the Light of the Menorah*, 134–142.

58. Fine and Zuckerman, "The Menorah as Symbol of Jewish Minority Status," 23–30.

59. *Sifre Zuta*, ed. H. S. Horovitz (Jerusalem: Wahrmann, 1966), Numbers 8: 2 and Fine, "When I Went to Rome."

60. Fine, *This Holy Place*, 114–17.

61. R. Brilliant, "Mythology," ed. K. Weitzmann, *The Age of Spirituality: Late Antique and Early Christian Cut, Third to Seventh Century* (New York: Metropolitan Museum of Art, 1979), 126.

62. Y. H. Yerushalmi, *Zakhor: Jewish History and Jewish Memory* (Seattle and London: University of Washington Press, 1982).

63. Hachlili, *AJAALI*, 1988, 255; L. I. Levine, *The Ancient Synagogue*, 149–53.

64. G. Foerster, "Decorated Marble Chancel Screens in Sixth Century Synagogues in Palestine and Their Relation to Christian Art and Architecture," *Actes du XIe Congres International d'Archeologie Chretienne* (Rome: École Francaise, 1989), 2: 1809–20; A. Ovadiah, "The Mosaic Workshop of Gaza in Christian Antiquity," *ASHAAD*, 2: 367–72.

65. Rutgers, *The Jews of Late Ancient Rome*, 81–5.

66. Urbach, "The Rabbinic Laws of Idolatry," 165, note 59.

67. Rutgers, *The Jews of Late Ancient Rome*, 83–5.

68. L. Y. Rahmani, *A Catalogue of Roman and Byzanatine Lead Coffins from Israel* (Jerusalem: Israel Antiquities Authority, 1999).

69. *Historia Ecclesiastica* 10.4.36–46, in L. M. White, *The Social Origins of Christian Architecture*, 2: 94–9. See also Branham, "Sacred Space under Erasure in Ancient Synagogues and Churches," 375–94.

70. J. H. Levy, *Studies in Jewish Hellenism* (Jerusalem: Bialik Institute, 1969), 255–8, in Hebrew, discusses Patristic sources for the disposition of the menorah through the eleventh century. See also Strauss, "The Date and Form of the Menorah of the Maccabees"; P. Bloch, "Seven-Branched Candelabra in Christian Churches," *Journal of Jewish Art*, 1 (1974), 46; M. Harrison, "From Jerusalem and Back Again: The Fate of the Treasures of Solomon," *Churches Built in Ancient Times: Recent Studies in Early Christian Archaeology*, ed. K. Painter (London: Society of Antiquaries of London: Accordia Research Centre, University of London), 239–48.

71. Bloch, "Seven-Branched Candelabra in Christian Churches," 46.

72. Discussed by H. Strauss, "The Date and Form of the Menorah of the Maccabees."

73. Negev, 1981, 28–9, 31–2; Hachlili, *The Menorah*, 272. A. Negev, *The Greek Inscriptions from the Negev* (Jerusalem: Franciscan Printing Press, 1981), following Avi-Yonah (cited by Goodenough) identifies this menorah as a palm branch. Reflecting the rarity of Christian menorahs, Negev writes (p. 28): "Note that the palm branch of seven leaves which is most unusual, and had it not been found in a church it would certainly have been considered as a menorah."

74. M. Simon, *Recherches d'Historie Judéo-Chrétienne* (Paris: Moulton, 1962), 181–87.

75. Hachlili, *The Menorah*, 271–2.

76. N. Bucaria (*Sicilia Judaica: Guida Alle Antichità Giudaiche Della Sicilia* [Palermo: Flaccovio, 1996], 54–5) suggests a possible fourth- to fifth-century date for this object, which is accepted by Hachlili (*The Menorah*, 272). Hachlili describes this object as a "five-armed menorah." Seven are visible, however, in the photograph published by Bucaria.

77. Hachlili, *The Menorah*, 273.

78. G. Galavaris, *Bread and the Liturgy; The Symbolism of Early Christian and Byzantine Bread Stamps* (Madison: University of Wisconsin Press, 1970), 34–6; D. M. Friedenberg, "The Evolution and Uses of Jewish Byzantine Stamp Seals," *Journal of the Walters Art Gallery*, 52–3 (1994–5), 17; Hachlili, *The Menorah*, 272.

79. Dothan, *Hammath Tiberias: Early Synagogues*, 33, pl. 9, no. 2.

80. Simon, *Recherches d'Historie Judéo-Chrétienne*, 187. See J. E. Taylor, "The Phenomenon of Early Jewish-Christianity: Reality or Scholarly Invention?" *Vigiliae Christianae*, 44 (1990), 313–34.

81. D. Barag, "Glass Pilgrim Vessels from Jerusalem, Part I," *Journal of Glass Studies*, 12 (1970), 48–63.

82. Ibid., 54.

83. Ibid., 46–8.

84. Ibid.

85. Barag ("Glass Pilgrim Vessels from Jerusalem, Part I," 61–2) posits that the Jewish bottles may have held earth from the Temple Mount.

86. Ibid., 53, ill. II.

87. Fine, *This Holy Place*, 114.

88. Barag, "Glass Pilgrim Vessels from Jerusalem, Parts II–III," *Journal of Glass Studies*, 13 (1971), 62–3.

89. I. Magen, "Samaritian Synagogues"; idem, "Samaritan Synagogues," *The Samaritans*, eds. E. Stern and H. Eshel (Jerusalem: Yad Izhak Ben Zvi Press and Israel Antiquities Authority, 2002), 405–6, 410, in Hebrew; idem, "The Areas of Samaritan Settlement in the Roman–Byzantine Period, *The Samaritans*, 262; Pummer, "Samaritan Material Remains and Archaeology"; idem, "Samaritan Synagogues and Jewish Synagogues: Similarities and Differences"; V. Sussman, "Samaritan Oil Lamps," *The Samaritans*, 342, 349–51; E. Ayalon, "Horbat Migdal (Tsur Natan) – An Ancient Samaritan Village," *The Samaritans*, 282.

90. Zori, "The Ancient Synagogue at Beth-Shean."

91. R. Jacoby, "The Four Species in Jewish and Samaritan Traditions," *FDS*, 225–30.

92. See, e.g., C. Roth, "Messianic Symbols in Palestinian Archaeology," *Palestine Exploration Quarterly*, 87 (1955), 151–64; D. Barag, "The Menorah in the Roman and Byzantine Periods: A Messianic Symbol," *Bulletin of the Anglo–Israel Archaeological Society*, 6 (1985–6), 44–7; Netzer and Weiss, *From Promise to*

Redemption, 36–7. For surveys of scholarly interpretation of "the meaning" of the menorah during late antiquity, see Levine, "The History and Significance of the Menorah in Antiquity," 147–8; Hachlili, *The Menorah*, 205–9.

93. See the commentary of Rabbenu Gershom, ad. loc. in the Vilna edition of the Babylonian Talmud; Ginzberg, *Legends of the Jews*, 6: 66, note 340; Brand, *Ceramics in Talmudic Literature*, 313.

94. Above, 100–101.

95. 11Q 18, Col. 8. *The Temple Scroll*, ed. Y. Yadin (Jerusalem: Israel Exploration Society, 1977–83), 2: 34–9.

96. See most prominently the *Baraita de-Melekhet ha-Mishkan* and R. Kirschner's introduction, pp. 1–11.

97. See P. R. Ackroyd, "The Temple Vessels – A Continuity Theme," *Studies in the Religion of Ancient Israel* (Supplements to Vetus Testamentum 23, Leiden: E. J. Brill, 1972), 166–81.

98. I discuss the notion of *zeman ha-zeh* as a significant category for interpreting rabbinic culture in Fine, *This Holy Place*, 21–3. See also Yerushalmi, *Zakhor*, 24.

99. As for, example, the Temple Institute in Jerusalem and its associated exhibition of "actual vessels that can be used in the third Temple." See *http://www.temple.org.il/*.

100. S. Brock, "A Letter Attributed to Cyril of Jerusalem on the Rebuilding of the Temple," *Bulletin of the School of Oriental and African Studies*, 40 (1977), 267–86.

101. Fine, "'When I Went to Rome."

102. See note 7 above.

103. *b. Menaḥot* 28b, *Rosh ha-Shanah* 24b, *Avodah Zarah* 43a, *Scolion to Megillat Taanit*, ms. Parma, Bibloteca Palatina, De Rossi 117, as cited by Noam, "The Miracle of the Cruse of Oil," 385, 390–1. See Sperber, "Shipudei ha-Makabim: Mah Hem?," 280–2.

104. In Jellenek, *Bet ha-Midrasch* 2: 88–91. See Lieberman's discussion in *Tosefta Ki-fshutah* to *t. Sotah* 13: 1. Compare *Avot de-Rabbi Nathan* (ed. S. Schechter [New York and Jerusalem: Jewish Theological Seminary, 1997] version A, 41 p. 133), which is far more ambiguous in this regard.

105. Ed. Rabinovitz, 2: 35–40. See Rabinovitz's full commentary on this text, ad. loc., and the comments of Lieberman, "Ḥazzanut Yannai," 241–2. It was partially translated and discussed by S. Schwartz, *Imperialism and Jewish Society*, 268–70.

106. See Psalm 68:14.

107. See Rabinovitz, ad. loc.

108. Another reference to the cult of the saints.

109. Klagsbald, "The Menorah as Symbol," correctly stresses the significance of light in general for the interpretation of the menorah.

110. 2: 242, lines 71–2.

111. See S. Elizur, "The Congregation in the Synagogue and the Ancient *Qedushta*," *Knesset Ezra: Literature and Life in the Synagogue, Studies Presented to Ezra Fleischer*, eds. S. Elizur, M. D. Herr, G. Shaked, and A. Shinan (Jerusalem: Yad Izhak Ben-Zvi Press, 1994), 171–90, in Hebrew; W. J. van Bekkum, "Hearing and Understanding Piyyut in the Liturgy of the Synagogue," *Zutot: Perspectives in Jewish Culture*, eds. S. Berger, M. Brocke, and I. Zwiep (Dordrecht, Boston, London: Kluger Academic Publishers, 2002), 1: 58–63.

112. *Pesiqta de-Rav Kahana*, 21, 3 (ed. B. Mandelbaum, 1: 320).

113. *Midrash Tanḥuma, Shemini* 8. See Rabinovitz's comment to Yannai's poem, p. 37, lines 12–13.

114. Leiden Papyrus X, in *Les Alchimistes grecs*, ed. R. Halleux (Paris: Belles Lettres, 1981), 1: 22, 40–1.

115. Israel Museum, Jerusalem, 180/52, folio 155v. Reproduced in Israeli, *In the Light of the Menorah*, 58. See also the menorah illustration in an Italian Bible dated 1300 at the British Library (Harley MS 5710, folio 136 recto).

116. *Pesiqta Rabbati*, ed. R. Ulmer, 1: xv–xvi, and note 18. See also Strack and Stemberger, *Introduction to the Talmud*, 322–9.

117. Ed. Ulmer, 1: xix.

118. Translations from *Pesiqta Rabbati* generally follow the Parma manuscript (3122, de Rossi 1240), with occasional references to other text traditions. See ed. Ulmer, 1: 101.

119. Ibid., 1: 107.

120. I consciously translate "base" (ירכה) and "shaft" (קנה) following Targum Neofiti and Targum Pseudo-Jonathan, as well as the *Revised Standard Version*, in order to maintain the single referent to קנה that is necessary for this midrash.

121. See ed. Friedman (Ish Shalom), (Vienna: s.n., 1880), 30a, note 29.

PART 4: READING HOLISTICALLY

1. S. Sinding-Larsen, *Iconography and Ritual: A Study of Analytical Perspectives* (Oslo: Universitetsforlaget As, 1984), 9.

2. Paulinus of Nola, *Paulinus' Churches at Nola: Texts, Translations and Commentary*, tr. R. C. Goldschmidt (Amsterdam: N. V. Nord-Hollandsche Untgevers Maatschappij, 1940), 4–5. On Paulinus and his building project, see D. E. Trout, *Paulinus of Nola: Life, Letters and Poems* (Berkeley, University of California, 1999).

3. Paulinus of Nola, *Paulinus' Churches*, 62–3.

4. P. Veyne ("Conduct Without Belief," 9) writes: "Let us suppose that the sculpted or painted decoration of churches has always been visible, that it has been understandable for the average spectator and that he took the trouble

to look at it. Even in this case, a church was not the 'catechism for the illiterate'. . . . Its imagery was for pleasure rather than instruction. . . ."

5. R. Webb, "The Aesthetics of Sacred Space: Narrative, Metaphor, and Motion in *Ekphraseis* of Church Buildings," *Dumbarton Oaks Papers*, 53 (1999), 61.

6. E.g. Wischnitzer, *The Messianic Theme in the Paintings of the Dura Synagogue*; Weiss and Netzer, *Promise and Redemption*, 38.

7. J. Wilkinson, "The Beth Alpha Synagogue Mosaic: Towards an Interpretation," *Jewish Art*, 5 (1978), 16–28.

8. See McLuhan's classic statement, *The Guttenberg Galaxy: The Making of Typographic Man* (New York: New American Library, 1962). See also Nelson, "To Say and to See: Ekphrasis and Vision in Byzantium," 148–9.

9. Weiss and Netzer, *Promise and Redemption*, 38.

10. In an e-mail dated January 26, 2004, Dr. Weiss informs me that this painting will be published in his forthcoming volume, *Deciphering an Ancient Message: The Sepphoris Synagogue in Its Archaeological and Socio-Historical Contexts* (Jerusalem: Israel Exploration Society).

11. This point is made regarding slides by R. Nelson, "The Slide Lecture, or, The Work of Art History in the Age of Mechanical Reproduction," *Critical Enquiry*, 26 (2000), 422.

12. *Microsoft Encarta Encyclopedia 99*, s.v. "Synagogue Ruins: Capernaum."

13. Nelson, *The Slide Lecture*, 434–5, reaches related conclusions.

14. T. F. Mathews, *The Early Churches of Constantanople: Architecture and Liturgy* (University Park, Penn.: Pennsylvania State University Press, 1971); P. Brown, "Art and Society in Late Antiquity," in *The Age of Spirituality: A Symposium*, ed. K. Weitzmann (New York: Metropolitan Museum of Art, 1980).

15. Under the influence of Catholic liturgists, Jewish liturgist L. A. Hoffman moved in this direction in his *Beyond the Text: A Holistic Approach to Liturgy* (Bloomington and Indianapolis: University of Indiana Press, 1989), 16–17.

16. K. Weitzmann, ed., *The Age of Spirituality: Late Antique and Early Christian Art, Third to Seventh Century* (New York: Metropolitan Museum of Art, 1979). For Weitzmann's perspective on this exhibition, see his *Sailing with Byzantium from Europe to America: The Memoirs of an Art Historian* (Munich: Editio Maris, 1994), 429–44.

17. See Weitzmann, *Sailing with Byzantium from Europe*, 439.

18. P. Brown, "Art and Society in Late Antiquity," *The Age of Spirituality: A Symposium*, 25. Veyne, "Conduct Without Belief," 4–6, also recognized the extent of Brown's innovation.

19. Brown has further developed this image, arguing that in the decoration of churches, "the entire Christian congregation, from the bishop downwards, wished to feel enveloped in a counter-*mundus*. To enter a church was to enter a *mundus* transformed." See Brown, "Images as a Substitute for Writing," 32.

20. See note 14 above and S. De Blaauw, "Architecture and Liturgy in Late Antiquity and the Middle Ages: Traditions and Trends in Modern Scholarship," *Archiv für Liturgie-Wissenschaft*, 33, no. 1 (1991), 1–34.

21. T. F. Mathews, *Byzantium from Antiquity to the Renaissance* (New York: Abrams, 1998), 97. See also my "A Liturgical Interpretation of Ancient Synagogue Remains in Late Antique Palestine," ed. L. I. Levine, *Continuity and Renewal: Jews and Judaism in Byzantine Christian Palestine* (Jerusalem: Dinur Center, Yad Izhak Ben-Zvi Press, 2004), 402–419, in Hebrew.

22. Mathews, *Byzantium*, 97–8.

23. Sinding-Larsen, *Iconography and Ritual*, 95; Gier Hellemo, *Adventus Domini: Eschatological Thought in 4th-Century Apses and Catecheses* (Leiden, 1989), esp. xx–xxi. Hellemo's corrective of Sinding-Larsen's disinterest in object-centered analysis is quite in order: "We agree with Sinding-Larsen's theoretical considerations but do, at the same time, maintain that the complicated 'dogmatical and doctrinal concepts expressed in the liturgy', can only be captured by a sort of iconological investigation" (p. xxi).

24. Sinding-Larsen, *Iconography and Ritual*, 38.

25. The opposite is the case with Galilean-type synagogues, particularly the Baram synagogue. At Baram, much of the facade and architectural shell are preserved, but few remains that tell us much about the religious life of the community are preserved. For that reason, I focus on extant mosaics in this chapter. For discussion of what may be learned from Galilean-type synagogues, see my *This Holy Place*, 105–21.

26. See, e.g., V. Tzaferis, *The Monastery of the Holy Cross in Jerusalem* (Jerusalem: E. Tzaferis, 1987).

CHAPTER 11: LITURGY AND THE ART OF THE DURA EUROPOS SYNAGOGUE

1. Goodenough, *Jewish Symbols*, 5: 4.

2. Kraeling, *The Synagogue*, 340.

3. Kayser, "Defining Jewish Art," 460.

4. Ibid.

5. Wharton, *Refiguring*, 38–51.

6. Fine, "Art and the Liturgical Context."

7. Goodenough, *Jewish Symbols*, 10: 198.

8. J. Gutmann, *The Dura-Europos Synagogue: A Re-evaluation* (Atlanta: Scholars Press, 1992), xx. See also idem, "Early Synagogue and Jewish Catacomb Art and Its Relation to Christian Art," *Aufstieg und Niedergang der Römische Welt* 2.21.2 (Berlin and New York: Walther de Gruyter, 1984), 1313–42; idem, "The Synagogue of Dura Europos: A Critical Analysis," *Evolution of the Synagogue: Problems and Progress*, eds. H. C. Kee and L. H. Cohick (Harrisburg: Trinity Press International, 1999), 83.

9. On the relationships between synagogue prayer and synagogue inscriptions, see Foerster, "Synagogue Inscriptions"; J. Yahalom, "Synagogue Inscriptions in Palestine."

10. *t. Shabbat* 14:3 and the parallels cited by Lieberman, *Tosefta Ki-fshutah*, 3:205–6.

11. The synagogue was a part of a group of contiguous buildings designated block L7 by the excavators. See Torrey, "Parchments and Papyri, 417; Kraeling, *The Synagogue*, 3.

12. See S. James, "Dura-Europos and the Chronology of Syria in the 250s AD," *Chiron*, 15 (1985), 111–24; D. MacDonald, "Dating the Fall of Dura-Europos," *Historia*, 35, no. 1 (1986), 45–68. These authors independently reach similar conclusions regarding the dating of the destruction of Dura Europos and the supposed Persian occupation of the city in 253 C.E.

13. The fragments are today preserved in the Beinecke Rare Book and Manuscript Library of Yale University, Inv. D. Pg. 25.

14. C. Torrey, "Parchments and Papyri," 417–19; Kraeling, *The Synagogue*, 259–60.

15. "Un Parchemin Liturgique Juif et la Gargote de la Synagogue a Doura-Europos," *Syria*, 20, no. 1 (1939), 23–34.

16. Sukenik, *The Synagogue of Dura-Europos*, 157–9.

17. S. Lieberman, *Yemenite Midrashim: A Lecture on the Yemenite Midrashim, Their Character and Value* (Jerusalem: Bamberger and Wahrmann, 1940), 40–1, in Hebrew; L. Ginzberg, *A Commentary on the Palestinian Talmud* (New York: Jewish Theological Seminary, 1941), 3: 355, in Hebrew.

18. Lieberman thanks Sukenik for bringing the parchment and Du Mesnil du Buisson's publication to his attention. Sukenik was apparently unaware of Ginzberg's comments.

19. "Ancient Eucharistic Prayers in Hebrew," *Jewish Quarterly Review*, 54 (1963–4), 100–9.

20. S. Laderman, "A New Look at the Second Register of the West Wall in Dura Europos," *Cahiers Archæologiques*, 45 (1997), 5–18.

21. C. B. Welles, R. O. Fink, and J. F. Gilliam, *Parchments and Papyri: The Excavations at Dura Europos, Final Report* V, Part 1 (New Haven: Yale University Press, 1959), 75.

22. *m. Megillah* 1:8, 2:2.

23. S. A. Birnbaum, *The Hebrew Scripts* (Leiden: E. J. Brill, 1971), 1:180–3.

24. See C. Sirat, *Les papyrus en caractères hébraïques trouvés en Egypte* (Paris: Editions du Centre national de la recherche scientifique, 1985), 27, pl. III.

25. B. Nitzan, *Qumran Prayer and Religious Poetry* (Leiden: E. J. Brill, 1994), 72–8, especially 76; J. Heinemann, *Prayer in the Talmud: Forms and Patterns*, tr. R. Sarason (Berlin: de Gruyter, 1977), 77–103.

26. *y. Berakhot* 9:1, 12d; *b. Berakhot* 40b. R. Kimelman, "Blessing Formulae and Divine Sovereignty in Rabbinic Literature," *Liturgy in the Life of the Synagogue*, eds. S. Fine and R. Langer (Winona Lake, Ind.: Eisenbrauns), forthcoming.

27. M. Beit Arie, "The Munich Palimpsest: A Hebrew Scroll Written Before the 8th Century," *Kirjat Sepher*, 43 (1967–8), 415, in Hebrew. The lone exception is Teicher, "Ancient Eucharistic," 100–9, who reads the X as representing *Christos*.

28. *Midrash Tehillim*, 136.

29. Lieberman, op. cit.

30. Published by A. Marmorstein, "*Shibolim*," *Ha-Zofeh: Quartalis Hebraica*, 10 (1926), 213. See also L. Finkelstein, "The Birkat Ha-Mazon," *Jewish Quarterly Review*, 8 (1928–9), 243, 246.

31. The most recent discussion of this prayer and parallel uses is by M. Bar-Ilan, "The Occurrence and Significance of Yoser ha'Adam Benediction," *Hebrew Union College Annual*, 56 (1985), 9–27, in Hebrew.

32. See Jeremiah 12:9, Ezekiel 31:6, 13.

33. Baer, *Seder Avodat Yisrael*, 75; D. de Sola Pool. *The Old Jewish–Aramaic Prayer: The Kaddish* (Leipzig: Rudolf Haupt, 1909), 17–18, 34, 61–2, which includes discussion of Hebrew versions.

34. C. Rabin, "The Linguistic Investigation of the Language of Jewish Prayer," *Studies in Aggadah, Targum and Jewish Liturgy in Memory of Joseph Heinemann*, eds. J. J. Petuchowski and E. Fleischer (Jerusalem: Magnes Press and Hebrew Union College Press, 1981), 163–71, in Hebrew.

35. J. T. Milik, "Parchemin judéo-araméen de Doura-Europos, an 200 ap. J.-C.," *Syria*, 45 (1968), 97–104. On languages used at Dura, see G. D. Kilpatrick, "Dura-Europos: The Parchments and the Papyri," *Greek, Roman and Byzantine Studies*, 5, no. 3 (1964), 215–25.

36. Torrey, "Parchments and Papyri," 419.

37. For the most recent edition, see Porphyry, *On Abstinence from Killing Animals*, tr. G. Clark (Ithaca: Cornell University Press, 2000).

38. Kraeling, *The Synagogue*, 259.

39. J. Neusner, *A History of the Jews in Babylonia* (Leiden: E. J. Brill, 1971), 1: 153. Taurobolium: The cultic slaughter of bulls.

40. On the relationships between the various religious buildings at Dura, see M. H. Gates, "Dura-Europos: A Fortress of

Syro–Mesopotamean Art," *Biblical Archaeologist*, 47, no. 3 (1984), 166–81.

41. The eating of animals does not seem to have been an issue at Dura or for most other residents of the Roman Empire. Within the Dura mithraeum itself, two graffiti listing foods and their costs were uncovered. Meat appears on both lists. See M. J. Vermaseren, ed., *Corpus Inscriptionum et Monumentorum Religionis Mithriacae* (The Hague: M. Nijhoff, 1956–60), nos. 64–5. One lists wine, meat, oil, wood, turnips . . . for prices that are illegible. The second lists meat for 19 dinars and 17 asses, a sauce for 1 dinar, paper for 1 ass, water and wood for 1 dinar each, and again wine for 28 dinars and 11 asses. Many thanks to Matthias Bode for this reference.

42. C. Osborne, "Ancient Vegeterianism," *Food in Antiquity*, eds. J. Wilkins, D. Harvey, and M. Dobson (Exeter: University of Exeter Press, 1995), 214–24, especially 218–23 on Porphyry. See also P. Garnsey, *Food and Society in Classical Antiquity* (Cambridge: Cambridge University Press, 1999), 16–17, 83–95.

43. R. Du Mesnil du Buisson, "Un Parchemin Liturgique Juif," 28. Translated by Teicher, *Eucharistic*, 102. Kraeling does not explain his implicit rejection of the interpretation of the fragment being related to the grace after meals. He seems to have been completely unaware of opinions of Lieberman, Ginzberg, and Sukenik.

44. Runesson, "The Synagogue at Ancient Ostia: The Building and Its History from the First to the Fifth Century," 46–9.

45. See Z. Safrai, "The Communal Functions of the Synagogue in the Land of Israel in the Rabbinic Period," *ASHAAD*, 1: 197.

46. Sukenik, *The Synagogue of Dura-Europos*, 158 (my translation).

47. C. Torrey, "The Aramaic Texts," in Kraeling, *The Synagogue*, 269; Naveh, *On Stone and Mosaic*, 133.

48. As I have demonstrated in *This Holy Place*, 80.

49. The designation used by Kraeling, west wall, band B, panel 4.

50. These images do not suggest the existence of an ornate ceremony for the entrance and removal of the Torah from the synagogue shrine. Cf. J. Gutmann, "Programmatic Painting in the Dura Synagogue," *The Dura Europos Synagogue*, ed. J. Gutmann (Missoula: Scholars Press, 1973), 147–8; idem, *The Dura-Europos Synagogue: A Re-evaluation (1932–1992)* (Atlanta: Scholar's Press, 1992), xxi. In the most recent version, "The Synagogue of Dura Europos," 81–2. On early Torah ceremonials, see Fine, *This Holy Place*, 77; R. Langer, "From Study of Scripture to a Reenactment of Sinai: The Emergence of the Synagogue Torah Service," *Worship*, 72, no. 1 (1998), 43–67.

51. *y. Taanit* 2:1, 65a. See my *This Holy Place*, 79–80, 145.

52. The conch was a form used to frame religious images during Greco–Roman antiquity. It appears often within other religious buildings of Dura Europos. See Kraeling, *The Synagogue*, 22–5, 55–61; S. Downey, *Mesopotamian Religious Architecture: Alexander through the Parthians* (Princeton: Princeton University Press, 1988), 89, 97, 107–8, 110, 113–14, 116, 118, 120, 128, and bibliography cited there. See M. Bratschkova, "Die Muschel in der antiken Kunst," *Bulletin de l'Institut Archeologique Bulgare*, 12, no. 1 (1938), 1–121.

53. Kraeling argues against this being an illustration of a Torah scroll on the basis that no supporting staves are visible (*The Synagogue*, 234, note 993). Such staves as are found on modern Torah scrolls are of later invention, and are not used by numerous Near Eastern communities. Note that Biblical scrolls at Qumran have no such staves.

54. The image is proportional to the size of the scroll that it holds. On scroll sizes, see S. Fine and M. Della Pergola, "The Ostia Synagogue and Its Torah Shrine," *The Jews of Ancient Rome*, ed. J. Goodnick Westenholz (Jerusalem: Bible Lands Museum, 1995), 42–57.

55. See R. Pfister and L. Bellinger, *The Textiles: The Excavations at Dura-Europos, Final Report IV, Part 2* (New Haven: Yale University Press, 1945), 10–12, especially tunic #1, pl. 5. Even as they provide concrete parallels to the garments illustrated in the wall paintings, our authors caution that the paintings "may be copied from earlier models" (p. 10). See B. Goldman, "The Dura Synagogue Costumes and Parthian Art," *The Dura-Europos Synagogue: A Re-evaluation*, ed. J. Gutmann, 52–77; idem, "Greco–Roman Dress in Syro–Mesopotamia," *The World of Roman Costume*, eds. J. L. Sebesta and L. Bonfante (Madison: University of Wisconsin Press, 1994), 163–81; L. A. Roussin, "Costume in Roman Palestine: Archaeological Remains and the Evidence of the Mishnah," *The World of Roman Costume*, eds. J. L. Sebesta and L. Bonfante (Madison: University of Wisconsin Press, 1994), 182–90.

56. Kraeling, *The Synagogue*, 81, note 239, suggests a Palmyrene parallel to the fringes, concluding that "in all probability those viewing the paintings would take the threads to represent the 'fringes,' but whether they were included by the artists for this purpose is not entirely clear."

57. S. Safrai and Z. Safrai, *The Haggadah of the Sages; The Passover Haggadah* (Israel: Carta, 1998), 133, note 14, in Hebrew, and the bibliography cited there.

58. Y. Yadin, *The Finds from the Bar Kokhba Period in the Cave of Letters*, 1: 226–58,

289–92; idem, *Bar-Kokhba: The Rediscovery of the Legendary*, 81–5. Identification of these mantles as Jewish prayer shawls is disputed by R. Arav, "Review of J. Magness, *The Archaeology of Qumran and the Dead Sea Scrolls* (Grand Rapids: Eerdmanns, 2002)," *Review of Biblical Literature*, 2003. http://www.bookreviews.org/pdf/2982_3085.pdf.

59. Kraeling, *The Synagogue*, 371–2. On the significance of hairstyles for art historical interpretation, see R. Brilliant, "Hairiness: A Matter of Style and Substance in Roman Portraits," *Eius Virtutis Studiosi: Classical and Postclassical Studies in Memory of Frank Edward Brown (1098–1988)*, eds. R. T. Scott and A. R. Scott (Washington, D.C.: National Gallery of Art, 1993), 303–14.

60. See Gutmann, "Early Synagogue and Jewish Catacomb Art and Its Relation to Christian Art," 1317.

61. L. Denqueker, "Le Zodiaque de la Synagogue de Beth Alpha et la Midrash," *Bijdragen, tijdschrift voor filospfie en theologie*, 47 (1986), 26. Denqueker further identifies the figure in wing panel 4 as Rabban Gamaliel proclaiming the lunar calendar.

62. Kraeling, *The Synagogue*, 234.

63. *m. Avot* 1:1. See G. D. Cohen's comments in his edition of Abraham Ibn Daud, *The Book of Tradition* (Philadelpha: Jewish Publication Society, 1967), xliii–lxii.

64. See most recently H. Najman, "Torah of Moses: Pseudonymous Attribution in Second Temple Writings," *Interpretation of Scripture in Early Judaism and Christiantiy: Studies in Language and Tradition*, ed. C. A. Evans (Sheffield: Sheffield Academic Press, 2000), 202–16. For Ezra in rabbinic literature, see Ginzberg, *Legends of the Jews*, 4: 354–9, 6: 441–9.

65. *Apion*, 2:175; *Acts* 15:21, *y. Megillah* 4:1, 75a; *b. Baba Qama* 82a. See I. Elbogen, *Jewish Liturgy: A Comprehensive History*, tr. R. P. Scheindlin (Philadelphia: Jewish Publication Society, 1993), 130, notes 3–6.

66. This literature on this type of projection is vast. For Josephus, see Feldman, *Josephus' Interpretation of the Bible*; for Targumic literature, Fine, "'Their Faces Shine with the Brightness of the Firmament.'" For medieval examples, see my "The Halakhic Motif in Jewish Iconography: Matzah-Baking in Late Medieval Southern Germany," *A Crown for a King: Studies in Memory of Prof. Stephen S. Kayser*, eds. S. Fine, S. Sabar, and W. Kramer (Berkeley: Magnes Museum and Jerusalem: Gefen, 2000), 111.

67. D. Flusser in H. Schreckenberg and K. Schubert, *Jewish Historiography and Iconography in Early and Medieval Christianity* (Assen/Maastricht: Van Gorcum and Minneapolis: Fortress Press, 1991), xvii. See also Jastrow, *Dictionary of the Targumim*, 642;

Sokoloff, *Dictionary of Jewish Palestinian Aramaic*, 260.

68. Incorporated into the Sabbath morning *Tefillah*. See, for example, *Seder Avodat Israel*, 219.

69. K. Baus, *Der Kranz in Antike und Christentum* (Bonn: P. Hanstein, 1940); R. E. Kolarik, "Wreath," *Oxford Dictionary of Byzantium*, ed. A. P. Kazhdan (New York: Oxford University Press, 1991), 2205.

70. The most recent discussion of this text is D. Stein, "Believing Is Seeing: Baba Batra 73a–75b," *Jerusalem Studies in Hebrew Literature*, 17 (1999), 9–32, in Hebrew.

71. Scholars have interpreted the covered structure to "Moses'" left as a scroll chest, which is possible, though not conclusive. See Kraeling, *The Synagogue*, 233–4.

72. Torrey, "The Aramaic Texts," 269.

73. Ibid., 270.

74. *Neophyti 1: Targum Palestinense Ms de la Biblioteca Vaticana*, ad. loc.; *Targum Pseudo-Jonathan of the Pentateuch: Text and Concordance*, ad. loc.

75. ובזעהי See *The Bible in Aramaic I: The Pentateuch According to Targum Onkelos*, ed. A. Sperber (Leiden: E. J. Brill, 1959), ad. loc.

76. Kilpatrick, "Dura-Europos: The Parchments and the Papyri," 216.

77. C. H. Kraeling, *The Christian Building*, with a contribution by C. Bradford Welles (New Haven: Dura Europos Publications, 1967), pl. xxxxvi, xxxxvii. Compare Kraeling's comments, p. 63. Kraeling suggests that the hands are "raised high in a gesture of astonishment and all face toward Christ and Peter in the lower zone." Even if he is correct, it seems to me that this "astonishment" (if that is what it is!) is expressed through a known liturgical form, superimposing the prayer stance of this community onto the Biblical scene.

78. See Welles's comments in Kraeling, *The Synagogue*, 266. Cf. Naveh, *On Stone and Mosaic*, 127–30.

79. Compare U. Ehrlich, *The Non-Verbal Language of Jewish Prayer* (Jerusalem: Magnes, 1999), 106–15, in Hebrew.

80. For the varied identifications of this image, Gutmann, *The Dura-Europos Synagogue: A Re-evaluation*, 142.

81. Gutmann, *The Dura-Europos Synagogue: A Re-evaluation*, 143; Ehrlich, *The Non-Verbal Language of Jewish Prayer*, 108–9.

82. Wharton, *Refiguring*, 43.

83. L. Dirven, *The Palmyrenes of Dura-Europos: A Study of Religious Interaction in Roman Syria* (Leiden: E. J. Brill, 1999), especially 67–98, 115–17. Wharton, *Refiguring*, 45. See Elsner, "Cultural Resistance and the Visual Image," 281. See also 282–99.

84. Wharton, *Refiguring*, 43.

85. M. Bregman, "The Darshan: Preacher and Teacher of Talmudic Times," *The Melton Journal*, 14 (1982), 3, 19, 26.

86. Wharton, *Refiguring*, 45–7; S. Fine, "Art and the Liturgical Context."

87. M. Kadushin, *The Rabbinic Mind* (New York: Jewish Theological Seminary, 1952) and *Worship and Ethics* (Chicago and London: University of Chicago Press, 1964); I. Heinemann, *Darkhei ha-Aggadah* (Jerusalem: Magnes, 1974).

88. J. Heinemann has demonstrated the close formal relationship between the grace after meals, the *Tefillah*, and other synagogue-related liturgical texts. See *Studies in Jewish Literature*, ed. A. Shinan (Jerusalem: Magnes, 1981), 3–11, in Hebrew.

89. For the purpose of this exercise, I will use the standard *Ashkenazi* version of the *Tefillah* as pronounced today, since I am interested in only general correspondences. Variance between the various versions, of course, is far less than the general agreement. See Baer, *Seder Avodat Yisrael*, 87–104.

90. David's role as messiah is emphasized in this panel and its inscription, "Samuel when he anointed (משח) David." See Torrey, *The Synagogue*, 273.

91. See Wharton, *Refiguring*, 43.

92. Kraeling, *The Synagogue*, 315. See also 264, cited by J. Gutmann, "The Synagogue of Dura Europos," 82. See the opinion of J. Greenfield and J. Naveh in his *On Stone and Mosaic*, 127, 131.

93. Page 183 above.

94. See Fine, "A Cosmopolitan 'Student of the Sages.'"

95. The fact that no image in the Dura church is drawn from the Old Testament sets a stark contrast between the fine quality of the synagogue paintings and the lower-quality New Testament images used by Christians. See Kraeling, *The Christian Building*, passim.

96. t. *Berakhot* 3:15–16, t. *Megillah* 2:18; Fine, *This Holy Place*, 45–6, 51–3, 112–17.

CHAPTER 12: SYNAGOGUE MOSAICS AND LITURGY IN THE LAND OF ISRAEL

1. L. Avrin, "Review of *The Frescoes of the Dura Synagogue and Christian Art*, by Kurt Weitzmann and Herbert L. Kessler," *Ars Orientalis*, 24 (1994), 162.

2. Sokoloff, *Dictionary of Jewish Palestinian Aramaic*, 3–28.

3. G. Foerster, "Synagogue Inscriptions and Their Relation to Liturgical Versions."

4. See Fine, *This Holy Place*, passim, especially 73, 88–9.

5. Foerster, "Synagogue Inscriptions," 23–6.

6. Hebrew Union College, Cincinnati, ms. 407, p. 23a. N. Wieder's transcription of this

text must be used with caution ("The Jericho Inscription and Jewish Liturgy," *The Formation of Jewish Liturgy in the East and the West: A Collection of Essays* [Jerusalem: Yad Izhak Ben-Zvi Press and Hebrew University of Jerusalem, 1998], 1: 128, in Hebrew).

7. Foerster, "Synagogue Inscriptions," 23–6; Wieder, "The Jericho Inscription," 141–4.

8. Page 183 above.

9. L. Y. Rahmani, "Mirror-Plaques from a Fifth-Century A.D. Tomb," *Israel Exploration Journal*, 14 (1964), 50–5.

10. On Christian parallels to the Beth Alpha "binding of Isaac," see J. Gutmann, "The Sacrifice of Isaac: Variations on a Theme in Early Jewish and Christian Art," *Sacred Images: Studies in Jewish Art from Antiquity to the Middle Ages, Thiasos ton Mouson: Studien zu Antike und Christentum. Festschrift für Josef Fink*, ed. D. Ahrens (Köln: Böhlau, 1984), 115–22.; idem, "Revisiting the Binding of Isaac Mosaic at Beth Alpha," *Bulletin of the Asia Institute* 6 (1992), 79–85.

11. Hachlili, *AJAALI*, 297–8. On the supposed identification of David in the Meroth mosaic, see Fine, *Sacred Realm*, 166–7.

12. Weiss and Netzer, *Promise and Redemption*, 24–5.

13. Ibid., 20–3.

14. G. Hanfmann, "The Continuity of Classical Art: Culture, Myth and Faith," *The Age of Spirituality: A Symposium*, ed. K. Weitzmann (New York: Metropolitan Museum of Art, 1980), 79–82.

15. On images of sacrifice at Dura, see H. Kessler in Weitzmann and Kessler, *The Frescos of the Dura Synagogue and Christian Art*, 156.

16. On pattern books, see B. Goldman, *The Sacred Portal: A Primary Symbol in Ancient Judaic Art* (Detroit: Wayne State University Press, 1966), 143–4; C. M. Dauphin, "Byzantine Pattern Books and 'Inhabited Scroll' Mosaics," *Art History*, 4 (1988), 401–23; L. A. Hunt, "The Byzantine Mosaics of Jordan in Context: Remarks on Imagery, Donors and Mosaicists," *Palestine Exploration Quarterly*, 126 (1994), 121–3, note 28.

17. G. Alon, *Studies in Jewish History* (Israel: Hakibbutz Hameuchad, 1967), 181–4, in Hebrew; Y. Deviri, *Light in the Sayings and Aphorisms of the Sages* (Holon, Israel: Y. Deviri, 1976), 112–15, in Hebrew; E. Zimmer, *Society and Its Customs: Studies in the History and Metamorphosis of Jewish Customs* (Ramat Gan: Bar Ilan University Press, 1996), 78–88, in Hebrew; D. Sperber, *The Customs of Israel* (Jerusalem: Mossad Harav Kook, 1994), 3: 88–91, in Hebrew.

18. J. Heinemann and J. J. Petuchowski, *The Literature of the Synagogue*, (New York: Behrman House, 1975). See A. Shinan's survey of this literature, "Synagogues in the Land of Israel:

The Literature of the Ancient Synagogue and Synagogue Archaeology," in Fine, *Sacred Realm*, 130–52.

19. For example, see *The Liturgical Poetry of Rabbi Yannai*, first fruits: 2: 175–82, menorah: 1: 340–5, zodiac: 1: 83–9, 2: 242.

20. *The Liturgical Poetry of Rabbi Yannai*, 2: 204.

21. Following *m. Rosh ha-Shanah* 3: 6 – "A shofar that is cracked and one stuck together is invalid. [If] one stuck together shards of shofars [to construct a composite shofar], it is invalid. [If] it was perforated and he filled [the hole], if [the filled hole] affects the sound of the shofar, it is invalid. If not, it is valid."

22. That is, not visible at the start of the new month. See Rabinovitz's comments, ad. loc.

23. Schechter, *Aspects of Rabbinic Theology*, 170–98; Moore, *Judaism*, 1: 538–46.

24. J. Wilkinson, *Egeria's Travels to the Holy Land* (Jerusalem: Ariel and Warminster: Aris & Phillips, 1981), 82–4.

25. Lewin, *Ozar ha-Gaonim*, 5: 51, no. 186; A. Yaari, *The History of the Festival of Simḥat Torah* (Jerusalem: Mosad ha-Rav Kook, 1964), 215, in Hebrew; Sperber, *The Customs of Israel* (1990), 1: 128–31, in Hebrew.

26. *Arba'ah Turim* (Jerusalem: Mosdot Shirat Devorah, 1993), *Orekh Ḥayyim* 610, and parallels.

27. See the sources cited by C. Adler and J. D. Eisenstein, "Flowers in the Home and the Synagogue," *JE*, 5: 420–1.

28. See C. Dauphin, "Mosaic Pavements as an Index of Prosperity and Fashion," *Levant*, 12 (1980), 112–134.

29. On Christian attitudes, see Tsafrir, *Eretz Israel from the Destruction of the Second Temple*, 416–17.

30. On remains of wall decoration, see Hachlili, *AJAALI*, 224.

31. Genizah documents speak of "reed mats" within Fatamid-period synagogues, some of which were "large" and used for seating on the floor. See S. D. Goitein, "Ambol – The Raised Platform in the Synagogue," *Eretz Israel*, 6 (1960), 166, in Hebrew; idem, "The Synagogue Building and Its Furnishings According to the Records of the Cairo Geniza," *Eretz Israel*, 7 (1964), 82, 90–2, in Hebrew; idem, *A Mediterranean Society* (Berkeley and Los Angeles: University of California Press, 1971), 1: 149–50.

32. W. A. Meeks and M. F. Meeks, "Vision of God and Scripture in a Fifth-Century Mosaic," *Reading in Christian Communities: Essays on Interpretation in the Early Church*, eds. C. A. Bobertz and D. Brakke (Notre Dame: Notre Dame University Press, 2002), 128.

33. *t. Megillah* 3: 21; Fine, *This Holy Place*, 30, 45–6.

34. For the earlier history of the Torah shrine, see Fine, *This Holy Place*, 30, 35–94.

35. See Fine, *This Holy Place*, 112–17 and the bibliography cited there; R. Hachlili, "Torah Shrine and Ark in Ancient Synagogues: A Reevaluation," *Zeitschrift des Deutschen Palästina-Vereins*, 116, no. 2 (2000), 146–83.

36. E. M. Meyers, J. Strange, and C. Meyers, "The Ark of Nabratein: A First Glance," *Biblical Archaeologist*, 44, no. 4 (1981), 237–43; E. M. Meyers and C. Meyers, "Finders of the Lost Ark," *Biblical Archaeology Review*, 7, no. 4 (1981), 29–39.

37. Birds atop aediculae appear with some frequency in late antique art. See, e.g., A. Gayet, *Les Monuments Coptes* (Paris: E. Leroux, 1889), pl. 24, fig. 29; pl. 86, fig. 97; Fine and Rutgers, "New Light on Judaism in Asia Minor during Late Antiquity," 18–19.

38. See, e.g., *y. Megillah* 3:1, 73d; *y. Yoma* 7: 1, 44b; *y. Megillah* 4:5, 75b; *y. Sota* 8:6, 22a.

39. See examples presented by A. Stauffer, ed., *Textiles of Late Antiquity* (New York: Metropolitan Museum of Art, 1995), especially 8, 10, 14, 24, 43.

40. Cf. D. Amit, "'The Curtain Would Be Removed for Them' (Yoma 54a): Ancient Synagogue Depictions," *FDS*, 231–4.

41. Lions: Hachlili, *AJAALI*, 322–5.

42. Fine, *This Holy Place*, 80.

43. I. M. Ta-Shma surveys the sources on lighting lamps in synagogues, "Synagogal Sanctity – Symbolism and Reality," *Knesset Ezra: Literature and Life in the Synagogue, Studies Presented to Ezra Fleischer*, eds. S. Elizur, M. D. Herr, G. Shaked, and A. Shinan (Jerusalem: Yad Izhak Ben-Zvi Press, 1994), 353–8, in Hebrew.

44. See Hachlili, *AJAALI*, 269–72.

45. L. Habas, "The *Bema* and Chancel Screen in Synagogues and Their Origin," *FDS*, 122–123, describes these objects as "incense cups."

46. As in the mosaic pavement of the baptistery at Skhira in Tunisia. See M. Fendri, *Basiliques Cretiennes de la Skhira* (Paris: Presses Universitaires de France, 1961), 50–3, who recognized the similarities between the representation at Na'aran and this image; Fine, *This Holy Place*, 116–17. A second such image appears on a Coptic stele. See Villa Hügel, *Koptische Kunst: Christentum m Nil* (Essen: Villa Hügel, 1963), 243, no. 98.

47. See Meyers and Meyers, "The Ark in Art," 1982.

48. "lamp for illumination." *Seder Avodat Yisrael*, 230; A. Yaari, "The *Mi'Sheberakh* Prayers: History and Texts," *Kirjath Sepher* 33, nos. 1–2 (1957–8), 118–30, 233–51, in Hebrew.

49. Many thanks to Richard Sarason for this report.

50. Poem 14, lines 98–103, *S. Pontii Meropii Paulini Nolani Opera, Corpus Scriptorum Ecclesiasticorum Latinorum*, ed. G. de Hartel (Vienna: Tempsky and Leipzig: G. Freytag, 1894), 30.3: 49; translated by M. McHugh in *The Poems of St. Paulinus of Nola*, ed. P. G. Walsh (New York and Paramus, N.J.: Newman Press, 1975), 80.

51. Poem 18, tr. R. Kalkman in Walsh, *The Poems of St. Paulinus of Nola*, 115.

52. Following Naveh, *On Stone and Mosaic*, 99.

53. See, e.g., Barag, Porat, and Netzer, "The Synagogue at En-Gedi," 117.

54. See Fine, *Sacred Realm*, 118.

55. Barag, Porat, and Netzer, "The Synagogue at En-Gedi," 117.

56. N. Zori, "The Ancient Synagogue at Beth-Shean," *Eretz Israel*, 8: 163, pl. 33, no. 3, in Hebrew.

57. Bahat, "A Synagogue at Beth-Shean," 83–4.

58. Fine, *This Holy Place*, 84–5; Ta-Shma, "Synagogal Sanctity," 353–8.

59. On the objects utilized, see Fine, *Sacred Realm*, cat. nos. 44, 50, 54, 55, 56, 57.

60. S. Saller and B. Bagatti, *The Town of Nebo (Khirbet El-Mekhayyat)* (Jerusalem: Franciscan, 1949), 30–9; M. Piccirillo, *Mount Nebo* (Jerusalem: Custodia Terra Sancta, 1987), 83–7; Foerster, "Christian Allegories and Symbols," 198–200.

61. Magen, "Samaritian Synagogues," 66–90.

62. Zori, "The Ancient Synagogue at Beth-Shean."

63. For example, the garden peristyle of the Villa of the Papyri in Herculaneum. See J. J. Deiss, *Herculaneum: Italy's Buried Treasure*, (Malibu: J. P. Getty Museum, 1989), 62–3.

64. *y. Taanit* 2:1, 65a.

65. Fine, *This Holy Place*, 88–90.

66. Naveh, "Aramaic and Hebrew Inscriptions," 307, and bibliography cited there.

67. J. Hoffman, "The Ancient Torah Service in Light of the Realia of the Talmudic Era," *Conservative Judaism*, 42, no. 2 (1989–90), 44.

68. Ehrlich, *The Non-Verbal Language of Jewish Prayer*, 106–15.

69. See Hachlili, *AJAALI*, 294–5 and pl. 26.

70. "Pass before the [Torah] chest." See the relevant bibliography cited by Z. Weiss, "The Location of the Sheliah Tzibbur during Prayer," *Cathedra*, 55 (1990), 9–21, in Hebrew; Regarding the situation in the Babylonian Talmud, see J. Hoffman, "Ancient Torah Service," 42–44.

71. *t. Berakhot* 3:6 and parallels.

72. For example, on the basket of *bikkurim*, birds appear on either side of the basket. This is not an unusual convention in Byzantine-period art, appearing, for example, in Ravenna.

What is unusual is that the doves are suspended upside down from their sides. This fits nicely with a early tradition (*baraita*) in *y. Bikkurim* 3:4, 65d, that suggests the birds were suspended "outside" the baskets in order to maintain the cleanliness of the first fruits. Our image of the *bikkurim* goes a step further: It seems that the birds are suspended upside down to ensure that the first fruits remain unsoiled. This observation was made to me in personal correspondence by Stuart Miller shortly after the discovery of the mosaic. Cf. Weiss and Netzer, *Promise and Redemption*, 24.

73. M. Swartz, "Sage, Priest and Poet: Typologies of Religious Leadership in the Ancient Synagogue," *JCP*, 109. J. Yahalom (*Poetry and Society in Jewish Galilee of Late Antiquity* [Tel Aviv: Hakibbutz Hameuchad, 1999], 111–16, in Hebrew) and others have recently asserted that Temple imagery in the Sepphoris mosaic suggests heightened social status of priests during the Byzantine period. I argue strenuously against this position, which assumes that the presence of Temple themes must, of necessity, reflect on the social status of priests. See my "Between Liturgy and Social History: Priestly Power in Late Antique Palestinian Synagogues?" *Journal of Jewish Studies*, 56, no. 1 (2005).

74. Z. Weiss and E. Netzer, *Promise and Redemption*, 30–1. See also J. Yahalom, *Poetry and Society*, 109–10.

75. *Genesis Rabba* 42, ed. J. Theodor and Ch. Albeck, 419, and the parallels cited there.

76. Fine, *This Holy Place*, 82–3.

77. *Hilkhot Eretz-Israel min ha-Geniza*, ed. M. Margoliot, brought to press by I. Ta-Shma (Jerusalem: Mossad Harav Kook, 1973), 131–2.

78. Cf. Z. Safrai, "From Synagogue to Little Temple," *Proceedings of the Tenth World Congress in Jewish Studies*, Division B (Jerusalem: World Union For Jewish Studies, 1990), 150–1.

79. J. Mann, "Anan's Liturgy and His Half-Yearly Cycle for Reading the Law," *Journal of Jewish Lore and Philosophy* 1, nos. 1–4 (1919), 344, note 26, in Hebrew. Al-Qumisi informs us that by analogy to the Temple, rabbinites would not enter synagogues in a state of impurity. See also M. Zucker, *Rav Saadya Gaon's Translation of the Torah* (New York: Jewish Theological Seminary, 1959), 171, note 666, in Hebrew.

80. *y. Megillah* 3:3, 74a. On ablution of hands and feet before prayer, see N. Wieder, "Islamic Influences on the Hebrew Cultus," *Melilah*, 2 (1946), 43, in Hebrew.

81. Barag, Porat, and Netzer, "The Synagogue at En-Gedi," 117.

82. Shinan, "Synagogues in the Land of Israel: The Literature of the Ancient Synagogue and Synagogue Archaeology."

83. Naveh, *On Stone and Mosaic*, 106–9; B. Mazar, "The Inscription on the Pavement of the Synagogue of Ein Gedi," *Tarbiz*, 40 (1970), 22–3, sets this invocation within the rhetoric of the entire inscription and suggests a parallel from *Song of Songs Rabba* 7:5.

84. O. G. von Simson, *Sacred Fortress: Byzantine Art and Statecraft in Ravenna* (Princeton: Princeton University Press, 1987), 25; Mathews, *Byzantium*, 103. See also J. Tuerk, "An Early Byzantine Inscribed Amulet and its Narratives," *Byzantine and Medieval Greek Studies*, 23 (1999), 34, who interprets the *orans* position as illustrated on an early Byzantine amulet.

85. On synagogue screens, see Foerster, "Decorated Marble Chancel Screens"; Branham, "Sacred Space under Erasure"; Fine, "'Chancel' Screens"; Habas, "The *Bema* and Chancel Screen," 111–130.

86. Foerster, "Decorated Marble Chancel Screens."

87. Cambridge University Library, T-S A45.6, fol. 1v, Ed. S. Hopkins, *A Miscellany of Literary Pieces from the Cambridge Genizah Collections* (Cambridge: Cambridge University Library, 1978), 12–14. For a detailed discussion of this text, see Fine, "'Chancel' Screens." Cf. Habas, "The *Bema* and Chancel Screen," 115, note 18.

88. The Genizah text actually reads *meturgaman mishpaḥah*. The notion of a "family translator" is unknown elsewhere in rabbinic literature.

89. G. M. Crowfoot, "Churches and Ecclesiastical Use," *Gerasa: City of the Decapolis*, ed. C. H. Kraeling (New Haven: Yale University Press, 1938), 175–6.

90. I. Sonne, "The Zodiac Theme in Ancient Synagogues and in Hebrew Printed Books," *Studies in Bibliography and Booklore*, 1 (1953–4), 4.

91. Dothan, *Hammath Tiberias: Early Synagogues*; R. Hachlili, "The Zodiac in Ancient Jewish Art: Representation and Significance," *Bulletin of the American Schools for Oriental Research* 228 (1977), 61–77; idem, "The Zodiac in Ancient Jewish Synagogal Art: A Review," *Jewish Studies Quarterly* 9, no. 3, (2002), 219–58; Weiss and Netzer, *Promise and Redemption*, 26–9.

92. K. Lehmann, "The Dome of Heaven," *Art Bulletin*, 27 (1945), 1–27.

93. Mathews, *The Clash of the Gods*, 142–76.

94. A. G. Sternberg, *The Zodiac of Tiberias/The Steps of Ahaz and the Steps of the Temple Mount* (Tiberias: Aharon G. Sternberg, 1972), 72–5, in Hebrew; Hanfmann, "The Continuity of Classical Art," 26–7. For other parallels, see Hachlili, "The Zodiac in Ancient Jewish Art: Representation and Significance," 61–3.

95. F. Boll, *Beiträge zur Ueberlieferungsgeschichte der griechischen Astrologie und Astronomie* (Munich: s.n., 1899), 126.

96. Hachlili, "The Zodiac in Ancient Jewish Art: Representation and Significance"; Weiss and Netzer, *Promise and Redemption*, 26–9.

97. H. G. Gundel, *Zodiakos: Tierkreisbilder im Altertum: Kosmische Bezüge und Jenseitsvorstellungen im antiken Alltagsleben* (Mainz am Rhein: Verlag P. von Zabern, 1992), no. 84.

98. Gundel, *Zodiakos*, no. 85.

99. I. Fishoff, ed. *The Realm of the Stars* (Jerusalem: Israel Museum, 2001), 29.

100. R. Jacoby, "The Four Seasons in Zodiac Mosaics: The Tallaras Baths in Astypalaea, Greece," *Israel Exploration Journal*, 51 (2001), 225–30.

101. See A. Shinan, *The Embroidered Targum, The Aggadah in Targum Pseudo-Jonathan to the Pentateuch* (Jerusalem: Magnes, 1992), 113–14, in Hebrew and Fine, *This Holy Place*, 15–16.

102. Alternatively, A. Mirsky, "Aquarius and Aries in the Ein Gedi Inscription and in Early *Piyyutim*" *Tarbiz* 40 (1970), 376–84, in Hebrew. Mirsky finds a parallel to this mirror imaging in extant *piyyutim*, which would suggest that the mirroring at Hammath Tiberias was intentional.

103. Dothan, *Hammath Tiberias: Early Synagogues*, 48.

104. As, for example, in the Monastery of the Lady Mary in Beth Shean. See G. M. FitzGerald, *A Sixth-Century Monastery at Beth Shan (Scythopolis)* (Philadelphia: University of Pennsylvania Press, 1939).

105. Naveh, *On Stone and Mosaic*, 106–8.

106. FitzGerald, *A Sixth-Century Monastery*.

107. Mathews, *The Clash of the Gods*, 149.

108. Hachlili, *The Zodiac in Ancient Jewish Art: Representation and Significance*, 63.

109. M. Avi-Yonah, "The Caesarea Inscription of the Twenty-Four Priestly Courses," *The Teacher's Yoke: Studies in Memory of Henry Trantham*, eds. E. J. Vardamon and J. L. Garrett (Waco, Tex.: Baylor University Press, 1964), 57.

110. See Sonne, "The Zodiac Theme," 4.

111. M. Avi-Yonah, "Ancient Synagogues," *Ariel*, 32 (1973), 43.

112. Avi-Yonah, "The Caesarea Inscription of the Twenty-Four Priestly Courses," 50–7.

113. G. Foerster, "The Zodiac Wheel in Ancient Synagogues and Its Iconographic Sources," *Eretz Israel*, (1986) 18: 380–91, in Hebrew; idem, "The Zodiac in Ancient Synagogues and its place in Jewish Thought and Literature," *Eretz Israel* 19 (1987), 225–234.

114. Weiss and Netzer, *Promise and Redemption*, 38–9.

115. For the latter Second Temple period, J. C. Vanderkam, *Calendars in the Dead Sea Scrolls: Measuring Time* (London and New York: Routledge, 1998).

116. S. Stern, *Calendar and Community: A History of the Jewish Calendar, Second Century BCE–Tenth Century CE* (Oxford and New York: Oxford University Press, 2001).

117. Ibid., 87–97, 146–53.

118. Ibid., 80–5.

119. S. Lieberman, "Neglected Sources," *Tarbiz*, 42, nos. 1–2 (1973), 54, in Hebrew.

120. Sukenik, *The Ancient Synagogue of Beth Alpha*, 57.

121. M. Narkiss, "The Zodiac in Jewish Art," *Kirjath Sepher*, 16 (1939–40), 513–19, in Hebrew; Fishhoff, *The Realm of the Stars*, passim, especially 44–7.

122. J. Yahalom, "Piyyut as Poetry," *The Synagogue in Late Antiquity*, ed. L. I. Levine (Philadelphia: American Schools for Oriental Research, 1987), 120. See also idem, "The Zodiac Wheel in Early Piyyut in Eretz-Israel," *Jerusalem Studies in Hebrew Literature*, 9 (1986), 313–22, in Hebrew; idem, *Poetry and Society*, 20–4.

123. M. Klein, "Palestinian Targum and Synagogue Mosaics," *Immanuel*, 11 (1980), 33–45.

124. G. Stemberger, "Die Bedeutung des Tierkreises auf Mosaikfussboden Spaetantiker Synagogen," *Kairos* 17 (1975), 34–44.

125. Pp. 187–189 above.

126. Discussed by Yahalom, "Piyyut as Poetry," 119–20.

127. *Aramaic Poetry of the Byzantine Period from Eretz-Israel*, eds. J. Yahalom and M. Sokoloff (Jerusalem: Israel Academy of Sciences and Humanities, 1999), no. 37, 230–4.

128. Variant reading cited by Yahalom and Sokoloff, ad. loc.

129. In the golden calf incident.

130. That is, that Moses broke on the seventeenth of Tammuz (*m. Ta'anit* 4:6).

131. A reference to Hanukkah.

132. The texts for Shevat and Adar are fragmentary. See Sokoloff and Yahalom, ad. loc.

133. A. J. Heschel, *The Sabbath: Its Meaning for Modern Man* (New York: Farrar, Straus and Young, 1951), 8.

134. T. M. Rudavsky, *Time Matters: Time, Creation and Cosmology in Medieval Jewish Philosophy* (Albany: State University of New York Press, 2000), 4; E. R. Wolfson, *Along the Path: Studies in Kabbalistic Myth, Symbolism, and Hermeneutics* (Albany: State University of New York Press, 1997), especially note 4.

135. *m. Berakhot* 1:1.

136. Baer, *Seder Avodat Yisrael*, 164.

137. Yannai, *piyyut* 140, lines 55–60, ed. Rabbiniwitz, 1: 143–4. See also 1: 66.

138. Rabbinowitz, *Yannai*, 65–8.

139. Sokoloff and Yahalom, *Aramaic Poetry of the Byzantine Period*, no. 37, 222–229. The translation makes use of A. S. Rodrigues Pereira, *Studies in Aramaic Poetry (c. 100 B.C.E.–600 C.E.): Selected Jewish, Christian and Samaritan Poems* (Assen, The Netherlands: Van Gorcum, 1997), 395–7 and 75–86. See also J. C. Greenfield and M. Sokoloff, "Astrological and Related Omen Texts in Jewish Palestinian Aramaic," *Journal of Near Eastern Studies*, 48, no. 3 (1989), 204–5.

140. Yahalom and Sokoloff (ad. loc.) note that "here the poet emphasizes the advantage of the month of Nisan over the other months."

141. The poem is an hourglass acrostic, reversing direction after reaching the last letter of the alphabet.

142. סימכ See Yahalom and Sokoloff, ad. loc., Sokoloff, *A Dictionary of Jewish Palestinian Aramaic*, 375.

CHAPTER 13: SANCTITY AND THE ART OF ANCIENT SYNAGOGUES

1. Fine, *This Holy Place*, vii.

2. Ibid., 159–62.

3. Ibid., 124.

4. M. Kadushin, *The Rabbinic Mind*, 167–93, and idem, *Worship and Ethics*, 216–34.

EPILOGUE

1. Slouschz was hailed as "the great Jewish archaeologist" in a solicitation letter dated July 20, 1923, following up on his recent fundraising mission to America on behalf of the Jewish Palestine Exploration Society. See Genazim: The Archives of the Hebrew Writers Association in Israel 35149–א. For Slouschz's correspondence with R. Y. Ben-Zvi, Genazim 27307–20א. I. Nimtzovich, "*Historian ha-Niskah: Prof. Nahum Slouschz ben 95*," ha-Umah November, 1966. idem, *Bez'ukhutam – D'muyoth Min Hapinkas: For Their Sake – Portraits form a Note-book* (Israel: Ministry of Defense, 1968), 227–30, in Hebrew.

SELECTED BIBLIOGRAPHY OF SECONDARY LITERATURE

Alon, Gedalyah. 1967. *Studies in Jewish History*. Israel: Hakibbutz Hameuchad. Hebrew.

Avigad, Nahman. 1954. *Ancient Monuments in the Kidron Valley*. Jerusalem: Mosad Bialik. Hebrew.

—— 1976. *Beth She'arim*. 3. New Brunswick: Rutgers University Press.

—— 1980. *Discovering Jerusalem*. Nashville: Thomas Nelson.

Avi-Yonah, Michael. 1981. *Art in Ancient Palestine*, eds. H. Katzenstein and Y. Tsafrir. Jerusalem: Magnes.

Ayali, Meir. 1987. *Workers and Craftsmen: Their Labor and Their Status in Rabbinic Literature*. Israel: Yad la-Talmud. Hebrew.

Barag, Dan. 1970. "Glass Pilgrim Vessels from Jerusalem, Part I." *Journal of Glass Studies* 12: 35–63.

—— 1971. "Glass Pilgrim Vessels from Jerusalem, Parts II–III." *Journal of Glass Studies* 13: 45–63.

—— 1987. "The Showbread Table and the Facade of the Temple on Coins of the Bar-Kokhba Revolt." *Qadmoniot* 20 (1–2): 22–5. Hebrew.

Barth, Frederik. 1969. *Ethnic Groups and Boundaries*. Boston: Little, Brown.

Baumgarten, Joseph M. 1999. "Art in the Synagogue: Some Talmudic Views." *JCP* 71–86. Updated from *Judaism* 19 (1970): 196–206.

Begg, C. T. 1997. "Solomon's Apostasy (1 Kgs. 11, 11–13) According to Josephus." *Journal for the Study of Judaism* 28 (3): 294–313.

Bekkum, W.-J. van. 2002. "Hearing and Understanding Piyyut in the Liturgy of the Synagogue." In *Zutot: Perspectives in Jewish Culture*, eds. S. Berger, M. Brocke, and I. Zwiep. Dordrecht, Boston, London: Kluwer Academic Publishers. 1: 58–63.

Ben Dov, Meir. 1982. *In the Shadow of the Temple: The Discovery of Ancient Jerusalem*. Jerusalem: Keter.

Ben Yehuda, Eliezer. 1980. *A Complete Dictionary of Ancient and Modern Hebrew*. Jerusalem: Makor. Hebrew.

Biale, David. 1979. *Gershom Scholem: Kabbalah and Counter-history*. Cambridge, Mass.: Harvard University Press.

Bland, Kalman P. 2000. *The Artless Jew: Medieval and Modern Affirmations and Denials of the Visual*. Princeton: Princeton University Press.

Blau, Ludwig. 1924. "Early Christian Epigraphy, Considered from the Jewish Point of View." *Hebrew Union College Annual* 1: 221–37.

—— 1926. "Early Christian Archaeology from a Jewish Point of View." *Hebrew Union College Annual* 3: 157–215.

Blidstein, Gerald J. 1968. *Rabbinic Legislation on Idolatry – Tractate Abodah Zarah, Chapter I*. Ph.D. dissertation. New York: Yeshiva University. Hebrew.

—— 1974a. "Prostration and Mosaics in Talmudic Law." *Bulletin of the Institute of Jewish Studies* 2: 19–39.

—— 1974b. "R. Yohanan, Idolatry, and Public Privilege." *Journal for the Study of Judaism* 5: 154–61.

—— 1975. "Nullification of Idolatry in Rabbinic Law." *Proceedings of the American Academy for Jewish Research* 41–2: 1–44.

Bloch, Peter. 1974. "Seven-Branched Candelabra in Christian Churches." *Journal of Jewish Art* 1: 44–9.

Boyarin, Daniel. 1990. "The Eye in the Torah: Ocular Desire in Midrashic Hermeneutic." *Critical Inquiry* 16 (3): 532–50.

Brand, Joshua. 1953. *Ceramics in Talmudic Literature*. Jerusalem: Mossad Harav Kook. Hebrew.

Brown, Peter. 1980. "Art and Society in Late Antiquity." In *The Age of Spirituality: A Symposium*, ed. K. Weitzmann. New York: Metropolitan Museum of Art. 17–28.

—— 1982. *Society and the Holy in Late Antiquity*. Berkeley and Los Angeles: University of California Press.

Brunner, Arnold W. 1907. "Synagogue Architecture." *The Brickbuilder: Devoted to the Interests of Architecture in Materials of Clay*. 16 (2–3): 20–4, 37–44.

Burford, Alison. 1974. *Craftsmen in Greek and Roman Society*. Ithaca: Cornell University Press.

Cohen, Anthony P. 1985. *The Symbolic Construction of Community*. Chichester: E. Horwood; London and New York: Tavistock Publications.

Cohen, Richard I. 1998. *Jewish Icons: Art and Society in Modern Europe*. Berkeley and Los Angeles: University of California Press.

Dauphin, Claudine. 1980. "Mosaic Pavements as an Index of Prosperity and Fashion." *Levant* 12: 112–34.

Dothan, Moshe. 1983. *Hammath Tiberias: Early Synagogues*. Jerusalem: Israel Exploration Society.

Elbogen, Ismar. 1993. *Jewish Liturgy: A Comprehensive History*, trans. R. P. Scheindlin. Philadelphia, New York, Jerusalem: Jewish Publication Society.

Eliav, Yaron Z. 1998. "Visiting the Sculptural Environment: Shaping the Second Commandment." In *Talmud Yerushalmi and Graeco–Roman Culture*, ed. P. Schäfer. Tübingen: Mohr Siebeck. 3: 411–33.

—— 2000. "The Roman Bath as a Jewish Institution: Another Look at the Encounter Between Judaism and the Greco–Roman Culture." *Journal for the Study of Judaism* 31 (4): 416–54.

Elizur, Shulamit. 1994. "The Congregation in the Synagogue and the Ancient Qedushta." In *Knesset Ezra: Literature and Life in the Synagogue, Studies Presented to Ezra Fleischer*, eds. S. Elizur, M. D. Herr, G. Shaked, and A. Shinan. Jerusalem: Yad Izhak Ben-Zvi. 171–90. Hebrew.

Elsner, Jás, ed. 1995. *Art and the Roman Viewer: The Transformation of Art from the Pagan World to Christianity*. Cambridge: Cambridge University Press.

—— 1998. *Imperial Rome and Christian Triumph: The Art of the Roman Empire AD 100–450*. Oxford: Oxford University Press.

2003. "Archaeologies and Agendas: Reflections on Late Ancient Jewish Art and Early Christian Art." *Journal of Roman Studie.* 93: 114–128.

Evans, Helen C., and William D. Wixom, eds. 1997. *The Glory of Byzantium: Art and Culture of the Middle Byzantine Era, A.D. 843–1261.* New York: Metropolitan Museum of Art.

Feldman, Louis H. 1996. *Studies in Hellenistic Judaism.* Leiden: E. J. Brill.

1998. *Josephus' Interpretation of the Bible.* Berkeley and Los Angeles: University of California Press.

Fine, Steven, ed. 1996. *Sacred Realm: The Emergence of the Synagogue in the Ancient World.* New York: Oxford University Press and Yeshiva University Museum.

1997. *This Holy Place: On the Sanctity of the Synagogue During the Greco–Roman Period.* Notre Dame, Ind.: University of Notre Dame Press.

1999a. "'Chancel' Screens in Late Antique Palestinian Synagogues: A Source from the Cairo Genizah." In *Religious and Ethnic Communities in Later Roman Palestine,* ed. H. Lapin. Potomac, Md.: University Press of Maryland. 67–85.

1999b. "Non-Jews in the Synagogues of Palestine: Rabbinic and Archaeological Perspectives." *JCP* 224–41.

2000. "A Note on Ossuary Burial and the Resurrection of the Dead in First Century Jerusalem." *Journal of Jewish Studies* 51: 69–76.

2002. 'Their Faces Shine with the Brightness of the Firmament': Study Houses and Synagogues in the *Targumim* to the Pentateuch," *Biblical Translation in Context,* ed. F. W. Knobloch. Bethesda, Md.: University Press of Maryland. 63–92.

2003. "Another View of Jerusalem's Necropolis During the First Century: A Decorated Ossuary from the Nelson and Helen Glueck Collection of the Cincinnati Art Museum." *Journal of Jewish Studies* 54 (2): 233–41.

2005. "Between Liturgy and Social History: Priestly Power in Late Antique Palestinian Synagogues?" *Journal of Jewish Studies* 56 (1).

Fine, Steven, and Leah Bierman Fine. 1999. *Where God Dwells: A Child's History of the Synagogue.* Los Angeles: Torah Aura.

Fine, Steven, and Leonard Victor Rutgers. 1996. "New Light on Judaism in Asia Minor during Late Antiquity: Two Recently Identified Inscribed Menorahs." *Jewish Studies Quarterly* 3 (1): 1–23.

Fine, Steven, and Bruce Zuckerman. 1985. "The Menorah as Symbol of Jewish Minority Status." In *Fusion in the Hellenistic*

East, ed. S. Fine. Los Angeles: University of Southern California Fisher Gallery. 23–30.

Finney, Paul Corby. 1994. *The Invisible God: The Earliest Christians on Art.* New York: Oxford University Press.

Fishoff, Iris, ed. 2001. *The Realm of the Stars.* Jerusalem: Israel Museum. Hebrew.

Fleischer, Ezra. 1975. *Hebrew Liturgical Poetry in the Middle Ages.* Jerusalem: Keter. Hebrew.

1988. *Eretz-Israel Prayers and Rituals as Portrayed in the Geniza Documents.* Jerusalem: Magnes Press. Hebrew.

Gilman, Sander. 1991. *The Jew's Body.* New York and London: Routledge.

Ginzberg, Louis. 1941–61. *A Commentary on the Palestinian Talmud.* New York: Jewish Theological Seminary. Hebrew.

1954. *Legends of the Jews.* Philadelphia: Jewish Publication Society.

Goitein, S. D. 1964. "The Synagogue Building and Its Furnishings According to the Records of the Cairo Geniza." *Eretz Israel* 7: 81–97. Hebrew. English summary, 169*–172*.

1971. *A Mediterranean Society.* 2. Berkeley, Los Angeles, and London: University of California Press.

Goodenough, Erwin R. 1953–68. *Jewish Symbols in the Greco–Roman Period.* New York: Pantheon.

Goodman, Martin. 1983. *State and Society in Roman Galilee, 132–212 C.E.* Totowa, N.J.: Rowman and Allanheld.

Gutmann, Joseph. 1971. "The Illustrated Jewish Manuscript in Antiquity: The Present State of the Question." In *No Graven Images: Studies in Art and the Hebrew Bible,* ed. J. Gutmann. New York: Ktav. 232–48.

1983. "The Illustrated Midrash in the Dura Synagogue Paintings: A New Dimension for the Study of Judaism." *Proceedings of The American Academy for Jewish Research* 50: 91–104.

1984. "Early Synagogue and Jewish Catacomb Art and Its Relation to Christian Art." *Aufstieg und Niedergang der Römische Welt* (Berlin and New York: Walther de Gryter, 1987) II 21.2: 1313–42.

Hachlili, Rachel. 1988a. *Ancient Jewish Art and Archaeology in the Land of Israel.* Leiden: E. J. Brill.

1988b. *Jewish Ornamented Ossuaries of the Late Second Temple Period.* Haifa: The Reuben and Edith Hecht Museum, University of Haifa.

1998. *Ancient Jewish Art and Archaeology in the Diaspora.* Leiden: E. J. Brill.

2001. *The Menorah, The Ancient Seven-Armed Candelabrum: Origin, Form and Significance.* Leiden: E. J. Brill.

Halbertal, Moshe, and Avishai Margalit. 1992. *Idolatry.* Cambridge, Mass.: Harvard University Press.

Hall, Jonathan. 1997. *Ethnic Identity in Greek Antiquity.* Cambridge: Cambridge University Press.

Hanfmann, George M. 1980. "The Continuity of Classical Art: Culture, Myth and Faith." In *The Age of Spirituality: A Symposium,* ed. K. Weitzmann. New York. 75–99.

Hellemo, Gier. 1989. *Adventus Domini: Eschatological Thought in 4th-Century Apses and Catecheses.* Leiden: E. J. Brill.

Heschel, Susannah. 1998. *Abraham Geiger and the Jewish Jesus.* Chicago: University of Chicago Press.

Hezser, Catherine. 1997. *The Social Structure of the Rabbinic Movement in Roman Palestine.* Tübingen: Mohr/Siebeck.

Hirschfeld, Yizhar. 1987. *Dwelling Houses in Roman and Byzantine Palestine.* Jerusalem: Yad Izhak Ben-Zvi Press. Hebrew.

Hoffman, Lawrence A. 1989. *Beyond the Text: A Holistic Approach to Liturgy.* Bloomington and Indianapolis: Indiana University Press.

Holtzman, Avner. 1999. *Aesthetics and National Revival – Hebrew Literature Against the Visual Arts.* Tel Aviv: Zmora-Bitan and Haifa University Press. Hebrew.

Horowitz, Elliot. 1994. "The Rite to Be Reckless: On the Perpetuation and Interpretation of Purim Violence." *Poetics Today* 15 (1): 9–54.

Ilan, Zvi. 1991. *Ancient Synagogues in Israel.* Israel: Ministry of Defense. Hebrew.

Ilan, Zvi, and Emmanuel Damati. 1987. *Meroth: The Ancient Jewish Village.* Tel Aviv: Society for the Preservation of Nature in Israel. Hebrew.

Israeli, Yael, ed. 1999. *In the Light of the Menorah: Story of a Symbol.* Jerusalem: Israel Museum and Philadelphia: Jewish Publication Society.

Jacob, Benno. 1992. *The Second Book of the Bible: Exodus,* trans. W. Jacob. Hoboken: Ktav.

Jacobs, Andrew S. 2004. *Remains of the Jews: The Holy Land and Christian Empire in Late Antiquity.* Stanford, CA: Stanford.

Jacobson, David M., and M. P. Weitzman. 1992. "What Was Corinthean Bronze?" *American Journal of Archaeology* 96 (2): 237–48.

Jacoby, Ruth. 2001. "The Four Seasons in Zodiac Mosaics: The Tallaras Baths in Astypalaea, Greece." *Israel Exploration Journal* 51: 225–30.

Jensen, Robin. 2000. *Understanding Early Christian Art.* London and New York: Routledge.

Jones, Sian. 1998. "Identities in Practice: Towards an Archaeological Perspective on

Jewish Identity in Antiquity." In *Jewish Local Patriotism and Self-Identification in the Graeco-Roman Period*, eds. S. Jones and S. Pearce. Sheffield: Sheffield Academic Press. 29–49.

Joselit, Jenna Weissmann. 1989. "Of Manners, Morals and Orthodox Judaism: Decorum Within the Orthodox Synagogue." In *Ramaz: School, Community, Scholarship and Orthodoxy*, ed. J. S. Gurock. Hoboken: Ktav. 20–39.

Kadushin, Max. 1952. *The Rabbinic Mind*. New York: Jewish Theological Seminary.

Kasher, Aryeh. 1985. *The Jews in Hellenistic and Roman Egypt*. Tübingen: Mohr.

Kaufmann, David. 1897. "Art in the Synagogue." *Jewish Quarterly Review*, Old Series 9: 254–69.

Kayser, Stephen S. 1953. "Defining Jewish Art." In *Mordecai M. Kaplan Jubilee Volume*. New York: Jewish Theological Seminary of America. 457–67.

Killebrew, Ann E., and Steven Fine. 1991. "Qatzrin-Reconstructing Village Life in Talmudic Times." *Biblical Archaeology Review* 27 (3): 44–56.

King, G. R. D. 1985. "Islam, Iconoclasm and the Declaration of Doctrine." *Bulletin of the School of Oriental and African Studies* 48, pt. 2: 267–77.

Kleeblatt, Norman L. 1996. *Too Jewish? Challenging Traditional Identities*. New York: Jewish Museum; New Brunswick, N.J.: Rutgers University Press.

Klein, Michael. 1980. "Palestinian Targum and Synagogue Mosaics." *Immanuel* 11: 33–45.

Kohl, Heinrich, and Carl Watzinger. 1916. *Antike Synagogen in Galilaea*. Leipzig: J. C. Hinrichs'sche Buchhandlung.

Kon, Maximilian. 1947. *The Tombs of the Kings*. Tel Aviv: Dvir. Hebrew.

Kotlar, David. 1971. *Art and Religion*. Jerusalem and Tel Aviv: M. Newman Publishing. Hebrew.

Kraabel, Alf Thomas. 1979. "The Diaspora Synagogue: Archaeological and Epigraphic Evidence since Sukenik." *Aufstieg und Niedergang der Römische Welt* (Berlin and New York: Walther de Gruyter) II 19 (1): 479–510.

Kraeling, Carl H. 1956. *The Synagogue. The Excavations of Dura Europos, Final Report VIII, Part 1*. New Haven: Yale University Press.

1967. *The Christian Building: Excavations at Dura-Europos, Final Report Vol. 8, Part 2*. New Haven: Dura Europos Publications.

Krauss, Samuel. 1921. "Die Galilaeischen Synagogenruinen und die Halakha." *Monatsschrift für Geschichte und Wissenschaft des Judentums* 65: 211–20.

1922. *Synagogale Altertümer*. Berlin and Vienna: B. Harz.

Krautheimer, Richard. 1967. "The Constantinian Basilica." *Dumbarton Oaks Papers* 21: 117–40.

Krinsky, Carol Herselle. 1985. *Synagogues of Europe: Architecture, History, Meaning*. New York: The Architectural History Foundation; Cambridge, Mass.: MIT Press.

Lerner, L. Scott. 2000. "Narrating the Architecture of Emancipation." *Jewish Social Studies* 6 (3): 1–30.

Levine, Lee I. 1975. "R. Abbahu of Caesarea." In *Christianity, Judaism and Other Greco-Roman Cults*, ed. J. Neusner. Leiden: E. J. Brill. 4: 56–76.

1989. *The Rabbinic Class of Roman Palestine*. Jerusalem: Yad Izhak Ben-Zvi Press.

1997. "The Revolutionary Effects of Archaeology on the Study of Jewish History: The Case of the Ancient Synagogue." In *The Archaeology of Israel: Constructing the Past, Interpreting the Present*, eds. N. A. Silberman and D. Small. Sheffield: Sheffield Academic Press. 166–89.

2000. *The Ancient Synagogue: The First Thousand Years*. New Haven: Yale University Press.

Levy, Johanan Hans. 1969. *Studies in Jewish Hellenism*. Jerusalem: Bialik Institute. Hebrew.

Levy, Moritz Abraham. 1862. *Geschichte der Jüdischen Münzen*. Leipzig: Nies'che Buchdruckerei (Carl B. Lorck).

Lieberman, Saul. 1940. *Yemenite Midrashim: A Lecture on the Yemenite Midrashim, Their Character and Value*. Jerusalem: Bamberger and Wahrmann. Hebrew.

1942. *Greek in Roman Palestine*. New York: Jewish Theological Seminary.

1946–7. "Palestine in the Third and Fourth Centuries." *Jewish Quarterly Review* 37: 31–54.

1955–88. *Tosefta Ki-fshutah: A Comprehensive Commentary on the Tosefta*. New York: Jewish Theological Seminary. Hebrew.

1962. *Hellenism in Jewish Palestine*. New York: Jewish Theological Seminary.

1991. *Studies in Palestinian Talmudic Literature*, ed. D. Rosenthal. Jerusalem: Magnes. Hebrew.

Lowenthal, David. 1990. *The Past Is a Foreign Country*. Cambridge: Cambridge University Press.

Luger, Yehezkel. 2001. *The Weekday Amidah in the Cairo Genizah*. Jerusalem: Orhot. Hebrew.

Magen, Itzhak. 1988. *The Stone Vessel Industry in Jerusalem During the Second Temple Period*. Israel: Society for the Preservation of Nature in Israel. Hebrew.

Magness, Jodi. 2001. "The Question of the Synagogue: The Problem of Typology."

In *Judaism in Late Antiquity, Part 3: Where We Stand: Issues and Debates in Ancient Judaism, Volume Four: The Special Problem of the Synagogue*. Leiden: E. J. Brill. 1–48.

Mathews, Thomas F. 1971. *The Early Churches of Constantinople: Architecture and Liturgy*. University Park, Penn.: Pennsylvania State University Press.

1993. *The Clash of the Gods: A Reinterpretation of Early Christian Art*. Princeton: Princeton University Press.

Mazar, Benjamin. 1973. *Beth She'arim. 1*. New Brunswick: Rutgers University Press.

Meshorer, Yaakov. 1997. *A Treasury of Jewish Coins from the Persian Period to Bar-Kochba*. Jerusalem: Yad Izhak Ben-Zvi Press. Hebrew.

Mettinger, T. N. D. 1995. *No Graven Image? Israelite Aniconism in Its Ancient Near Eastern Context*. Stockholm: Almsquist and Wiksell International.

Meyers, Carol. 1976. *The Tabernacle Menorah: A Synthetic Study of a Symbol from the Biblical Cult*. Missoula: Scholars Press.

Meyers, Carol L., and Eric M. Meyers. 1982. "A Ceramic Rendering of the Torah Shrine from Nabratein." *Eretz Israel* 16: 176*–185*.

1987. *The Anchor Bible: Haggai, Zechariah 1–8: A New Translation with Introduction and Commentary*. Garden City: Doubleday.

1993. *The Anchor Bible: Zechariah 9–14: A New Translation with Introduction and Commentary*. Garden City: Doubleday.

Meyers, Eric M. 2001. "Dating of the Gush Halav Synagogue: A Response to Jodi Magness." *Judaism in Late Antiquity, Part 3: Where We Stand: Issues and Debates in Ancient Judaism, Volume Four: The Special Problem of the Synagogue*. Leiden: E. J. Brill. 49–63.

Meyers, Eric M., A. Thomas Kraabel, and James F. Strange. 1976. *Ancient Synagogue Excavations at Khirbet Shema', Upper Galilee, Israel, 1970–1972*. Durham: Duke University Press.

Meyers, Eric M., Carol L. Meyers, and James F. Strange. 1990. *Excavations at the Ancient Synagogue of Gush Halav*. Winona Lake, Ind.: Eisenbrauns.

Meyers, Eric M., James F. Strange, and Carol L. Meyers. 1981. "The Ark of Nabratein: A First Glance." *Biblical Archaeologist* 44 (4): 237–43.

Mildenberg, Leo. 1984. *The Coinage of the Bar Kokhba War*. Aarau: Verlag Sauerländer.

Miller, Stuart S. 1999. "The Rabbis and the Non-Existent Monolithic Synagogue." *JCP* 57–70.

2005. *Sages and Commoners in Late Antique 'Erez Israel*. Tübingen: Mohr Siebeck.

Mirsky, Aharon. 1970. "Aquarius and Aries in the Ein Gedi Inscription and in Early Piyyutim." *Tarbiz* 40: 376–84. Hebrew.

Mishory, Alek. 2000. *Lo and Behold: Zionist Icons and Visual Symbols in Israeli Culture*. Tel Aviv: Am Oved. Hebrew.

Moore, George Foot. 1927–30. *Judaism in the First Centuries of the Common Era*. Cambridge, Mass.: Harvard University Press.

Najman, Hindy. 2000. "Torah of Moses: Pseudonymous Attribution in Second Temple Writings." In *Interpretation of Scripture in Early Judaism and Christiantiy: Studies in Language and Tradition*, ed. C. A. Evans. Sheffield: Sheffield Academic Press. 202–16.

Narkiss, Bezalel. 1974. "A Scheme of the Sanctuary from the Time of Herod the Great." *Journal of Jewish Art* 1: 6–15.

Narkiss, Mordecai. 1939–40. "The Zodiac in Jewish Art." *Kirjath Sepher* 16: 513–19. Hebrew.

Naveh, Joseph, ed. 1978. *On Stone and Mosaic: The Aramaic and Hebrew Inscriptions from Ancient Synagogues*. Israel: Maariv. Hebrew.

—— 1989. "The Aramaic and Hebrew Inscriptions from Ancient Synagogues." *Eretz Israel* 20: 302–10. Hebrew.

Naveh, Joseph, and Shaul Shaked. 1975. *Amulets and Magic Bowls: Aramaic Incantations from Late Antiquity*. Jerusalem and Leiden: E. J. Brill.

—— 1985. *Magic Spells and Formulae: Aramaic Incantations of Late Antiquity*. Jerusalem: Magnes Press.

Nelson, Robert S. 2000. "The Slide Lecture, or, The Work of Art *History* in the Age of Mechanical Reproduction." *Critical Enquiry* 26: 414–34.

Netzer, Ehud. 1998. "The Enchanted Palace Built by Hyrcanus the Tobiad in Transjordan." *Qadmoniot* 36 (2): 117–22. Hebrew.

Neusner, Jacob. 1988. "Introduction" to E. R. Goodenough, *Jewish Symbols in the Greco–Roman Period: Abridged Edition*. Princeton: Princeton University Press. ix–xxxvii.

—— 1998. "The Iconography of Judaisms." *Approaches to Ancient Judaism*. New Series 13. Atlanta: Scholars Press, 1998. 139–56.

Noam, Vered. 2002–3. "The Miracle of the Cruse of Oil: Questioning Its Use as a Source for Assessing the Sages' Attitude Toward the Hasmoneans." *Zion* 67: 382–400. Hebrew.

Olin, Margaret. 2001. *A Nation Without Art*. Omaha: University of Nebraska Press.

Ovadiah, Asher. 1969. "Excavations in the Area of the Ancient Synagogue at Gaza (Preliminary Report)." *Israel Exploration Journal* 19 (4): 193–8.

—— 1977. "The Reciprocal Relationship between Synagogues and Churches in the Byzantine Period." In *Between and Sinai: Memorial to Amnon*, ed. M. Broshi. Jerusalem: Yedidim. 163–70. Hebrew.

Paul, Shalom M. 1967. "Jerusalem – City of Gold." *Israel Exploration Journal* 17: 257–63.

—— 1977. "Jerusalem of Gold – A Song and an Ancient Crown." *Biblical Archaeology Review* 3 (4): 38–40.

Pfanner, Michael. 1983. *Der Titusbogen*. Mainz am Rhein: Philipp von Zabern.

Picard, Gilbert Charles. 1957. *Les Trophées Romains: Contribution à l'historie de la Religion de le'Art de Rome*. Paris: E. De Boccard.

Pummer, Reinhard. 1989. "Samaritan Material Remains and Archaeology." In *The Samaritans*, ed. A. D. Crown. Tübingen: J. C. B. Mohr. 135–77.

—— 1999. "Samaritan Synagogues and Jewish Synagogues: Similarities and Differences." *JCP* 118–60.

Rahmani, L. Y. 1960. "The Ancient Synagogue of Maon (Nirim): The Small Finds and Coins." *Louis M. Rabinowitz Fund for the Exploration of Ancient Synagogues Bulletin* 3: 14–19.

—— 1967. "Jason's Tomb." *Israel Exploration Journal* 17: 61–100.

—— 1994. *A Catalogue of Jewish Ossuaries in the Collections of the State of Israel*. Jerusalem: Israel Antiquities Authority.

Rajak, Tessa. 1998. "The Rabbinic Dead and the Diaspora Dead at Beth She'arim." In *The Talmud Yerushalmi and Graeco-Roman Culture I*, ed. P. Schäfer. Tübingen: Mohr Siebeck. 349–66.

—— 1999. "Jews and Greeks: The Invention and Exploitation of Polarities in the Nineteenth Century." In *The Uses and Abuses of Antiquity*, eds. M. Biddiss and M. Wyke. Bern: Peter Lang. 57–77.

Reich, Ronny. 1980. "Mishnah Sheqalim 8:2 and the Archaeological Evidence." In *Jerusalem in the Second Temple Period: Abraham Schalit Memorial Volum*, eds. A. Oppenheimer, U. Rappaport, and M. Stern. Jerusalem: Yad Izhak Ben-Zvi Press. 225–56. Hebrew.

Reif, Stefan C. 1993. *Judaism and Hebrew Prayer*. Cambridge: Cambridge University Press.

Reifenberg, Adolf. 1950. *Ancient Hebrew Arts*. New York: Schocken.

Richardson, Peter. 1996. *Herod: King of the Jews and Friend of the Romans*. Columbia: University of South Carolina Press.

Romanoff, Paul. 1944. *Symbols on Ancient Jewish Coins*. Philadelphia: Dropsie College for Hebrew and Cognate Learning.

Rosenfeld, Ben-Zion. 1997. *Lod and Its Sages in the Period of the Mishnah and the Talmud*. Jerusalem: Yad Izhak Ben-Zvi Press. Hebrew.

Rostovtzeff, M. I., R. Bellinger, C. Hopkins, and C. B. Welles, eds. 1936. *The Excavations at Dura-Europos: Preliminary Report of the Sixth Season of Work October 1932–March 1933*. New Haven: Yale University Press.

Roth, Cecil, ed. 1971. *Jewish Art*. 2nd ed. rev. by B. Narkiss. London: Vallentine, Mitchell.

Roth-Gerson, Leah. 1987. *Greek Inscriptions in the Synagogues in Eretz-Israel*. Jerusalem: Yad Izhak Ben-Zvi Press.

Roussin, Lucille A. 1981. "The Beit Leontis Mosaic: An Escathological Interpretation." *Jewish Art* 8: 6–19.

—— 1994. "Costume in Roman Palestine: Archaeological Remains and the Evidence of the Mishnah." In *The World of Roman Costume*, eds. J. L. Sebesta and L. Bonfante. Madison: University of Wisconsin Press. 182–90.

Runesson, Anders. 2001. "The Synagogue at Ancient Ostia: The Building and Its History from the First to the Fifth Century." In *The Synagogue of Ancient Ostia and the Jews of Rome: Interdisciplinary Studies, Skifter Utgivna av Svenska Institutet I Rome 4, LVII*, eds. B. Olsson, D. Mitternacht, and O. Brandt. Stockholm: Paul Aströms. 29–99.

Rutgers, Leonard V. 1995. *The Jews of Late Ancient Rome: An Archaeological and Historical Study on the Interaction of Jews and Non-Jews in the Roman-Diaspora*. Leiden: E. J. Brill.

—— 1998. *The Hidden Heritage of Diaspora Judaism*. Leuven: Peeters.

Safrai, Samuel. 1965. *Pilgrimage at the Time of the Second Temple*. Jerusalem: Akadamon. Hebrew.

Safrai, Ze'ev. 1987. "Financing Synagogue Construction in the Period of the Mishna and the Talmud." In *Synagogues in Antiquity*, eds. A. Kasher, A. Oppenheimer, and U. Rappaport. Jerusalem: Yad Izhak Ben-Zvi Press. 77–96. Hebrew.

—— 1989. "Dukhan, Aron and Teva: How Was the Ancient Synagogue Furnished?" In *Ancient Synagogues in Israel*, ed. R. Hachlili. London: BAR International. 69–83.

St. Hart, H. 1952. "Judaea and Rome: The Official Commentary." *Journal of Theological Studies*. New Series 3: 172–97.

Sanders, E. P. 1992. *Judaism: Practice and Belief 63 BCE–66 CE*. London and Philadelphia: Trinity International.

Schäfer, Peter. 1998. "Jews and Gentiles in Yerushalmi Avodah Zarah." In *Talmud Yerushalmi and Graeco-Roman Culture*, ed. P. Schäfer. Tübingen: Mohr Siebeck. 3: 335–52.

Schiffman, Lawrence H. 1987. "The Conversion of the Royal House of Adiabene in Josephus and in Rabbinic Sources." In *Josephus, Judaism and Christianity*, eds. L. H. Feldman and G. Hata. Detroit: Wayne State University Press. 293–312.

Scholem, Gershom. 1978. "The Star of David: History of a Symbol." In *The Messianic Idea in Judaism and Other Essays on Jewish Spirituality*. New York: Schocken. 257–81.

Schwabe, Moshe, and Baruch Lifshitz. 1974. *Beth She'arim*. 2. New Brunswick, N.J.: Rutgers University Press.

Schwartz, Seth. 2001. *Imperialism and Jewish Society, 200 B.C.E. to 640 C.E.* Princeton: Princeton University Press.

Seager, Andrew R. 1972. "The Building History of the Sardis Synagogue." *American Journal of Archaeology* 76: 425–35.

Shavit, Yaakov. 1997a. "Archaeology, Political Culture and Culture in Israel." In *The Archaeology of Israel: Constructing the Past, Interpreting the Present*, eds. N. A. Silberman and D. Small. Sheffield: Sheffield Academic Press. 48–61.

1997b. *Athens in Jerusalem: Classical Antiquity and Hellenism in the Making of the Modern Secular Jew*. London and Portland, Ore.: Littman Library of Jewish Civilization.

Shinan, Avigdor. 1992a. "The Aramaic Targum as a Mirror of Galilean Jewry." In *The Galilee in Late Antiquity*, ed. L. I. Levine. New York and Jerusalem: Jewish Theological Seminary of America 241–51.

1992b. *The Embroidered Targum: The Aggadah in Targum Pseudo-Jonathan of the Pentateuch*. Jerusalem: Magnes Press. Hebrew.

Siegel, J. P. 1972. "The Alexandrians in Jerusalem and Their Torah Scroll with Gold Tetragrammata." *Israel Exploration Journal* 22: 39–43.

Silberman, Neil A. 1993. *A Prophet Amongst You: The Life of Yigael Yadin: Soldier, Scholar and Mythmaker of Modern Israel*. Reading, Mass.: Addison-Wesley.

Sinding-Larsen, S. 1984. *Iconography and Ritual: A Study of Analytical Perspectives*. Oslo: Universitetsforlaget As.

Slouschz, Nahum. 1921. "The Excavations in Hammat of Tiberias (General Survey)." *Hashiloach* 38: 546–51. Hebrew.

Smallwood, E. Mary. 1976. *The Jews under Roman Rule: From Pompey to Diocletian*. Leiden: E. J. Brill.

Smith, Morton. 1967. "Goodenough's Jewish Symbols in Retrospect." *Journal of Biblical Literature* 86: 53–68.

Soussloff, Catherine. 1999. *Jewish Identity in Modern Art History*. Berkeley and Los Angeles: University of California Press.

Sperber, Daniel. 1965. "The History of the Menorah." *Journal of Jewish Studies* 16: 171–204.

1993. *Material Culture in Eretz-Israel during the Talmudic Period*. Jerusalem: Yad Izhak Ben-Zvi Press and Ramat Gan: Bar Ilan University Press. Hebrew.

Stern, Menachem. 1980. "Jerusalem, the Most Famous of the Cities of the East (Pliny, *Natural History* V, 70)." In *Jerusalem in the Second Temple Period: Abraham Schalit Memorial Volume*, eds. A. Oppenheimer, U. Rappaport, and M. Stern. Jerusalem: Yad Izhak Ben-Zvi Press and Ministry of Defense. 257–70. Hebrew.

Stern, Sacha. 1996. "Figurative Art and *Halakha* in the Midrashic–Talmudic Period." *Zion* 61: 379–419. Hebrew.

2001. *Calendar and Community: A History of the Jewish Calendar, Second Century BCE–Tenth Century CE*. Oxford and New York: Oxford University Press.

Sternberg, Aharon Genossar. 1972. *The Zodiac of Tiberias / The Steps of Ahaz and the Steps of the Temple Mount*. Tiberias: Aharon G. Sternberg. Hebrew.

Stow, Kenneth. 2001. *Theater of Acculturation: The Roman Ghetto in the Sixteenth Century*. Seattle and London: University of Washington Press.

Strother, Z. S. 1998. *Inventing Masks: Agency and History in the Art of the Central Pende*. Chicago: University of Chicago Press.

Strauss, Heinrich. 1960a. "The Date and Form of the Menorah of the Maccabees." *Eretz Israel* 6: 122–29. Hebrew.

1960b. "Jewish Art as a Minority Problem." *Journal of Jewish Sociology* 2: 147–71.

Stroumsa, Gedaliahu G. 1989. "Religious Contacts in Byzantine Palestine." *Numen* 36 (1): 16–42.

Strzygowski, Josef. 1901. *Orient oder Rom: Beitrage zur Geschichte der Spatantiken und Fruhchristlichen Kunst*. Leipzig: J. C. Hinrichs'sche Buchhandlung.

Sukenik, E. L. 1932. *The Ancient Synagogue of Beth Alpha*. Jerusalem: Hebrew University.

1934. *Ancient Synagogues in Palestine and Greece*. London: Oxford University Press.

1947. *The Synagogue of Dura Europos and Its Frescoes*. Jerusalem: Mosad Bialik. Hebrew.

1949. "The Present State of Synagogue Studies." *Louis M. Rabinowitz Fund for the Exploration of Ancient Synagogues* 1: 8–23.

Sukenik, E. L., and L. A. Mayer. 1930. *The Third Wall of Jerusalem; An Account of Excavations, Hebrew University, Jerusalem*. Jerusalem: Hebrew University; London: Oxford University Press.

Sussman, Jacob. 1973–4, 1974–5. "A Halakhic Inscription from the Beth-Shean

Valley." *Tarbiz* 43: 88–158, 44: 193–5. Hebrew.

Sussman, Varda. 1982. *Ornamented Jewish Oil-Lamps: From the Destruction of the Second Temple Period through the Bar Kokhba Revolt*. Warminster: Aris & Phillips; Jerusalem: Israel Exploration Society.

Ta-Shma, Israel M. 1994. "Synagogal Sanctity – Symbolism and Reality." In *Knesset Ezra: Literature and Life in the Synagogue, Studies Presented to Ezra Fleischer*, eds. S. Elizur, M. D. Herr, G. Shaked, and A. Shinan. Jerusalem: Yad Izhak Ben-Zvi. 351–64. Hebrew.

Tcherikover, Victor. 1959. *Hellenistic Civilization and the Jews*. Philadelphia: Jewish Publication Society of America.

Tryster, Hillel. 1995. *Israel Before Israel: Silent Cinema in the Holy Land*. Jerusalem: Steven Spielberg Jewish Film Archive.

Tsafrir, Yoram. 1984. *Eretz Israel from the Destruction of the Second Temple to the Muslim Conquest, Art and Archaeology*. Jerusalem: Yad Izhak Ben-Zvi Press. Hebrew.

1987. "The Byzantine Setting and Its Influence on Ancient Synagogues." In *The Synagogue in Late Antiquity*, ed. L. I. Levine. Philadelphia: American Schools for Oriental Research. 147–56.

Urbach, Ephraim E. 1958. "The Rabbinical Laws of Idolatry in the Second and Third Centuries in Light of Archaeological and Historical Facts." *Eretz Israel* 5: 189–205. Hebrew. Trans. and abridged in *Israel Exploration Journal* 9, 3–4 (1959): 149–65, 229–45.

1975. *The Sages – Their Concepts and Beliefs*. Trans. I. Abrahams. Jerusalem: Magnes Press.

Urman, Dan. 1995. "The House of Assembly and the House of Study: Are They One and the Same?" *ASHAAD* 1: 232–55.

Veyne, Paul. 1988. "Conduct Without Belief and Works of Art Without Viewers." *Diogenes* 143: 1–22.

Vikan, Gary. 1982, 1998. "Byzantine Pilgrims' Art." In *Heaven on Earth: Art and the Church in Byzantium*, ed. L. Safran. University Park, Penn.: Pennsylvania State University Press. 229–66.

Ville-Patlagean, Evelyne. 1962. "Une Image de Salomon en Basileus Byzantin." *Revue des Études Juives* 121 (1–2): 9–33.

Vincent, L. H. 1961. "Un sanctuaire dans la region de Jericho, la synagogue de Na'arah." *Revue Biblique* 68: 161–73.

Vitto, Fanny. 1995. "The Interior Decoration of Palestinian Churches and Synagogues." *Byzantinische Forschungen* 21: 283–300.

Webb, Ruth. 1999. "The Aesthetics of Sacred Space: Narrative, Metaphor, and Motion in *Ekphraseis* of Church Buildings." *Dumbarton Oaks Papers* 53: 60–74.

Weiss, Ze'ev 1989. *The Jewish Cemetery in the Galilee in the Period of the Mishnah and the Talmud: An Archaeological Investigation with the Aid of Talmudic Sources*. M.A. thesis. Jerusalem: Hebrew University.

Weiss, Ze'ev, and Ehud Netzer. 1996. *Promise and Redemption: A Synagogue Mosaic from Sepphoris*. Jerusalem: Israel Museum.

Weitzmann, Kurt. 1971. "The Question of the Influence of Jewish Pictorial Sources on Old Testament Illustration." In *No Graven Images: Studies in Art and the Hebrew Bible*, ed. J. Gutmann. New York: Ktav. 309–28.

——— ed. 1979. *Age of Spirituality*. New York: Metropolitan Museum of Art; Princeton: Princeton University Press.

——— 1994. *Sailing with Byzantium from Europe to America: The Memoirs of an Art Historian*. Munich: Editio Maris.

Weitzmann, Kurt, and Herbert L. Kessler. 1990. *The Frescoes of the Dura Synagogue and Christian Art*. Washington, D.C.: Dumbarton Oaks.

Wertheimer, Jack. 1994. *Tradition Renewed: A History of the Jewish Theological Seminary of America*. New York: Jewish Theological Seminary.

Wharton, Annabel Jane. 1995. *Refiguring the Post Classical City: Dura Europos, Jerash, Jerusalem, and Ravenna*. Cambridge: Cambridge University Press.

White, L. Michael. 1997. *The Social Origins of Christian Architecture, Volume II*. Valley Forge, Penn.: Trinity Press International.

Wieder, Naphtali. 1998. "The Jericho Inscription and Jewish Liturgy." In *The Formation of Jewish Liturgy in the East and the West: A Collection of Essays*. Jerusalem: Yad Izhak Ben-Zvi Press and Hebrew University of Jerusalem. 1: 126–51. Hebrew.

Wiegand, Theodor, and Hans Schrader. 1904. *Priene: Ergebnisse der Ausgrabungen und Untersuchungen in den Jahren 1895–1898*. Berlin: Georg Reimer.

Wilson, C. W., and H. H. Kitchener. 1881. "Synagogues." *Survey of Ancient Palestine Special Papers on Topography, Archaeology, Manners and Customs, Etc.* London: Committee of the Palestine Exploration Fund. 294–305.

Yaari, Abraham. 1964 *The History of the Festival of Simhat Torah*. Jerusalem: Mossad Harav Kook. Hebrew.

Yadin, Yigael. 1963. *The Finds from the Bar Kokhba Period in the Cave of Letters*. Jerusalem: Israel Exploration Society. Hebrew.

Yahalom, Joseph. 1980. "Synagogue Inscriptions in Palestine – A Stylistic Classification." *Immanuel* 10: 47–57.

——— 1986. "The Zodiac Wheel in Early Piyyut in Eretz-Israel." *Jerusalem Studies in Hebrew Literature* 9: 313–22. Hebrew.

——— 1987. "Piyyut as Poetry." In *The Synagogue in Late Antiquity*, ed. L. I. Levine. Philadelphia: American Schools for Oriental Research. 111–26.

Yarden, Leon. 1991. *The Spoils of Jerusalem on the Arch of Titus: A Re-Investigation*. Stockholm: Svenska Institutet i Rom; Göteborg: P. Åströms.

Yeivin, Ze'ev. 2000. *The Synagogue of Korazim: The 1962–1964, 1980–1987 Excavations*. Jerusalem: Israel Antiquities Authority. Hebrew.

Zanker, Paul. 1997. "In Search of the Roman Viewer." In *The Interpretation of Architectural Sculpture in Greece and Rome*, ed. D. Buitron-Oliver. Washington, D.C.: National Gallery of Art. 179–92.

Zevulun, Uza, and Y. Olenik. 1979. *Form and Function in the Talmudic Period*. Tel Aviv: Haaretz Museum. Hebrew and English.

Zori, N. 1966. "The House of Kyrios Leontis at Beth Shean." *Israel Exploration Journal* 16: 123–34.

——— 1967. "The Ancient Synagogue at Beth-Shean." *Eretz Israel* 8: 149–67. Hebrew.

Zulay, Menahem. 1995. "Rabban shel ha-Paytanim." In *Eretz Israel and Its Poetry*, ed. E. Hazan. Jerusalem: Magnes. 85–94. Hebrew.

INDEX OF PRIMARY SOURCES

GENERAL INDEX